Governance, Regulation, and Privatization in the Asia-Pacific Region

NBER–East Asia Seminar on Economics
Volume 12

National Bureau of Economic Research
Korea Development Institute
Chung-Hua Institution for Economic Research
Tokyo Center for Economic Research
Hong Kong University of Science and Technology
Productivity Commission, Australia

Governance, Regulation, and Privatization in the Asia-Pacific Region

Edited by **Takatoshi Ito and Anne O. Krueger**

The University of Chicago Press

Chicago and London

TAKATOSHI ITO is professor at the Institute of Economic Research at Hitotsubashi University and a research associate of the National Bureau of Economic Research. ANNE O. KRUEGER is first deputy managing director of the International Monetary Fund and a research associate of the National Bureau of Economic Research. Together they have edited the eleven previous volumes in the NBER-East Asia Seminar on Economics series; Krueger has also been the editor or coeditor of eight other books published by the Press.

The University of Chicago Press, Chicago 60637
The University of Chicago Press, Ltd., London
© 2004 by the National Bureau of Economic Research
All rights reserved. Published 2004
Printed in the United States of America
13 12 11 10 09 08 07 06 05 04   1 2 3 4 5
ISBN: 0-226-38679-1 (cloth)

Library of Congress Cataloging-in-Publication Data

NBER-East Asia Seminar on Economics (12th : 2001 : Hong Kong, China)
    Governance, regulation, and privatization in the Asia-Pacific Region / edited by Takatoshi Ito and Anne O. Krueger.
        p. cm. — (NBER-East Asia seminar on economics ; v. 12)
    "This volume contains edited versions of papers presented at the NBER's East Asia Seminar on Economics twelfth annual conference, held in Hong Kong, June 28–30, 2001"—Ackn.
    Includes bibliographical references and index.
    ISBN 0-226-38679-1 (cloth : alk. paper)
    1. Privatization—East Asia. 2. Corporate governance—East Asia. 3. Trade regulation—East Asia.   4. Industrial policy—East Asia. I. Ito, Takatoshi, 1950– II. Krueger, Anne O. III. Title. IV. NBER-East Asia seminar on economics (Series) ; v. 12.

HD4310.5.N34 2001
338.095—dc22

                                                                    2003053377

Relation of the Directors to the
Work and Publications
of the NBER

1. The object of the NBER is to ascertain and present to the economics profession, and to the public more generally, important economic facts and their interpretation in a scientific manner without policy recommendations. The Board of Directors is charged with the responsibility of ensuring that the work of the NBER is carried on in strict conformity with this object.

2. The President shall establish an internal review process to ensure that book manuscripts proposed for publication DO NOT contain policy recommendations. This shall apply both to the proceedings of conferences and to manuscripts by a single author or by one or more co-authors but shall not apply to authors of comments at NBER conferences who are not NBER affiliates.

3. No book manuscript reporting research shall be published by the NBER until the President has sent to each member of the Board a notice that a manuscript is recommended for publication and that in the President's opinion it is suitable for publication in accordance with the above principles of the NBER. Such notification will include a table of contents and an abstract or summary of the manuscript's content, a list of contributors if applicable, and a response form for use by Directors who desire a copy of the manuscript for review. Each manuscript shall contain a summary drawing attention to the nature and treatment of the problem studied and the main conclusions reached.

4. No volume shall be published until forty-five days have elapsed from the above notification of intention to publish it. During this period a copy shall be sent to any Director requesting it, and if any Director objects to publication on the grounds that the manuscript contains policy recommendations, the objection will be presented to the author(s) or editor(s). In case of dispute, all members of the Board shall be notified, and the President shall appoint an ad hoc committee of the Board to decide the matter; thirty days additional shall be granted for this purpose.

5. The President shall present annually to the Board a report describing the internal manuscript review process, any objections made by Directors before publication or by anyone after publication, any disputes about such matters, and how they were handled.

6. Publications of the NBER issued for informational purposes concerning the work of the Bureau, or issued to inform the public of the activities at the Bureau, including but not limited to the NBER Digest and Reporter, shall be consistent with the object stated in paragraph 1. They shall contain a specific disclaimer noting that they have not passed through the review procedures required in this resolution. The Executive Committee of the Board is charged with the review of all such publications from time to time.

7. NBER working papers and manuscripts distributed on the Bureau's web site are not deemed to be publications for the purpose of this resolution, but they shall be consistent with the object stated in paragraph 1. Working papers shall contain a specific disclaimer noting that they have not passed through the review procedures required in this resolution. The NBER's web site shall contain a similar disclaimer. The President shall establish an internal review process to ensure that the working papers and the web site do not contain policy recommendations, and shall report annually to the Board on this process and any concerns raised in connection with it.

8. Unless otherwise determined by the Board or exempted by the terms of paragraphs 6 and 7, a copy of this resolution shall be printed in each NBER publication as described in paragraph 2 above.

Contents

III. Sectoral Privatization and Regulation

Acknowledgments

This volume contains edited versions of papers presented at the NBER's East Asia Seminar on Economics twelfth annual conference, held in Hong Kong on 28–30 June 2001; the Hong Kong University of Science and Technology was the local host. The conference arrangements coordinated by Kirsten Foss Davis and Brett Maranjian and the local hosts were excellent.

We are indebted to members of the program committee who organized the conference, and to Chung-Hua Institution, Taipei; the Hong Kong University of Science and Technology; Korea Development Institute, Seoul; Productivity Commission, Australia; and the Tokyo Center for Economic Research. All the participants enjoyed the venue and the wonderful facilities in which the conference was held.

The National Bureau of Economic Research provided logistical support. We are greatly indebted to the NBER and to the Asian institutions that supported the research and the conference.

Introduction

Takatoshi Ito and Anne O. Krueger

After several decades in which public-sector enterprises (PSEs) played large and often increasing roles in national economies in most countries in the world, the past two decades have seen a reversal. In industrial countries, privatization efforts started in the late 1970s and 1980s as concerns with the efficiency and cost-effectiveness of state-owned enterprises mounted. During that same period, it was becoming increasingly evident that PSEs in many developing countries were not fulfilling their intended roles—they were high-cost monopolies, often greatly overstaffed as politicians used them to provide employment for friends and relatives. Privatization began tentatively in a few countries, and then picked up momentum in both the pioneers and others. The original motives were buttressed by the need for revenues from privatization and from elimination of PSE losses to reduce fiscal deficits, as the costs of inflation became increasingly evident. Then, in the early 1990s, the collapse of the command economies of the former Soviet Union and of Eastern Europe resulted in strong pressures for rapid privatization in those countries. By the late 1990s, increased appreciation of the importance of the financial sector's efficient operation led to intensified efforts for privatization of financial institutions, as well.

Privatization did not always proceed smoothly, however. There were questions associated with methods of privatization, as well as with the structuring of the environment for operation of newly privatized firms. With regard to the former, governments found themselves under attack because public enterprises had been "given away" or sold too cheaply, or

Takatoshi Ito is professor at the Institute of Economic Research, Hitotsubashi University, and a research associate of the National Bureau of Economic Research. Anne O. Krueger is first deputy managing director of the International Monetary Fund and a research associate of the National Bureau of Economic Research.

because ownership had been granted to cronies rather than to the most deserving. When, in Eastern European countries, citizens were given shares in individual enterprises, concerns arose that there would be no effective ownership control over management; when enterprises were instead sold to a few large buyers (especially if they were foreign), allegations of monopoly power were made. Questions also arose as to the desirable degree of restructuring of PSEs that should occur prior to privatization. Controversies also surrounded efforts to shed excess manpower, either while enterprises were still in the public sector or when new owners attempted to reduce costs.

Moreover, it became clear that it was not enough to transfer ownership to the private sector, even if the problems enumerated above were satisfactorily addressed. Once firms were no longer publicly owned, key issues arose with respect to corporate control of management and the environment in which the newly privatized enterprises functioned. Some enterprises were privatized with owners who had little control over managements, which continued to run their firms in the same ways as before. Some privatized firms were natural monopolies, and where regulatory frameworks (or competition) were not provided, the new owners simply reaped monopoly profits (although there is evidence that many of these owners did reduce costs at least to a degree).

As if these problems were not enough, it quickly became evident that for markets to function well, an appropriate infrastructure is necessary. This infrastructure requires a legal framework in which corporate governance, a commercial code, and other rules of the game are elaborated and enforced. Corporate governance entails not only the relations of owners to managers, but the rights of minority shareholders, regulations governing accounting procedures and the provision of information to shareholders, and accountability of boards of directors. Commercial codes enforce contracts and enable transactions to take place over time. Bankruptcy laws provide creditor protection and enable preservation of value or orderly exit, whichever is appropriate.

Most of the lessons learned to date have come through experience. Privatizations deemed no more than partially successful have resulted in greater appreciation of the legal environment and infrastructure in which private enterprises have functioned in many market economies. Features—such as bankruptcy and minority shareholder rights—previously taken for granted have been better understood as analysts have examined the implications of their absence or malfunctioning. As experience with privatization has grown, so has appreciation and understanding of the issues involved in successful privatization. Successful outcomes depend not only (and perhaps least) on the successful sale of the company, but more importantly on the rights of owners, the legal framework in which corporate governance functions, and the ways in which incentives are provided for the privatized firms to respond as competitors rather than as monopolists.

In this volume, some of the main lessons from privatization in the East Asian region are brought together and analyzed. The first three papers provide overviews of key aspects of the process.

In chapter 1, Simon Johnson and Andrei Schleifer note that "[p]rivatized firms with weak corporate governance have repeatedly demonstrated weak performance and have frequently been 'tunneled' by their management. . . . The lesson from postcommunist countries is that effective investor protection needs to accompany privatization." They then proceed to analyze the appropriate forms of corporate governance, addressing in particular the question as to whether market participants can for themselves work out appropriate contracts for corporate governance (with the government relegated to the role of contract enforcement) or whether a more active governmental stance protecting shareholder rights is appropriate.

Johnson and Shleifer then review the growing body of empirical evidence that has emerged on this issue. They provide a concise overview of much of that empirical evidence, showing the ways in which economists have been able to provide answers to the basic question as to whether the legal framework matters. They conclude that "[t]he evidence that legal rules matter is overwhelming." While private contracts can to some degree compensate for the absence of an appropriate legal framework, Johnson and Shleifer show that the degree to which they can do so is far from adequate. When protection of shareholder rights is in itself weak, stronger investor protection in stock markets can partially compensate.

Chapter 2, by Philip L. Williams and Graeme Woodbridge, analyzes Australia's merger policy and the lessons it may provide for other countries. They focus on those instances in which there is a trade-off between efficiency and competition because of economies of scale. In Australia, there were a significant number of cases in which mergers would have resulted in greater efficiency, but would simultaneously have reduced competition. Williams and Woodbridge believe that appropriate merger policy must weigh the trade-offs between the benefits to society of lower costs and the associated costs of greater concentration of economic power. Moreover, there are benefits to speed in evaluating mergers, and the authorities must be able to form their judgments based on secret information. These requirements, in turn, render it difficult to achieve a transparent and fair process for evaluating mergers. The authors show how Australia's law governing mergers was insufficiently cognizant of these requirements, and how the process of approval therefore became informal and secretive in order to avoid the high costs of public knowledge of the relevant information, and suggest that a more transparent and fairer process could be devised that has legal standing.

In chapter 3, John McMillan provides a framework for evaluation of the use of markets to solve economic policy problems. His analysis focuses on what he regards as the "middle ground" between government ownership and purely private governance, which arises when government permits an activity to be conducted privately but maintains substantial control rights. To illustrate his points, McMillan uses four examples: emissions trading (for environmental protection); spectrum auctions (in which public policy designs the market); electricity regulation (where Californian efforts at deregulation were badly designed); and fisheries (where the government sets the quota to protect the "tragedy of the commons" and overfishing). McMillan argues that markets generate information, otherwise unavailable to governments, that can be used in the appropriate regulatory environment if governments use markets to induce the revelation of needed information. But, at the same time, markets cannot by themselves solve public policy problems, and regulation (and information) continues to be needed (as with the fisheries quota). McMillan concludes, after examining the four cases, that improper regulation can lead to results as bad as, or worse than, the market outcome. By the same token, however, appropriate regulation can in many instances achieve an outcome superior to that attainable in an unfettered private market.

These three papers provide an overview and framework of the theme and issues of the rest of the volume. They provide important theoretical and practical insights for individual cases and sectors in different countries. The rest of the volume consists of empirical investigations of particular industries in a particular country.

The next group of papers examines individual experiences in East Asian countries. In chapter 4, the first paper of this section, Il Chong Nam surveys Korea's policy toward privatizing the large PSEs. He shows that, until the 1990s, there was no effort to do so. Then, starting in 1994, a privatization movement developed, which culminated in a 1997 law to privatize large public-sector corporations. This was possible because of a change in the political regime at that time. Divestitures started after the passage of the 1997 law. Nam shows that the divestitures were not sufficiently extensive to prevent the government from intervening in the enterprises. He believes that limited success resulted from insufficient attention to competition policy, the regulatory framework, and industry structure. He also notes the linkages between treatment of the to-be-privatized PSEs and treatment of the *chaebol:* they were not initially permitted to bid to take ownership of any of the PSEs, but they are so important in the Korean economy that their absence was critical. Further progress in privatization almost certainly will entail an integration of competition policy, policy toward the *chaebol,* and divestiture, illustrating yet again the importance of the infrastructure and environment in which individual enterprises are privatized.

Korean corporate governance is the focus of Sung Wook Joh's chapter 5.

She analyzes the financial difficulties of Korean firms in the run-up to 1997, noting the incentives to borrow and the falling profitability of firms prior to the outset of the crisis. She then links the financial performance of different enterprises with the control and ownership rights prevailing before the crisis. She found that, controlling for other variables, firms with a high controlling-shareholder ownership had better profitability and financial performance than did those with much less concentrated financial interest. When the disparity between controlling and small shareholder interest was sufficiently large, however, controlling shareholders followed their own self-interest and "expropriated small shareholders." In her words, "Korean firms' low profits persisted because the corporate governance system did not induce firm management to maximize firm value." Joh believes that the absence of a credible exit threat, inadequate financial information (including the absence of financial institutions monitoring performance), the virtual absence of minority shareholder rights, and weak boards of directors all contributed to poor corporate performance, which in turn triggered the Korean financial crisis of 1997. She concludes that, in the aftermath of 1997, the Korean government has been altering incentives to align the interests of major shareholders more closely with those of maximizing the value of the firm.

Youngjae Lim, in chapter 6, argues that corporate governance fundamentally changed after the economic crisis of 1997 in Korea. Using a firm-level data set, he shows that after the crisis, the largest firms are leaving banks and switching their financing to capital markets, while the small and medium-sized firms are increasing their dependence on bank financing. A gap in corporate profits has widened after the crisis. Since banks are losing their best customers, the future profitability of the bank may be questioned. Also, changes in the corporate finance may affect corporate governance in the future, but it is too early to make definite statements on these points.

Chong-Hyun Nam was a conference participant and made excellent comments during the conference. Since Dr. Lim adopted most of the comments that were suggested by Dr. Nam, we did not include Dr. Nam's comments in this volume. This is a rare instance where a discussant is so perceptive that his comments are fully adopted and he becomes a "victim of his own success." We appreciate Dr. Nam for his appropriate and constructive suggestions for improving the paper.

In chapter 7, Chen Chien-Hsun and Shih Hui-Tzu examine the relationship between initial public offerings (IPOs) and corporate governance in China during the transition. Chen and Shih find that IPOs resulted in little, if any, change in the performance of companies having undergone IPOs in industries other than public utilities, transportation, and finance. They find a number of reasons for this. First of all, they note that companies planning to list an IPO may be tempted to inflate earnings or balance-sheet figures pre-IPO, thus leading to statistically poor performance after the IPO. But they also note that "there is too much insider trading, the responsibilities of the boards of directors are not sufficiently defined, there is too much administrative interference, too many problems of internal control, and so on." They conclude by noting that the quality of listed companies is a major factor in determining the health of capital markets in any country, and that measures that result in improvements in the quality of IPOs are therefore an important part of the development of China's capital markets.

Chapter 8, by David D. Li and Frances T. Lui, seeks to ascertain the determinants of the kinds of state economic enterprises in China that are privatized. They explore the incentives confronting the government and the workers that would lead them to decide to privatize. One hypothesis focuses on the desire, by the government, for greater economic efficiency. Another is the need to reduce the fiscal burden of individual enterprises when the subsidies from the government get too large.

The authors carry out a probit estimation to examine whether the conditions derived from their theoretical model indeed predict the probability of privatization or liquidation. Various factors that may contribute to the probability of privatization/liquidation are analyzed and interpreted. The authors find that their efficiency measures did not have a statistically significant impact on the decision. They interpret their results to mean that governments privatize state-owned enterprises (SOEs) in order to increase government revenue and reduce the size of subsidies. Governments are more reluctant to privatize when there is likely to be larger resulting unemployment or when the loss of political control will be more significant. The authors conclude that first-best (from the economist's viewpoint) privatizations may not be feasible, and that policymakers seeking to improve economic welfare may be well advised to seek second-best solutions that take government objectives into account, reducing the size of layoffs and generating large revenues.

In chapter 9, Tetsushi Sonobe and Keijiro Otsuka contrast the town and village enterprises (TVEs) and SOEs in China. They first note that until the early 1990s, the dominant move away from state ownership was through the establishment and growth of TVEs; it was only in the 1990s that privatization of SOEs began to take place. They hypothesized that (1) intervention in the management of TVEs by local governments became less productive in the 1990s because of the declining importance of SOEs for the operation of TVEs and (2) recent privatization improved the productive efficiency of TVEs without sacrificing marketing efficiency. They use a unique data set, with information on the garment and casting industries for the greater Yangtze region.

Using econometric methods and their rich data set, the authors obtained results that they interpret to relate primarily to the short-run effects of privatization. They conclude that privatization yielded positive significant effects on productivity in both industries. Privatization and its accompanying benefits accelerated in the mid-1990s, as the relative importance of SOEs declined and that of free market transactions increased. That, in turn, made interventions by local governments less productive. They believe that the greater competition resulting from privatization will continue to lead to productivity growth over the medium and longer terms.

Reform of the SOEs is one of the most important policy priorities. Yang Yao's chapter 10 investigates privatization in China. It shows that politicians' commitment to reform is important in improving economic performance in the private sector. The fewer the political rent-seeking activities, the better the private-sector performance. Privatization is viewed as the additional incentive to engage in reform. The case study of the Shunde region is presented to show how the reform was successfully implemented in the region. Government commitment was shown by the reforms in the government sector—consolidation of the government agencies and reduction in the number of government employees. The efficiency and transparency of the government led to better firm performance.

The next set of papers focuses on issues of sectoral privatization and regulation. The first, chapter 11 by Helen Owens, covers the behavior of the Australian railroad industry under various regimes. Alternative methods of dealing with railroads, as Owens notes, include downsizing by separation of activities, corporatization, privatization, and renting out the tracks to competitive service providers. Owens points out that no single method always works, and that each method has its drawbacks. There is no one right method for all time. In part, this is a consequence of the fact that railroads had a large element of natural monopoly (although that element has diminished in recent years), which means that whatever method is used, a simulation of competition must be achieved by some means. But there is also the consideration that railroads relieve some of the (untaxed) congestion from highways. To the extent that they do that, they are offsetting a negative externality. In addition, timetables must be coordinated (for safety reasons), and technological change (such as air freight) can change the environment.

Owens offers some tentative conclusions (at least for existing technology): If there is sufficient competition between transport modes and competition among railroads is possible, vertical separation may be appropriate. If, however, there is little possibility of competition among railroads, vertical integration makes more sense, accompanied by promotion of competition for the market. When there is market power in a network, vertical integration is also appropriate, but awarding contracts on the basis of the lowest rates and periodic recontracting can reduce monopoly rents. She concludes, however, that the situation must be judged on a case-by-case basis, and that there is no universal rule.

In chapter 12, Fumitoshi Mizutani and Kiyoshi Nakamura discuss the Japanese experience with railways. They start by providing background for the privatization decision, which was based on a desire to reduce both the government subsidies to railroads (which were one of the three largest in the 1980s) and the political constraints on railroad operations that contributed to operating deficits. Once privatized, the railroads improved their performance.

The paper examines the performance of national rail privatization in several dimensions. First, overall performance is examined. Performance improved after privatization. Second, the effect of horizontal separation is evaluated. The sizes of the divided companies are examined by comparing them to privately owned rail companies. Third, vertical integration was maintained in Japan, while separate infrastructure was created in the United Kingdom. The authors judge that the vertical integration is economically more efficient. Functional separation (freight is separated) also improves performance. Railroad privatization increases competition in the market and efficiencies of the privatized companies.

In chapter 13, Tsuruhiko Nambu analyzes developments in the Japanese telecommunications industry since 1985, when privatization and deregulation began. The author argues that privatization with incomplete deregulation has resulted in an unsatisfactory situation in Japan. In part, this is because the rate structure was left intact at the time of privatization: there was no attempt to permit competition in some parts of the system with access fees to the trunk lines, nor was there any rate rebalancing (as was undertaken in the United Kingdom). Only three long-distance carriers entered the market, and they earned high rates of return. However, one of those three has exited the industry, while a second is being acquired by Vodafone. Nambu argues that some of the additional reform measures, such as further dividing local companies into regionals, do not make sense, while some others, such as competition policy with wireline and wireless, may be beneficial for the economy.

The last two papers focus on the financial industry. Charles Calomiris and Joseph Mason, in chapter 14, consider the policy issues arising from distressed banks: should they be rescued? On what terms should resources be transferred to banks? What lessons can be drawn from the experiences in the past (in particular those in the United States in the 1930s) for Japan and other Asian countries? With respect to the first question, the authors regard bank finance as crucial for financial intermediation of funds from savers to investors, especially in countries without strong capital markets, such as in Asia, and conclude that public policy to intervene in the process of bank failures (or prevent them) is called for. However, the design of intervention is important in order not to give wrong incentives to banks. The bank supervision framework should encourage market discipline to reward value creation and prudent risk management. Although costs may be quite high, such as 20 percent of gross domestic product in recent Asian currency crisis countries, the bank should be helped. The authors observe that costs of bank rescues depend on the choice of which banks to rescue and the means by which rescue is effected. Not all banks may be rescued, and foreign banks may be encouraged to enter the market, although they are not perfect substitutes for domestic banks. The rescue efforts should be focused on relatively solvent banks and those with high franchise values. Costs of partial bailout should be considered. The rescue efforts should minimize moral hazard, and that would reduce costs substantially. For example, high-risk lending should not be allowed after infusion of government capital. The U.S. experience in the 1930s, especially the role of the Reconstruction Finance Corporation, is reviewed and contrasted to the Japanese experiences of government loans and preferred stock purchases in 1998 and 1999. The authors recommend combining subsidized preferred stock purchases with mandatory matching contributions of common stock, limits on bank dividend payments, and reforms of bank capital regulation to use market discipline.

The final paper, chapter 15, by Aaron Tornell, analyzes the role of bailout guarantees that accompany bank privatization and financial liberalization in many episodes over the past decade. He argues that where firms are constrained in bank credit, bailout guarantees can encourage banks to lend and enhance long-run growth, provided that they are accompanied by appropriate policies, such as undertaking bailouts only in cases of systemic crisis and establishing an efficient regulatory framework. The cost of pursuing higher long-run growth is an increased vulnerability to crises. However, the chance of an actual crisis should be small to avoid the unintended effect of reducing productive investment. The model analysis is accompanied by a case of policy dilemma caused by the Mexican banking crisis that followed the currency crisis of 1994–1995.

I

Overview

Privatization and Corporate Governance

Simon Johnson and Andrei Shleifer

1.1 Introduction

Privatization is at the top of the political agenda in Asia. In China, the state sector has failed to wither and continues to consume a large amount of state resources (Steinfeld 1998, 2000). In Korea, the state has acquired substantial banking assets through bailout programs and now faces the serious issue of how to dispose of these assets (Chopra et al. 2001). In Malaysia, there is the beginning of a real discussion about how best to manage the relationship between the state and previously state-owned enterprises (Gomez and Jomo 1998). Throughout Asia, strong interest is developing in whether further privatization will speed up the economic recovery and sustain growth.

The early enthusiasm for privatization, however, has worn off since the 1980s and there is a general feeling of caution. Recent experience, particularly in Eastern Europe and the former Soviet Union, has demonstrated that simply privatizing is often not enough. As a result, there is a new emphasis on various complementary measures, such as stimulating competition. These complementary measures are often quite distinct from privatization itself and require separate political initiatives. In this paper we focus on one important issue that has emerged over the past decade: corporate governance of privatized firms.

Privatized firms with weak corporate governance have repeatedly

Simon Johnson is the Ronald A. Kurtz Associate Professor at the Sloan School of Management, Massachusetts Institute of Technology, and a faculty research fellow of the National Bureau of Economic Research. Andrei Shleifer is the Whipple V. N. Jones Professor of Economics at Harvard University and a research associate of the National Bureau of Economic Research.

demonstrated weak performance and have frequently been "tunneled" by their management. In the Czech Republic, management of newly privatized firms conspired with the managers of investment funds to strip assets and siphon off cash flow (Coffee 1999b). Belated attempts by the Czech authorities to control this process have proved difficult. The lesson from postcommunist countries is that effective investor protection must accompany privatization.

But how exactly should corporate governance be implemented? In particular, is it necessary or even helpful for the government to pass and enforce laws or legal regulations? Or can the private sector achieve all its desired outcomes simply by relying on private contracts, in which case all the government needs to do is to ensure that such contracts are enforced?

Ronald Coase (1960) explained the conditions under which individuals and private firms should be able to make contracts as they please. As long as the enforcement costs of these contracts are nil, individuals do not need statutory law or can find ways to contract around the law. There remains strong support in both law and economics for three important Coasian positions: law does not matter; law matters, but other institutions adapt to allow efficient private contracts; and finally, while law matters and domestic institutions cannot adapt enough, firms and individuals can write international contracts that achieve efficiency.

Coasian arguments have had great influence on discussions about corporate finance, and in this paper we focus on this literature, emphasizing points that seem particularly relevant for thinking about privatization. In the spirit of this general position, Easterbrook and Fischel (1991) argue that firms wishing to raise external finance can commit themselves to treat investors properly through a variety of mechanisms. Law may restrict the scope of these mechanisms, but firms and investors can always reach efficient arrangements. If this view is taken to the extreme, all countries that have a good judicial system should be able to achieve similar and efficient financial arrangements for firms. In this view, all privatization needs to do is to transfer property rights to private investors and the market will take care of the rest.

Also in the Coasian spirit, Berglof and von Thadden (1999) argue that civil-law countries in Europe have developed institutions that allow companies to enter enforceable contracts with investors. In their view, law may matter and have shortcomings, but the political process and firm-specific actions can generate other ways of offering effective guarantees to investors—for example, by mandating certain forms of government intervention or establishing a particular ownership structure and dividend policy. As a consequence, bringing U.S.-type institutions into Europe would not be helpful and could even be disruptive. In this view, the arrangements may differ across countries, but in many cases firms should be able to access external finance. The implication is that while privatization should be accompanied by institution building of some form, it does not need U.S.-style investor protection in order to be effective.

Even among the scholars who are convinced that legal rules matter, there is a Coasian skepticism about whether changing rules can have large effects. Coffee (1999a, b) argues that while U.S. firms derive important advantages from the U.S. legal system, other countries are not converging through changing their rules, presumably because this is politically difficult. Instead, there is a process of "functional" convergence, through which firms choose to adopt U.S.-type private contracts with their investors—for example, by issuing American Depositary Receipts (ADRs). In this view, corporate governance of privatized firms can be assured through the issue of ADRs or through otherwise listing in a stock market with a high level of investor protection.

These Coasian arguments are extremely powerful. However, they are rejected by the data. Recent research shows that the legal rules protecting investors matter in many ways, that other institutions cannot adapt sufficiently, and that changing domestic legal rules can have a big impact. We are also moving closer to a theoretical understanding of why exactly these Coasian positions are not correct and what this implies for standard models of economics and finance. The implication is that unless privatization is accompanied by enforceable investor protection, its benefits for firm performance will be limited because of severe agency problems, including various forms of expropriation or "tunneling" by management.

The evidence that legal rules matter is overwhelming. Protection of minority shareholders is weaker in countries with a civil law tradition. In many countries, the judiciary cannot be counted on to enforce contracts between investors and firms. Countries with less protection for minority shareholders have smaller equity markets, other things equal (La Porta et al. 1997a). Firms in countries with less investor protection use less outside finance (La Porta et al. 1997a) and have higher debt-equity ratios, making them more vulnerable to collapse (Friedman, Johnson, and Mitton 2003). Countries and companies with weak corporate governance can also suffer larger collapses when hit by adverse shocks (Johnson, Boone, et al. 2000; Mitton 2002; Lemmon and Lins 2003). Countries with weaker institutions have experienced greater output volatility over the past forty years (Thaicharoen 2001) and have suffered larger exchange rate crises (Pivovarsky and Thaicharoen 2001).

Other domestic institutions can adapt to some extent, but not enough to offset weak legal protection. The government has only limited ability to act directly to compensate for weak investor protection. Private companies in civil-law countries have developed various mechanisms to improve their investor relations, but these mechanisms are far from perfect. In many civil-law countries there are significant loopholes through which value can be tunneled legally out of a company (Johnson, La Porta, et al. 2000). An important complement of effective privatization is the effective legal protection of investors.

Laws and other institutions providing investor protection are persistent and hard to change. But this does not mean that legal reform is ineffective. Among countries with relatively weak legal systems, the evidence indicates that strong stock market regulation can to a large degree act as an effective substitute for judicial enforcement of contracts (Glaeser, Johnson, and Shleifer 2001). Poland provides a clear example of conditions under which a strong, independent stock-market regulator can create a well-functioning stock market, despite a weak judiciary. In all the success cases of capital market development and privatization through public sale of shares, good legal rules are of paramount importance.

Shleifer and Vishny (1997b) review the literature on corporate governance before the recent wave of findings from comparative research. La Porta et al. (2000b) describe the first wave of this research, which constitutes about twenty papers written through the early fall of 1999. However, the pace of activity in this area is accelerating. We cover about thirty new papers not included in either of these previous surveys.

Sections 1.2, 1.3, and 1.4 review the evidence against each of the Coasian positions, with particular emphasis on recent experience with privatization. Section 1.5 reports recent theoretical analysis based on this evidence. Section 1.6 concludes.

1.2   Law Matters

The strongest Coasian position is that law does not matter. If this were true, we should expect to see no significant correlation between legal rules and economic outcomes around the world. The evidence decisively rejects this hypothesis.

1.2.1   Investor Protection

The new literature on the importance of law begins with La Porta et al. (1998), who show there are systematic differences in the legal rights of investors across countries. An important explanatory factor of these differences is the origin of the legal system.

La Porta et al. (1998) propose six dimensions to evaluate the extent of protection of minority shareholders against expropriation by the insiders, as captured by a commercial code (or company law). First, the rules in some countries allow proxy voting by mail, which makes it easier for minority shareholders to exercise their voting rights. Second, the law in some countries blocks the shares for a period prior to a general meeting of shareholders, which makes it harder for shareholders to vote. Third, the law in some countries allows some type of cumulative voting, which makes it easier for a group of minority shareholders to elect at least one director of their choice. Fourth, the law in some countries incorporates a mechanism which gives the minority shareholders who feel oppressed by the board the right to sue or otherwise get relief from the board's decision. In the United States, this oppressed minority mechanism takes the very effective form of a class action suit, but in other countries there are other ways to petition the company or the courts with a complaint. Fifth, in some countries, the law gives minority shareholders a preemptive right to new issues, which protects them from dilution by the controlling shareholders who could otherwise issue new shares to themselves or to friendly parties. Sixth, the law in some countries requires relatively few shares to call an extraordinary shareholder meeting, at which the board can presumably be challenged or even replaced, whereas in other cases a large equity stake is needed for that purpose. La Porta et al. (1998) aggregate these six dimensions of shareholder protection into an anti–director rights index by simply adding a 1 when the law is protective along one of the dimensions and a 0 when it is not.

The highest shareholder-rights score in the La Porta et al. (1998) sample of forty-nine countries is 5. Investor protection is significantly higher in common-law countries, with an average score of 4, compared with French-origin civil-law countries, with an average score of 2.33. There is significant variation within legal origin, however. In the La Porta et al. data, there is no association between a country's level of economic development and its anti–director rights score, but a strong association between the score and the size of its stock market relative to gross national product (GNP).

La Porta et al. (1998, 1999) also find that the legal enforcement of contracts is weaker in countries with a civil-law tradition. For example, the efficiency of the judicial system on average is 8.15 in English-origin countries (on a scale of 1 to 10, where 10 means more efficient), but only 6.56 in French-origin countries. Legal origin therefore affects investor protection both through the rights available in the laws and the ease of enforcement of these rights.

Glaeser, Johnson, and Shleifer (2001) look in more detail at Poland and the Czech Republic, which were not included in the original La Porta et al. (1998) sample. They find that the Polish commercial code protected investors more than did the Czech code, but the most important difference was in the design and implementation of securities law. As Pistor (1995), Coffee (1999a), and Black (2000) also argue, protection under the commercial code is complementary to protection under securities law.

Slavova (1999) extends the La Porta et al. (1998) work to twenty-one formerly communist countries of Eastern Europe and the former Soviet Union. Rather than looking directly at the laws, she uses a survey to ask local legal professionals what specific rules are in place and how they are enforced. Her work confirms the analysis of La Porta et al. on the general relationship between shareholder protection and stock market development and the detailed assessment of Glaeser, Johnson, and Shleifer (2001) on Poland and the Czech Republic. For postcommunist countries, privatization has proved much more effective where capital markets have also developed at least to some extent.

Recent research has focused on some additional determinants of investor protection (Bebchuk and Roe 1999; Roe 2000, 2003; Stulz and Williamson 2003). Rajan and Zingales (2003) maintain that there is an important underlying political process. Berkowitz, Pistor, and Richard (2003) argue that the way in which legal systems were transplanted to other countries is more important than legal origin. However, Acemoglu, Johnson, and Robinson (2001) confirm that legal origin has explanatory power with respect to current institutions. They find that additional explanatory power lies with the way in which countries were colonized, and particularly whether the disease environment favored early settlers, but legal origin remains important. Using the pattern of colonization to generate a set of plausible instrumental variables, they show that institutions have a major impact on gross domestic product (GDP) per capita today (see also Acemoglu, Johnson, and Robinson 2002).

1.2.2 Outcomes

Measures of investor protection matter for economic outcomes. There is a direct effect of investor protection on the development of external capital markets. Both stock markets and debt markets are less developed in French origin countries (La Porta et al. 1997a). This is evident both in outside capitalization (measured as market capitalization owned by outsiders relative to GNP), domestic listed firms per capita, and initial public offerings per capita. For a sample of the largest firms in each country in 1996, La Porta et al. (1997a) find that French legal origin countries have significantly lower market capitalization relative to sales and to cash flow.

Subsequent work has found that lower stock market development can reduce growth (Levine and Zervos 1998), that financial development is correlated with growth (Beck, Levine, and Loayza 2000), and that the availability of external finance determines whether a country can develop capital-intensive sectors (Rajan and Zingales 1998a). Wurgler (2000) finds there is a better allocation of capital to industries in countries with more financial development.

Countries with weaker investor protection suffer more adverse consequences when hit by a shock. Johnson, Boone, et al. (2000) present evidence that the weakness of legal institutions for corporate governance had an adverse effect on the extent of depreciations and stock market declines in the Asian crisis. Corporate governance provides at least as convincing an explanation for the extent of exchange rate depreciation and stock market decline as any or all of the usual macroeconomic arguments. These results hold more generally for exchange rate crises and output volatility over the past forty years (Pivovarsky and Thaicharoen 2001; Thaicharoen 2001).

Firm-level evidence supports this view. Mitton (2002) looks at five Asian countries most affected by the 1997–1998 crisis, and finds that firms with larger inside ownership and less transparent accounting suffered larger falls in stock price. He also finds that more diversified firms suffer a greater fall, particularly if they have more uneven investment opportunities (measured in terms of Tobin's Q). This is consistent with, although it does not prove, the view that firms with weaker corporate governance faced a larger loss of investor confidence. It may also be the case that more diversified firms are less able to allocate investment properly due to internal politics, as suggested by Scharfstein and Stein (2000), and that these political problems become worse in a downturn.

Nalbantoglu and Savasoglu (2000) find similar results for Turkey in the late 1990s. Lemmon and Lins (2003) confirm Mitton's (2002) findings using the separation of control and cash-flow rights to measure the extent of agency problems. Firms in which controlling shareholders had less cash-flow rights suffered larger stock price declines in the Asian crisis. Over longer periods of time, Lins and Servaes (2002) also find a discount for diversified firms in seven emerging markets. Claessens et al. (2003) find a diversification discount for East Asian firms and worse performance for conglomerates during the East Asian crisis.

1.3 Other Institutions

The second Coasian view is that even if legal rules matter and are weak in some countries, other governmental or private institutions should adapt to protect investors. The political process or even private negotiation between firms and investors can deliver investor protection. Three main mechanisms have been suggested.

First, the government may put pressure on firms to treat investors properly, even though the law does not require it. If firms expropriate investors, they can lose other rights, such as favorable tax treatment or even the right to operate. This is the argument made by Berglof and von Thadden (1999) for many European countries. The government could try to ensure that firms behave by directly owning and running banks. In fact, government ownership of banks is significantly higher in French-origin legal systems (La Porta, Lopez-de-Silanes, and Shleifer 2002).

This approach requires an honest and effective government, but this is itself an endogenous outcome. La Porta et al. (1999) show that countries with a civil-law tradition are likely to have higher corruption and less effective government administration. Governments may also say that they want to protect investors, but in a sharp downturn find that they would rather protect entrepreneurs. This is one interpretation of what happened recently in some Asian countries, for example, Malaysia (Johnson and Mitton 2003).

Second, ownership may develop in a different way from the United States and the United Kingdom. In particular, concentrated outside ownership may allow more effective control over management. In fact, most civil-law countries have concentrated ownership. La Porta, Lopez-de-Silanes, and Shleifer (1999) show that groups of connected firms are much more usual than stand-alone firms in most countries. These groups typically include at least one company that is publicly traded or otherwise raises funds from outside investors, as well as a number of additional companies that are completely privately held. Some valuable assets are usually kept private.

This type of organization is particularly common in emerging markets where the legal protection of minority shareholder rights and creditors is weaker (La Porta et al. 1998). With the exception of Chile, the Latin American countries for which data are available have higher than average ownership concentration (La Porta and Lopez-de-Silanes 1998). Concentrated ownership also plays an important role in some European countries. For example, Gorton and Schmid (2000) find that firms are more highly valued when large shareholders own more shares in Germany. In eighteen emerging markets, Lins (2003) finds that large blockholders generally increase firm value.

The trouble with this approach is that there are still small minority shareholders in most countries with stock markets (see the data in table 2 from La Porta et al. 1997a). If large shareholders actually control management, small shareholders are not protected from expropriation. In fact, what happened in the Czech Republic over the past decade suggests that in an environment of weak legal protection, it is easy to gain control over a privatized firm and then strip it of value (Coffee 1999b; Glaeser, Johnson, and Shleifer 2001). Hellwig (2000) explains clearly the deficiencies of protection for small shareholders in Germany and Switzerland.

Third, there may be some reputation building by firms. For example, by paying higher dividends, companies in civil-law countries could establish a reputation for treating shareholders properly. In principle, repeated interaction between managers and shareholders could establish that management can be trusted, and this should increase their ability to raise more capital.

Theoretically, this argument has an important weakness. Managers may be happy to treat shareholders well when the economy is growing fast, but this does not imply anything about how they will be treated in a downturn (Johnson, Boone et al. 2000). It is very easy to expropriate shareholders for a few years and then return to the capital markets. Not surprisingly, the empirical evidence does not support the view that there is more reputation building through dividend policy in civil-law countries. In fact, La Porta et al. (2000a) show that companies in common-law countries pay higher dividends.

1.4   Legal Reform

Coffee (1999a) argues that there is an important movement toward "functional convergence," through which firms around the world are adopting U.S.-type mechanisms to protect investors. There is certainly a move toward issuing ADRs, and these seem to improve access to external capital markets. Lins, Strickland, and Zenner (2002) show that the sensitivity of investment to cash flow falls when an ADR is issued by a company from a country with a weak legal system and a less developed capital market (as defined by La Porta et al. 1997a). Reese and Weisbach (2002) show that companies in civil-law countries are more likely to list ADRs on an organized exchange in the United States, thus committing themselves to greater disclosure. All of this work supports the third Coasian view, that international contracts can get around some of the deficiencies of domestic investor protection. The implication is that while law may matter and domestic institutions cannot adapt, domestic legal reform is inessential.

The trouble is that ADRs may help companies opt into a regime of greater disclosure, but they do not stop expropriation as long as it is disclosed. The substitutes for the law thus do not work perfectly. For example, privatized Italian companies over the past decade have often issued ADRs, but there is an active debate about whether this has proved effective. ADRs have had at best limited positive effects for Mexican firms in the 1990s (Siegel 2002).

There are important processes of legal reform at work in many countries, and the evidence suggests that some of these efforts have important effects on investor protection and the financing of firms. In countries with weak legal systems, the expropriation of outside investors takes place through relatively open forms of outright theft, transfer pricing, related lending, failure to disclose relevant information when issuing securities, and failure to report earnings properly. What can prevent this when the courts are weak? Recent work suggests that in such financial markets a strong regulator can protect the property rights of outside investors and thereby improve welfare. This may be particularly important where privatization is being attempted.

The idea of focusing the regulation of securities markets on intermediaries is sometimes credited to James Landis, a contributor to the 1933 and 1934 Securities Acts in the United States (McCraw 1984). Landis reasoned that the U.S. Securities and Exchange Commission by itself could monitor neither the compliance with disclosure, reporting, and other rules by all listed firms; nor the trading practices of all market participants. Rather, the commission would regulate intermediaries, such as the brokers, the accounting firms, the investment advisors, and so on, who would in turn attempt to assure compliance with regulatory requirements by the issuers and the traders. Moreover, by maintaining substantial power over the intermediaries through its administrative relationships, including the power to issue and revoke licenses, the commission could force them to monitor market participants.

Glaeser, Johnson, and Shleifer (2001) find that the stringent—and stringently enforced—regulations in Poland, expressed in both company and securities laws, have stimulated rapid development of securities markets and enabled a large number of new firms to go public. It has also greatly facilitated the privatization of state-owned firms. The expropriation of investors has been relatively modest, and the qualitative evaluations of the Polish market have been very positive as well. In contrast, the lax—and laxly enforced—regulations in the Czech Republic have been associated with the stagnation of markets, the delisting of hundreds of privatized companies from the stock exchange, and no listing of new private companies. The expropriation of investors has apparently been rampant, and has acquired a new Czech-specific name: *tunneling*. Consistent with these concerns, the qualitative assessments of the Czech market have been poor. Starting in 1996, the Czech Republic has sharply tightened its regulations. These findings suggest that even countries with relatively weak legal systems can improve the protection of investors, and that this improvement will help firms to obtain external finance.

Poland also demonstrates the value of regulating intermediaries, particularly investment funds and brokers. When these organizations are tightly regulated, it is possible to suspend or revoke their licenses for inappropriate actions. These intermediaries then have a strong interest in ensuring both internal compliance and external vigilance. It is helpful that everyone involved with the securities market watch out for the misbehavior of others.

1.5   Theory

The Coasian argument seems extremely powerful. Why does it fail? How does this affect standard models of finance? What is the right way to model firms in countries with weak legal institutions?

1.5.1   Law and Regulation

The Coasian argument, in all three versions reviewed here, relies on the crucial assumption that the judiciary is able to enforce both existing property rights and the efficiency-enhancing contracts. But what if the courts are not efficient enough to perform this role, because they are underfinanced, unmotivated, unfamiliar with the economic issues, or even corrupt? At the least, it may then be necessary to provide a detailed legal framework to facilitate the work of the courts. In some cases, it may be necessary to go further and create a regulatory framework, which empowers a regulator to provide and enforce rules that promote more efficient outcomes. This case for regulation is stronger when the government is more interested in public welfare than in catering to incumbent firms. Glaeser, Johnson, and Shleifer (2001) and Glaeser and Shleifer (2002) discuss the incentives to enforce alternative laws and regulations more generally.

It is quite possible for a country to get stuck in an equilibrium with weak law enforcement. For example, Johnson, Kaufmann, and Shleifer (1997) argue that many countries in the former Soviet Union drove firms underground with high taxation, corruption, and regulation. This undermined the tax base of the government and made it harder to provide reasonable rule of law. Without rule of law, there is much less incentive to become a registered firm and pay taxes. Thus most of the former Soviet Union, but not the better parts of Eastern Europe, is trapped with weak law enforcement, a large unofficial economy, and a low tax base. In this environment, it proved difficult to privatize without creating widespread possibilities for tunneling.

1.5.2   Tunneling, Propping, and Debt

While the evidence reviewed above suggests that expropriation of shareholders is endemic, it is not the case that there is a zero cost of stealing in most countries. In fact, we need to understand how standard finance results are modified as the cost of stealing varies.

The original model of expropriation by managers is Jensen and Meckling (1976). Burkhart, Gromb, and Panunzi (1998) introduce the assumption that most diversion by management is costly, because (for example) it involves legal maneuvers. La Porta et al. (2002) show how to think about the cost of stealing across countries in a simple static framework. This approach has been developed further by Johnson, Boone, et al. (2000) and more recently by Friedman, Johnson, and Mitton (2003) and Shleifer and Wolfenzon (2002).

Johnson, Boone, et al. (2000) present a new theoretical explanation for the effects of corporate governance on macroeconomic outcomes. If stealing by managers increases when the expected rate of return on investment falls, then an adverse shock to investor confidence leads to increased theft and to lower capital inflow and greater attempted capital outflow for a country. These, in turn, translate into lower stock prices and a depreciated exchange rate.

The model in Friedman, Johnson, and Mitton (2003) puts ideas from Jensen (1986), Myers (1977), and La Porta et al. (2002) into a dynamic setting. The key assumption is that entrepreneurs not only can take from the firm, but they can also give. There is substantial evidence that in moments of crisis, entrepreneurs in some legal systems prop up their firms in order to keep them going (Hoshi, Kashyap, and Scharfstein 1991; Kim 2003).

Friedman, Johnson, and Mitton (2003) find that some debt finance is generally optimal because it reduces theft and induces propping in some states of the world. Thus debt can serve the role proposed by Jensen (1986) in reducing agency costs, even if there is no enforceable debt contract (i.e., effectively no collateral). However, in other states of the world, a debt over-hang may induce entrepreneurs to loot the company. Thus there can de-velop an overhang of debt with the negative consequences analyzed by Myers (1977). When the legal system is weaker, Friedman, Johnson, and Mitton show that the debt-equity ratio will usually be higher, even though this increases the probability that the firm will collapse. In weaker legal sys-tems, entrepreneurs also make investments that increase the cost of rene-gotiation, because this raises the cost of defaulting on a loan and thus in-creases the feasible amount of debt.

In this model, weaker legal institutions lead to the financing of fewer projects. But weak legal institutions can also contribute to economic crises. Weak protection of investor rights does not make shocks more likely, but it does mean that negative shocks have larger effects on the overall econ-omy. Institutions matter for a particular aspect of volatility—whether countries can suffer large collapses (Acemoglu et al. 2003). Reasonable cap-ital structures in a weak legal environment can lead to a bimodal distribu-tion of outcomes.

The data are broadly supportive. Friedman, Johnson, and Mitton (2003) show that Asian firms with weaker corporate governance were more highly indebted before the financial crisis of 1997–1998. Kim and Stone (1999) find that countries with more corporate debt suffered larger falls in output during the Asian crisis of 1997–1998. Other work suggests both that ag-gregate corporate debt is higher in countries with weaker corporate gover-nance (Demirguc-Kunt and Maksimovic 1999) and that it was higher within Asian countries for firms with weaker corporate governance. Lee, Lee, and Lee (2001), for example, demonstrate that corporate leverage was higher for *chaebol* companies than for non-*chaebol*, and highest for the top few *chaebol*.

More work is needed to link the debt findings more precisely to corpo-rate governance and macroeconomic outcomes. Caballero and Krishna-murthy (1999) is one early attempt to formalize these ideas, emphasizing implications of underinvestment in appropriate collateral that occurs due to legal problems in some countries.

This research is part of a broader movement looking at the macroeco-nomic implications of institutions. Blanchard and Wolfers (2000) argue that labor market institutions in Western Europe were appropriate, but could not handle the shocks they received in the 1970s and 1980s. In this view a functional set of institutions became dysfunctional because of a par-ticular set of shocks. More generally, Blanchard argues that macroeco-nomic dynamics may depend on institutional structures: "Institutions also matter for short-run fluctuations, with different mechanisms across coun-tries. . . . Identifying the role of differences in institutions in generating differences in macroeconomic short- and medium-run evolutions is likely to be an important topic of research in the future (2000, p. 1404).

1.6 Conclusions

A great deal of research suggests that privatization can be helpful for economic development. But the effectiveness of privatization is greater when corporate governance works well. This paper has reviewed recent evidence showing that effective laws are an important requirement for corporate governance. Without enforceable investor protection, privatization is less likely to succeed.

Law definitely matters. Countries with better investor protection have better developed financial markets and more growth. The determinants of law are complex, but the origin of the legal system is an important factor.

Legal origin is not destiny. Laws can be changed and other institutions can adapt to some extent. Civil-law European countries have become rich with more government ownership and more concentrated ownership than is seen in common-law countries. But it is a fallacy to infer that compensating institutions fully compensate for the shortcomings of the law.

Legal reform works. Countries as diverse as Chile, Germany, Poland, and South Korea have all made progress recently with changing the rules for investor protection. There are many different ways to change the rules, and the required changes vary by country. But investor protection is advancing in many countries, precisely because people have learned that it matters for economic development.

We are not arguing that all countries could or should become just like the United States. But in important dimensions we see countries around the world adopting investor protection measures that are modeled on U.S. law. The evidence suggests that when these measures are implemented in an enforceable way, they can change both the extent of investor protection and the ability of firms to obtain external finance. Properly designed U.S.-type innovations can work even in countries with quite different legal origins, such as Germany and Poland.

Of course, confidence in the United States has been shaken recently by corporate scandals, particularly concerning accounting issues. But, at least so far, there have been only four major scandals: Enron, WorldCom, Tyco, and Adelphia, and the U.S. regulatory system is responding (see Coffee 2003). It is important not to exaggerate the dimensions of the U.S. problems with corporate governance. At the same time, we do not think that the United States has ideal or even best practices on all dimensions of accounting, regulations, and corporate governance. There is clearly a need for the reforms now underway (and perhaps more).

By giving us a clear framework to think about contracts, Ronald Coase shed a great deal of light on many issues, including comparative corporate governance and privatization. It is an indication of the power of his approach, that research is now advancing by trying to augment Coasian arguments about how firms are financed around the world. The Coasian idea that private contracts can attain efficient outcomes is powerful and in many instances correct. The right question is how to make it easier for the private sector to write its own efficient contracts. In many cases, this can be achieved only through changing the broader legal rules that underpin capital and other markets.

References

Acemoglu, Daron, Simon Johnson, and James A. Robinson. 2001. Colonial origins of comparative development: An empirical investigation. *American Economic Review* 91:1369–401.

———. 2002. Reversal of fortune: Geography and institutions in the making of the modern world income distribution. *Quarterly Journal of Economics* 117:1231–94.

Acemoglu, Daron, Simon Johnson, James A. Robinson, and Yunyong Thai-charoen. 2003. Institutional causes, macroeconomic symptoms: Volatility, crises, and growth. *Journal of Monetary Economics* 50 (1): 49–123.

Bebchuk, Lucian Ayre, and Mark J. Roe. 1999. A theory of path dependence in corporate ownership and governance. *Stanford Law Review* 52 (52): 127–170.

Beck, Thorsten, Ross Levine, and Norman Loayza. 2000. Finance and the sources of growth. *Journal of Financial Economics* 58 (1–2): 261–300.

Berglof, Erik, and Ernst-Ludwig von Thadden. 1999. The changing corporate governance paradigm: Implications for transition and developing countries. SITE manuscript. Stockholm: Stockholm School of Economics.

Berkowitz, Daniel, Katharina Pistor, and Jean-Francois Richard. 2003. Economic development, legality, and the transplant effect. *European Economic Review* 47 (1): 165–195.

Black, Bernard S. 2000. The core institutions that support strong securities markets. *Business Lawyer* 55:1565–607.

Blanchard, Olivier. 2000. What do we know about macroeconomics that Fisher and Wicksell did not? *Quarterly Journal of Economics* 115 (4): 1375–410.

Blanchard, Olivier, and Justin Wolfers. 2000. The role of shocks and institutions in the rise of European unemployment: The aggregate evidence. *Economic Journal* 110 (March): 1–33.

Burkhart, Mike, Denis Gromb, and Fausto Panunzi. 1998. Why higher takeover premia protect minority shareholders. *Journal of Political Economy* 106:172–204.

Caballero, Ricardo, and Arvind Krishnamurthy. 1999. Emerging markets crises: An asset markets perspective. Department of Economics, unpublished manuscript. Cambridge: MIT.

Chopra, Ajai, Kenneth Kang, Meral Karasulu, Hong Liang, Henry Ma, and Anthony Richards. 2001. From crisis to recovery in Korea: Strategy, achievements, and lessons. IMF Working Paper no. 01/154. Washington, D.C.: International Monetary Fund, Asia Pacific Department.

Claessens, Stijn, Simeon Djankov, Joseph P. H. Fan, and Larry H. P. Lang. 2003. The benefits and costs of internal markets: Evidence from Asia's financial crisis. World Bank manuscript. Available at http://www1.fee.uva.nl./fm/papers/ Claessens/benefits.pdf.

Coase, Ronald. 1960. The problem of social cost. *Journal of Law and Economics* 31–44.

Coffee, John C., Jr. 1999a. The future as history: The prospects for global convergence in corporate governance and its implications. *Northwestern University Law Review* 93:631–707.

———. 1999b. Privatization and corporate governance: The lessons from securities market failure. *Journal of Corporation Law* 25:1–39.

———. 2003. What caused Enron? A capsule social and economic history of the 1990s. Columbia Law and Economics Working Paper no. 214. Columbia University, January.

Demirguc-Kunt, Asli, and Vojislav Maksimovic. 1999. Institutions, financial markets, and firms' debt maturity. *Journal of Financial Economics* 54:295–336.

Easterbrook, Frank H., and Daniel R. Fischel. 1991. *The economic structure of corporate law.* Cambridge: Harvard University Press.

Friedman, Eric, Simon Johnson, and Todd Mitton. 2003. Tunneling and propping. *Journal of Comparative Economics*, forthcoming.

Glaeser, Edward, Simon Johnson, and Andrei Shleifer. 2001. Coase versus the Coasians. *Quarterly Journal of Economics* 116 (August): 853–899.

Glaeser, Edward, and Andrei Shleifer. 2002. Legal origins. *Quarterly Journal of Economics* 117 (November): 1193–230.

Gomez, Edmund Terence, and K. S. Jomo. 1998. *Malaysia's political economy: Politics, patronage, and profits.* Cambridge: Cambridge University Press.

Gorton, Gary, and Frank Schmid. 2000. Universal banking and the performance of German firms. *Journal of Financial Economics* 58 (1–2): 29–80.

Hellwig, Martin. 2000. On the economics and politics of corporate finance and corporate control. In *Corporate governance,* ed. X. Vives, 95–134. Cambridge: Cambridge University Press.

Hoshi, Takeo, Anil Kashyap, and David Scharfstein. 1991. Corporate structure, liquidity, and investment: Evidence from Japanese industrial groups. *Quarterly Journal of Economics* 106:33–60.

Jensen, Michael C. 1986. Agency costs of free cash flow, corporate finance, and takeovers. *American Economic Review* 76:323–329.

Jensen, Michael C., and William H. Meckling. 1976. Theory of the firm: Managerial behavior, agency costs, and ownership structure. *Journal of Financial Economics* 3:305–360.

Johnson, Simon, Peter Boone, Alasdair Breach, and Eric Friedman. 2000. Corporate governance in the Asian financial crisis. *Journal of Financial Economics* 58:141–186.

Johnson, Simon, Daniel Kaufmann, and Andrei Shleifer. 1997. The unofficial economy in transition. *Brookings Papers on Economic Activity,* Issue no. 2:159–239. Washington, D.C.: Brookings Institution.

Johnson, Simon, Rafael La Porta, Florencio Lopez-de-Silanes, and Andrei Shleifer. 2000. Tunneling. *American Economic Review* 90 (2): 22–27.

Johnson, Simon, and Todd Mitton. 2003. Cronyism and capital controls: Evidence from Malaysia. *Journal of Financial Economics* 67 (2): 351–382.

Kim, Se-Jik. 2003. Bailout and conglomeration. *Journal of Financial Economics*, forthcoming.

Kim, Se-Jik, and Mark R. Stone. 1999. Corporate leverage, bankruptcy, and output adjustment in post-crisis East Asia. IMF Working Paper no. WP/99/143. Washington, D.C.: International Monetary Fund, October.

La Porta, Rafael, and Florencio Lopez-de-Silanes. 1998. Capital markets and legal institutions. In *Beyond the Washington consensus: Institutions matter,* ed. Shadid Burki and Guillermo Perry, Washington, D.C.: World Bank.

La Porta, Rafael, Florencio Lopez-de-Silanes, Andrei Shleifer, 2002. Government ownership of banks. *Journal of Finance* 57:265–302.

La Porta, Rafael, Florencio Lopez-de-Silanes, Andrei Shleifer, and Robert Vishny. 1997a. Legal determinants of external finance. *Journal of Finance* 52:1131–50.

———. 1997b. Shareholders' rights: Appendix. Unpublished appendix to "Law and finance," *Journal of Political Economy* 106:1113–55.

———. 1998. Law and finance. *Journal of Political Economy* 106:1113–55.

———. 1999. The quality of government. *Journal of Law, Economics, and Organization* 15:222–279.

———. 2000a. Agency problems and dividend policies around the world. *Journal of Finance* 55 (February): 1–33.

———. 2000b. Investor protection and corporate governance. *Journal of Financial Economics* 58 (1–2): 3–28.

———. 2002. Investor Protection and Corporate valuation. *Journal of Finance* 57:1147–70.

Lee, Jong-Wha, Young Soo Lee, and Byung-Sun Lee. 2001. The determination of corporate debt in Korea. *Asian Economic Journal* 14 (4).

Lemmon, Michael L., and Karl V. Lins. 2003. Ownership structure, corporate governance, and firm value: Evidence from the East Asian financial crisis. *Journal of Finance*, forthcoming.

Levine, Ross, and Sara Zervos. 1998. Stock markets, banks, and economic growth. *American Economic Review* 88:537–558.

Lins, Karl. 2003. Equity ownership and firm value in emerging markets. *Journal of Financial and Quantitative Analysis,* forthcoming.

Lins, Karl, and Henri Servaes. 2002. Is corporate diversification beneficial in emerging markets? *Financial Management* 31 (2): 5–31.

Lins, Karl, Deon Strickland, and Marc Zenner. 2002. Do non-U.S. firms issue stock on U.S. equity markets to relax capital constraints? Manuscript. August. University of North Carolina and Ohio State University.

McCraw, Thomas K. 1984. *Prophets of regulation.* Cambridge, Mass.: Belknap Press.

Mitton, Todd. 2002. A cross-firm analysis of the impact of corporate governance on the East Asian financial crisis. *Journal of Financial Economics* 64:215–242.

Myers, Stewart C. 1977. Determinants of corporate borrowing. *Journal of Financial Economics* 5:147–175.

Nalbantoglu, Osman, and Serkan Savasoglu. 2000. Impact of corporate governance and foreign trading on firm returns during crises: The case of Turkey. Harvard University, Department of Economics. Manuscript, April.

Pistor, Katharina. 1995. Law meets the market: Matches and mismatches in transition economies. Harvard University Manuscript.

Pivovarsky, Alexander, and Yunyong Thaicharoen. 2001. Institutions and the severity of currency crises. Manuscript, May. MIT and Harvard University.

Rajan, Raghuram, and Luigi Zingales. 1998a. Financial dependence and growth. *American Economic Review* 88 (3): 559–586.

———. 1998b. Which capitalism? Lessons from the East Asian crisis. *Journal of Applied Corporate Finance* 11:40–48.

———. 2003. The politics of financial development. *Journal of Financial Economics,* forthcoming.

Reese, William A., Jr., and Michael S. Weisbach. 2002. Protection of minority shareholder interests, cross-listings in the United States, and subsequent equity offerings. *Journal of Financial Economics* 66:65–104.

Roe, Mark J. 2000. Political foundations for separating ownership from corporate control. *Stanford Law Review* 53 (December): 539–606.

———. 2003. *Political determinants of corporate governance.* Oxford: Oxford University Press.

Scharfstein, David S., and Jeremy C. Stein. 2000. The dark side of internal capital markets: Divisional rent-seeking and inefficient investment. *Journal of Finance* 55:2537–64.

Shleifer, Andrei, and Robert Vishny. 1997a. The limits of arbitrage. *Journal of Finance* 52 (1): 35–55.

———. 1997b. A survey of corporate governance. *Journal of Finance* 52 (2): 737–783.

Shleifer, Andrei, and Daniel Wolfenzon. 2002. Investor protection and equity markets. *Journal of Financial Economics* 66:3–27.

Siegel, Jordan. 2002. Can foreign firms bond themselves effectively by renting U.S. securities laws? MIT, Sloan School of Management. Unpublished manuscript.

Slavova, Stefka. 1999. Law and finance in transition economies. Financial Markets Group Special Paper no. 121. London: London School of Management, December.

Steinfeld, Edward S. 1998. *Forging reform in China.* Cambridge: Cambridge University Press.

———. 2000. AMCs in China. CLSA Emerging Markets: China Research. London: CLSA, October.

Stulz, René M., and Rohan Williamson. 2003. Culture, openness, and finance. *Journal of Financial Economics,* forthcoming.

Thaicharoen, Yunyong. 2001. Institutions and output fluctuations. MIT, Department of Economics. Manuscript, May.

Wurgler, Jeffrey. 2000. Financial markets and the allocation of capital. *Journal of Financial Economics* 58:187–214.

Comment   Cassey Lee Hong Kim

The early literature in privatization focused on the importance of private ownership for efficiency as well the role of competition in soliciting behavior that would benefit consumers. In the past few years, the emphasis in the privatization literature has shifted to the issue of corporate governance. What brought about this change? Were private ownership and competition themselves insufficient to ensure that the full benefits of privatization will materialize? The gap that corporate governance fills in the privatization literature can be seen from figure 1C.1.

Private ownership provides incentives for firms to operate efficiently

Cassey Lee Hong Kim is head of the department of applied economics at the University of Malaya.

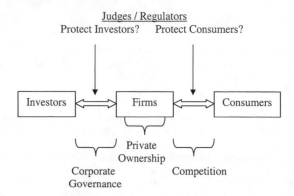

Fig. 1C.1   Agents and institutions in privatization

while competition ensures that such efficiency gains are passed on to the consumers. Corporate governance looks at the missing link between investors (suppliers of finance) and those who control the firms (management). More specifically, it addresses the question of how investors can get a return on their investments (Shleifer and Vishny 1997). Will this come about "naturally" (emerge spontaneously) or do we need to enact effective laws that protect investors?

Johnson and Shleifer attribute to Coase (1960) the idea that private contracts can be written between investors and managers such that the former's interests are safeguarded. In their paper, Johnson and Shleifer argue that, contrary to Coase, law matters. The authors also review the evidence against two weaker variants of the Coase argument. The first variant involves the emergence of spontaneous actions by governments or private institutions (e.g., concentrated shareholders) to protect the interests of investors in the presence of weak legal rules. The second variant goes one step further by postulating the emergence of capital markets outside the country with weak legal system to overcome this problem.

Coase I

Johnson and Shleifer marshal a wide range of empirical evidence involving many different levels of analysis to support their argument that law matters (fig. 1C.2). The strongest evidence comes from country case studies involving Poland and the Czech Republic (Glaeser, Johnson, and Shleifer 2001) that directly attempt to link stock market development to legal institutions that protect investors. The authors also cite numerous papers by La Porta et al. that found relationships between legal traditions and legal institutions for investor protection, and between legal institutions and economic performance. Compared to all these areas, the least developed area is the evolution of legal traditions (Glaeser and Shleifer 2000 is an example). It is not very clear from the literature why private contracts cannot be written to solve principal-agent problem under corporate gov-

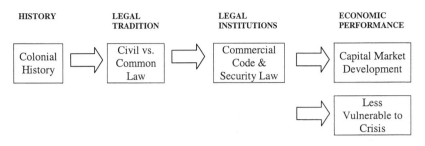

Fig. 1C.2   How law matters in corporate governance

ernance. Is it simply because the Coasian assumption about zero transactions cost does not exist? Or is something more fundamental happening here?

It is plausible that there are circumstances where the gains that a manager can obtain from an action that works against the owner's interest exceed any amount the latter can compensate the former. A private contract between such parties can of course involve some form of agreed-upon punishment. But there are limits to such punishment without infringing on a person's fundamental rights. Severe punishments such as imprisonment can only be enforced in the realm of the law and not private contracts. In this sense, it is not just that law matters, but rather that law complements private contracts. For matters of a smaller scale, such as a firm's quarterly performance, contracts are still effective.

Coase II

What if law matters, as Johnson and Shleifer argue, but is too weak in a given country? Can institutions—both public and private—overcome this by taking over the financing and management of corporations? The first option is tantamount to renationalization—an action that fundamentally transforms the objective of the firm from a profit-oriented to a public or politically oriented one. Once this is done, we are back where we started: namely, the preprivatization situation. Hence, the problem with this is not (as Johnson and Shleifer argue) that the state—the new owner—may not be honest or effective but rather that it has a different objective from private institutions. Very often, renationalization of privatized entities is undertaken to avoid political fallout. One way to look at this problem is to apply Coase's (1937) theory of the firm to the state. As long as private ownership best serves the state's objective, it is upheld. Otherwise, the boundary of the state is re-enlarged by renationalizing the firm, perhaps at least until the legal institutions pertaining to corporate governance are strengthened.[1] To

---

1. There are other problems when this occurs. When privatization exercises are accompanied by liberalization via market entry, renationalization of the incumbent poses considerable regulatory problems.

further complicate matters, the evolution of such institutions is, as Johnson and Shleifer put it, "an endogenous outcome" (albeit in a different context).

In the second option, when the legal rules are weak, private institutions can take over the management of the firm, possibly via concentrated ownership. The empirical evidence that Johnson and Shleifer discuss is intriguing. For example, they allude to the importance of relationship-based (bank) financing. It is not clear, however, whether relationship-based financing is an adaptation to weak investor protection by legal institutions or whether this is inferior to the Anglo-Saxon, arm's-length type of equity financing. Finally, the authors highlight interesting evidence on the impact of large shareholding. Firms are more highly valued when large shareholders own more shares in Germany (and emerging markets), while large shareholders can lead to expropriation at the expense of small holders in the Czech Republic. Do these findings contradict each other, or does it mean large shareholding is beneficial only if some form of protection is accorded to minority shareholders?

Coase III

The problem of weak domestic-investor protection is overcome in the third Coasian argument through bypasses via sourcing funds in international markets. In other words, there is no need to improve domestic investor protection since firms can source funds from outside the domestic capital markets. Is this second-best, and is constrained efficiency achieved? Johnson and Shleifer give the impression that there is very little empirical work that addresses these questions. Instead, the authors argue that legal reforms are beneficial. One such reform—for countries with strong legal systems (the Neuer Markt)—involves the formation of a new segment of the capital market for start-ups with higher degrees of investor protection. This could be perceived as supporting the third Coasian argument if the argument is construed as involving external contracts rather than international contracts. After all, markets such as the Neuer Markt appear to have an "enclave" characteristic (i.e., a different set of rules seems to apply). For countries with weak legal systems, Johnson and Shleifer propose a different type of reform that focuses on regulating financial intermediaries. The effectiveness of this will, of course, depend on whether the political system is conducive to the establishment of an independent and effective regulator. In this regard, the political economy of corporate governance reform seems to be the next important research agenda.

References

Coase, Ronald. 1937. The nature of the firm. *Economica* 4:386–405.
———. 1960. The problem of social cost. *Journal of Law and Economics* 3:1–44.

Glaeser, Edward, Simon Johnson, and Andrei Shleifer. 2001. Coase versus the Coasians. *Quarterly Journal of Economics* 116 (3): 853–899.

Glaeser, Edward, and Andrei Shleifer. 2002. Legal origins. *Quarterly Journal of Economics* 117 (November): 1193–1230.

Shleifer, Andrei, and Robert Vishny. 1997. A survey of corporate governance. *Journal of Finance* 52 (2): 737–783.

Comment   Richard H. Snape

Many of us would agree with Johnson and Shleifer that the 1990s have shown that institutions do matter, as do transaction and agency costs; that vacuums are not necessarily filled by socially useful activities; that governments do not necessarily pursue the general good; and that they are often weak and captive. Legal systems matter.

A great deal of recent research work is drawn upon in this paper. Efficiently operating capital markets matter for development and even if efficient institutions may develop endogenously in the long term, a great deal may be wasted in the meantime. But, it is suggested, countries can be stuck in an equilibrium of weak law enforcement, a large unofficial (gray) economy, and a low tax base. Such an economy is very difficult to privatize without "tunneling," which does not just have distributional effects, but efficiency and development effects also.

If legal systems are weak, how does one move to give confidence to investors—particularly small investors? There is an endorsement of Poland compared with the Czech Republic, for example—a strong and independent regulator of the stock market, despite a weak judiciary. The stock market is not the only institution, of course. There is a case for regulation and prudential requirements on a whole range of financial intermediaries. These intermediaries can be large enough to monitor those in whom they invest, but they in turn need to be monitored and, if necessary, disciplined.

Of course, we quickly hit the problem of who regulates or monitors the regulators.

We can specify good principles of regulation, but how can they be legislated or enforced if the government is weak, populist, complicit, or even corrupt?

What perhaps could be developed further in the paper is an examination of how to move to better regulation. There are two questions:

1. What are good principles for regulation?
2. How do we introduce them?

Richard H. Snape was deputy chairman of the Productivity Commission, Australia, and emeritus professor at Monash University. He passed away in the fall of 2002.

We have some examples of change provided—Chile, Germany, Poland, and South Korea—but there is more to be pursued here. We can hardly expect civil-law countries to change their legal systems without revolution (and, incidentally, Malaysia is not a civil-law country). Perhaps we can take some lessons from trade policy.

Why did countries move from inward-looking to outwardly oriented policies? Partly from empirical evidence, partly from change in development theory; partly from external pressures (from the International Monetary Fund or the World Bank); partly from crises. Governments were also required to stand up to protected interests, and this of course is the critical factor.

The important literature drawn upon in the paper is part of the empirical work that can facilitate the change. It can be compared with work by Anne Krueger and others in the 1970s and 1980s in the trade policy area. Crises can help, and the Asian financial crises have brought the lesson home to some. But as was mentioned by Mari Pangestu, we need the substance of good regulation and not just institutions with fine-sounding names. Moreover, we cannot develop appropriate institutions, including institutions to regulate, without developing a framework for acceptance of them. Knowing the right rules is one thing; knowing how to introduce them is another.

Public education is crucial in getting the framework to introduced good regulation for corporate governance as well as good trade policy.

Why did trade policy change in Australia?

There was education, measurement of costs of protection, a perceived crisis, and a government that took an economy-wide perspective—and a parliamentary opposition that did not oppose the changes. But populism is always present and education is an ongoing requirement.

Antitrust Merger Policy
Lessons from the
Australian Experience

Philip L. Williams and Graeme Woodbridge

2.1 Introduction

Antitrust policy is one branch of public policy that may be used to limit the market power of deregulated and privatized public utilities. The experience over the last two decades or so of the telecommunications and airlines industries in the United States and of many of the deregulated utilities in the United Kingdom is that the opening to competition of monopolies that were previously protected by statute or regulation led initially to entry; but, after a period of a few years, there were strong incentives for these new enterprises to merge. This experience suggests that countries contemplating privatization and deregulation of public utilities should consider whether their antitrust regimes (and, in particular, their merger policies) are appropriate to the period of privatization and deregulation.

The current provisions of Australia's antitrust merger regime have remained virtually unchanged since 1974. Australia's experience with these provisions in the subsequent quarter of a century yields some useful lessons for countries that are contemplating the introduction, or reform, of their antitrust policies in preparation of greater reliance on market constraints on their public utilities. This paper assesses the Australian experience and

Philip L. Williams is executive chairman of Frontier Economics Pty Ltd and a professorial fellow of Melbourne Business School, University of Melbourne, Australia. Graeme Woodbridge is senior industry analyst with CommSec. He wrote this paper while he was a consultant with Frontier Economics Pty Ltd.

We would like to thank Maureen Brunt, Charles Calomiris, Frances Hanks, Chong-Hyun Nam, Chander Shekhar, members of the Economics-COPS seminar at Monash University, referees of the National Bureau of Economic Research and University of Chicago Press, and the editors of this volume for comments on an earlier draft.

argues that certain features of the Australian regime are useful contributions to the international stock of regulatory design, whereas other features of the Australian regime are best not replicated.

Any assessment of public policy must ultimately depend on the social welfare function that one adopts. This paper will adopt as a definition of *value* the difference between willingness to pay and opportunity cost; and anything that enhances value will be regarded as good. Like much economic activity, mergers are undertaken because they enhance the value that accrues to the parties to the merger. But value may accrue to a person either because more value has been created or because he or she is able to gain a larger share of the value that exists. It is common to label behavior that creates value as *efficient,* and to label behavior that merely enhances bargaining power as *monopolization* or *rent seeking.*[1] If we adopt the value standard in assessing public policy, monopoly is neither uniformly good nor uniformly bad. Nevertheless, antitrust policy carries a general presumption against monopoly because one classic way in which a monopolist increases its bargaining power with respect to its customers is by limiting the amount of output it is prepared to supply. That is, the monopolist deliberately destroys value in order to increase its bargaining power with respect to its customers. This paper accepts this presumption. It accepts that a public policy motivated by the maximization of value will seek to prevent mergers that enhance monopoly power because, in general, the enhancement of monopoly power will diminish value.

Mergers and takeovers involve the sale of assets. Like other forms of trade, mergers occur because the buyer's willingness to pay for the assets exceeds the seller's opportunity cost of the sale. The gains from trade can derive from three principal sources: an increase in economic efficiency, an increase in monopoly power, or an increase in the scope for rent seeking more broadly. The increase in economic efficiency can take many forms; but these generally can be classified as either identifying assets that the market has previously undervalued, or taking advantage of some type of synergy that can better be realized within a merged entity than by means of trade between the activities of the two enterprises. The increase in monopoly power is generally a result of an increase in concentration in a particular market, which may lead to problems of monopoly either because of increased likelihood of collusion (see Stigler 1964; Green and Porter 1984) or because of independent behavior (Cournot 1929; Cowling and Waterson 1976). In addition to seeking monopoly rents, mergers and acquisitions can be motivated by other forms of rent seeking. For instance, parties

---

1. According to Buchanan (1980), economic rent "is that part of the payment to an owner of resources over and above that which those resources could command in any alternative use" (3). As monopoly profits are payments above opportunity costs, they are economic rents. They are not the only form of economic rents, however. For instance, economic rents can be achieved by those favored by government licences or from favorable government contracts.

with close alignments with the government may find it profitable to acquire a firm whose profits are driven by success in gaining government contracts.

Antitrust merger policy that aims to maximize value should distinguish between mergers with these motivations. Putting the matter crudely, it should allow to proceed those mergers that are motivated by economic efficiency and it should disallow those mergers that are motivated by an increase in monopoly power or rent seeking. In practice, a particular merger can rarely be placed neatly into these boxes. For instance, real-life mergers have the uncomfortable habit of straddling efficiency and monopoly power—with one foot firmly in one box and the other foot more or less firmly in the other. The task of the regulator or the court is to decide what is going on. If the merger is clearly all about increasing the monopoly power of the parties or rent seeking, it should be stopped. If there are clear efficiency advantages or if it is not clear which of the considerations predominates, the merger should be allowed to proceed on the ground that regulators and courts should place the onus of proof (as a lawyer would put it) on the party that is advocating interference in the freedom of the market.

This paper will return to the point of onus of proof toward the end. It is clearly important in the rules and operation of any antitrust policy. It also biases many judgments within transition economies as to whether antitrust policy should be adopted. Even if one adopts the standard of value as one's standard of public policy, one may still be opposed to antitrust policy on the ground that the overwhelming majority of all mergers are value enhancing. This presumption would have particular appeal in an economy, such as Hong Kong, where international trade and investment flows are relatively free. But even in Hong Kong one can readily observe economic activities, such as rail links and transport tunnels, where monopoly power might be used to destroy value. It is appropriate to ask how antitrust policy might be structured so as to enhance the value that is created by industries such as these. That is the question that is addressed by this paper: If a nation is contemplating antitrust merger policy, does the experience of Australia offer any guidance as to how value might be maximized? In drawing on Australia's experience we primarily focus on the success of Australian policy in distinguishing between mergers that enhance efficiency and mergers that enhance monopoly power. Although mergers may be enhanced by rent seeking, this is currently not a major driver of mergers or acquisitions in Australia. We do, however, make some comments at the end of the paper on how changes in the Australian merger laws could reduce the incentive for rent seeking.

The distinction between conduct prompted by economic efficiency and conduct prompted by monopoly power is fundamental to antitrust policy. But merger policy has a very particular set of issues that sets it apart from other elements of antitrust policy: timeliness and secrecy are most often crucial for its successful implementation. Timeliness is related to secrecy in some obvious ways: The longer the regulator delays dealing with a confidential matter, the greater is the danger that information will leak to the market. The leaking of information may raise the price of the target and thereby reduce the gains to the bidder (Schwert 1996). If gains to the bidder are reduced by the processes of the law, there is a danger that the incentives for enterprises to seek out efficiency-enhancing mergers will be reduced. Even in a public process, such as a trial, timeliness is related to efficiency, not via secrecy but through the spread of information. A long trial may make efficiency-enhancing opportunities disappear because the world changes or because a more attractive bidder may appear, or because the second most attractive bidder loses interest. To repeat, the danger with these happenings is not that they discourage mergers that are motivated by increasing monopoly power. The danger is that delays and consequent flows of information may discourage enterprises from searching out efficiency-enhancing merger opportunities. This is not to imply that process must be kept secret once the merger has been made public. To do so runs the danger of undermining confidence in the decision-making process.

These reflections lead us to propose that two criteria are necessary if antitrust merger policy is to enhance value. In the first place, the criteria for assessing mergers should direct the regulators or the courts to allow those mergers that promote economic efficiency and to disallow those mergers that promote monopoly power. Second, the process of assessment should be able to be conducted in a way that maintains confidentiality (until the merger is made public by the firms involved) and is speedy.

This paper explains the formal processes of Australian antitrust merger policy and how it performs against these twin sets of criteria. The experience over the last quarter of a century is that Australia's formal, statutory processes have been quite unsuitable when assessed against these criteria. The paper explains why the delay and public nature of these processes have made them quite unsuitable. These problems with the formal, statutory processes have led to the evolution of a process of confidential, informal clearance of mergers. This process has no basis in any Australian statute. Confidential, informal clearance of mergers has satisfied the criterion of a speedy and confidential process, but it has not enabled the proper weighing of efficiency and monopoly. The process of informal clearance of mergers has led, in turn, to two other problems: a lack of formal guidance by means of precedent, and the assumption by the antitrust regulator of an unhealthy degree of power to extract concessions from the enterprises that wish to merge. In brief, Australia's reliance on discretion over rules has limited the extent to which its merger policy has been able to enhance the value generated by the Australian economy.

This criticism applies to antitrust merger policy in other jurisdictions. Antitrust merger policy in both the United States and Europe has become an administrative rather than a court-centered process. This has caused lawyers to raise questions about appropriate processes and the development of the law. As noted by Sims and Herman,

> [B]ecause ... most merger objections are resolved by consent decree; merger litigation (at least outside the hospital industry) has become a rare beast. Given that consent decree negotiations are private, and confidentiality rules (and sometimes agency prudence) limit what can be disclosed about why the agency did what it did, it is increasingly difficult for those who are not interacting regularly with the agency and other merger lawyers to be fully informed about how the agencies (and, to an even greater degree, particularly staffers) are approaching specific types of problems. (1997, 883)

2.2 Proscribed Behavior

2.2.1 The Wording of Section 50

The principal proscription of mergers in Australia's antitrust law is to be found in s. 50 of the Trade Practices Act. Its present wording is (in part) as follows:

> s. 50 Prohibition of acquisitions that would result in a substantial lessening of competition
> (1) A corporation must not directly or indirectly:
>   (a) acquire shares in the capital of a body corporate; or
>   (b) acquire any assets of a person;
>   if the acquisition would have the effect, or be likely to have the effect, of substantially lessening competition in a market.
> (2) A person must not directly or indirectly:
>   (a) acquire shares in the capital of a corporation; or
>   (b) acquire any assets of a corporation;
>   if the acquisition would have the effect, or be likely to have the effect, of substantially lessening competition in a market.
> (3) Without limiting the matters that may be taken into account for the purposes of subsections (1) and (2) in determining whether the acquisition would have the effect, or be likely to have the effect, of substantially lessening competition in a market, the following matters must be taken into account:
>   (a) the actual and potential level of import competition in the market;
>   (b) the height of barriers to entry to the market;
>   (c) the level of concentration in the market;
>   (d) the degree of countervailing power in the market;
>   (e) the likelihood that the acquisition would result in the acquirer being able to significantly and sustainably increase prices or profit margins;
>   (f) the extent to which substitutes are available in the market or are likely to be available in the market;

(g) the dynamic characteristics of the market, including growth, innovation and product differentiation;

(h) the likelihood that the acquisition would result in the removal from the market of a vigorous and effective competitor;

(i) the nature and extent of vertical integration in the market.

The principal mergers that have been dealt with under s. 50 are listed after the references and summarized in the appendix to this paper. The appendix summarizes the cases in diagrams that have been constructed similar to the trees used in the extended form of game theory for games that take place over time. The decisions closer to the top of the page occurred prior to the decisions lower on the page. At any moment, the player who has to make the decision is confronted with the options that are outlined. The option that was, in fact, selected is that which is indicated by an arrow.

Some of the cases summarized in the appendix were dealt with under a version of s. 50 whose criterion differed from that which is quoted above. The original proscription was similar to the present. The first merger that came before the courts was the attempted acquisition of Avis Rent-a-Car by Ansett Transport Industries (*Ansett Avis*). This was tried following the amendments to the Trade Practices Act in 1977 in which the test of substantial lessening of competition was amended to that of an acquisition by a corporation that would be, or would be likely to be, in a position to control or dominate a market. The trial judge in *Ansett Avis* considered the phrase "control or dominate." He found "that the word 'dominate' is to be construed as something less than 'control'" (*Ansett* Avis at 17717) and, because of this, the word "control" was redundant. It was removed.

The only other three mergers to be tried under the section—Australian Meat Holdings' attempt to acquire Thomas Borthwick and Sons (*AMH*), the attempt by Arnotts to acquire the biscuit business of Nabisco Australia (*Arnotts*), and the attempt by Davids Holdings to take over QIW Retailers (*QIW v. Davids*)—were assessed according to the criterion of dominance of a market.

The present section came into effect on 21 January 1993. Although proceedings have been issued under the current section, no cases have resulted in judgment. The reasons for the lack of litigation under the section will be explored in section 2.2.2 of this paper.

The current (and original) test of substantial lessening of competition uses words that appear elsewhere in the antitrust provisions of the Trade Practices Act. This means that we are able to speak confidently of the meaning of the test without the aid of a decision in a trial under the section. The seminal authority for the phrase is to be found in a case under s. 47 involving exclusive dealing: the decision of the full federal court in *Outboard Marine v. Hecar* appeal. In that decision, the full federal court held

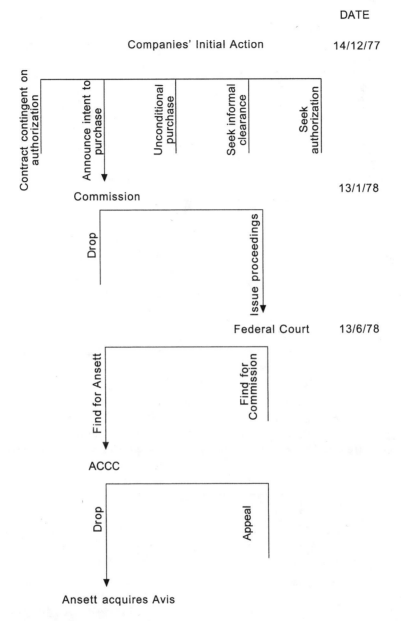

DATE

Companies' Initial Action   14/12/77

Contract contingent on authorization

Announce intent to purchase

Unconditional purchase

Seek informal clearance

Seek authorization

Commission   13/1/78

Drop

Issue proceedings

Federal Court   13/6/78

Find for Ansett

Find for Commission

ACCC

Drop

Appeal

Ansett acquires Avis

Fig. 2.1 *Ansett Avis*

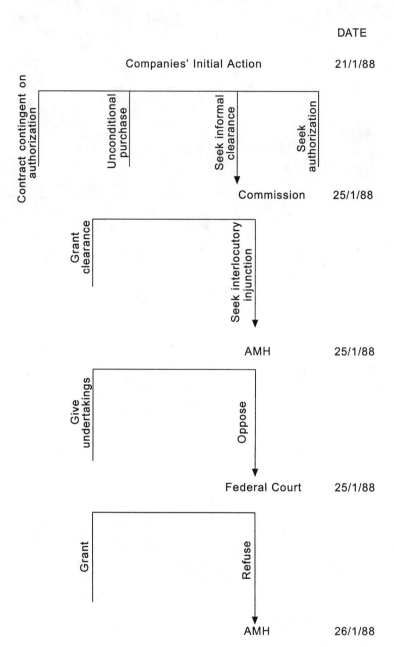

DATE

Companies' Initial Action   21/1/88

Contract contingent on authorization

Unconditional purchase

Seek informal clearance

Seek authorization

Commission   25/1/88

Grant clearance

Seek interlocutory injunction

AMH   25/1/88

Give undertakings

Oppose

Federal Court   25/1/88

Grant

Refuse

AMH   26/1/88

Fig. 2.2   *AMH*

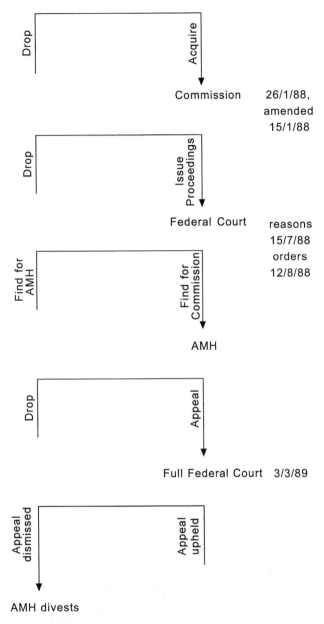

Drop

Acquire

Commission   26/1/88,
              amended
              15/1/88

Drop

Issue
Proceedings

Federal Court   reasons
                 15/7/88
                 orders
                 12/8/88

Find for
AMH

Find for
Commission

AMH

Drop

Appeal

Full Federal Court   3/3/89

Appeal
dismissed

Appeal
upheld

AMH divests

Fig. 2.2   (cont.)

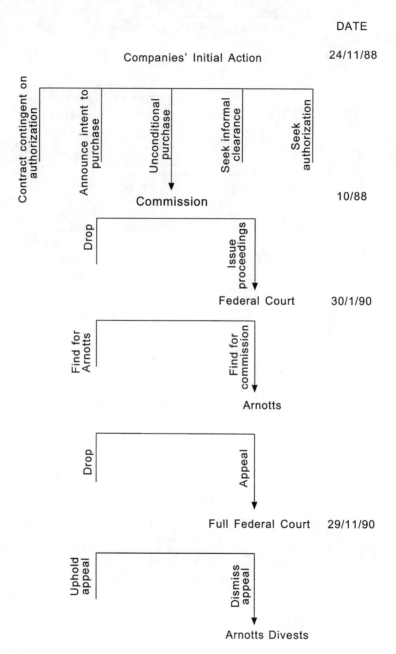

DATE

Companies' Initial Action   24/11/88

Commission   10/88

Federal Court   30/1/90

Arnotts

Full Federal Court   29/11/90

Arnotts Divests

Fig. 2.3 *Arnotts*

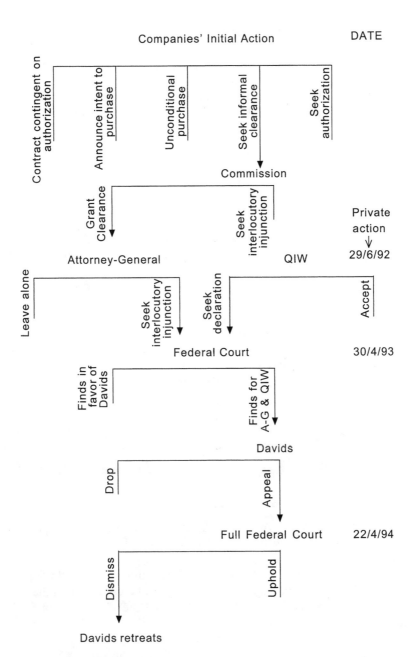

Fig. 2.4   *QIW v. Davids*

that the state of competition depended on the structure of the market, so a substantial lessening of competition involved a change in the structure of the market. To prove a substantial lessening of competition, one had to prove that the structure of the market with the conduct in question would be less conducive to competitive behavior than would be the structure of the market without the conduct in question. The full court put it in these words:

> More assistance [in defining competition] can be gleaned from the decision of the Trade Practices Tribunal with Woodward J. presiding, in *Re Queensland Co-Operative Milling Association Limited; Re Defiance Holdings Limited* (1976) ATPR 40-012; (1976) 8 A.L.R. 481. There an economic concept of competition was adopted. Five elements of market structure were noted by the Tribunal as being relevant to the determination of the state of competition in a market. Of those, the most important factor was said to be the height of barriers to entry, that is, the ease with which new firms might enter and secure a viable market. . . .
>
> It would seem that "competition" for the purposes of sec. 47(10) must be read as referring to a process or state of affairs in the market. In considering the state of competition a detailed evaluation of the market structure seems to be required. In the *Dandy* case *Smithers J.* regarded as necessary an assessment of the nature and extent of competition which would exist therein but for the conduct in question, the operation of the market and the extent of the contemplated lessening.
>
> Two other decisions of the Trade Practices Tribunal are relevant here— *Ford Motor Co. of Australia Limited v. Ford Sales Co. of Australia Limited* (1977) ATPR 40-043; and *Southern Cross Beverages Pty. Limited* (1981) ATPR 40-200. In both cases, the Tribunal undertook a detailed analysis of the market, the state of competition therein and the likely effect of the conduct upon competition in the market. In our opinion, the same type of approach should have been adopted in the present case. (*Outboard Marine v. Hecar* appeal at 43983).

A further gloss on the notion of substantial lessening of competition has been the gradual emergence of the future-with-and-without test. The test makes it clear that the substantial lessening does not involve a comparison of the future with the past. Rather, it is a forward-looking test. In particular, it involves a comparison of the future state of competition in the market if the merger were to occur with the future state of competition in the market if the merger were not to occur.

The future-with-and-without test is at least implicit in the tribunal's decision of *Re QCMA,* which has as one of its subheadings "The Future of Barnes without Merger." The test has been quite explicitly adopted by the full court of the federal court in *Stirling Harbour Services* appeal (at 41267):

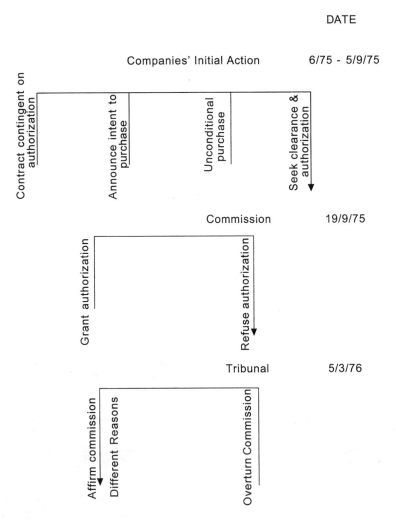

Fig. 2.5 *Re QCMA*

There was no dispute but that in determining whether the proposed conduct has the purpose, or has or is likely to have the effect, of substantially lessening competition in the relevant market, the Court has to:
- consider the likely state of future competition in the market "with and without" the impugned conduct; and
- on the basis of such consideration, conclude whether the conduct has the proscribed purpose or effect

Dandy Power Equipment Pty Limited v Mercury Marine Pty Limited (1982) ATPR 40-315 at 43,887; (1982) 64 FLR 238 at 259; *Outboard Marine Australia Pty Limited v Hecar Investments No 6 Pty Limited* (1982)

ATPR 40-327 at 43,982; (1982) 44 ALR 667 at 669–670. The test is not a "before and after" test, although, as a matter of fact, the existing state of competition in the market may throw some light on the likely future state of competition in the market absent the impugned conduct.

The reference by the tribunal in *Re QCMA* and by the full federal court in *Outboard Marine v. Hecar* to the primacy of the condition of entry in considering the extent to which a market is competitive gives a clear hint as to the time horizon over which competition is to be assessed. If one gives primacy to the condition of entry, there is a clear indication that one is assessing competitive forces over a long time horizon. The point is made in Brunt (1990, 96) as follows:

> Competition is a process rather than a situation. Dynamic processes of substitution are at work. Technological change in products and processes, whether small or large, is ongoing and there are changing tastes and shifting demographic and locational factors to which business firms respond. Profits and losses move the system: it is the hope of supernormal profits and some respite from the "perennial gale" that motivates firms' endeavours to discover and supply the kinds of goods and services their customers want and to strive for cost-efficiency. Such a vision tells us that effective competition is fully compatible with the existence of strictly "limited monopolies" resting upon some short run advantage or upon distinctive characteristics of product (including location). Where there is effective competition, it is the on-going substitution process that ensures that any achievement of market power will be transitory.

The paucity of litigation under s. 50 has meant that there are many questions over which the courts have given companies and their legal advisers little guidance—simply because the issues have not arisen during the course of litigation. One such area of uncertainty is the relevance of arguments to do with efficiency under s. 50. In section 2.1 of this chapter, we argued that mergers could be motivated either by prospective enhancements in economic efficiency or by prospective increases in monopoly power. The words of the test as set out in s. 50 make no explicit reference to economic efficiency, so the extent to which argument over economic efficiency would be relevant to a case tried under s. 50 has not been decided.

The issue did arise in the *Arnotts* litigation. Both the judgment at the trial and the full court on appeal make the point that there are substantial economies of scale in the production and distribution of biscuits. The courts found the point to go to market power; but it could have been interpreted as an efficiency explanation of the merger. The appeal judgment was in no doubt as to the importance of economies of scale for Arnotts Limited:

> Arnotts' economies of scale flow, of course, from its market share. Once again, more detail would have been helpful. But it is clear that Arnotts does enjoy substantial economies of scale. Its volume provides flexibility

in the use of factory ovens and warehouses and unit economies in advertising, with emphasis upon the name and tradition of Arnotts. Its great product range minimises seasonal sales fluctuations, with resulting benefits to cash flow, the efficient use of manufacturing and distribution resources and retention of supermarket shelf space allocations.

Similarly, there are economies of scale in distribution costs. A company which accounts for 65% of all biscuit sales must have a marked advantage, in terms of unit distribution costs, over companies which have only 13% or 8% of the market. All three companies distribute directly to the retail stores but the Arnotts' truck must be off-loading many more biscuits at each stop. Again, there must be an advantage to Arnotts in spreading the cost of a sales representative's visit to a store amongst 65 units, as against Weston's 13 units or Nabisco's 8. (*Arnotts* appeal, at 51791–92).

If a merger enhances economic efficiency, that may be relevant to argument under s. 50 because the enhancements may enhance the ability of the merged entity to survive in a competitive market. Alternatively, arguments and evidence concerning economic efficiency could be introduced under the rubric of substantiality. For example, a merger may lessen competition, but may enhance efficiency. The efficiency considerations may be relevant to a court's consideration as to whether the lessening of competition is substantial.

To repeat, these arguments have not been considered by a judge in proceedings under s. 50. Until the courts consider more cases, many questions of this kind will remain unresolved. Certainly, it is not clear whether or in what way efficiency arguments can be considered by the courts under s. 50. To the extent that there is uncertainty, the principal issues that, as a matter of economic policy, should be considered in the antitrust treatment of mergers may not be able to be considered by the Australian courts. The principal issues should be whether the merger is primarily motivated by increases in economic efficiency or by increases in monopoly power. To the extent that s. 50 makes it likely that these issues cannot be considered, the Australian model provides a lesson as to what other jurisdictions should avoid.

The courts in New Zealand have had more opportunities to consider the relevance of efficiency to the ways in which mergers might result in the lessening of competition. In an unreported case involving a strike-out application,[2] the high court (per Justice Gallen and Dr. M. Brunt) had this to say:

In applying s. 27, counsel for Clear invites us to disregard any positive contribution that efficiencies may make to the competitive process. He

---

2. *Clear Communications Limited v. Sky Network Television Limited and others* (1996, 66–67), High Court of New Zealand CP.19/96. Judgment of 1 August 1997.

says the existence of authorisation in the New Zealand Act makes efficiencies relevant only in so far as they give rise to heightened barriers to
entry and hence an enhancement of market power.

We cannot accept this contention. It is contrary to a well-established
line of authority in New Zealand law that receives its latest statement
in *Port Nelson Limited v Commerce Commission* (1996) 7 TCLR 217 in
relation to s. 27 (at p. 228):

> "The relevant inquiry is as to substantially lessening competition.
> That is not the same as substantially lessening the effectiveness of a
> particular competitor. Competition in a market is a much broader
> concept. It is defined in s. 3(1) as meaning 'workable and effective
> competition.' That encompasses a market framework which partici-
> pants may enter and in which they may engage in rivalrous behaviour
> with the expectation of deriving advantage from greater efficiency.
> There appears to have been consistent acceptance of the elements of
> competition in *Re Queensland Co-operative Milling Association Lim-
> ited; Re Defiance Holdings Limited* [(1976) 25 FLR 169; 8 ALR 481,
> 517; 1 ATPR 40-012, 17, 247] at p188; p515; p 17,246, and further quo-
> tation is unnecessary."

2.2.2   Reasons for Lack of Litigation

As was noted in the preceding section of this paper, in the first quarter of
a century of the Trade Practices Act, only four mergers have been litigated
to judgment. Although private parties have the right to issue proceedings
for breach of s. 50, private parties cannot apply for an injunction to prevent a merger from occurring. However, a company that is faced with an
unwanted offer of takeover can apply for a declaration that the takeover
would infringe s. 50. Broken Hill Proprietary Co. Ltd. (BHP) made an application of this type when faced with the unwanted attentions of Robert
Holmes a Court's Bell Resources Group. Similarly, QIW made an application for a declaration of breach of s. 50 when it was faced with the unwanted attention of Davids Holdings, and the Australian Competition and
Consumer Commission (ACCC)[3] was reluctant to apply for an injunction.
However, even in this situation, QIW managed to persuade the commonwealth attorney general to apply for an injunction to prevent the merger.

Apart from the possibility of an application for a declaration, the only
action a private party can take to obtain an injunction to prevent a merger
is to lobby the commission or the attorney general to apply for an injunction. All four mergers that have been litigated to a decision under s. 50 have
involved applications by the commission or (in the case of *QIW v. Davids*

---

3. The Australian Competition and Consumer Commission is the general antitrust regulator in Australia. In addition to its roles in mergers and acquisitions, the commission has roles
in a range of antitrust matters, including anticompetitive conduct, consumer safeguards, and
the regulation of access to essential facilities.

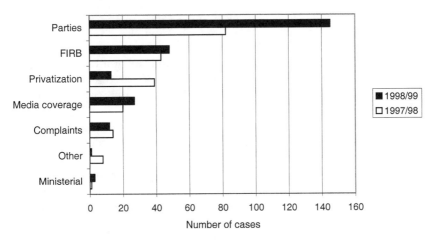

Fig. 2.6   Merger and acquisition matters referred to the commission
Source: ACCC (2000, 73).

trial) by the attorney general for injunctions or orders to divest. In the cases of *AMH* trial and *Arnotts* trial, the application had to be for divestiture because the acquisition had been already been undertaken.

Unlike some other jurisdictions, Australia does not compel parties to a merger to notify the regulator of their intentions. In its first three years, the Trade Practices Act provided for the clearance of mergers. This was abolished from 1 July 1977. Since then, the act has provided for two ways in which parties contemplating a merger may deal with the commission: they may apply for authorization (see section 2.3) or they may consummate the merger and dare the commission to litigate. Between 1 July 1977 and the development of the present system of informal clearances, parties had little incentive to notify the commission of their intentions, so there was much discussion of a system of compulsory notification. Indeed, New Zealand (which incorporated Australia's antitrust provisions into its Commerce Act pursuant to the Australia–New Zealand Closer Economic Relations Agreement of 1983) added a compulsion to notify.

In recent times, there has been little or no discussion in Australia of compulsory notification. It appears that the commission gets to hear of all significant mergers prior to their consummation.

From figure 2.6, it is clear that, although the vast majority of matters are referred to the commission by the parties, there is a range of other avenues, including other regulators (such as the Federal Investment Review Board [FIRB]), the selling of public assets (such as electricity generators), media reports, and complaints by affected parties. In a number of cases, matters are referred to the commission by more than one source.

From the preceding discussion, it should be clear that the Australian experience yields few lessons as to the need for a system of compulsory notification. Under the present Australian system, there is no need for compulsory notification. The regulator gains the information that it needs to enable it to perform its task, and the parties are prepared to approach the commission because of the development of the nonstatutory process of informal clearances.

It is hardly surprising that litigation as a means of implementing antitrust merger policy is unpopular with the regulator and with the parties. It is time consuming and it involves considerable uncertainty. The processes of litigation may discourage and ultimately prevent anticompetitive mergers and acquisitions; but they may also delay or discourage efficiency-enhancing mergers and acquisitions. This is particularly the case for mergers and acquisitions for which the window of opportunity is small or the major efficiency benefits are immediate. Litigation may deter efficiency-enhancing mergers and result in economic loss in a number of different ways.

Delay probably constitutes the most significant potential for economic loss. In some mergers and acquisitions the economic synergies are of most value in the current market environment. Delay, by reducing these efficiencies, may destroy the economic gains from the acquisition. The window of opportunity may pass during the process.

Even if the acquisition ultimately does proceed, the economic benefits of the acquisition may not accrue to the offeror. For example, it is commonly said that many mergers between banks are motivated by a more-efficient bank's ability to use its systems to identify underperforming assets in other banks. If a lengthy court process occurs prior to the consummation of the merger, the problem of the underperforming assets may have been addressed so that the bank that identified the problem is unable to gain a return for its efforts.

The cost of delaying a merger or acquisition has been recognized by the courts. This was the subject of comment by Justice Wilcox in his decision in *AMH* trial (at 49479):

> It is for me a matter of concern that the crucial determination of the limits of a market—about which question I assume commercial people frequently make almost intuitive judgements—should be seen as requiring the time, effort and expense involved in this case. My concern is intensified by the circumstances that, almost by definition, proceedings to prevent a breach of sec. 50, or to reverse the effects of an antecedent breach, will always involve a measure of urgency.

The courts have made similar remarks when assessing the balance of convenience relevant to applications for interlocutory injunctions in merger cases. In *Santos* (at 40637), Justice Hill said that a court must weigh up the real consequences to each party, taking in mind not only the public interest but also the private interests involved. There is, in my view, no presumption that an interim injunction should be granted.

Similarly, in *Rank Commercial,* Justice Davies observed the following:

A court cannot hold the underlying commercial situation in a state of status quo during the lengthy period in which preparation for a trial might ordinarily be expected to take. In this period the facts, including share values, will change.

Furthermore, delay combined with the publication of the proposed acquisition may allow a competing bidder to acquire the target firm. The recent proposed mergers between Taubmans and Wattyl, on the one hand, and Santos/Sagasco, on the other, show that the delay caused by the processes of litigation may enable a rival suitor to appear and so the proposed acquirer may withdraw the offer and sell the shares to the new suitor.

It may be argued that the delay did no harm—that the delay enabled the appearance of a new suitor that enabled the generation of more efficiencies or less monopoly power than would have been generated by the original proposal of marriage. It may be thought that this is the explanation as to why these mergers were not consummated. However, this characterization may be a distortion. Litigation is expensive and the prospects of victory in complex commercial litigation are always uncertain. An alternative characterization would be that an offeror enmeshed in complex litigation might prefer to accept the certain money offered by the new suitor to the prospect of pursuing the uncertain prize of consummation of its original desires.

2.3   Authorization

2.3.1   The System

Authorization is a process by which the parties to a merger or acquisition may be granted immunity for breaching s. 50 or s. 50A of the Trade Practices Act. This immunity is given if the commission[4] forms the view that the merger or acquisition will be of net benefit to the public—s. 90. In considering net benefits, the commission can consider efficiencies. So, in contrast to the process of a trial under s. 50, the process of authorization explicitly allows for the consideration of efficiencies. Authorization is initiated by one of the parties to the merger. It is not initiated by the commission.

An authorization decision by the commission can be appealed to the tribunal.[5] A review by the tribunal is a rehearing of the matter. Whereas the

4. The ACCC was known as the Trade Practices Commission until 1995.
5. The Australian Competition Tribunal was known as the Trade Practices Tribunal until 1995.

commission is an administrative body, the tribunal is a quasi-judicial body. It is chaired by a judge of the federal court, who sits with two other members, one of whom is usually an economist and the other, a person with business experience.

Once a merger or acquisition has been authorized (by either the commission or, on appeal, by the tribunal), parties to the merger or acquisition are granted immunity from breaching s. 50 so long as the conditions pertaining to the authorization are not breached.

Section 90 purports to limit the time that the commission has to determine applications for authorization. Section 90 (11) states that, if the commission does not determine an application for authorization within thirty days from its receipt, the commission shall be deemed to have granted the application. However, s. 90 (11A) provides that this period may be extended to forty-five days if the commission notifies the applicant that it considers the matter to be complex. Furthermore, the period can be extended if the commission requires extra information, if a person (such as an objector) wishes the commission to hold a conference, or if the applicant agrees to a request by the commission to an extension of time. (It may be supposed that an applicant who wishes an application to succeed is unlikely to refuse such a request.)

Section 102 imposes a sixty-day limit on the tribunal in its review of determinations by the commission. But this period can be extended at the discretion of the tribunal if the tribunal considers that, for reasons such as the complexity of the matter, the matter cannot be dealt with properly within the period of sixty days.

Applications for authorization are not only time consuming, they are also public. In processing applications, the commission feels the need to undertake research, and the commission's research generally involves asking competitors, suppliers, and purchasers what they think of the proposed merger. Furthermore, those who have been notified of the merger by the commission may request a conference, which provides extra publicity.

As was noted in section 2.1, the future-with-and-without test was first articulated by the tribunal. This implies that it was first articulated in the context of an appeal from an authorization decision of the commission. So in weighing the benefit to the public against the detriment caused by the lessening of competition, the tribunal (and the commission) compare the future with and without the merger.

Like the process of litigation, the process of authorization is public and, although there are time limits as explained above, both processes are relatively time consuming. A key difference between the two processes is that the process of authorization explicitly allows for the weighing of detriment caused by any lessening of competition against any offsetting benefit to the public.

The explicit consideration of benefits to the public under the process of authorization includes, of course, the consideration of economic efficiency. Although the commission has, on occasion, demanded that benefits be "passed on" to final consumers if they are to be considered (see Officer and Williams 1995) this is not because of the wording of the statute.

Indeed, in the seminal decision by the tribunal, in the merger case of *QCMA,* the tribunal went out of its way to state that all benefits, no matter to whom they accrue, should be counted as benefits to the public for the purpose of consideration of an application for authorization:

> One question that arises is whether by the public is meant the consuming public. One submission to us was that, in the context of the objectives of the Act, we should direct our attention to that part of the public concerned with the use or consumption of flour in the Queensland market. This would be to interpret the phrase as pointing to much the same considerations as those raised by sec. 21(1)(b) of the British *Restrictive Practices Act* 1956, which asks whether withholding approval would "deny to the public as purchasers, consumers or users . . . specific and substantial benefits or advantages . . .". However this is not what the Australian Act says; and we cannot but think that the choice of a wider expression was deliberate, as pointing to some wider conception of the public interest, though no doubt the interests of the public as purchasers, consumers or users must fall within it and bulk large.
>
> Another question raised is whether public benefit must be contrasted with private benefit. Can a benefit to some of the private parties to the merger—for example the shareholders of Barnes—be claimed as a public benefit? . . . [W]e would not wish to rule out of consideration any argument coming within the widest possible conception of public benefit. This we see as anything of value to the community generally, any contribution to the aims pursued by the society including as one of its principal elements (in the context of trade practices legislation) the achievement of the economic goals of efficiency and progress. (*Re QCMA,* at 17242)

2.3.2   Applications for Authorization of Mergers

Given the clear mandate of the commission to consider the key issues of both the increase in monopoly power and the effects of the merger on efficiency following an application for authorization, one might predict that parties would far prefer to apply for authorization than to risk litigation in the courts. However, their revealed preferences are that they avoid applications for authorization as much as they avoid the courts. Table 2.1 shows the number of applications lodged during the last six years for authorization of mergers and acquisitions recorded in the public register of the commission.

Table 2.1 suggests that very few parties apply for authorization of mergers. Given the open process and its time-consuming nature, perhaps the real puzzle is why there are any applications at all. The explanation lies in

Table 2.1   **Applications for Authorizations of Acquisitions Registered with the Commission**

Year	No. of Applications
1995	3
1996	2
1997	1
1998	0
1999	2
2000	0
2001 (to date)	0

Source: Public Register of Applications for Authorisation, Australian Competition, and Consumer Commission Web site (www.accc.gov.au).

the features of any particular merger that distinguish it from the vast majority of mergers for which applications are not made. An example may be found in *Re QIW* decision. As was noted in section 2.2, immediately prior to this application for authorization QIW was a party to s. 50 litigation, when it successfully used the courts to thwart the unwanted advances of Davids Holdings (*QIW v. Davids*). In that litigation, the courts found in favor of QIW that the product dimension of the relevant market was confined to the wholesaling of groceries to independent retailers—that is, that the integrated grocery chains were not participants in the relevant market. That finding, if it were transported to other factual situations, would effectively have precluded further mergers among specialist grocery wholesalers. The authorization was an attempt by Davids to clear the way for its acquisition of Composite Buyers Limited (CBL). Davids clearly reasoned that, unless the acquisition was authorized, it would run the risk of a private application for divestiture for breach of s. 50 immediately after the acquisition had been consummated. The commission granted the authorization; and this decision was upheld (in its principal elements) on appeal by the tribunal.

An interesting feature of the merger was that Davids did not proceed to acquire CBL. QIW was also interested in acquiring CBL. Immediately prior to the decision of the commission, QIW increased its offer for CBL and succeeded in acquiring a controlling interest in CBL.

The delay, and the subsequent possibility of a counteroffer, are two respects in which the process of authorization is similar to that of litigation under s. 50. The public nature of the process is another. The delay and lack of secrecy of these two statutory processes explain their lack of appeal to merging parties and, one may guess, to the commission. The result has been the development in Australia of a quick and secret process that has no foundation in the antitrust statute. This process is generally known as the *process of informal clearance.*

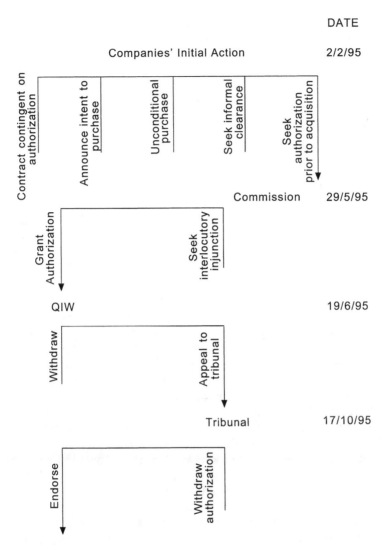

Fig. 2.7 *Re QIW*

2.4 Informal Clearances

2.4.1 The Process

The costs and risks associated with the statutory processes combined with the powers of the commission to seek an injunction to prevent a merger or acquisition have seen an informal notification and clearance process develop in Australia. The informal notification and clearance process is not based in the statute. Although the commission has published *Merger Guidelines,* which inform parties of the informal process, the guidelines have no statutory basis. As a result, the commission has significant discretion in how it goes about assessing proposed mergers and acquisitions and the conditions it endeavours to impose on the acquirer. The informal clearance process consists of three major parts:

- Notification,
- Assessment; and
- Outcome.

As was noted in section 2.1 above, parties to a proposed merger or acquisition are not obligated under the Trade Practices Act to notify the commission of their proposal. However, many do. As shown in figure 2.1, well in excess of half of the mergers and acquisitions notified to the commission over the last two years have been notified by the parties. This is done on either a public or a confidential basis.

The reason parties notify the commission is to gain some comfort as to whether the commission will seek an injunction if they proceed with the acquisition. If the commission indicates it will seek an injunction if the acquisition proceeds, the notification process allows the party or parties to explore with the commission options for changing the proposed acquisition to address the competition concerns. This process enables the commission to make the parties aware of its view of an acquisition and merger before the matter reaches the court.

The informal process by which the commission assesses merger and acquisitions is described in its *Merger Guidelines.* The process aims to consider the matters a court would consider under s. 50.

A major issue affecting the process and how the commission conducts its investigation is whether the merger or acquisition is notified to the commission on a confidential basis. Maintaining confidentiality restricts the commission's ability to seek the views of, and to acquire information from, other parties such as competitor suppliers and buyers—that is, the confidentiality limits the commission's opportunity to conduct market inquiries.

In some cases this may not matter. For example, the commission has indicated that it will not oppose mergers and acquisitions that fall below a certain concentration threshold. As noted by the commission in its *Merger Guidelines* (ACCC 1999, 44):

> The Commission has adopted concentration thresholds below which it is unlikely to intervene in a proposed merger. The thresholds have been established on the basis of the Commission's historical experience of mergers and knowledge of current market structures. . . .
>
> If the merger will result in a post-merger combined market share of the four (or fewer) largest firms (CR4) of 75 per cent or more and the merged

firm will supply at least 15 per cent of the relevant market, the Commission will want to give further consideration to a merger proposal before being satisfied that it will not result in a substantial lessening of competition. In any event, if the merged firm will supply 40 per cent or more of the market, the Commission will want to give the merger further consideration. The two thresholds reflect concerns with the potential exercise of both coordinated market power and unilateral market power.

Below these thresholds, the Commission is unlikely to take any further interest in a merger.

In other cases, especially where the likely effects of a merger or acquisition are complex, the commission's market inquiries may be extremely important. As a result, the commission may not be able to form a final view on the matter until the proposal has been made public.

In the case of the merger proposed between Santos and Sagasco, the commission granted an informal clearance and then changed its mind. The behavior of the commission is readily explained: If, for reasons of secrecy, they are unable to make any inquiries other than of the parties, the information they may be relying on may be biased, partial, or even misleading. In such circumstances, it is clear that the commission must be able to change its mind when it is able to make open inquiries.

The criteria employed in the process of informal clearance, while set out in detail in the *Merger Guidelines,* are based on the commission's own interpretation of s. 50. The process of informal clearance refers to s. 50 in that, if the applicant is given an informal clearance, it is given an assurance that, on the basis of the information available to it, the commission will not issue proceedings for breach of s. 50 should the proposed merger proceed. Accordingly, the commission must satisfy itself that the merger will not breach s. 50.

One important feature of the commission's interpretation of s. 50 in its processing of informal clearances is the very limited role it allows for consideration of economic efficiency. As was noted in section 2.1 above, the place of efficiency arguments under s. 50 has never been explicitly considered by the courts—because it has not arisen in any of the four cases that have run to judgment.

The extent to which the commission is prepared to consider economic efficiency within the context of an informal application for clearance is set out in paragraphs 5.159 and following of the commission's *Merger Guidelines.* There is a marked similarity between these provisions and those of the *Horizontal Merger Guidelines* issued by the U.S. Department of Justice and the Federal Trade Commission. The ACCC (1999, 59–60) guidelines read, in part:

5.171   As discussed in paragraphs 5.16–5.17, although s. 50 is concerned with the level of competition in markets and not the competitiveness of individual firms, and while efficiencies are more generally relevant in the context of authorisation, the extent to which any efficiency enhancing aspects of a merger may impact on the competitiveness of markets is relevant in the context of s. 50.

5.172   Where a merger enhances the efficiency of the merged firm, for example by achieving economies of scale or effectively combining research and development facilities, it may have the effect of creating a new or enhanced competitive constraint on the unilateral conduct of other firms in the market or it may undermine the conditions for coordinated conduct. Pecuniary benefits, such as lower input prices due to enhanced bargaining power, may also be relevant in a s. 50 context.

5.173   If efficiencies are likely to result in lower (or not significantly higher) prices, increased output and/or higher quality goods or services, the merger may not substantially lessen competition.

5.174   While recognising that precise quantification of such efficiencies is not generally possible, the Commission will require strong and credible evidence that such efficiencies are likely to accrue and that the claimed benefits for competition are likely to follow.

Paragraph 5.172 indicates that the role of any consideration of economic efficiency within the context of an application for an informal clearance is highly circumscribed. In particular, if a firm with a large market share believes that it can gain access to efficiencies through merger, that consideration will be ruled by the commission to be irrelevant to an application for informal clearance. Indeed, the commission may well follow the lead of the full federal court in *Arnotts* appeal, as quoted above, and say that to the extent that a merger enhances the efficiency of a firm with a large market share, it is likely to lessen competition.

This interpretation by the commission means that the commission elects to rule as irrelevant many arguments of economic efficiency in the context of applications for informal clearance. The commission will normally respond to such arguments by informing the parties that, if they wish to put such arguments, they must submit an application for authorization—with its attendant delays and publicity. This response is usually sufficient to persuade the parties to drop the submissions.

It is clearly unsatisfactory that issues of economic efficiency cannot be fully considered under the procedure by which the mergers are dealt with by the Australian antitrust authority. This problem could be remedied if s. 50 were to be amended to invite the courts and, therefore, the commission in its processing of applications for clearance, to consider the trade-offs between considerations of competition and efficiency. Such a change would enable the efficiency implications of a merger to be considered. Under the present Australian arrangements they are only considered very rarely because the statutory option of an application for authorization is no real option for the great bulk of mergers.

One model as to how the Australian statute could be changed is provided by Canada's Competition Act (1985). The principal merger provision is found in s. 92(1), which proscribes mergers that prevent or lessen competition substantially. This is qualified by s. 96(1), which provides an efficiency defence. It is worth quoting in full (in its English version):

> The Tribunal shall not make an order under section 92 if it finds that the merger or proposed merger in respect of which the application is made has brought about or is likely to bring about gains in efficiency that will be greater than, and will offset, the effects of any prevention or lessening of competition that will result or is likely to result from the merger or proposed merger and that the gains in efficiency would not be likely be attained if the order were made.

From 1991 until very recently, the *Merger Enforcement Guidelines* of the Canadian commissioner had indicated that the effects of an anticompetitive merger were to be assessed by estimating the aggregate effect of the merger on social surplus. A recent decision on appeal from a decision of the tribunal (Superior Propane) makes it clear that this approach was an incorrect interpretation of the law. Under the previous approach of the commission, it had focused solely on aggregate surplus and had ignored other factors, such as the distribution of the surplus. The court found that the correct approach is not to disregard any of the effects of the lessening of competition that would be likely to result from a merger.

Although some may consider this judgment a setback for the cause of economic efficiency, the decision in *Superior Propane* merely brings the Canadian standard into line with the standard applied by the Australian tribunal in merger cases. As the tribunal has said since the earliest of cases, the public interest is sufficiently broad to enable all considerations to be argued before the tribunal. In effect, the decision in *Superior Propane* establishes that Canada has a statutory standard that is very similar to that which would be applied by the tribunal in its consideration of the authorization of a merger—if such a case were to come to it for consideration. If the statute is to reflect a proper weighing of competition and efficiency considerations, the same standard should be incorporated in s. 50.

2.4.2   Outcomes of an Informal Clearance

The commission has a number of options after it has assessed a proposed merger. It can

- indicate that it will not oppose the merger or acquisition,
- indicate that it will oppose the merger or acquisition unless the or parties agree to certain conditions or to act in a certain manner, or
- indicate it will oppose the merger or acquisition under any conditions.

As shown in table 2.2, the majority of matters that reach a final decision by the commission are not opposed. A range of other proposals are withdrawn before the commission reaches its final view.

Table 2.2   Outcomes of Mergers before the Commission

	Matters Decided	Matters Not Opposed	Matters Resolved with Conditions	Matters Opposed
1993–1994	77	71	1	5
1994–1995	113	101	5	7
1995–1996	117	105	3	9
1996–1997	147	140	2	5
1997–1998	176	165	6	5
1998–1999	185	168	10	7
1999–2000	208	199	5	4

Sources: ACCC (2000) and Section 50 Mergers and Acquisitions Register, Australian Competition and Consumer Commission Web site (www.accc.gov.au, http://accc.gov.au).

The table suggests that the commission imposes, or attempts to impose, conditions on a number of mergers. These are the circumstances in which efficiency-enhancing acquisitions are most likely to be inhibited. The commission has significant bargaining power to "encourage" the party or parties to significantly alter the form of the proposal or to impose conditions on the parties if the proposal proceeds.

If the commission indicates that it is likely to seek an injunction from the courts if the proposal proceeded in its submitted form, the parties have a number of options:

1. Proceed with the proposal and most likely contest the matter or an injunction before the Court.
2. Seek authorization of the proposed merger or acquisition from the commission, and if rejected, appeal to the tribunal.
3. Alter the proposal in a manner to address the concerns of the commission.
4. Address any anticompetitive consequences of the merger or acquisition by making undertakings under s. 87B of the Trade Practices Act.
5. Decide not to proceed with the proposal.

The first and second options follow the statutory processes described in the previous sections of this chapter. The third and fourth options are informal processes that give the commission significant discretion. The major difference between these options is whether the altered proposal is subject to legally enforceable undertakings.

2.4.3   Section 87B Undertakings

Under s. 87B of the Trade Practices Act, the commission, subject to the approval of the courts, is allowed to accept written undertakings in connection with its power and functions under the act. Undertakings are legally enforceable guarantees that the parties will or will not undertake certain actions following the merger or acquisition.

For instance, say the commission is concerned that a merger will substantially lessen competition in some geographic markets, but not others. The commission may accept undertakings by the merged entity to divest itself (postmerger) of certain assets in those markets.

Undertakings also provide the parties with some flexibility where the timeliness of the merger or acquisitions is paramount. Undertakings have been used by parties to guarantee divestiture if the commission forms the view that the merger or acquisition would substantially lessen competition. In this case, undertakings have allowed the transaction to proceed while giving the commission time to assess the transaction.

Probably the most detailed undertakings to be given by parties during a merger application to the commission were those given to the commission by Pioneer International Limited, Caltex Australia Limited, and Ampol Limited on 28 March 1995. On 3 November 1994, the parties informed the commission that they were considering a merger. This was announced to the public on 14 December 1994. The commission quickly formed the view that the merger was likely to infringe s. 50. The parties disagreed. Nevertheless, they gave numerous undertakings to address the concerns raised by the commission. These undertakings were clearly directed to ensure that independent oil companies prospered. The merged entity undertook

- to sell particular terminals to independents by particular dates;
- to facilitate access by independents to the terminals that were retained;
- during the first six years, to offer at least 1,000 megaliters of petrol to independents each year on reasonable terms;
- during the first two years, to use its best endeavors to sell on reasonable terms thirty-five retail sites in metropolitan areas with an aggregate volume of 50 megaliters; and so on.

In short, Caltex and Ampol felt that they could prevent the commission from initiating proceedings under s. 50 only by offering to sell quite substantial assets by which the commission could pursue a restructuring of Australia's wholesaling and retailing of petrol. The commission has substantial power in its granting of informal clearances.

2.4.4 Shortcomings of the Informal Process

Although this informal process has the scope to reduce some of the delay and publicity associated with a proposed merger, it has three major problems.

First, the informal processes are not based in the statute. Although the commission's *Merger Guidelines* inform parties of the informal process, the guidelines have no statutory basis. This creates uncertainty: There are no rules governing the processes that the commission can use following an application for an informal clearance.

Table 2.3   Duration of Matters Informally Assessed by the Commission

	1997–1998	1998–1999
Less than 2 weeks	36	48
2–3 weeks	57	56
4–6 weeks	22	41
7–9 weeks	3	11
More than 9 weeks	18	22

Source: ACCC (2000, 70).

Second, the process lacks formal guidance by means of precedent. As the commission does not publish the reasons for its decision, there are no formal precedents to guide future decisions and to subject the decisions to peer review. This lack of precedent is another factor that increases the discretion that is exercised by the commission in any particular case. The corollary is that the uncertainty confronting the parties to a merger is increased.

Finally, it provides the commission with significant bargaining power to extract concession from the parties. These problems create a risk that efficiency-enhancing mergers will be unnecessarily altered or deterred. Noah (1997) characterises this behavior as "administrative arm-twisting."[6]

It might be thought that the need for confidentiality and for speed mean that the process cannot be combined with review processes. This is not the case—providing the commission gives reasons for its decisions and any reviews occur after the merger has been announced. This could be provided for in legislation. Any review on the merits would clearly be problematic if the commission has been unable to gather information. However, if the process were governed by statute, parties would be able to appeal if the commission violated the requirements of the statute.

The number of matters dealt with in table 2.3 points to the popularity of the process of informal clearance compared with authorization or litigation. It also points to the speed of the process compared with the processes set out in the statute.

2.5   Lessons from the Australian Experience

Lessons can be drawn from the Australian experience both for how Australia should reform its own statute and procedures, and for other jurisdictions that may be reconsidering their own commitment to antitrust merger policy if those countries wish to maximize value.

6. Noah (1997, 874) defines administrative arm-twisting as "a threat by an agency to impose a sanction or withhold a benefit in hopes of encouraging 'voluntary' compliance with a request that the agency could not impose directly on a regulated entity." We are indebted to Robertson (2001) for this reference.

The key lessons from the Australian experience that might be drawn for other jurisdictions that wished to maximize value are the following:

1. The criteria for assessing mergers must explicitly provide for an assessment as to whether the merger is primarily motivated by an increase in monopoly power or an increase in economic efficiency.

2. The process must be quick and must allow for secrecy (up the point that the merger is made public by one of the parties).

If the Australian legislature wished to maximize value, it should

1. give the present clearance process a statutory basis, so that parties can go to the commission with the knowledge that there are some constraints on what it may do;

2. legislate by amending to provide that the commission weighs up monopoly and efficiency considerations in considering whether it should grant a clearance; and

3. require the commission to publish its reasons as soon as the merger is public.

If applied in less developed countries, these principles will increase the prospect that the regulator will allow value-enhancing mergers. Furthermore, by increasing the transparency of the decisions of the regulator, they will minimize the scope for mergers or acquisitions motivated by rent seeking and improve certainty in the regulatory processes.

References

Australian Competition and Consumer Commission (ACCC). 1999. *Merger guidelines.* Canberra: ACCC, June.

————. 2000. Merger and acquisition matters referred to the commission. *ACCC Journal* 25 (February): 73.

Brunt, Maureen. 1990. "Market Definition" issues in Australian and New Zealand trade practices litigation. *Australian Business Law Review* 18:86–128.

Buchanan, James M. 1980. Rent seeking and profit seeking. In *Toward a theory of the rent-seeking society,* ed. J. M. Buchanan, J. D. Tollison, and G. Tullock, 3–15. College Station: Texas A&M Press.

Canada, Director of Investigation and Research. 1991. *Merger enforcement guidelines.* Information Bulletin no. 5, March.

Cournot, Antoine-Augustin. 1929. *Researches into the mathematical principles of the theory of wealth.* English ed. Translated by Nathaniel T. Bacon. 1838. New York: Macmillan.

Cowling, Keith, and Michael Waterson. 1976. Price-cost margins and market structure. *Economica* 43:267–274.

Green, Edward J., and Robert H. Porter. 1984. Noncooperative collusion under imperfect price information. *Econometrica* 52:87–100.

Noah, Lars. 1997. Administrative arm-twisting in the shadow of congressional delegations of authority. *Wisconsin Law Review,* Issue 5:873–894.

Officer, Robert, and Philip Williams. 1995. The public benefit test in an authorisation decision. In *The law and the market,* ed. Megan Richardson and Philip L. Williams, 157–165. Leichhardt, New South Wales, Australia: Federation Press.

Robertson, Donald. 2001. Comment on "The evolution of antitrust law in the United States. In *Trade Practices Act: A twenty-five year stocktake,* ed. Frances Hanks and Philip Williams, 15–21. Leichhardt, New South Wales, Australia: Federation Press.

Schwert, G. William. 1996. Markup pricing in mergers and acquisitions. *Journal of Financial Economics* 41:153–192.

Sims, Joe, and Deborah P. Herman. 1997. The effect of twenty years of Hart-Scott-Rodino on merger practice: A case study in the Law of Unintended Consequences applied to antitrust legislation. *Antitrust Law Journal* 77:865–903.

Stigler, George. 1964. A theory of oligopoly. *Journal of Political Economy* 72:44–61.

Merger Cases Referenced in Text

In all cases, references are to the *Australian Trade Practices Reporter.*

Re QCMA: Re Queensland Co-operative Milling Association Ltd., Defiance Holdings Ltd. (Proposed Mergers with Barnes Milling Ltd.) (1976) ATPR 40-012, 17,223–17,270.

Ansett Avis: Trade Practices Commission v. Ansett Transport Industries (Operations) Pty Ltd & Ors (1978) ATPR 40-071, 17,705–17,732.

AMH trial: *Trade Practices Commission v. Australian Meat Holdings & Ors* (1988) ATPR 40-876, 49,465–49,651.

AMH appeal: *Australian Meat Holdings Pty Ltd v. Trade Practices Commission* (1989) ATPR 40-932, 50,082–50,111.

Arnotts trial: *Trade Practices Commission v. Arnotts Limited &Ors* (1990) ATPR 41-062, 51,815–51,888.

Arnotts appeal: *Arnotts Limited & Ors v. Trade Practices Commission* (1990) ATPR 41-061, 51,767–51,814.

DIW v. Davids trial: QIW Retailers Limited v. Davids Holdings Pty Limited & Ors; Attorney-General of the Commonwealth v. Davids Holdings Pty Limited & Anor (1993) ATPR 41-226, 41,101–41,145.

QIW v. Davids appeal: *Davids Holdings Pty Limited & Ors v. Attorney-General of the Commonwealth & Anor* (1994) ATPR 41-304, 42,066–42,099.

Re QIW decision: *Davids Limited* (1995) ATPR (Com) 50-185, 55,602–55,672.

Re QIW appeal: *Re Queensland Independent Wholesaler Limited* (1995) ATPR 41-438, 40,914–40,967.

Outboard Marine v. Hecar: Outboard Marine Australia Pty Ltd v. Hecar Investments (No 6) Pty Ltd (1982) ATPR 40-327.

Santos: Trade Practices Commission v. Santos LTD (1992) ATPR 41-195.

Rank Commercial: Trade Practices Commission v. Rank Commercial LTD (1994) ATPR 41-343.

Superior Propane: Commissioner of Competition v. Superior Propane Inc. and ICG Propane Inc. (2001) FCA 104.

Stirling Harbour Services appeal: Stirling Harbour Services Pty Limited v. Bunbury Port Authority (2000) ATPR 41-783.

Comment   Charles W. Calomiris

The paper by Williams and Woodbridge provides a useful review of antitrust law as it is practiced in Australia. The authors begin by positing two criteria that are necessary "if antitrust merger policy is to enhance value." First, mergers that promote efficiency must be permitted and those that promote monopoly power disallowed. Second, the merger approval process should be speedy and confidential. They then hold up the experience of Australia to the mirror of their two-part objective function. They find Australian practice wanting in important respects and propose some modifications that they believe would improve regulatory performance.

It is hard to find fault with the twin objectives the authors propose, except in the incompleteness of the list of objectives, and in the failure to fully consider ways in which broad differences in approach to regulation might affect the likelihood of meeting either the objectives they propose or others that might be added to their list. In my comments, I will add a third criterion to the Williams-Woodbridge list—a criterion that is already implicit in their discussion of the flaws of the current system—and propose changes in regulatory process that would likely improve performance according to all three criteria. Specifically, I will argue that an approach to antitrust regulation that relies more on specific rules defining the criteria for permissible mergers, and that provides prospective merger counterparties with clear safe harbors from regulators' blocking mergers, would improve regulatory performance in comparison with the current approach, which relies almost entirely on discretionary, case-by-case judgments in the form of "informal notifications and clearances."

The objective I would add to the Williams-Woodbridge list for measuring regulatory performance is avoiding "stealth regulation." Stealth regulation refers to the practice of using antitrust authority as an extortionist device for coercing firms to do things that they are not legally required to do, but that the bureaucrat entrusted with regulating them wishes them to do. Stealth regulation is a serious problem in the United States, especially in the regulation of telecommunications and banking.[1] In telecommunications and banking, permission for acquisitions are withheld on flimsy legal

Charles W. Calomiris is the Henry Kaufman Professor of Finance and Economics, Columbia University, Graduate School of Business; Arthur F. Burns Scholar and codirector of the Financial Deregulation Project at the American Enterprise Institute for Public Policy Research; and a research associate of the National Bureau of Economic Research.

1. "Separate Statement of Commissioner Harold Furchtgott-Roth Concurring in Part, Dissenting in Part" Re: Applications of Ameritech Corp., Transferor, and SBC Communications, Inc., Transferee, For Consent to Transfer Control of Corporations Holding Commission Licenses and Lines Pursuant to Sections 214 and 310(d) of the Communications Act and Parts 5, 22, 24, 25, 63, 90, 95, and 101 of the Commission's Rules, CC Docket 98-141.

grounds, including alleged antitrust concerns, until firms "voluntarily" offer to institute new policies, which are touted as providing some program alleged to benefit the "community." Given the legal costs and time lost in fighting the regulators, firms often give in to this extortion, which, of course, encourages it. In some cases, regulatory extortion serves the political goals of ambitious bureaucrats; in other cases, it has a corrupt purpose, as money is channeled to favored recipients. Whatever its purpose, stealth regulation is a highly inappropriate use of regulatory discretion. I do not know the extent to which this problem is present in Australia, and the evidence in table 2.2 on the use of conditions in the merger approval process suggests that stealth regulation is less a problem in Australia than in the United States (at least so far). But, assuming that the dictum "power corrupts" applies around the globe, it should also be a policy concern there. Williams and Woodbridge seem to agree that this has been a problem in Australia, when they write that "Australia's reliance on discretion over rules" has granted the antitrust regulator "an unhealthy degree of power to extract concessions from the enterprises that wish to merge." That is the sense in which their discussion implicitly recognizes the need to avoid regulatory abuse; but they should elevate this concern to the status of an important and explicit goal for the regulatory process.

Let me turn to the question of how the extent of regulatory discretion affects regulatory performance according to all three criteria. First, as the authors note, the legal standard used to judge whether a merger is appropriate is quite vague—whether competition in the relevant market would be worsened by the merger, based on the "future-with-and-without test." That vagueness, and the desire to preserve confidentiality during the merger approval process, has encouraged the reliance on informal, secret regulatory deliberations to decide whether to permit or to challenge a merger. But as the authors recognize, this informality (especially when combined with the admitted necessity of secrecy) invites ineffective and abusive policy, and it may not be sufficiently speedy in reaching a result. That is, there is no reason to believe that the efficiency criterion is being satisfied or that the process is sufficiently speedy, and there is great opportunity for abuse.

How could speed and confidentiality be preserved while also ensuring greater effectiveness and less abuse? Williams and Woodbridge suggest that the answer is to mandate that regulators weigh efficiency and monopoly when deciding whether to approve a merger. No doubt the authors are right to argue that it is appropriate to weigh efficiency gains against lessening of competition. But, as a recipe for reform, this is a thin gruel. Their proposed criterion is still extremely vague. And it accomplishes little in the way of making the merger approval process predictable to prospective counterparties, which Williams and Woodbridge rightly emphasize as desirable. I see no reason to believe that this new mandate will add rationality or predictability to the process, hasten regulatory action, or avoid stealth regulation. All it would likely accomplish is the relabeling of the jargon used by bureaucrats to explain their protracted, results-oriented, discretionary decisions. Requiring that the Australian Competition and Consumer Commission publish its reasoning sounds like a good idea, but published opinions are not necessarily clear or defensible ones.

Ideally, to make antitrust adjudication more effective, speedy, and predictable, one would bind the commission's decisions so that they were derived in predictable ways from observable criteria. Furthermore, one would put in place firm time deadlines for first- and second-stage decisions by the commission (i.e., first, with respect to the decision to hear a merger case, and second, regarding the time before a decision must be reached). The ideal rules-based approach would have two parts. First, it would establish safe harbor rules. A good starting place would be to offer safe harbor to all mergers unless they are challenged by a third party. Challenged mergers should also enjoy safe harbor if, according to some prespecified set of objective, quantifiable criteria, a merger does not violate a given threshold of anticompetitiveness. Mergers enjoying safe harbor would be protected from regulatory risk by being automatically approved. For firms that fail the automatic approval test, the commission's deliberations should also be transparent, predictable, based on objective preannounced criteria, and subject to hard time limits.

With respect to safe harbor, the concentration ratio could serve as a possible criterion. Any mergers that would result in small industrial concentration or little price impact would not be subject to further review by the commission. Enforcing even this simple first-stage rule would require that the commission explicitly define the industry for which the calculation is relevant. This is tricky, but it could be handled in various ways. One possibility would be assigning all firms, ex ante, to an industry, so that the combination resulting from any proposed merger would have a predefined effect on the concentration in one or more industries. Another possibility would be allowing the commission to define the relevant industry concept ex post, but require that this definition be defensible on objective grounds.[2] Whatever the safe harbor rule chosen, it is essential that it be observable and known to all participants ex ante. I rely on concentration ratios in my example of a proposed safe harbor rule not because they are precise measures of market power but because a minimal degree of market concentration is a necessary condition for market power, and because they are relatively easy to define. Of course, even this simple approach to a safe harbor rule must admit some discretion, if only because statistical data and econometric estimation will always permit some manipulation. Nevertheless, this approach would be a huge step in the right direction.

2. For example, if the firms placed in the industry concept do not exhibit sufficiently positive cross-price elasticities, the definition would not be deemed acceptable.

For firms that do not receive automatic safe harbor, a second, more complicated set of rules would apply to the process for considering the merger. It would be useful here to vary the burden of proof according to prima facie evidence about some criteria. For example, for firms that have concentration ratios only slightly above the safe harbor maximum, the burden of proof would be on the commission, and the criteria that would have to be satisfied to bar the merger would be relatively demanding. The commission would have a specific evidentiary burden. The criteria for the decision would, as before, be prespecified and quantitative. For mergers that would result in substantial industrial concentration, the burden of proof would shift to the firms, in the sense that the criteria necessary for denying the merger would be less demanding. As before, the rules would be prespecified, including rules that determine the means of weighing the estimated monopoly costs and efficiency gains from the merger. With such rules in place, the job of the commission largely would be (1) to refine the rules over time, and (2) to ensure that the rules are executed properly. Discretion on a case-by-case basis would be kept to a minimum.

Of course, some discretion would remain no matter how one tried to limit it. But if the commission were subject to specific evidentiary burdens, and were required to prespecify detailed empirical criteria for denying mergers, the opportunities for delay and abuse would be substantially reduced. Furthermore, being forced to adopt specific criteria and to announce objective functions that weigh the estimated effects of the merger on efficiency and monopoly power, improves the likelihood that the decisions will do a better job balancing opposing considerations.

None of this would be easy to implement. Besides the tricky technical issues of deciding on reasonable criteria and weights to attach to them, there is an even bigger impediment to this sort of reform. Politicians tend not to like proposals like this, partly because such folk tend to overvalue the benefits of discretion and undervalue the benefits of predictable rules and constraints on the abuse of power. For Australia, the United States, and other countries to arrive at this sort of rational process it may be necessary for power to be placed more in the hands of people who think like economists. We can all look forward to that distant happy day.

Comment   Chong-Hyun Nam

This paper is very informative and is useful for policymakers both in Australia and in many other countries. The paper addresses at the outset a sort of ideal set of criteria under which antitrust merger policies should be

Chong-Hyun Nam is professor of economics at Korea University.

formed and operated. In brief, it states that antitrust merger policies should be designed in such a way as to allow those mergers and acquisitions (M&As) that promote economic efficiency while discouraging those M&As that promote monopoly power. At the same time, it says that the process of assessing M&As needs to be conducted in a speedy and confidential manner so that social costs involved with the M&As can be minimized. In light of these criteria, the paper then makes a very careful review of Australian antitrust laws and their applications in practice for recent years.

To summarize the highlights of the paper: The most important finding is that the antitrust laws, as set out in s. 50 of the Trade Practice Act, are grossly inadequate to deal with mergers because they make no explicit reference to economic efficiency. The paper also finds that the authorization process seems a little bit better than the litigation process based on s. 50, since it allows the commission to make decisions based on net economic benefits, which means that economic efficiency can be taken into consideration in the decision-making process.

Both litigation and authorizing processes, the two statutory processes, suffer, however, from delay and lack of secrecy, and therefore have been least popular among parties to the mergers. As a natural consequence, parties to the mergers relied heavily on a more quick and secret process, namely, the informal clearance process. As was already discussed by the authors, the informal clearance process has no foundation in the antitrust statute, and hence cannot be used as a precedent: the reasons for its decision cannot be made public. Moreover, there is a danger that the commission may exercise too much discretionary or bargaining power to extract concessions from parties to the mergers.

In the end, the paper suggests three major reform agendas for possible legislation. They are as follows: (1) give the present informal clearance process a statutory basis; (2) require the commission to access potential efficiency gains from the mergers, and use them in weighing trade-offs between efficiency gains and monopoly-power increases when considering whether to grant a clearance; and (3) require the commission to publish its reasons for decision as soon as the merger becomes public. Among these three points, I have no disagreement with the first and the third, but I have some reservations about the second.

I think it is too tall an order—if not an impossible task—for the commission to measure economic efficiency gains from the mergers. It will be not only time consuming but also inaccurate, at best. Further, I am not sure if it is necessary for the commission to assess the efficiency gains in order to be able to make the right decision when granting a clearance. What I have in mind is that most of the merger cases are likely to be efficiency enhancing. Otherwise, they would not have been tried in the first place.

However, the economic efficiency gains should by no means be used as compensation for the negative effects that may result from increased monopoly power. In other words, the negative effects originating from increased monopoly power should be prevented in any circumstance, regardless of the magnitude of expected efficiency gains from the mergers. From the social welfare point of view, the negative effects of increased monopoly power can best be assessed in terms of price changes of the concerned products, not by changes in the number of firms or by changes in their market shares. As long as prices of concerned products remain unchanged, or are lower than before the mergers take place, there is no reason for the commission not to grant a clearance.

Therefore, I think, the commission's effort needs to be focused on the price effects of the mergers, and that should be used as a major criterion when considering whether to give a clearance. If we accept this simple principle, the antitrust merger rules and the commission's duty can be made a lot simpler than they are now. For example, the commission does not need to intervene at all in private M&A activities as long as international competition is guaranteed for the concerned products, which are tradable goods in nature. Parties to the mergers do not even need to notify the commission under these kinds of circumstances. However, the commission needs to intervene in private M&A activities when the concerned products are characterized by nontradable goods, or when natural or artificial trade barriers are so high that effective competition cannot be guaranteed simply by exposing them to international competition only. Even in this case, the commission's burden can be reduced substantially if the commission makes use of price-undertakings whenever it seems appropriate. When granting a clearance, the commission needs to make sure that domestic prices of the concerned products do not rise as a result of M&As. In any event, making rules and regulations simpler and clearer is a job best left for economists, not for lawyers.

3

Using Markets to Help
Solve Public Problems

John McMillan

Governments around the world have begun using markets as means to policy ends. Pollution control has been assigned to a market in emissions allowances. The right to use the electromagnetic spectrum for telecommunications has been auctioned off. In electricity supply, markets have replaced allocation by state agencies or regulated monopolies. In fishery management, tradable quotas have started to be used instead of direct regulation.[1]

Using markets to allocate public resources represents a middle ground between privatization and government control. It is not privatization because the government retains substantial control rights. It is not government control of the traditional kind because part of the decision-making over how the resources are employed takes place in markets rather than in the bureaucracy.

Controversy has dogged the adoption of markets by governments. Emissions trading is immoral, say some environmentalists, for it legitimates polluting. Critics of the spectrum auctions, like the technology guru Nicholas Negroponte (quoted in *Financial Times,* 8 June 2000, p. 5), say they amount to "an economically unsustainable tax" on the telecommunications industry, bringing high prices for consumers and stifling innovation. The high electricity prices in California following deregulation prompted

John McMillan is the Jonathan B. Lovelace Professor of Economics at the Graduate School of Business, Stanford University.

I thank Kyoji Fukau, Takatoshi Ito, Anne Krueger, Tsuruhiko Nambu, Tetsushi Sonobe, Dale Squires, and an anonymous referee for comments, and the Stanford Graduate School of Business for support.

1. Another such use of markets is in restructuring publicly owned railroads (see chap. 11 in this volume). Yet another is the proposal by the U.S. Shadow Financial Regulatory Committee (2000) that bank regulators create a new high-risk bond, the price of which would provide input into the regulators' decisions.

calls to reregulate the industry. With the advent of tradable fishery quotas, says Greenpeace, "corporate interests are about to gobble up the rights to species of fish and turn them into private property. With privatization we lose our rights to have a say about how the oceans—something we all share—are being treated" (www.greenpeaceusa.org/features/itq.htm).

The case for using markets is a pragmatic one: They are justified only if they work better than the feasible alternatives. Do they? In what follows I ask what can be learned from these experiences in the use of markets as policy tools.

Governments can successfully use markets. Information is the key (as is elaborated in my recent book, McMillan 2002). The market process—where it works well—generates information on which of the firms are able to put scarce resources to the best use and on what the highest value use is. This information is unlikely to be revealed via a political or administrative procedure. Well-functioning markets remove the need, in other words, for the government to pick winners.

The public sector's ability to use markets, however, is constrained. The very reasons that certain activities have historically been placed in the public sector—natural monopoly, externalities, common property—make implementing markets for them difficult. "Leave it to the market" is usually bad advice.

There are two senses in which markets are a limited tool (as is also explained in McMillan 2002). First, a market does not automatically work as it is supposed to. The design of the market matters. With an ordinary private-sector market, the rules and procedures that govern it have evolved over years of trial and error. A public-sector market, by contrast, is judged by how well it works from its inception. Its rules and procedures, therefore, must be exhaustively thought through in advance. For a market to deliver on its public-policy promise, the government must design it skillfully.

Second, a market can provide only part of the solution to a public problem. With spectrum rights, pollution rights, electricity, and fisheries, the market does its job only within a framework of continued government action. Where there are elements of common property, externality, or natural monopoly, regulation continues to be needed even after a market has been introduced. The role of the market is to help the regulators do their job more effectively.

3.1 Spectrum Licenses

Auctions have been used by numerous governments to allocate licenses to use the electromagnetic spectrum for telecommunications, starting in New Zealand in 1990 and then the United States in 1994 and followed by countries such as Australia, Mexico, Canada, the United Kingdom, Germany, Hong Kong, and Singapore. The *Financial Times* (2 November 2000) called the spectrum auctions "the world's largest concerted transfer of money from the corporate sector to state coffers." As of 2001 the U.S. auctions had fetched a total of $42 billion. In 2000, an auction of spectrum licenses in the United Kingdom yielded $34 billion, and one in Germany went to $46 billion.[2]

Before auctioning, spectrum licenses had been given away for free. Who received the right to use the spectrum was decided by administrative hearings, or, in the case of some U.S. cellular telephone licenses, by lottery. Spectrum auctions, it is sometimes claimed, have the drawback of raising the prices that consumers ultimately pay for services. Janice Hughes, of Spectrum Strategy Consultants, said of Hong Kong, "An auction would push the price of a single license to at least US$1 billion per operator and, there is no question about it, those costs would be passed on to consumers in the form of substantially higher prices" (*South China Morning Post,* 21 August 2000, p. 3).

To argue this, however, is to confuse fixed and variable costs. A firm that cares about its profits bases its price on its marginal cost: that is, the cost of supplying an additional customer with the service. The auction price is paid before any service is provided—it is a fixed cost—so it is not part of the marginal cost of supplying the service and does not affect the price charged to customers. There is a caveat to this fixed-cost argument. If capital-market frictions mean that the more the firm borrows, the higher the interest rate it must pay, then the extra debt added by the auction price could result in the firm's investing less and having a higher marginal cost. This caveat aside, the auction revenue is a pure transfer from the firm's profits to the government. The price to users would be almost the same whether the government sold the spectrum or gave it away.

Yet another complaint is that auctions favor large bidders with deep pockets, so new entrants find it hard to compete. Against this view is the fact that the 1990s, the period in which market forces came into the telecommunications industry, in fact saw far more entries than before. The alternative to auctions, administrative processes, are not notably open to outsiders. It may be easier for a new firm to raise money to bid in an auction than to become a player in the political process. Governments that use so-called beauty contests to assign spectrum often favor the incumbents. When South Korea awarded two mobile licenses by an administrative procedure in 2000, for example, it selected from several applicants the two that were already the most entrenched: SK Telecom, Korea's biggest mobile provider, and Korea Telecom, which is state run. Auctions are more transparent than most administrative procedures. (This is another aspect of the information-provision feature of auctions: they enable the public to see how the decision is made.) This transparency puts a brake on government favoritism.

Mexico provides evidence against the doomsayers. The auctioning of

2. On the European experience with spectrum auctions, see Klemperer (2002).

spectrum licenses, from 1996 on, began a transformation of the telecommunications industry. Telephones for the first time became accessible to those other than the rich. By 2001, there were more subscribers to wireless phone lines than fixed-wire lines (16 million and rising vs. 12 million; *San Diego Mercury News,* 19 July 2000, p. 1C). The wireless services were supplied competitively by a half-dozen firms, while the fixed-wire services were provided by the incumbent monopolist, Telefonos de Mexico SA. As a result of the competition, consumers paid far less for wireless services than for fixed-wire services. The sums the wireless firms paid for their licenses—totaling over $1 billion—were no impediment to entry and did not keep the price of consumer services high.

3.2   Electricity

California's electricity deregulation was supposed to create "a market structure that provides competitive, low cost, and reliable electric service" (*Los Angeles Times,* 11 January 2001), according to the State Assembly bill that initiated it. But it didn't. The price of wholesale electricity rose to ten times what it had been. Governor Gray Davis labeled the move to markets "a colossal and dangerous failure" (*Los Angeles Times,* 14 January 2001).

Elementary supply and demand were at the heart of the crisis. Electricity supply was inadequate. Economic growth had brought increases in California's electricity usage, but few new generating plants had been built. Exacerbating the supply problem, at the time of deregulation unusually low rainfall and snowfall meant low water levels for hydro-generation and increased the need to use natural gas to generate electricity. At the same time there was a big increase in the price of natural gas.

In the old system, utilities operated as regulated monopolies: they could pass any cost increases on to their customers in higher rates and so had little incentive to hold their costs down. Deregulation meant wholesale electricity prices were set by competition rather than by a regulator. But the deregulation did not extend to retail prices, which continued to be held fixed, which meant that, when wholesale prices rose above retail prices, the utilities made losses. It also meant that demand-side pressures were lacking. Consumers had no price-based incentive to cut back at times when supply was short.

"We are so far into the realm of extraordinary gouging we are orders of magnitude off the chart," California Assembly Speaker Fred Keeley told the Federal Energy Regulatory Commission (FERC) in 2001 (*San Jose Mercury News,* 11 April 2001, p. 1A). Why did deregulation raise prices, rather than lowering them as it was intended to?

The special features of electricity make the performance of the market unusually sensitive to its design (Wilson 2002). Since electricity is costly to store, it must be produced as needed. Demand fluctuates. At peak demand times, all but a handful of generators are operating at their maximum capacity, and at such times those marginal producers can bid the price high.

The high prices were in part an ordinary market response to high demand, when it is the high-cost gas-fired plants, and not the low-cost hydro plants, that are the marginal suppliers. When demand hits a peak, therefore, marginal cost is high. Moreover, the price of natural gas rose dramatically in 2000. The price of electricity was driven up by the cost of generation.

At times, however, prices rose far above the generation costs. "There is evidence that some generators may be withholding electricity," Governor Davis said, "to create artificial scarcity and drive up the price astronomically" (*San Jose Mercury News,* 11 April 2001, p. 1A). Such manipulation of the market would have been illegal. It may not have been unnecessary for the generators to illicitly collude, however. At peak demand, most generators cannot expand their output because they are already producing at their full capacity. For the few remaining generators, the bidding incentives can drive prices high even without coordinated bidding.

One company, Enron, used complex schemes with names like Fat Boy, Ricochet, and Death Star to manipulate prices by tens of millions of dollars. The state of California estimated the power suppliers overcharged it to the extent of $9 billion during the crisis. The FERC agreed that overcharging had occurred, but disagreed about the amount: FERC ruled that the overcharging totaled $1.8 billion (*New York Times,* 23 March 2001, p. A14; *Financial Times,* 13 December 2002, p. 8).[3]

3.3   Pollution Control

The U.S. government in 1990 introduced a new technique to reduce sulfur dioxide emissions, the main cause of acid rain. Replacing command and control, under which each polluting firm had been directly regulated by the Environmental Protection Agency (EPA), the act created a market in the rights to pollute. It defined emissions allowances, that is, licenses allowing the holder to emit one ton of sulfur dioxide in one year. The allowances were tradable: they could be bought, sold, or banked for future use.

To reduce its emissions of sulfur dioxide, a coal-burning electricity producer either installs scrubbers or switches to cleaner fuel. The costs of cleanup differ among plants, depending on location and the age and type of their equipment. Implementing command and control effectively would have required considerable knowledge on the part of the EPA of each individual plant.

---

3. For estimates of the gap between price and marginal cost, see Borenstein, Bushnell, and Wolak (2000) and Joskow and Kahn (2002).

Tradable emissions allowances, by contrast, achieve pollution control flexibly. The total nationwide level of emissions is set by the government, which prints a total number of licenses equal to the target level of emissions. How much each plant cuts back is then set by the market. Those firms that find it relatively inexpensive to reduce their emissions sell some of their allowances and use the revenue to pay for their abatement activities (and have some profit left over). Those that find abatement relatively costly buy extra allowances. As a result, the target reduction in total emissions is achieved at the lowest possible cost to the industry.

The emissions-allowances program has been a success, according to various studies. The Environmental Defense Fund, an environmental group, said in its March 1995 newsletter that emissions trading "is cleaning up acid rain faster and far more cheaply than skeptics had predicted. The market system is unleashing inventiveness and showing that the cleanup need not put a heavy burden on the economy" (www.edf.org). The pollutants emitted fell below the ceiling the government had set. This was achieved at a cost to industry of billions of dollars less than the estimated cost of command and control. Air quality measurably improved.[4]

3.4   Fisheries

Fisheries are chronically overexploited. "The global marine fish catch is approaching its upper limit," according to an article in *Science* magazine (Botsford, Castilla, and Peterson 1997, 509). "Almost a half of the individual fish stocks are fully exploited, and another 22 percent are overexploited." The management of marine ecosystems "has failed to achieve a principal goal, sustainability."[5]

The overfishing results from the open-access nature of the fishery. In the absence of rules, the individual fishers have no incentive to conserve, because any fish they leave are taken by someone else. They cannot individually ensure the fish stocks are maintained.

Informal solutions to the open access problem work in certain circumstances. There are numerous examples of communities that have devised collective mechanisms to counter overfishing (Sethi and Somanathan 1996). Informal solutions, however, work only within tight-knit fishing communities. With large, anonymous groups of fishers that outsiders can enter, social sanctions hold little sway and so some kind of government intervention may be needed to prevent overfishing.

To regulate fisheries, governments have imposed controls, each of which has led to distortions. Regulatory controls on the number of boats have

---

4. For more on evaluating the program, see Ellerman et al. (2000), Bohi and Burtraw (1997), and EPA (1999). See also the EPA Web site, www.epa.gov/acidrain. For other environmental programs that use market incentives, see Daily and Ellison (2002) and Goldberg (2001).

5. For an excellent account of the fisheries crisis, see Grafton, Squires, and Kirkley (1996).

brought bigger boats with extra equipment and crew. Restrictions on the length of the vessels have induced companies to build wider, heavier boats. Restrictions on the number of crew have resulted in investment in high-tech fishing gear (adding electronic devices for locating fish increase a vessel's catch dramatically). Restrictions on equipment have meant the hiring of extra crew. Regulations specifying that fishing can take place only within a certain season induce firms to invest in high-capacity boats, so they can catch as much as possible in the time allowed; the investments sit idle for the rest of the year (Grafton, Squires, and Kirkley 1996; Grafton, Squires, and Fox 2000). And even with these regulations, the overfishing has continued.

Some governments have switched to a new, more market-based method of fish conservation. The regulators assign to each fishing vessel a quota, defining how much it is allowed to catch. Quotas directly address the basic issue—that overfishing is a consequence of the fact that no one owns the fish—by establishing property rights.

The New Zealand government introduced tradable quotas in the mid-1980s. The aim was to reduce catches to sustainable levels. Quotas were allocated to individual fishers based on their prior investments in equipment. The quotas may be bought and sold. A new entrant or an incumbent wanting to expand needs to buy quotas. This means the quotas tend to end up with the most efficient producers.

When the New Zealand government wanted to reduce the total catch because of what it judged to be overfishing, it used a market process. It called for tenders from the fishers. A bid stated how much money the fisher would accept to reduce the allowed catch by a specified amount. The government accepted the lowest bids up to its target catch reduction, and paid each successful bidder the market-clearing price per ton of quota reduction (Sharp 1996, 442).

The tradable-quota system is an application of the idea of Ronald Coase (1960) of defining property rights so as to solve an externality. The system works effectively (Grafton, Squires, and Fox 2000; Straker, Kerr, and Hendy 2002). Fish stocks been conserved and fishers' profits have risen. Quota-holders have a stake in preserving the fishery in order to maintain the value of their quotas. In New Zealand, the fishers have formed associations to fund research aimed at conserving the stocks of scallops, snapper, and orange roughy. The creation of property rights has resulted, as Coase said it would, in the open-access externality's being internalized.

3.5 Lessons on Markets as Policy Tools

Some lessons can be drawn from these experiences in the use of markets by governments. Markets can be useful policy tools, primarily because they reveal information that otherwise might be unobtainable. But there are two crucial caveats, which seem obvious but are often overlooked. Markets can solve only certain kinds of problems, and they need to be implemented well.

3.5.1   Markets Reveal Information

The emissions-allowance market, like any other competitive market, generates information.[6] It reveals how to allocate pollution reduction across firms in the way that brings the lowest total cost. It also reveals what the costs of reducing pollution actually are. Bureaucrats could, in principle, control pollution as cost effectively as the market by requiring extra reduction from those plants that have lower abatement costs. Realistically, however, they do not know where abatement costs are high and where they are low. It is the firms themselves that best understand how much it would cost them to cut their own pollution.

The EPA can know a firm's abatement costs only if the firm itself volunteers the information. The incentives under command and control worked against this. Managers, negotiating with the EPA, might exaggerate their firms' abatement costs in order to be assigned easier cleanup targets. The managers may even not have known how low their abatement costs could be driven, for under command and control they had little incentive to find out. Bureaucracy-run pollution controls are hindered by a lack of information.[7] Under the market, by contrast, firms with low cleanup costs have a profit-based incentive to reveal this fact, by selling their allowances.

Before emissions trading began, the EPA estimated it would cost $750 to clean up a ton of sulfur dioxide. The electric-power firms claimed it would cost them up to $1,500. The average price at which the allowances actually traded over 1994–1999 was about $150.[8] By selling an allowance for $150, a firm was in effect saying that cutting its emissions would cost it no more than $150 per ton. In other words, the market revealed cost of cleanup to be five to ten times less than had been previously suggested.

The spectrum auctions, similarly, revealed information. The multibillion-dollar prices reached seemed too high to some observers at the time,

6. For an overview of markets as information providers, see McMillan (2002).

7. It is theoretically possible to devise a centralized mechanism that induces firms to reveal their private information, along the lines of Baron and Myerson (1982). This would involve subsidizing the plants that reveal themselves to be low cost (and so are asked to do the most cleanup) and taxing the others. Such a mechanism is, however, difficult if not impossible to implement in practice.

8. The $1,500 figure was stated in the 1990 Clean Air Act as the price of direct sales of allowances by the EPA, and the $750 figure was cited by the EPA in 1990 as its best guess of the price at which allowances would trade (Bohi and Burtraw 1997, 8). The allowances prices ranged between $70 and $220 over 1994–1999 (see www.epa.gov/acidrain/ats/prices). The price of low-sulfur coal fell in a way that could not have been anticipated, and this explains part of the five- to tenfold difference between actual and predicted prices (Bohi and Burtraw; Ellerman et al. 2000). Much of it, though, is due to information generation. (Although pricing rules of the EPA auction tend to induce low prices, as I will discuss, this is not the explanation, for most of the transactions occur in the private market.)

and even more so with the benefit of hindsight. In the frenzy of the bidding, the critics say, the telecommunications executives bid far above their estimates of value. If that were true, we should question their competence (as should their shareholders). But it isn't likely to be the correct interpretation. The auction prices revealed the industry's best current estimate of the value of the spectrum. Before there was competition, that knowledge stayed with the firms. The arrival of competition forced the insiders to reveal the value of the spectrum rights, and to pass much of that value on to the government.

The competitive process reveals information. After an auction, the seller knows which of the bidders values the item the most, and the price gives an estimate of value. There is a twist, however. The bidders are in part all trying to estimate the same thing, the future profitability of running mobile telecommunications services. This common-value feature means the bidders risk falling into the trap of the "winner's curse": that is, learning, too late, that the price has gone higher than the item is worth. If they are all knowledgable, then the best estimate is something like the average of their valuations. The winning bid, of course, is higher than the average bid. The winner is likely to be the bidder whose estimate is the most optimistic, probably overoptimistic.

In any auction, unwary bidders risk overestimating the value of winning. Bidders sometimes get caught up in the excitement of an auction and pay too much. But they need not be fooled. Experienced bidders avoid the winner's curse by bidding cautiously: They recognize they will win only if they have relatively high value estimates and bid accordingly lower. Alert winners need not be cursed.[9] It is not especially difficult to avoid being subject to the winner's curse. All you have to do is understand precisely why there is a risk of bidding too high. The phrase "winner's curse" has in fact become common parlance in the telecommunications industry, suggesting the bidders did understand it.

The wisdom of hindsight is a different matter. Changes in the telecommunications industry subsequent to the auctions in some cases, such as the German and U.K. auctions, caused a rethinking of the value of the spectrum; but that is an ordinary business risk. In the optimistic late 1990s, the industry set a high value on spectrum, anticipating vast profits in the near future from mobile telecommunications. In the pessimistic years of 2000–2003, those profits failed to materialize, and the bid prices were seen to have overvalued the spectrum. But that is an ordinary business misjudgment, not something inherent in the auction process. Ironically, the telecommunications industry, long the recipient of government handouts, gave something back via the spectrum auctions to taxpayers.

---

9. On bidding to avoid the winner's curse, see Wilson (1969) and Milgrom and Weber (1982). On experiments with common-value auctions, see Garvin and Kagel (1994).

In California's electricity deregulation, the market's information revelation was thwarted. Because wholesale prices sometimes far exceeded marginal production costs, they provided no useful information about the supply side of the market. And because retail prices were fixed, they were prevented from providing information about the demand side.

3.5.2   Markets Must Be Well Designed

The California electricity market tripped up on an elementary feature of market design. Prices were not allowed to do their job. Although the wholesale price at which the utilities bought power was market-set, the regulators fixed the retail price the utilities charged their customers. If the retail price had varied month by month to reflect wholesale prices, not only could the utility have avoided indebtedness, but consumers would have been motivated to conserve electricity. For business customers sophisticated meters allowing real-time pricing could have been installed. Businesses could shut down when prices were high, and run extra shifts when they were low. Peak-time power would thus be saved for other uses such as in homes. With the retail price fixed, the system had no way of responding to shortages.

Some critics say California's deregulation did not go far enough; it should have moved to fully free markets. Others say there should have been no deregulation, for markets for electricity cannot work. Both sides oversimplify. The deregulation fell short in retaining retail price controls and preventing prices from signaling scarcity; it went too far in eliminating restraints on overpricing by the generating companies. The problem was not too much or too little use of markets, but poor market design.

In its spectrum auctions the U.S. government adopted a novel form of auction, the *simultaneous ascending auction,* designed to address the specific features of the spectrum market. (For details of the market design, see McAfee and McMillan 1996 and Milgrom 2000.) The success of the spectrum auctions justified the choice of auction form.

With the tradable pollution licenses, by contrast, the market-design issue was not fully faced. The government put in place an auction for the allowances that was flawed—in a way that shows the importance of apparently innocuous features of the rules of the market game. (Cason and Plott 1996 pointed out this flaw in the EPA auction.) The market process was a double auction: potential sellers submitted price-quantity offers, and potential buyers submitted price-quantity bids. The rules for setting the prices unintentionally had the effect of giving not only buyers but also sellers incentives to bid low.

The poor auction design could have been a dampener on emissions trading. By luck, however, it turned out to have no ill effects. Bottom-up market creation compensated for flaws in the top-down market design. The emissions-allowances program was rescued by the emergence of a private market alongside the EPA auction. (In fact, the EPA envisaged its auction as a way of jump-starting the private market, and in this it succeeded.) Intermediaries took on the role of market makers, buying and selling allowances on behalf of clients and sometimes speculating on their own account. Although sellers may be deterred by the prospect of low prices from offering their allowances in the EPA auction, they have the alternative of the private market. The private market handles most of the transactions.

The secondary market in emissions allowances is easy to operate. One allowance is identical to another: it is simply the right to emit one ton of sulfur dioxide in a year. Because of the simplicity of what is being traded, it was not difficult to create a smoothly operating secondary market in emissions allowances. For this reason, in the case of emissions allowances, getting the market design wrong turned out to be inconsequential. With the emissions allowances, it was just a matter of leaving it to the market.

We cannot usually rely on secondary markets, however, to rescue a badly designed primary market. In the case of the spectrum auctions, a spontaneously developed secondary market could not be expected to operate efficiently (at least without a lengthy period of evolution). The very reasons why designing the spectrum auctions was nontrivial—the complementarities among the licenses—meant the secondary market would be plagued by high transaction costs and resulting inefficiencies. Because the secondary market could not be relied on, it was important to get the initial auction design right.

Emissions allowances are an exception that proves the rule. Generally, the design of a market must be watertight, especially when large sums of money are at stake. Any oversight in market design can have harmful repercussions, as bidders can be counted on to seek ways to outfox the mechanism. A newly instituted market achieves what it is supposed to only if it is well designed. The rules of the market matter.[10]

3.5.3   Markets Do Not Supersede Regulation

Emissions allowances do not take the government out of pollution control, but help it control pollution more efficiently. The government hands over to the market a part of its role: deciding how the emissions cutbacks are to be shared among the firms. But it retains its primary roles: assessing how much pollution in total is to be allowed, checking compliance, and fining any firms that break the rules.

In deregulated electricity markets also, government oversight continues to be needed. The transmission grid—the web of high-voltage lines that carry the power—is by its nature a monopoly, and so cannot be left to an unregulated market. Because of the physics of electricity, the operator of

---

10. For more on how the rules of market matter to its efficient operation, see McMillan (2002).

the grid must constantly monitor it to ensure its reliability. The amount of power being pumped into the grid by the generators must always equal the amount being tapped by electricity users. The transmission system would be destabilized, bringing blackouts around the state, if there were a sudden uncompensated surge in the amount of electricity either being put in or drawn out. No matter how smoothly the retail and wholesale electricity markets operate, therefore, the grid needs continuing regulation.

Electricity-market regulation is needed also for competition-policy reasons. Because demand is insensitive to price and the consequences of a supply shortfall are severe, a few producers are, in periods if peak demand, in the position of being able to bid prices far above production costs. These high prices do not immediately call forth new sources of supply, since new-generation facilities take years to come online. Unlike the case of the pollution allowances, private-sector intermediaries cannot step in to correct the official market's failings by starting their own marketplaces, for all the power must travel through the grid. Competition by itself cannot always be relied on to hold the price down close to generation costs. There continues to be a role for regulatory oversight of pricing.

With spectrum auctions, similarly, a role for the government remains. It continues to coordinate the usage of the spectrum by defining the purposes each wavelength band can be put to—broadcasting or various specific telecommunications applications. Some of this coordination role can in principle be passed on to the market: New Zealand is going the farthest in considering passing some of the spectrum management to the private sector. But the government still does the waveband equivalent of land-use zoning. The ultimate decision on how the publicly owned spectrum is to be used remains with the government. This is because there are externalities: users of adjacent wavebands might cause interference with each other. And reassigning spectrum as new technologies arise might require some central coordination.

With fisheries, also, creating and enforcing workable property rights requires ongoing government action. Quotas do not eliminate the need for regulatory supervision. The regulator must decide what level of total catch is sustainable. It must devise rules on who initially receives the quotas. Dividing up the rights to the catch is a source of contention among the fishers.

No system of monitoring, moreover, is infallible. New Zealand goes to great lengths to prevent out-of-quota fishing. It insists on full documentation, with paperwork recording each step of the fishes' journey from point of landing to final consumption or export. Fishers may not sell fish to anyone other than a licensed fish receiver. Catch reports, licensed-fish-receiver receipts, cold-storage records, and export invoices are all collated and checked for discrepancies. Overfishing and misreporting are criminal offenses.[11]

11. On monitoring, see Batkin (1996) and Squires, Kirkley, and Tisdell (1995).

Property rights are not a free lunch. Transaction costs must be faced, as Coase (1960) stressed. Quota oversight is expensive. With a fishery, as with the other public-sector applications, resorting to markets does not remove the need for government action.

3.6   Competition as a Tool of Redistribution

In 1961 President John F. Kennedy issued an executive order requiring government contractors to "take affirmative action to ensure that applicants are employed and employees are treated during employment without regard to their race, creed, color, or national origin." Since then, affirmative action policies have waxed and waned. Of necessity, given the nature of the task, they have mostly taken the form of administered policies, including court-mandated correction of inequities in employment and university-admission rules favoring minority applicants. But market-based policies have also been used, particularly in government contracting and procurement.

Blacks and Hispanics have historically been underrepresented among owners of U.S. businesses. In part this was because of discrimination in the credit market. Studies of loan patterns have found that, controlling for factors like credit ratings and previous bankruptcies, blacks are less likely to receive bank credit than other entrepreneurs. Even in the absence of discrimination, underrepresentation can be self-perpetuating. In industries like construction, when an upcoming job is announced, some preselected firms are invited to bid for it, based on their having done good work in the past. For minority-owned firms this was a catch-22. They could not bid for a contract, because they were not put on the list of invitees, because they had not had a contract.

Affirmative action in government contracting was intended to increase the disproportionately small share of government contracts going to minority-owned firms. It has been a success, as measured by a markedly increased share of contracts held by minority firms and an increase in black employment. The evidence on the program's costs is sketchy, but what there is suggests that they have been low (despite some fraud, with phony minority-owned firms being created as a front for white-owned firms in order to receive the preferences). The price paid relative to the government's prior cost estimate has been on average little different for minority firms benefiting from preferences than for others. In New Jersey, the introduction of preferences sharply increased the share of contracts going to minority firms, but their cessation a few years later brought no reduction in the share, suggesting that the minority firms had been given a jump start by the program and then had been able to stand on their own.[12]

---

12. The foregoing draws on Holzer and Neumark (2000).

The U.S. government, as well as state and local governments, used two kinds of affirmative-action policies in contracting. One was to guarantee that certain contracts went to minority-owned firms. A contract was offered to a single minority firm without competitive bidding, or the contract was put up for bidding on a set-aside basis, meaning that only minority-owned firms could bid for it. An alternative policy, that of price preferences, consisted of designing the market's rules so as to achieve the policy goal. Contracts were put up for bid in the normal way, but with the difference that minority-owned firms received a price break. Before the government compared the bids, it subtracted a specified amount from the minority-owned firms' bids, usually 10 percent, meaning a minority firm could win if its bid was higher, by no more than 10 percent, than a nonminority firm's bid.

Mayor David N. Dinkins introduced a 10 percent price preference for firms owned by minorities or women into New York City's municipal contracting in 1993. One year later, according to a report issued by the Dinkins administration, minority- and women-owned companies' share of the contracts had risen sharply, from 9.0 percent to 17.5 percent. The cost of the program through not selecting the lowest bids, the report said, was $2.7 million, or 1 percent of the total contracting budget. The city of Los Angeles implemented a similar price-preference program.

Government preferences were controversial. The New York program was abolished by Mayor Rudolph W. Giuliani, not only on the grounds of cost but also from a philosophical objection to affirmative action. California voters voted in a 1996 ballot initiative to end affirmative action programs. Los Angeles then replaced its affirmative action program with a 5 percent price preference for any small firm. Since many of the small businesses are owned by minorities and women, however, the small-business price break meant that the Los Angeles contracts were still steered toward them (the share of city spending going to minority firms rose from 12 percent in 1996 to 15 percent in 2000; *New York Times,* 2 February 1994, p. B2; *San Jose Mercury News,* 4 December 2000, p. 1A).

Setting aside a contract for one or a few bidders necessarily increases the price paid by the government, since, with bidding competition eliminated or reduced, there is no reliable way of identifying which firm would have the lowest cost of doing the job. A price preference, by contrast, can be a free-lunch policy. It not only addresses the public-policy goal of increasing the number of contracts going to the minority firms, but it also could actually sometimes lower the average price the government pays its contractors.[13] With price preferences, a minority firm would win if its bid was no more than 10 percent higher than the lowest bid from a nonminority firm. The minority firms typically have a higher cost of carrying out the con-

13. This piece of theorizing is from McAfee and McMillan (1987, 714–16).

tracted work than the nonminority firms (because of lack of access to capital and lack of experience). They would therefore impose little competitive pressure on the nonminority firms, which could, if there were little competition among themselves, get away with bidding relatively high. A price preference for the minority firms stimulates the bidding competition, forcing the nonminority firms to bid lower. Depending on the level of the price preference, its price-lowering effect (from the lower bids from the nonminority firms) could sometimes outweigh its price-raising effect (from the chance that a minority firm wins and must be paid a relatively high price). The price preferences, therefore, should not much increase the government's overall contracting bill; they are more cost effective than the alternative of earmarking some contracts for minority firms. Price preferences can help level an unlevel playing field.

This logic came to play in the designing of the spectrum auctions. Congress required the Federal Communications Commission (FCC) to "ensure that small businesses, rural telephone companies, and businesses owned by members of minority groups and women are given the opportunity to participate in the provision of spectrum-based services" (U.S. Congress 1993). The first two FCC auctions included price preferences, of as much as 40 percent. FCC chairman Reed E. Hundt described the preferences as offering "the single most important economic opportunity made available to women and minorities in our country's history" (McAfee and McMillan 1996, p. 167). They were controversial, however. "We want a guarantee of spectrum competition," wrote William Safire in the *New York Times*. "The criterion to determine competition must be scrupulously economic, not jiggered by the Government to introduce sexual or racial or ethnic or ideological favoritism" (*New York Times*, 16 March 1995). Despite revealing a misunderstanding of the effects of price preferences—as just argued, they could actually make the bidding more competitive—such views became dominant. When the mood in Washington turned against affirmative action, the FCC scrapped the preferences from subsequent auctions. Nevertheless, where they were used they succeeded in their policy aim of helping some minority-owned firms enter the mobile telecommunications industry.

Market mechanisms, then, can in some circumstances be called upon to help with redistribution toward the disadvantaged—and can achieve it more cost effectively than administrative methods.

3.7 Conclusion

In picking winners, governments have a poor track record. Picking winners is exactly what the government is called upon to do when it makes allocation decisions such as which firm gets the right to use a publicly owned resource. A market-based allocation leaves the government to do what only it can do, while turning over to the market the job of picking winners.

Competitive markets, if well designed, can reveal the information that is needed for allocating the resources efficiently. Markets do not replace the government's regulatory role, but in the right circumstances they can be an effective instrument of regulation.

References

Baron, David P., and Roger B. Myerson. 1982. Regulating a monopolist with unknown costs. *Econometrica* 50:911–930.

Batkin, Kirsten M. 1996. New Zealand's quota management system: A solution to the United States' Federal Fisheries Management crisis? *Natural Resources Journal* 36 (4): 855–880.

Bohi, Douglas R., and Dallas Burtraw. 1997. SO_2 allowance trading: How experience and expectations measure up. Discussion Paper no. 97-24. Washington, D.C.: Resources for the Future, February.

Borenstein, Severin, James Bushnell, and Frank Wolak. 2000. Diagnosing market power in California's restructured wholesale electricity market. NBER Working Paper no. 7868. Cambridge, Mass.: National Bureau of Economic Research, September.

Botsford, Louis W., Juan Carlos Castilla, and Charles H. Peterson. 1997. The management of fisheries and marine ecosystems. *Science* 277 (July): 509–515.

Cason, Timothy N., and Charles R. Plott. 1996. EPA's new emissions trading mechanism: A laboratory evaluation. *Journal of Environmental Economics and Management* 30:133–160.

Coase, R. H. 1960. The problem of social cost. *Journal of Law and Economics* 3:1–44.

Daily, Gretchen C., and Katherine Ellison. 2002. *The new economy of nature.* New York: Island Press.

Ellerman, A. Denny, Paul L. Joskow, Richard Schmalensee, Juan-Pablo Montero, and Elizabeth M. Bailey. 2000. *Markets for clean air.* New York: Cambridge University Press.

Environmental Protection Agency (EPA). 1999. *Progress report on the EPA acid rain program.* Washington, D.C.: EPA. Available at www.epa.gov/acidrain.

Garvin, Susan, and John H. Kagel. 1994. Learning in common-value auctions. *Journal of Economic Behavior and Organization* 25 (December): 351–370.

Goldberg, Beth. 2001. Auctioning CO_2 permits: A business-friendly climate policy. In *Redefining Progress* [booklet]. Oakland, Calif.

Grafton, R. Quentin, Dale Squires, and Kevin J. Fox. 2000. Private property and economic efficiency: A study of a common-pool resource. *Journal of Law and Economics* 43:679–714.

Grafton, R. Quentin, Dale Squires, and James E. Kirkley. 1996. Private property rights and crises in world fisheries. *Contemporary Economic Policy* 14:89–99.

Holzer, Harry, and David Neumark. 2000. Assessing affirmative action. *Journal of Economic Literature* 38:483–568.

Joskow, Paul, and Edward Kahn. 2002. A quantitative analysis of pricing behavior in California's wholesale electricity market during summer 2000. *Energy Journal* 23 (4): 1–35.

Klemperer, Paul. 2001. What really matters in auction design. *Journal of Economic Perspectives* 16 (1): 169–189.

McAfee, R. Preston, and John McMillan. 1987. Auctions and bidding. *Journal of Economic Literature* 25 (2): 699–738.

———. 1996. Analyzing the airwaves auction. *Journal of Economic Perspectives* 10:159–176.

McMillan, John. 2002. *Reinventing the bazaar: A natural history of markets.* New York: Norton.

Milgrom, Paul. 2000. Putting auction theory to work: The simultaneous ascending auction. *Journal of Political Economy* 108:245–272.

Milgrom, Paul R., and Robert J. Weber. 1982. A theory of auctions and competitive bidding. *Econometrica* 50:1089–1122.

Sethi, Rajiv, and E. Somanathan. 1996. The evolution of social norms in common property resource use. *American Economic Review* 86:766–788.

Sharp, Basil M. H. 1996. Natural resource management. In *A study of economic reform: The case of New Zealand,* ed. B. Silverstone, A. Bollard, and R. Lattimore, 425–429. Amsterdam: North-Holland.

Squires, Dale, James Kirkley, and Clement A. Tisdell. 1995. Individual transferable quotas as a fisheries management tool. *Reviews in Fisheries Science* 3:141–169.

Straker, Gina, Suzi Kerr, and Joanna Hendy. 2002. *A regulatory history of New Zealand's quota management system* [booklet]. Wellington, N.Z.: Motu Economic and Policy Research, August. Available at www.motu.org.nz/nz_fish.htm.

U.S. Congress. 1993. Omnibus Budget Reconciliation Act of 1993 Conference Report [HR 2264], Title VI, "Communications Licensing and Spectrum Allocation Improvement." Report 103-213, August.

U.S. Shadow Financial Regulatory Committee. *Reforming bank capital regulation.* Washington, D.C.: AEI Press.

Wilson, Robert B. 1969. Competitive bidding with disparate information. *Management Science* 15:446–448.

———. 2002. Architecture of power markets. *Econometrica* 70:1299–340.

Comment   Kyoji Fukao

As I am not an expert on industrial organization, my comments will be of a general nature.

This paper reviews four examples of public-sector uses of markets and derives several important lessons; for example, markets reveal information and markets must be well designed. I found the paper quite informative, because the author provides very clear explanations of complicated issues such as electromagnetic-spectrum auctions and the retail market for electricity. Moreover, I basically agree with the author's argument on the lessons to be learned. I have four comments.

My first comment is on theory. The author argues that the desirability of the introduction of a market and optimal market design depend crucially on the characteristics of the goods that will be traded. However, these issues are not addressed systematically. If the author provided us with a gen-

Kyoji Fukao is professor at the Institute of Economic Research, Hitotsubashi University.

eral theory on the use of the market, this would be very helpful. Let me give an example. Important characteristics of goods can be classified into several factors. First, difficulties in establishing and protecting property rights are an important factor. In the case of fisheries and pollution, monitoring the property rights is expensive. Second, difficulties in storage and elasticity of intertemporal substitution are another important factor. If it is difficult to store goods, as in the case of electricity, we will have quite volatile spot prices and the introduction of forward markets will be an important issue. Third, the risk of market power abuses is another important factor. If the author drew a figure, or table, in which each axis denotes one of these characteristics, and located each good in this figure, the theoretical analysis of the paper would become clearer.

My second comment is on the relationship between the use of markets and privatization. The author does not show us explicitly how his argument is related to the privatization issue. If the author elaborated on this issue, the reader would be able to better understand the close relationship between this and other papers presented at this seminar. Let me give an example. In the case of industries in which networks for transmission and distribution are important, such as electricity, telecommunications, and railroads, it is sometimes desirable to continue regulating the "wires" business, and to privatize the industry through vertical separation. In such cases, the design of the wholesale market is a very important issue.

My third comment regards data on market prices. If some data on market prices were provided in the paper, the author's argument would become more persuasive. For example, I would like to see some figures for the wholesale price of electricity. International or interregional comparisons of price levels also would be informative. If the author could compare the average price level for the electromagnetic spectrum among countries and analyze what market characteristics affect the price level, this would enhance the study.

My last comment regards international aspects. I think that whether foreigners are permitted to participate in a new market or not, and whether goods are internationally tradable or not, are pertinent topics. I would like to ask the author to consider these issues in his future work.

Comment   Tsuruhiko Nambu

This paper is quite insightful; it gives us an opportunity to rethink the tide of deregulation or join a chorus for market mechanisms. As far as there exist public policy goals, a third party must remain to solve this task. With-

Tsuruhiko Nambu is professor of economics at Gakushuin University.

out this entity, one variable is missing for solving the overall social system. This is common sense, but its meaning is clearly verified by considering four episodes: pollution control, electricity, spectrum allocation, and fishery management. In three cases of the four, market mechanisms worked to a remarkable extent to help government realize public goals. But in one case, electricity, we witnessed a total failure in California.

In the first three cases, the task of government is to assign property rights: to give proper incentives to realize public objectives. In the last case, government intervened in the old market paradigm, namely vertical integration, to create an unbundled system. I think the cases of pollution and fisheries are readily understandable because they are based upon approving vested interests without asking for distributional fairness at the start. If the eventual result is acceptable from the viewpoint of public policy, then the initial distribution of rights does not matter: this is a pragmatic approach.

Less convincing is the case of spectrum auctions. It is true that auctions reveal the value of spectra, but I wonder whether they offer an efficient solution. Let us look at the U.S. telecommunications industry, where entry into local markets used to be forbidden by the consent decree. Long-distance carriers wished to enter the local market. They employed a strategy to make use of cellular telephony to beat regional Bell operating companies (RBOCs). Because of the constraints on long-distance carriers, their willingness to pay for an electromagnetic spectrum might be greater than without constraints. It may have pushed up prices more than necessary. The move of RBOCs to defend their markets may have accelerated this price increase. Summing up, I wish to say that institutional bias surrounding the telecommunications industry would harm the auction results. Looking at the reality that AT&T is said to divest its cellular division may help us understand the situation.

I fully agree with the discussion on electricity failure in California. One comment may be in order when we remember the bad relationship between the Public Utility Commission and electricity companies in California. In transition from the old system to new, some constructive talks were necessary, especially when knowledge was owned one-sidedly by the incumbent firms. If regulated firms do not have any incentive to collaborate with regulators who impose transition costs on them, they will not teach their secrets, later possibly inducing a breakdown of the system. In my guess, this was the case of mustrun electric power–generating plants sold off by the electric power utilities. Many experts say that these should not have been allowed to be sold off so as to maintain voltage control. But California utilities, it seems, did not pay attention to this problem. There may have been discussion over these matters if there had existed smoother communication between regulated firms and the regulator. This kind of relationship is dependent on history, and I think we need to be sensible of this path dependence.

II

Country Studies

4

Recent Developments in the Public-Enterprise Sector of Korea

Il Chong Nam

4.1 Introduction

The government has always been the dominant figure in the corporate landscape of Korea. This is not surprising, considering that Korea has a relatively short history of capitalism and that the government played a decisive role in the fast industrialization process that began in the 1960s. An important aspect of the economic development strategy of the successive administrations was the creation of large firms in modern industries that realize economies of scale and scope. Many large commercial Korean firms were established by the *chaebol* system, which crucially depended on the government's intervention in the financial market. Following the heavy and chemical industry drive of the mid-1970s, the automobile, shipbuilding, electronics, chemical, and oil refinery industries, as well as a host of others (including construction), were erected in this manner.[1]

The government's involvement has been more direct in the remaining industries that require large amounts of capital to start and maintain the business. The government owned and operated all of the major network industries, including telephony, postal services, electricity, gas, water, and rail transportation. It also owned and operated other large firms in manufacturing industries such as the tobacco and steel industries. All of these industries began virtually as government monopolies. The government also owned and operated monopolistic suppliers in minting, textbook publish-

Il Chong Nam is professor at the Korea Development Institute School of Public Policy and Management.

1. For a discussion on the *chaebol* system and industrial policies of past governments, see Nam, Kang, and Kim (2001) and Nam et al. (2001).

ing, and several other industries whose main customer was the government itself. In addition, the government owned or invested in a score of firms in competitive industries such as newspapers, venture capital, coal mining, and chemicals. Furthermore, some bankrupt private firms were acquired by public enterprises and became public enterprises themselves. Finally, the government controlled and partly owned much of the financial sector for a long period before it nationalized much of the industry in the aftermath of the recent economic crisis.

The above-listed commercial businesses owned and controlled by the government took several different legal forms: government agencies, public corporations, and *gongdan*.[2] For instance, rail transportation has been operating as a government agency within the transportation department, while telecommunications was transformed from a similar government agency into a public corporation. However, almost all of the commercial businesses owned and controlled by the government were perceived mainly as policy instruments rather than money-making firms, regardless of the form they took.

One consequence of such a command-and-control approach was the lack of separation among public enterprises' conflicting objectives. Policy objectives were generally not clearly separated from commercial goals. For network industries, separation among industrial policies, regulatory functions, and commercial operation was generally absent. Thus, the line ministry was charged with regulatory power on the one hand and the authority to make key business decisions for the monopolistic supplier under its control on the other.[3] Further, it pursued a wide range of industrial policy objectives that were often in conflict with the other two objectives.

Although no rigorous empirical analysis has been conducted, it is widely believed that most of the public enterprises had serious problems in managerial efficiency due to conflicting goals and absence of clear accountability for various cost-inducing activities. Casual observation and scattered pieces of information all suggest that there were serious irregularities within most public enterprises.[4] Scandals involving the procurement practices of public enterprises were not infrequent. Decisions on hiring, appointment of employees to various positions, promotions, and rewards

---

2. A *gongdan* is a nonprofit public foundation based on public laws.

3. The *line ministry* of a public enterprise is the ministry that is in charge of the industry to which the public enterprise belongs as well as policies relevant to the industry. Every public enterprise has its line ministry. The line ministry of a public enterprise has a wide range of authority over the relevant industry, including policy development, regulation of firms in the industry, and the control of the public enterprise.

4. It is interesting to note that while it is hard for anyone familiar with public enterprises to deny that they were inefficient, it is also hard to establish that large private firms were more efficient than public enterprises. Comparison of various indices on the financial performance of public enterprises and large private firms generally indicates that the latter fared worse. In fact, more than one-third of large *chaebol* firms have ended up bankrupt since 1997.

were often made based on factors that were seldom related to the profitability of the public enterprises.

There have been two waves of reform efforts aimed at privatizing the public-enterprise sector. In late 1997, the Kim Young Sam administration introduced the Act for Privatization and Improvement of the Efficiency of Large Public Enterprises, generally referred to as the "Special Act on Privatization," to promote privatization of four large public enterprises.[5] The act aimed at reforming corporate governance structures of commercial public enterprises to be privatized, while at the same time preventing takeover by *chaebols* during their privatization. The second wave of reform, initiated by the current administration that came to power at the peak of the economic crisis, is still unfolding. The current administration turned over large shares of public enterprises to private hands. It is also transforming the electricity industry from a vertically integrated public-enterprise monopoly into a competitive industry operated by private interests. However, full privatization of a large public enterprise has yet to occur.

In short, privatization is still proceeding and is far from complete. Thus, it is too early to quantitatively evaluate the outcome of the policies toward state-owned enterprises (SOEs) being privatized with any precision.[6] Instead, our goal in this paper is to give an accurate description of the key aspects of the public-enterprise sector in Korea, as well as the privatization process, and to identify the remaining issues. In addition, this paper deals with the *chaebol* problem that worked as a barrier to privatization.

The paper proceeds as follows. Section 4.2 provides an overview of the public-enterprise sector, encompassing the institutional frameworks governing public enterprises and their characteristics and positions in relevant markets. Section 4.3 provides key financial information on public enterprises, including revenues, profits, and debt-equity ratios. This section also compares the performance of large SOEs with that of *chaebol* firms. One notable finding is that large SOEs are generally more efficient than *chaebol* firms. Section 4.4 describes the main elements of the 1997 Special Act on Privatization and analyzes the factors that led to the introduction of the act as well as its effect. Section 4.5 summarizes the privatization policies of the new administration and their results. This section deals with both institutional changes and divestiture of the government's shares and also provides analysis of some of the crucial events. Sections 4.2 through 4.5 are devoted

5. Nam and Kang (1998) offer an extensive analysis of the Special Act and of other key issues regarding the public-enterprise sector in Korea.

6. For instance, comparison of costs before and after privatization is not possible for most large commercial SOEs because they have been only partially privatized and are generally still controlled by the government. There are several small SOEs that have been completely privatized and are now controlled by private investors, but a meaningful quantitative comparison of efficiency before and after privatization is also difficult since they have been privatized only recently.

to twenty-six nonfinancial corporations in which the government is the dominant shareholder or in a controlling position. Section 4.6 explains other forms of commercial organizations owned and controlled by the government, and the final section draws conclusions.

4.2   An Overview of the Public-Enterprise Sector Prior to 1998

4.2.1   Institutional Environment

At the end of September 1997 there were twenty-six nonfinancial corporations in which the government was the sole owner or had controlling interests.[7] Many of them had several subsidiaries in which they held controlling interests.[8] Most of the twenty-six corporations had strong commercial elements in the nature of their business. Some of them, such as Korea Telecom (KT) and Korea Tobacco and Ginseng (KT&G), started as government agencies and were later transformed into corporations. Some others, such as Pohang Steel Co. (POSCO), were established as corporations from the beginning. Korea Heavy was established as a result of the merger among three ailing private firms, which were acquired by a consortium headed by Korea Electric Power Corporation (KEPCO).[9]

The twenty-six public enterprises were perceived by the government primarily as policy instruments rather than profit-seeking business organizations. Consequently, the shareholders' rights of each of them were given to a line ministry, which put priority on policy considerations in exercising the rights.[10] Some of the public enterprises had their own corporation acts, such as the KEPCO Act and KT&G Act, which made it clear that they were established to serve public policy objectives and explicitly gave the line ministry control of the respective public enterprise. All of the govern-

7. 1997 is a good year for comparison with the current year because it is the last year of the old regime, which had been quite stable since the late 1980s. The public-enterprise sector began to change in a fundamental way in November 1997, after the newly introduced Special Act on Privatization took effect.

8. Some of the twenty-six corporations are subsidiaries of one of the twenty-six public enterprises, at least in terms of ownership. For instance, Korea Electric Power Corporation (KEPCO), the vertically integrated monopoly in the electricity industry, was the second-largest shareholder of Korea Heavy, which was the monopolist in the generator industry. KEPCO was also the second-largest shareholder, after the government, of Korea Gas Corporation (KOGAS), the monopolist in the importing stage as well as in the wholesale stage of the gas industry. However, it should also be noted that KEPCO did not exercise or attempt to exercise control of these two public enterprises; the government maintained exclusive control of them.

9. Korea Heavy is not the only firm to become a public enterprise as a result of rationalization measures for bankrupt private firms. For instance, Hanyang, which was once a leading construction company, went bankrupt and was acquired by the Korea Housing Corporation as a part of the rationalization measures applied to Hanyang and its stakeholders.

10. For instance, the Ministry of Commerce, Industry, and Energy (MOCIE) used its control over KEPCO to pursue its own policy objectives, while the Ministry of Information and Communications (MIC) exercised its control over Korea Telecom.

ment-owned corporations had such acts,[11] while among the government-invested corporations, only Korea Broadcasting System, Korea Chemical, and KTB were subject to such acts.[12] Whereas the rest of the government-invested corporations were not subject to such individual corporation acts, they were still controlled by their respective line ministries, although to a lesser degree.[13]

Some of the twenty-six corporations were also subject to the industry acts that govern the firms in an industry to which a public enterprise belonged. Public enterprises that were monopolistic or dominant in their industries were significantly affected by the industry acts, as they constituted all or much of the relevant industries. In addition, some of the twenty-six public enterprises that were classified as government-owned corporations by the Framework Act were subject to additional constraints set by that act.

Corporations in which the government had a controlling interest were, and still are, classified into two groups: government-owned corporations (GOCs, or *tooja-gigwan*) and government-invested corporations (GICs, or *choolja-gigwan*), depending on whether they were subject to the Framework Act for GOCs. The general rule that differentiated GOCs from GICs was government ownership. In October 1997, all of the twenty-six corporations (except Korea Broadcasting System) in which the government's share was 50 percent or higher were subject to the Framework Act. The reason that Korea Broadcasting System, which was and still is 100 percent owned by the government, was exempt from the Framework Act is not clear.

Government-owned corporations were generally perceived as more closely related with public policy objectives. In other words, GICs were viewed as having stronger commercial elements by the government and were thus allowed to enjoy greater freedom in their operations. In particular, GOCs were subject to the restrictions set by the Framework Act, which was similar in many respects to the set of restrictions applied to government agencies. The Framework Act basically perceives a GOC as a subsidiary of the line ministry and tries to constrain the management of the GOC to achieve the policy objectives set by the line ministry with as little cost as possible.

Table 4.1 summarizes the main businesses and market positions of twenty-six GOCs and GICs. As one can see from the table, almost all GOCs are monopolies in their respective markets. Most GOCs sell their goods or services mostly to the government. On the other hand, all of the GICs sell their goods or services to nongovernment consumers.

11. For instance, KT was subject to the KT Act, and KEPCO was subject to the KEPCO Act.

12. Explained further in the next paragraph.

13. For instance, POSCO was controlled by MOCIE, which used its control over POSCO to keep domestic steel prices from exceeding a certain level.

Table 4.1   Main Business and Market Position of Government-Owned and Government-Invested Corporations (October 1997)

Classification	Company	Main Business	Main Consumer	Market Position
Government-owned corporation (*tooja gigwan*)	Korea Minting and Security Printing Corp.	• Minting and printing of Korean currency and securities	Government	Monopoly
	Agricultural and Fishery Marketing Corp.	• Promotion of the agroprocessing industry and operation of the government's price stabilization program	Government	Monopoly
	Rural Development Corp.	• Large-scale comprehensive agricultural development • Southwestern coast reclamation project	Government	Monopoly
	KEPCO	• Integrated electric utility service	General	Monopoly
	Korea Coal Corporation	• Operation and development of coal mines	Government	Monopoly
	Korea Resources Corp.	• Integrated support to the mining industry • Securing stable supply of overseas mineral resources	Government	Monopoly
	Korea National Oil Corp.	• Exploration and development of domestic and overseas oil resources • Construction, management, operation, and lease of petroleum storage facilities	Government	Monopoly
	Korea Trade Investment Promotion Agency	• Collection and provision of overseas market information to the government and private firms	Government	Monopoly
	Korea National Housing Corp.	• Housing construction for low-income households	General	Nondominant firm in a competitive industry
	Korea Highway Corp.	• Construction, maintenance, and traffic management of expressways	Government	Monopoly
	Korea Water Resources Corp.	• Management and construction of multipurpose dams and multiregional water supply systems	Local Government	Monopoly
	Korea Land Corp.	• Land resource acquisition, management, development, and supply	Government	Monopoly

	Korea National Tourism Org.	• Overseas promotion of the Korean tourism industry	Government	Monopoly
		• Development of tourist resorts		
	KT&G	• Cigarettes and ginseng manufacturing	General	Monopoly
	KT	• Principal licensed supplier of fixed-link local telephone service and domestic and international long-distance telecommunications services	General oligopoly	Dominant firm in
	KOGAS	• Importer and wholesale distributor of natural gas	General	Monopoly
Government-invested corporation (*choolja gigwan*)	Korea Appraisal Board	• Provision of valuation services	General	Monopoly
	Daehan Oil Pipeline Corp.	• Pipeline construction, operation, transportation, and storage of oil products	General	Monopoly
	Seoul Shinmun	• Newspaper publishing	General	Nondominant firm in a competitive industry
	Korea Broadcasting System	• Broadcasting	General	Dominant firm in oligopoly
	Korea District Heating Corp.	• Operation of district heating system	General	Monopoly
	POSCO	• Largest fully-integrated steel producer in Korea	General	Dominant firm in oligopoly
	Korea General Chemical Co.	• Producer of aluminum and other by-products thereof	General	Dominant firm in oligopoly
	Korea Heavy Industries and Construction Co.	• Manufacturer of power generators and industrial and marine engines	General	Monopoly
	Korea Technology Banking Corporation	• Financial services provider, especially of venture capital financing	General	Nondominant firm in a competitive industry
	National Textbook Co.	• Textbook publishing	General	Monopoly

Source: Korea Development Institute.

Notes: KEPCO = Korea Electric Power Corp.; KOGAS = Korea Gas Corp.; KT = Korea Telecom; KT&G = Korea Tobacco and Ginseng; POSCO = Pohang Iron and Steel Co.

4.2.2   Governance of Public Enterprises Prior to November 1997

Who are the stakeholders of SOEs? Who controls them, and to what ends? Stakeholders of SOEs include employees and managers, just as in private firms. But the most important stakeholders are the bureaucrats and politicians. Bureaucrats and politicians control SOEs, as they control the government, who owns SOEs. The nature of ownership and control of an SOE differs fundamentally from that of a private firm in two respects. First, as the owner or a dominant shareholder, the government pursues not only financial return but policy objective as well. Second, bureaucrats and politicians who control SOEs on behalf of the general public have no personal financial stake in SOEs, unlike shareholders of private firms.

Pursuing two potentially conflicting goals often led to suboptimal outcomes in the overall performance. Designing proper incentive mechanisms that motivate managers and employees of SOEs to try to hit the right balance between policy goals and financial goals became increasingly difficult as the size of the operation of SOEs became larger, while the overall economy became larger and more sophisticated. Properly allocating authority over SOEs among various government branches became increasingly difficult. As a result, the governance structure of SOEs has evolved over time, responding to the changes in economic conditions.

The governance of a public enterprise before the introduction of the 1997 Special Act on Privatization depended on whether it was subject to the Framework Act. The Framework Act required that a GOC board consist of a member from the line ministry and another from the then–Economic Planning Board,[14] and the rest from outside the government. The board members who were not from the government were mainly lawyers and professors appointed by the government. The board reviewed and made decisions on the issues of importance, such as key investment decisions and appointment of executives. In reviewing and making decisions on the agenda, the board was required by the act to put priority on public policy considerations.

Although there were nine board members, the one from the line ministry played a decisive role. The board member from the economic planning board played a secondary role of checking for wasteful activities. The remaining members from outside the government generally were not expected to play a significant role and usually approved an agenda that had already been negotiated by the two members from the government. The board member from the line ministry intervened heavily with the management of a GOC. The board members were paid only token amounts of

---

14. The Economic Planning Board was charged with the task of planning and budgeting as well as that of coordinating economic policies of various ministries. The board later merged with the Ministry of Finance.

money for their services and did not have any monetary incentives in the financial performance of the public enterprise for which they worked.

The chief executive officers of the GOCs were selected by the government without active participation of the board. Political appointment was not rare. The rest of the top executives were usually selected from the bureaucracy of the GOCs themselves. Appointment of ex–government officials to a GOC position other than chief executive officer was barred by law. Executive pay was generally lower than that in private firms. Incentive-based management contracts were not used. Top executives, in particular the chief executive officers, usually considered themselves as bureaucrats belonging to the government rather than executives of a business organization.

The GOCs had to submit annual budget plans to the government, which regularly evaluated their performance. In addition to being subject to a strict quota on the number of employees and the number of managerial positions, they were also regularly audited by the Office of the Inspector General and the National Assembly.

The corporate governance of GICs was similar to that of GOCs, although GICs were not subject to any law that specified a particular governance model. However, they were granted more autonomy compared with GOCs. The line ministry generally was given shareholder's rights and could successfully control a GIC in a way that suited its policy objectives.

One peculiar aspect of the public enterprises in Korea is that, although they were officially treated as policy instruments, many of them had private shareholders. The best example is KEPCO, which was and still is a GOC subject to the Framework Act as well as the KEPCO Act and the Electricity Industry Act. The three acts all stipulate that KEPCO should be run primarily as an instrument that the government could use in pursuing its policy objectives related to the electricity industry. In reality, KEPCO has indeed been run basically as a policy instrument, as the acts intended; but the government sold its shares of KEPCO in several tranches to private investors, including a large number of foreign investors. Korea Telecom is another example. The first tranche of KT shares was sold to domestic investors in 1994 while KT was a GOC. Sales of GOC shares to private investors raise the question about the nature of those GOCs.[15]

4.3   Sizes and Financial Performance of Public Enterprises

4.3.1   Size of Operation and Financial Performance of Public Enterprises

This section attempts to describe SOEs in key aspects, such as size, profitability, and financial stability. After summarizing key statistics for large

---

15. It is not clear to me why the investors purchased the shares of KT and KEPCO at the time.

SOEs, we compare the performance of commercial SOEs with that of *chaebol* firms.

Table 4.2 contains key statistics for the twenty-six GOCs and GICs. For most GOCs that sell their services almost exclusively to the government, profits do not seem to be an important measure of managerial efficiency. Revenues of these public enterprises may be viewed as budgets allocated to them by the government for certain activities they perform on behalf of the government. Korea Coal Corporation kept accumulating large amounts of losses, as it was supposed to subsidize failing coal mines. Such large losses are not a result of internal inefficiency of Korea Coal. Similarly, large revenues or profits of GOCs such as Korea Trade Investment Promotion Agency, Korea National Housing, Korea Highway Corporation, and Korea Land Corporation are not likely to be a result of their internal efficiency.

Some GICs that look promising in table 4.2 may not be profit-oriented, efficient business organizations. For instance, Korea Broadcasting System is not considered to be a profit-oriented business organization, although it has enjoyed the status of a GIC for quite a while. Its stable profitability comes mainly from a guaranteed source of revenue, fees collected from all television owners.[16] The other two network broadcasting companies (Munhwa Broadcasting Corporation and Korea Broadcasting System) are not entitled to the TV viewing fees. Korea Broadcasting System is also competing with the other two networks in the market for advertisement time.[17]

The public enterprises for which meaningful discussions on commercial performance can be made are the "Big Six" and a handful of GICs. The Big Six are KEPCO, KT, KT&G, POSCO, Korea Gas Corporation (KOGAS), and Korea Heavy. Among the Big Six commercial public enterprises, KOGAS and Korea Heavy did not earn as much profit as the other four. KOGAS is still in the stage of building a national transmission network and has been investing more cash than it has generated. Korea Heavy depends on KEPCO, one of its major shareholders, for a large part of its revenue. As a consequence, its accounting profits are believed to depend heavily on the terms that govern its contracts with KEPCO.

It will be interesting to compare operating efficiency of various SOEs as well as that of SOEs and large private firms, almost all of which were *chaebol* affiliated until very recently. However, direct comparison of, say, costs of operation turned out to be quite complicated and seems beyond the scope of this paper.[18] Comparison of profitability based upon accounting data

16. Fees are for watching TV programs produced and aired by Korea Broadcasting System.
17. Korea Broadcasting System offers two main channels, one of which provides advertisements.
18. In almost all cases, SOEs operate in completely different industries. Further, most commercial SOEs are monopolistic and do not have private competitors providing the same services competing with them. In addition, cost data of many *chaebol* firms turned out to be false, and are being corrected. An empirical analysis of the comparative efficiency of SOEs and *chaebol* firms that takes these factors into account is beyond the scope of this paper.

Table 4.2   Key Statistics on Government-Owned and Government-Invested Corporations

Classification	Company	No. of Employees		Government's Share (%)		Sales[a]		Profit (Loss)[a]	
		1997	2000	1997	2000	1997	2000	1997	2000
Government-owned corporation (*tooja gigwan*)	Korea Minting and Security Printing Corp.	2,634	1,450	100	100	1,967	2,142	158	251
	Agricultural and Fishery Marketing Corp.	948	500	100	100	1,825	947	6	32
	Rural Development Corp.	2,478	6,031	100	100	7,947	18,935	272	23
	KEPCO	39,454	33,745	69.8	52.2	131,162	182,528	5,606	17,926
	Korea Coal Corp.	4,072	2,694	98.3	98.8	2,110	1,694	-833	-740
	Korea Resources Corp.	431	328	98.1	98.3	550	547	-23	7
	Korea National Oil Corp.	949	774	100	100	3,841	4,595	150	478
	Korea Trade Investment Promotion Agency	649	565	100	100	784	1,223	0	114
	Korea National Housing Corp.	5,914	2,991	98.1	73.2	38,224	31,599	733	-2,485
	Korea Highway Corp.	5,178	3,704	89.5	82.6	14,778	19,366	448	253
	Korea Water Resources Corp.	4,162	3,167	91.8	79.8	16,169	11,783	450	626
	Korea Land Corp.	2,490	1,820	92.9	72.1	32,706	33,845	5,207	1,160
	Korea National Tourism Org.	984	680	56.1	55.2	2,118	3,342	134	377
	KT&G	7,680	4,467	89.2	13.8	42,434	45,686	2,258	2,704
	KT	59,491	46,095	71.2	58.9	77,852	103,221	797	10,101
	KOGAS	2,891	2,386	50.2	26.8	29,266	61,119	-3,355	945
Government-invested corporation (*choolja gigwan*)	Korea Appraisal Board	1,120	789	49.3	49.4	816	598	22	-467
	Daehan Oil Pipeline Corp.	386	378	52.7	46.5	336	721	-443	-286
	Seoul Shinmun	1,077	n.a.	50.0	50.0	1,840	1,050	-173	105
	Korea Broadcasting System	5,741	5,049[b]	100	100	9,999	9,503[b]	686	956[b]
	Korea District Heating Corp.	1,015	752	46.1	46.1	2,026	3,461	7	940
	POSCO	19,294	19,275	19.6	0	97,181	116,920	7,290	16,970
	Korea General Chemical Co.	263	n.a.	0	0	150	793[b]	-566	107[b]
	Korea Heavy Industries and Construction Co.	7,851	6,322	0	0	30,070	24,091	453	-249
	Korea Technology Banking Corp.	163	231	10.2	0	4,384	4,967	24	1,509
	National Textbook Co.	1,120	847	40.0	0	517	1,030	38	17
Total		178,435	145,040	68.2	57.0	521,012	685,706	19,346	51,374

Source: Companies' annual reports.

Note: n.a. = not available. See table 4.1 for explanation of other abbreviations.

[a] 0.1 billion won.

[b] 1999.

Table 4.3   Profit Leaders among Listed Companies (unit: 0.1 billion won)

Rank	Company	Profit
1	Samsung Electronics	60,145
2	KEPCO	17,925
3	POSCO	16,369
4	KT	10,101
5	SK Telecom	9,506
6	Hyundai Motors	6,678
7	Samsung SDI Co.	5,439
8	LG Electronics	5,021
9	Kia Motors	3,307
10	LG Chemical	3,248
11	LG Chemical Investment	3,248
12	KT&G	2,704
13	Shinhan	2,631
14	Hanil Synthetic Fiber	2,592
15	SK Telecom	1,447
16	LG Construction	1,235
17	Hyundai Mobis	1,131
18	Anam Electronics	1,081
19	Hanwha	1,056
20	Dongbu Construction	1,039
21	KOGAS	944
22	PacInd	847
23	LG Industrial System	823
24	Hyundai Dept. Store	801
25	Samsung Corp.	750
26	Pungsan	729
27	HITE Brewery	701
28	Shinsegae	697
29	Kumkang Korea Chemical	677
30	Inchon Iron and Steel	635

Source: Korea Stock Exchange (December 2000).
Note: See table 4.1 for explanation of abbreviations.

also has its limitation, as most SOEs are monopolistic while most of *chaebol* firms face competition in their industries. In this paper, we will not attempt to directly compare operating efficiency of SOEs and *chaebol* firms and will only compare various financial ratios, which can serve as indirect signals.[19]

The "Big Four" (the Big Six minus KOGAS and Korea Heavy) are the most important commercial firms owned by the Korean government. They consistently turn out large profits and generally sustain stable growth. Table 4.3 shows the profits earned by the top thirty performers among the

19. We believe that a meaningful analysis can be accomplished by comparing Korean firms with their counterparts in other countries. Such a comparative study seems to be appropriate for a separate research.

listed companies in 2000. KEPCO, POSCO, and KT ranked second, third, and fourth after Samsung Electronics. Table 4.3 may be biased in favor of nonpublic enterprises because it is based upon accounting reports of the listed companies. It has been discovered in the aftermath of the economic crisis that accounting reports of many private companies contained serious flaws. Accounting reports from public enterprises have never been subject to allegations of serious wrongdoing. Thus, the Big Four could be in an even more dominant position if standard accounting practices had been used.

As of April 2001, KT ranked fourth after Samsung Electronics, SK Telecom, and Korea Exchange Bank in terms of the size of the market capitalization among listed firms.[20] KEPCO ranked fifth and was immediately followed by POSCO. KT&G and KOGAS ranked fourteenth and twenty-seventh, respectively. In terms of the percentage of market capitalization to the total market capitalization of all listed firms, KT, KEPCO, POSCO, KT&G, and KOGAS recorded 8.6, 6.4, 4.1, 1.3, and 0.5 percent, respectively.[21]

Combined, the Big Six, and certainly the Big Four, fared better than the market average in terms of their financial performance. Table 4.4 compares the returns on investment, interest coverage ratios, and debt-equity ratios of the Big Six public enterprises with the market average of the listed companies. Earnings per share for the Big Six were consistently higher than the market average of the listed companies, both before and after the economic crisis. Weak performance of KEPCO and KOGAS in 1997 is due to the large appreciation of the dollar against the Korean won that occurred that year during the economic crisis. KEPCO had a large portion of loans expressed in foreign currencies, while KOGAS imports all of the natural gas it sells from abroad.

With respect to interest coverage ratios and debt-equity ratios, which began receiving increasing attention as key financial indices since the onset of the crisis, the public enterprises fared significantly better than their counterparts in the private sector. Four public enterprises show debt-equity ratios that are far below the market average.[22] The high debt-equity ratio of KOGAS is due to the high rate of investment using borrowed money that resulted from expansion of the national gas transmission network. Interest coverage ratios of the public enterprises have been much higher than the market average. Weak performance of KEPCO in 1997 is due to the rapid

20. SK Telecom used to be a subsidiary of KT, but became a subsidiary of SK Group after 1994.

21. Samsung Electronics, SK Group, and Korea Exchange Bank recorded 16.2, 8.8, and 8.7 percent, respectively.

22. The *interest coverage ratio* of a firm is defined to be the amounts that the firm has to pay as interest on its debts divided by the operating profit (before paying interests) in a given year. A firm earns a gross profit that is just enough to pay interests when its interest coverage ratio is equal to 1.

Table 4.4   **Financial Ratios of the Big Six Public Enterprises**

Classification/Company	1996	1997	1998	1999	2000
Net income to stockholder's equity ratio					
KT&G	8.63	9.24	11.23	11.01	9.76
POSCO	9.49	−2.27	9.87	17.15	17.36
KOGAS	16.36	−48.76	13.03	10.14	4.04
KT	0.21	0.60	2.93	2.81	8.84
KEPCO	3.15	−3.62	6.29	4.84	5.63
Doosan Heavy Industries and Construction Co.	15.21	−7.90	4.41	1.56	−1.49
Weighted average of listed companies	2.96	−16.04	−8.69	−8.17	0.25
	(627)	(630)	(625)	(570)	(628)
Weighted average, excluding Big Six firms	1.9	−22.74	−15.25	−15.08	−3.41
Interest coverage ratio					
KT&G	469.21	467.03	443.77	1729.72	912.41
POSCO	2.75	0.97	3.13	8.07	7.60
KOGAS	3.09	−1.55	1.78	2.49	1.50
KT	3.27	2.11	3.02	4.01	4.80
KEPCO	2.02	−0.16	2.91	3.23	2.95
Doosan Heavy Industries and Construction Co.	4.91	0.67	2.18	1.27	0.50
Weighted average of listed companies	1.31	0.36	0.75	0.70	1.30
	(627)	(630)	(625)	(570)	(628)
Weighted average, excluding Big Six firms	1.18	0.34	0.62	0.48	1.04
Debt-equity ratio					
KT&G	24.79	31.53	24.85	29.01	38.08
POSCO	118.50	160.48	118.85	89.59	88.41
KOGAS	230.23	555.79	273.70	184.22	259.02
KT	189.34	223.98	192.33	75.69	103.32
KEPCO	112.89	185.23	175.23	111.50	102.70
Doosan Heavy Industries and Construction Co.	186.91	243.66	127.35	139.11	113.50
Weighted average of listed companies	265.31	415.35	316.43	199.73	205.52
	(627)	(630)	(625)	(570)	(628)
Weighted average, excluding Big Six firms	326.41	532.08	382.75	246.20	253.14

Source: Korea Development Institute.

Notes: Numbers in parentheses are the number of firms in the sample. See table 4.1 for explanation of abbreviations.

depreciation of the Korean won. Thus, the public enterprises do not seem to be facing the possibility of serious financial trouble, which has threatened a large part of the corporate sector since the mid-1990s.

4.4   1997 Special Act on Privatization: A First Step toward Privatization

Most of the large SOEs that exist today were formed in 1980s or earlier. The system by which SOEs operate was also formed in the mid-1980s and remained unchanged until the end of the Roh Tae Woo administration. There did not exist significant demand for privatization either; reason for this low demand can be summarized as follows. First, there was a general consensus that SOEs were the only feasible, and probably the most efficient, way to build much-needed infrastructure, such as national telecommunications, electricity, gas networks, and highway networks. Second, *chaebols* that had been given various subsidies from the government concentrated on expanding their territory in export industries as well as some domestic industries that lay outside of the domains of SOEs. Third, there was little understanding of how different economic systems worked at the time. There were few bureaucrats or politicians who could distinguish between commercial objectives and the public goals of an SOE. Fourth, there was no political pressure to privatize SOEs.

In 1994, the Kim Young Sam administration, during its second year in power, commissioned a comprehensive study of several public enterprises, including KEPCO, KT, POSCO, and KT&G. It is not clear what motivated the study. However, one can point out the following changes in the economic environment, which appear to have affected the change in the government's attitude toward SOEs. First, most of the basic infrastructure investment was completed in most of the industries mentioned above. Second, *chaebols* had been given a more favorable and generous treatment from the Roh administration, and gained freer access to the financial market. Third, privatization somehow became one of the key economic policies of the Kim Young Sam administration, which kept pushing for a tangible outcome. It is worth noting that financial losses of SOEs were not a factor behind the push for privatization, as all SOEs subject to the study, except for Korea Heavy, were very profitable.

The study reviewed, among other things, the possibility of privatizing each of the public enterprises. The results of the studies for KT&G, POSCO, and KT generally concluded that a significant degree of loss of efficiency existed due to their governance structures and that privatization would produce more efficient outcomes. By the end of 1996, a consensus was building up within the government that privatization was needed for some of the commercial public enterprises.

The possibility of privatizing large public enterprises immediately raised the question of whether *chaebols* should be allowed to purchase controlling interests. At that time, the problem with selling public enterprises to *chaebols* seemed only political in nature, as there existed a widespread strong sentiment against handing over the large, commercial public enterprises to *chaebols*.[23] It appears that most policymakers at the time believed that it

23. At that time, there were few, if any, who expected that the economic crisis was on its way. The economic crisis revealed that *chaebol* were able to set up and maintain control of large firms only by heavy government intervention in the financial market. It also revealed that *chaebol* were neither particularly efficient nor able to raise capital needed to purchase controlling interests of large firms on their own through proper market mechanisms. In fact, many *chaebol* went bankrupt. After the economic crisis, the *chaebol* issue began to be analyzed from a very different angle.

was politically unfeasible to allow *chaebols* to acquire controlling interests.[24] Thus, it was decided that *chaebols* would not be allowed to take control of the public enterprises to be privatized.

The government forecast quite correctly that a large-scale sale of the shares of large public enterprises to domestic investors would be difficult to achieve. Large-scale sale to foreign investors was also excluded from consideration for a variety of reasons. As a consequence, it appeared inevitable that the government had to maintain dominant ownership of large public enterprises for quite a while. Thus, there arose the question about the governance of the commercial public enterprises that would eventually be privatized during the period in which the government remained a major shareholder. The need for the separation of public policy objectives from the commercial operation of the public enterprises was also acknowledged for the first time. The 1997 Special Act on Privatization was introduced to address these issues.

The act targeted four public enterprises, KT&G, KT, KOGAS, and Korea Heavy, and had two main elements. First, it put restrictions on the ownership of all four public enterprises in order to prevent *chaebols* from acquiring controlling interests. Specifically, the act required that the combined share of any investor, including the shares held by the parties who are in intimate relations with the investor, should not exceed 15 percent of each of the four public enterprises.

Second, the act prescribed an Anglo-Saxon-style corporate governance structure for the four public enterprises. The act stipulated that the board must consist of only civilians, thus removing the presence of the line ministry as well as the Ministry of Finance and Economy[25] from the board. It also gave the board power similar to that of a typical board in large firms in the United Kingdom or United States. The act even contained detailed procedures for selecting chief executive officers, which were aimed at guaranteeing transparency in the selection process.

In addition, the Framework Act was amended to exempt KT&G, KT, and KOGAS from the application of the act, thus making them GICs, even though the government's share in each of these companies exceeded the 50 percent benchmark. Further, the KT Act and KT&G Act were abolished. These two measures removed many of the constraints rooted in the policy-related concerns of the line ministry that bound the commercial operation of KT and KT&G, thus basically making them private common-stock companies subject to company laws. Legally, they differed from a private company only to the extent that they were subject to the Special Act and

24. Their assessment seems to have correctly reflected the political reality.
25. There was a change in the government itself in which the Economic Planning Board merged with the Ministry of Finance to form the Ministry of Finance and Economy. The authority of the old Economic Planning Board concerning public enterprises was passed on to the newly formed ministry.

the industry acts. The KOGAS Act was left intact because its line ministry (the Ministry of Commerce, Industry, and Energy, or MOCIE) successfully argued that the KOGAS Act was needed to enable MOCIE to complete the national gas-transmission network within the target period. Thus, KOGAS was freed from the constraints given by the Framework Act, but was left to the control of the line ministry and its policy concerns.

The spirit of the act was clear. The act envisaged that the four public enterprises would develop into large, commercial, private firms to be run by professional managers who strive to maximize the shareholders' monetary interests. It also recognized the need for the separation of policy concerns from commercial operation and attempted to restrain the line ministries in their dealings with the public enterprises. The act was quite successful in achieving the goals that were the motivation behind the act. By prohibiting *chaebols* from acquiring controlling interests of the four public enterprises, it ended a long dispute that worked as a barrier to privatization, and thus enabled privatization to proceed.[26] The act also allowed the three former GOCs, in particular KT and KT&G, to be run basically as profit-seeking firms. Finally, it installed a corporate governance mechanism that was in line with large profit-oriented firms, at least on the surface.

However, the Special Act and the other privatization measures introduced in 1997 were far from a complete privatization package and even contained some crucial flaws. The act failed to completely sever the ties with policy consideration and allowed the line ministry to maintain shareholders' rights. It also contained a clause that explicitly stated that the management of the public enterprises must consider public policy objectives when making decisions. Such clauses are not consistent with the rest of the act or its spirit. The clause that leaves the shareholders' rights in the hands of the line ministry left the door open for the line ministry to intervene in the management of public enterprises to promote its policy concerns. The act also left the four public enterprises subject to audits by the Office of the Inspector General and the National Assembly.[27]

Another criticism directed at the privatization measures taken in 1997 concerned the target firms. It was difficult to understand why POSCO was not included in the list of target firms, while KT&G and Korea Heavy were included, as there were few public policy objectives with which one could identify POSCO.[28] Exclusion of KEPCO also was hard to understand considering that KT and KOGAS were included and that KEPCO

---

26. I believe that it also provided part of the solution to the *chaebol* problems, although few were aware of the issue at the time, and the act did not intend to solve the fundamental problems associated with the *chaebol*. It was revealed later on that the expansion of the *chaebol* groups, based upon financial transactions that lack transparency and accountability, was one of the main culprits for the recent economic crisis.

27. Private firms are not subject to such audits.

28. For instance, one of the functions KT&G performed on behalf of the government was subsidizing the tobacco-growing farmers in Korea.

had the highest proportion of private ownership among the three network giants.

It is also worth noting that regulatory reforms accompanying the partial privatization of KT by the Special Act have not occurred. The Communications Commission had existed not as an independent regulatory body, but as a part of KT's line ministry, the Ministry of Information and Communications (MIC). The commission was not even given the authority over regulating rates and access charges, which was handled directly by the MIC. Little changed on the regulation front after the Special Act took effect. The same was true for the gas and electricity industries.

Overall, the special act was incomplete as a privatization measure. It even failed to secure logical consistency in some respects, as mentioned above. As a result, it was only half successful in inducing the effect of privatization. However, it was the greatest step in the direction of privatization ever taken by Korea until that time. It also opened a new chapter in corporate governance of large, commercial enterprises in Korea, as it was the first-ever attempt in Korea at installing an advanced form of corporate governance in large firms. At the time, corporate governance was not even an issue for private firms as most people took for granted the absolute control by dominant shareholders of *chaebol* firms.

4.5   Privatization Drive after the Economic Crisis

4.5.1   Privatization Plan of 1998

In March 1998, a new government succeeded the Kim Young Sam administration at the peak of the economic crisis. The new government had to implement measures aimed at reducing employment and the size of operations of many private firms and financial institutions that were bankrupt to rehabilitate them. There was political pressure from labor and *chaebols* alike that the bureaucracy should share the pain as well. At the time, it was generally acknowledged that SOEs had sizable room for improving efficiency, although they were in good financial health, unlike private firms. Thus, the new government introduced measures aimed at restructuring public enterprises in its early days in power. The focus was given to reduction in unneeded workers, removal of redundant operations, and sales of assets and businesses of public enterprises that were not essential for operation.

Privatization received secondary attention as it was acknowledged to be more difficult than restructuring, involving plans on market structures and regulatory frameworks. However, some within the new government expected that they would eventually have to sell SOEs to raise money to cover the costs of corporate and financial restructuring. There was also a need to raise foreign capital to increase the foreign currency reserve, the depletion of which was believed by many to have caused the economic crisis.[29] Contrary to what many believe, neither the International Monetary Fund nor the World Bank played a significant role in shaping policies on public enterprises in Korea.

The Budget and Planning Commission, a new government agency created by the new administration, announced an ambitious privatization and restructuring plan that covered 108 public enterprises.[30] The 1998 plan classified public enterprises into three groups and prescribed different solutions for each of them.

The first group is the set of public enterprises to be privatized. POSCO, Korea Heavy, Korea Chemical, KTB, and Korea Textbook were included in this group, along with twelve subsidiaries of various GOCs and GICs. The second group consists of the public enterprises that eventually need to be privatized, but would not be privatized in the near future. It includes KT, KT&G, KEPCO, KOGAS, Daehan Oil Pipeline, and Korea District Heating, as well as twenty-eight subsidiaries of GOCs and GICs. The third group is the set of public enterprises that would not be privatized. Thirteen GOCs were included as well as fourteen subsidiaries of some GOCs and GICs.

The Ministry of Planning and Budget's (MPB's) prescription for the first group of public enterprises was to turn the shares of each over to private hands and let the new owners run them based upon profit incentives. It is noteworthy that, in the case of Korea Heavy, the government changed the previous administration's policy on *chaebol* ownership of large public enterprises. The government subsequently amended the Special Act and excluded Korea Heavy from the list of public enterprises covered by the act. The main reason for this change was the government's realization that the best and probably the only feasible way to privatize Korea Heavy was through a trade sale or sale of controlling interests to a single party.

For the second group, gradual privatization was proposed as the solution. The meaning of "gradual privatization" was unclear from the moment it was announced and has never been well understood. The GOCs and GICs belonging to the second group were all monopolistic firms in network industries, except for KT&G. Privatization of monopolistic public enterprises in the network industries requires a wide range of changes in regulatory and industrial policies. It could also lead to fundamental changes in the organization of the line ministries. Privatization of KT&G also inevitably entails a fundamental change in the industrial policies for the tobacco-growing industry, which could prove to be a difficult task. It seems that the MPB acknowledged the need to privatize those public en-

29. Even many *chaebol* firms tried to sell assets and businesses of some of their firms to meet the demands by the government to increase liquidity, reduce debts and costs, and raise foreign capital.
30. The commission changed its name to the Ministry of Planning and Budget a year later.

terprises, but also realized that their privatization requires complex and far-reaching changes in regulatory and industrial policies that were beyond its control when it announced "gradual privatization" as the solution to the second group of public enterprises.

For the third group of public enterprises, privatization was not an option. The MPB's solutions for the third group of public enterprises were internal restructuring or liquidation. Some public enterprises were determined to lack public policy concerns that could justify their existence as public enterprises as well as any marketable commercial value. Hanyang was the best example. It was determined to be liquidated. Most other public enterprises belonging to the third group were allowed to continue to operate as before, but were subject to a heavy dose of the internal restructuring program, which entailed a large reduction in employment and in the scope of the business.[31]

The 1998 privatization plan (see table 4.5) was far more comprehensive in scope and depth than any other privatization effort by the previous administrations. The 1998 privatization plan has changed considerably in the implementation stage. However, it served as the skeleton of the new administration's policy for public enterprises.

4.5.2   Other Measures and Recent Developments in Privatization

Special Act

The new government left most of the contents of the Special Act intact.[32] Thus, the ceiling on the ownership of some of the large public enterprises was left unchanged, as was the governance structure for them. The shareholders' rights of the government in the public enterprises covered by the act were still left to the line ministries. The government kept making changes to the list of public enterprises to be covered by the act. Korea Heavy was later dropped, as mentioned above, while some smaller public enterprises were added.

Framework Act

The new administration amended the Framework Act and changed the governance structure of GOCs to the one specified by the Special Act. Thus, GOCs are now governed by a board whose members are recruited from outside the government. The new governance structure could be con-

---

31. Intense shake-ups also fell on most of the public enterprises belonging to the other groups as well. To a certain degree, such shake-ups were taken to cut unnecessary costs that were due to inefficient management of the public enterprises. The scope and depth of restructuring of the public enterprises also appear to have been affected by the onset of the economic crisis.

32. Korea Heavy was excluded from the act, as mentioned earlier. There also were some other relatively minor changes.

Table 4.5   **Privatization Plan of 1998**

Solutions/Targeted GOCs and GICs	Targeted Subsidiaries of GOCs and GICs
Complete privatization	
Pohang Iron and Steel Co.	12 subsidiaries, including KT Card Co. and
Korea Heavy Industries and Construction Co.	Hanyang Wood Co.
Korea General Chemical Co.	
Korea Technology Banking Corp.	
National Textbook Co.	
Subtotal = 5	
Gradual privatization	
KT	28 subsidiaries, including KT Powertel Co.,
KT&G	Korea Liquefied Natural Gas Co., and Korea
KEPCO	Power Engineering Co.
KOGAS	
Daehan Oil Pipeline Corp.	
Korea District Heating Corp.	
Subtotal = 6	
Restructuring	
Agricultural and Fishery Marketing Corp.	Restructuring
Korea Coal Corp.	6 subsidiaries, including KT Freetel Co. and
Korea Highway Corp.	Korea Nuclear Fuel Co.
Korea Land Corp.	
Korea National Housing Corp.	
Korea National Oil Corp.	
Korea Resources Corp.	
Korea Security Printing and Minting Corp.	Liquidation or merger
Korea National Tourist Org.	8 subsidiaries, including Hanyang Corp. and
Korea Trade and Investment Promotion Agency	Korea Real Estate Trust Co.
Korea Water Resources Corp	
Rural Development Corp.	
Korea Appraisal Board	
Subtotal = 13 (14 subsidiaries)	
Total = 24 (54 subsidiaries)	

Source: Ministry of Planning and Budget.

Notes: GOC = government-owned corporation; GIC = government-invested corporation. See table 4.1 for explanation of other abbreviations.

flicting with the other aspect of the Framework Act that is based upon the idea that a GOC is a policy instrument of its line ministry rather than a profit-oriented firm. It is not clear to us how the board, which consists of those outside the government, can make sure that GOCs are run smoothly to achieve the policy objectives of the line ministry.

Regulatory and Industrial Policies

Not a great deal of changes occurred in the way line ministries go about their business of promoting policy objectives since the privatization began.

Separation of commercial elements of commercial public enterprises and regulatory functions of the government from the industrial policies of the line ministries in network industries has not even been discussed much. In particular, the regulatory environment for the telecommunications and gas industries has little changed. Further, the communications commission has not been granted independence. The MIC, which also assumes the role of the dominant shareholder of KT, still has the authority to regulate rates and access charges. The market structure and regulatory scheme of the gas industry have not changed much either.

However, there has been a significant change in the policies toward the electricity industry and KEPCO. After two years of study and debates, the government successfully passed the Act for the Restructuring of the Electricity Industry. As a result, KEPCO was split into six generating companies (gencos), a monopolistic firm vertically integrated in the transmission and distribution stages, usually called "post-KEPCO"[33]; and the pool market. The government also made public its intention to ultimately split post-KEPCO into one monopoly for the transmission stage and several local monopolies for the distribution stage.

Finally, a regulatory body—the Electricity Commission—has been established within the line ministry, MOCIE, and was given the authority to regulate the electricity industry. Although the commission is not independent of MOCIE, it was charged with the responsibility to regulate rates. Thus, the Electricity Commission appears, at least on the surface, to be a quite legitimate regulator, unlike the Communications Commission.

The restructuring is still in its early stage. Sales of *gencos* to a third party independent of post-KEPCO have yet to occur either. Thus, it is too early to tell whether the reform of the electricity industry is a success. It is also too early to tell whether the Electricity Commission, which is only two months old, will perform properly and independently as a regulator.

Recent Developments in Tobacco, Telecom,
Oil Pipeline, and District-Heating Industries

The 1998 privatization plan went through a few changes in the implementation stage. The biggest changes were made with regard to KT&G and KT, both of which had been classified as public enterprises to be gradually privatized. The government changed its plan and added those two, as well as two other smaller public enterprises (Daehan Pipeline and Korea District Heating) initially classified as those for gradual privatization, to the list of firms to be fully privatized.

The government also made changes aimed at separating industrial policy concerns from the commercial operation of KT&G. The government

---

33. The official name of the monopoly is still KEPCO, but many call it "post-KEPCO" to distinguish it from the old monopoly, vertically integrated in all stages of the industry.

abolished the statutory ban on entry into tobacco manufacturing and is scheduled to open the market in late 2001.[34] Thus, foreign as well as domestic competitors will be able to compete with KT&G on more level terms in Korea. At the same time, the government also gave up the right to control the prices of cigarettes produced by KT&G so that the prices of cigarettes would be determined in the market.

These liberalization measures and privatization of KT&G would undoubtedly have significant impact on the tobacco-growing industry of Korea. KT&G is expected to reduce purchase of tobacco leaves from domestic growers each year until its purchase from domestic growers drops to a certain level. It will also reduce the subsidies that it has given to the association of tobacco-growing farmers for a long time. KT&G and the association of tobacco growers are currently working on a deal that will require KT&G to make a lump-sum donation to a foundation to compensate for the losses to the association and tobacco growers, resulting from privatization and liberalization of the tobacco industry.

The change in policies toward KT came about as a result of a string of events that few had anticipated. The twist began in 1999 when the government announced its plan to grant three licenses to operate G-3 mobile services, usually called IMT-2000 in Korea, in 2000. The announcement catapulted the five mobile operators, of which four were suffering from losses while the incumbent SK Telecom was earning huge profits, into an intriguing game of mergers and acquisitions played out by competitors in a tight oligopoly. Shinsegi and Hansol ended up offering themselves as merger and acquisition targets. SK Telecom successfully acquired Shinsegi Telecom. Korea Telecom Freetel, a subsidiary of KT, and LG Telecom, affiliated with the LG Group (the fourth largest *chaebol* group in Korea), competed fiercely to acquire controlling interests of Hansol. Korea Telecom offered more attractive terms than LG and eventually bought 44.1 percent of the shares of Hansol, thus becoming an undisputed second after SK Telecom in the mobile market.[35]

Purchase of controlling interests in Hansol Telecom by KT was probably the first-ever case of a public enterprise voluntarily acquiring a major private firm that was not bankrupt, and thus became the subject of an intense controversy. The criticism directed at KT was that it was not even classified by the government as an enterprise to be privatized and should not be allowed to purchase control of a private operator, as there was a

---

34. Conditions for a license to operate a manufacturing facility in the tobacco industry are being drawn up.

35. Becoming the largest and second-largest operators in terms of revenue or, equivalently, the number of subscribers, was considered by many to be a key factor in winning a license for 3G services at the time. SK Telecom and KT came out as winners in reality. They won the two licenses for users of the asynchronous-mode standard. LG competed with the two for a license for asynchronous-mode standard operators and failed. LG has not won a license yet.

private suitor willing to purchase Hansol. On the other hand, if the government prohibited KT from making bids on Hansol, it would almost certainly cause serious damage to the competitiveness of KT and its market value, while at the same time forcing Hansol to sell its shares to LG at less favorable terms. In the end, the government decided to allow KT to go ahead and make a bid on Hansol. At the same time, the government announced that it would completely privatize KT by mid-2002.[36]

Thus, KT is to be privatized earlier than any other large, commercial public enterprise. However, there have not been fundamental changes in the regulatory frameworks or in the way industrial policies are promoted by the line ministry.

4.5.3   Divestitures and Ownership Distributions

For all the GOCs except KEPCO, the government is essentially the sole owner. In cases where the government's share is below 100 percent, the shares not owned by the government are owned by other public institutions controlled by the government. The government did not own a single share in Korea Chemical and Korea Heavy in 1997, nor does it now; but these two firms were classified in 1997 as GICs by the government as their dominant shareholders were public institutions that the government could easily control. The government's shares in POSCO, KTB, and Korea Textbook were reduced to zero between 1997 and 2000. KTB and Korea Textbook have been completely privatized. However, POSCO is not generally viewed as a fully privatized company because its largest shareholder is the Industrial Bank of Korea, which is a public enterprise controlled by the government.

Table 4.6 summarizes the ownership distributions for the Big Six as of December 2000. KEPCO is still 52.2 percent owned by the government. Of the remaining shares, 26 percent are owned by foreign investors. Further dilution of the government's share is not likely to occur for a while because most of the loans that KEPCO borrowed from foreign creditors have a condition in the loan contracts that allows the creditors to call for early payments if the government's share falls below 50 percent. There is no major investor other than the government.

The government's share in KT is 59 percent. However, it will drop to less than 30 percent if the current efforts by the government to sell additional shares to foreign investors succeed. The government is also planning to sell off the remaining shares by 2002. Kookmin Pension, the largest pension in Korea, is the second largest shareholder after the government. The remaining shares are owned by a few financial institutions as well as many small investors. Foreign ownership stands at 19.4 percent.

---

36. The discussions above suggest that KT was already an operator that was as commercial in nature as any others in the telecom business were. The government may have simply ignored this obvious fact until it was too awkward to continue to ignore it.

Table 4.6   **Main Shareholders of the Big Six and Their Shares (December 2000)**

Company	Main Stockholders
KOGAS	Korean government: 26.9% KEPCO: 24.5% Local government: 9.8% Daeshin Securities: 7.2% Foreigners: 2.1%
KT&G	Korean government: 13.8% Industrial Bank of Korea: 35.2% The Export-Import Bank of Korea: 7.0% Daehan Investment Trust: 7.0% Foreigners: 5.0%
POSCO	Industrial Bank of Korea: 4.9% Foreigners: 48.6%
KT	Korean Government: 59.0% Foreigners: 19.4%
KEPCO	Korean Government: 52.2% Korea Deposit Insurance Corp.: 5.1% Foreigners: 26.0%
Korea Heavy Industries and Construction Co., Ltd. (Doosan Heavy Industries and Construction Co., Ltd.)	Doosan Corp.: 36.0% Korea Development Bank: 12.6% KEPCO: 11.7%

Source: National Information and Credit Evaluation.
Note: See table 4.1 for explanation of abbreviations.

Korea Tobacco and Ginseng

The government's share in KT&G was close to 100 percent before the onset of the crisis. Its ownership kept decreasing after the onset of the economic crisis to the current level of 13.8 percent, as a result of a series of government investments in several banks using the KT&G shares. The purpose of the investments was to increase the size of the equities as well as the Bank for International Settlements ratios of the banks and other financial institutions, which were necessary from the perspective of financial and corporate restructuring. The banks that own KT&G shares were not expected to actively exercise their rights as major shareholders, and the government can still control 53 percent of the shares. Small investors and various financial institutions own around 15 percent.

Pohang Steel Company

The government sold its remaining 3 percent in 2000 and currently does not own a single share in POSCO. But it is believed to be able to control POSCO through its influence over the Industrial Bank of Korea, which is the largest single shareholder with 4.9 percent. It is not clear at this point whether the corporate governance of POSCO will remain as it is or whether a *chaebol* would be allowed to take control. POSCO has not been subject to the Special Act.

Korea Gas Corporation

KOGAS used to be owned by the government, KEPCO, and various local governments, which initially owned 50.2, 35.5, and 14.3 percent, respectively. KOGAS became listed after a public offering in which 38.8 percent was sold to institutional investors and small investors.[37] The shares held by the government, KEPCO, and local governments were reduced to 26.8, 24.4, and 9.8 percent, respectively, as a result of the offering. KOGAS is still controlled by the government.

Korea Electric Power Corporation

The Korean government owned more than 70 percent of the shares of KEPCO until 1996. An additional sale of KEPCO shares in 1998 lowered the government's share to 58.2 percent, while it increased the shares held by general investors to 36.4 percent. The government sold an additional 5 percent of depository receipts (DRs) for US$750,000,000 in 1999, further reducing its share to 53.2 percent. The shares held by foreign investors were a meager 1.14 percent in 1992, but increased to 10.99 percent in 1995 and 26.11 percent in 2000.

Korea Heavy

Korea Heavy used to be owned by KEPCO, Korea Development Bank, and Korea Exchange Bank, with 40.5, 43.8, and 15.7 percent, respectively. The government fully controlled Korea Heavy using its dominant position in all of the three public enterprises. In 2000, the government forced KEPCO and Korea Development Bank to sell 28.8 percent and 31.2 percent, respectively, of Korea Heavy (a total of 60 percent of the outstanding shares) to a *chaebol* consortium, the employees' ownership program, and the general investors. Doosan Group purchased 36 percent, while the Employee Ownership Plan (EOP) and the general investors purchased 10 percent and 14 percent, respectively. Doosan appears to be in a position to wield control of Korea Heavy.

Korea Telecom

Divestiture of KT started in 1993. During the 1993–1996 period, the government attempted to sell 49 percent of KT shares, but were able to sell only 28.8 percent for 2.751 trillion Korean won to domestic investors. In

37. Daeshin Securities ended up owning 7.2 percent of KOGAS since it was the main broker in the last public offering of KOGAS and had an obligation to maintain the share price above a certain level.

1999, the government sold 14.4 percent to foreign investors through issuing DRs that were listed on the New York Stock Exchange and London Stock Exchange and reduced its shares from 71.2 percent to 56.8 percent.[38] The sales brought in US$2.48566 billion, of which US$1.14723 billion went into the government coffer. Another effort at selling additional shares domestically early in 2001 was unsuccessful. As of July 2001, the government was trying to sell up to 15 percent of shares to a foreign strategic investor and an additional 17.8 percent to investors in the international market through issuing DRs. The government sold the remaining shares to private investors in 2002.

The largest shareholder after the government is Kukmin Pension, with 3 percent. No other shareholder owns more than 1 percent. There are two restrictions on the ownership of KT shares in addition to the 15 percent ceiling for any single party. First, the Telecommunications Industry Act puts a ceiling on the combined ownership in KT by foreign investors at 49 percent. Second, the act also forbids a foreigner to become the largest shareholder of KT. The last restriction on the ownership of KT was introduced to maintain KT as a Korean firm. But no such restriction exists for SK Telecom or any other telecom operator in Korea.

Other, Smaller Public Enterprises

Of the smaller GOCs and GICs, four relatively small GICs have been completely privatized since the privatization drive of the current administration began in early 1998. All of the government's shares of KTB and Korea Textbook have been sold to a venture capital and a private textbook company, respectively. Korea Chemical was not sold as a whole. Instead, the government forced Korea Chemical to sell its major business unit, Namhae Chemical, which was also the only unit within Korea Chemical that had any economic value, to Farmers' Association (*Nonghyup*).[39] Daehan Pipeline has also been sold to a consortium of investors headed by the SK Group, which has a refinery and oil distribution subsidiary.

The results of the new administration's privatization program are far more extensive and thorough compared with those of preceding administrations. However, the privatization process is far from complete and is still unfolding. Large public enterprises are not fully privatized. Although a few small public enterprises are fully privatized, they have been in private hands for less than three years. Thus, it is not possible to conduct a meaningful evaluation of the effects of privatization in Korea, similar to the one offered by Galal et al. (1994).

38. Of the 14.4 percent, 6.7 percent were old shares, while the remaining 7.7 percent were newly issued ones.

39. There is the question of whether this was a bona fide privatization. Farmers' Association is a nonprofit organization and is considered by many to be no better than other public enterprises in terms of efficiency.

4.6   Other Government Involvement in Commercial Activities and in the Financial Market

The public enterprises that we have covered thus far in this paper comprise only a fraction of the larger set of commercial organizations that are owned and controlled by the government. The government fully owns and runs the postal service and rail transportation as government agencies. The postal service is a part of the MIC organization. Korea Rail, the monopoly in the rail and rail transportation industry, is an agency within the Ministry of Construction and Transportation. Local governments have set up a large number of local public enterprises. The best known example is City Rail of Seoul, which continually posted large losses.

The area in which the government's ownership and control is the most crucial, but has been neglected in this paper, is the financial sector. The government has been the dominant player in the financial sector over the past four decades, frequently allocating financial resources to the projects that it favored. The government actually owned and directly controlled many financial institutions, including several banks and their subsidiaries, even before the economic crisis hit Korea in 1997. The government had a controlling interest in Korea Development Bank, Korea Housing Bank, Kookmin Bank, and Industrial Bank of Korea. It utilized these banks and their subsidiaries as instruments for its policies toward the financial market.

The government also was somehow able to wield tight control over the banks in which it had no or few shares. Most of the commercial banks and their subsidiaries had been tightly controlled by the government, despite the fact that *chaebols* were the largest shareholders of the banks prior to the onset of the economic crisis.[40] It is worth noting that although *chaebols* owned a large share of banks, they were not allowed to wield control of the banks. However, the *chaebols* ended up being able to obtain large amounts of loans from the banks anyway, as they were aided by government that intervened in the management of the banks. It was revealed later on that a large proportion of the loans made to many *chaebols* this way turned out to be lost in unprofitable projects. The result was the massive bankruptcies of large firms, which immediately translated into deep financial difficulty of many banks and financial companies. Roughly one-third of the *chaebol* firms became insolvent or fell in deep financial trouble since 1997.[41]

Many banks and nonbank financial institutions have been closed since

40. There was a 5 percent ceiling on the individual ownership of commercial banks before the onset of the crisis. Major *chaebol,* such as Samsung or Hyundai, owned large shares of the banks while meeting the 5 percent constraint. The government somehow succeeded in preventing large shareholders from participating in the governance of the banks, taking on the role itself.

41. The list of casualties includes such well-known names as Hanbo, Kia, Dong A Construction, Halla, Jinro, and many Daewoo firms (including Daewoo Motors and Daewoo Corporation). Recently, Hyundai Construction was also added to this list.

1998. Most of those that survived had to be recapitalized by the government's money and ended up being mostly owned by the government. Thus, much of the financial sector has been nationalized, while parts of the corporate sector dominated by public enterprises have been privatized. Further, most of the large *chaebol* firms that went bankrupt or fell into serious financial trouble ended up being owned by the banks or placed in court receivership. Large firms in which the banks became major shareholders suffer from the absence of a proper governance mechanism, as the banks themselves are not equipped with a well-functioning governance mechanism.

Firms in court receivership are basically governed by the judges and run by trustees who are appointed by the judges. While judges in Korea are generally trustworthy and competent in enforcing laws, they are not businessmen and have little incentive, other than their sense of responsibility to society, to try to make the firms commercially successful. Trustees also appear to face an incentive structure that often leads them to enjoy the perks of a chief executive officer rather than to try to turn the firms around and sell them to prospective investors. Firms in court receivership sometimes appear to be another breed of public enterprise that lacks a proper corporate governance structure based upon well-defined profit motives.

The banks and other financial institutions that have been nationalized, as well as the bankrupt firms that are in court receivership or are controlled by creditor institutions, need to be recognized as public enterprises that should be privatized. Thus far, the government has privatized only First National Bank, which essentially became nationalized after going through bankruptcy and recapitalization with the government's money. In addition, a sizable proportion of shares of some banks, including Kookmin Bank, was sold to foreign investors. However, it will take quite a while to completely privatize the banks and establish a well-functioning system of financial regulation. Privatization of the firms in court receivership or in workout programs is not an easy task, either.

4.7 Concluding Remarks

Korea has made significant progress in privatizing the commercial businesses owned by the government. Korea's approach to commercial public enterprises and their privatization differs, in several respects, from that of New Zealand and the United Kingdom or other European countries that are going through large-scale privatization. In those countries, the government separated the policy concerns from the public enterprises to be privatized. However, that was not the case in Korea. Rather, privatization policies were mostly focused on divestiture and often lacked concrete plans on a broader set of issues concerning industrial organization of the relevant markets and the policies thereupon.

In network industries, privatization policies focused on partial sales of the shares owned by the government and did not pay much attention to the industry structure, competition policies, or regulatory frameworks. The policy environment was, by and large, left intact, as were the functions and organizations of the line ministries. These differences are probably due to the way the government is organized and operates in Korea. Line ministries of commercial public enterprises in Korea have long been granted the authority to intervene in the relevant industries to promote a wide range of policy objectives. Separation among commercial operation of the public enterprises to be privatized, regulatory functions of the government, and the industrial policies of the government probably require a fundamental change in the way the line ministries operate, and more generally in the way the government is organized and operates. It appears that Korea was not ready to make such a change in the way the government is organized and operates with regard to privatization.

Another crucial factor that affected the privatization path of Korea is the absence of a properly functioning financial market and adequate corporate governance systems for large firms. Extensive reliance on the *chaebol* system and the accompanying heavy government intervention in the financial market during the past four decades deprived the financial sector of a fair chance of developing into a well-functioning market. The only governance systems that existed in Korea for large firms were essentially ownership and control by the government or control by *chaebol* families that depended crucially upon heavy government intervention in the financial market.

In fact, the *chaebol* system can be viewed as a device that uses a handful of families as artificial corporate-governance agents. Key *chaebol* firms were established with the money borrowed from banks as a result of intervention by the government in the banking sector. Thus, it was eventually the government and not the *chaebol* families who took the risks in investing key *chaebol* firms. Actually, it turned out after the onset of the economic crisis that the government indeed covered the losses of the banks and the *chaebol* firms when *chaebol* firms went bankrupt.

It would be unrealistic to expect the *chaebol* system, which is based on a government-controlled financial sector and lack of transparency and accountability, to produce an efficient outcome. In fact, section 4.3 showed that *chaebol* firms performed quite poorly. It seems quite clear that the *chaebol* system is not a plausible alternative for privatizing large SOEs in Korea. In fact, *chaebol* firms, which are already heavily leveraged, do not have enough money to purchase controlling interests in large SOEs. The only way to sell SOEs to *chaebols* would be by lending them money and letting them play the role of artificial corporate-governance agents. This is actually the way *chaebol* families obtained control of the firms under their control now.

A more proper mode of privatization needs to be developed. Developing a new mode of privatization requires establishing a new mode of corporate governance in large firms and financial institutions in Korea. Korea has yet to come up with a model of corporate governance for large, commercial firms that can be relied upon by a majority of investors. For this to occur, the financial market must be made to work based upon sound profit incentives of banks and other financial companies as well as effective prudential supervision.

The financial market in Korea is going through a fundamental change after the recent economic crisis, which was caused at least in part by the lack of proper governance systems in large firms and financial institutions. Korea's chance of successful privatization crucially depends on whether and how fast it can turn around its financial market, which in turn demands the adoption of a stable and efficient governance model by large corporations in the real as well as financial sectors.

References

Galal, Ahmed, Leroy Jones, Pankaj Tandon, and Ingo Vogelsang. 1994. *Welfare consequences of selling public enterprises: An empirical analysis.* New York: Oxford University Press.

Nam, Il Chong, and Yung Jae Kang. 1998. *Privatization strategy* (in Korean). *KDI Journal of Economic Policy* 20 (3–4): 111–165.

Nam, Il Chong, Yung Jae Kang, and Joon Kyung Kim. 2001. Corporate governance trends in Asia. In *Corporate governance in Asia: A comparative perspective,* ed. Stilson Nestor and Takahiro Yasui, 85–115. Paris: Organization for Economic Cooperation and Development.

Nam, Il Chong, Yung Jae Kang, Joon Kyung Kim, Jun Il Kim, and Sung Wook Cho. 2001. Corporate governance in Korea. In *Corporate governance in Asia: A comparative perspective,* ed. Stilson Nestor and Takahiro Yasui, 155–216. Paris: Organization for Economic Cooperation and Development.

Comment   Cassey Lee Hong Kim

Nam's ambitious survey paper succeeds in discussing the different types of public enterprises that exist in South Korea and the reforms that these entities have undergone in the past four years. I will confine my comments to the reform process because the paper raises several interesting questions in this area. The most obvious one has to do with the question of why South

Cassey Lee Hong Kim is head of the department of applied economics at the University of Malaya.

Korea took so long to implement economic reforms in the public enterprise sector. Compared to other countries, South Korea is a relative latecomer to the economic reform scene. While many countries have embarked
on privatization programs since the early 1980s, South Korea only began
privatizing its public enterprises in 1997.

The first question brings us to a second related question: that is, what
were the main driving forces underlying these reforms? There is some evidence that efficiency gain was an important motivating factor. For example, one piece of legislation that made reforms possible in 1997 was an
act that had the revealing title the "Act for Privatization and Improvement
of the Efficiency of Large Public Enterprises" (or the Special Act on Privatization). But it is hard to believe that efficiency gains alone could con-
vince politicians to undertake reforms. Economic reforms of public enterprises require tremendous political willpower for the simple reason that
they generate significant public concern. In the case of some countries, economic reforms could take place only with the emergence of strong new
political leadership, as was the case with Britain (under Thatcher) and
Malaysia (under Mahathir). In the case of South Korea, were there any
changes in its political regime that made possible these reforms of its public
enterprises?[1]

The author identifies two waves of reform of public enterprises in South
Korea. Each episode of reform was undertaken by a new political administration. The first wave began in 1994 when the government commissioned
a study of several public enterprises. This culminated in the passage of the
Special Act on Privatization in 1997. The seed for the first wave of reform
was planted as far back as 1993, when Kim Young Sam became the first
democratically elected civilian president since the military coup d'etat of
1961. Kim Young Sam rode in on a reform ticket during the election and,
a month after coming to power, the newly elected president unveiled two
reform packages: the One Hundred–Day New Economy Plan and the Five-
Year Plan for the New Economy. Even though these plans did not recommend privatization of public enterprises, they inevitably led to it, because
the central motto of both plans was "small government" and "respect for
the private sector's creativity and vitality."

How successful was the first wave of reform? The main objective of the
first wave was to transform a few selected public enterprises into profit-
oriented firms with good (read: Anglo-Saxon) governance structure. Even
though Nam's paper does not explicitly take a stand on this issue, one gets
the distinct feeling that the reforms were of limited success on several accounts: public policy continued to exert influence in the selected firms; too
few firms were involved; and no regulatory reforms were carried out. In the

---

1. One would think politics assume an even greater role in countries with strong workers'
representation (unions).

paper, Nam does mention two major constraints to reforms: the desire to exclude *chaebol* participation and limited equity-acquisition capacity of domestic investors. Aside from this, one is left to wonder about the bureaucratic and political constraints as well.

By 1997, the political support for the Kim administration began to unravel with industrial unrest, economic crisis, and political scandals. This culminated in South Korea's seeking an emergency loan package of US$21 billion from the International Monetary Fund (IMF) in November 1997. It is under this scenario that the veteran opposition leader Kim Dae Jung won the December 1997 election. Thus, the second wave of reforms that began in 1998 was undertaken under a very different environment—a new political administration, economic crisis, and the IMF. I think it would be interesting to know how each of these factors influenced the extent and speed of reforms of public enterprises after 1998. For example, was privatization an issue on Kim Dae Jung's election agenda? Was privatization perceived as having a role to play in the resolution of the economic crisis? Did the reforms demanded by the IMF agreement include reform of public enterprises?[2] On the last question, there is some evidence that suggests that privatization in the immediate aftermath of the economic crisis in 1997 was not affected by the standby agreement between the South Korean government and the IMF. A perusal of the letter of intent that the South Korean government sent to the IMF, dated 7 February 1997, shows that it concentrated on issues such as macropolicies, financial restructuring, capital account liberalization, trade liberalization, labor market reform, and corporate governance reforms.[3]

The second wave of reform remains unfinished. But in the three years since its commencement, the privatization record has been a mixed one. Nam's paper shows that the divestitures carried out were not sufficiently extensive to reduce the government's ability to intervene in companies. Nam points out that the limited success of recent reforms arises from not having paid attention to issues pertaining to industry structure, competition policies, and regulatory frameworks. But looking at Korea's development experience, one would imagine that an extensive change in a short time would not have been possible without tearing apart the country's social and economic fabric.

Many of the economic problems that South Korea faces today are a legacy of a very comprehensive and consistent implementation of a state-led industrialization policy for at least three decades (since the 1960s). The government essentially took control and harnessed the resources of both

2. It was reported in the media that the IMF had actually demanded that all the three major candidates in the 1997 election pledge support for terms in the IMF agreement to be signed.

3. Privatization initiatives only appeared later in the letters of intent to the IMF in March and November 1999.

the financial sector and public enterprises to support the development of large conglomerates (*chaebols*). In Nam's paper, it is evident that *chaebols* remain an important factor even when we discuss the reforms of public enterprises. Because they have such a strong presence in the economy it is difficult to see how they can be excluded unless a long-term policy of reducing their role in the Korean economy is undertaken. For example, if further reforms of public enterprises require a move away from a bank-based to a financial-market-based financial system, then parallel changes in corporate finance will be required. But such changes are far from easy to carry out. South Korea's recent experience is an example. It appears that during the first wave of reform (1994–1997), the *chaebols* were excluded from participating in the reforms of public enterprises partly on account of their dismal track record and their involvement in political scandals in the previous political regimes. But after this period, it is possible that politicians and policymakers have increasingly realized that these entities are too important to exclude unless one can muster enough sustainable political support to alter the role of *chaebols* in the Korean economy. Recent developments, such as relaxation of the ownership limit on *chaebols* in financial institutions, seem to indicate this to be the case. Hence, *chaebol* reform lies at the heart of successful reforms in both the financial system and the public-enterprise sector. All this will depend on the emergence of a political environment that is supportive of the implementation of extensive reforms that incurs the risk of de-industrialization and reduced competitiveness.

5

The Korean Economic Crisis and Corporate Governance System

Sung Wook Joh

5.1 Introduction

After Korea's being touted as one of Asia's economic tigers, the country's 1997 economic collapse shocked many people. Many argued that after other Asian country crises, the massive creditor and investor flight from the Korean currency market caused Korea's high-debt economy to collapse. However, this argument ignores both Korea's low corporate profitability over the last decade, and the fundamental causes of the financial sector's weakness. Following a discussion on how high debt-equity ratios and low profitability helped cause the 1997 Korea economic crisis, I will examine their determinants, and how poor corporate governance allowed such low profitability to occur for so long. Finally, I will discuss recent reforms and their preliminary results.

Advocates of the currency-flight view point to Korea's high-debt economy over the past decade to support their argument. Compared to other countries, Korea's debt-equity ratio was very high. Furthermore, high debt-equity ratios in Korea have been the norm for many years. In the currency-flight view, although these high debt-equity ratios spurred high growth, they also left Korean firms vulnerable to fickle creditors and investors. When other Asian economies such as Thailand and Indonesia collapsed, creditors and investors pulled their money out of Korean firms. The

Sung Wook Joh is professor in the business school at Korea University.

I am grateful to the participants at the 12th Annual NBER seminar on the East Asian Economics for their helpful comments on the earlier version of the paper. I am especially grateful to Anne Krueger, Mario Lamberte, Philip Williams, and an anonymous referee for their detailed and helpful comments.

ensuing liquidity crisis forced many firms to default on their loans. Thus, many firms failed, and the Korean economy collapsed.

Criticism of the above argument includes (1) the absence of high profits, (2) the many firm failures before the collapse of other Asian economies, and (3) the argument's dependence on creditor and investor irrationality. With high debt-equity ratios, Korean firms were expected to yield high profits on their equity. However, the average rate of return on equity was often *lower* than the prevailing interest rates for loans (Joh 2003), and the return on capital had been lower than the opportunity cost. Krueger and Yoo (2001) showed that the rate of return on assets (ROA) of the Korean manufacturing sector has been lower than that of other countries such as Japan, Germany, the United States, and Taiwan. So, on average, the capital used in the corporate sector was wasted on unprofitable projects.

Korea's weak corporate governance allowed this low profitability to continue for almost ten years before the crisis. Many firms, including six of the thirty largest conglomerates, failed before the collapse of other Asian economies simply because their low profits fell short of their required loan payments (Joh 2002). The failure of many large firms severely weakened financial institutions. Rationally concerned about their investments and loans, foreign investors sold their Korean stocks, and foreign banks demanded repayment of the short-term loans given to Korean financial institutions rather than rolling them over to the following year, which had been the usual practice. Foreign banks and investors exacerbated the crisis; they did not cause it.

5.2   Crisis and Corporate-Sector Problems

High debt-equity ratios and low firm performance helped trigger failures of large *chaebols* even before the 1997 economic crisis. In this section, we review the causes of the corporate-sector problems.

5.2.1   High Corporate Debt

As figure 5.1 shows, the average debt-equity ratio of Korean firms has been very high for a long time and did not rise before the crisis. In 1997, Korean firms' average debt-equity ratio was higher than those of other countries' (Korea, 396 percent; United States, 154 percent; Japan, 193 percent; Taiwan, 86 percent.[1]

When six of the thirty largest *chaebols* (business groups) went bankrupt *before* the currency crisis, it triggered a cascade of nonperforming loans. Starting with the default by Hanbo (ranked fourteenth) in January 1997 well before the Asian crisis, a series of large *chaebol* defaults raised suspicion regarding conglomerates' survival and the fundamental soundness of

---

1. For Taiwanese firms, the figure is based on 1996 data (Bank of Korea 1997).

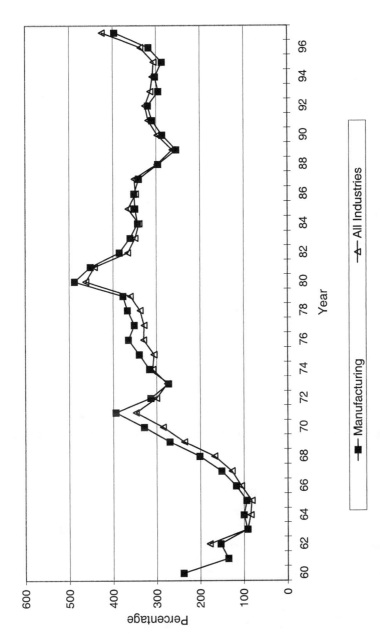

Fig. 5.1   Debt-equity ratio of Korean firms
Source: Bank of Korea (various issues).

Table 5.1   Six Bankrupt Conglomerates among the Thirty Largest *Chaebol* (all defaulted in 1997)

	Hanbo	Sammi	Jinro	KIA	Haitai	New-Core
Default date	23 January	19 March	21 April	15 July	1 November	4 November
Ranking	14th	25th	19th	8th	24th	28th
Debt (trillions of won)	4.42	2.43	3.23	9.57	2.52	1.85
Debt-equity ratio	648%	3,333%	4,836%	522%	669%	1,253%

Sources: Default date and ranking are from Shin and Hahm (1998). Debt size and debt-equity ratio are from Korea Fair Trade Commission (1999).

the corporate sector. The total debt of these bankrupt conglomerates alone amounted to 24.02 trillion won (see table 5.1), 35.5 percent and 5.3 percent of the government budget and gross national product (GNP), respectively, in 1997. Although the money for bailout would be smaller than the size of debt, large debt of the failed *chaebols* in 1997 implied that bailout would cost more than earlier bailouts. For example, during the financial crisis in the middle of 1980s, the Bank of Korea provided six commercial banks with 1.7 trillion won between 1985 and 1987 to rescue many debt-ridden firms that became insolvent (see Joh 2001). Because the debt of the *chaebol* became too large for the economy, and other firms were doing so poorly that they could not easily acquire the firms with such high levels of debt, it was extremely difficult for the government to rescue the firms in trouble in 1997.

Due to their size and importance in subcontracting,[2] the failure of these *chaebols* had a devastating impact on the economy, leading to a series of bankruptcies. When we consider bankruptcy of subcontractors, the impact of the failure of these conglomerates would be too large for the government to handle. Table 5.2 shows the rapid increase in the ratio of nonperforming loans from 1997 to 1998.[3]

Causes of High Debt-Equity Ratio

During the early high-growth period, the government provided large firms with capital at low interest rates. Because large firms were more likely to receive government-subsidized capital and the government's implicit guarantees, firms had an incentive to increase their size by using crossholdings and cross-debt guarantees. Moreover, creditors were not provid-

2. Chung and Yang (1992) report that the shares of the top five and top thirty *chaebol* in GNP were 9.2 percent and 16.3 percent, respectively. The Korea Economic Research Institute reports that in 1995 the shares of the top four and top thirty were 9.2 percent and 16.2 percent, respectively.

3. Many criticize that these official numbers underestimated the true size of nonperforming loans. Some estimate that nonperforming loans reached somewhere between 200 and 300 trillion won.

Table 5.2   **Nonperforming Loans (end of period)**

	December 1997	March 1998	June 1998	September 1998	December 1998
Precautionary loans	42.8	57.7	72.5	n.a	n.a.
Substandard loans or below (A)	43.6	59.6	63.5	64.0	60.2
Bank	31.6	38.8	40.0	35.0	33.6
NBFI	12.0	20.8	23.5	29.0	26.6
Total loan (B)	647.4	668.7	624.8	614.3	576.5
A/B (%)	6.7	8.9	10.2	10.4	10.5

Sources: Financial Supervisory Commission (various press releases).

Notes: Precautionary loans were overdue for more than three months, and substandard loans were overdue for more than six months. Loan classification has changed since 1999. Amounts are in trillions of won.

ing a monitoring role to failing firms. Rather, banks continued to provide loans to failing firms. These factors helped cause high debt-equity ratios.

Government-Provided Incentives and Bailouts for Large Firms. Since the 1960s, past Korean governments have mobilized and allocated scarce capital to firms and industries (such as light-export-oriented industries and heavy and chemical industries) based on an assessment of their contribution to the nation's industrialization and modernization. The government used a compliance mechanism that effectively guided the behavior of major businesses (Jones and SaKong 1980). Through nationalized banks, the government provided targeted firms with capital at lower interest rates than time deposit rates or inflation rates until the beginning of the 1980s. Financial institutions simply implemented the government decisions and made no independent decisions. Lee (1992) argued that the Korean government operated an internal capital market and channeled subsidized credit to carefully targeted firms and industries.

When the government subsidized debt during the high-growth period, it was a rational decision for firms to increase their levels of debt. As table 5.3 shows, until 1981 borrowing money from the national investment fund, or borrowing for export, was lucrative because the borrowing interest rate was lower than the interest rate on one-year time deposits or the inflation rate. After 1981, interest rates on bank loans became greater than interest rates on savings in time deposits. This was possible because the earlier Korean government nationalized and owned the banks and regulated the interest rates. It also practically dictated the credit allocation. This credit policy affeted the corporate sector: firms formed a large business group to expropriate cheap loans. Creditors in credit allocation decisions favored business groups because subsidiaries could provide debt payment guarantees and the government implicitly guaranteed them when they were in financial distress.

With subsidized debt, firms were encouraged to invest in labor-intensive

Table 5.3   **Interest Rates, 1964–1981**

Year	Inflation (CPI)	Time Deposit[a]	Bank Loans General	NIF	Export	Curb Market
1964	—	15.0	16.0	—	8.0	61.8
1965	—	30.0	26.0	—	6.5	58.9
1966	11.2	30.0	26.0	—	6.0	58.7
1967	10.9	30.0	26.0	—	6.0	56.7
1968	10.8	26.0	25.2	—	6.0	56.0
1969	12.3	24.0	24.0	—	6.0	51.4
1970	15.9	22.8	24.0	—	6.0	50.2
1971	13.5	22.0	22.0	—	6.0	46.4
1972	11.7	15.0	15.5	—	6.0	39.0
1973	3.1	12.6	15.5	—	7.0	33.2
1974	24.3	15.0	15.5	12.0	9.0	40.6
1975	25.3	15.0	15.5	12.0	9.0	47.9
1976	15.3	15.6	18.0	14.0	8.0	40.5
1977	10.1	15.8	16.0	14.0	8.0	38.1
1978	14.4	16.9	19.0	16.0	9.0	41.7
1979	18.3	14.4	19.0	16.0	9.0	42.4
1980	28.7	19.5	20.0	19.5	15.0	44.9
1981	21.3	16.2	17.0	17.5	15.0	35.3

Sources: Cho and Kim (1997; original source, Bank of Korea, *Economic Statistics Yearbook,* various issues).

Notes: CPI = consumer price index; NIF = National Investment Fund. Dash indicates data are not available.

[a]One-year time bank deposit.

exporting industries, or the heavy and chemical industry,[4] in the 1960s and 1970s, respectively. The return from investment in these industries resulted partly from lower capital costs and/or lower corporate income taxes and the like.[5] Therefore, at the individual level, each firm had an incentive to invest in these industries, and may have made a rational choice of investment, other things being equal. Consequently, investment in these industries in the aggregate may have exceeded the socially optimal level as resources shifted from other, more socially profitable industries.

Moreover, with huge debt, firms were vulnerable to drops in demand and macroeconomic shocks. Each time many large firms faced financial distress, the government intervened and rescued them.[6] During the debt crisis

---

4. These industries include power-generating equipment, cars, engines, heavy electric equipment, telephone-switching systems, refined copper, etc.

5. Kim (1997) reports that President Park Chung Hee held monthly cabinet meetings that decided policy measures to facilitate exports. Kim also reports that exporting firms received credits at a lower interest rate and paid corporate income tax at 50 percent of the usual corporate income tax rate.

6. See Joh (2001) for more discussion on this issue.

of 1972, the government froze their debts and gave bailout loans[7] to firms in financial distress. From 1979 to 1983, firms again suffered from over-investment and depression following the second oil shock (Lee 1995). To deal with insolvency problems associated with excessive capacity, the government gave financial subsidies and consolidated firms to create more concentrated markets. In the 1980s, the government adopted some liberal procompetition policies, privatizing commercial banks during 1981–1983, and reducing the gap in interest rates between industrial policy loans and general loans. During 1984–1988, many debt-ridden firms became insolvent, only to have the government intervene yet again.[8] By providing creditor banks with special 3 to 6 percent interest rate loans (the general bank loan rate was about 12 percent; see Lee 1995), the government allowed these banks to write off bad debts, extend debt maturities, and replace existing debt with longer-term debt at a lower rate.[9] In short, the government had repeatedly given large firms preferential subsidies and bailed them out during times of financial distress.

Firms Inflate Size with Cross-Holdings and Cross-Debt Guarantees. Large firms received both low-cost capital for undertaking large projects and implicit guarantees from the government. Thus, firms had incentives to exaggerate their true size and performance. This was particularly easy for business group firms that engaged in intragroup transactions and interlocking ownership.[10] For example, through interlocking ownership, a firm A invests its assets in an affiliated firm B. Through double-counting of these investments, the sum of the assets of A and B can exceed the total assets of the group.

Chaebols also can borrow more money through cross-debt payment guarantees. On average, a few large and better-performing firms in a *chaebol* typically guaranteed 80 percent of the *chaebol* firms' total debt. Moreover, *chaebols* with higher debt payment guarantees managed to borrow more money, resulting in higher debt-to-equity ratios at the group level (Lee 1998). Using debt payment guarantees, even poorly operating subsidies managed to borrow money. The total debt payment guarantees often far exceeded their total equity, raising doubts on their validity (see table 5.4).

Loans to Failing Firms. Banks continued lending to high debt-equity firms, as table 5.5 shows. The largest thirty *chaebols* had very high debt-equity

---

7. For more of the 1972 government emergency measure, see Cho and Kim (1997).

8. The government revised its tax exemption law to facilitate the insolvency procedure in December 1985.

9. See Cho and Kim (1997). In total, acquiring firms and consolidating firms received subsidies worth 7.28 trillion won (Lee 1995).

10. At least 60 percent of firms subject to external auditing report that they have legally affiliated firms. See Joh (2003).

Table 5.4   Debt Payment Guarantees of the Thirty Largest *Chaebol* (trillions of won)

Year	Equity (A)	Restriction (B)	No Restriction (C)	Sum (B + C)	B/A	(B + C)/A
		Amount of Debt Payment Guarantee			Ratio (%)	
1993	3.52	12.06	4.49	16.55	342.4	469.8
1994	4.28	7.25	3.82	11.07	169.3	258.1
1995	5.07	4.83	3.38	8.21	95.2	161.9
1996	6.29	3.52	3.23	6.75	55.9	107.3
1997	7.04	3.36	3.13	6.49	47.7	92.2

Source: Korea Fair Trade Commission (various dates).

Table 5.5   High Debt-Equity Ratios and Accounting Profitability of Thirty Large *Chaebol*

	1995	1996	1997	1998	1999	2000
Average debt-equity ratio	347.5	386.5	519.0	369.1	306.6	218.7
Groups with debt-equity ≥ 1,000%	3	3	4	2	2	2
Groups with negative equity	0	0	2	8	5	3
Groups with loss	13	12	18	n.a.	n.a.	n.a.

Sources: Korea Fair Trade Commission (various dates) and Choi (1996, 1997, 1998).
Notes: n.a. = not available. *Chaebol* with negative equity were not included in calculating the average debt-equity ratio.

ratios (348 percent in 1995, 519 percent in 1997), some exceeding 1,000 percent. Moreover, before the crisis occurred, more than 40 percent of the largest thirty *chaebols* experienced losses. For example, thirteen out of thirty *chaebols* exhibited losses in 1995. Beginning in 1997, some *chaebols* showed that the accumulated losses eroded their paid-in capital completely, resulting in negative equity. However, these *chaebols* managed to maintain their debt levels, or borrowed more, resulting in a higher level of debt-to-equity ratios. The continuing flow of capital to large conglomerate firms suggests that financial institutions were not making lending decisions based on monitoring *chaebol* finances.

5.2.2   Low Corporate Firm Performance

With high debt-equity ratios, Korean firms were expected to yield high performance on their equity. When highly profitable firms borrow money to exploit their investment and growth opportunities, a high debt level might not be a serious problem. However, as figure 5.2 shows, the average rate of return on equity was often *lower* than the prevailing interest rates for loans. On average, the return on capital had been lower than its

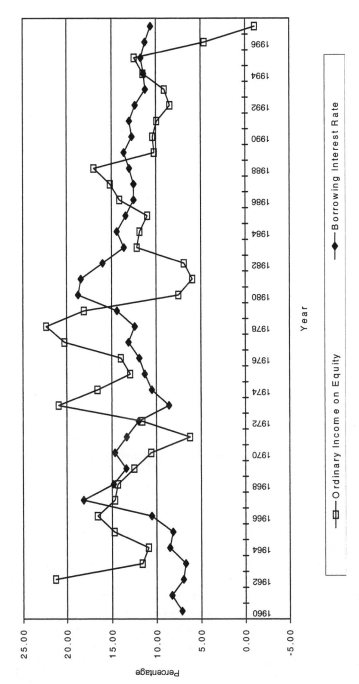

Fig. 5.2 Profitability of Korean firms
Source: Bank of Korea (various issues).

opportunity cost for almost ten years before the crisis. So, the capital was, on average, wasted on unprofitable projects.

Moreover, the return in the stock market also shows that shareholders on average did not receive high returns either. Shareholders received very small dividends as firms did not make much profit, and on average they did not make capital gains either. The monthly Korean stock price index in figure 5.3 shows large ups and downs in the return on stocks. For almost five years after the stock market opened, the stock price index hardly changed. Starting in the middle of the 1980s, the stock price increased fast and reached its peak in 1989. However, in the 1990s the index was below the peak in the 1980s, except for a few observations. In addition, after the peak of October 1994 the average stock index already had started to decline before the economic crisis.

From these two figures, it is clear that firm performance was weak and shareholders did not receive high returns. Why was the performance of the corporate sector so low? There are several factors to examine. First, large, poorly performing firms did not exit the market; and second, controlling shareholders did not increase firm value. Rather, they diverted firm resources.

To examine the causes of the low performance of Korean firms, I analyze panel data on publicly traded firms' ownership and financial data compiled by National Information Credit Evaluation, Inc. (NICE). Due to ownership data availability, I examine firm data from 1993 to 1997. For the analysis of Korean data, accounting profitability rather than stock market–based performance is likely a better performance measure for a couple of reasons. First, developing countries show stock market inefficiency, so stock prices in Korea are not likely to reflect all available information. Second, a firm's accounting profitability is more directly related to its financial survivability than stock market value is (Mossman et al. 1998). Many studies used accounting measures to predict bankruptcy (Altman 1968, Takahashi, Kurokawa, and Watase 1984) or financial distress (Hoshi, Kashyap, and Sharfstein 1991).

After excluding financial institutions and state-controlled firms from the analysis, the data set includes 4,702 observations between 1993 and 1997. I examine whether owners with more control rights than ownership rights expropriated firm resources before the crisis. As Jensen and Meckling (1976) argue, a controlling shareholder has an incentive to expropriate firm resources when his or her control rights exceed ownership rights because his or her private benefits exceed their costs. Concentrated ownership means less discrepancy of interests under the assumption that the control level is very high. This assumption is likely to hold because the control and influence of controlling shareholders is very high in Korea. Korea suffers from a poor corporate governance system, as the legal institutional environment does not protect minority shareholders and the controlling

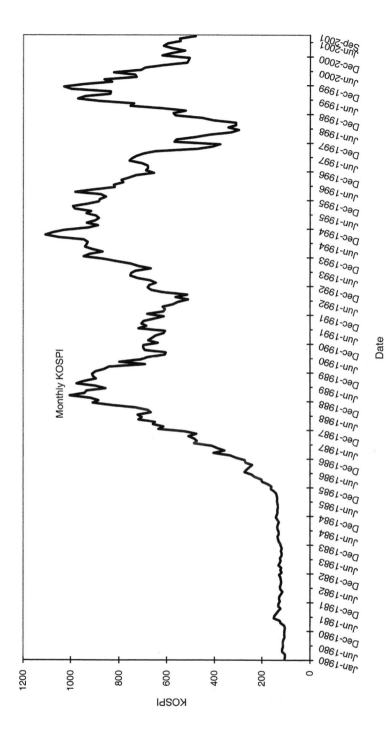

Fig. 5.3   Monthly stock price index, 1980–2000
Source: Korea Stock Exchange, monthly stock price index.

Table 5.6   Determinants of Profitability among Publicly Traded Firms

	Ordinary Income/Sales	
	(1)	(2)
Ownership	0.0505	
	(9.84)	
Control and ownership-rights difference		−0.0205
		(−3.99)
Debt ratio	−0.0272	−0.0257
	(−7.40)	(−6.94)
Chaebol dummy	−1.3473	−1.5620
	(−3.52)	(−3.95)
Log (asset)	0.1408	−0.3097
	(0.95)	(−2.16)
R&D/sales	−0.0605	−0.0766
	(−1.20)	(−1.50)
Export/sales	0.0126	0.0120
	(2.14)	(2.01)
Advertisement/sales	−0.0281	−0.0048
	(−0.38)	(−0.06)
Market share	0.0675	0.0794
	(3.90)	(4.56)
Industry and year dummies	Included	Included
No. of observations	4,702	4,702
Adjusted R^2	0.3673	0.3560

Notes: The regression tests the determinants of accounting profitability based on listed firms between 1993 and 1997. Ownership measures the controlling shareholder and his or her family member's ownership excluding the intragroup shareholding. Control and ownership-rights difference is measured as the sum of all institutional and intragroup ownership minus controlling shareholder and his or her family member's ownership. An industry dummy is assigned for each five-digit Korean standard industrial classification code. The *chaebol* dummy takes a value of 1 when a firm belongs to one of the largest seventy *chaebol.* Numbers in parentheses are *t*-values controlling for heteroskedasticity.

shareholders' position is secured. Using ownership that is the stake of the largest shareholder and his or her family members, the empirical result is presented in column (1) in table 5.6. However, ownership is not a direct measure of the discrepancy between control rights and ownership rights unless controlling shareholders' control is more or less similar. To incorporate the referee's concern, I also use the difference between control rights and ownership rights in the analysis. I include the results in column (2) in table 5.6.

Controlling firm size, capital structure, and firm- and industry-specific characteristics,[11] I found that firms with high controlling shareholder ownership outperformed those with low controlling shareholder ownership, as the first column shows. In the second column, firms with high discrepancy between control rights and ownership rights show lower profitability. Like-

11. For a brief summary of how these variables affect firm performance, see Martin (1993).

wise, independent firms outperformed *chaebol*. The results are consistent with the argument that controlling shareholders with a large disparity between control and ownership rights pursue their own private interests at the expense of other shareholders. For more on this, see Jensen and Meckling (1976) and Joh (2003).

Cause of Low Firm Performance

The above results show that controlling shareholders have expropriated small shareholders, lowering corporate performance. In other words, Korean firms' low profits persisted because the corporate governance system did not induce firm management to maximize firm value.

According to Shleifer and Vishny (1997), corporate governance defines the ways in which the suppliers of finance to corporations are assured of getting a return on their investment in a firm. By defining firm rules, incentives, and goals, the management, capital suppliers, and other stakeholders affect the mechanisms by which capital and resources are allocated, profits are distributed, and performance is monitored. In a corporate governance system that operates for the benefit of all shareholders,[12] management pursues maximization of firm value.

This section examines the factors that contribute to poor corporate governance systems. In particular, we examine factors including (1) no credible exit threat, (2) lack of financial-institution monitoring, (3) few legal rights or types of protection for minority shareholders, (4) a negligent board of directors, and (5) inadequate financial information.

No Credible Exit Threat. Ideally, the market continuously revolutionizes from within, incessantly destroying the old firms and creating new ones, according to Schumpeter (1952). As weak firms fail, new, strong firms will replace them and employ people who lost jobs. Resources are released and shifted from the dying factories and firms to entering producers. In Korea, this "creative destruction" process was so weak for large firms that resources were not efficiently allocated.

Using the annual census data, Joh (2000) showed that the Korean manufacturing sector has high turnover (see table 5.7). The annual output by new and dying plants over total economy output was high, 4.1 percent and 5.4 percent, respectively. Between 1990 and 1998, the output ratios of entering and exiting plants, including switching plants, exceed 12.0 percent and 16.9 percent of total output, respectively. The entering and exiting plants over total plants were even higher, reaching 14.4 percent and 17.7 percent, respectively. When switching plants were included, the ratio jumped to 24 percent and 32 percent. These turnover rates are higher than

---

12. With financial market liberalization and globalization, shareholders' interests become most important.

Table 5.7   **Output by Plants with Different Turnover Status, 1990–1998 (%)**

	Continuing Plants	New Plants	Switch-Ins	Dying Plants	Switch-Outs
1990				3.7	18.8
1991	69.3	4.3	11.7	4.4	10.3
1992	70.2	3.8	5	7.4	13.6
1993	70.9	6.4	9.5	4.9	8.3
1994	75.5	3.1	5.1	5.7	10.6
1995	74.7	4.0	6.9	5.5	8.9
1996	74.0	3.8	6.1	5.1	11
1997	71.9	3.7	7.4	6.2	10.8
1998		3.9	11.4	n.a.	n.a.
Mean	72.4	4.1	7.9	5.4	11.5

Source: Joh (2000).

Notes: n.a. = not applicable. The mean is a simple average over time.

those in most countries. The exit rates measured by percentage of producers for the United States, the United Kingdom, Germany, and Canada are 7.0 percent, 11.5 percent, 4.6 percent, and 4.8 percent, respectively (Joh 2000).

However, turnover rate varies depending on the plant size. For larger plants, turnover is much lower. While small plants exit the market when they fail, large plants often do not. Table 5.8 summarizes the effects of size on turnover. Panel A shows the effect of number of employees, panel B shows effects of asset size, and panel C shows the effects of capital equipment ratio on turnover. All panels show very similar results. Birth and death rates are lower in the group of plants with the most employees, greatest assets, or greatest capital ratio. These findings imply that the exit threat for large firms was not as effective as that for small plants. Without a credible threat to firm survival, managers of large firms had less incentive to improve firm performance. In addition, large, failing firms continued to operate, taking away resources from profitable firms.

Large firms faced a weak exit threat for three reasons. The first of these was *lengthy bankruptcy* proceedings. There were three formal bankruptcy procedures: liquidation, composition, and corporate reorganization (similar to Chapter 11 of the U.S. bankruptcy code). However, these formal insolvency procedures for large firms were rarely used in Korea until 1997. Lengthy proceedings, often lasting several years, invited strategic and opportunistic debtor behavior, thus reducing the attractiveness of bankruptcy alternatives for creditors (see table 5.7). Although more than 17,000 cases of insolvency were reported in 1997, only 490 were filed before the court. Of these, only thirty-eight liquidations were filed (Organization for Economic Cooperation and Development [OECD] 1998). Moreover, the

Table 5.8   **Output Ratios by Plant Turnover Status When Size is Measured through Employees, Assets, and Capital Equipment, 1990–1998 (%)**

	Continuing	New Plants	Switch-Ins	Dying Plants	Switch-Outs
		A. Number of Employees			
Top 20%	76.9	2.5	7.3	3.3	10.0
20–40%	73.0	5.2	6.7	6.8	8.3
40–60%	67.3	8.3	7.0	8.9	8.5
60–80%	57.5	11.5	8.2	12.6	10.2
80–100%	45.8	17.2	8.2	20.0	8.8
		B. Asset Size			
Top 20%	77.1	2.6	7.3	3.2	9.8
20–40%	72.6	4.8	6.8	6.6	9.2
40–60%	69.2	6.8	6.7	8.8	8.5
60–80%	56.8	10.8	8.7	13.3	10.4
80–100%	46.2	17.9	7.5	18.8	9.6
		C. Capital Equipment Ratio			
Top 20%	76.8	3.1	7.5	3.2	9.4
20–40%	74.6	3.6	7.2	5.0	9.6
40–60%	75.0	3.5	6.5	5.5	9.5
60–80%	70.5	5.0	6.5	7.8	10.2
80–100%	54.5	11.5	8.6	13.3	12.2

Source: Joh (2000).

Table 5.9   **Number of Cases and Duration of Bankruptcy Proceedings (1993–1995)**

	Number of Years						
	≤3	4–5	6–7	8–10	11–15	16–20	Total
Successful turnaround, conclusion	1	1	2	6	7	1	18
Failure, termination	17	12	10	8	5	0	52

Source: Court Administration Agency, recited from Koo (1998).

law allowed firms that owed less than 250 billion won to use a settlement procedure in which the court played a rather minor role while the debtor retained possession of its estate. Composition offered few guarantees to creditors, and 65.7 percent of insolvent firms (322 out of 490 cases) applied for this settlement procedure. The remaining firms applied for corporate reorganization, but their financial conditions often had deteriorated too far to restructure successfully. Koo (1998) showed that the average debt-equity ratio of these firms was 1,200 percent. See table 5.9 for a summary of the number of cases and duration of the proceedings.

The second cause of the weak exit threat companies faced was the *underdeveloped corporate control market.* Government regulations on mergers and acquisitions (M&As) and ownership structure also weakened the

Table 5.10   **In-Group Ownership Trends of the Thirty Largest *Chaebol* (%)**

	1989	1990	1991	1992	1993	1994	1995	1996	1997
30 largest *chaebol*	31.5	31.7	33.0	33.5	33.1	33.0	32.8	33.8	34.5
5 largest *chaebol*	35.7	36.3	38.4	38.6	37.2	35.0	n.a.	n.a.	36.6

Source: Korea Fair Trade Commission (1999).
Note: n.a. = not available.

exit mechanism. Until recently, hostile mergers and acquisitions were not allowed, and even friendly M&As were limited to small firms.[13] Any M&A by foreigners involving over two trillion won in assets required government approval. The mandatory-tender-offer system required investors who bought over 25 percent of a firm's shares to publicly purchase over 50 percent of the shares. In addition, the ownership structure of *chaebol,* with large interlocking ownership by affiliated firms as shown in table 5.10, obstructed takeovers by outside investors. Controlling shareholders with less than 10 percent direct ownership have control through interlocking ownership by other firms in the same *chaebol* group. Therefore, corporate raiders needed to buy the sum of the incumbent controlling owners' shares, the interlocking firms' shares, and one more share.

Finally, *government support for weak, large firms* was an additional cause of the weak exit threat. Before the crisis, large firms hardly faced any exit threats because of the government's implicit guarantee.[14] As discussed earlier, the government had repeatedly rescued many failing *chaebol.* Because of the debt payment guarantees, poorly performing subsidiaries can cause financial distress for high-performing subsidiaries. So the failure of a few subsidiaries in a large conglomerate can cause a chain reaction of failures and devastate the economy. Partially due to its impacts on employment and on the overall economy, the government arranged for some banks to lend more money to these failing firms. This government behavior led to the belief that *chaebols* were "too big to fail."

Lack of Financial-Institution Monitoring. Financial institutions as creditors should monitor their borrowing firms to insure their lending. However, financial institutions in Korea have not provided adequate monitoring, even though Korean firms rely heavily on debt for their financing. There are at least two reasons. Although once-nationalized commercial banks were privatized in the 1980s, the legacy of government control remained through interest rate regulation, credit policies, and government-appointed top executives. As a result, banks did not develop suitable credit

13. In May 1998, six months after the 1997 crisis, the Korean government removed all restrictions on M&A activities.
14. Kukjae's failure in 1984 was a politically motivated exception.

evaluation and risk management techniques to make informed loan decisions. Banks did not have an incentive to monitor or discipline managers. Often, they gave loans to large firms with implicit government guarantees or cross-debt guarantees, as discussed earlier. Moreover, the linkage between *chaebols* and financial institutions exacerbated the problems. According to Kim (1999), *chaebol* with nonbank financial institutions show a high debt-equity ratio while those *chaebol*-controlled financial institutions show a lower ROA. These results suggest that *chaebols* were transferring resources from financial institutions to poorly performing industrial firms.

Few Legal Rights or Types of Protection for Minority Shareholders. As equity holders, shareholders have incentives to induce firm management to pursue value maximization. However, effective monitoring activity is underprovided, as it has public-good properties. While a monitoring shareholder pays all costs, he or she cannot monopolize the benefit of monitoring but shares it with other shareholders. When a shareholder overcame free-rider problems associated with the public-good property of monitoring, the shareholder was likely to face difficulty in actively engaging in monitoring because most shareholder rights required a minimum 5 percent ownership that few shareholders had. Shareholders needed at least 5 percent ownership to do any of the following: remove a director, file an injunction, file a derivative suit, demand a convocation, inspect accounting books, inspect corporate affairs and company property, or request a removal of liquidation receiver. Over 97 percent of shareholders lacked these rights as they were small investors with less than 1 percent ownership. Even when small shareholders do not have certain rights, minority shareholders as a group could be better protected when class action suits are introduced and fiduciary duty is imposed on directors and managers.[15] However, neither class action suits nor fiduciary duty was introduced. Therefore, minority shareholders had few legal rights or types of protection. So they had difficulty preventing controlling shareholders and firm managers from pursuing wasteful projects.

Negligent Board of Directors. Without a significant exit threat and little financial-institution monitoring, internal monitoring and discipline become more important. The board of directors should monitor and discipline managers, thereby mitigating the opportunistic behavior of controlling shareholders. However, boards of directors did not. We have indirect evidence that boards did not represent all the shareholders' interests, and did not monitor controlling shareholders. Before the crisis occurred, over 75 percent of firms polled said that they rarely or never con-

---

15. See Johnson et al. (2000) for more discussion on fiduciary duty and duty of care for managers and directors.

Table 5.11   **Frequency of Considering Minority Shareholder Opinion in Selecting Directors and Auditors (%)**

Type of Firm	Always	Often	Sometimes	Rarely	Never
Owner-manager	6.2	6.2	12.5	31.3	43.8
Hired manager	2.9	5.7	14.3	40.0	37.1

Source: Jun and Gong (1995).

Table 5.12   **Outside Directors' Attendance and Approval Rates (%)**

Agenda Approval	Board Attendance	Other Involvement
99.3	66.0	6.2

Source: Jang (2000).

sidered the minority shareholders' opinion in selecting directors and auditors (Jun and Kong 1995). Because board members were elected through separate majority votes, controlling shareholders were able to elect all directors they recommended. On average, the controlling shareholders could control more than 40 percent of shares in the largest thirty *chaebols* as they controlled not only their family ownership but also in-group ownership, as shown in table 5.10. Therefore, the controlling shareholders were able to select all directors and, hence, have all the control (see table 5.11).

Moreover, once directors and auditors were elected, they did not have to represent the firm value or shareholder groups' interest. The legal responsibilities of directors are based on the principle of *duty of care.*[16] Under this principle, directors are given the benefit of the doubt when conflicts of interest are in question. Otherwise, their willfulness or negligence is to be proved legally. Consequently, board members were accountable only to the controlling shareholders, as small shareholders with less than 5 percent of ownership could not remove them. The extremely high agenda approval rate of outside directors after the crisis (see table 5.12) implies that directors did not hinder controlling shareholders from pursuing private benefits.

Inadequate Financial Information. Inadequate financial information hinders management evaluation, thereby obstructing rewards for good managers and removal of poor managers. The market lacked accurate and reliable information on firm performance and management due to low accounting standards, lack of transparency, and government-triggered incentives for firms to exaggerate their size. Accounting standards in Korea

16. See n. 15.

Table 5.13   **Review of Auditing Firms' Financial Statements, 1998–2000**

	Firms (A)	Improper Auditing (B)	Ratio (B/A)
Regular auditing (listed firms)	97	29	29.9%
Irregular/frequent auditing	6	3	50%
Special auditing	48	46	96%
Consigned auditing	118	116	98%
Total	269	194	72%

Source: Financial Supervisory Service (2000).

Table 5.14   **Large *Chaebol* under Insolvency Procedures, As of August 1999**

	Daewoo	Donga	Halla	Kohap	Jinro	Anam	Haitai	Kangwon	Shinho
Type	w/o	w/o	r/o	w/o	c/o	w/o	c/o	w/o	w/o
Rank in 1996	2	11	17	18	22	23	24	26	29

Source: Ministry of Finance and Economy (1999).
Notes: w/o = workout; r/o = reorganization; c/o = composition.

did not meet accepted international standards, so poor auditing hindered efforts to monitor and evaluate firm performance. For example, when firm A guarantees debt payment to firm B, A need not report such action accurately, thereby hiding A's higher risk. Furthermore, with easy access to debt financing, *chaebols* need not attract and retain equity investors through financial transparency. Indeed, withholding information from other shareholders facilitates firm control by the dominant shareholder.

It is difficult to measure how opaque the financial statements were before the crisis. However, recent auditing of financial statements by the Financial Supervisory Service reveals many flaws. On average, the review found that 72 percent of audits had flaws. Improper auditing ranges from minor errors to fraud. So firm financial statements in earlier years facing less scrutiny were likely more flawed and misleading (see table 5.13).

5.3   Effects of Recent Corporate Governance Reforms

5.3.1   Major Changes

Since the crisis occurred, several measures have been introduced to improve the corporate governance system, including more credible exit threats for large firms, strengthened minority shareholders' rights, mandated outside directors, and increased roles for boards of directors.

Many large conglomerates, including Daewoo, which was ranked second in 1999, have fallen to insolvency procedures (see table 5.14). Although the government continues to try to rescue some *chaebols* (e.g.,

Table 5.15   M&A Trends before and after the Crisis

	Total Cases	Cases by Foreigners	Amount by Foreigners ($ billions)
1997	418	19	0.84
1999	557	168	8.80
Change	139	149	7.86
	(33.2%)	(784%)	(935%)

Source: Korea Fair Trade Commission (1998, 2000).

Table 5.16   Key Items of Minority Shareholders' Rights (%)

	Former Commercial Code	Amendments	Securities and Exchange Act
Requesting removal of a director	5	3	0.5 (0.25)
Right to injunction	5	1	0.5 (0.25)
Derivative suit	5	1	0.01
Shareholder's proposal	n.a.	3	1 (0.5)
Demand for convocation	5	3	3 (1.5)
Inspect account books	5	3	1 (0.5)
Inspect affairs and property	5	3	3 (1.5)
Request a new liquidation receiver	5	3	0.5 (0.25)

Source: Joh (2001; original source, Ministry of Finance and Economy).

Notes: n.a. = not applicable. Appraisal rights of general shareholders' meeting convocation and shareholder proposals estimated on the basis of voting stocks. Numbers in parentheses show cases of corporations with more than 100 billion won in paid-in capital at the end of the most recent business year.

Hyundai), these failures signal a new government policy of nonintervention in the corporate sector. So many failing *chaebols* were losing so much money that the government may have lacked the funds to save them from bankruptcy.

In addition, all M&As, including hostile takeovers and foreign takeovers, have been legalized. Compared to 1997, the number and amount of M&As, especially by foreign firms, had skyrocketed in 1999 (see table 5.15). In short, large, failing firms face more credible exit threats than before.

The government has lowered the minimum shareholding requirements for many shareholder rights (see table 5.16). Now any shareholder with 0.01 percent of firm ownership can file a derivative suit. Despite such changes, monitoring by individual small shareholders remains unlikely,

Table 5.17   **Selection of Outside Directors**

	Recommending Party			
	Controlling Shareholder	Main Creditor	Employee	Others
Ratio	343	25	20	77
	(73.8%)	(5.3%)	(4.3%)	(16.6%)

Source: Jang (2000).

Table 5.18   **Directors' Attendance Rate Classified by Agenda Category (%)**

Immediate Public Disclosure	One-Day Disclosure	Transactions with Controlling Shareholders	Others
61.4	52.7	36.6	47.5

Source: Jang (2000).

mostly due to the free-rider problems associated with the public-good property of monitoring.

Now, after the crisis, outside directors are mandated, and their role has been strengthened. But the situation has not changed much. In 1999, more than 73 percent of board members selected were recommended by the controlling shareholders (see table 5.17). Moreover, the overall activity of directors is disappointing. As discussed earlier, their agenda approval rate is very high, exceeding 99 percent. Further, when the boards have to approve transactions involving controlling shareholders, the attendance rate is very low (see table 5.18). In short, the oversight role of boards of directors is still limited.

5.3.2   Effects of Reform

It is too early to evaluate the full effects of corporate governance reforms on the corporate sector. Nevertheless, some of the early results imply changes in the corporate sector. Joh (2002) argues that the corporate sector shows improved profitability in 1999 and 2000 compared with the precrisis periods. In particular, surviving *chaebols* show higher profitability.

Chiu and Joh (2003) try to evaluate how the crisis and corporate reform affect the structure of *chaebols*. They argue that a firm's rate of return depends on market risk, firm idiosyncratic risk, and group risk. Through an internal capital market, *chaebol* structure enables firms to transfer idiosyncratic risks to other firms and exposes them to other firms' risks as well. Facing transferred risk and common group risk, *chaebol*-affiliated firms show synchronicity in their stock market rates of return. Using the daily stock market data between 1996 and 2001, Chiu and Joh measure the strength of business group structure through risk transfer and synchronicity. The risk transfer of small *chaebols* has increased compared to the precrisis period. However, the risk transfer of large *chaebols* has decreased below the precrisis level during the crisis and post-Daewoo-collapse periods (Daewoo was second-largest *chaebol* in 1999). While the level of synchronicity remains above the precrisis level, the synchronicity of large *chaebols* decreased below the precrisis level. Using firm-level panel data, they show that the effect of group risk is high during the crisis and reform periods. But it becomes smaller than its precrisis level for large *chaebols* during the post-Daewoo-collapse period.

Joh and Ryoo (2000) examined the extent of a controlling shareholder's private gains. Since they are difficult to detect, the *proportional voting rights premium* (*PVRP*) is used. PVRP is the difference in common stock price and preferred stock price divided by the preferred stock price. Common stocks have voting rights and lower dividends. In contrast, preferred stocks have no voting rights but receive higher dividends. Thus, the premium increases during corporate-control contests over a firm (e.g., M&As) when control rights are sought, or when a shareholder can reap private gains through control-ownership disparity. Otherwise, the PVRP will be smaller. For example, average PVRPs in the United States, Sweden, and the United Kingdom are 5.3 percent, 6.5 percent, and 13.3 percent, respectively.

In contrast, the PVRP in Korea has been very large with wide fluctuations. The average PVRP was around 95 percent of a common share in 1996. Because takeover threats were almost nonexistent due to legal constraints, the premium before the crisis mostly represents private benefits. The average PVRP in 1999 after restructuring was lower than in 1996, but still around 81 percent. In contrast, this result suggests that investors believe controlling shareholders' private gains are still high, but smaller than before the crisis.

5.4   Conclusion

High debt-equity ratios, low long-term firm profitability, and weak corporate governance helped cause Korea's 1997 economic crisis. High debt-equity ratios stemmed from government policy, firms' inflation of their reported size, and negligent bank lending. Government industrial policy pushed development of specific industries and gave special incentives to large firms. Firms then inflated their apparent size through cross-holdings and cross-debt guarantees. Moreover, government-directed banks continued lending money to low-profitability firms. As a result, many large firms had huge debt-equity ratios.

Low firm profits were caused partially by unprofitable investment in affiliated firms. Control-ownership disparity and *chaebol* organization correlated with low profitability, suggesting that controlling shareholders exploited these unprofitable investments for private gains. Moreover, Korea's weak governance system allowed such low profitability to persist for nearly ten years. Factors that contribute to the failure of corporate governance include the following: (1) no credible exit threat, (2) lack of financial-institution monitoring, (3) few legal rights or types of protection for minority shareholders, (4) negligent boards of directors, and (5) inadequate financial information.

After maintaining high debts and low profitability for a long time, the Korean corporate sector experienced massive failures in 1997. Partially prompted by changes in government policies regarding the corporate governance system, including allowing many of the largest *chaebols* to fail, the corporate sector has been under pressure to change its structure and goals from size maximization to value maximization.

References

Altman, Edward. 1968. Financial ratios, discriminant analysis, and the prediction of corporate bankruptcy. *Journal of Finance* 4:589–609.

Bank of Korea. 1997. *Financial statement analysis.* Seoul: Bank of Korea.

———. Various issues. *Economic statistics yearbook.* Seoul: Bank of Korea.

———. Various years. *Financial statement analysis.* Seoul: Bank of Korea.

Chiu, Ming Ming, and Sung Wook Joh. 2003. The effects of the economic crisis and corporate reform on business groups: Evidence from Korea. Paper presented at the third Asian Corporate Governance Conference. May, Seoul.

Cho, Yoon Je, and Joon Kyung Kim. 1997. *Credit policies and the industrialization of Korea: Lessons and strategies.* Seoul: Korea Development Institute.

Choi, Sung Noh. 1996, 1997, 1998. *The largest thirty chaebols in Korea.* Seoul: Free Enterprise Institute.

Chung, Byong Hyou, and Young Shik Yang. 1992. *Korean chaebols.* Seoul: Korea Development Institute.

Financial Supervisory Service. 2000. Press release on the review of auditing firms' financial statements, 1998–2000. Seoul: Financial Supervisory Service.

———. Various issues. Press release on nonperforming loans. Seoul: Financial Supervisory Service.

Hoshi, Takeo, Anil Kashyap, and David Scharfstein. 1991. Corporate structure, liquidity, and investment: Evidence from Japanese industrial groups. *Quarterly Journal of Economics* 106:33–60.

Jang, Ha Sung. 2000. A study on the effects of the post-crisis corporate reform. Korea University. Mimeograph.

Jensen, Michael, and William Meckling. 1976. Theory of the firm: Managerial behavior, agency costs, and ownership structure. *Journal of Financial Economics* 3:305–360.

Joh, Sung Wook. 2000. Micro-dynamics of industrial competition: Evidence from Korean manufacturing plants. KDI Policy Study no. 2000-5. Seoul: Korea Development Institute.

———. 2001. The Korean corporate sector: Crisis and reform. In *Korea's economic prospects: From financial crisis to prosperity,* ed. Yul Kwon and William Shepherd, 116–132. Cheltenham, U.K.: Edward Elgar.

———. 2002. *Chaebol* reform and structural changes in the corporate sector. Paper presented at conference, The Korean Economy: Beyond the Crisis. October, Seoul.

———. 2003. Corporate governance and firm profitability: Evidence from Korea before the economic crisis. *Journal of Financial Economics* 68:287–322.

Joh, Sung Wook, and Sang Dai Ryoo. 2000. Evaluation of changes in the corporate governance system of Korean *chaebols.* Paper presented at the twelfth Pacific Asia Free Trade and Development Conference. May, Seoul.

Johnson, Simon, Rafael La Porta, Florencio Lopez de Silanes, and Andrei Shleifer. 2000. Tunneling. *American Economic Review Papers and Proceedings* 90:22–27.

Jones, Leroy, and Il SaKong. 1980. *Government, business, and entrepreneurship in economic development: The Korean case.* Cambridge: Harvard University Press.

Jun, In Woo, and Byeong-Ho Gong. 1995. *Corporate governance in Korea.* Seoul: Korea Economic Research Institute.

Kim, Chung-Yum. 1997. *Policymaking on the front lines: Memoirs of a Korean practitioner, 1945–1979.* Seoul: Jung-Ang Daily Press.

Kim, Joon Kyung. 1999. *Chaebols'* ownership of NBFIs and related problems. *KDI Economic Outlook* 1 (4): 83–94.

Koo, Bonchun. 1998. *Reform measures for Korean bankruptcy reorganization and composition.* Seoul: Korea Development Institute.

Korea Fair Trade Commission. 1998, 2000. *White book for Fair Trade Commission.* Seoul: Korea Fair Trade Commission.

———. 1999. Press release on the thirty largest *chaebols'* ownership structure. Seoul: Korea Fair Trade Commission, April.

———. Various dates. Press releases on equity investment and debt payment guarantees of the thirty largest *chaebol.* Seoul: Korea Fair Trade Commission.

Krueger, Anne, and Jungho Yoo. 2001. Falling profitability, higher borrowing costs, and *chaebol* finances during the Korean crisis. Paper presented at the Conference on the Korean Crisis and Recovery. 17–19 May, Seoul.

Lee, Byong Ki. 1998. *Debt payment guarantees of Korean chaebols.* Seoul: Korea Economic Research Institute.

Lee, Chung H. 1992. The government, financial system, and large private enterprises in the economic development of South Korea. *World Development* 20:187–197.

Lee, Soon Woo. 1995. *Reorganization of failing firms.* Seoul: Jilritamgoo.

Martin, Stephen. 1993. *Advanced industrial economics.* Oxford, U.K.: Blackwell.

Ministry of Finance and Economy. 1999. Press release on corporate restructuring. Seoul: Ministry of Finance and Economy.

Mossman, Charles, Geoffrey Bell, Mick Swartz, and Harry Turtle. 1998. An empirical comparison of bankruptcy models. *Financial Review* 33:35–54.

Organization for Economic Cooperation and Development (OECD). 1998. *OECD economic surveys.* Paris: OECD.

Schumpeter, Joseph A. 1952. *History of economic analysis.* New York: Oxford University Press.

Shin, Inseok, and Joon-Ho Hahm. 1998. The Korean crisis: Causes and resolution. KDI Working Paper no. 9805. Seoul: Korea Development Institute.

Shleifer, Andrei, and Robert Vishny. 1997. A survey of corporate governance. *Journal of Finance* 52:737–783.

Takahashi, Kichinosuke, Yukiharu Kurokawa, and Kazunori Watase. 1984. Corporate bankruptcy prediction in Japan. *Journal of Banking and Finance* 8:229–247.

Comment   Mario B. Lamberte

Up until the East Asian financial crisis, many observers had admired the rapid growth of the Korean economy. Of course, there were those who doubted the sustainability of Korea's economic growth by comparing its industrial strategy, which relied so much on the *chaebols*, with that of Taiwan's, which nurtured small and medium enterprises. The criticisms were somewhat muted by Korea's hosting of the summer Olympics and admission to the Organization for Economic Cooperation and Development. In the 1990s, Korea's exports and foreign direct investment to its neighboring countries started to compete with those of Japan's. Korea also started to behave itself like a donor country, at least for Asian countries.

The Korean economy's sterling performance in the last two decades prior to the regional crisis had convinced many that the Korean economic model works and can be applied to their countries. In the Philippines, for example, many (including policymakers) believe that the best way for the country to grow rapidly is to choose a few winning industries, limit the number of large players within each industry, and pour all the necessary government support into those industries. The Philippine president ought to emulate what President Park Chung Hee did to boost exports. Interestingly, the Korean economy's quick recovery from the crisis seemed to have strengthened Philippine resolve to adopt the Korean model. This only goes to show how observers and policymakers in the region have regarded Korea's successful economic model. Indeed, Joh's present paper and her earlier works referred to in that paper are important reading materials for all because they shed light on why the formidable Korean economy collapsed during the East Asian financial crisis.

Joh's main thesis is that the Korean economy's collapse was actually an accident waiting to happen long before the regional financial crisis. The Korean corporate sector, which had been dominated by *chaebols*, carried very high debt-equity ratios for almost three decades, dwarfing those that can be observed in developed economies. Contrary to expectations, firms' rates of return on equity had been dismally low, and this persisted for a long time. This has made the Korean economy very fragile. A collapse of a few *chaebols* that had made large contributions to the domestic economy created a ripple effect, causing similarly situated firms to default, and ultimately sending the economy into a tailspin.

Joh's explanations of the causes of the high debt-equity ratios and low performance of the corporate sector certainly deserve greater attention, especially since she backs them up with hard data. She attributes the persist-

Mario B. Lamberte is president of the Philippine Institute for Development Studies.

ence of high debt-equity ratios to the government's generous incentives and bailout arrangements for large, failing firms; banks' continued lending to highly indebted, poorly performing firms; and very lax rules on firms' cross-holdings and cross-debt guarantees. Controlling shareholders caused the low profitability of firms, which had been sustained because of weak corporate governance, inadequate financial information of firms, failure of banks to act as effective monitors of corporate governance, weak protection systems for minority shareholders, and negligent boards of directors. She has noted some of the recent measures adopted by the Korean government to improve corporate governance, such as instituting more credible exit threats for large firms, mandating outside directors, and increasing roles for boards of directors. It is still too early to evaluate the effectiveness of these measures, but the initial results seem to have been mixed.

As the author noted, the recent crisis is not the first time that the Korean corporate sector encountered a crisis in the last thirty years. There were in fact several crises in the 1970s and the 1980s. Perhaps, the author can elaborate more on what makes the recent crisis different from the previous ones. Is it the extent of participation of foreign investors and lenders, who fled in droves when they saw their interests about to be eroded by the impending crisis? Is it because the same crisis occurred at a time when the political and economic environment could no longer accommodate the solutions used in the past in dealing with similar crises? Or is it the sheer size of the cost of bailing out ailing corporations? It would certainly help if there were information on the costs incurred by the government in bailing out failed corporations in the 1970s and 1980s. The Philippines encountered a severe economic crisis in the mid-1980s. The magnitude of the costs absorbed by the government in cleaning up nonperforming assets of private and government-owned corporations that lent to failed "crony" firms made the public sensitive to any discussion about bailing out another corporation. I wonder if the ailing corporations in the 1970s and 1980s that received substantial assistance from the Korean government in various forms are the same corporations that faced financial distress during the East Asian financial crisis.

One of the things that puzzled me (which, by the way, was partly explained by the author) was the persistently low rate of return on equity despite the high debt-equity ratios of firms. Why would both majority and minority shareholders continue to keep their money in these corporations when "the return on capital had been lower than its opportunity cost"? I am not too familiar with the Korean capital market, but I wonder if the prevailing interest rate on loans has been generally accepted as the indicator of the cost of capital in the country.

Developing countries in the region are keenly watching the progress of Korea's efforts in reforming corporate governance because of the important lessons it brings to them. The trends in mergers and acquisitions are particularly interesting, especially after hostile takeovers and foreign takeovers have been legalized in Korea. However, this is only one part of the story. The other part of the story is whether the corporate sector, in general, and the newly merged or acquired corporations, in particular, have instituted measures to improve corporate governance.

The reforms instituted by Korea in enhancing the rights and protection of minority shareholders are indeed commendable. However, as the author noted, "[d]espite such changes, monitoring by individual small shareholders remains unlikely, mostly due to the free-rider problems associated with the public-good property of monitoring." This is one of the instances in which outside directors can be counted upon. However, the performance of outside directors has so far been generally disappointing. This raises two issues. One pertains to the rules in selecting outside directors. Having outside directors would be rendered futile if controlling shareholders had the unquestioned authority to select them. Even if their role was strengthened, outside directors would still feel beholden to the controlling shareholders. The other issue is the limited market of outside directors in developing economies. I wonder if, in the case of Korea, the corporation code allows foreigners to sit as outside directors, at least in big corporations, to make up for the lack of such capacity at home. I would hasten to add, however, that the monitoring system being developed in Korea to assess performance of outside directors is something that could be emulated by other countries in the region that have mandated the inclusion of outside directors.

Finally, I would like to raise two minor points. One is that it would greatly help the reader to interpret table 5.5 if the author explained how the variable "ownership" is measured and whether the variable "*chaebol* dummy" refers to the holding companies or to all of the 552 corporations identified as belonging to *chaebols*. The other is that the author should have briefly discussed the method used in estimating the parameters of the same table.

Comment   Philip L. Williams

The Paper

Economists, as a profession, are notoriously cynical. We tend to analyze the behavior of individuals and groups by attributing to them the basest of

Philip L. Williams is executive chairman of Frontier Economics Pty Ltd and is a professorial fellow of Melbourne Business School, University of Melbourne.

motives. Our analysis repeats, with interest, the Christian doctrine of original sin.

The cynicism of the economist is perhaps most pronounced among those of us who devote our professional careers to the analysis of public policy; and this cynicism is constant across time and space. For the past three centuries and across all continents, economists have expressed this cynicism (with very little adaptation to allow for differences in institutions or culture).

This paper, by Sung Wook Joh, is very much in this tradition of extreme cynicism toward government policy. It presents a picture of government policy prior to the currency crisis that is truly alarming. The crisis in Korea is shown to be far more fundamental than a flight of capital caused by foreign providers of funds. Rather, the large Korean conglomerates (the *chaebols*) were starting to fail some years prior to the currency crisis, but the weakness of these conglomerates was hidden for many years by the government's pressuring the banks to keep lending.

The paper ends on a note of cautious optimism. Recent reforms (allowing conglomerates to fail, legalizing mergers and acquisitions, increasing rights to small shareholders) are worthwhile improvements in corporate governance; but, as always, more remains to be done.

Although the matters rehearsed in the preceding section are the themes of the paper, its chief contribution lies in its detailed empirical analysis. This gives rise to two reflections.

The Korean Enterprise

The first reflection is stimulated by "Causes of Low Firm Performance," in section 5.2.2, and, in particular, by table 5.7. Table 5.7 suggests that (despite the behavior of government in ensuring the conglomerates get their share of soft loans), Korea has a high rate of turnover of plants. The paper comments that this rate of turnover is much higher for smaller plants than for larger plants.

These observations immediately raise the question of how to map from data relating to plants to data relating to enterprises and, indeed, whether Korean data relating to enterprises are available. Indeed, there is a prior, and much more intractable, issue: where to draw the boundaries to an enterprise if separate legal entities are linked together by intragroup transactions, cross-ownership of shares, common directors, and cross-guarantees of debt.

Rate of Return on Shareholders' Funds

My second reflection is stimulated by a number of observations in the paper about rates of return on equity compared with rates of return on debt. The paper states (section 5.1 and section 5.2.2) that high debt-equity ratios would lead one to expect high rates of return on equity. This makes good intuitive sense: If one is providing equity funds, the more dollars of debt that are standing ahead of me in the queue, the higher is the risk to me if the corporation is in trouble and so the higher will be my average return *ex post.*

But the paper presents evidence that seems to contradict this story: the data presented show that the average rate of return on equity has frequently been below the prevailing rate of interest. This is an obvious puzzle: If a saver has a dollar, why would he or she transfer this to a corporation in the form of equity (lower returns and higher risk) when it could be transferred in the form of debt?

I shall address my remarks to the rate of return on funds, not to the rate of return on sales, which is the dependent variable in the regression reported in table 5.6. I think, subject to what I am about to say, that the regression could be made more relevant to the argument of the paper by re-running it with the dependent variable as the rate of return on shareholders' funds.

My observations are these. In the first place, one must question the data of the rates of return on shareholders' funds. The paper tells of alarming problems with the recording of assets and liabilities in the balance sheets of the various legal entities that make up each *chaebol.* For example, we are told (in "Causes of Low Firm Performance") that if firm A invests in affiliated firm B, there may be double-counting of the investments so that the sum of the assets of A and B can exceed the total assets of the group. Similarly, we are told (in "Inadequate Financial Information") that debt payment guarantees by a larger corporation to a smaller corporation within a *chaebol* can increase the amount of aggregate borrowing because the guarantee is not recorded as a liability in the balance sheet of the larger corporation. These problems suggest that any numbers based on accounting data are likely to be extremely suspect.

The second observation that should be made about the comparison of rates of return on equity compared with debt is that, even if the figures in the company accounts can be used as indicative, the recorded rates of interest cannot be used without adjustment because they hide the large subsidies that were provided to debt finance. A recent paper (Krueger and Yoo 2001) attempts to estimate the magnitude of these subsidies.

Implications for Policy

These reflections on data impel me to question the (admittedly guarded) optimism of the conclusions of the paper. Governance demands the gathering of information and an ability to react to it. This paper argues overwhelmingly that the information available to providers of funds to Korean companies is grossly distorted. The chief culprits seem to be two: (1) government-promoted distortions through control of the banks and (2) poor accounting standards.

These two problems seem to be quite fundamental to the issue of corporate governance in Korea. Until they are addressed, investors will continue to treat Korean corporations with cynicism. Indeed, the cynicism of the investors will match the cynicism of the economists.

Reference

Krueger, Anne O., and Jungho Yoo. 2001. *Chaebol* capitalism and the currency-financial crisis in Korea. NBER Conference Paper. Cambridge, Mass.: National Bureau of Economic Research, February.

Sources of Corporate Financing and Economic Crisis in Korea
Micro-Evidence

Youngjae Lim

6.1 Introduction

Using a firm-level data set[1] in Korea during the 1992–2000 period, this paper attempts to examine the dynamic patterns in the allocation of credit across firms. Supposedly, in Korea, the economic crisis in 1997 had a significant impact on the pattern in the allocation of credit across firms. In particular, this paper aims to examine these dynamic patterns across large and small firms after the crisis.

Corporate financing issues are intimately related to the cause of the Korean crisis. For instance, the indebtedness of *chaebol* to banks is viewed as having contributed much to the crisis.[2] Among others, Krueger and Yoo (2001) demonstrate that *chaebol* indebtedness is indeed the chief culprit of the crisis. In this regard, since the outbreak of the financial crisis in 1997, the government has undertaken various reform measures to restructure the financial and corporate sectors.[3] The new regulatory system is now underway to induce the financial institutions to change their imprudent lending practices, and the capital market began to force the *chaebol* to correct their incentive structure. Supposedly, these postcrisis developments in Korea have caused the *chaebol* and financial institutions to change their previously imprudent (borrowing and lending) practices.

The paper suggests that large firms, to some extent, are leaving banks

Youngjae Lim is a fellow at the Korea Development Institute.

The author wishes to thank Chong-Hyun Nam for his helpful suggestions for the paper.

1. The data set covers most of the Korean firms except for extra-small ones.

2. The failure of the corporate governance of *chaebol* exacerbated the situation. For the failure of *chaebol* corporate governance before the crisis, see Joh (2003).

3. Bankruptcy policy reform was one of the essential elements in these structural reforms. Lim (2002) studies empirically the post-crisis bankruptcy policy reform in Korea.

and going to the capital market for their financing after the crisis.[4] The paper also suggests that profitable small firms are gaining easier access to credit from financial institutions after the crisis. There has been a shift in the allocation of bank credit from large firms to small firms. Is this shift due to lenders' choice or due to borrowers' changed incentives? The paper suggests that the improved lending practices of banks contributed at least partially to this shift of bank credit from large firms to small firms.[5]

This paper is organized as follows. Section 6.2 provides the aggregate data on the corporate financing sources in Korea during the 1992–2000 period. Section 6.3 explains the firm-level data set. Section 6.4 examines the dynamic patterns in the allocation of credit across firms, and section 6.5 concludes the paper with agenda for future research.

6.2   Aggregate Patterns in the Corporate Financing Sources

Table 6.1 shows the aggregate data for the sources of corporate financing before and after the economic crisis. The numbers in table 6.1 are calculated from the information given in various publications by the Bank of Korea.[6]

The main reason we present this table is that it decomposes indirect finance further into detailed sources—commercial banks, insurance companies (including pension funds), short-term finance companies (e.g., merchant banks), and other nonbank financial intermediaries. Another point concerning the table is that it has been constructed by aggregating all the financial transactions for all the firms in the Korean economy. Hence, we could use this table to check the consistency in the firm-level data, for example, whether there is any systematic bias in the firm-level data due to the exclusion of extra-small firms.

After the crisis, in 1998–1999, the share of external finance in the total finance sharply declines to 50 percent from about 70 percent, throughout the 1990s until 1997.[7]

In 1998, as expected, the crisis completely changes the table for

---

4. Shortly after the crisis, the corporate bond market took off with the weak regulatory infrastructure. This immature expansion led to liquidity crises in 1999 and 2001. See Lim (2002) as well as Oh and Rhee (2002).

5. Borensztein and Lee (2002) examine the microdata on Korean listed firms in 1996–1998. They suggest that *chaebol*-affiliated firms lost the preferential access to credit and that credit was reallocated in favor of more efficient firms.

6. The *Economic Statistics Yearbook, Flow of Funds, Monthly Bulletin,* and Web site (www. bok.or.kr).

7. Although not shown in the table, the share of external finance in the total finance declined steadily throughout the 1970s and 1980s, and until 1988. During this period (except for the period of oil shocks), overseas export markets, together with emerging domestic markets, helped Korean firms to realize large profits. The ratio of internal finance to total finance was less than 20 percent in 1975, but it continued to grow to a level of more than 40 percent in 1988.

Table 6.1 Sources of Corporate Financing (flows) for All Firms in the Korean Economy, 1992–2000 (%)

	1992	1993	1994	1995	1996	1997	1998	1999	2000
Total finance	100.0	100.0	100.0	100.0	100.0	100.0	100.0	100.0	—
Retained earnings	28.7	30.0	27.3	27.9	22.6	27.1	50.0	49.4	—
External finance	71.3	70.0	72.7	72.1	77.4	72.9	50.0	50.6	—
External finance	100.0	100.0	100.0	100.0	100.0	100.0	100.0	100.0	100.0
Indirect finance	36.3	31.4	44.5	31.8	28.0	36.8	-57.3	4.1	17.1
Commercial banks	15.1	13.1	20.7	14.9	14.0	12.9	2.5	29.2	35.2
Insurance companies	3.9	3.1	2.4	2.7	2.8	2.3	-20.8	0.5	3.1
Short-term finance companies (e.g., merchant banks)	-0.4	2.4	4.3	0.5	-0.4	1.8	-22.4	-2.6	-6.8
Other nonbank financial intermediaries	17.7	12.8	17.1	13.7	11.5	19.8	-16.7	-22.9	-14.4
Direct finance	38.9	49.1	36.5	48.1	47.2	37.4	178.9	46.8	28.6
Government bonds	3.3	3.4	0.4	-0.9	0.3	0.5	2.0	0.0	-2.2
Commercial paper	7.6	13.9	4.9	16.1	17.5	3.7	-42.2	-30.4	-1.7
Corporate bonds	12.1	14.5	14.2	15.3	17.9	23.3	165.9	-5.3	-3.2
Equity	15.9	17.3	17.0	17.6	11.6	9.9	53.2	82.6	35.6
Foreign borrowing	7.1	1.5	6.6	8.4	10.4	5.6	-35.5	24.1	23.7
Borrowing from government	1.0	-0.2	0.2	0.2	-0.2	1.4	5.8	3.6	7.4
Interfirm credit	8.9	9.0	6.9	5.0	6.8	10.6	-27.2	10.2	6.8
Other	7.9	9.2	5.3	6.5	7.8	8.4	35.3	11.1	16.5

Source: Author's own calculations from the information in the various publications by the Bank of Korea (*Economic Statistics Yearbook, Flow of Funds,* and *Monthly Bulletin* [various issues of each], and Web site www.bok.or.kr).

Note: Dashes indicate the data are not yet available.

corporate financing sources. However, in 2000, when the crisis phases out, the table for corporate financing sources takes a somewhat different composition compared to before the crisis.

First of all, the share of indirect finance does not recover the level before the crisis. A look into the components of indirect finance is necessary. The nonbank financial intermediaries, except for insurance companies, lose their share significantly, compared with before the crisis. On the other hand, the share of commercial banks increases to almost double the average level before the crisis. Second, in 2000, the composition of direct finance changes compared to before the crisis. Equity takes away the share of the borrowing from financial markets (commercial paper, bonds, etc). Finally, foreign borrowing increases its share significantly.

6.3   The Firm-Level Data

This study uses detailed financial information on the firms that have external audit reports. According to the Act on External Audit of Joint-Stock Corporations, a firm with assets of 7 billion won or more must issue audited financial statements. The data thus include all the firms with assets of 7 billion won or more. The total number of firms in the data is about 11,000.

The Financial Supervisory Commission is responsible for establishing accounting and auditing standards, and the Securities and Futures Commission is then responsible for the review of the audited financial statements issued by firms. Finally, National Information and Credit Evaluation, Inc. (NICE) codes this public information into its database after checking the consistency of the reported financial statements.

From the NICE data, we can estimate only the borrowing from all financial intermediaries, not the borrowings from the detailed components of indirect finance. However, table 6.2 shows that after the crisis, most of the new lending by financial intermediaries is, in fact, from commercial banks, not from nonbank financial institutions.

Table 6.2   **Summary Statistics of Firm-Level Data (simple mean, %)**

	All Firms in the Sample		
	1992–1996	1997–1998	1999–2000
EBIT/Asset	6.61578	3.79944	4.62773
Borrowing/Asset	0.38655	0.43713	0.37910
Loans from financial institutions/Borrowing	0.76436	0.80880	0.83345
Bond financing/Borrowing	0.07573	0.07605	0.05752

Note: Number of observations in sample is 11,026.

6.3.1   Summary Statistics

Table 6.2 presents sample means for the key variables in the empirical analysis. It divides the sample period into the three subperiods around the crisis: 1992–1996, 1997–1998, and 1999–2000. Note that the financial crisis broke out in 1997 and that the economy began to recover in 1999 after the crisis. Profitability is measured by earnings before interest and tax payments (EBIT) divided by total assets. After the crisis, the share of loans in asset increases compared with the precrisis period; on the other hand, the weight of bond financing decreases.

The financing pattern varies according to the size of firms. For example, the empirical distribution of the loans' share in total asset has a different shape according to the size of firms. For this reason, we divide all individual firms into ten groups based on the distribution of asset size, and select three representative size cohorts for presenting the empirical results. The results are robust to minor changes in the thresholds. We employ the following three size cohorts: (1) the largest firms (top 1 percent in asset size),[8] (2) the medium-sized firms (middle 10 percent in asset size), and (3) the smallest firms (bottom 10 percent in asset size).

For the three size cohorts, table 6.3 provides sample means for the key variables in the empirical analysis. It also divides the sample period into the three subperiods around the crisis.

The statistics in table 6.3 present a different picture compared to the one in table 6.2. The aggregate numbers in table 6.2 do not fully capture the changes in the financing pattern experienced by heterogeneous firms during this period. Profitability evolves differently according to size groups. Profitability worsens for large and small firms, whereas it rebounds for medium-sized firms. While the share of loans in asset decreases for large firms, the opposite is the case for the other groups. After the crisis, large firms finance more in the bond market, but the other groups have more limited access to the bond market compared to the precrisis period.

6.3.2   Firm Size Distribution

Figure 6.1 shows the yearly firm-size distributions for all the firms in the sample before and after the crisis. Before the crisis, the distribution shifts to the right-hand side—implying on average an increase in firm size. The shape of the distribution gets skewed to the right gradually over time until 1997. We find relatively fewer small firms over time in the yearly distributions.

After the crisis, it is hard to find a clear pattern in the shift of the

8. For the case of large firms, we present the results using this particular cohort, but defining the largest firms differently (e.g., the top 5 percent, or top 10 percent) does not change the qualitative results of the paper.

Table 6.3   Summary Statistics for the Three Size Cohorts in Firm-Level Data (simple mean, %)

	Large Firms (top 1% in asset size, N = 81)			Medium-Sized Firms (middle 10% in asset size, N = 1,039)			Small Firms (bottom 10% in asset size, N = 1,967)		
	1992–1996	1997–1998	1999–2000	1992–1996	1997–1998	1999–2000	1992–1996	1997–1998	1999–2000
Asset	3,111.022	5,552.276	6,424.852	12.114	16.539	18.960	3.986	5.636	4.590
EBIT/Asset	7.15573	3.31644	1.83426	6.84442	5.62404	7.34264	4.50535	-0.02398	-4.61268
Borrowing/Asset	0.493031	0.575053	0.471116	0.409815	0.430318	0.376597	0.274567	0.437087	0.340989
Loans from financial institutions/Borrowing	0.644068	0.559247	0.495934	0.805886	0.831305	0.864931	0.646217	0.848398	0.846132
Bond financing/Borrowing	0.2922	0.4305	0.4808	0.0372	0.0416	0.0214	0.0137	0.0218	0.0174

Note: Asset in billions of won. N = no. of observations.

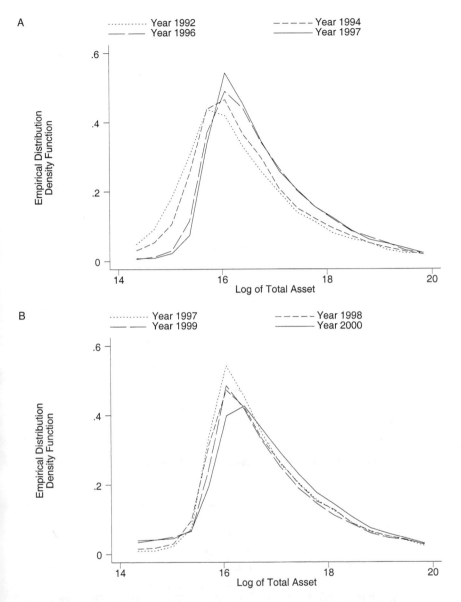

Fig. 6.1   All sample firms, log of total asset: *A,* **before the crisis, 1992–1997;** *B,* **after the crisis, 1997–2000**

Source: Author's calculation for all the firms in the NICE data.

distribution itself. However, the left-hand tail of the distribution—the smallest firms in the sample—becomes thicker after the crisis. The relative frequency of the smallest firms in the sample increases after the crisis. This thicker left tail could occur either from an increased number of new entrants or from the inclusion of extra-small firms that were previously excluded from the sample. Note that we observe the opposite before the crisis—the left-hand tail of the distribution getting thinner.

6.3.3   Firm Profitability Distribution

Figure 6.2 presents the yearly profitability distributions for all the firms in the sample before and after the crisis. The yearly distributions remain the same before the crisis. The crisis significantly affects the profitability distribution in 1997, indicating, on average, a decrease in firm profitability. After the crisis, the profitability distribution shifts much to the right or left depending on the macroeconomic situation. In fact, after the crisis, the magnitude of the business cycle becomes larger than compared to the precrisis period.[9]

Figure 6.3 shows that the small and medium-sized firms have more dispersed distributions in 1992–2000. Since this pattern remains the same in the sample period, we do not present the yearly distributions here. Large firms are more homogeneous in terms of profitability compared to the other size cohorts.

Figure 6.4 shows that the crisis had an impact on the shape of profitability for small firms. After the crisis (1997–2000), the distribution gets more dispersed over time. After the crisis small firms become a more heterogeneous group compared to the precrisis period.

6.4   Financing Pattern and the Crisis: Micro-Evidence

In section 6.3.1, the summary statistics of key financing variables hint that the heterogeneity of firms is important in understanding the evolution of the financing pattern after the crisis. The sample means of key financing variables also hint at the following pattern around the crisis: the largest firms are leaving financial intermediaries and switching directly to the financial markets for their financing, whereas the small and medium-sized firms are increasing their dependency on financial intermediaries for financing. In this section, we test these hypotheses rigorously. To get genuine cross-sectional results, we must control for the effect of the business cycles.

The empirical distributions of key financing variables have different shapes according to the size of firms and evolve differently after the crisis.

---

9. The annual growth rates of GDP after the crisis are 5.0 percent (1997), –6.7 percent (1998), 10.9 percent (1999), and 8.8 percent (2000), whereas, before the crisis, the difference between the high and low peak years does not exceed 4 percent.

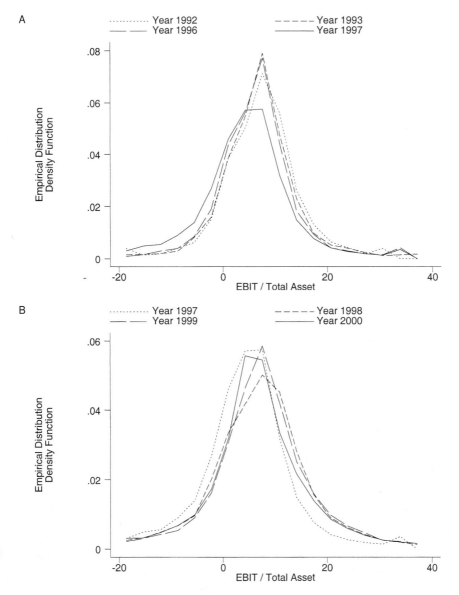

Fig. 6.2   All sample firms, EBIT/total asset: *A*, **before the crisis, 1992–1997;** *B*, **after the crisis, 1997–2000**

Source: Author's calculation for all the firms in the NICE data.

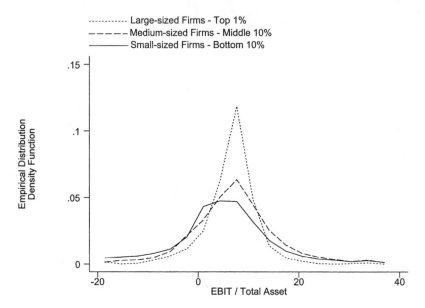

Fig. 6.3   All sample firms, EBIT/total asset: sample period, 1992–2000
Source: Author's calculation for all the firms in the NICE data.

In this section, therefore, we also present the result from comparing the empirical distributions of key financing variables.

6.4.1   Loans from Financial Institutions

Table 6.4 shows the regressions of the loan-borrowing ratio (defined as the borrowing from financial intermediaries divided by total borrowing) on the dummy variables denoting the size cohort interacted with year dummies and on the macrovariables (growth rate of gross domestic product [GDP], interest rate). The macrovariables control for the effect of the business cycles. In table 6.4, therefore, the reported coefficient for the specific year indicates the loan-borrowing ratio's difference between the size cohort in that specific year and all the other firms in the whole sample period. Table 6.4 shows the regression results for the three size cohorts (top 1 percent, middle 10 percent, bottom 10 percent).

After the crisis (in 1998–2000), the largest firms significantly decrease the share of loans in total borrowing. The coefficients for 1998–2000 are larger than 0.3 (all significant), whereas the coefficients for 1992–1997 are smaller than 0.2 (also all significant). That is, after the crisis, the largest firms are leaving financial intermediaries for their financing.

For the small firms this share jumps to a higher number from 1995 and stays more or less there even after the crisis. The coefficients for 1992–1994 are smaller than –0.2 (all significant), whereas the coefficients for

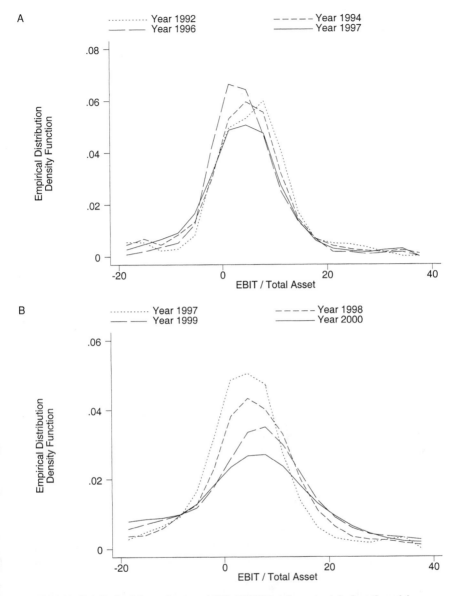

Fig. 6.4 Small-sized firms (bottom 10%), EBIT/total asset: *A,* **before the crisis;** *B,* **after the crisis**

Source: Author's calculation for all the firms in the NICE data.

Table 6.4   **The Effect of the Crisis on the Loan-Borrowing Ratio for Each Size Cohort**

Independent Variable[a]	Dependent Variable[b]		
	Large Firms (top 1% in asset size)	Medium-Sized Firms (middle 10% in asset size)	Small Firms (bottom 10% in asset size)
1992	−0.092114**	0.038763**	−0.238474**
	(−2.62)	(2.87)	(−13.00)
1993	−0.158658**	−0.023511*	−0.290327**
	(−4.55)	(−1.84)	(−18.11)
1994	−0.142179**	0.025618**	−0.228863**
	(−4.14)	(2.16)	(−14.64)
1995	−0.129324**	0.059797**	−0.030198**
	(−3.79)	(5.29)	(−1.99)
1996	−0.167552**	0.030885**	0.053789**
	(−4.91)	(2.77)	(3.42)
1997	*−0.167804** *	*0.044728** *	*0.045980** *
	(−4.96)	*(4.27)*	*(4.15)*
1998	−0.301641**	0.042048**	0.070248**
	(−8.87)	(3.67)	(5.88)
1999	−0.321025**	0.057508**	0.044566**
	(−9.54)	(5.51)	(4.97)
2000	−0.329379**	0.045512**	0.012498
	(−9.84)	(4.06)	(1.21)
GDP growth rate	−0.003067**	−0.003040**	−0.002224**
	(−10.53)	(−9.93)	(−7.36)
Yields to corporate bonds	−0.016176**	−0.015893**	−0.013788**
	(−20.77)	(−19.42)	(−17.11)
No. of observations	56,990	56,990	56,990

Notes: Numbers in parenthesis are *t*-values. Loan-borrowing ratio refers to the borrowing from financial markets divided by total borrowing.

[a]Dummy variable denoting a specific cohort interacted with year dummies.

[b]Borrowing from financial intermediaries/total borrowing.

**Significant at the 5 percent level.

*Significant at the 10 percent level.

1996–2000 are larger than zero (in 1995, −0.03); these coefficients are all significant except in 2000. The small firms did not have much access to financial intermediaries in 1992–1994, but they have better access to the loans from financial intermediaries afterward.

For the medium-sized firms, the share of loans in total borrowing does not show any marked trend around the crisis. Note that the summary statistics in section 6.3.1 suggested a different interpretation for the behavior of medium-sized firms.

Empirical Distribution of Loans for Different Cohorts

Figure 6.5 shows the distribution of the loan-borrowing ratio for the largest cohort (top 1 percent of firms in asset size) before and after the cri-

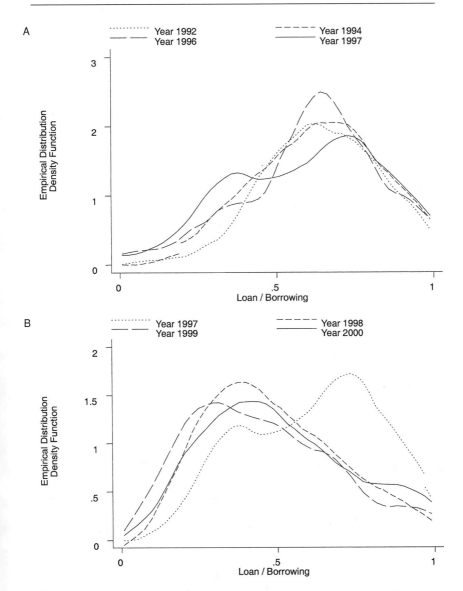

Fig. 6.5   Largest firms (top 1%), loan/borrowing: *A,* **before the crisis;** *B,* **after the crisis**

Source: Author's calculation for all the firms in the NICE data.

sis. After the crisis (in 1998–2000), the loan-borrowing ratio distribution for the largest firms clearly shifts leftward, as seen in panel B. This leftward shift starts partly in 1997 during the crisis.

For the small firms (bottom 10 percent firms in asset size) the distribution of the loan-borrowing ratio shifts to the right markedly in 1996 (actually in 1995, although not shown in the paper) and maintains more or less this pattern even after the crisis (fig. 6.6).

In figure 6.6, panel A, we note that, until 1994, a certain portion of the firms in our database lacks access to financial intermediaries for their corporate financing. One could see a certain density around zero. However, after 1994, this pattern changes: the density around zero continues to disappear until 1997, and, after the crisis, appears again, but on a much smaller scale than before 1995. Panels A and B in figure 6.6 make another interesting point. After 1994, we continue to see a peak at 1 and a certain mass around 1, which indicates that these firms depend (or do not depend) completely on the loans from financial intermediaries for their borrowing.

For the medium-sized firms, the share of loans in total borrowing does not show any marked changes before or after the crisis, except that, after the crisis, we could see more cluster around 1 (fig. 6.7).

6.4.2 Determinants of the Changes in the Allocation of Loans

Why do we observe such shifts in the allocation of loans by financial institutions as documented in section 6.4.1? Are they reflecting the firms' spontaneous choice for financing sources as a result of corporate restructuring, or did the financial reform cause financial institutions to shift their lending patterns? To see whether this is the case, we attempt to test the effect of individual firm profitability on the shift in allocation of loans by financial institutions.

Table 6.5 shows the regressions of the change in loans on firm profitability (interacted with year dummy) for small firms. We also test the effect of the affiliation with *chaebol* on the access to loans. The *chaebol* dummy distinguishes the top thirty *chaebol* from the others.

Table 6.5 suggests the interpretation that, for the small firms, profitability is an important factor in determining access to loans by financial institutions after the crisis.[10] Financial institutions actively search for profitable small firms to provide loans after the crisis. In section 6.3.4, we pointed out that the crisis had an impact on the shape of the profitability for small firms. The profitability distribution becomes more dispersed after the crisis. It means that selecting efficient small firms became more difficult after the crisis.

Before the crisis, profitability was not a factor in the access of small firms to loans; on the contrary, inefficient small firms did have more access to loans by financial institutions. This reflects the fact that small firms were protected through various regulations by the government before the crisis. Note that the affiliation with *chaebol* has a negative effect on access to loans. In Korea, small firms affiliated with *chaebol* usually do not get

---

10. For medium-sized and large firms, the regression of the change in loans on firm profitability did not produce meaningful results.

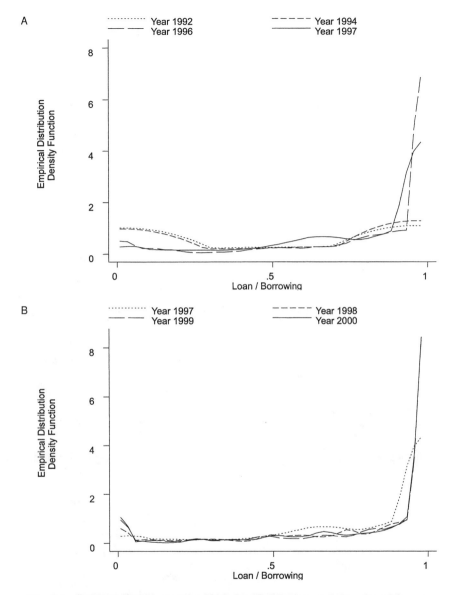

Fig. 6.6   Small-sized firms (bottom 10%), loan/borrowing: *A,* before the crisis; *B,* after the crisis

Source: Author's calculation for all the firms in the NICE data.

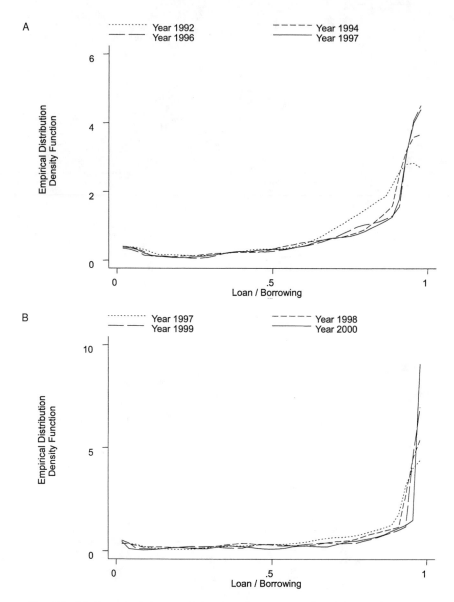

Fig. 6.7   Medium-sized firms (middle 10%), loan/borrowing: *A,* **before the crisis;** *B,* **after the crisis**

Source: Author's calculation for all the firms in the NICE data.

Table 6.5   **Determinant of Loans for Small Firms**

Independent Variable	Dependent Variable[a]
Profitability · 1993 Dummy	−6.27416**
	(−4.87)
Profitability · 1994 Dummy	−4.56897**
	(−4.23)
Profitability · 1995 Dummy	−2.20905**
	(−2.03)
Profitability · 1996 Dummy	−2.24397**
	(−2.00)
Profitability · 1997 Dummy	*3.39365**
	(3.36)*
Profitability · 1998 Dummy	−1.68222**
	(−2.41)
Profitability · 1999 Dummy	1.09281**
	(2.76)
Profitability · 1000 Dummy	1.01871**
	(2.84)
Chaebol Dummy · (1993–1997) Dummy	−86.47024**
	(−2.37)
Chaebol Dummy · (1998–2000) Dummy	−85.39975*
	(−1.73)
GDP growth rate	−4.84860**
	(−5.33)
Yield to corporate bonds	2.47850
	(0.93)
No. of observations	4,388

Notes: Unit of loans = 10 million won. Numbers in parentheses are *t*-values. Profitability refers to the EBIT divided by total assets.

[a]Change in loans.

**Significant at the 5 percent level.

*Significant at the 10 percent level.

protection but rather face tight regulations to the effect of protecting other independent small firms. This kind of regulation has been gradually shrinking since the crisis.

6.4.3   Total Borrowing

In section 6.4.1, it is suggested that the largest firms are leaving financial intermediaries for their corporate financing after the crisis. Then, the question arises: do the large firms decrease investment and scale down their business? Otherwise, do they find other sources of financing after the crisis? To check this, we look at total borrowing before and after the crisis.

Table 6.6 shows the regressions of the borrowing-dependency ratio (defined as total borrowing divided by total assets) on the dummy variables denoting the size cohort interacted with year dummies and on the macro-

Table 6.6   Test of Borrowing-Dependency Ratio for Size Cohorts

Independent Variable[a]	Dependent Variable[b]		
	Large Firms (top 1% in asset size)	Medium-Sized Firms (middle 10% in asset size)	Small Firms (bottom 10% in asset size)
1992	0.065951*	0.002772	−0.147234**
	(1.83)	(0.20)	(−9.24)
1993	0.087718**	0.000540	−0.131432**
	(2.46)	(0.04)	(−9.44)
1994	0.100312**	0.008327	−0.149869**
	(2.82)	(0.71)	(−11.53)
1995	0.098005**	0.023694**	−0.108633**
	(2.77)	(2.08)	(−8.28)
1996	0.133107**	0.032537**	−0.108653**
	(3.76)	(2.92)	(−8.22)
1997	*0.194158**	0.054186**	0.041092**
	(5.57)*	*(5.16)*	*(3.72)*
1998	0.132828**	−0.021260*	0.001323
	(3.79)	(−1.86)	(0.11)
1999	0.077798**	0.002175	−0.009230**
	(2.21)	(0.20)	(−9.72)
2000	0.099435**	−0.015028	−0.104478**
	(2.84)	(−1.29)	(32.23)
GDP growth rate	−0.001729**	−0.002001**	−0.001364**
	(−5.93)	(−6.53)	(−4.49)
Yields to corporate bonds	0.002870**	0.002403**	0.002480**
	(3.64)	(2.91)	(3.03)
No. of observations	61,732	61,732	61,732

Notes: Numbers in parentheses are *t*-values. Borrowing-dependency ratio refers to the total borrowing divided by total assets.
[a]Dummy variable denoting a specific cohort interacted with year dummies.
[b]Total borrowing/total asset.
**Significant at the 5 percent level.
*Significant at the 10 percent level.

variables (growth rate of GDP, interest rate). In table 6.6, the reported coefficient for the specific year indicates the borrowing-dependency differences between the size cohort in that specific year and all the other firms in the whole sample period. Table 6.6 shows the regression results for the three size cohorts (top 1 percent, middle 10 percent, bottom 10 percent).

The crisis affected the borrowing-dependency ratio of all the cohorts only during the crisis. When the crisis died out, the borrowing-asset ratio returned to the previous trend. The share of borrowing in total assets went up much more for small firms during the crisis than for the other size cohorts. Unlike the others, small firms had no other cushions (e.g., equity, retained earnings) to absorb the adverse effect of the crisis.

Table 6.7   The Effect of the Crisis on the Bond-Borrowing Ratio for Each Size Cohort

Independent Variable[a]	Dependent Variable[b]		
	Large Firms (top 1% in asset size)	Top 6–10% in Asset Size	Top 11–20% in Asset Size
1992	0.160692**	0.103350**	0.047441**
	(2.62)	(11.35)	(6.94)
1993	0.185830**	0.132925**	0.073764**
	(4.55)	(14.98)	(11.17)
1994	0.245725**	0.150490**	0.077310**
	(4.14)	(17.09)	(11.96)
1995	0.248630**	0.156919**	0.075703**
	(3.79)	(17.78)	(11.76)
1996	0.266046**	0.172363**	0.084974**
	(4.91)	(19.57)	(13.27)
1997	*0.297227** *	*0.171449** *	*0.087462** *
	(4.96)	*(19.65)*	*(13.98)*
1998	0.421412**	0.178142**	0.067650**
	(8.87)	(19.35)	(9.98)
1999	0.446375**	0.196404**	0.049279**
	(9.54)	(21.32)	(7.50)
2000	0.393401**	0.160074**	0.033200**
	(9.84)	(17.17)	(4.79)
GDP growth rate	0.000144**	0.000067	–0.000009
	(–10.53)	(0.39)	(–0.05)
Yields to corporate bonds	0.003134**	0.002853**	0.002246**
	(–20.77)	(6.21)	(4.67)
No. of observations	56,990	56,990	56,990

Notes: Numbers in parentheses are *t*-values. Bond-borrowing ratio refers to the borrowing from financial markets divided by total borrowing.
[a]Dummy variable denoting a specific cohort interacted with year dummies.
[b]Borrowing from financial markets/total borrowing.
**Significant at the 5 percent level.

6.4.4   Financing in the Bond Market

The above result implies that the large firms moved to some other sources of financing after the crisis. This section will show that the large firms went to the bond market to compensate for the decrease in loans by financial institutions. This was hinted in section 6.2.1. We test it formally in the following.

Table 6.7 shows the regressions of the bond-borrowing ratio (defined as the borrowing from financial markets divided by total borrowing) on the dummy variables denoting the size cohort interacted with year dummies and on the macrovariables (growth rate of GDP, interest rate). In table 6.7, the reported coefficient for the specific year indicates the bond-borrowing ratio's differences between the size cohort in that specific year and all the other firms in the whole sample period. Table 6.7 shows the regression results for the three size cohorts (top 1 percent, top 6–10 percent, top 11–20 percent). The reason for choosing a different set of cohorts for table 6.5 is that, for the sample period, the small and medium-sized firms (the cohorts we used in the regression analysis before) do not have access to borrowing from financial markets.

After the crisis (in 1998–2000), the largest firms markedly increase the share of bond financing in total borrowing. The coefficients for 1998–2000 are around 0.4 (all significant), whereas the coefficients for 1992–1997 are smaller than 0.3 (also all significant).

For all the size cohorts, the share of bond financing in total asset increases gradually from 1992 to 1996. This is due to the financial liberalization policy gradually taken by the government since the early 1990s. During this period the size of the bond market in Korea gradually expanded. The bond market developed more rapidly with the speed-up of financial liberalization policy after the crisis.

Empirical Distribution of Bond Financing for Different Cohorts

Figure 6.8 shows the bond-borrowing ratio distributions before and after the crisis for the largest cohort. After the crisis (in 1998–2000), the bond-borrowing ratio distribution for the largest firms shifts clearly to the right (panel B).

In figure 6.9 we show the similar figures for another size cohort (top 11–20 percent of firms in asset size). This cohort includes, in fact, the smallest firms to have any access to the bond market at all in the sample period. For this cohort, the bond-borrowing ratio distribution shifts to the right marginally before the crisis. After the crisis, however, the distribution shifts back to the left. There is a large peak around zero in 1999 and the distribution becomes degenerate in 2000 (i.e., this cohort does not have any access to the bond market). A large proportion of the bonds that were issued during the crisis were at risk of default, especially after the demise of the Daewoo group (one of the top four *chaebol* at that time in Korea) in 1999. This, in turn, put the whole market for corporate bonds into a state of malfunction in 1999 and in 2000.

6.5   Concluding Remarks

The paper documents that large firms, to some extent, are leaving banks and going to the capital market for their financing after the crisis.[11] The

11. Clearly, the liberalization of financial markets, which happened at an accelerating rate after the crisis, contributed to broaden the supply base of various corporate financing sources. But, for further deepening of the supply base of various corporate financing sources, Korea needs better protection of investors' rights.

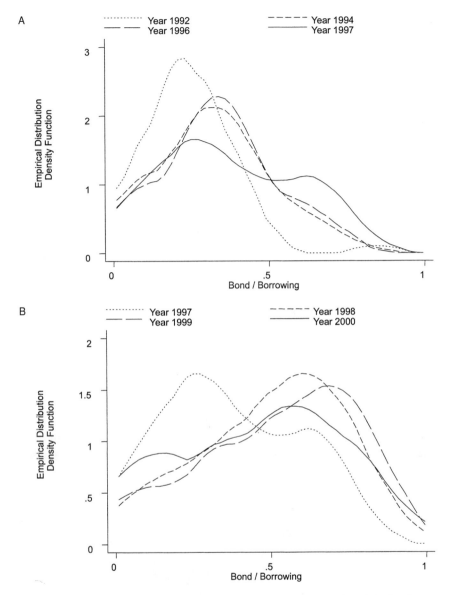

Fig. 6.8   Large-sized firms (top 1%), bond/borrowing: *A*, before the crisis; *B*, after the crisis

Source: Author's calculation for all the firms in the NICE data.

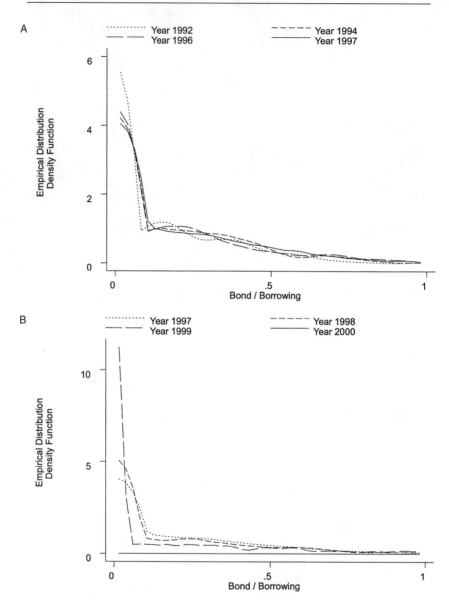

Fig. 6.9   Large firms (top 10%–top 20%), bond/borrowing: *A,* before the crisis; *B,* after the crisis

Source: Author's calculation for all the firms in the NICE data.

paper also shows that profitable small firms are gaining easier access to credit by financial institutions after the crisis. Financial institutions are reallocating their credit from large firms to small firms after the crisis. Why do we observe such shifts in the allocation of loans by financial institutions? Are they reflecting the firms' spontaneous choice for financing sources as a result of corporate restructuring? Otherwise, did the financial reform cause financial institutions to change their lending practices? The paper suggests that the banks' improved lending practices contributed at least partially to this shift.

References

Bank of Korea. Various issues. *Economic statistics yearbook.* Seoul: Bank of Korea.
————. Various issues. *Flow of funds.* Seoul: Bank of Korea.
————. Various issues. *Monthly bulletin.* Seoul: Bank of Korea.
Borensztein, Eduardo, and Jong-Wha Lee. 2002. Financial crisis and credit crunch in Korea: Evidence from firm-level data. *Journal of Monetary Economics* 49 (4): 853–875.
Joh, Sung Wook. Forthcoming. Corporate governance and firm profitability: Evidence from Korea before the crisis. *Journal of Financial Economics.*
Krueger, Anne O., and Jungho Yoo. 2002. Falling profitability, higher borrowing costs, and *chaebol* finances during the Korean crisis. Chapter 5 in *Korean crisis and recovery,* ed. David T. Coe and Se-Jik Kim. Washington, D.C.: International Monetary Fund.
Lim, Youngjae. 2002. Hyundai crisis: Its development and resolution. *Journal of East Asian Studies* 2 (February).
————. 2003. The corporate bankruptcy system and the economic crisis. Chapter 8 in *Economic crisis and corporate restructuring in Korea: Reforming the chaebol,* ed. Stephan Haggard, Wonhyuk Lim, and Euysung Kim. New York: Cambridge University Press.
Oh, Gyutaeg, and Changyong Rhee. 2002. The role of corporate bond markets in the Korean financial restructuring process. Chapter 7 in *Korean crisis and recovery,* ed. David T. Coe and Se-Jik Kim. Washington, D.C.: International Monetary Fund.

Comment   Francis T. Lui

The Asian financial crisis of 1997 and 1998 has caused such enormous losses for the economies involved that it is important for them to learn from what has happened so that similar mistakes can be avoided in the future.

Francis T. Lui is professor of economics and director of the Center for Economic Development at Hong Kong University of Science and Technology.

Among the many possible causes of the crisis, imprudent lending to corporations, induced by various kinds of moral hazard behavior, often has been regarded as a main culprit. Arguably, this turned on the whole chain of events that started in Thailand. In Korea, where *chaebol* indebtedness was also a big issue, the economy quickly was affected by the crisis.

With this background, it is natural for economists to ask some compelling questions. What was the nature of corporate financing before the crisis? How did corporations finance their investments? How did the corporate financial structures change after the crisis? How did the size of the firms affect their profits and financial structures? What lessons can we learn from the events? These questions should be addressed both empirically and theoretically. Youngjae Lim's paper, using a large database on Korean firms, is an attempt to answer some of these questions from an empirical perspective. Specifically, it focuses on what happened to the sources of corporate financing of firms of different sizes. Since papers of this kind can provide us with useful information on what actually happened, they should be very much welcome by the profession.

The approach used in the paper basically involves the following. First, with occasional minor deviations, it classifies firms into three major categories: the largest firms, those of medium size, and the smallest ones. Second, it examines the sources of financing of each of these firm categories in different years from 1992 to 2000. The comparison therefore can be done both cross-sectionally and longitudinally. Sources of funds being studied include borrowing from financial intermediaries and borrowing from financial markets. The paper also compares profitability of the three categories of firms over time.

Three methods are used to organize the data. First, descriptive statistics, including the means and standard deviations of the variables involved, are presented for every category of firm before, during, and after the Asian financial crisis. The main variables are "borrowing from financial intermediaries" and "borrowing from financial markets," each divided by total borrowing. Second, the density functions of these variables for different types of firms in different years are presented. Readers can inspect the graphs to arrive at their conclusions. Third, a more formal statistical approach involving different sources of financing or profitability as dependent variables is used. The main explanatory variables are dummies representing different types of firms in different years. In addition, GDP growth rates and yields to corporate bonds are used to isolate the effects of business cycles.

These three ways of organizing the data essentially yield the same results. To some extent, there is redundancy in employing all three methods in the paper. Since the first two cannot control for the influences of business cycles, which obscure the effects of the crisis on the financial structure, they are inferior to the third, which is already sufficient to tell the main stories of this paper. Readers can go through it much more efficiently by just paying attention to the part on statistical tests.

One may complain that the reliance on many dummy variables may introduce too much arbitrariness in the regression model. There are various ways to reduce the number of dummies. For example, one can construct continuous variables based on the sizes of the firms, as measured by the values of their assets. This probably will not generate major improvements, but the author may know better how robust his results are.

Another drawback of the paper is the short time-series of data, which last from 1992 to 2000, just a couple of years after the Asian financial crisis. Although there is an attempt to control for business cycles, it is not clear that the duration of the data is long enough to tell whether the post-crisis changes in financial structures are permanent or transitory. This problem cannot be resolved until more data are available over time.

What are the main findings of the paper? After the crisis, the largest firms have big declines in their borrowing from financial intermediaries. There is, however, no major change in total borrowing. The declines in loans by intermediaries are compensated for by sizable increases in corporate bond financing. While there are no obvious changes in the sources of financing for medium-sized firms, new patterns for the smallest ones have emerged. Before the crisis, small firms were less dependent than medium firms on loans by financial intermediaries. However, after the crisis, their borrowing from intermediaries exhibits significant increases. Because of the small size of these firms, they typically have no access to financing through corporate bonds. It should also be noted that the profitability of the small firms has been declining over time. The distributions of profits both across the entire sample of firms, and across the smallest firms, appears to be widening after the crisis. The small firms seem to have become both riskier and less profitable.

These results, while valuable for their own sake, are descriptive in nature. They tell us what happened, but not the reason it happened. Hence it is rather difficult to directly infer any major lessons from them. In a sense, they raise more questions than have been answered. For instance, the paper does not let us know whether the decline in loans provided by financial intermediaries to large corporations is due to the reluctance of these intermediaries to lend them money, or due to the voluntary choice of the firms to choose other means of financing. Has the cost of financing by intermediaries been raised enough to correct for moral hazard? Do financial markets in Korea possess better information than banks, so that the former can provide cheaper loans to the large firms? Is it true that bond financing has become more important only because the financial markets in Korea are now more developed? Is the Asian financial crisis just a historical coincidence, having nothing to do with the changing financial structures for the large firms? As for the small firms, is it true that intermediaries are more willing than before to lend them money? Are the decline in profitability and the increase in risks caused by worsening of the investment environment? Alternatively, are these simply due to the entry of many inexperienced small firms? The last question can be answered partially if data on the number of newly registered firms are available.

One can continue to lengthen the list of questions related to the changes in sources of corporate financing in Korea. Clearly, no one author is responsible for answering all the questions. This being said, the paper would make a better contribution had the author been able to provide more institutional details on the Korean financial markets and to offer coherent explanations for his descriptive empirical findings. There is need for more theoretical papers in this area.

Initial Public Offering and Corporate Governance in China's Transitional Economy

Chen Chien-Hsun and Shih Hui-Tzu

7.1 Introduction

During periods of institutional transformation—given that informal constraints such as culture, rules, and values are difficult to change once formed, and that the transformation may result in the development of an inefficient system—there could be obstacles to transformation that lock the institution into its original path of evolution. Other institutions displaying better performance consequently would be unable to emerge (North 1991, 1994). An efficient institution thus can be beneficial to institutional transformation and to the spontaneous evolution of society (Hayek 1960).

In the process of institutional transformation, whereby China gradually has moved away from a centrally planned economy toward a market economy, the emphasis has been on the establishment of a sound system of property rights and a stable financial system. The reform of the financial system has attracted the most attention. The financial system is closely bound up with the reform of state-owned enterprises (SOEs) and of the fiscal system; thus the reform of the financial system will have a significant impact on the institutional transformation of China's economy as a whole. The establishment of the Shanghai Stock Exchange in December 1990 was a landmark in the development of the stock market in China. As the necessary infrastructure was established, the calls for a direct-financing market grew louder. The stock market began to blossom, and there was rapid development within a relatively short period of time.

Chen Chien-Hsun is a research fellow at the Chung-Hua Institution for Economic Research. Shih Hui-Tzu is a research fellow at the Chung-Hua Institution for Economic Research.

The types of shares traded in China's stock market can be divided into three main categories: A-, B-, and H-shares. A-shares are available to domestic holders, B-shares are available exclusively to foreign investors and certain authorized domestic securities firms, and H-shares are listed on the Hong Kong Stock Exchange.[1] Since 1987, A-shares have steadily become more popular; as of December 2000, the total amount raised through the issuing of new shares and allotment shares came to 324.213 billion renminbi (RMB). As regards B-shares, since they were first issued in 1992, they have become one of the main means by which China secures its foreign investment. However, the amount of money raised through B-shares has been less than the amount raised from A-, H-, or N-shares (N-shares are listed on the New York Stock Exchange). H-shares were first issued in 1993 as another means by which the stock markets could secure foreign capital. By 2000, the total amount of funds secured by the issuing of new shares and allotment shares came to RMB 225.226 billion (see the China Securities Regulatory Commission Web site: www.csrc.gov.cn).[2]

Several recent empirical studies have provided evidence of the performance of initial public offerings (IPOs) for China's stock markets; for example, Mok and Hui (1998) found that A-share IPOs in Shanghai were 289 percent underpriced between 19 December 1990 and 31 December 1993, due to the excessive demand for the limited supply of negotiable shares. B-share IPOs were only 26 percent underpriced. Different ownership structures, a long time-lag between offering and listing, and information asymmetry all contributed to IPO underpricing. Using data on 308 firm-commitment IPOs from 1 January 1987 through to 31 December 1995, Su and Fleisher (1999) found that IPO underpricing was a strategy for firms to signal their value to investors. From a sample of eighty-three IPOs completed between 1992 and 1995, Aharony, Lee, and Wong (2000) found that the median firm return on assets (ROA) peaked in the IPO year and declined thereafter. The post-IPO decline in ROA is statistically insignificant in protected industries such as petrochemicals, energy, and raw materials; firms in the protected industries are favored by the Chinese government in the selection process. Chen, Firth, and Kim (2000) considered 277 A-share and 65 B-share IPOs during the 1992–1995 period, with their results showing that B-share IPOs underperformed A-share IPOs during the postissue periods for up to three years.

In this paper, we extend the prior works on Chinese IPOs and empirically examine IPO performance. Our sample consists of 437 companies listed on the Shanghai Stock Exchange, and 447 companies listed on the Shenzhen exchange (for a longer time period) from 1995 to 1999. Investigation of China's IPOs is appealing and timely, since most of the listed companies are

1. From 20 February 2001, B-shares were made available to domestic residents.
2. Xu (2000) indicates there is no significant evidence of any causal relationship between volume and volatility for Shanghai B-shares. Sun and Tong (2000) also find foreign investors are more sensitive to currency risk.

SOEs, and establishing effective corporate governance of SOEs has become a key priority for China's policymakers during the transitional period.

The remainder of the paper is organized as follows. Section 7.2 contains a discussion on equity structure and the corporate governance mechanism. Section 7.3 establishes financial indicators to evaluate the operational performance of listed companies. The empirical results of IPOs' performance are reported in section 7.4, with section 7.5 providing concluding remarks to this study.

7.2   Equity Structure and Corporate Governance

The methods by which stocks are listed and shares issued in China's stock markets violate the market principle. Equity in listed companies is artificially divided into different categories of shares in the same stock that have different rights: state shares, legal person shares, public shares, and internal employee shares. State shares are held by the state and its varied ministries, bureaus, and regional governments; legal person shares are kept by other SOEs; public shares are retained by individuals or private entities; and internal employee shares are maintained by managers and employees. For example, holders of state shares can transfer their allotment rights in part or in whole to the holders of public shares; while holders of state shares can maintain their right to share in the benefits from share allotment, or choose not to participate in share allotment, thereby transferring the risk onto the shoulders of the holders of public shares. By contrast, the holders of public shares can buy and sell shares only on the secondary market.

Table 7.1 provides details of the equity structure of listed companies in China and the changes to that structure during the period from the end of 1992 to the end of 2000.

State shares remained the dominant proportion of total shares, but the proportion of state shares in the equity structure of listed companies fell from 41.38 percent to 38.90 percent, a decrease of 2.48 percent. The reasons for this decline were as follows: (1) Owing to the fall in central government revenue, China stopped increasing the capitalization of SOEs; however, listed companies were constantly implementing capital increments to increase the proportion of public shares, which therefore caused the proportion of state shares to fall. (2) In the last few years there has been a series of cases of state shares' being privately transferred to legal persons, which has increased the proportion of legal person shares.

The reform of SOEs is nevertheless still making use mainly of state-owned holding companies, with the government insisting that listed companies must still be subsidiaries of a state-owned holding company. The reform of the SOEs therefore does not involve wholesale privatization, and state shares therefore continue to play an important role.

As far as founders' stocks are concerned, the proportion of domestic legal person shares has risen from 13.14 percent to 16.94 percent, an increase

Table 7.1   Equity Structure of Stocks Listed on China's Stock Markets

Share Type	End 1992 Billions of Shares	End 1992 %	End 1997 Billions of Shares	End 1997 %	End 1998 Billions of Shares	End 1998 %	End 1999 Billions of Shares	End 1999 %	End 2000 Billions of Shares	End 2000 %
Shares not yet in circulation	4.769	69.25	127.124	65.44	166.485	65.89	200.71	65.02	243.743	64.28
Founder's stock	4.035	58.59	107.826	55.50	142.934	56.57	174.709	56.60	216.54	57.11
State shares	2.850	41.38	61.228	31.52	86.551	34.25	111.607	36.16	147.513	38.90
Domestic legal person shares	0.905	13.14	43.991	22.64	52.806	20.90	59.051	19.13	64.255	16.94
Foreign legal person shares	0.280	4.07	2.607	1.34	3.577	1.42	4.051	1.31	4.62	1.22
Fund-raising legal person shares	0.649	9.42	13.049	6.72	15.234	6.03	19.01	6.16	21.421	5.65
Internal employee shares	0.085	1.23	3.962	2.04	5.170	2.05	3.671	1.19	2.429	0.64
Other (transferred allotment)	0.00	0.00	2.287	1.18	3.147	1.25	3.32	1.08	2.462	0.65
Shares in circulation	2.118	30.75	67.144	34.56	86.194	34.11	107.965	34.98	135.427	35.72
Domestically listed Renminbi shares (A-shares)	1.093	15.87	44.268	22.79	60.803	24.06	81.318	26.34	107.817	28.44
Domestically listed foreign capital shares (B-shares)	1.025	14.88	11.731	6.04	13.396	5.30	14.192	4.60	15.157	4.00
Overseas-listed foreign capital shares (H-shares)	0.00	0.00	11.145	5.74	11.995	4.75	12.454	4.03	12.454	3.28

Sources: China Securities Regulatory Commission (CSRC; 2000, 189) and the CSRC Web site (www.csrc.gov.cn).

Note: Each share has a face value of RMB 1.00.

of 3.80 percent, while the proportion of fund-raising legal person shares has fallen from 9.42 percent to 5.65 percent, a decrease of 3.77 percent. The reasons for this are as follows:

1. Most listed companies have been transformed from SOEs; listing is usually implemented as part of the restructuring of SOEs, and the proportion of total capitalization accounted for by the former SOEs' internal reserves is defined as founder's stock after listing.

2. Many listed companies are the profitable parts of SOEs which were spun off, with the SOEs retaining founder's stock; this has led to a significant increase in the proportion of founder's stock.

3. Owing to the general decline in enterprise performance over the last few years, and the restrictions on the circulation of legal person shares, the market for legal person shares is not sufficiently lively and market prices are unattractively low; as a result, there has been a general decrease in mutual investment between unrelated legal persons, so that the proportion of fund-raising legal person shares has fallen gradually.

The proportion of employee shares in unlisted companies rose from 1.23 percent to 2.04 percent, and then declined to 0.64 percent. This reflects the way in which, during the process of institutional transformation, enterprises have used employee stock options as a means of improving employee welfare.

With regard to the proportion of total equity accounted for by the various types of shares, the continual implementation of capital increments to increase the number of public shares and the private transfer of state shares to legal persons has caused the proportion of listed company equity accounted for by state shares to fall from 41.38 percent in 1992 to 38.0 percent in 2000. State shares are, however, still the most numerous category of shares. At the same time, because shares that cannot be traded freely (including state shares) account for 60 percent of total equity, company managers do not have to worry that poor management may cause their enterprises' stock prices to fall, or that their company will be faced with the threat of being taken over. In other words, holders of public shares cannot "vote with their feet" and managers are not concerned about the rights of public shareholders (Xu and Wang 1999).

In 2000, the Chinese government began undertaking reform of its SOEs in the petrochemical,[3] communications,[4] rail transport, and electric power

---

3. China Petroleum and Natural Gas Ltd. implemented an IPO using H-shares and American depository receipts (ADR) in both Hong Kong and New York in March 2000, after which the state shares in the company held by its parent company, China National Petroleum Corporation (CNPC), was reduced to 90 percent (Wu 2001).

4. In June 2000, following reorganization, Zhong Lian Tung secured a stock market listing in both Hong Kong and New York using "red chip" shares and ADR. The amount of capital raised was US$6.278 billion, making this the largest IPO ever involving an Asian company (other than Japanese companies). Following the IPO, the shares in Zhong Lian Tung held by the state fell by 80 percent (Wu 2001).

sectors, seeking to reorganize the entire industry and establish a regulated company system. The aim was to have these reorganized companies listed on the domestic and overseas stock markets, establishing a regulated framework for corporate governance and turning the old SOEs into real businesses.

The developing capital markets can, on the one hand, enable enterprises to increase their capitalization; while at the same time change in enterprises' equity and corporate governance structures can be used to create a solid foundation for dealing with the underlying causes of indebtedness. However, China's capital markets have not had long to develop, and their overall level of development is still low. Too little in-depth thinking has gone into directing the course of their development, and various levels of disparity exist in certain areas. Furthermore, theoretically speaking, the corporate governance structure requires a separation between investors and managers; a set of incentive mechanisms and restrictive mechanisms need to be developed to reduce agency costs and ensure that the investors receive a return on their investment. However, there are inherent weaknesses in the governance structure of China's SOEs. First of all, as far as incentive mechanisms are concerned, despite twenty years of reform there has been no systematic improvement in the incentive mechanisms of China's SOEs, and their attempts to imitate the incentive mechanisms of private enterprises have run into two major problems. First of all, it is very difficult to find suitable indicators for implementing rewards and punishments in SOEs, wherein both the starting point and the policy burden are different; and second, there is a lack of faith in the commitments made. The SOEs' restrictive mechanisms are characterized by excessive administrative interference and the simultaneous existence of excessive internal controls.[5] As a result, enterprise management tends to become divorced from the owners' interest. It is therefore not enough to rely on the capital markets alone to transform the SOEs; a strategic withdrawal is needed from state involvement in the economy, and a favorable environment for privatization has to be created. This is the only way in which the reform of the SOEs can really be facilitated (Wu and Zhao 2000).

7.3   The Operational Performance of Listed Companies

We will explore the operational performance of listed companies in China in terms of the growth, profitability, and stability of these companies, taking into consideration differences between stock exchanges and industries. The selection of financial indicators is based on (1) the use of

5. One example is Zhonguo Yituo Ltd. in Henan Province. Although Zhonguo Yituo succeeded in securing RMB 1.6 billion through the stock market in 1997, the lack of sound management mechanisms led to errors being made with respect to the company's expansion, and consequently, the company's operational performance was poor.

listed companies' operating revenue and net profit growth rates to explore the performance of listed companies in terms of growth, as well as the differences between stock exchanges and industries; (2) the use of listed companies' earnings per share (EPS) and return on equity (ROE, which equals net profit/shareholders' equity) to explore listed companies' performance in terms of profitability, as well as the differences between stock exchanges and industries; and (3) the use of listed companies' quick ratios ([current asset – inventory]/current ratio) and current ratio (current asset/ current liability) to explore listed companies' performance in terms of stability, as well as the differences between stock exchanges and industries. Empirical verification is then undertaken with regard to the impact of IPOs on the operational performance of listed companies, to determine the impact of the stock market on China's economic development as it progresses through this period of institutional transformation.

7.3.1   Data Description and Methodology

Listed companies' interim financial reports for 1999 published by China Securities Regulatory Commission (CSRC) were used for empirical estimation. The data given covered the period from mid-1995 to mid-1999. The CSRC data include listed companies' operating revenue, net profit rates, EPS, ROE, quick ratio, and current ratio. The sample consisted of 884 companies (including both A-shares and B-shares); 437 of the companies were listed on the Shanghai Stock Market and 447 were listed on the Shenzhen Stock Market.

As regards industry classification, the Shanghai Stock Market divides all listed companies into five categories: industrial, commercial, real estate, public utilities, and general. The Shenzhen Stock Market divides all listed companies into six categories: industrial, commercial, financial, real estate, public utilities, and general. Such classifications are inappropriate, partly because the two stock exchanges use different classification systems, and partly because the classifications are not sufficiently precise. If the industry data produced by the Shanghai and Shenzhen stock markets are used, not only is the classification too precise, but the disparity between the numbers of enterprises in each category is too obvious. To facilitate comparison, for the purposes of this study all listed companies were divided into twenty-one industries: agriculture; mining; food, textiles, and garments; printing and papermaking; metals and metal products; chemical industry; pharmaceuticals; construction materials; machinery; electronics and electrical appliances; precision instruments; vehicles; miscellaneous; public utilities; transportation; finance; real estate and construction; travel and hotels; commerce; foreign trade; and information (see table 7.2).

The data cover the period 1995–1999, during which both the Asian financial crisis and China's economic recovery occurred. Therefore it is inappropriate to compare the data for different years. In addition, regarding

Table 7.2   Sample Data Industry Categories

Industry Category	Original Category	Industry Category	Original Category
Agriculture	Agriculture	Commerce	Commerce
	Forestry		Rental
	Fisheries		Packaging
	Livestock		General
Mining	Mining	Information	Computers
Machinery	Agricultural machinery		Communications
	Machinery	Foreign trade	Trade
	Milling machines and	Food, textiles, and	Food
	materials	garments	Textiles
	Textile machinery		Garments
Electronics and	Electromechanical	Printing and	Printing
electrical appliances	Electronic appliances	papermaking	Paper industry
	Wire and cable	Chemical industry	Chemicals
	Refrigeration		Artificial fiber
	equipment		Paints
	Home appliances	Construction materials	Glass
Precision instruments	Instruments and meters		Construction
	Medical instruments		materials
Vehicles	Bicycles		Cement
	Motorcycles	Real estate and	Materials
	Auto accessories	construction	Ceramics
	Auto manufacturing		Basic construction
	Shipbuilding		Highway construction
	Aircraft manufacturing		Harbor construction
Metals and metal	Iron and steel	Public utilities	Industrial districts
products	Metallurgy		Real estate
Pharmaceuticals	Pharmaceuticals		Building contractors
	Biotechnology		Public utilities
Miscellaneous	Pens		Energy
	Toys		Water supply
	Jewelry	Transportation	Warehousing
	Sports		Transportation
	Industrial		Containers
Travel and hotels	Travel	Finance	Finance
	Hotels		
	Brewing		

the comparison of financial indicators between listed companies, a reasonable level of comprehension already has been achieved with respect to listed companies' financial statements; thus the main emphasis in the following analysis will be on the comparison of industry performance in each year and on industry performance within the sample as a whole.

The industries to which listed companies belong are grouped into five categories: (1) those industries that have performed very well by comparison with the average for all industries (e.g., the financial indicator for the industry in question was 50 percent higher than the average for all industries for that year or period); (2) those industries that performed better than the average for all industries (e.g., the financial indicator for the industry in question was higher than—but less than 50 percent higher than—the average for all industries for that year or period); (3) those industries that performed worse than the average for all industries (e.g., the financial indicator for the industry in question was lower than—but less than 50 percent lower than—the average for all industries for that year or period); (4) those industries that performed significantly worse than the average for all industries (e.g., the financial indicator for the industry in question was less than 0.5 percent of the average for all industries for that year or period); (5) those industries that performed markedly worse than the average for all industries (e.g., the financial indicator for the industry in question was less than 0.1 percent of the average for all industries for that year or period).

To assess the pre- and post-IPO operational performance of listed companies, according to Greene (1993), the analysis of variance (ANOVA) tests the null hypothesis that all coefficients of the regression other than the intercept are zero; the ANOVA test rather than regression method can be used to conduct empirical assessment. Therefore, the ANOVA method was utilized to verify the impact of the IPOs on the operational performance of listed companies, to determine whether the null hypothesis could be accepted—the null hypothesis was that a listed company's operational performance would not change after its IPO; namely, there would be no difference in the financial indicators between the average values of the IPO year and the average values of the subsequent three years.

We begin by analyzing the overall operational performance of the industries to which China's listed companies belong, from the points of view of growth, profitability, and stability. First, we conduct a combined analysis of operating revenue and profitability by industry. Then we calculate the overall financial indicator ratings for each stock exchange and each industry, in order to evaluate the overall relative operational performance of listed companies in China.

Regarding the analysis of overall industry operating revenue and profitability, the financial indicators that can best represent a listed company's operating revenue and profitability are the operating revenue growth rate and ROE (Li 1999). The industry's growth rate in operating revenue is taken as the horizontal axis, with ROE as the vertical axis, and the relevant values from the Shanghai and Shenzhen stock exchanges are then plotted on the graph. The average value for all companies listed on the two exchanges is taken as the demarcation point, and all industries are divided into four categories: (1) industries with high growth and high profits (the first quadrant on the graph); (2) industries with low growth but high profits (the second quadrant); (3) industries with low growth but low profits (the third quadrant); and (4) industries with high growth and low profits (the fourth quadrant). Those industries with high growth and high profits have the highest overall revenue and profitability; those industries with low growth and low profits have the lowest overall revenue and profitability; those industries with high growth and low profits or low growth and high profits lie between the two (see figs. 7.1 and 7.2).

Industries with High Growth and High Profitability

This category includes public utilities and trade. Their chief characteristics are that they have a large potential market and good development potential.

Industries with Low Growth and High Profitability

This category includes transportation, pharmaceuticals, agriculture, and mining. These industries have stable market prices, and while they do experience temporary slumps, overall they are stable, mature industries with high profitability.

Industries with High Growth and Low Profitability

On the Shanghai Stock Exchange, this category includes a total of six industries: precision instruments, information, electronics and electrical appliances, the chemical industry, commerce, and miscellaneous. On the Shenzhen Stock Exchange it includes a total of five industries: food, textiles, and garments; pharmaceuticals; printing and papermaking; machinery; and information. The chief characteristic of these industries is that competition is very fierce within each industry. Although overall demand is still increasing, the rate of increase in supply is far higher than the rate of increase in demand. As a result, price-cutting competition is causing earnings to fall, and there is market polarization in the performance of companies in the industry. However, the prospects for the industry as a whole are still good, and there is considerable potential for development in the medium and long terms.

Industries with Low Growth and Low Profits

On the Shanghai Stock Exchange this category includes a total of nine industries: real estate and construction; travel and hotels; construction materials; metals and metal products; finance; vehicles; machinery; food, textiles, and garments; and printing and papermaking. On the Shenzhen Stock Exchange, it includes a total of fourteen industries: real estate and construction, travel and hotels, construction materials, metals and metal products, finance, vehicles, electronics and electrical appliances, the chemical industry, commerce, miscellaneous, agriculture, precision instruments, trade, and transportation. The main characteristic of these industries is that many of them are primary industries. In recent years, the prices of raw materials and energy in China have risen, but the price of finished

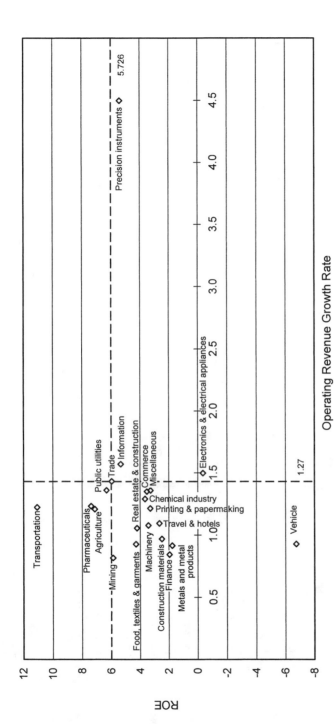

Fig. 7.1   Distribution of ROE and operating revenue growth rate for companies listed on the Shanghai Stock Exchange, by industry

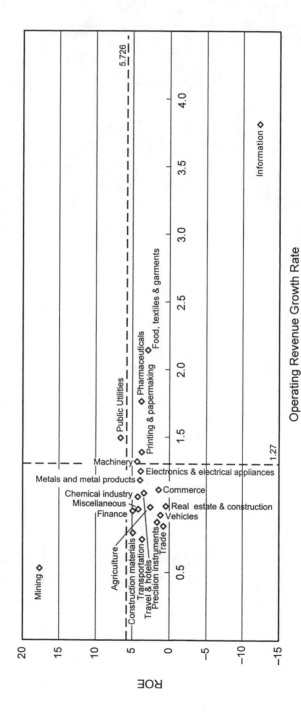

Fig. 7.2   Distribution of ROE and operating revenue growth rate for companies listed on the Shenzhen Stock Exchange, by industry

products has fallen. As a result, the market has contracted, competition has become much fiercer, and overall industry performance has fallen.

Finally, we calculate the overall financial indicator scores for each stock exchange and each industry in order to evaluate the overall relative operational performance of listed companies in China. The standard for evaluation is based on the principles of analysis described above. Those industries displaying good performance are awarded 5 points, those displaying acceptable performance are awarded 4 points, those displaying relatively poor performance are awarded 3 points, those displaying bad performance are awarded 2 points, and those displaying very bad performance are awarded just 1 point.

The only industries to display good overall performance (with a total score of 4 or higher) are the public-utility, transportation, and finance industries. In terms of the stock exchange, for the Shanghai Stock Exchange those industries that displayed relatively good performance were the public-utility, chemical, trade, and precision instruments industries; for the Shenzhen Stock Exchange they were the transportation and finance industries. Clearly, the overall operational performance of most industries is poor, and those that demonstrate better performance are China's "sunrise" industries. Furthermore, of the companies listed on the Shanghai Stock Exchange, the overall performance of those in agriculture; food, textiles, and garments; metals and metal products; chemical industry; pharmaceuticals; precision instruments; miscellaneous; public utilities; real estate; commerce; trade; and information is superior to that of those listed on the Shenzhen Stock Exchange (see tables 7.3–7.5).

7.4 The Impact of IPOs on Listed Companies

In the previous section, we undertook structural analysis of the financial indicators of listed companies in China. However, more analysis is needed to determine whether an IPO does in fact have a positive impact on a company's operations.[6] In this study, we use the ANOVA method, which is applied to the data for the year of IPO and the subsequent three years, to undertake a mean value parity assumption verification analysis with respect to companies' operating revenue growth rate, net profit growth rate, EPS, and ROE. The results are shown in table 7.6. The results of the ANOVA analysis show that following IPO, the only financial indicators in which there is any statistically significant change are ROE and EPS (for companies listed on the Shanghai Stock Exchange only); in other words, only in the profitability indicators is there any change.

6. According to Chinese Company Law, the stock shares of listed companies shall not be less than 5,000 shares. If they reach 5,000 shares, there is no need to issue new shares; therefore, a dilution effect by IPOs does not exist. Otherwise, if there were less than 5,000 shares, the dilution effect may be pervasive.

Table 7.3   **Overall Financial Indicator Ratings, Listed Companies in China**

Name of Industry	Operating Revenue	Net Profit Rate	ROE	EPS	Quick Ratio	Current Ratio	Average
Agriculture	3	3	3	3	4	4	3.33
Mining	2	3	5	4	4	3	3.50
Food, textiles, and garments	2	3	3	3	4	4	3.17
Printing and papermaking	2	3	3	3	4	4	3.17
Metals and metal products	5	4	3	3	3	3	3.50
Chemical industry	4	4	3	3	4	4	3.67
Pharmaceuticals	3	3	3	3	4	3	3.17
Construction materials	2	3	3	3	3	3	2.83
Machinery	3	3	3	3	3	4	3.17
Electronics and electrical appliances	5	5	3	4	3	3	3.83
Precision instruments	2	4	3	5	4	4	3.67
Vehicles	5	3	2	3	3	3	3.17
Miscellaneous	2	3	4	4	4	4	3.50
Public utilities	3	5	4	4	4	4	4.00
Transportation	4	3	4	4	5	5	4.17
Finance	4	5	4	5	3	3	4.00
Real estate and construction	3	4	3	3	3	3	3.17
Travel and hotels	3	4	3	4	4	4	3.67
Commerce	3	3	5	3	3	3	3.33
Foreign trade	5	3	3	4	4	4	3.83
Information	3	4	2	4	4	4	3.50

Notes: Those industries displaying superior performance are given 5 points; those displaying reasonable performance are given 4 points; those displaying relatively poor performance are given 3 points; those displaying poor performance are given 2 points; and those displaying very bad performance are given 1 point.

We further classify the industry into six subcategories: agriculture, manufacturing, public utilities, real estate and construction, finance and commerce, and general. The results of ANOVA in table 7.7 indicate that following IPO, the financial indicators in which there are statistically significant changes are ROE for manufacturing and for finance and commerce, since they are state monopolies. If the listed companies are grouped by share classes (as in table 7.8), the results of ANOVA indicate that only ROE has any significant change for both A-shares and B-shares.

If the financial indicators for listed companies before and after IPO are grouped in sets of two years, regardless of whether the company is listed on the Shanghai or Shenzhen Stock Exchange, we can see from the results that (1) operating revenue growth rate tends to decline sharply after IPO, with a clear disparity with the annual statistics reported at the time of IPO; (2) net profit growth rate tends to decline sharply after IPO, with a clear disparity with the annual statistics reported at the time of IPO; (3) ROE tends

Table 7.4   **Overall Financial Indicator Ratings, Companies Listed on the Shanghai Stock Exchange**

Name of Industry	Operating Revenue	Net Profit Rate	ROE	EPS	Quick Ratio	Current Ratio	Average
Agriculture	3	4	4	4	4	4	3.83
Mining	2	3	4	3	3	3	3.00
Food, textiles, and garments	2	3	4	4	4	4	3.50
Printing and papermaking	2	3	3	3	3	3	2.83
Metals and metal products	5	4	3	3	3	3	3.50
Chemical industry	5	5	4	3	4	4	4.17
Pharmaceuticals	3	3	4	4	3	3	3.33
Construction materials	2	2	3	2	3	3	2.50
Machinery	3	3	3	3	3	4	3.17
Electronics and electrical appliances	4	4	3	4	3	3	3.50
Precision instruments	3	3	4	4	5	5	4.00
Vehicles	4	3	2	3	3	3	3.00
Miscellaneous	2	3	4	4	4	4	3.50
Public utilities	3	5	5	4	4	4	4.17
Transportation	3	3	5	4	4	4	3.83
Finance	2	5	4	5	3	3	3.67
Real estate and construction	3	4	4	4	3	3	3.50
Travel and hotels	2	3	3	3	4	4	3.17
Commerce	3	3	4	4	3	3	3.33
Foreign trade	5	4	4	5	4	4	4.33
Information	3	4	4	4	3	3	3.50

Notes: See table 7.3.

to fall sharply after IPO, with a clear disparity with the financial statements submitted at the time of IPO; and (4) EPS tend to fall sharply after IPO; in the case of companies listed on the Shanghai Stock Exchange, there is a clear disparity with the financial statements submitted at the time of IPO, while for companies listed on the Shenzhen Stock Exchange this is not the case, and some improvement can be seen in the tendency for earnings per share to fall.

The above analysis shows that for enterprises in China's stock markets, IPO does not present any marked benefits with respect to operational performance, and in fact performance tends to worsen. One of the reasons for this is that in order to implement the IPO and secure a stock market listing, companies tend to submit inflated figures in the financial statements that they are required to provide; the real situation is reflected gradually after the company has secured a listing. In addition, the state still retains a majority share in most listed SOEs in China; thus, the fundamental character of these enterprises is unchanged and the influence of the original SOE

Table 7.5   Overall Financial Indicator Ratings, Companies Listed on the Shenzhen Stock Exchange

Name of Industry	Operating Revenue	Net Profit Rate	ROE	EPS	Quick Ratio	Current Ratio	Average
Agriculture	3	2	2	3	4	4	3.00
Mining	2	3	5	4	5	4	3.83
Food, textiles, and garments	2	2	2	2	3	3	2.33
Printing and papermaking	3	3	2	3	4	4	3.17
Metals and metal products	5	4	2	3	3	3	3.33
Chemical industry	4	3	3	3	3	3	3.17
Pharmaceuticals	3	2	2	3	4	4	3.00
Construction materials	3	3	3	4	4	4	3.50
Machinery	4	3	3	4	3	4	3.50
Electronics and electrical appliances	5	5	3	4	3	3	3.83
Precision instruments	2	4	2	5	4	4	3.50
Vehicles	5	4	2	3	3	3	3.33
Miscellaneous	2	3	4	5	3	3	3.33
Public utilities	3	5	3	4	4	4	3.83
Transportation	4	4	3	4	5	5	4.17
Finance	5	5	4	4	3	3	4.00
Real estate and construction	3	4	2	3	3	3	3.00
Travel and hotels	3	5	3	4	4	4	3.83
Commerce	3	2	5	3	3	3	3.17
Foreign trade	3	2	2	2	3	3	2.50
Information	3	4	1	4	4	4	3.33

Notes: See table 7.3.

Table 7.6   Empirical Results of ANOVA, by Stock Exchange

	Shanghai		Shenzhen	
Financial Indicator	F value	Pr $>$ F value	F value	Pr $>$ F value
Operating revenue growth rate	0.16	0.926	0.86	0.4600
Net profit growth rate	0.16	0.926	1.07	0.3602
EPS	8.10	0.0001*	1.15	0.3340
ROE	9.12	0.0001*	10.55	0.0001*

*Significant at the 1 percent level.

systems and structures is not erased. In particular, the government still directly appoints, or interferes in the appointment of, senior managers for some companies; a company chairman or president is frequently appointed by government authorities. In their governance structure, therefore, many listed companies retain an agency relationship within the company, rather than a property-ownership relationship. At best, governance

Table 7.7   **Empirical Results of ANOVA, by Industry**

Financial Indicator	Agriculture		Manufacturing		Public Utilities		Real Estate and Construction		Finance and Commerce		General	
	F	Pr > F	F	F	Pr > F	F	Pr > F	Pr > F	F	Pr > F	F	Pr > F
Operating revenue growth rate	3.34	0.048	1.26	0.2860	0.43	0.732	0.51	0.677	0.234	0.878	0.06	0.981
Net profit growth rate	0.75	0.480	0.50	0.6570	1.28	0.297	0.91	0.442	0.79	0.502	0.41	0.743
EPS	1.51	0.229	0.82	0.4850	1.79	0.162	4.01	0.011	1.50	0.215	2.83	0.042
ROE	1.24	0.310	10.59	0.0001*	0.78	0.511	3.64	0.017	5.47	0.001*	0.07	0.977

Notes: Agriculture includes the agriculture, forestry, fisheries, and livestock sectors. Manufacturing includes the mining; food, textiles, and garments; printing and papermaking; chemical industry; pharmaceuticals; construction materials; machinery; electronics and electrical appliances; precision instruments; vehicles; metals and metal products; information; and miscellaneous sectors. General includes the transportation, travel and hotels, and foreign trade sectors.

*The null hypothesis is rejected within a 1 percent level of significance.

Table 7.8   Empirical Results of ANOVA, by Share Class

	A-Share		B-Share	
Financial Indicator	F	Pr > F	F	Pr > F
Operating revenue growth rate	0.83	0.478	0.53	0.595
Net profit growth rate	1.55	0.200	0.61	0.552
EPS	2.49	0.059	3.20	0.034
ROE	15.93	0.001*	6.83	0.001*

*The null hypothesis is rejected within a 1 percent level of significance.

in these companies is a mixture of political interest and economic interest. What's more, the control that holders of "state shares" exercise over the company tends to be weak in economic terms but strong in political terms. As a result, in their role as "agents," the managers tend to be opportunistic with respect to political matters, and to be affected by moral hazard with respect to economic matters. Using firm-level data from over 300 stock companies from 1993 to 1995, Xu and Wang (1999) found that there was a relationship between ownership structure and corporate performance, indicating the positive role of legal person shares and the negative role of state shares. Chen (2001) used a sample of 434 manufacturing firms listed on the Chinese stock exchange; his findings showed that state shares play a negative role in corporate governance, while domestic institutional and managerial shareholdings improve firm's performance.

Owing to the dual identity of the manager-agent, the mechanism for encouragement and sanction by the company's managers cannot lead to the maximization of benefits for the company. There are further serious problems, such as the fact that internal control of company personnel is not kept within reasonable limits (Li and Huang 1999). In other words, the inherent defects of the governance structure of Chinese companies led to poor operational performance (He and Liu 2000; Wu and Zhao 2000). For example, it is unclear how much control the ownership of "state shares" confers, there is too much insider trading, the responsibilities of the boards of directors are not sufficiently defined, there is too much administrative interference, too many problems of internal control, and so on. As a result, although working capital may have increased after listing, there has been no corresponding improvement in operational management. Consequently, the improvement in the company's operational performance as a result of IPO is not that dramatic. Of course, operational performance is also affected by other factors not directly related to the company itself, such as the business cycle, the government's industrial policy, and developments in related industries; that is to say, the fact that the Asian financial crisis and a weakening of demand in China occurred during the period covered by the sample is another reason for the sudden fall in the financial indicators.

7.5 Conclusions

Whether one looks at growth, profitability, and stability individually or all together, it can be seen that the only industries in China in which listed companies display strong performance are the public utilities, transportation, and finance; that is to say, China's "sunrise" industries. The overall operational performance of all other industries is clearly unsatisfactory, and poor performance is particularly widespread with respect to growth. Owing to the weak demand within China, there is excessive supply, intra-industry competition has become increasingly fierce, and enterprises' profit margins have been squeezed. In reality, the majority of enterprises in most industries have lost their ability to secure further financing, making it difficult for them to develop their operations further. In other words, listed companies have been willing to trade reduced profits for increased operating revenue and market share, which has affected their ability to secure financing.

An examination of the changes in listed companies' financial indicators following IPO reveals that, with the exception of earnings-related indicators (EPS and ROE), there is no significant change. What's more, the financial indicators tend to fall rapidly year on year. This means that the IPO is of little obvious help to companies' operational performance, and may actually make it worse. One of the reasons for this is that, in order to implement the IPO and secure a stock market listing, companies tend to submit inflated figures in the financial statements they are required to provide; the real situation is only gradually reflected after the company has secured a listing. Another possible factor is the poor corporate-governance characteristics of Chinese enterprises. For example, it is unclear how much control the ownership of "state shares" confers, there is too much insider trading, the responsibilities of the boards of directors are not sufficiently defined, and there is too much administrative interference and too many problems of internal control. As a result, although working capital may increase after listing, there is no corresponding improvement in operational management. Consequently, the improvement in the company's operational performance as a result of IPO is not that dramatic. Of course, another factor causing the financial indicators to fall rapidly is the fact that the Asian financial crisis and a falling-off in domestic demand occurred during the period covered by the sample.

The quality of listed companies is a prerequisite and a foundation for the development of capital markets. Only when listed companies display strong performance and growth can the ongoing development of the market be maintained. One of the things that needs to be done in order to improve the quality of listed companies is to select for listing those companies that display strong performance, have strong development potential, and occupy a leading or advantageous position within their industries, encouraging hi-tech enterprises and companies in other emerging industries to make use of the capital markets. The second task is to ensure that the capital raised through IPO is used more efficiently; companies' listing plans should be in conformity with their inventory and asset adjustment and their technology upgrading. Third, listed companies need to thoroughly transform their management mechanisms, establishing efficient corporate governance structures and corresponding stock option incentive mechanisms. Furthermore, the operations of listed companies need to be improved. Support can be provided for listed companies to improve their asset and liability structures through debt-for-equity swaps and refinancing, and the Chinese government could encourage interregional, cross-industry mergers; acquisitions; and asset reorganization between listed companies as well as between listed and nonlisted companies, and between companies with different ownership structures. In this way, it will be possible to improve the operational efficiency of listed companies, cultivating a group of large listed companies with strong capabilities that will be competitive in international markets, making listed companies the core element in the market and allowing them to exercise the function of market stabilization.

References

Aharony, J., C. W. J. Lee, and T. J. Wong. 2000. Financial packaging of IPO firms in China. *Journal of Accounting Research* 38 (Spring): 103–126.

Chen, G., M. Firth, and J. B. Kim. 2000. The post-issue market performance of initial public offerings in China's new stock markets. *Review of Quantitative Finance and Accounting* 14 (June): 319–339.

Chen, J. 2001. Ownership structure as corporate governance mechanism: Evidence from Chinese listed companies. *Economics of Planning* 34:53–72.

China Securities Regulatory Commission. 2000. *China securities and futures statistical yearbook, 2000.* Beijing: Zhongguo Caizheng Jingji Press.

Greene, W. H. 1993. *Econometric analysis.* New York: Macmillan.

Hayek, F. A. 1960. *The constitution of liberty.* Chicago: University of Chicago Press.

He, Shunwen, and Xing Liu. 2000. Problems relating to the control and equity structure of listed companies in China. *Xin Bao,* 18 May.

Li, Geping, and Bin Huang. 1999. The improvement of transferring state shares and listed companies governance. *Caimao Jingji* 8:36–42.

Li, Kan. 1999. *Zhongguo Gushi Bodong Guilu Jiqi Fenxifangfa* (China's stock price fluctuation and analysis method). Beijing: Jingji Kexue Press.

Mok, H. M. K., and Y. V. Hui. 1998. Underpricing and aftermarket performance of IPOs in Shanghai, China. *Pacific-Basin Finance Journal* 6 (November): 453–474.

North, D. C. 1991. *Institutions, institutional change, and economic performance.* New York: Cambridge University Press.

———. 1994. Economic performance through time. *American Economic Review* 84 (June): 359–368.

Su, D., and B. M. Fleisher. 1999. An empirical investigation of underpricing in Chinese IPOs. *Pacific-Basin Finance Journal* 7 (May): 173–202.

Sun, Q., and W. H. S. Tong. 2000. The effect of market segmentation on stock prices: The China syndrome. *Journal of Banking and Finance* 24 (December): 1875–1902.

Wu, Jinglian. 2001. China's financial sector: Perfecting the governance structure of listed companies. *Da Gong Bao,* 20 February.

Wu, Youchang, and Xiao Zhao. 2000. Debt-to-equity swap: A theoretical and policy analysis based on corporate governance. *Jingji Yanjiu* 2:26–33.

Xu, C. K. 2000. The microstructure of the Chinese stock market. *China Economic Review* 11:79–97.

Xu, X., and Y. Wang. 1999. Ownership structure and corporate governance in Chinese stock companies. *China Economic Review* 10:75–98.

Comment   Deunden Nikomborirak

The objective of this paper is to determine, with the use of empirical data on listed companies, whether getting listed in the stock market improves the financial performance of enterprises. The conclusion reached is that financial performance actually deteriorates after the listing year for four main reasons:

1. Initial figures tend to be inflated.

2. Despite privatization, state corporate control remains.

3. Listed companies in the Chinese stock markets are not subject to market discipline since equity shares in listed companies are divided up into state shares, legal person shares, public shares, and internal employee shares. Public shares can be traded only in the secondary market and state shares are not traded freely.

4. The Asian crisis may have contributed to the overall inferior financial performance of listed companies.

While these are valid reasons for explaining the lack of improvement in the financial performance of listed companies, they are not supported by the empirical tests undertaken. This is because the empirical study fails to disaggregate each of these effects. It simply confirms that there is a negative change in the EPS and ROE after the listing. On this note, I would like to make some suggestions with regard to how the effects may be disaggregated so that the authors' conclusions may be better supported.

Deunden Nikomborirak is research director for economic governance in the Sectoral Economics Program at the Thailand Development Research Institute.

First, to examine the extent of the inflation of the initial figures, one may use the difference in the financial figures (i.e., the ROE and EPS) of newly listed companies and those of the incumbents in the market in a similar industry. Second, to isolate the impact of sustained state control of former SOEs, dummies may be introduced for listed companies that are former SOEs. Third, to determine whether the listed company is subject to sufficient market discipline, the proportion of equity shares that are traded on the stock exchange may be used as a proxy. Finally, the impact of the Asian crisis may be isolated by using the average industry's performance as a benchmark.

Comment   Changqi Wu

This is an interesting and timely paper addressing an important issue in the process of China's economic development, namely, the role of stock markets. In China's effort to establish a market economy in the last two decades, hardly any other industry or institution has caught so much attention and debate as the development of stock markets. It has been more than ten years since China reestablished its first stock exchange. China's two stock exchanges in Shanghai and Shenzhen are featured permanently in Asia's financial market. But the problems abound. From the very beginning of the economic reform, the role of the stock market has been controversial. This is also a thorny and hotly debated issue within China.

In the industrialized economies, stock markets are an important component of the overall market institutions. As part of the financial system, stock markets facilitate resource allocation within the economy and help companies to raise capital. In addition, the stock prices transmit and reflect information on firms' performance to the general public. Stock markets also impose discipline on managers' behavior.

In the case of China and other emerging markets, because of underdevelopment of the market institutions and lack of sophisticated and transparent financial systems, the stock markets may not be able to play those roles. The two authors address some of those problems in their paper.

The authors try to assess the impact of stock listing on the performance of the listed companies in two stock exchanges in China. They find that the performance of those companies depends critically on industrial characteristics. Those firms operating in less competitive industries perform better than others. The authors do not find any significant improvement in performance before and after the stock listing. Instead, the listed firms'

Changqi Wu is professor of strategy and public policy at Guanghua School of Management, Peking University.

performance deteriorated across the board after their IPOs, despite the injection of new capital into those companies. The authors suggest that the deterioration in performance may be attributable to manipulation of accounts and bad corporate governance. They argue that improving corporate governance is essential to improving the performance of listed companies.

My comments on this paper are focused on three issues: measurement, data methodology, and results. I hope that my comments can be useful to the authors.

Measurement

The authors have used three indicators to measure the performance of companies immediately before and after the IPOs: growth of net profit, ROE, and quick ratio. These indicators are all calculated based on accounting information available. They are clearly useful and reflect the performance of those companies to a large extent, although attention is called to a few specific factors that are unique in the operating environment in China.

For instance, the authors use ROE as the performance of the listed companies. As is well known, ROE is influenced strongly by the debt-equity ratio. Moreover, ROE may not reflect the efficient use of total capital employed by the company. As in the case of China, the SOEs benefit from indirect government subsidies through subsidized loans from the state-owned banks. That may distort the measure of ROE. One should also note that China experienced double-digit inflation in the first half of 1990s; using the ROE as the performance measure in the high inflation environment may build in an upward bias.

The authors use the quick ratio and the current ratio as firms' stability measures. Both ratios measure the possibility of default of the listed companies. A unique feature of listed companies in China's stock markets is that the majority of the listed companies are SOEs. Those SOEs often are under the protection of the various levels of government. Although it is theoretically possible for an SOE to go under, practically speaking it is very difficult for this to happen because the government agencies will try all means to keep the company afloat.

Data and Methodology

The authors examine the performance of listed companies using data from the China Securities Regulatory Commission, covering a five-year period from 1995 to 1999. The advantage of skipping the early period of IPO data is obvious. The nature of the emerging stock markets in China may not warranty the availability and quality of the data. It is up to the authors to choose which time period to use in their study. There are other databases available in the market. For instance, the electronic database developed by the *Taiwan Economic Journal* covers a longer period, 1991 to 2000. That database also contains financial market information, such as stock prices and trading volumes.

The authors use the ANOVA method to detect the impact of IPO on performance with panel data. An alternative is to use the event-study method that can capture the impact of IPOs. For instance, if the performance data cover a six-year period, with the first three years covering the operations prior to the time of the IPO and the second three years covering data after the IPO, that may make the results more significant.

The Results

In the introduction and conclusion, the authors interpret the better performance of listed companies in industries such as utilities and finance as the result of their being "sunrise" industries. The reason is that those industries are underdeveloped; therefore the early movers can enjoy a better return. I would consider that the term "sunrise industry" is not a good explanation for those companies' outperformance of the others. An alternative explanation that is plausible is that, because those sectors are protected by the government, those firms are enjoying the monopoly rent.

The authors construct figure 7.1 to map the clusters of companies in the coordinates with the vertical axis denoting ROE, representing current performance, and the horizontal axis, growth rate of profit, representing the future growth potential. When the authors calculate the industry average, the means of all listed companies of both variables are used. This runs the risk of possible selection bias. A better benchmark is the average of all firms in China, not only the listed companies, which are not representative of all enterprises in China. Moreover, alternative combinations can be made between current profitability and Tobin's Q-ratio. The latter may reflect the monopoly rent or future unrealized profit.

Tables 7.3 to 7.5 show how the industry proxy is calculated. We must be very careful when summing measures of different natures together. Because of incompatibility among these individual measures, it is hard to make meaningful adjustments for the weight in each category. The equal-weight method looks arbitrary.

The authors report that the statistically significant indicators are EPS and ROE. That result is expected, because IPOs of an ongoing concern will introduce a dilution effect on both EPS and ROE because more shares are being issued. The result essentially indicates that an IPO has no economically significant impact on the performance of the privatized firms.

I now come back to the question in the title of the paper: What is corporate governance? In its narrow sense, the question of corporate governance should include the following issues: What is the composition of the board and the voting rules? Who are the board members? How are decisions made? How can the small shareholder's interests be protected? The authors do not address this problem directly.

The authors point out that corporate governance of those listed companies does not change much despite the so-called partial privatization. It is largely because the core of corporate governance does not change. The large shareholders are still government agencies and other SOEs. Only when ownership and corporate governance are changed fundamentally can one hope that China's stock markets will function as they should.

To sum up, the authors have done some interesting work. They show that stock market listings without fundamental change in the nature of the enterprises may not induce improvement in efficiency and performance of enterprises in China. Given that the majority of listed firms in China is still state owned and operated, this result does not seem surprising. Nevertheless, the results call for an effort to reform those enterprises.

Why Do Governments Dump State Enterprises?
Evidence from China

David D. Li and Francis T. Lui

8.1 Introduction

Should governments privatize state-owned enterprises (SOEs)? What is the impact of existing privatization programs? These are important research questions that have motivated an enormous amount of economic research during the past decade. According to a few recent literature surveys (Djankov and Murrell 2002; Megginson and Netter 2001; Toninelli 2000), the accumulated research seems to have converged on the view that privatization is critical to reform SOEs and many of the implemented privatization programs have had a positive impact on enterprise performance. Thanks to this research, our knowledge on these important questions has greatly improved.

But why do governments choose to privatize SOEs? More generally, why do governments choose to part with, or dump, SOEs by either transferring their ownership to private hands or liquidating the enterprises? In many ways, these are even more important and relevant questions than the opening questions that have generated the huge privatization literature. After all, there are no obvious reasons to believe that in reality governments faithfully follow economists' advice on major economic policy issues such as privatization. Policymakers often seem to have their own considerations and agenda. With a better understanding of why governments (do not) choose to privatize, the obstacles to efficiency-enhancing privatization might be

David D. Li is associate professor of economics and associate director of the Center for Economic Development at Hong Kong University of Science and Technology. Francis T. Lui is professor of economics and director of the Center for Economic Development at Hong Kong University of Science and Technology.

We thank Songnian Chen for helpful discussions and Tao Li for competent research assistance. All errors are our own.

identified and resolved and our economic analysis of privatization put to better use.

Unfortunately, there is a very limited literature on why governments choose to dump SOEs, although one can identify a few general streams of thinking on this issue. In some cases, there is limited formal research, especially empirical research, along each of the streams.

The first group of general theories argues that governments dump SOEs in order to enhance enterprise efficiency. In fact, most theoretical research on privatization simply starts from this premise and derives various predictions. Underlying this thinking is the belief that, somehow, the political marketplace is efficient and the equilibrium of the political game is economically efficient. In a larger context, Glaeser, Johnson, and Shleifer (2001) call this the Coasian theory of institutions. But why, in reality, does there seem to be a common phenomenon—that many efficiency-enhancing privatization programs fail to be implemented due to government objections? At least, we need empirical tests of such theories of government decisions of privatization.

The second line of thinking explains that governments dump state enterprises in order to enhance their revenue rather than efficiency.[1] Privatization or liquidation of SOEs may bring in sales revenues to the government. Privatization also may increase the future flow of tax revenue when the efficiency of the privatized enterprises increases enough and tax enforcement is strong enough. Finally, in the case of profit-losing SOEs, privatization or liquidation of such enterprises relieves governments of the burden of financial subsidies. In the Chinese context, Cao, Qian, and Weingast (1999) argue that governments privatize due to their facing harder budget constraints. However, without enterprise-level data, they cannot directly test this hypothesis. Using a data set of China's township and village enterprises, Brandt, Li, and Roberts (2001) find that when local banks faced tighter liquidity constraints, it was more likely that local collective enterprises were privatized. It is interesting to test this line of thinking against the first one.

The third line of thinking is that governments dump SOEs as a strategic move in political games. For example, it is often suggested that reformist politicians in Eastern Europe and the former Soviet Union chose mass privatization in order to secure political support for further reforms (see, e.g., Shleifer and Treisman 2000). In the context of Western Europe, it might be that conservative parties in power use privatization or liquidation of SOEs in order to weaken labor unions and therefore the political basis of the labor party of social democrats. For example, Biais and Perotti (1998) model

---

1. Under a set of strict conditions (including a perfect capital market, nondistortionary taxes, and a fully competitive product market), maximizing privatization revenue or government tax revenue or stopping financial losses is equivalent to maximizing social efficiency. We certainly do not think these conditions are satisfied in the economies we are concerned with.

how a right-wing government can use mass privatization to get reelected. Plausible as it is, this explanation for the motivation of privatization has yet to be put to systematic empirical tests.

The purpose of this chapter is to fill the gap in the literature by empirically testing competing theories of why governments dump (i.e., privatize or liquidate) SOEs. We are able to do this thanks to a unique data set of Chinese state enterprises, in which some were privatized or liquidated while the rest remained state owned. The focus of the test is on the first two groups of theories of government motivations of privatization, since in the Chinese context, political moves are often covert and we do not have reliable information on them. However, we are able to estimate the relative level of the political benefit of control to the government with SOEs.

In order to facilitate the test, we first set up a simple theoretical model that is general enough to incorporate various explanations as special cases. We then derive predictions of the simple model, linking them to the hypothesized government preference. Empirical estimations of the underlying parameters provide us with inferences on government preferences and therefore yield tests of different theories of why governments privatize.

Our simple model of privatization is based on a bargaining game between a government and the workers of the SOE. The government is assumed to have a general objective function consisting of the enterprise's efficiency and revenue contribution and the political benefit of control to the government. The issue of the burden of financial subsidies to poorly performing SOEs is also modeled by allowing the government to treat negative revenue asymmetrically from positive revenue. The workers care about employment (or unemployment) and total wages. Privatization or liquidation of SOEs may cause changes in efficiency, in total revenue to workers and the government, in employment, and in the political benefit of control of the government. These changes are anticipated by both parties when they negotiate the decision to privatize or liquidate, so that the equilibrium takes these factors into account.

The simple model predicts when privatization or liquidation is implemented based on the underlying parameters of the government objective function as well as changes to the SOE due to privatization. By testing this prediction against observed data on privatization, we are able to estimate the parameters of the government's objective function and therefore test different theories of privatization.

The empirical tests reject the efficiency theory while supporting the revenue theory. They show that none of the alternative measures of efficiency increases has predictive power with regard to the privatization-or-liquidation decision. On the other hand, increases in revenue to the government are important in predicting the decision. In particular, a significant factor inducing the privatization-liquidation decision is delayed loan and interest payment *when it becomes a financial burden to the government.*

That is, delayed loan and interest payment alone is not important. Moreover, other things being equal, the more surplus workers there are and the greater the government's political benefit of control of the enterprise, the less likely is the SOE to be privatized or liquidated. Overall, the main message of the tests is that governments dump SOEs not for the purpose of increasing efficiency but for enhancing tax revenue, or for relieving themselves of the financial burden of subsidizing profit-losing state enterprises.

Section 8.2 of the paper describes the simple model of privatization and its predictions. Section 8.3 explains the design of the empirical tests and measurement of variables. Test results are presented in section 8.4, and section 8.5 summarizes the paper with discussions on some policy implications.

8.2   A Simple Model of Privatization

Two parties are most critical in the privatization decision of a state enterprise, and the model focuses on them. The first is the government agency, which is in control of the senior managers of an SOE. The government agency and the senior managers of an SOE who are government officials can be viewed as one entity and have important decision rights in privatizing of the enterprise. The other party is the workers, who have been offered long-term employment by the SOE and can demand compensation when they become unemployed. For simplicity, we assume that both parties have to agree before a privatization decision can be made.

To be general, we suppose that the government may be concerned with three possible objectives associated with an enterprise: economic efficiency of the enterprise, revenue contribution from the enterprise to the government, and political benefit of control from the enterprise. The possible concern for efficiency comes from the government's desire to seek the society's economic prosperity. The preference for tax revenue is often argued to be common among bureaucrats of various kinds. Finally, government officials derive the political benefit of control by gaining direct control of an SOE, as many have illustrated (e.g., Kornai 1978, 1992). The general preference of the government is the same regardless of whether an SOE is privatized or not. But each of the entries in the objective function may change after privatization. In particular, the political benefit of control is supposed to be zero when the firm is private. We assume the relative weight on each of the three elements to be α, β, and 1, respectively. We can write the objective function of the government as

(1) $$W_G = \alpha t + \beta T + B,$$

where e is a measure of economic efficiency of the enterprise (whether it is state owned or privatized); T is the equivalent of per-period revenue the government gets, and B is the political benefit of control (which is zero when the enterprise is private).

A potentially important factor we need to model is the so-called *soft budget constraint,* which refers to the phenomenon that SOEs expect to be bailed out when in financial difficulty. An alternative way to interpret the soft budget constraint is that the government tolerates negative revenue, T, from the operation of the enterprise. The opposite of the soft budget constraint is the *hard budget constraint,* which makes the government feel extra pain with negative T and thus makes it likely to make changes in the operation of the enterprise rather than passively subsidize it. Based on this analysis, we introduce an extra term to equation (1) to capture the softness of the budget constraint:

$$(2) \qquad W_G = \alpha e + \beta T + \beta_S D(T)T + B$$

where $D(T) = 1$ if $T < 0$, and $D(T) = 0$ otherwise. The coefficient β_S is meant to capture the phenomenon of the soft budget constraint. The lower the value of β_S, the softer the budget constraint is. Intuitively, β_S is the extra pain a single unit of loss of profit causes to the government.

Turning to workers' objectives, we focus on two concerns. First, they are concerned with layoffs. Second, other things being equal, an increase in the total wage bill benefits all workers. Thus, a reduction in employment must be compensated by an increase in the total wage bill paid to the same group of workers in the form of wages and unemployment compensation. Let the size of employment be L and the per-period wage bill be W, and let the relative weights on them be 1 and γ, respectively. We write down the objective function of the workers as

$$(3) \qquad W_L = L + \gamma W.$$

An interpretation of the objective of the workers is that if the privatization results in the layoff of one worker, then the extra compensation paid to the worker must be γ.

We are now ready to analyze the conditions under which privatization may occur. Obviously, such a decision is an outcome of negotiations between the government and the workers, and compensation from the government to workers may be necessary. Suppose that M is the monetary equivalent of the monthly perpetual amount of transfer from the government to workers needed in order for the latter to agree to privatization.

In order for the workers to agree to a plan of privatization, it must be that

$$(4) \qquad \Delta W_L = \Delta L + \gamma(\Delta W + M) > 0,$$

where the differences are taken between the value of privatization and no privatization.

At the same time, the government must also find privatization to be worthwhile, i.e.,

$$(5) \qquad \Delta W_G = \alpha \Delta e + \beta(\Delta T - M) + \beta_S \Delta[D(T)T] + \Delta B > 0.$$

Multiplying equation (4) by β and equation (5) by γ and adding up the two multiplied inequalities, we have

(6) $\alpha\gamma\Delta e + \beta\Delta L + \beta\gamma(\Delta W + \Delta T) + \gamma\beta_S[\Delta D(T)T] + \gamma\Delta B > 0.$

We define

$$R = W + T,$$

which is the total amount of cash flow of the enterprise that can be divided among government and workers. Equation (6) can be rewritten as

(7) $\alpha\gamma\Delta e + \beta\Delta L + \beta\gamma\Delta R + \gamma\beta_S[\Delta D(T)T] + \gamma\Delta B > 0.$

We make two assumptions to further simplify equation (7). First, we assume that after privatization, there is no need for the government to bear a negative loss of the enterprise (i.e., T is always positive after privatization). We use T_S to denote the value of government revenue collection from SOEs. Second, the political benefit of control to the government after privatization is zero. We denote the political benefit of control associated with SOEs as B_S. Equation (7) can be simplified as

(8) $\alpha\gamma\Delta e + \beta\gamma\Delta R - \gamma\beta_S D(T_S)T_S + \beta\Delta L - \gamma B_S > 0.$

A simple interpretation of equation (8) is that in order for an SOE to be privatized, a combination of the efficiency gain, the increase in cash flow R, and the preprivatization profit-loss must be high enough to overcome the combination of the layoff of workers and the loss of political benefit of control of the government. Another way to interpret equation (8) is to look at the impact of the government's and the workers' preferences on the privatization decision. Other things being equal, a higher α (i.e., government's putting more weight on efficiency) makes privatization more likely to happen, since Δe is positive. When $\gamma\Delta R + \Delta L$ is positive, i.e., when the increase in cash flow from privatization is sufficient to compensate layoff of workers so that a surplus is left for the government, a higher β also makes privatization more likely to happen. Finally, so long as γ is not zero, a higher β_S (i.e., a harder budget constraint) makes privatization more plausible.

Notice that equation (8) is general enough for us to test various hypotheses of why privatization was implemented. Although we may not be able to identify each of the parameters of α, β, and γ, we will be able to estimate the coefficients on each of the variables of Δe, ΔR, $D(T_S)$, T_S, ΔL, and B_S. The hypothesis that efficiency gain is a cause of privatization can be tested by estimating the coefficient of Δe; the estimated coefficients of ΔR and $D(T_S)T_S$ are the bases for testing the hypotheses that increasing revenue, or hardening the budget constraint, are causes of privatization, respectively.

8.3   The Data and Design of the Empirical Tests

8.3.1   The Data Set

The data set we use is based on three surveys of several hundred Chinese SOEs covering the 1980–1999 period. The first survey was conducted in 1990 by a research team consisting of economists from the Chinese Academy of Social Sciences (CASS), Oxford University, and the University of Michigan. The survey has information on 769 SOEs from 1980 to 1989. The second survey was implemented in 1995 by researchers from the CASS and the University of Michigan, and collected information on the same group of enterprises from 1990 to 1994. Of the original 769 sample enterprises, 680 remained valid in the second survey. The third survey was sponsored by a consortium of researchers from mainland China, Hong Kong, and the United States. Carried out in early 2000, the survey obtained information retrospectively on the sampled enterprises from 1994 to 1999 (with overlapping information of 1994 for the purpose of quality control). Putting all three surveys together, we have a data set of a substantial number of China's SOEs throughout the twenty years of reform.

The sample of the enterprises came from four provinces and five sectors and represented mostly manufacturing firms. Unlike surveys of the SOEs conducted by government agencies, the two surveys were carefully designed and pilot-tested by economics researchers. The data set contains detailed information on the operations and financial information of the SOEs in the sample. It also contains qualitative information from the senior managements of the SOEs. The first part of the data set was widely used in studies such as Groves et al. (1994), Groves et al. (1995), and Li (1997).

What makes our empirical test possible is that in the third enterprise survey, conducted in 2000, about 200 of the original sample of 680 "disappeared"; i.e., these enterprises no longer existed at the time of survey in early 2000. Subsequently, the survey team made major efforts in finding out what happened to most of these enterprises. It turned out that the majority of these former SOEs were either privatized or liquidated (i.e., "dumped") by their supervising government agencies. The rest, of course, were still SOEs but were merged with other state enterprises and therefore disappeared from the sample.

The dumped SOEs fell into two large categories: privatization and bankruptcy/liquidation. There were several cases of privatization, including sales to private individuals (often, the chief manager) or private enterprises, mergers with township and village enterprises (TVEs), and takeovers by foreign enterprises. Figure 8.1 provides a breakdown of the major categories of the cases.

Regarding the dumped SOEs, the survey team could not get as detailed

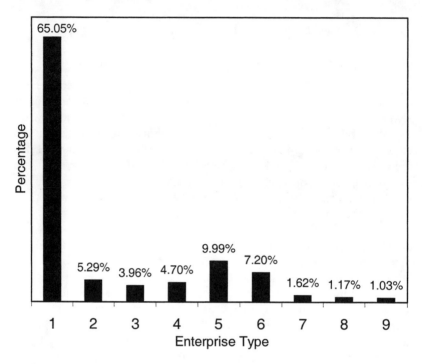

Fig. 8.1   Type distribution (all 681 enterprises)

Notes: 1 = SOEs without ownership changes; 2 = SOEs merged or acquired by other SOEs; 3 = SOEs acquired by foreign invested firms; 4 = SOEs acquired by urban collective enterprises; 5 = SOEs that were liquidated; 6 = SOEs in bankruptcy procedures; 7 = SOEs auctioned or leased out; 8 = SOEs that become share-holding cooperatives; 9 = SOEs that disappeared and could not be identified. We treat cases 3 to 8 as privatization or liquidation.

information about their operation after the ownership change as from before the change. The survey provides information on when the identity change happened, who bought the ownership shares of the enterprise (when relevant), and what happened to the workers (in many but not all cases).

8.3.2   The Design of the Econometric Test

Our empirical tests closely follow the theoretical model as summarized in inequality (8). Let y_i be the dependent variable, which is equal to 1 if enterprise i was dumped by the government between 1995 and 2000; otherwise it is zero. In our empirical tests, we do not distinguish the two subcategories of privatization and bankruptcy/liquidation, since the theoretical model is applicable to both cases. Our econometric model is

$$(9) \qquad \text{prob}\{y_i = 1\} = \text{prob}[\alpha\gamma\Delta e_i + \beta\gamma\Delta R_i - \gamma\beta_s D(T_{Si})T_{Si} \\ + \beta\Delta L_i - \gamma B_{Si} + \varepsilon_i > 0],$$

where all the variables are the same as those explained before and the error term ε_i is introduced due to omitted variables that we cannot observe. We assume that the error term follows a normal distribution. Due to the wide variations in the size of enterprises in the sample, it is unreasonable to assume that the error term has the same standard deviation across different enterprises. Instead, we believe that for larger firms, the privatization decision invokes more considerations not captured by the model. Therefore, we assume that the error term for large firms has a larger standard deviation than for small firms. In particular, we assume that the standard deviation of the error term is proportional to the size of the labor force of the firm. This means that in the actual implementation, we divide all of the independent variables by the size of the employment of the enterprise.

8.3.3   Measurement of Variables

The dependent variable y_i is zero for enterprises that remained state-owned by early 2000, including those that were merged with other SOEs. The variable y_i is equal to 1 if the ith enterprise had been either privatized or bankrupt/liquidated by 2000—corresponding to categories 3 to 8 in figure 8.1. From the point of view of the theory, both cases are the same, representing the situation that the government decided to get rid of control of the enterprise.

We measure the efficiency gain Δe_i in two alternative ways. First, we use an estimated increase in the gross rate of return on total assets of the enterprise after the identity change, whether it is actual or counterfactual. The gross rate of return on total assets is defined as the total amount of value-added of the enterprises (which is available to pay wages and bonuses, taxes, bank interest, etc.) divided by the total value of the assets. Unfortunately, we do not have data on the gross rate of return for those privatized SOEs. Neither do we have observations on the counterfactual cases of privatization for those unprivatized SOEs. Fortunately, in the last survey (conducted in 2000), we have a sample of about 300 non-state-owned enterprises. We calculate the average rate of return on assets for industry groups of these firms and use the averages for privatized SOEs. That is, Δe_i was constructed as the difference between the industry average gross rate of return on assets of non-state-owned enterprises and the average of SOEs from 1990 to 1994.

Alternatively, we measure Δe_i by potential increases in labor productivity when a privatized enterprise lays off those surplus workers while maintaining the same production level as before. In the surveys, enterprise managers provided information on the maximal amount of workers who could be laid off without affecting current production of the enterprise. In the case of liquidation, we still calculate the index. Under the assumption that productive workers (not including surplus workers) of the liquidated enterprise are transferred to a similar production facility in the same industry, the index also captures the potential productivity increase.

ΔR_i, which is the increase in total cash flow of the enterprise due to privatization or liquidation, cannot be fully observed in the data set due to the lack of information on the operation of privatized enterprises. By definition, ΔR_i is not a measure of social-welfare or social-efficiency gain, since it only affects the welfare of the government and workers. For example, cutting a surplus worker does not change ΔR_i, since the saved wage bill for the government comes from the same amount of loss of the affected worker. Cutting a surplus worker does increase social efficiency, as captured by Δe_i.

In order to implement the econometric model, we partially parameterize ΔR_i. We assume that ΔR_i consists of two parts: observed and unobserved. The observed part is based on the information of how the enterprise was losing profit before its potential identity change. The data set describes the percentage of the output that is losing profit. It is reasonable to assume that after being privatized or liquidated, the enterprise will sell the part of the asset that produces such outputs. The value of the assets, which is assumed to be proportional to the profit-losing output, constitutes part of the source of enhanced revenue for the government and workers. Using an interest rate of 5 percent, we convert the one-time increase in cash flow to perpetual increase in cash flow and define this as S_i. Moreover, through other channels, the privatization can also increase the total amount of cash flow for the government and workers to share. Not being able to observe it, we suppose it is proportional to the total value of the remaining asset. The proportion depends on observed attributions of the enterprise before being privatized, such as which industry the enterprise is in and how much reform it had implemented as an SOE. In summary, we assume

$$\Delta R_i = S_i + (a_1 \text{ industry}_1 + a_2 \text{industry}_2 + \ldots + a_j \text{industry}_j + b_1 \text{ reform}_1$$
$$+ \ldots a_R \text{ reform}_R) A_i + \eta_i,$$

where S_i is immediate and observable cost saving obtainable through privatization or liquidation; a_1 industry$_1$ . . . are industry dummies; reform$_1$ . . . are reform dummies, preprivatization; A_i is the value of asset of the enterprise; and η_i is the error term due to omitted variables, which is assumed to follow a normal distribution with standard deviation proportional to employment of the enterprise (an index of enterprise size), since for larger firms the estimation formula is likely to be disproportionately inaccurate.

T_i, which is the negative cash flow of the SOE borne by the government before privatization or liquidation, is estimated by two methods. The first alternative uses the average negative profit plus sale tax incurred by the enterprise for three years, 1992 to 1994. The other alternative is the total accumulated delayed bank loan and interest payment, which is a measure of cumulative poor financial performance. The advantage of using delayed bank loan and interest payment is that this reflects a longer-run problem than negative profit.

After using each of these variables in the regressions, we redo the regressions, multiplying them by an index of how much burden the poor performance of the enterprise created for the government. We call this sbc_i, which takes a value of zero if the manager of the SOE enterprise said that he did not get any help from the government in the case of dealing with delayed payment of bank loan. This is a case in which accumulated financial loss had not become a problem for the government. The value of sbc_i is 4 if the manager answered that he had obtained the most important help from the government on the issue. It takes a value of 1, 2, or 3 in the intermediate cases. The higher the value of sbc_i, the more burden the government felt facing each unit of financial loss of the enterprise.

ΔL_i, which is the reduction in employment due to the privatization or liquidation of the state enterprise (thus, it is mostly negative), can be calculated based on observed variables. For each case of privatization and liquidation, the survey has specific information on what happened to the workers; e.g., a certain percentage of workers were transferred to a unemployment agency and a certain percentage of workers were provided with new employment in the privatized enterprise. For those enterprises without identity changes, we use the total number of surplus workers as a proxy of ΔL_i, since those workers would most likely have been cut had the SOE been dumped.

Finally, for the political benefit of control associated with an SOE, B_i, we again have to parameterize due to the inability to observe. We suppose that B_i depends on the preprivatization size of employment, total value of fixed asset, and the level of the supervising government agency (central, provincial, or county). That is, we assume

$$B_i = c_i L_i + c_i V_i + c_i \text{Central}_i + c_i \text{Province}_i + c_i \text{County}_i + \rho_i,$$

where L_i is employment; V_i value of fixed asset; $\text{Central}_i, \ldots,$ are government-level dummies; and ρ_i is the error term due to omitted variables, which we assume to have a standard deviation proportional to the size of employment.

In summary, we estimate the following probit regression:

$$(10) \quad \text{prob}\{y_i = 1\} = \text{prob}\{\alpha\gamma\Delta e_i + \beta\gamma[S_i + (a_1\text{industry}_1$$
$$+ a_2\text{industry}_2 + \ldots + a_j\text{industry}_j + b_1\text{reform}_1$$
$$+ \ldots a_R\text{reform}_R)A_i] - \gamma\beta_S D(T_{Si})T_{Si} + \beta\Delta L_i$$
$$- \gamma(c_i L_i + c_i V_i + c_i \text{Central}_i + c_i \text{Province}_i$$
$$+ c_i \text{County}_i) + \delta_i > 0\},$$

where δ_i is the combined error term, which still follows a normal distribution with standard deviation proportional to the size of the enterprise (indexed by the size of employment).

122 Privatized or Liquidated Enterprises

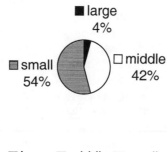

■ large □ middle ▨ small

559 Remaining State Enterprises

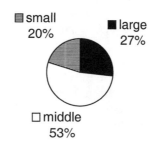

■ large □ middle ▨ small

Fig. 8.2   The sample distribution

8.4   Results of the Empirical Test

Among the 681 sample enterprises, 122 were either privatized or liquidated at any time between 1995 and 2000. The rest remained SOEs (see fig.
8.2 for details). Comparing the two groups of sample enterprises, one major difference is size. Among those privatized or liquidated, about 4 percent
were large enterprises, while 27 percent of those remaining SOEs were
large enterprises. This is consistent with the government policies of "let go
the small and medium and grab tight the large," which has been implemented since the early 1990s with regard to SOE reform. Our test takes this
into account.

Table 8.1 lists the summary statistics of the independent variables. Sev-

Table 8.1   **Summary Statistics of Regression Sample**

	Mean	SD
Privatized or liquidated enterprises		
Difference in rate of return on assets with/without privatization	0.07	0.28
Labor productivity improvement by cutting surplus labor	0.54	0.57
Difference in total employment with/without privatization	−234	1,049
Total assets used in unprofitable production	583.50	2871.40
Delayed loan and interest payment	133.14	365.49
(Index of the burden of subsidies) * (delayed loan and interest payment)	318.78	854.64
Profit loss	75.90	105.65
(Index of the burden of subsidies) * (profit loss)	130.59	236.06
Total employment, preprivatization	822	1,039
Total output, preprivatization	1,781.66	3600.84
Net fixed asset, preprivatization	913.76	1438.90
No. of observations	122	
Remaining state enterprises		
Difference in rate of return on assets with/without privatization	−0.07	0.26
Labor productivity improvement by cutting surplus labor	1.56	11.35
Difference in total employment with/without privatization	−641	1,192
Total assets used in unprofitable production	1,076.39	3,474.93
Delayed loan and interest payment	241.90	1,006.94
(Index of the burden of subsidies) * (delayed loan and interest payment)	450.10	1,904.59
Profit loss	96.66	261.81
(Index of the burden of subsidies) * (profit loss)	146.73	466.08
Total employment	2,214	3,740
Total output	10,633	32217
Net fixed asset	5,363.9	2,230.9
No. of observations	559	

Note: Unit = RMB 10,000 (wherever applicable). SD = standard deviation.

eral patterns are noticeable. Total employment, value of output, and fixed asset value are bigger for an average remaining SOE than for a privatized or liquidated enterprise. Likewise, the same pattern holds for such variables as change of employment, delayed loan payments, and total wage bill of surplus workers. However, the difference in the latter set of variables between the two groups of sample enterprises is proportionately much less than those of the former set of variables. Intuitively, using one of the former sets of variables as the weight, a regression using the latter group of variables should provide predicative powers. This is the statistical essence of the test results, which we explain below.

The estimation results of the probit regressions are given in table 8.2. There are a few consistent findings across the regressions. First, the results show that efficiency, whether measured by increases in the rate of return on assets or by improvements in labor productivity, is not a significant factor in the decision on privatization or liquidation. Second, the variables

Table 8.2 **Heteroskedastic Probit Regressions: The Determinants of State Enterprises' Privatization or Liquidation Decisions**

	Regression 1	Regression 2	Regression 3	Regression 4
Difference in rate of return on assets with/without privatization	−222.20*** (1.64)	−222.20***	−222.22*** (1.45)	−222.22***
Labor productivity improvement by cutting surplus labor		0.95 (0.19)		1.34 (0.26)
Difference in total employment with/ without privatization	1.37*** (4.38)	1.42*** (4.56)	1.32*** (4.18)	1.28*** (4.05)
Corporatization-reform dummy	0.11 (0.69)	0.12 (0.75)	0.11 (0.69)	0.13 (0.79)
Mining and utility industry	0.04 (0.21)	−0.03 (−0.13)	0.08 (0.35)	0.02 (0.08)
Light manufacturing industry	0.24 (1.32)	0.22 (1.27)	0.27 (1.45)	0.27 (1.46)
Chemical industry	−0.22 (−1.04)	−0.25 (−1.18)	−0.24 (−1.09)	−0.24 (−1.11)
Heavy manufacturing industry	0.01 (0.07)	−0.006 (−0.03)	0.05 (0.29)	0.06 (0.35)
Enterprise-size dummy	0.30*** (2.58)	0.33*** (2.77)	0.33*** (2.79)	0.36*** (3.01)
Total assets used in unprofitable production	0.11* (1.86)	0.12** (1.98)	0.05 (0.81)	0.04 (0.65)
Delayed loan and interest payment	−0.47 (−1.35)	−0.48 (−1.37)		
(Index of the burden of subsidies) · (delayed loan and interest payment)	0.35** (2.26)	0.35** (2.29)		
Profit loss			−0.82 (−0.79)	−0.37 (−0.39)
(Index of the burden of subsidies) · (profit loss)			0.93* (1.88)	0.86* (1.78)
Total employment, preprivatization	−0.37** (−2.15)	−0.29* (−1.73)	−0.39** (−2.22)	−0.38** (−2.15)
Total output, preprivatization	−0.16*** (−4.38)	−0.18*** (−4.81)	−0.15*** (−4.02)	−0.16*** (−4.25)
Net fixed asset, preprivatization	−0.34* (−1.81)	−0.31* (−1.73)	−0.39** (−2.03)	−0.39** (−2.05)
Central-government dummy	−67.10 (−0.27)	−88.27 (−0.36)	−74.77 (−0.31)	−72.05 (−0.30)
Province-government dummy	−328.55** (−2.14)	−318.44** (−2.14)	−370.02** (−2.43)	−364.83** (−2.47)
City-government dummy	−58.80 (−0.58)	−70.83 (−0.70)	−84.57 (−0.84)	−93.26 (−0.93)
Constant	417.09*** (3.91)	400.32*** (3.75)	443.86*** (4.21)	429.15*** (4.07)
No. of observations	652	657	652	651
R^2	0.2889	0.2864	0.2842	0.2824

Notes: Dependent variable = 1 if privatized or liquidated, 0 otherwise. We assume the standard deviation of the error term is proportional to size of employment. Z-ratios are in parentheses.

***Significant at the 1 percent level.

**Significant at the 5 percent level.

*Significant at the 10 percent level.

Table 8.3   **Increases in the Probability of Privatization or Liquidation Due to Increments in Independent Variables**

	Regression 1	Regression 2	Regression 3	Regression 4
Difference in total employment with/ without privatization	0.6127	0.5901	0.5962	0.5732
Enterprise-size dummy (from large to small or medium)	0.0002	0.0001	0.00005	0.00005
Total assets used on unprofitable production	0.0827	0.1042		
(Index of the burden of subsidies) · (delayed loan and interest payment)	0.0555	0.0340	0.0493	0.0405
Total employment, preprivatization	−0.0663	−0.0441	−0.0758	−0.0610
Total production value, preprivatization	−0.0681	−0.0466	−0.0774	−0.0621
Net fixed assets, preprivatization	−0.0681	−0.0466	−0.0774	−0.0621
Province-government dummy (from having a nonprovincial to a provincial supervising government agency)	−0.0388	−0.0275	−0.0475	−0.0391

Notes: Probability change under standard normal distribution assumption. Omitted are those independent variables which are not statistically significant. Except for the dummy variables, the amount of increase in all independent variables is 1 standard deviation of the variable.

measuring changes in available cash flow for the government and workers are mostly positive and statistically significant, supporting the hypothesis that the privatization or liquidation decision is driven by increasing government revenue. Third, although the total delayed loan plus interest payment is not statistically significant, it becomes significant when multiplied by the index of the burden of financial subsidies, which is zero if the enterprise obtained no help from the government in dealing with loan payment and 4 if it received the most important help from the government. In other words, the accumulated dept per se is not a cause pushing for privatization or liquidation. But when a high level of bad debt becomes a major financial burden to the government, it is effective in inducing the privatization or liquidation decisions of the government. Finally, the regressions show that the larger the unemployment associated with privatization or liquidation, the less likely the government will be to dump the SOE, as the coefficients on the unemployment term are negative and statistically significant.

How economically significant are the variables in affecting the decision of privatization or liquidation? Table 8.3 calculates the increases in the probability of privatization or liquidation due an increase in those statistically significant variables. It shows that a 1-standard-deviation increase in layoff due to privatization or liquidation decreases the probability of privatization or liquidation by 57 to 61 percent. A similar change in total assets used in unprofitable production increases the probability by 8 to 10 percent. Similar changes in delayed loan and interest payment multiplied by the index of the burden of subsidies increases the probability by 3 to 5 percent.

8.5   Concluding Remarks

The enormous amount of literature on privatization has mostly focused on the question of whether and how governments should privatize SOEs as well as on the impact of existing privatization programs. We argue that an equally important question is why governments in reality (do not) choose to dump SOEs through privatization or liquidation. The lack of research on this question leaves us with three general theories, explaining that governments dump SOEs in order to maximize economic efficiency, government revenue, and political benefits.

Utilizing panel data from China, in which some SOEs were dumped and others remained state owned, we are able to test the efficiency and revenue theories of why governments privatize or liquidate SOEs. The tests reject the efficiency theory and provide support for the revenue theory. In addition, the findings reveal that the motive of getting rid of the financial burden of subsidizing poorly performing SOEs is important. Moreover, we find that avoiding unemployment and losing the government's political benefits of control of SOEs are important considerations preventing privatization or liquidation decisions.

On privatization issues, economists tend to propose the first-best programs, aiming at maximizing social efficiency. However, the findings in the paper show that, in reality, the key decision maker, the government, takes revenue maximization as an objective and is concerned with unemployment. First-best programs are often blocked by the government. Therefore, in order for a privatization program to be feasible, it might be sensible to advocate second-best programs of privatization or liquidation that take government concerns into account while enhancing social efficiency.

References

Biais, B., and E. Perotti. 1998. Machiavellian underpricing. Institut d'Economie Industrielle. Mimeograph.

Brandt, Lauren, Hongbin Li, and Joanne Roberts. 2001. Why do governments privatize? University of Toronto, Department of Economics. Mimeograph.

Cao, Yuanzheng, Yingyi Qian, and Barry Weingast. 1999. From federalism, Chinese style to privatization, Chinese style. *Economics of Transition* 7 (1): 103–131.

Djankov, Simeon, and Peter Murrell. 2002. Enterprise restructuring in transition: A quantitative survey. *Journal of Economic Literature* 40 (September): 739–792.

Glaeser, Edward, Simon Johnson, and Andrei Shleifer. 2001. Coase v. the Coasians. *Quarterly Journal of Economics* 16 (3): 853–899.

Groves, Theodore, Yongmaio Hong, John McMillan, and Barry Naughton. 1995. China's evolving managerial labor market. *Journal of Political Economy* 103 (4): 873–892.

Groves, Theodore, Yongmaio Hong, Barry Naughton, and John McMillan. 1994. Autonomy and incentives in China's state enterprises. *Quarterly Journal of Economics* 109 (1): 183–210.

Kornai, Janos. 1978. The firm: Budget constraint and profit. Chapter 13 in *Economics of shortage.* Amsterdam: North-Holland.

———. 1992. *The socialist system.* New York: Cambridge University Press.

Li, Wei. 1997. The impact of economic reform on the performance of Chinese state enterprises, 1980–1989. *Journal of Political Economy* 105 (5): 1080–106.

Megginson, William L., and Jeffry M. Netter. 2001. From State to market: A survey of empirical studies on privatization. *Journal of Economic Literature* (June): 321–389.

Shleifer, Andrei, and Daniel Treisman. 2000. *Without a map: Political tactics and economic reform in Russia.* Cambridge: MIT Press.

Toninelli, Pier Angelo. 2000. *The rise and fall of state-owned enterprise in the Western world.* Cambridge: Cambridge University Press.

Comment   Deunden Nikomborirak

This paper tries to explain the underlying governments' motivation in privatizing public enterprises by using empirical data from over 600 SOEs, about 120 of which "disappeared" during the 1994–2000 period. The conclusion is that governments privatize SOEs mainly to generate revenue rather than to promote efficiency and that the government is particularly concerned about the loss of political benefits associated with public enterprises. While I find the attempt to conduct empirical tests on government motivation for privatization interesting, the lack of sufficient data on post-privatization enterprises renders the empirical support for said conclusions quite weak.

First, one must be careful in trying to form conclusions with regard to *ex ante* motivation by using *ex post* data. Motivations are based on expected rather than actual results. Second, the classification of privatized enterprises on the basis of state equity shares may not be appropriate. According to the authors, privatized enterprises include state enterprises that are liquidated, bankrupt, or sold to private individuals. It is not certain, however, whether the selling of state enterprises always translates into transfer of corporate control to the private sector. For example, if the government retains a minority share, does that mean that the privatized entity functions completely like a private enterprise? If not, we cannot expect the privatized entity to operate any differently simply from the partial transfer of

Deunden Nikomborirak is research director for economic governance in the sectoral economics program at the Thailand Development Research Institute.

state equity ownership to the private sector. Third, proxies used to capture the three different motives for privatization—namely, efficiency, revenue generation, and political benefits—have several flaws, as will be elaborated below.

The use of financial performance (i.e., gross rate of return) as a proxy for efficiency may not be appropriate if the market is not competitive such that higher profit does not mean lower cost. It is also possible that the privatized state enterprises lose their privileges so that, while they may become more efficient, their profit levels fall as a result of greater competition. Due to the lack of information on the privatized enterprises, the paper assumes that the ex-SOEs' level of efficiency matches those of competing private companies. This is quite a strong assumption given that former SOEs may retain some of their former privileges or corporate practices.

The paper also tries to estimate the change in the size of cash flow as a proxy for the revenue-generation motive. Again, due to the absence of data on privatized companies, the authors assume that extra revenue is generated from the one-time sale of the loss-generating portion of the business, which is estimated by the percentage of output associated with losses. For example, if 20 percent of the output constitutes the loss-generating portion, it is assumed that 20 percent of the asset will be sold off. The additional revenue, then, is generated by the perpetual flow of interest earnings from the asset sale. I find this method of estimating additional cash flow rather crude. First, for firms that produce many products or services, it is almost impossible to determine which products or services generate losses. Second, assuming that assets can be divided up in proportion to output is unrealistic. Finally, asset valuation is one of the most difficult processes. Thus, one should avoid using asset values as proxies unless a very thorough method of asset evaluation is undertaken.

Besides the sale of assets, the authors assume that there are unobserved flows of additional revenues generated from privatization that are proportional to the remaining assets. The proportion depends on the observed attributes of the enterprise, such as the industry to which it belongs and how much reform has been implemented before. These are extremely vague proxies and there are no clear explanations of how these variables add to the additional flow of revenue.

Another variable that represents the revenue motivation is the reduction in government subsidies. Two proxies were used: One is the average actual subsidy during 1992–1994, which is valid; the other is the accumulated bank loan and interest payment, which is supposed to reflect the level of financial burden of the government. The latter is multiplied by an "index of burden to the government." This index takes the value of zero if the manager of the particular SOE claims that the enterprise does not receive assistance from the government in case of delayed payments of loan, and a value of 4 if the manager claims that government financial assistance is readily available. I find this method of estimating government perceived financial burden rather arbitrary and subjective, undermining the validity of statistical results.

Finally, the proxies used for the political benefits associated with an SOE include the size of employment, total value of fixed assets, and level of supervising government agency. While regression results show that these variables are statistically significant, it is not certain that the chosen variables necessarily contribute to political benefits. For example, the fact that large SOEs are less likely to be privatized may be because of the more complicated nature of the privatization, the limited size of the capital market, or the government's unwillingness to generate large-scale unemployment, rather than the loss of political benefits.

The final point I would like to comment on is the lack of time dimension. All variables are estimated and compared on a per-period basis, while in reality government needs and demands are more immediate, due to future uncertainties and various short-run constraints. In fact, short-sightedness has been quoted as one of the reasons governments are likely to forgo potential long-term efficiency gains that are uncertain and dispersed, while favoring immediate financial gains from sales of SOEs by ensuring that the privatized SOEs maintain privileges that they used to enjoy.

Comment   Yun-Wing Sung

The authors of the article have a unique data set covering Chinese SOEs throughout twenty years of the reform era (1980–1999). The data are used to test two theories of privatization: whether governments privatize to enhance enterprise efficiency (efficiency theory) or to increase government revenue (revenue theory). The test rejects the efficiency theory and supports the revenue theory. The authors have used a unique data set to address the *positive* question, "Why do governments privatize?" It is a very valuable contribution to the literature.

The authors distinguish between enterprise efficiency and government revenue enhancement, which are quite different. However, the authors do not distinguish between enterprise efficiency and social efficiency, which also can be quite different, especially under the conditions in China. For instance, given arbitrary prices, which were quite prevalent in China in the 1980s, an enterprise suffering losses nevertheless may be socially efficient. The losses may be due to artificially inflated prices of input, or depressed

Yun-Wing Sung is professor in and chairman of the department of economics at the Chinese University of Hong Kong.

prices of output. In such a case, closing down the enterprise may lead to a loss of social welfare.

For the purpose of the paper, enterprise efficiency is the appropriate concept to use. As the authors have correctly argued, gains in enterprise efficiency are reflected in increase in rates of return to total assets after privatization. Unfortunately, the authors have a tendency to use the concepts of "enterprise efficiency" and "social efficiency" interchangeably. For instance, in their discussion on the measurement of "efficiency gain, which should refer to gains in enterprise efficiency, the authors argued that "Cutting a surplus worker does increase *social efficiency* [italics added], as captured by Δe_i." Cutting a surplus worker will increase enterprise efficiency. Whether it increases social efficiency is quite uncertain. If the worker remains unemployed after layoff, there is no change in social efficiency.

In the concluding section of the paper, the authors again refer to social efficiency. They seemed to have assumed that gains in enterprise efficiency would automatically lead to gains in social efficiency. The authors should have distinguished between the two concepts and spelled out the conditions under which gains in enterprise efficiency would lead to gains in social efficiency.

9

Productivity Effects of TVE Privatization
The Case Study of Garment and Metal-Casting Enterprises in the Greater Yangtze River Region

Tetsushi Sonobe and Keijiro Otsuka

9.1 Introduction

Until the 1980s, China's miraculous economic growth had been led by publicly owned township and village enterprises (TVEs), which may be more accurately termed township- and village-*run* enterprises, or TVREs (Chen, Jefferson, and Singh 1992; Jefferson, Rawski, and Zheng 1996; Otsuka, Liu, and Murakami 1998).[1] In the 1990s, however, the private sector emerged to become the leading sector of the economy in China. In the southeastern part of Jiangsu province, where the successful record of economic development based on TVREs in the 1980s was dubbed the "Sunan Model of Industrial Development," the privatization of TVREs was taking place in the late 1990s. Further, the growth rate of the Zhejiang province, which depended consistently on the growth of the private sector beginning in the 1980s, outweighed that of most other provinces, including Jiangsu, in the 1990s (Zhang 1999).

By now it is well known that privatization has been taking place rapidly and widely in China, but it is much less well known whether, and to what extent, privatization has improved resource allocation and productivity.[2] The major question addressed in this study is, what are the productivity

Tetsushi Sonobe is professorial fellow at the Foundation for Advanced Studies on International Development and professor at the National Graduate Research Institute for Policy Studies. Keijiro Otsuka is professorial fellow at the Foundation for Advanced Studies on International Development and professor at the National Graduate Research Institute for Policy Studies.

We would like to thank Yang Yao, Yun-Wing Sung, John McMillan, and Simon Johnson for helpful comments.

1. Note that TVEs include both TVREs and private enterprises.
2. An exceptional and pioneering study is Li and Rozelle (2000).

effects of TVE privatization? If the recent privatization results in the improvement of production efficiency, then why did it not take place earlier? Also, it is interesting to ask why TVREs prospered in Jiangsu in the 1980s. These issues are critically important in understanding the growth performance of the Chinese economy in the 1990s and in assessing its future growth potential for the early decades of the twenty-first century.

As a first step toward a fuller understanding of the effects of TVE privatization on productivity, this study looks at the garment and metal-casting enterprises in the Greater Yangtze River Region, extending from the suburbs of Shanghai to the western border of Anhui province. Among the common and important characteristics of TVREs in the suburbs of Shanghai and southern Jiangsu are their dependence on state-owned enterprises (SOEs) in technology, management, and marketing (Otsuka, Liu, and Murakami 1998). Some TVREs used to be cooperative TVEs or "branch factories" of urban SOEs; managers were sent from SOEs and the profits were shared between them in accordance with their investment shares (Fudan University Economic Research Center 1988). "Putting-out contracts" frequently were made, not only between SOEs and their branches but also between SOEs and independent TVREs. Moreover, TVREs often purchased second-hand machines used by SOEs and employed retired SOE workers in order to acquire the technology and management know-how of the SOEs (Murakami, Liu, and Otsuka 1994, 1996). It seems that township and village governments supported such transactions and cooperation through their direct involvement in enterprise management.[3]

Our maintained hypothesis is that this cooperation between TVREs and SOEs was mutually beneficial, at least in the light industries during the 1980s.[4] TVREs faced largely unregulated management environments, but lacked technology, management know-how, and marketing capacity. In contrast, the management of SOEs was tightly regulated, even though they had decent management, technology, and marketing knowledge. In the 1990s, two major changes seem to have taken place, which eroded the advantage of the TVRE-SOE cooperation. First, TVREs absorbed the production knowledge and capacity of SOEs, so that the payoff to maintaining cooperative relationships with SOEs gradually declined (Liu and Otsuka 1998). Second, a free-market system developed, so that direct government support for inter-enterprise transactions, particularly face-to-face transactions between TVREs and SOEs in our context, tended to lose significance (Li 1996; Hsiao et al. 1998; Jin and Qian 1998; Chen and Rozelle 1999). Therefore, we hypothesize that privatization in the late 1990s re-

3. This view is consistent with the justification of TVREs by Che and Qian (1998), who argue that the advantage of local government ownership lies in reduction of state predation.
4. Lin and Yao (2001) contend that the development of the SOE sector tended to help the development of the TVE sector in the light industries, whereas the opposite was the case in the heavy industries.

sulted in significant improvements in production efficiency by enhancing management incentives without sacrificing marketing efficiencies.

The organization of this paper is as follows. In the next section, our sampling scheme is explained, and the basic statistics of our sample enterprises, such as the growth rate of valued-added, are presented. In section 9.3, we examine the changing importance of subcontracting transactions with SOEs and the changing distribution of stock ownership by the local government vis-à-vis private owners. Then we assess the impacts of privatization on productivity by estimating a function that explains the growth rate of per-worker value-added, separately for the garment and metal-casting industries, in section 9.4. The implications of this study are discussed in the final section.

9.2 Data

To analyze the determinants and consequences of TVRE privatization, we use data collected by a rural-enterprise survey conducted in 1999 and 2000 in the Greater Yangtze River Region, from the suburbs of Shanghai to about 650 kilometers upstream. The study includes five counties in the suburbs of Shanghai, nineteen counties in the south of the Yangtze River in Jiangsu province, and twenty-nine counties between the Yangtze and the Huai He rivers in Anhui province. These areas are connected by an expressway that goes from Shanghai along the Yangtze River to Nanjing, the capital city of Jiangsu, crosses the river from south to north, and then goes west up to and beyond Hefei, the capital city of Anhui. The sample enterprises were selected randomly from the enterprise lists compiled by the local governments of twenty-eight counties selected randomly from the fifty-three counties. The garment and casting samples consist of seventy-eight and eighty enterprises, respectively.

We chose specific industries for our case studies, partly because the productivity impacts of privatization cannot be assessed unless we can reasonably assume identical production function parameters among sample enterprises. We chose the Greater Yangtze River Region because the influence of SOEs in Shanghai, a center of the state industrial sectors in China, tends to decline with distance from Shanghai, so there are sufficient geographical variations of the influence of SOEs. The garment and the casting industries were chosen partly because they have numerous enterprises over wide areas and partly because their dependence on SOEs is so different: As of 2000, the metal-casting enterprises depend wholly on SOEs in both input and output transactions, whereas the garment enterprises are far more independent of SOEs.

The retrospective survey of enterprises provides information on production and costs as well as on changing distributions of ownership shares during the 1995–1998 period, and information on equipment and market-

Table 9.1   **Average Annual Growth Rates of Real Value-Added by Study Area, 1995–1998 (%)**

	Shanghai (1)	Southeast Jiangsu (2)	Southwest Jiangsu (3)	Anhui (4)	Total (5)
Garment industry					
Growth rate	8.8	9.4	13.5	25.9	15.4
No. of observations	8	14	18	16	56
Casting industry					
Growth rate	−13.0	2.2	−3.2	7.5	1.1
No. of observations	4	14	20	20	58

ing channels in 1995 and 1998. Table 9.1 shows the growth rate of real value-added of the sample enterprises and the number of observations by area. In this study, value-added was calculated as the gross value of output minus material cost, energy cost, and payments to shipping agencies and wholesalers. We applied the method of double deflation to the survey data on nominal value-added, in order to obtain real value-added at the 1998 price.[5] The data of real value-added in both 1995 and 1998 are only complete for fifty-six enterprises in the garment industry and fifty-eight in the casting industry, particularly because of the entry of new enterprises after 1995.[6] For descriptive exposition, we classified the study areas into four regions: the suburbs of Shanghai, southeast Jiangsu, southwest Jiangsu, and Anhui.

Southeast Jiangsu is a traditionally fertile granary area and is close to Shanghai. With these geographical advantages, the economy in this area started to grow rapidly with the development of TVREs, as soon as the central government began the economic reforms of the late 1970s. By the early 1990s, the successful TVRE-led development strategy pursued in this area became widely known under the name "Sunan Model of Industrial Development." Since the early 1990s, however, the Sunan model has been chal-

5. The price indexes of products of the Garment and Other Fiber Products industry and the Smelting and Pressing of Ferrous Metals industry, assessed at the factory gate by the State Statistical Bureau (various years), were used as deflators for garment and casting products, respectively. Since price data on shipping and marketing services are not available, we applied the same deflator as the output to these services. As deflators for materials in the garment and the casting industries, we used the factory price index of products of the Textile industry and the Smelting and Pressing of Ferrous Metals industry, respectively. As a deflator for energy cost, we used the electricity price data in the case of the garment sample and the coal price data in the case of the casting sample, both of which are provided by the State Statistical Bureau (various years).

6. Each sample includes several new entrants established in 1995, 1996, or 1997. Those firms established in 1998 were excluded from the sample. The production data in the first year of operation of new entrants were not used in the analysis because variables in the first year have incomparably greater variances than those in subsequent years.

lenged by another model of industrial development formed in and around the city of Wenzhou in Zhejiang province, where the economy has been catching up with southeast Jiangsu despite starting from a much lower level of development (Zhang 1999; Sonobe, Hu, and Otsuka 2002a). In this "Wenzhou Model of Industrial Development," high economic growth is driven by private enterprises and "disguised" TVREs, which were essentially private but disguised themselves as TVREs because private enterprises were treated unfavorably by various regulations.

TVREs were also developed in southwest Jiangsu, including in Nanjing. Probably because Nanjing is the capital of Jiangsu province, there were a larger number of SOEs and urban collective enterprises in this area than in southeast Jiangsu. Accordingly, the relative importance of the TVRE sector was smaller in this area than in southeast Jiangsu. In Anhui, where manufacturing was least developed among the areas we study, the share of the SOE sector in gross industrial output was greatest, although the absolute size of the SOE sector was much smaller than in the other areas of study.[7] It is interesting to note that the share of private enterprises and self-employed, small-scale family enterprises in Anhui province was greater than in the other areas we study in 1995 and earlier.[8] This is consistent with the hypothesis that the development of the private sector predominated in poor areas with few SOEs because local governments in those areas could not afford to establish a large number of TVREs in cooperation with SOEs.

As shown in table 9.1, the average size of enterprises, in terms of their real value-added, grew in all areas in the garment sample but declined in Shanghai and southwest Jiangsu in the casting sample from 1995 to 1998.[9] One factor that made the casting industry stagnant or declining was the antipollution regulation in urbanized areas. The regulation was most stringent in Shanghai, where the municipal government prohibited the expansion and renewal of foundries. Customers shifted orders away from foundries in Shanghai to other areas where environmental regulations were looser, especially to southeast Jiangsu. As a result, casting enterprises in southeast Jiangsu had a much better growth record than their counterparts in southwest Jiangsu as well as in Shanghai. However, casting enterprises in Anhui were growing even faster. In the garment sample, the average growth rate increases with distance from Shanghai. Thus, in both the casting and garment samples, enterprises in Anhui were growing faster than in any other areas we study. This suggests that patterns of compara-

---

7. Data of industrial output and its composition by sector, aggregated at the provincial level, are available from the statistical bureaus of Jiangsu and Anhui provinces (various years).

8. The self-employed enterprises are those with seven or fewer workers.

9. In a discussion of growth performance, attention should be paid to effects of business cycles.

tive advantage in the coastal and central regions were changing significantly within labor-intensive industries (such as the garment industry) and polluting industries (such as the casting industry).

A unique feature of our enterprise survey is that it traces the changing distribution of ownership within each sample enterprise since its establishment. Officially registered ownership types (such as TVRE, shareholding, joint share, foreign joint venture, and private) could be misleading, as the episodes of numerous "disguised" TVREs in Wenzhou suggest. Such enterprises also existed in Jiangsu, according to our own survey. Moreover, such categorization offers no information on increases in private ownership shares if the registered ownership type of the enterprise remains the same. Thus, for the purpose of measuring the extent of privatization, it is more desirable to use continuous indicators of ownership rather than categorical variables. In practice, the privatization of an enterprise begins with an estimate of the capitalized value of its assets. Then, the shares of various owners (e.g., the township government, which invested primarily at the time of the enterprise's establishment, and the enterprise itself, which reinvested profits) are determined according to their previous investments and services. Hence, the ownership distribution becomes clear after capitalization. To trace the ownership distribution before capitalization, we simply relied on the subjective assessment of key informants, who were usually general managers.

As shown in table 9.2, we classified owners into five types: (1) local government, (2) SOEs, (3) workers, (4) joint ventures with foreign enterprises, and (5) private owners. In this classification, SOEs include urban collective enterprises. Private owners include, most importantly, the general manager and other leaders within the enterprise, and a relatively small number of individuals and enterprises outside the enterprise except SOEs and joint ven-

Table 9.2   Changing Distribution of Ownership Shares, 1995–1998 (%)

	Local Government (1)	SOEs (2)	Workers (3)	Foreign and Joint Ventures (4)	Private Owners (5)	Total (6)
Garment industry						
1995	59.6	5.0	0.5	11.3	23.6	100
1996	54.9	5.3	0.5	11.5	27.7	100
1997	42.5	6.4	2.4	12.0	36.7	100
1998	28.6	5.5	2.7	12.0	51.2	100
Casting industry						
1995	77.4	4.1	0.6	2.0	15.9	100
1996	65.7	5.0	1.5	3.3	24.5	100
1997	48.7	6.3	4.6	2.8	37.6	100
1998	28.5	7.1	9.2	2.1	53.1	100

tures. In the garment sample, there were a number of enterprises that had experienced partial privatization before 1995, as reflected in private ownership of as high as 23.6 percent. In the casting sample, most enterprises were 100 percent owned in 1995 by the local government, at least nominally; there were also a small number of completely private enterprises, most of which were outgrowths of self-employed, family enterprises. Thus, the average ownership share of local governments was much higher in the casting sample in 1995. In both samples, however, the pace of privatization accelerated, and the average ownership share of local governments decreased to less than 30 percent and that of private owners increased to more than 50 percent in 1998. Presumably, this is not a mere coincidence but a result of the increasing pressure that the central government put on local governments to fully privatize their TVREs.

In the literature on ambiguous property rights in China, a central question is why TVREs could achieve remarkable growth performance in the 1980s and the early 1990s, despite the disincentive effect of the ambiguous ownership of TVREs on enterprise management. A plausible answer to this question is that the market in this period in China was characterized by high transaction costs, which could be reduced by the intervention of local governments (Li 1996; Hsiao et al. 1998; Jin and Qian 1998; Chen and Rozelle 1999). We emphasize that such transaction costs were particularly high when transactions were made with SOEs (although that is not mentioned in this literature). As free-market transactions developed, however, it is likely that the government support for transactions and the cooperation between TVREs and SOEs gradually have lost significance. If this is the case, privatization ought to increase the production efficiency of rural enterprises. In order to examine the relevance of these arguments, we look more carefully at the production data in the next two sections.

9.3 Privatization and Growth in the Garment Industry

Garment enterprises in our sample produce a variety of products ranging from cheap underwear to expensive and technically difficult products such as men's suits. In view of the presumed importance of marketing channels, we classify these products into original products, which are designed and marketed by the sample enterprises themselves, and those produced under subcontracting with large enterprises, such as SOEs and foreign joint ventures. Although many of the sample enterprises in southeast Jiangsu used to be cooperative TVEs or branch factories of SOEs in Shanghai before free-market transactions were developed, they are now transacting with a number of SOEs and other enterprises. While subcontracting has several forms, such as "putting out" and original equipment manufacturing (OEM), we do not distinguish them because such distinctions are prac-

Table 9.3   Composition of Sales Revenue, Garment Industry, 1995 and 1998 (%)

	Original Products	Subcontracting		Total
		With SOEs	With Other Enterprises	
1995				
Shanghai	23.8	22.9	53.3	100
Southeast Jiangsu	18.0	45.6	36.4	100
Southwest Jiangsu	26.8	32.1	41.1	100
Anhui	29.4	49.0	21.6	100
Total	24.9	39.0	36.1	100
1998				
Shanghai	23.7	17.9	58.4	100
Southeast Jiangsu	15.7	37.2	47.1	100
Southwest Jiangsu	25.4	28.3	46.3	100
Anhui	26.4	38.7	34.9	100
Total	23.1	32.0	44.9	100

tically impossible for some sample enterprises. Instead, we distinguish subcontracting with SOEs from subcontracting with other types of enterprises.

Table 9.3 shows the composition of original products, and subcontracting with SOEs and other enterprises, in sales revenues by study area in 1995 and 1998. Compared with Zhejiang province, in our study areas the garment enterprises, especially those in southeast Jiangsu, have high skills and use expensive equipment to produce high-quality products, but they are behind in establishing their own marketing networks. Consistent with this argument, the proportion of original products to sales revenue in southeast Jiangsu in 1995 is as low as 18 percent, and that of subcontracting with SOEs is as high as 45.6 percent. One possible explanation for such marked differences between this area and Zhejiang is that the garment enterprises in southeast Jiangsu could afford to invest in expensive machines by taking advantage of their geographical proximity to Shanghai to receive subcontracting orders from SOEs and foreign ventures. Although the garment enterprises in Anhui did not have an advantage in this respect, they did have high shares of subcontracting with SOEs because they tended to follow the Sunan model; that is, they had a high propensity to subcontract with relatively small local SOEs and urban collectives.

Table 9.4 compares the ownership shares of the local government between enterprises heavily dependent on SOE subcontracting and the other sample enterprises. In 1995, SOE subcontracting accounted for more than half of the sales revenue at twenty-four sample enterprises; they had a much higher average ownership share of the local government and a lower average share of private owners than the other sample enterprises. This suggests that the local government's involvement in enterprise manage-

Table 9.4   **Ownership Share by Transaction Mode, Garment Industry, 1995 and 1998 (%)**

	Enterprises with >50% SOE Subcontracting in 1995 (1)	Enterprises with ≤50% SOE Subcontracting in 1995 (2)	Total (3)
1995			
Local government's ownership share	73.1	49.2	59.6
Private share	15.5	29.6	23.6
1998			
Local government's ownership share	27.9	28.5	28.6
Private share	55.1	48.3	51.2
No. of observations	24	32	56

ment was helpful in making and maintaining subcontracting contacts with SOEs in 1995. By 1998, however, there was a reversal in the relationship between ownership pattern and transaction mode, in which those enterprises heavily dependent on SOE subcontracting tended to have lower government shares and higher private shares. This reversal is consistent with our maintained hypothesis that the local government's support for subcontracting with SOEs lost its significance in this industry during the period under study.

Privatization, which clarifies ambiguous property rights by increasing managers' ownership shares, would enhance the profit-seeking incentives of managers. If the local government's support for subcontracting with SOEs lost its importance, then privatization would improve production efficiency without sacrificing transaction efficiencies. To date, however, few empirical studies have assessed the productivity effects of TVRE privatization or even confirmed its existence. On the contrary, some theoretical studies presume that the productive efficiency of a rural enterprise does not depend on the type of enterprise ownership (e.g., Weitzman and Xu 1994). One exception is the pioneering work by Li and Rozelle (2000); they find that although positive productivity effects exist, they are not realized right after privatization but with adjustment lags of a few years.[10]

To assess the productivity effect of privatization, we specify a growth function of the following general form:

(1) $G(V) = f[G(K), G(L), PS_{1995}, \Delta PS_{1996}, \Delta PS_{1997}, \mathbf{X}],$

where $G(V)$, $G(K)$, and $G(L)$ are growth rates of real value added, real capital stock, and the number of workers, respectively, from 1995 to 1998; PS_{1995}

---

10. Their use of dummy variables to represent the privatization is questionable in view of the continuous process of privatization.

is the ownership share of private owners in 1995, which is intended to capture the effect of privatization that took place before 1996; ΔPS_{1996} and ΔPS_{1997} are increases in the share of private owners during the entire year of 1996 and 1997, respectively; and X is a vector of other independent variables. To estimate the real capital stock, we first estimate nominal net investment from the survey data on the nominal capital stock, and then use the factory price index of machinery products as our deflator.[11] The estimated real values of net investments are added to the real value of the initial investment to obtain the real values of the capital stock in 1995 and 1998.

Since the dependent variable in equation (1) is the growth rate of value-added rather than physical quantity, it is affected not only by production efficiency but also by transaction efficiency. If privatization enhanced production efficiency without sacrificing transaction efficiency, then it would have a significantly positive effect on output growth. To the extent that the role of the local government in supporting TVE-SOE transactions was important, however, privatization would reduce transaction efficiency and cancel part of the positive productivity effect. We focus on the privatization that took place before 1998 because it is unlikely that privatization in 1998 immediately affected the productivity growth during the 1995–1998 period. Vector X includes the proportion of SOE-subcontracting to sales revenue in 1995, three provincial dummies (with southwest Jiangsu being the default), the road distance from Shanghai, the road distance from the nearest exit of the expressway, and the years of operation. If subcontracting with SOEs helped a TVE learn technology, marketing, or management from SOEs, the proportion of SOE subcontracting would have a positive effect on labor productivity growth.

To avoid possibly serious multicollinearity between $G(K)$ and $G(L)$, and to control for the effect of enterprise specific unobservables, we modify equation (1) into the following estimable form:

$$(2) \qquad G(V/L) = a_0 + a_1 PS_{1995} + a_2 \Delta PS_{1996} + a_3 \Delta PS_{1997} + a_4 X$$
$$+ a_5 G(K/L) + u,$$

where u is an error term. Since the growth rate of the capital-labor ratio, $G(K/L)$, on the right-hand side of equation (2) is likely to be endogenous, we instrument it with $\ln(L)$, $\ln(K/L)$, and $\ln(V/L)$ in the base year (i.e., 1995) and the growth rate of average annual wage earnings per worker in the county during the 1995–1998 period.[12] Although there is a possibility

11. Through our survey, we obtained nominal values of initial investments in equipment at the time of enterprise establishment, and nominal stock values of equipment in 1995 and 1998. We assumed that equal amounts of nominal net investment were made each year between enterprise establishment and 1995 and between 1995 and 1998. In this way, we estimated annual values of nominal net investment.

12. The data of average labor earnings by county were taken from the statistical bureaus of Shanghai municipality and of Jiangsu and Anhui provinces (various years).

Table 9.5   Estimates of Growth Functions, Garment Industry, 1995–1998

	$G(K/L)$ 3SLS (1)	$G(V/L)$ 3SLS (2)	$G(V/L)$ OLS (3)
PS_{1995}	0.019 (0.135)	−0.077 (0.115)	−0.132 (0.152)
ΔPS_{1996}	0.029 (0.284)	0.783** (0.254)	0.780** (0.319)
ΔPS_{1997}	0.023 (0.225)	0.069 (0.207)	0.076 (0.252)
Proportion of SOE subcontracting in 1995	−0.162 (0.114)	−0.196* (0.108)	−0.309** (0.127)
Shanghai dummy	0.393* (0.230)	−0.132 (0.203)	0.210 (0.258)
Southeast Jiangsu dummy	0.065 (0.157)	−0.099 (0.142)	−0.040 (0.176)
Anhui dummy	0.286 (0.243)	0.408* (0.213)	0.581* (0.273)
ln(distance from Shanghai)	−0.0003 (0.001)	−0.001 (0.001)	−0.001 (0.001)
ln(distance from highway)	0.004* (0.002)	−0.002 (0.002)	−0.001 (0.002)
ln(years of operation)	0.171** (0.055)	−0.011 (0.050)	0.106* (0.062)
$G(K/L)$		0.667** (0.149)	
Growth rate of average wages	0.649 (0.862)		1.076 (1.001)
$\ln(L_{1995})$	0.042 (0.052)		−0.008 (0.061)
$\ln(K_{1995}/L_{1995})$	−0.320** (0.068)		−0.219** (0.078)
$\ln(V_{1995}/L_{1995})$	−0.061 (0.053)		−0.088 (0.062)
Constant	−0.686 (0.424)	0.428 (0.225)	0.006 (0.490)
R^2	0.505	0.508	0.486

Notes: The sample size is 56. Numbers in parentheses are standard errors.
**Significant at the 1 percent level (one-sided test).
*Significant at the 5 percent level.

that the choice of the extent of privatization by the local government is affected by the labor productivity growth of the enterprise, ΔPS and PS are treated as exogenous variables at this stage of our study.

Table 9.5 reports three-stage least squares (3SLS) estimates of the capital-labor ratio (K/L) growth function and the labor productivity (V/L) growth function. For comparison, the ordinary least squares (OLS) estimates of the reduced form are also shown. In column (1), the K/L ratio level in 1995 has a negative and significant effect on its subsequent growth, serving as an instrumental variable. The years of operation have a positive and significant effect on the K/L ratio growth, which suggests that older enterprises tended to have had large labor employment before 1995 and then hastened to adjust their labor and capital inputs to the soaring wage rate during the study period. The private ownership share as of 1995 and the subsequent privatization do not have any significant effect on the K/L ratio growth in the garment sample.

In columns (2) and (3), privatization in 1996 has a positive and significant effect on the growth of labor productivity, which strongly supports the hypothesis that privatization improves production efficiency. In both columns, the productivity effect of privatization in 1997 is positive but insignificant. These results are consistent with the finding by Li and Rozelle (2000) that the productivity effect is realized not right after privatization but with an adjustment time lag of a few years. The result, that the proportion of SOE subcontracting has a negative and significant effect on labor productivity growth, suggests that the sample enterprises already had absorbed technologies and management know-how from SOEs by the sample period, and that transactions with technologically more advanced enterprises, such as foreign joint ventures, or the establishment of own marketing channels were becoming important for productivity growth. As shown in column (2), the estimate of the coefficient, a_5, of $G(K/L)$ in equation (2) is 0.667. This is reasonably close to the sample average of $(1 - $ labor share), where the labor share is measured as the ratio of nominal wage payments to nominal value-added.

9.4   Privatization and Growth in the Casting Industry

Unlike subcontracting in the garment industry, casting subcontracting was done almost exclusively with SOEs, especially those in and around Shanghai. Even in the case of original products manufactured and sold freely by TVEs, major buyers were mostly SOEs, and suppliers of important inputs, such as coal and pig iron, were also SOEs. Thus, transactions and cooperation with SOEs were indispensable for casting enterprises. Moreover, the quality of cast products is difficult to observe visually, especially in the case of complicated shapes and large sizes. Hence, the cost of inter-enterprise transactions tended to be high in this industry, even though free-market transactions were developed in the 1990s. Therefore, it is likely that the role of the local government in supporting transactions with SOEs was greater in this industry than in the garment industry.

According to table 9.6, original products accounted for a large part of sales revenue in Anhui but much less in areas closer to Shanghai. Enterprise managers told us that original products tended to be parts for light consumer goods and relatively simple machines, such as small pumps and

Table 9.6   **Composition of Sales Revenue, Casting Industry, 1995 and 1998 (%)**

	Original Products	Subcontract	Total
1995			
Shanghai	15.0	85.0	100
Southeast Jiangsu	33.0	67.0	100
Southwest Jiangsu	57.6	42.4	100
Anhui	64.3	35.7	100
Total	51.0	49.0	100
1998			
Shanghai	15.5	84.5	100
Southeast Jiangsu	25.3	74.6	100
Southwest Jiangsu	59.5	40.5	100
Anhui	60.0	40.0	100
Total	48.4	51.6	100

Table 9.7   **Ownership Share by Transaction Mode, Casting Industry, 1995 and 1998 (%)**

	Enterprises with >50% Original Products in 1995 (1)	Enterprises with ≤50% Original Products in 1995 (2)	Total (3)
1995			
Local government's ownership share	79.0	75.8	77.4
Private share	15.8	16.1	15.9
1998			
Local government's ownership share	36.4	20.6	28.5
Private share	46.4	59.8	53.1
No. of observations	29	29	58

tractor engines, while parts for heavy equipment, such as huge engines for large ships, were produced under subcontracts with SOEs. The heavy concentration of large SOEs in Shanghai and its immediate vicinity seems to explain the finding from table 9.6 that the proportion of subcontracting decreases as the distance from Shanghai increases. As shown in table 9.7, the ownership structure of original product-oriented enterprises was similar to that of subcontracting-oriented enterprises in 1995. In 1998, the difference in ownership structure between these two types of enterprises was a little greater than in 1995, but it was not statistically significant.

Table 9.8 reports the estimation results of the K/L ratio function and the labor productivity growth function for the casting sample. This table is organized in the same way as table 9.5 except that the proportion of SOE-subcontracting to sales revenue in table 9.5 is replaced by the proportion of

Table 9.8   **Estimates of Growth Functions, Casting Industry, 1995–1998**

	$G(K/L)$ 3SLS (1)	$G(V/L)$ 3SLS (2)	$G(V/L)$ OLS (3)
PS_{1995}	−0.298*	0.0005	−0.104
	(0.145)	(0.199)	(0.242)
ΔPS_{1996}	0.069	0.421*	0.480
	(0.182)	(0.249)	(0.304)
ΔPS_{1997}	0.339*	−0.435*	−0.166
	(0.189)	(0.238)	(0.315)
Proportion of original product in 1995	−0.069	0.014	−0.002
	(0.103)	(0.137)	(0.172)
Shanghai dummy	−0.042	−0.309	−0.294
	(0.393)	(0.522)	(0.272)
Southeast Jiangsu dummy	0.134	0.023	0.117
	(0.186)	(0.250)	(0.310)
Anhui dummy	0.444**	0.425*	0.618*
	(0.166)	(0.207)	(0.277)
ln(distance from Shanghai)	−0.258	−0.196	−0.294
	(0.163)	(0.208)	(0.272)
ln(distance from highway)	−0.011	0.097	0.084
	(0.046)	(0.062)	(0.077)
ln(years of operation)	0.110*	−0.056	−0.015
	(0.065)	(0.087)	(0.108)
$G(K/L)$		0.533*	
		(0.256)	
Growth rate of average wages	0.749		0.616
	(0.583)		(0.975)
$\ln(L_{1995})$	0.111**		0.072
	(0.039)		(0.066)
$\ln(K_{1995}/L_{1995})$	−0.138*		0.021
	(0.065)		(0.109)
$\ln(V_{1995}/L_{1995})$	−0.202*		−0.224
	(0.091)		(0.152)
Constant	−0.767	0.769	0.890
	(0.960)	(1.177)	(1.603)
R^2	0.397	0.302	0.254

Notes: The sample size is 56. Numbers in parentheses are standard errors.
**Significant at the 1 percent level.
*Significant at the 5 percent level.

original products in table 9.8. In column (1), the private ownership share as of 1995 had a negative and significant effect on the growth of the K/L ratio during the 1995–1998 period, whereas privatization that took place in 1997 had a positive and significant effect on the K/L ratio growth. These results suggest that privatized enterprises at first reduced excess capital more than labor but then increased it as production efficiency was expected to improve. The Anhui dummy has a positive and significant effect on the K/L ratio growth; this is likely to be a reflection of the tendency toward geographical growth convergence. The K/L ratio, labor productivity, and labor employment size in 1995 in column (1), which are excluded from column (2), have positive and significant effects on the subsequent growth of the K/L ratio. Hence they serve as instrumental variables.

The most important result shown in table 9.8 is that privatization in 1996 had a positive and significant effect on labor productivity growth, even though the productivity effect of privatization was weaker in the casting industry than in the garment industry. Interestingly, privatization in 1997 has a negative and significant effect on labor productivity growth. These results are consistent with our arguments that the temporarily detrimental effect of privatization on transaction efficiency was more substantial in the casting industry than in the garment industry, and that the productivity effect of privatization was realized with time lags. The Anhui dummy has a positive and significant effect on labor productivity as well as on K/L ratio growth, which supports the hypothesis that the center of gravity in the casting industry was shifting from the coastal region, such as the suburbs of Shanghai, to the central region, including Anhui province.

9.5   Concluding Remarks

In this study, we find that privatization of TVREs has been taking place rapidly in the Greater Yangtze River Region since the middle of the 1990s. Although this rapid privatization was due partly to the policy of the central government, we argue that it was related closely to the increasing importance of free-market transactions which made the intervention of local governments in the management of TVREs less productive. Thus, we advance the hypothesis that the recent privatization improved the production efficiency of enterprises. Our hypothesis clearly is supported by the three-stage estimation of the capital-labor ratio growth and labor productivity growth functions for both the garment and metal-casting industries. This indicates that productivity was enhanced significantly by privatization with a few years' time lag. The estimation results suggest that the productivity effect of privatization was greater in an industry where products and materials were more efficiently sold and bought in free markets.

At this point, we must emphasize that in all likelihood, our analysis has identified mere short-run effects of privatization on productivity. In the longer run, privatization will have greater effects on productivity than estimated in this study, as free markets of products and materials develop. In our observation, enormous differences still exist between private enterprises in Zhejiang province and the Greater Yangtze River Region. First, current competition among enterprises in Zhejiang province centers around the production of differentiated, improved products, often with brand names, and the establishment of a nationwide marketing network. In Jiangsu, however, competition through brand names and the establishment of own marketing networks began late and has taken place only among a small number of leading enterprises. Second, closely related industries tend to be clustered in Zhejiang province in order to enjoy the so-called "localization economies" arising from information externalities, the division and specialization of labor among enterprises, and possibly the formation of skilled labor markets (see, e.g., Zhang 1999; Sonobe, Hu, and Otsuka 2002a,b). Such industrial clusters seem to have been formed gradually through free-market competition over the last two decades. In contrast, industrial clusters have been less developed in the Greater Yangtze River Region except in the Sunan area near Shanghai. It is likely that in the longer run, the improvement of products and marketing capacity and the geographical concentration of industries will take place in the Greater Yangtze River Region as well.

The upshot is that we have to distinguish carefully between the short-run effects of privatization, which would have arisen from improved management incentives, and its longer-run effects, which would arise from investments in the development of improved products and the establishment of marketing systems, as well as from the formation of industrial clusters. Our result, that the short-run incentive effect of privation is significantly positive, strongly indicates that privatization can be a driving force leading to the continued improvement of productivity over long periods, so far as privatization enhances market competition among enterprises across wide areas.

References

Anhui Province Statistical Bureau. Various years. *Statistical yearbook of Anhui.* Beijing: China Statistics Press.

Che, Jiahua, and Yingyi Qian. 1998. Insecure property rights and government ownership of firms. *Quarterly Journal of Economics* 113 (May): 467–496.

Chen, Hongyi, and Scott Rozelle. 1999. Leaders, managers, and the organization of township and village enterprises in China. *Journal of Development Economics* 60 (December): 529–557.

Chen, Kang, Gary H. Jefferson, and Inderjit Singh. 1992. Lessons from China's economic reform. *Journal of Comparative Economics* 16 (June): 201–225.

Fudan University Economic Research Center. 1988. *The new avenue for enterprise reform and development: Survey report on horizontal cooperation of industrial enterprises in Shanghai* (in Chinese). Shanghai: Fudan Daxue Chubansha.

Hsiao, Cheng, Jeffrey Nugent, Isabelle Perringne, and Jicheng Qiu. 1998. Shares versus residual claimant contracts: The case of Chinese TVEs. *Journal of Comparative Economics* 26 (June): 317–337.

Jefferson, Gary H., Thomas G. Rawski, and Yuxin Zheng. 1996. Chinese industrial productivity: Trends, measurement, and recent developments. *Journal of Comparative Economics* 23 (October): 146–180.

Jiangsu Province Statistical Bureau. Various years. *Statistical yearbook of Jiangsu.* Beijing: China Statistics Press.

Jin, Hehui, and Yingyi Qian. 1998. Public versus private ownership of firms: Evidence from rural China. *Quarterly Journal of Economics* 113 (August): 773–808.

Li, David D. 1996. A theory of ambiguous property rights in transition economies: The case of the Chinese non-state sector. *Journal of Comparative Economics* 23 (August): 1–19.

Li, Hongbin, and Scott Rozelle. 2000. Saving or stripping rural industry: An analysis of privatization and efficiency in China. *Agricultural Economics* 23 (September): 241–252.

Lin, Justin Y., and Yang Yao. 2001. Chinese rural industrialization in the context of the East Asian Miracle. In *Rethinking the East Asian Miracle,* ed. J. Stiglitz and S. Yusuf, 143–195. Washington, D.C.: World Bank.

Lin, Justin Y., Fang Cai, and Zhou Li. 1996. *The China Miracle: Development strategy and economic reform.* Hong Kong: Chinese University Press.

Liu, Deqiang, and Keijiro Otsuka. 1998. Township-village enterprises in garment sector of China. In *Toward the rural-based development of commerce and industry: Selected experiences from East Asia,* ed. Y. Hayami, 161–186. Washington, D.C.: World Bank Institute.

Murakami, Naoki, Deqiang Liu, and Keijiro Otsuka. 1994. Technical and allocative efficiency among socialist enterprises: The case of the garment industry in China. *Journal of Comparative Economics* 19 (December): 410–433.

———. 1996. Market reform, division of labor, and increasing advantages of small-scale enterprises: The case of the machine tool industry in China. *Journal of Comparative Economics* 23 (December): 256–277.

Otsuka, Keijiro, Deqiang Liu, and Naoki Murakami. 1998. *Industrial reform in China: Past performance and future prospects.* Oxford, U.K.: Clarendon Press.

Shanghai Municipality Statistics Bureau. Various years. *Statistical yearbook of Shanghai.* Beijing: China Statistics Press.

Sonobe, Tetsushi, Dinghuan Hu, and Keijiro Otsuka. 2002a. *From inferior to superior products: An inquiry into the Wenzhou model of industrial development in China.* Tokyo: Foundation for Advanced Studies on International Development. Manuscript.

———. 2002b. Process of cluster formation in China: A case study of a garment town. *Journal of Development Studies* 39 (October): 118–139.

State Statistical Bureau. Various years. *China statistical yearbook.* Beijing: China Statistics Press.

Tao, Zhigang, and Tian Zhu. 2000. Agency and self-enforcing contracts. *Journal of Comparative Economics* 28 (March): 80–94.

Weitzman, Martin L., and Chenggang Xu. 1994. Chinese township-village enterprises as vaguely defined cooperatives. *Journal of Comparative Economics* 18 (April): 121–145.

Zhang, Renshou. 1999. *The systematic review of economic transition in Zhejiang rural area* (in Chinese). Hangzhou, China: Zhejiang Renming Chuban She.

Comment   Yun-Wing Sung

This paper draws on a unique data set on TVEs of the garment and metal-casting enterprises in the Great Yangtze River Region from 1995 to 1998, and presents evidence that productivity of TVEs was significantly en-

Yun-Wing Sung is professor in and chairman of the department of economics at the Chinese University of Hong Kong.

hanced by privatization. Despite ambiguous property rights (TVEs are owned by lower-level local governments), TVEs achieved remarkable growth in the 1980s and early 1990s. However, since the early 1990s, the growth performance of TVEs deteriorated sharply and fell behind that of private enterprises. Privatization of TVEs occurred on a large scale in the mid-1990s.

The contrasting performance of TVEs in two different periods of China's reform era remains a puzzle in transition economics that has not been studied adequately. Sonobe and Otsuka explain the puzzle by the "plausible hypothesis" that, in the first stage of the reform era, China's market was characterized by high transaction costs, which could be reduced by the intervention of local governments. Such transaction costs were particularly high when transactions were made with SOEs. However, as China's market matured with economic reforms, government support for transactions between TVEs and SOEs lost its significance. The plausible hypothesis is very interesting in transition economics as it provides a credible argument that gradualism is superior to a big bang.

While the article has presented persuasive evidence that productivity of TVEs was significantly enhanced by privatization since 1995, it provides only an indirect test of the plausible hypothesis. The authors argue that, as transactions with SOEs account for a bigger share of sales in the metal-casting industry than the garment industry, reduction of transaction costs through government intervention should be more significant in the metal-casting industry. The test shows that privatization has a weaker effect on productivity in metal casting than in garment. This result is consistent with the plausible hypothesis because privatization would reduce transaction efficiency more substantially in metal casting than in garment. However, as the casting industry is quite different from the garment industry, there can be many other explanations of the weaker effect of privatization on productivity in metal casting. The test of the plausible hypothesis is not conclusive.

The plausible hypothesis is very interesting, but also difficult to test. As the data set only involves two industries during 1995–1998, conclusive testing of the plausible hypothesis is not possible. A longer time span, more industries, or both would be required.

Despite the inconclusive test of the plausible hypothesis, the article is valuable in a lot of ways. The enterprise survey is very carefully done. For instance, it traces the changing distribution of ownership of capital stock for each sample enterprise. To tackle the problem that private TVEs had an incentive to be politically correct by disguising themselves under collective ownership, the authors also rely on the subjective assessment of key informants, usually general managers. The survey also has detailed information on composition of sales by mode of transaction (i.e., original product versus subcontracting with SOEs), which provides some data for indirectly testing the plausible hypothesis. As a whole, the article is a very valuable contribution to the literature on transition economics.

Comment   Yang Yao

This paper provides an empirical assessment of the productivity effects of TVE privatization in China. The results are illuminating and provide useful policy implications. Although privatization has converted almost all the TVEs and most of the small and medium SOEs into private firms, the word "privatization" is still a kind of taboo in Chinese mainstream publications, so empirical studies on privatization are still scant both inside and outside China. The evidence provided by this paper thus is both timely and informative. It is especially interesting that privatization is found to be the most effective for firms that are more involved in free-market transactions. Privatization in China has taken a bottom-up approach and has been induced by economic forces. There have been both theories and anecdotal evidence showing that the spontaneous privatization in China has been induced by market liberalization of the Chinese economy, but there has been no systematic evidence to prove it. This paper's finding partly fills the gap by providing indirect evidence (direct evidence would have shown that firms more involved in free-market transactions are more likely to be privatized, which is not done in this paper).

While the paper is well done, I would like to point out two areas that further work can improve upon.

The authors have a large data set, but they use only two sectors for their study, which seriously limits the sample size. The authors argue that they have done so because different industries use different technologies. However, this issue can be taken care of by estimating a different production function for each industry and then adding industrial dummies in their analysis.

The authors use the change of the private share in a firm as the indicator of the extent of privatization of the firm. There are several issues surrounding this definition. First, there are both initially private and privatized TVEs in the sample. By the authors' definition of privatization, an initially private firm has a value of zero for this variable. This considerably weakens the implications of this variable because it actually measures an adjustment of the ownership structure in the firm regardless of the direction of the adjustment. A possible improvement is to assign a value of 1 to those initially private firms so the direction of the adjustment is pinned down toward privatization. Second, the starting year of 1995 is not the

Yang Yao is professor at the China Center for Economic Research, Beijing University.

starting year for privatization, I suppose, at least not for most firms. As a result, the current definition of privatization would be biased for firms that had started privatization before 1995, pretty much like those initially private firms. Third, the lack of an effect of privatization in the year 1996–1997 may just be a reflection of the problem, since in those two years privatization might well have finished so there is not much variation in the data.

10

Government Commitment and the Outcome of Privatization in China

Yang Yao

If there was any significant change in the Chinese economic structure in the 1990s, it had to be privatization. By one report, 80 percent of the firms at or below county level were privatized by the end of 1998 (Zhao 1999).[1] Privatization also spread to large state-owned enterprises (SOEs) in large cities. A recent study (International Finance Corporation [IFC], forthcoming) found that 70 percent of the SOEs in the eleven sample cities had taken some form of privatization. However, the performance record of privatization varied from city to city. A question then arises as to why such performance disparity occurred. In this paper, we first use recent survey data to assess the regional performance disparity and then explain it. We ascribe the disparity to the different degrees of local government commitment to privatization.

Privatization transfers the legal ownership of a public firm to private hands, making the latter the residual claimant. However, privatization by no means binds the government's hand from intervening, nor does it bind bureaucrats' hands from grabbing. One serious problem that private firms encounter in China is the excessive and irregular charges imposed by local governments. For example, the survey that this study will draw data from found that the amount of fees is equivalent to the amount of regular taxes among the surveyed firms (Garnaut et al. 2001). Privatization cannot exempt a firm from the excessive charges. In other words, privatization does not mean the establishment of the rule of law. The lack of rule of law has been identified by some authors as the most important factor that led to

Yang Yao is professor at the China Center for Economic Research, Beijing University.

1. A county-level unit does not necessarily mean a rural area. Many counties have turned into urban areas and changed their administrative status to "city," although they are still regarded as county-level administrative units.

Russia's economic failures (e.g., Shleifer 1997). However, the establishment of rule of law is not always in the politician's interests; and, even if it is, it may turn out not to be time-consistent for the politician. On the other hand, having been through frequent policy changes by the government, the manager of the firm may not trust it even if the establishment of the rule of law is in the politician's interests. Therefore, the politician has to establish a credible commitment at the time of privatization just to induce good performance or even to make privatization happen in the first place.

The paper is organized as follows. Section 10.1 presents a brief review of the Chinese government's policy toward privatization in the last twenty years. Section 10.2 shows the regional disparity in firm performance by presenting the econometric results on six cities. Section 10.3 constructs a theoretical model to explain the relationship between government commitment and post-privatization performance. Section 10.4 presents the government reform experience in Shunde, Guangdong province, to provide an illustration of the theory. Section 10.5 concludes the paper with a discussion of the implications of the study.

10.1   Government Policy toward Privatization

Reform of the SOEs has been a major theme of China's reform efforts since the urban reform was launched in 1984. Throughout the 1980s, although there were calls for privatization, government emphasis was on how to improve the performance of the SOEs by changing their internal governance. Inspired by the success of the household responsibility system in the countryside, one major effort was to introduce a contracting system into the SOEs. In such a system, the manager signed a contract with the government on specific terms. The manager promised to maintain a certain record of the firm's financial position, including sales, profitability, capital accumulation, and so on. In return, the government promised the manager certain returns, such as a commission, out of the profit. One problem with the contracting system was that the manager's terms were asymmetric: the manager would be rewarded for his successes, but would not be punished credibly for his failure. As a result, personal collateral was introduced into the system.

A further development was to adopt a lease contract: the manager leased the firm by paying the government a fixed proportion of the firm's profit. The first significant case of a lease contract was the Wuhan Motor Engine Factory in 1986, wherein three people invested 34,000 yuan as collateral to lease the factory. By the end of the 1980s, lease contracts were encouraged by the government as a means of reforming small SOEs. A State Council regulation regarding the lease of small SOEs was issued in May 1988.[2] One

---

2. "Tentative Regulations on the Lease of Small State-Owned Industrial Enterprises," the State Council, 20 May 1988.

direct consequence of the adoption of the lease contract was the introduction of private entrepreneurs into the management of SOEs, because managers could be recruited from outside the enterprise. When it proliferated into the countryside, leasehold in many cases led to the privatization of township and village enterprises (TVEs). This happened when the managers could retain the ownership of the capital accumulated during the lease period. After the manager leased the firm for several years, his own capital would overwhelm the capital owned by the local government, and the firm would effectively be owned by the manager himself.

In addition to contracting and leasing, other reform measures that would potentially lead to privatization were also adopted. Among them, incorporation was the most significant. In the beginning, the government restricted incorporation to be conducted only among SOEs themselves. However, private shares soon appeared. The first case of private shares occurred in three Guangzhou SOEs in 1986. In those three firms, employees bought 30 percent of the total assets of each firm. The first case of incorporation of a large SOE was in August 1988 when Shengyang Motor Corporation was transformed into Shengyang Jinbei Motors Incorporated through the issue of shares to the general public.

The opening of the Shenzhen Stock Exchange in 1990 and the Shanghai Stock Exchange in 1991 enabled SOEs to issue shares to the public widely. However, the Chinese government implemented restrictive measures to prevent the state from losing control of the newly listed SOEs. For example, it required that a certain proportion of a firm's shares not be sold.

Real privatization began after Deng Xiaoping's visit to the south in 1992. As with many other reform initiatives, privatization began with localities and was then sanctioned by the central government. The most important impetus for local privatization was the large amount of debt accumulated in the state sector. This was a more pressing problem in small cities because of their smaller economies. For example, in Zhucheng city, Shandong province, among the 150 city-owned enterprises, 103 were in the red, and the total loss was 147 million yuan, equivalent to the city government's revenue for 1.5 years (Zhao 1999). Shunde of Guangdong province had the same problem when it first started its privatization program in 1992. The solution reached by the localities was to privatize small firms, but Shunde and Zhucheng were more radical, privatizing almost all of their state and collective firms. In 1995 the central government, after several rounds of investigation and discussion, formed a policy called *zhuada fangxiao,* or "keep the larger and let the smaller go," which limited the state's authority to 500 to 1,000 large state firms and allowed smaller firms to be leased or sold.[3]

3. In 1994, as the ministry in charge of the government's economic affairs, the State Economic and Trade Commission sent a report, "Suggestions on Revitalizing Small State-Owned Enterprises," to vice premier Wu Banguo, who was in charge of enterprise reforms. In September 1995, the policy was formally announced by the central committee of the CCP in one of its plenaries and was put into the suggestions to the ninth five-year plan.

The government had a good reason for implementing this policy. In 1997, the 500 largest state firms had 37 percent of the assets held by state industrial firms, contributed 46 percent of the taxes collected on all state firms, and accounted for 63 percent of the total profit in the state sector. On the other hand, smaller firms owned by local governments had worse performance than those owned by the central government. In 1995, 24.3 percent of the central firms were in the red, but 72.5 percent of the local firms were in the red (Zhao 1999). Therefore, "Control of the (500) largest firms means we have control of the largest chunk of the state economy."[4]

From the "let the smaller go" part of the policy came the word *gaizhi,* meaning "changing the system." Starting in 1994, *gaizhi* began to spread to the whole country. The content of *gaizhi* included contracting and leasing, the two methods used before, as well as new methods such as selling to private owners, employee-holding, incorporation, listing on the stock market, restructuring of internal and external governance, and bankruptcy. By international standards, *gaizhi* really is privatization.

One aspect of *gaizhi* was to remove the "red hat" for red-hat firms—that is, firms with a collective face that were actually run privately. In March 1998, the government issued a directive requiring all red-hat firms to take off their hats by November 1998.

Sichuan provides an example of *gaizhi.* In 1994, the provincial government began to implement *gaizhi,* starting with county-owned enterprises. By the end of 1998, the province ended *gaizhi* for 68.6 percent of the 42,681 firms that were targeted for *gaizhi.* Among those transformed, 35.1 percent were transformed into employee-owned companies, 11 percent were transformed into employee-owned cooperatives, 14.3 percent were sold, 7 percent were contracted out to individuals, 8.5 percent were leased out, 7 percent were bankrupt, and 5 percent were taken over by other firms.

Privatization in general was more popular in the countryside. After 1993, many localities that had been renowned for their development of the collective economy, including Shunde and southern Jiangsu, began to implement massive privatization. TVEs used to have vaguely defined property rights that did not maintain clear-cut definitions of who—the entrepreneur or the government or both—owned the enterprises. Because of their marvelous growth records, TVEs have been hailed by some authors as posing a challenge to the neoclassical doctrine of clearly defined ownership (e.g., Weitzman and Xu 1994). However, as TVE growth slowed down in the 1990s, the disadvantages of their vaguely defined property rights were acknowledged by academic researchers. Like their urban counterparts, the SOEs, TVEs suffered a soft-budget problem (Zhang 1998). Local governments felt the problem earlier because they shouldered a con-

---

4. Vice premier Wu Banguo's speech in the national conference on economy, 20 December 1997. Quoted in Zhao (1999).

siderable amount of debts accumulated by their TVEs' nonperforming loans. Financial crisis led the government to seek institutional change (e.g., North and Weingast 1989). Li, Li, and Zhang (2000) showed with a theoretical model that financial competition among local governments was a major cause of China's local privatization initiatives. The evolution of government policy toward privatization in China, especially in the 1990s, exemplified the theory.[5]

However, the wave of privatization initiated by *gaizhi* in 1998 met the criticism that it led to the loss of state assets. The government also lowered its tone on privatization. Some localities stopped their privatization programs; more of them lowered their profiles to avoid being subject to the criticism. The new constitutional amendment enacted in early 1999 elicited a new round of privatization. It was estimated that 70 percent of the SOEs had been privatized by the end of 2002 (IFC, forthcoming). By international standards, *gaizhi* thus qualifies as a property-rights revolution, although this revolution has been largely silent.

10.2 Regional Disparity in Firm Performance

Although privatization has spread cross the country, its outcome is not uniform. Liu, Wang, and Yao (2001) showed that many privatized firms in southern Jiangsu, a region once famous for its collective firms, had problems. On the one hand, asset stripping was rampant in newly privatized firms; on the other hand, the local economy had regressed to one based on small, family workshops. Qin (1998) found a similar phenomenon in this region. However, there were better performers, too. Zhucheng of Shandong province and Shunde of Guangdong province have performed quite well. In this section, we use firm-level data from a 1999 survey to assess the post-privatization performance in six cities: Beijing, Chengdu, Wenzhou, Shunde, Deyang, and Mianyang.[6] Beijing is the national capital; Chengdu is the capital of the Sichuan province, located in southwest of China; Wenzhou is a prefecture-level city in southern Zhejiang province; Shunde is located in the Pearl River delta, close to Macao; and Deyang and Mianyang are two cities in Sichuan province. Except for Beijing, all the other cities are renowned for their recent development of private firms, many of which are privatized firms. The survey was designed to study China's emerging private sector, so firms included in the survey are mostly private firms. This makes the study of post-privatization performance easier, because it controls for within-firm incentive problems that frequently are found in public firms. Data on firm performance and other relevant information were col-

---

5. In this respect, Zhao (1999) is a nice reference.
6. The survey was organized by IFC in 1999. For a description of the survey, see Garnaut et al. (2001).

lected for 1995 and 1998. The total number of firms covered by the survey was 629. However, this study is limited to the firms that provided valid information, so the sample size is smaller.

We study three performance indicators: value-added, pretax return to capital, and the growth of capital stock in the period 1995 to 1998. We use value-added instead of output because the former is a better measure of performance; besides, we do not have enough valid data for intermediate inputs. Confined by data availability, we have to limit the study of value-added and pretax profit rates to the year 1998. The study of the growth of the capital stock is especially interesting because it reflects entrepreneurs' confidence in the local economy. The aim of the study is to assess the performance difference between the six cities after firm-level characteristics are controlled for.

For value-added, we first run a Cobb-Douglas value-added production function with labor and capital as inputs. Value-added is measured in 10,000 yuan, labor is the number of employees of a firm, and capital is the original value of the capital stock at the end of 1998 (measured in 10,000 yuan). We do not have good data on capital depreciation so we cannot use net capital value.

In addition to the two inputs, we use other variables to control for firm efficiency. These variables can be assigned to three groups. The first is firm characteristics. These include ratio of college-and-above graduates in management, the percentage of self-finance when the firm was first established, the degree of competition in the industry, whether there are entry barriers to the industry, whether the firm is an exporter, and the firm's ownership status. The ratio of college-and-above graduates measures the stock of human capital in management and thus (partly) controls for the firm's innovative capacity. Self-finance is relative to borrowing from formal financial institutions; it includes owners' own savings and borrowing from friends and relatives. On the one hand, it controls for the constraints that a firm faces in the financial market; therefore, more self-finance may entail smaller chances of success. However, more self-finance also imposes more self-discipline on the firm and forces it to use funds more wisely. Therefore, the sign on the effect of this variable is undetermined.

Degree of competition takes three values: 1 = heated competition, 2 = modest competition, and 3 = no competition. Less competition in the industry implies a stronger monopoly position for the firm in the market; we expect this variable to have a positive effect on productivity. Entry barrier is a dummy variable with a value of 1 indicating that the barrier exists, and a value of zero meaning no barrier. Entry barrier takes the form of licensing and other government approvals. Firms in an industry with entry barrier enjoy more monopoly power, so we expect that this variable would contribute positively to a firm's productivity.

Export status controls for a firm's international linkage, and it is expected that an exporter will perform better than a nonexporter. Ownership is grouped into three categories: domestic SOEs and collective firms, domestic private firms, and foreign firms and joint ventures. The first category is used as the reference group in the regressions.

The second group of variables is city dummies. If not otherwise defined, Shunde is used as the reference city in the regressions. For the purpose of the current study, this group of variables is key to our understanding of regional performance disparities.

The third group of variables is industrial dummies. We grouped the firms into six large industries: primary (mining, logging, and agriculture); light manufacturing (food, garments, furniture, and sports and office supplies); heavy manufacturing (chemicals, metal and nonmetal refinement and manufacturing); machinery; electronics; and others. The last industry is used as the reference group.

There are 247 firms with valid data. Distribution of those firms is as follows: Beijing 116, Shunde 24, Chengdu 36, Wenzhou 32, Deyang 10, and Mianyang 29. Beijing turns out to have more firms with valid data. This is because Beijing had better organizational arrangements when the survey was implemented.

The results of the value-added production function are presented in column (1) of table 10.1. To save space, the results for the industrial dummies are not reported. The output elasticities for labor and capital are 0.99 and 0.20, respectively, indicating weak increasing returns to scale. Among the firm characteristics, only the percentage of self-finance is significant. It has a positive sign, showing that the effect of financial discipline outweighs the effect of financial constraint. Among the city dummies, all but Deyang have a negative sign, and the coefficient for Beijing is significant. This shows that firms in Shunde might be more efficient than those in the other cities. To further explore this possibility, we rerun the regression by grouping all five cities except Shunde into one group and studying their difference from Shunde. The results are reported in column (2) of table 10.1. Although the estimate for Shunde is not statistically significant, the size of the difference is large. Firms in Shunde are 46.5 percent more efficient than firms in the other cities.

The third and fourth columns in table 10.1 report two more regressions on value-added. The dependent variable is value-added per yuan of capital. This time, a new variable—capital per worker—is added to the regression. The first regression takes Shunde as the reference city and puts in all the other city dummies. Now, all the cities except Deyang are shown to be significantly inferior to Shunde. The difference ranges from 10.4 yuan (1.25 dollars) to 12.5 yuan (1.50 dollars), which is substantial. The second regression then takes the previous approach, to group all the other cities together. The estimation puts the difference between Shunde and the other cities at 11.5 yuan (1.39 dollars), which is highly significant. Therefore, Shunde is far more efficient than the other cities in utilizing its capital.

Table 10.1   Determinants of Firm Performance: 1998

Variables	Log Value-Added		Value-Added/Capital		Profit/Capital	
	(1)	(2)	(1)	(2)	(1)	(2)
Constant	-0.875	-1.845*	0.595	-10.576	-7.087	-11.289**
	(1.031)	(0.902)	(10.710)	(9.249)	(7.545)	(6.521)
Log number of workers	0.995*	1.070*	4.339*	4.311*	1.480**	1.510*
	(0.107)	(0.097)	(1.187)	(1.075)	(0.836)	(0.758)
Log capital stock (10,000 yuan)	0.203*	0.207*	-2.430*	-2.461*	0.041	-0.029
	(0.056)	(0.056)	(0.672)	(0.652)	(0.474)	(0.460)
Capital per worker (10,000 yuan)			0.017	0.019**	0.001	0.003
			(0.012)	(0.011)	(0.008)	(0.008)
Ratio of college-and-above graduates in management	0.202	0.284	-0.880	-0.724	1.279	1.323
	(0.288)	(0.283)	(2.981)	(2.904)	(2.100)	(2.047)
Percentage of self-finance when firm was established	0.395**	0.329	3.311	3.294	2.801	2.830
	(0.242)	(0.241)	(2.512)	(2.471)	(1.769)	(1.743)
Degree of competition	-0.065	-0.030	1.041	1.220	1.190	1.425
	(0.168)	(0.164)	(1.738)	(1.679)	(1.224)	(1.184)
Barrier to entry	0.419	0.397	-0.507	-0.432	-1.821	-1.743
	(0.266)	(0.266)	(2.759)	(2.730)	(1.944)	(1.925)
Exporter	-0.673	-0.518	-4.090	-3.713	-6.841*	-6.397*
	(0.425)	(0.417)	(4.423)	(4.312)	(3.116)	(3.040)

	(1)	(2)	(3)	(4)	(5)	(6)
Domestic private firm	−0.137	−0.079	2.831	2.427	−0.089	−0.654
	(0.661)	(0.650)	(6.848)	(6.663)	(4.825)	(4.698)
Joint venture or foreign firm	−0.939	−0.977	−4.444	−4.554	−3.136	−3.871
	(0.913)	(0.892)	(9.466)	(9.165)	(6.669)	(6.462)
Beijing	−0.800*		−11.613*		−4.562	
	(0.398)		(4.135)		(2.913)	
Chengdu	−0.140		−10.380*		−2.892	
	(0.451)		(4.704)		(3.314)	
Wenzhou	−0.305		−12.541*		−4.834	
	(0.473)		(4.910)		(3.459)	
Deyang	0.004		−9.968		−4.393	
	(0.634)		(6.582)		(4.637)	
Mianyang	−0.308		−12.053*		−5.457	
	(0.480)		(4.981)		(3.509)	
Shunde		0.465		11.466*		4.382**
		(0.370)		(3.797)		(2.677)
R^2	0.609	0.599	0.138	0.137	0.093	0.090

Notes: 247 firms. Standard errors are reported in parentheses.

**Significant at the 5 percent level.

*Significant at the 10 percent level.

This is shown further by the estimation of pretax profit per yuan of capital. The results of two regressions are reported in the last two columns in table 10.1. The definitions of the two regressions are the same as before. In the first regression, all the other cities are shown to be slightly less efficient than Shunde. The second regression then shows that the difference between Shunde and the other cities is 4.38 yuan (53 cents), which is significant at the 10 percent significance level. It is noteworthy that an exporter is significantly less efficient than a nonexporter in terms of profitability, a result contrary to our expectation. One explanation is that Chinese exporters frequently are engaged in price competition, so their profit margins are narrowed. However, the fact that firms are still engaged in exporting shows that they might get indirect benefits such as tax returns and foreign currency retention.

Finally, the results on capital growth are presented in table 10.2. Growth is defined as (capital stock of 1998 – capital stock of 1995)/(capital stock of 1995). Because of the limitation of valid data, the sample size shrinks to sixty-three firms. On average, the firms grew 8.43 times in the three-year period. However, the variation is large. The distribution, from the highest to the lowest, is as follows: Deyang, 21.5 times (six firms), Shunde, 15.5 times (six firms), Beijing, 6.4 times (fourteen firms), Mianyang, 8.1 times (seventeen firms), Wenzhou, 4.1 times (fourteen firms), and Chengdu, 3.9 times (six firms). To maintain degrees of freedom, industrial dummies are

Table 10.2   Growth of Capital Stock: 1995–1998

Variables	Estimates
Constant	18.935*
	(7.515)
Capital in 1995 (10,000 yuan)	–0.0018**
	(0.0011)
Ratio of college-and-above graduates	–1.181
in management	(5.138)
Percentage of self-finance when	–3.087
firm was established	(5.003)
Degree of competition	–6.117*
	(2.938)
Barrier to entry	–2.462
	(6.476)
Exporter	23.222*
	(7.595)
Shunde	11.762**
	(6.951)
R^2	0.267

Notes: 63 firms. Standard errors are reported in parentheses.
**Significant at the 5 percent level.
*Significant at the 10 percent level.

excluded. In addition, we only explore the difference between Shunde and the other cities as a whole. However, we add the capital stock in 1995 to control for initial firm size. Understandably, the results show that capital stock in 1995 has a significantly negative effect on capital growth. Another significant result is that exporters have experienced much higher growth. Less comprehensible is the result that a firm in a less competitive industry tends to have a smaller growth rate. The most important result in terms of our concern is that Shunde has a significantly higher growth rate than other cities, with the difference being 11.8 times.

To summarize these empirical results, we find that Shunde has been consistently doing better than the other cities. The task remaining is to explain Shunde's better performance. In the regressions, we relied on the city dummies to assess regional differences, but the dummies can carry the effects of a lot of uncontrolled regional characteristics. Here we would like to concentrate on a single aspect of the problem, that is, the regularity of government administration. Privatization gives private owners legal ownership of the firm, but does not automatically guarantee that the government will protect that ownership. In this respect, Shunde has done much better than the other cities. It conducted a radical government reform concurrently with its privatization program. In the next section, we present a theoretical model to show that government commitment to the protection of private ownership is the key to successful privatization. The commitment is shown by the government's stripping of its own power. In section 10.4, we come back to the case of Shunde by presenting a description of its government reform.

10.3   A Model of Government Commitment and Privatization

In this section, we present a formal model explaining the relationship between government reform and firm performance. First, however, we provide a verbal description of the ideas behind the model.

Consider an economy composed of a firm, a politician, and a firm manager. The firm initially is publicly owned. The manager is delegated to managing the firm with a fixed wage, so he also provides a fixed amount of effort. A politician leads a bureaucracy of many bureaucrats and delegates to them the regulations of the firm. In the Chinese context, regulations include project approval and direct intervention into the firm's management affairs (such as employment target, wage determination, investment decisions, etc.) as well as other regular regulatory activities such as taxation, standard enforcement, and so on. However, if they are unregulated, these bureaucrats tend to be corrupt and to grab from the firm, and these regulatory functions provide a vehicle for that grab. The politician needs these functions to achieve particular goals that are valuable to him. One example is that maintaining full employment increases his popularity among a certain portion of the population. Another example is that implementing a specific industrial policy drives out some industries (like those creating heavy pollution) that he thinks are bad for the local economy. In addition, the politician cares about the opinion of the general public and the support of his subordinates. The general public cares about the revenue of the firm, and the bureaucrats care about their "grabbing capacities." Therefore, the profit of the firm, intervention power, and the bureaucrats' grabbing capacities all enter his utility.

A governance reform is defined as the establishment of the rule of law that eliminates the bureaucrats' grabbing from the firm. The reform is different from eliminating government intervention into the firm. Under certain circumstances (such as the Mao Zedong era in China), government intervention does not necessarily lead to corruption. However, it facilitates, if not directly causes, corruption in most cases. We assume that it is at the politician's discretion whether to take the reform and eliminate his subordinates' grabbing power. Under public ownership of the firm, the manager's supply of effort does not respond to the grab, so corruption is not harmful to the politician and he will not undertake the reform.

Privatization is a shift in ownership that makes the manager the residual claimant. It does not guarantee that government intervention disappears along with the ownership shift, though. Because the manager begins to respond to the severity of the grabbing hand, corruption becomes costly to the politician, and it may be an efficient decision for him ex ante to conduct the governance reform along with privatization. More importantly, the manager will not take the firm in the first place, and privatization will fail if the governance reform is not undertaken. Therefore, the two reforms are preconditions for each other. Nevertheless, there is a critical difference between them: While the ownership reform is irreversible, the governance reform has a time-consistency problem. If the manager believed the politician and provided effort, it would be in the politician's interest to renege, in other words, to let loose the corruption. But the manager can envision this reneging behavior perfectly and will take precautions in advance, probably providing the effort that he provided under public ownership. As a result, privatization will not be an attractive choice for either the politician or the manager. This is a typical time-inconsistency and subsequent inefficiency problem in which a player cannot make a binding commitment.

However, this problem may merely arise as a result of the limited number of choices that are available to the players. In the real world, the number of choices that a player can choose from is large and once they have been made, some of them become binding constraints on the player (he may be held legally responsible to keep the choices). Even a government in a totalitarian state cannot be totally free of observing its choices. In our case, removing government intervention can be made a binding constraint (probably through the privatization contract) on the politician; if this is done, it can serve as a credible commitment for the politician to stick to the governance reform because, by removal of the intervention, corruption becomes more visible and its cost to the politician becomes higher.

The commitment mechanism discussed here is different from those frequently appearing in recent literature that concentrates on the decentralization of decision making (e.g., North and Weingast 1989; Qian and Weingast 1996, 1997; and Zhang and Li 1998). Here the commitment can be termed "burning the bridge," a military tactic that can be traced back to Chinese Han dynasty two thousand years ago. In one battle, General Han Xin brought his army to a big river, crossed it, and burned down the bridge over it, so that no retreating route was left for his men and the only hope for them to survive was to defeat the enemy. They did that. In this story, Han Xin had another choice: taking the army over the river (and burning down the bridges over it), in addition to killing retreating soldiers himself. The former was an automatic binding constraint on his men and himself, because retreating into the river would mean immediate death; the latter, however, was not, because even he wanted to kill all the cowards, many of whom would succeed in escaping from the messy battlefield.

10.3.1   Settings

The economy is composed of a firm, a politician, and a firm manager. The firm is initially publicly owned. The manager is delegated to manage the firm. We assume that public ownership makes an incentive contract infeasible for the manager. This assumption can be justified on the grounds of the soft budget constraint first proposed by Kornai (1979) and later refined by Qian (1994) and Dewatripont and Maskin (1995). Therefore, we assume that the manager provides a fixed amount of effort, e_0, for firm management. At this level of effort, the disutility to the manager is zero. Consistently, the wage that the manager gets is also normalized to zero.

In the meantime, the politician maintains a certain level of intervention $s \in [0, 1]$, say, that is delegated to the bureaucrats to implement on the firm. However, the bureaucrats tend to grab from the firm if they are not properly checked. We assume that their total grab is proportional to the firm's revenue, with the proportion being $t \in [0, 1]$. The grab also brings a deadweight loss to the firm. In summary, we can specify the firm's net revenue as

$$(1) \qquad\qquad R = \theta e_0 - at,$$

where $\theta \geq 1$ is a parameter representing the firm's market conditions, and a is a positive number measuring the intensity of the deadweight loss brought about by the grabbing. A larger θ implies a stronger local economy. To structure the discussion, we set a boundary condition that R is nonnegative for any t and s.[7]

---

7. This assumption is inessential to our results; but since the revenue function and the politician's utility to be introduced later are both linear, we need this assumption as a boundary condition. With this boundary condition, our analysis will be simplified technically.

The politician cares about the general public's interest, the support of the bureaucrats, and the result of the intervention. The public's interest can be represented by the size of R,[8] the support of the bureaucrats by t, and the result of the intervention by s. However, corruption also has a cost to the politician, and the cost is likely to increase as t becomes larger. Nevertheless, government intervention can serve as a disguise and a damage-control device and mitigates the cost. These concerns are best represented in the politician's utility function (all in monetary terms)

$$U = R + \alpha_1 t + \beta s - (\alpha_2 - \gamma s)t,$$

where α_1, α_2, β, and γ are all positive numbers. In the equation, β represents the weight that the politician puts on the result of the intervention, α_1 represents the support of the bureaucrats, and the sum $\alpha_2 - \gamma s$ represents the cost of corruption. Collecting and rearranging terms, we have

(2) $U = R + \alpha t + \beta s + \gamma t s,$

where $\alpha = \alpha_1 - \alpha_2$. Then $\alpha t + \gamma t s$ is the net gain from granting the bureaucrats the grabbing power. We assume that β is larger than 1, that is, that the politician values more of the special interests achieved by intervention than the general public's interest.

Governance reform is defined as the politician's elimination of the corruption and setting t equal to zero. As the setup shows, the interests involved may prevent it from happening.

10.3.2   Public Ownership

Governance reform may not be desirable for the politician under public ownership of the firm. Because his utility increases monotonically with s, the politician will set s equal to 1. He will also set $t = 1$ because his utility is linear in t. If that is the case, his utility is

(3) $U_0^c = \theta e_0 - a + \alpha + \beta + \gamma.$

With governance reform, t is set equal to zero, and his utility is

(4) $U_0^* = \theta e_0 + \beta.$

However, setting $t = 0$ may not be compatible with the politician's incentive if the following condition holds:

(5) $\alpha + \gamma > a$

It is noteworthy that this condition has nothing to do with θ, so the government of a city with a stronger economy does not have a stronger incentive to engage in governance reform than the government of a city with a weaker economy. We will show that with privatization, governance reform could oc-

---

8. Alternatively, one can also interpret this assumption as the politician's concern on tax revenue—a larger economy implies more tax revenue to the government.

cur even when equation (5) holds; that is, privatization would give the politician an extra incentive to engage in the reform. On the other hand, only when the reform is carried out and committed to by the politician will privatization be a Pareto improvement to both the politician and the manager.

10.3.3 Governance Reform and Privatization

Privatization shifts the ownership of firm from the government to the firm manager and makes the latter the residue claimant.[9] We let the politician and the manager play the following game.

On day 1, the politician announces whether to privatize the firm and determines the level of intervention in the firm. On day 2, the manager decides whether to accept the offer of privatization and, if he does, how much effort to put into the firm. On day 3, the politician decides whether to engage in governance reform and the production is carried out.

We assume that privatization and the politician's decision about intervention in the firm are irreversible and observable by the manager. We put the politician's decision about governance reform after the manager's effort to capture the nonenforceability of the reform. To wit, it may be an ex ante optimal decision for the politician to engage in the reform (i.e., to set t be zero), but if the manager believed the politician and acted accordingly, it would be in his interest to renege and give up the reform afterward (i.e., to revert to corruption). However, the manager can well envision the politician's time-inconsistency problem and act accordingly. Like the feature shared by the time-consistency literature, this will result in inefficient outcome. In what follows, we will first replicate this standard result and then propose two commitment mechanisms that the politician can use to commit himself to his ex ante efficient decisions.

We start with the politician's ex ante efficient decisions on day 1. In making these decisions, he takes into account the manager's response to the grabbing hand because the latter now becomes the residual claimant of the firm. For any level of effort e, the disutility (in monetary terms) to the manager is $(1/2)\mu(e - e_0)^2$, where μ is a positive number. He maximizes his net profit $\pi = (1 - t)(\theta e - at) - (1/2)\mu(e - e_0)^2$ by choosing his effort e. This immediately gives us a solution to e, $e(t) = \theta(1 - t)/\mu + e_0$. Taking this for granted, the politician maximizes his utility by choosing t and s, that is, he solves the following problem:

$$(6) \qquad \max_{s,t} U = [\theta e(t) - at] + \alpha t + \beta s + \gamma ts$$

The optimal solution to s is still 1. To make governance reform (i.e., $t = 0$) attractive to the politician, we need that the marginal utility of t be negative, that is,

9. Implicitly, we assume that the firm is given to the manager for free. While it could be justified by empirical findings on Russia and to some extent, on China (Garnaut et al. 2001), this assumption is made to simplify our analysis and allows us to concentrate on the incentive effect of privatization.

(7)
$$\alpha + \gamma < \frac{\theta^2}{\mu + a}.$$

The left-hand side of this condition is the marginal benefit of corruption, and the right-hand side is the marginal cost of corruption that includes the deadweight loss and an extra cost due to the manager's lost incentive. The inequality may hold even if equation (5) holds. Therefore, governance reform is easier with privatization than under public ownership. This is because now the manager's effort responds to the grabbing hand and an increase in t causes an extra cost of a factor θ^2 due to the manager's lost incentive. It is noteworthy that government reform is easier under a larger θ, in other words, a city with a more prosperous local economy will be more likely to take the reform.

If equation (7) holds, t is set to 0 at which the manager's supply of effort is $e^* = \theta/\mu + e_0$, and the politician's utility is

(8)
$$U^* = \frac{\theta^2}{\mu} + \theta e_0 + \beta.$$

Obviously, U^* is greater than U_0^*. Under equation (7), U^* is also greater than U_0^c. Therefore, privatization makes the politician better off if he can commit himself to the governance reform. On the other hand, the surplus left to the manager is all the firm's revenue $\theta^2/\mu + \theta e_0$, so his net utility is $\theta e_0 + 0.5\theta^2/\mu$, which is positive. Finally, the general public is also pleased because the firm's revenue increased from $\theta e_0 - a$ to $\theta^2/\mu + \theta e_0$. Therefore, we have the following proposition:

PROPOSITION 1. *If the politician can commit to governance reform, privatization will be a Pareto improvement to the politician, the manager and the general public.*

However, governance reform may not be time consistent for the politician, because if the manager spent e^* on day 2, he might gain by loosening his control on his subordinates on day 3. To examine this possibility, we note that the marginal utility of t on day 3 is the same as in the case before privatization, which is positive by equation (5). Therefore, sticking to governance reform is not an ex post optimal choice for the politician. Of course, the manager can readily envision the politician's opportunist behavior and would have not provided e^* on day 2. Since the tax rate under corruption is 1 when the number of bureaucrats is large, the manager will provide e_0, exactly what he did under public ownership. Hence, both the manager and the politician are made indifferent between public ownership and privatization. Therefore, we have the following proposition:

PROPOSITION 2. *Without commitment to governance reform, privatization will not be a better choice for both the politician and the manager.*

Propositions 1 and 2 create a dilemma for the politician. To resolve the dilemma, the politician has to make a credible commitment on day 1 assuring the manager that he will stick to governance reform. This can be done by setting s equal to zero. When s is zero, the marginal utility of t on day 3 becomes $-a + \alpha$, which is negative if

$$(9) \qquad\qquad \alpha < a.$$

This condition implies that the weight of the bureaucrats' support is less than the intensity of deadweight loss caused by grabbing if corruption is exposed because of open government intervention. Whether this is true depends on the politician's preference and the severity of the deadweight loss, yet it is clear that it can happen even when equation (5) holds. The politician's utility under commitment is

$$(10) \qquad\qquad U^{*\prime} = \frac{\theta^2}{\mu} + \theta e_0,$$

which is smaller than U^*. That is, commitment is costly to the politician. However, his utility still can be larger than the most he can get under public ownership, U_0^c, if the following condition holds

$$(11) \qquad\qquad \alpha + \beta + \gamma < \frac{\theta^2}{\mu} + a.$$

The left-hand side is the cost of privatization and commitment, and the right-hand side is the gain from it. So the condition requires that the gain be larger than the cost. If this condition holds, the manager still gets $\theta e_0 + 0.5\theta^2/\mu$, the same as what he gets when there is no commitment problem. The revenue of the firm also reaches the highest $\theta e_0 + \theta^2/\mu$.

This is a good time to reiterate the conditions under which the commitment problem arises and can be overcome. They are conditions in equations (5), (9), and (11). The permissible parameter region defined by these three conditions is shown in figure 10.1. Notice that the size of the region depends on the relative sizes of θ^2 and β. If the latter is greater than the former, then the permissible region vanishes. Therefore, the robustness of the local economy and the weight that the politician puts on special interests and goals are critical. Thus, we have the following proposition:

PROPOSITION 3. *Commitment to governance reform can happen only if the local economy is robust and/or the politician cares less about special interests.*

10.4   Government Reform in Shunde

The government reform in Shunde began in 1993 and ended in 1999. It was radical by any measure. It was a top-down reform starting with the municipal government itself. It downsized the government by nearly half

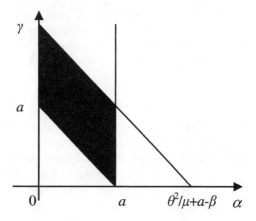

Fig. 10.1   Permissible parameter region for proposition 3

in terms of the number of government agencies and by a quarter in terms of the number of employees, transformed the functions of the government, increased the transparency of government administration, and enhanced the rule of law. In this section, we first provide a description of the reform, and then analyze the factors leading to its success, putting the emphasis on its linkage with privatization. At the end of the section, we conclude with a discussion of future problems.

10.4.1   Accomplishments of the Reform

The major pieces of the Shunde government reform are consolidation of government agencies and downsizing, transformation of government functions, establishment of administrative transparency, and enhanced efficiency and rule of law. Before the reform, there were 62 regular government agencies and more than 100 temporary agencies in the municipal government. The reform trimmed the number of regular agencies to 36 and eliminated 80 temporary agencies (Jiang 1999). All the intermediary committees between bureaus and the mayor were eliminated, and many bureaus with similar functions were combined. The most radical act was to combine the parallel departments in the government and the party organ. For example, the government secretary office was combined with the party secretary office; the Department of Organization and the Department of Veteran Leaders in the party organ were combined with the Department of Personnel in the government; and the party discipline committee was combined with the Bureau of Inspection in the government. The party organ is an indispensable entity in Chinese politics and government administration. Important government policies and directives are determined by the standing committee of the Communist Party, and the government's responsibility is only implementation. The consolidation of government and party departments enhances the characteristics of a party-state and its long-term merits can be much disputed, but it is a practical choice to downsize the government precisely because the Shunde reform was confined by China's party-state establishment.

In addition to cutting the number of government agencies, Shunde's government reform also took a tough position on government employees. Before the reform, there were 1,235 employees in the municipal government; the reform made a 25.8 percent cut and downsized the government to only 916 employees. This is really a small government in terms of the city's own population of 1.2 million and a similar population of migrants. However, the 319 employees who left the government were not simply laid off; 284 of them were transferred into newly founded businesses that had been transformed from government agencies, 15 people took early retirement, 8 people were transferred to townships, and only 12 people found their own employment. As a result, the resistance to the reform was lessened considerably. The real test, however, was the 123 officials whose ranks were lowered or even stripped off (Jiang 1999).

The downsizing not only could meet the resistance of those who lost their privileges, but also constituted a potential conflict with higher government establishments. A standard practice in China is that lower-level governments have to have the same, if not more, departments that a higher government has. The elimination and consolidation of departments in Shunde thus raised potential conflicts with the Guangdong provincial government. The way that this problem was solved was that each remaining department assumed more responsibilities and the work intensity of the remaining employees increased dramatically.

Downsizing the government cannot be sustained if its functions are not transformed. Shunde teaches us a lesson on that. In 1984, it had a government reform that cut nine government agencies and 171 people. However, because the government was still deeply involved in the management of the economy, the size of government quickly increased again. By 1987, the number of agencies increased by ten, to sixty-six, and the number of employees increased by 378, to 1,299 (Jiang 1999). The 1993 reform not only consolidated government agencies but also stripped many functions once assumed by the old agencies. This was made possible by the ownership reform. Before the reform, the government needed one bureau to manage the municipal-level firms and another bureau to provide administrative guidance to firms at the township and village levels. It also had separate bureaus in charge of domestic trade, international trade and cooperation, customs, rural trade, and tourism. After the reform, the two bureaus in charge of industry were combined into the Bureau of Industrial Development, and the other bureaus in charge of trade issues were combined into the Bureau of Trade Development. Together with the consolidation, the functions of these bureaus were reduced considerably. For example, the new industrial bureau no longer had the power to interfere with the internal management affairs of the old municipal firms, most of which have been privatized. Since their functions have been reduced, the industrial and trade bureaus are in the process of merging into one bureau.

The reform has reduced the government's role in economic management to a minimum, but the government has not become a figurehead. The Shunde government still maintains an active role in attracting investments, creating jobs, enforcing government regulations, providing local public goods, and managing an active industrial policy. This last function is directed mainly toward environmental protection. Shunde has large textile, dyeing, and tile industries that pollute heavily. As income increases, public demand for clean water and air has increased considerably. The Shunde government consciously rejects projects in these industries and uses taxation to force small labor-intensive and polluting firms out of business. This definitely affects employment, but it is unknown how serious the adverse effect is.

One striking change after the reform is the increase in transparency and efficiency in the Shunde government's administration. This is exemplified by its reform of its project approval process. The rule in China is that the government has the power to determine whether a project is worthwhile for the economy. The provincial-level government and cities designated to have separate fiscal plans can approve a domestic project with an investment of less than 30 million yuan renminbi, or a foreign direct investment project with an investment of less than 30 million U.S. dollars; beyond that, the project has to be approved by the central government. To get a project approved and the firm established, the owner has to have the patience to go through the maze-like government bureaucracy, spending considerable amounts of time and financial resources. The Shunde government cannot break the rule of approval, but has substantially increased the transparency and effectiveness of the approval process. Their innovation was to establish one approval office that provides "one-stop" approval for a project: it has the power to hand over the approval and is also responsible for preparing all the necessary documents for the project. This saves tremendously on the owner's efforts and increases the transparency of the approval process.

Another sign of transparency is the monthly administrative bulletin *Shunde Administrative Affairs,* published by the government. The bulletin publishes the newest laws and regulations issued by various levels of government and is sent to larger firms as well as to public venues, like hotels. This bulletin is unique among Chinese cities and serves as a bridge between the government and the private sector.

In relation to economic performance, the most important change brought about by Shunde's government reform is the increased regularity of government administration and the enhanced rule of law. This is shown in the IFC survey. To the question of how many major changes to laws, regulations, or policies took place in the last three years that affected a firm's business, the average answer in Shunde was 0.36 while the average for all the six surveyed cities was 2.54. In particular, Beijing had 6.19 times. Although Shunde's government levies were not the lowest among the six cities, they were certainly the most stable. For example, for fees (the most variable part of government levies), its coefficient of variation was 0.84 for Shunde, but in the range of 1.30 to 1.77 for the other five cities (Zhi 2001). Therefore, the policy environment is much more predictable in Shunde than in other cities. In addition, more people in Shunde than in other cities trusted the court when they had a dispute. There were 40.6 percent of the firms in Shunde that checked "going to the court" as a solution to a dispute, while the average for all the cities was 30.7 percent.

10.4.2   Factors Leading to the Success of the Reform

The success of the Shunde government reform is closely tied to its ownership reform, a visionary and strong leadership, a prosperous local economy, and meticulous design of the reform. As the review in the last section showed, the ownership reform was brought about by the financial problems faced by the public firms. Our theoretical model in section 10.3 then showed that ownership reform creates conditions for government reform. This is because, on the one hand, ownership reform makes firm managers the residual claimants, so they become sensitive to irregularities in government administration and law enforcement. On the other hand, ownership reform dispenses with many government functions. Both increase the politician's costs to maintaining a large and loosely controlled government, so his incentive to launch government reform is enhanced. In return, government reform sets down a credible commitment to better state governance and reduced corruption, so privatization results in good firm performance. As a result, government reform and privatization create a synergy for a better economy.

In addition to the conditions created by privatization, the role played by Shunde's leadership was also indispensable in bringing about the government reform. Our theoretical model predicts that the politician's preference is an important factor in determining the possibility of the reform. In Shunde, the reform-oriented leadership played a pivotal role in its ownership and government reforms. The party secretary is young, open-minded, and determined to engage in reform. Under his influence, the whole leadership team adopted a new philosophy toward government administration; that is, the government should draw away from direct engagement in economic affairs and instead should concentrate on the provision of public goods (including the provision of a fair, just, and open competitive environment) and implementation of the law. After several years of reform efforts, this new philosophy has gained popularity in the government and provided an important informal constraint on the behavior of government officials. No matter how thorough the reform is, the formal rules thus established still would be incomplete and government officials still would be empowered with a considerable degree of discretion in their decision making. Under this situation, informal constraints such as the new philosophy established in Shunde become important. One example of the effect of this informal constraint is the failure of the Bureau of Industrial Development to establish a small and medium-sized enterprise (SME) service center that was to provide charged services to SMEs. The bureau sent the proposal to the government office for screening before it was sent to the mayor for approval. The government office, staffed with junior officials, rejected the proposal and did not send it to the mayor. The message was simple: charged services could become a jumping-off board for corruption and should not be encouraged. The decision of the government office was not consistent with the rule of hierarchy commonly found in the Chinese bureaucracy, but instead was consistent with the new philosophy in Shunde.

The third factor contributing to Shunde's success is that it has a viable local economy. Although many firms were in the red when Shunde's privatization program began in the early 1990s, their losses were not created by their nonviability in the market, but rather by their mismanagement. Shunde is a production base for China's home electronics, an industry with continuously expanding domestic and international demand. Governance reform involves a trade-off between decreasing bureaucratic support and increasing social output. But a better local economy makes it easier for social output to increase, so, as our theoretical model predicts, the politician's willingness to engage in the reform is enhanced. In addition, a better local economy also makes layoffs easier as the private sector is more capable of absorbing the laid-off workers.

The last factor contributing to Shunde's success is its well-designed reform plan. This plan was not formed from the very beginning, but has been revised and enhanced in the course of the reform. Laid-off workers were not simply thrown out of the government; instead, they were first put into government-supported companies in the transition period. Afterward, these companies were privatized and the workers gradually were absorbed by the private sector. For workers remaining in the government, a major measure for boosting their morale was to increase their wages. The income of a government employee is now above the average in the private sector. However, even this wage is not enough to balance a person's desire for corrupt income. As a complement, the Shunde government maintains an active promotion system that puts able officials into important positions. In addition, the new administrative philosophy gives government officials a sense of honor as well as responsibility, which plays an important role in guarding the integrity of the administration.

10.5   Conclusions

The transition from a planned economy to a market economy is not merely a transformation of ownership, but also a transformation of state governance. In Eastern Europe and the former Soviet Union, the transformation of ownership was accomplished almost overnight, but initial performance records were uniformly bad. After almost a decade, some countries (such as Poland and the Czech Republic) have improved their performance records, but many of them (especially those in the former Soviet Union) are still in deep trouble. As Shleifer (1997) pointed out, the diverse performance records in Poland and Russia were a result of their different types of state governance, especially in the area of rule of law. The Shunde experience provides yet another example.

The problem with Russia is not so much with its economy, but rather with its state governance. In particular, the dissolution of the Soviet Union and the fall of the communist regime created a power vacuum. In the process of filling this vacuum, special-interest groups and monopolists have captured the state. China is luckier than Russia for not having gone through the destruction of the state apparatus. The danger, of course, is that without that destruction, China may be stuck with the old system and may never be able to build a sound state governance structure. In this regard, privatization as forced by financial problems may well provide an opportunity for China to take on serious governance reform, starting with the government itself. Right now, government reform at the central level is finished; the central government has reduced its size by 15 percent, and twenty ministries have been eliminated. Reform at the local level is underway and radical downsizing is expected. With China's economy being privatized continuously, the government reform may well be sustainable, so the synergy of a private-ownership-based economy and a sound state governance structure can be formed.

References

Dewatripont, Mathias, and Eric Maskin. 1995. Credit and efficiency in centralized and decentralized economies. *Review of Economic Studies* 62 (4): 541–555.

Garnaut, Ross, Ligang Song, Xiaolu Wang, and Yang Yao. 2001. *Private enterprise in China.* Canberra: Asia Pacific Press at Australian National University.

International Finance Corporation. Forthcoming. *Privatization in China.* Washington, D.C.: World Bank.

Jiang, Zhongzuo. 1999. *Institutional change in economic development: Theoretical and empirical studies based on Shunde's experience.* Ph.D. diss. College of Economics and Trade, Agricultural University of Southern China, Guangzhou.

Kornai, Janos. 1979. Resource-constrained versus demand-constrained systems. *Econometrica* 47 (4): 801–819.

Li, Shaomin, Shuhe Li, and Weiying Zhang. 2000. The road to capitalism: Competition and institutional change in China. *Journal of Comparative Economics* 28 (2): 269–292.

Liu, Yigao, Xiaoyi Wang, and Yang Yao. 2001. *The social and economic dynamics of the Chinese village.* ShijiaZhuang, China: Hebei Renmin Press.

North, Douglass, and Barry Weingast. 1989. Constitutions and commitment: The evolution of institutions governing public choice in seventeenth-century England. *Journal of Economic History* 49 (4): 803–832.

Qian, Yingyi. 1994. A theory of shortage in socialist economies based on the "soft budget constraint." *American Economic Review* 84 (1): 145–156.

Qian, Yingyi, and Barry Weingast. 1996. China's transition to markets: Market-preserving federalism, Chinese style. *Journal of Policy Reform* 1 (2): 149–185.

———. 1997. Federalism as a commitment to reserving market incentives. *Journal of Economic Perspectives* 11 (4): 83–92.

Qin, Hui. 1998. *Case studies on TVE privatization in Juangsu and Zhejiang.* Hong Kong: Chinese University of Hong Kong Press.

Shleifer, Andrei. 1997. Government in transition. *European Economic Review* 41 (3–5): 385–410.

Weitzman, Martin, and Chenggang Xu. 1994. Chinese township village enterprises as vaguely defined cooperatives. *Journal of Comparative Economics* 23 (1): 121–145.

Zhang, Gang. 1998. *A study on township and village enterprises.* Ph.D. diss. Stockholm School of Economics, Stockholm, Sweden.

Zhang, Weiying, and Shuhe Li. 1998. Regional competition and the privatization of Chinese SOEs. *Economic Research* 1998 (12): 13–22.

Zhao, Xiao. 1999. Competition, public choice, and privatization in China. China Center for Economic Research Working Paper Series C1999025. Beijing University, Beijing, China.

Zhi, Zhaohua. 2001. Privatization, government reform, and regional economic development. Master's thesis, China Center for Economic Research, Beijing University, Beijing, China.

Comment   David D. Li

This paper addresses the issue of when privatization works or fails to work. This is a very important issue because in reality, privatization programs often fall short of expectations in improving enterprise performance and in enhancing social welfare, and may even backfire and lead to back-sliding of the overall reform program. More importantly, the issue is more relevant than the issue of whether privatization should be implemented but has attracted less research so far. Understanding the issue well is critical to better design of privatization programs.

David D. Li is associate professor of economics and associate director of the Center for Economic Development at Hong Kong University of Science and Technology.

The issue of when privatization works arises from the fact that privatization is only a nominal transfer of ownership from the government to private hands. There is no guarantee that after privatization, the government, being the strongest player in most economies, continues to lend a heavy hand in the actual decisions of the private enterprises. Neither is there assurance that other parties, for instance, managers of enterprises who are not owners, take advantage of the retreat of the government and encroach on the control rights of the new owners.

Existing wisdom points to three general sets of conditions that induce success of a privatization program. The first is solid legal institutions that help define the rights of property owners. With the benefit of such institutions, new owners of privatized enterprises can expect to exercise their control rights in order to implement necessary changes for improving the performance of the enterprise. Of course, emerging market economies, which usually hope to establish functioning legal institutions via rapid privatization, can only wish such mechanisms were in existence.

Without the benefit of the rule of law, one alternative is to select suitable new owners to take over the privatized enterprises from the government. Suitable owners are ones who are strong enough to fend off postprivatization government interventions and guard against managerial abuses. One class of candidate is foreign corporations that are large and mobile and therefore are better positioned than domestic owners.

This paper provides a new perspective on this issue. The central message is that the government can and should precommit to certain mechanisms before privatization. With the precommitted mechanism, it is more difficult for the government to interfere in the operation of privatized enterprises and therefore improved performance of the privatized enterprises is more likely.

At an abstract level, the message makes a lot of intuitive sense and it is interesting to see it delivered in a coherent theoretical framework. We often do see that successful privatization is preceded or accompanied by major reforms of the government. Failed privatization programs are often those that were single-mindedly intended to privatize enterprises without concurrent reforms.

However, what exactly are the commitment mechanisms? This paper stops short of making this explicit. From the context of the discussion, these mechanisms might include shrinking the scope of control of the government, reducing the size of the government, simplifying regulatory setup of the government, and others. Yet, in reality, these different measures of reform have different implications for the post-privatization operation of enterprises. It helps sharpen the predictions of the theoretical model if the paper makes explicit the assumptions of which mechanisms it refers to.

The thrust of the theoretical model comes from the assumption that the commitment that the government makes and the difficulty with which the government interferes in the operation of the privatized enterprise are complementary. That is, the more commitment the government makes, the more difficult for the government to interfere. Again, it helps to be specific on this assumption. What kind of interference does the paper refer to? Why does such interference become more difficult for the government to make? Why, with stronger precommitment, is the interference more costly to the government?

The power of a theory lies in its ability to generate testable predications. This paper is no exception. By raising the issue of precommitment before privatization, the paper makes intuitive appeals but lacks a sequence of predictions for the reader to chew on and for future empirical work to test. The lack of more specific reference to the key assumptions leads to the lack of specific predictions. I believe that future research in this area will benefit from this line of exploration.

III

Sectoral Privatization and Regulation

Rail Reform Strategies
The Australian Experience

Helen Owens

11.1 Introduction

Railways began operating in Australia in the 1850s and, in many ways, they transformed transport in the country. They became vital links between Australia's cities and ports and the rural hinterland, facilitated export expansion, and were used by governments to pursue social and political objectives (Productivity Commission [PC] 1999).

However, much has changed since those early days. As more air, land, and sea transport options have developed, so the role of rail has changed. Although railways in Australia still play a significant role in the intrastate transport of bulk commodities and general freight along major corridors, and in urban transport, they are not as successful in other areas. Changing modal shares with the decline of rail in part reflect inherent advantages of other transport modes, particularly technological improvements. However, there have also been concerns that the poor performance of rail contributed to its own decline. Indeed, one Australian state government told the PC during its 1999 inquiry into rail reform in Australia that a lack of rail (and maritime) productivity has resulted in an overreliance on air and road transport in Australia (PC 1999, 1).

Concerns about the performance of rail led to a number of railway reforms and inquiries into the industry in the 1990s. However, it is not just in

Helen Owens is a commissioner on the Australian Productivity Commission and presided on the commission's 1999 inquiry into progress in rail reform.

This paper is based on the report of an inquiry into progress of rail reform undertaken by the Productivity Commission (PC) for the Australian government in 1999 (PC 1999). However, some views expressed in this paper do not necessarily reflect those of the PC. I am grateful to John Salerian, Kim Gusberti, the seminar discussants and referees for comments and assistance.

Australia that reforms have occurred. Railways in many countries have undergone significant changes in aspects of their organizational structures, ownership, and access arrangements over this period. Widely differing approaches to rail reform are evident, both across countries (discussed briefly below) and in different jurisdictions in Australia (the focus of this paper).

Reforms have included structural separation (both vertical and horizontal), the introduction of commercial disciplines (corporatization and privatization), and arrangements for third-party access to track infrastructure.

The wide range of reforms being implemented raises the question of whether one approach is superior to another. Using Australian railways as an example, this paper argues that because rail networks differ in terms of their economic characteristics and the challenges they face, it is important that individual reform packages be tailored to each network.

11.2   International Reforms

During the 1990s, reforms in some countries, such as Great Britain (England, Scotland, and Wales), New Zealand, and Argentina, involved increased private-sector participation.[1] In Great Britain, for example, twenty-five passenger service operations were established under franchising arrangements and the track, signals, and stations were sold to the private sector.[2] Structural reform across these countries has involved different combinations of vertical and horizontal separation (table 11.1).

Other countries have adopted reforms that change structures within government-owned railways. For instance, in 1994 the publicly owned Netherlands Railway was separated vertically into track infrastructure and train operations, with the latter divided into four commercial business units (passenger, freight, stations, real estate). Some new private entrants have also entered the Dutch market.

Table 11.2 provides an overview of the structure and ownership of the railways in selected countries.[3]

Many teething problems have been associated with these reforms. A notable example has been Great Britain. An apparent deterioration of services and major safety problems—as evident from several rail crashes in the 1990s, as well as the Hatfield rail crash in October 2000—led experts to blame the fragmentation of the system. One transport specialist suggested

1. Discussion of rail reform in Argentina, Australia, Great Britain, Germany, Sweden, and other European countries can be found in World Bank (1996), PC (1999), Kain (1998), Bowers (1996), Jansson and Cardebring (1989), and European Conference of Ministers of Transport ([ECMT] 2001).

2. The British government released a white paper in 1992 proposing changes to the railways. The Railways Act of 1993 allowed the structural reform of the railways, which were sold or franchised in 1997.

3. PC (1999) benchmarked Australia's railways with selected systems in Europe, America, and Japan. Railways in other Asian countries were not examined.

Table 11.1   **Definitions Relating to Structural Separation**

	Definition
Structural separation	Separation of businesses into discrete legal entities.
Horizontal separation	Occurs either by product (freight and passenger services) or by geographic area (interstate, regional, and urban railways).
Vertical separation	Separation of functional levels (track infrastructure and train operations).
Above track, or train operations	Provision of rail freight and passenger transport services involving locomotives and other rollingstock.
Below track, or track infrastructure	Physically fixed rail facilities such as track, sleepers, signals, terminals, and yards.

Table 11.2   **Overview of Structure and Ownership of Overseas Railways, 1999**

Country	Structure	Train Operator	Track Infrastructure
Argentina	Horizontally separated and vertically integrated	Franchisees	Government
Canada	Horizontally separated (by function) and vertically integrated with access for passenger services	Various private	Various private
Germany	Horizontal and vertical separation of accounts	Governments and private	Government
Great Britain	Horizontally and vertically separated	Franchisees	Private
Japan	Horizontally separated (by function) and vertically integrated with access for freight services	Franchisees and government freight operator	Government with franchisees having control of track
The Netherlands	Horizontally and vertically separated	Government and various private	Government
New Zealand	Horizontally and vertically integrated	Private	Government (leased for nominal rent)
Sweden	Horizontally and vertically separated	Government and various private	Government
United States	Horizontally separated (by function) and vertically integrated with access for passenger services	Various private	Various private

Source: PC (1999, E2).

that the complex structures created by privatization generated some problems, particularly relating to lines of accountability (Grayling 2000). Others have noted problems such as the setting of inappropriate benchmarks, shortcomings in liability regimes, and weak investment incentives (*The Economist,* 3 July 1999, 57–60; Trace 1999).

11.3   Australian Reforms

The development of railways in Australia since the 1850s[4] reflects the fact that Australia is a federation of states. There is a national (commonwealth) government and eight state and territory governments.[5]

Historically, railways have been (and many are today) under the jurisdiction of state governments. At the start of the 1990s the Australian rail system was characterized by integrated (state-owned) railways providing passenger and freight services in their respective jurisdictions.

Australian National (AN; owned by the commonwealth government) provided long-distance passenger services on the mainland, freight services across jurisdictions, and intrastate freight services in South Australia and Tasmania.

The state systems accounted for most rail freight transported. Of the more than 66 billion net-ton kilometers of rail freight transported in 1996–1997, for example, about three-quarters were accounted for by state railways. Queensland was the largest individual freight carrier, transporting about 43 percent of the total in that year. The busiest routes (in terms of net-ton kilometers) tended to be along the north-south corridor, that is, between Melbourne and Sydney and between Brisbane and Melbourne. However, rail had the most significant *share* of freight transport on the route between Perth and Adelaide (Industry Commission [IC] 1991).

One of the legacies of the historical pattern of development of the railways was a degree of parochialism that resulted in a lack of standardization of rail gauges. Standardization of the interstate network was only completed in 1995 when the Melbourne-to-Adelaide broad-gauge route was converted to standard gauge.

A number of factors drove reform in Australian railways in the 1990s. These included the following:

- Increasing pressure on government budgets to finance railway deficits, subsidies, and investment (the total amount of explicit subsidies paid to railways by state governments in 1997–1998, e.g., exceeded Australian $2.3 billion, representing 4 to 5 percent of the outlays of some

4. Rail reform in Australia is discussed further in PC (1999), Salerian (1999), and Scrafton (2001).

5. The states and territories of Australia are New South Wales, Victoria, Queensland, South Australia, Western Australia, Tasmania, Northern Territory, and Australian Capital Territory.

governments; PC 1999, 263). In 1996–1997, the rail deficit was A$1.36 billion (House of Representatives Standing Committee on Communications, Transport, and Microeconomic Reform [HORSCCTMR] 1998, 110), and total commonwealth, state, and local government investment in rail was about A$1.6 billion (HORSCCTMR, 112).

- Pressure on railway freight rates arising from increasing intermodal competition (this increased competition was due to the removal of the legislated monopoly previously given to rail for the carriage of certain bulk commodities,[6] and improvements in road transport technology and infrastructure).
- Pressure on railway freight rates from increasing competition in downstream markets for some commodities.
- The introduction of a National Competition Policy.[7]

A wide range of different structural, ownership, and access arrangements was introduced by the states in the 1990s (table 11.3). Queensland has retained a single, government-owned railway that provides freight and passenger services and maintains rollingstock and track infrastructure. This entity was, however, corporatized in 1995–1996. New South Wales (NSW), on the other hand, structurally separated its State Rail Authority in 1996, initially into four government-owned businesses (with responsibility for urban and nonurban passenger services, freight, track infrastructure, and track maintenance), of which three were corporatized.

In other states, reforms have led to greater participation by the private sector through franchising of urban and nonurban passenger rail services (Victoria) and privatization of freight operations (Victoria, Western Australia). The commonwealth government privatized parts of the AN railways and has plans to sell the National Rail Corporation (NRC), which assumed responsibility for AN's interstate freight operations in 1993. The interstate track was transferred to a new federal authority, the Australian Rail Track Corporation (ARTC), in 1998. On the east-west corridor across Australia, private operators now compete directly with the government operator in niche markets.[8] Overall the number of private railways rose from six in 1991 to nineteen in 1999.

6. Industry Commission (1991) and PC (1999) discuss the restrictions that existed on the intrastate carriage of particular commodities. For example, rail was required to transport coal (in NSW and Queensland) and domestic grains and petroleum (in Victoria, Queensland, and Western Australia).

7. In 1995 the Council of Australian Governments agreed to implement a package of measures to extend competition policies to previously exempt sectors of the economy. A Competition Principles Agreement established principles for structural reform of public monopolies, competitive neutrality between the public and private sectors, prices oversight of government business enterprises, regimes to provide access to essential facilities, and reviews of legislation restricting competition.

8. The former AN system now consists of two private operators (Australia Southern Railroad, Australian Transport Network), a corporatized government freight operator (NRC), a private passenger-train operator (Great Southern Railway), and a government track authority (ARTC).

Table 11.3   Structure and Ownership of Australian Railways, 1999

Jurisdiction	Structure	Train Operator	Track Infrastructure
Commonwealth	Vertically separated	Government and various private	Government
New South Wales	Horizontally and vertically separated	Government and various private[a]	Government
Victoria	Horizontally separated and vertically integrated	Private	Government (lease urban and nonurban)
Queensland	Horizontally and vertically integrated (with access for third parties)	Government	Government
Western Australia	Horizontally separated and vertically integrated (with access for third parties)	Government and private	Government (lease nonurban)
South Australia	Horizontally separated and vertically integrated	Government and private[a]	Government (lease nonurban)
Tasmania	Horizontally and vertically integrated	Private	Private

Source: PC (1999).

[a]NSW's FreightCorp has won a major coal haul contract in South Australia and NRC is operating intrastate services in NSW.

As with the experience overseas, these reforms have not been without problems. In particular, problems similar to those in Great Britain seem to have arisen following structural reforms in NSW, where a series of rail accidents and concerns over track maintenance standards resulted in an inquiry into the safety of the network. This safety audit, released in April 2000, noted that poor coordination among the new government-owned rail agencies had impeded the system's safety performance, and that a cultural change was required to allow the "effective delivery" of safety initiatives (D. Humphries, "Safety Gets Back Seat on Trains, Audit Finds," *Sydney Morning Herald,* 5 April 2000). In 2001, the businesses responsible for track access (Rail Access Corporation) and maintenance (Rail Services Australia) were merged into a single entity, the Rail Infrastructure Corporation, subject to direction from the NSW transport minister.

Until recently, attempts to privatize the NRC and the NSW Freight Rail Corporation (FreightCorp) had stalled. The sale of NRC was complicated by the fact that three governments—the commonwealth, NSW, and Victoria—had joint ownership of the corporation.[9] Disputes over access to Victorian terminals and tracks initially delayed privatization (M. Skulley,

9. NRC is 70 percent owned by the commonwealth, with minority stakes held by NSW (20 percent) and Victoria (10 percent).

"Full Steam Ahead: Rail Freight Sell-Off," *Australian Financial Review,* 1 March 1999, p. 3). These issues were resolved in 1999. In NSW, the Labor government faced opposition (particularly within its own party) to a proposal, made in September 2000, to privatize FreightCorp in parallel with the NRC. Concerns were mainly related to job losses and the possible impact of the sale on the regions. The NSW government eventually received support for the privatization proposal from an Upper House committee of Parliament and a Country Labor Party conference.[10]

The commonwealth and relevant state governments have now agreed to link the two businesses before selling them by the end of 2001. It is intended that the merged entity would have two divisions—a bulk haulage arm (FreightCorp's business) and an intermodal arm for NRC's interstate freight services. However, concerns have been expressed that the twin sale could substantially lessen competition, with the merged entity holding a high proportion of standard-gauge rollingstock. The governments have indicated that any competition issues raised by the Australian Competition and Consumer Commission (ACCC) would be addressed through the sale process (Batchelor et al. 2001).[11]

11.4 Performance of Australia's Railways

Reforms in the 1990s transformed the structure and operations of Australia's railways. There is now greater competition between railways and more private-sector participation in some corridors. The PC (1999) found that there were significant improvements in the productivity of (government-owned) railways providing freight and passenger services over the period 1989–1990 to 1997–1998.

Figure 11.1 indicates that the average annual growth in (total factor) productivity of Australia's railways of around 8 percent was greater than that of Canada, Japan, and the United States.

Freight customers benefited from this improvement in productivity. Real freight rates fell 30 percent between 1990 and 1998. This is comparable

10. The NSW Labor government support for the sale of FreightCorp was based on commonwealth government decisions to privatize NRC but prohibit the sale of NRC to Freight-Corp. The NSW government argued that the privatization of NRC would have left Freight-Corp vulnerable to "cherry-picking" of its most profitable contracts by NRC. After much debate, the NSW Country Labor Conference in November 2000 voted to condemn the privatization of NRC, but to make it a condition of sale of FreightCorp that it be sold to the same bidder as NRC (D. Murphy, "FreightCorp Sell-Off Wins Crucial Labor Support," *Sydney Morning Herald,* 13 November 2000). An Upper House committee of the NSW Parliament also made several recommendations about conditions to be attached to the privatization, which were incorporated in legislation (NSW Legislative Council 2001).

11. The Trade Practices Act of 1974 prohibits mergers and acquisitions that have the effect or likely effect of substantially lessening competition in a substantial market. The ACCC has the power to reject mergers that would substantially lessen competition, but can also authorize these where there is sufficient public benefit.

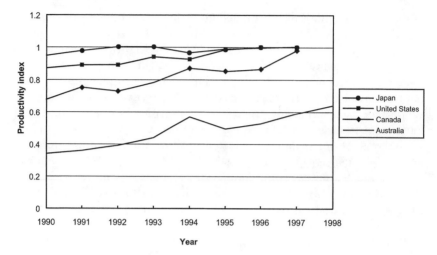

Fig. 11.1   Productivity levels of freight and passenger systems
Source: PC (1999, xxiv).

with decreases in Canada (33 percent) and the United States (26 percent) between 1990 and 1997.

However, while Australia has narrowed the gap in productivity, there remains a significant difference. Australia's level of productivity in 1998 was about two-thirds that of the best-performing countries (in 1997).

Some of the difference is due to factors that inherently disadvantage Australia, such as scale of operation. However, technical efficiency (productivity adjusted for the effect of scale) remains 30 percent below that of the best-performing countries.

11.5   Future Reforms

As discussed in section 11.4, improvements in the productivity of Australian railways had occurred in the 1990s but there was room for further improvement. Reforms during the decade had contributed to the improved performance but the PC inquiry report (PC 1999) considered that more needed to be done to ensure further productivity gains in Australia. It argued that a greater commercial focus and the harnessing of competitive forces were the keys to ensuring further productivity gains. Numerous participants to the inquiry agreed with this view.

While steps had been taken to corporatize the remaining government-owned railways, the ongoing problems for these railways appear to reflect the way the corporatization model has been implemented. Corporatization aims to provide a public enterprise with similar objectives, incentives, and sanctions to those of a private-sector firm (Hilmer, Rayner, and Taperell

1993, 300). The Hilmer Report noted five basic principles for the effective implementation of corporatization. These were clarity and consistency of objectives, management authority, performance monitoring, effective rewards and sanctions, and competitive neutrality.[12]

However, governments still subject their rail operators to multiple, often conflicting objectives relating to social welfare, regional development, and employment. Governments as shareholders face budget constraints and are often reluctant to provide equity funding or to allow railways to borrow on their own behalf, even if justified commercially. Further, governments are often reluctant to maintain an arm's-length relationship with their railway boards because of political and community pressures.

Even in theory, limitations apply to the corporatization model. In particular, public ownership subjects governments and taxpayers to considerable commercial risks.

Thus, private-sector alternatives to government provision have an important role to play in overcoming these problems. These alternatives can include contracting out and franchising. Competitive tendering and contracting (CTC) allows the introduction of competition into the provision of certain services and has been used increasingly by Australian railways, particularly in areas such as maintenance. Competition is introduced through the bidding process and so encourages providers to adopt efficient service-delivery methods. The main benefits of CTC are seen to include lower costs, improved service, and greater flexibility (King 1994). However, contract specification is an important determinant of the success of CTC. As well as specifying price, contracts need to contain incentives or conditions to maintain service quality.

Franchising involves the government granting a franchisee the right to operate a service for a fixed period. It can generate further gains because franchisees bear revenue risks, thus strengthening their incentives to improve service quality and expand the size of the market.

Full privatization can, in theory, offer a number of benefits over public ownership. Privately owned firms are said to have greater incentives and ability than public enterprises to be cost efficient, to make productive investments, and to be innovative and customer focused (see, e.g., Asterisis 1994). Privatization thus provides opportunities to change the leadership and culture of rail enterprises and transfer risk fully to the private sector.

In Australia, the Tasmanian rail system and interstate nonurban passenger systems have been privatized. The experience of privatization with these systems is encouraging and supports privatizing freight railways

---

12. In October 1992, a committee inquiry was established by the prime minister, with the support of state and territory governments, on the need for a national competition policy and its basic principles. The report of the inquiry (Hilmer, Rayner, and Taperell 1993) became known as the Hilmer Report, after the committee's chairman Frederick G. Hilmer.

Table 11.4   **Definitions Relating to Competition**

	Definition
Intermodal competition	Competition between rail and other modes of transport, such as road and coastal shipping.
Competition "for" the market	Competition between bidders tendering for the exclusive right to provide a specified service over a given period of time.
Competition "in" the market	Competition between train operators for the same customers on a given network (rail-on-rail competition).
Competition for train schedules	Competing demands by train operators for access to the track infrastructure. This can occur between train operators serving different markets (e.g., freight and passenger services), between operators competing for the same customers, or between trains with different origins/destinations wishing to travel over common segments of the network.
Competition in downstream markets	Competition in markets that railways serve.
Yardstick competition	Involves comparing the performance of organizations with similar objectives operating in separate geographic markets.

operating in competitive markets, such as NRC and NSW's Freight-Corp.[13] Scrafton (2001) argued that new entrants in freight and urban passenger rail appeared to be turning around markets that previously had been declining, with commitments to investment, new services, and courageous targets. For example, since purchasing Tasrail in 1997, the private owners have increased traffic volumes significantly, winning major contracts to haul logs and containers. Tasrail's revenue increased, while costs fell, making the railway profitable for the first time in 130 years. The private owners have invested heavily in new sleepers, communications systems, and replacement of the aging rollingstock. Likewise, some interstate passenger routes began to generate positive margins following privatization (PC 1999).

Competition can improve performance further. There are a number of forms competition can take—both "in" the market and "for" the market. Much of the rail network is already subject to intermodal competition from road, air, or coastal shipping, or competition in downstream markets. The different forms of competition are summarized in table 11.4.

13. The PC inquiry report recommended privatizing all remaining government-owned freight operations, with special arrangements for the rollingstock on the main coal lines (PC 1999, 145–151).

Competition can be facilitated by structural reform (e.g., vertical or horizontal separation; table 11.1) and the introduction of regulatory arrangements to enable access to track infrastructure. However, no single structure or access regime is appropriate for all networks.

11.6   Decision-Making Framework

So how do governments decide which approach is appropriate in reforming their rail networks? The specification of objectives and examination of the characteristics of the rail network can help in the decision-making process. Taking these steps allows identification of the forms of competition and structural reform that may be appropriate in each market.

Specifying the objectives of reform at the outset helps to identify the rationale for reform, and hence provides guidance on how best to implement reform (and, indeed, helps to identify whether reform is needed at all). For instance, the overarching objective of reform may be to have an efficient transport system meeting the freight and transport needs of a country, not to raise revenue from the private sector or to increase the aggregate level of service from railways. This implies that the extent to which each transport mode is used in the transport system would depend on its economic merit. Railways simultaneously compete with and complement other modes in providing a seamless transport service.

The efficient operation of railways is an important contributor to an efficient transport system. The sources of improved efficiency in railways—as in other industries—are static and dynamic efficiency gains. Static gains are achieved through one-off improvements to eliminate the sources of x-inefficiency. This can involve making better use of existing labor, equipment, and infrastructure. Dynamic efficiency gains involve continual improvement through innovation and, in the case of rail, continually optimizing its position in the transport logistics chain.

In most instances rail reform packages implemented across countries have delivered static efficiency gains. In New Zealand, for example, there were significant improvements in labor productivity, asset utilization, traffic levels, and profit in the five years following privatization (PC 1999, 149). To some extent these are the "easy" gains. But dynamic efficiency is likely to be more important to rail in the long run. Achieving greater dynamic efficiency is more difficult as it is likely to involve fundamental changes to the culture and operations of railways.

It is also important to understand the differing economic characteristics of individual rail networks. In a few markets, such as the transportation of bulk commodities such as coal, railways are able to exercise market power and extract monopoly rents from users. For other freight operations, railways may generate just sufficient earnings to be commercially viable and support future investment. Urban passenger rail services tend to be loss-making and rely on government subsidies for survival.

In addition, network interface issues, which occur when a train from one network needs access to another network, can potentially impede the efficiency of train operations and influence the appropriateness of different policy options. The extent of interface issues will depend on several factors, including the number of trains from other networks seeking access, the complexity of the network, and the level of traffic density.

Having identified objectives and network characteristics, the forms of competition likely to be effective in each network can be identified. Competition "for" the market, as occurs with franchising, is typically suited to natural monopoly situations where it is most cost effective to have only one provider of the rail service. In other markets, it may be possible to have multiple train operators competing for the same customers—that is, competition "in" the market (e.g., long-distance rail lines). This can encourage market segmentation and product diversity. In other markets, intermodal competition or competition in downstream markets may be sufficient to promote operational efficiency.

Finally, the emphasis in rail reform on promoting various types of competition is underpinned by structural reform. In essence, structural reform involves breaking up established railways into separate entities, with separation occurring on a geographic, functional (track, rollingstock, maintenance), and/or product (passenger or freight) basis.

The potential benefits of structural separation may include the promotion of competition, facilitation of the regulation of natural monopoly elements of the track, and the implementation of appropriate policies in different markets (PC 1999).

Separating train operations from the track (vertical separation) is designed to facilitate competition between train operators for the same customers and competition for train schedules. But vertical separation may not be effective in markets where there is limited scope for more than one operator, or there is already effective competition from other modes of transport or competition in downstream markets (Organization for Economic Cooperation and Development [OECD] 1999). It may also result in coordination and safety problems.

Separating railways by function or geography (horizontal separation) can improve the effectiveness of policies and regulatory regimes relating to different rail businesses. Contractual arrangements to meet noncommercial objectives (social, regional, or environmental) can also be implemented more readily. It also enables services to be franchised in order to introduce competition "for" the market through periodic competitive bidding.

The potential benefits of structural separation need to be balanced against the costs. The costs of structural separation potentially can include loss of economies of scope, interface problems between networks, loss of commercial sustainability, adverse effects on safety, and adjustment costs.[14]

11.7   Applying the Decision-Making Framework

The PC (1999) inquiry report into progress in rail reform applied this decision-making framework to the Australian railway system. Based on their economic characteristics, four different types of rail network can be identified in Australia—urban passenger, regional, main coal lines, and the interstate network. For each network the problems to be addressed and the impediments to improved performance differ, requiring differing policy solutions.

11.7.1   Urban Rail Passenger Networks

Urban rail passenger networks exist in the mainland state capital cities of Sydney, Melbourne, Brisbane, Perth, and Adelaide. These networks are noncommercial and exist in their current form only because of continued government support. In the markets served by these networks there is strong intermodal competition from private motor vehicles and from alternative public transport modes in some instances. There is no rail-on-rail competition.

Urban rail passenger networks pose a variety of challenges to governments and their operators. These railways are often criticized for their deficiencies in productive efficiency, large financial deficits, and poor service quality. These problems are further compounded by the fact that urban rail passenger services are highly visible to the public, often in need of capital investment, and subject to industrial disputes.

Given the loss-making nature of these networks, governments ultimately decide which services will be provided and the contribution users make toward the cost of provision. The performance of the urban transport system can be improved by ensuring that urban rail services fulfill an appropriate role within the system (improving allocative efficiency) and then that those services are provided at least cost to taxpayers (improving operational efficiency).

Allocative efficiency can be improved through the rigorous application of the purchaser-provider framework. The purchaser-provider framework separates the responsibility for deciding which goods and services are provided to the community from the responsibility for delivering the services (PC 1999). Governments consider and decide on the choice and mix of

---

14. PC (1999, 107–108) discusses the potential costs of vertical separation in more detail. Further information can also be obtained from Kessides and Willig (1995); Brooks and Button (1995); Thompson (1997); King (1997); OECD (1998); van de Velde and van Reeven (1998); and OECD (1999).

transport services purchased to promote stated objectives, rather than leaving such decisions to railway management.[15]

Greater operational efficiency can be encouraged by generating competition for the market through contracting or franchising. This approach is preferred to promoting competition between train operators. Urban rail passenger services require that trains run frequently and to a complex timetable. Coordination of services to meet the timetable is likely to be more effectively undertaken by one operator. In addition, the relatively small size of many urban passenger networks in Australia limits the scope for competition between train operators for the same customers.

Vertical integration can facilitate the franchising process and operational efficiency of urban passenger networks. Vertical separation is not warranted because there are no benefits to be obtained (through competition between train operators) to offset the costs of separation. In addition, accountability is also likely to be weakened in such a structure. If service standards are not achieved or if accidents occur, a regulator will be required to apportion responsibility and impose sanctions. As noted by Kain (1998), apportioning blame for poor performance may require considerable information and administration on the part of the regulator.

Horizontal separation of urban rail passenger networks from other rail networks can facilitate the application of the purchaser-provider framework by clearly delineating those services requiring government support from other commercial rail operations and networks. In addition, it may be worthwhile to horizontally separate the networks further into two or more geographically based franchises to promote "yardstick" competition, provided the population size is sufficient to support such separation.[16]

The benefits of further horizontal separation need to be balanced against potential interface and coordination issues that may occur between operators over shared segments of the network.[17] It has been argued, including by participants to the PC's inquiry into rail reform (PC 1999), that in some instances the horizontal separation of urban rail passenger networks from other rail networks is impracticable due to the interface issues between them. However, there are examples both in Australia and overseas of the use of contractual arrangements to overcome such problems. In Vic-

15. The PC identified five stages in the implementation of the purchaser-provider framework, including the specification of policy objectives, specification of rail services required to promote the objectives, determination of the level and form of subsidy, delivery of specified services, and costing of rail services (PC 1999, 12–16).

16. The establishment of the twenty-five horizontally separated passenger franchises in the United Kingdom is an example. In Victoria, the U.K. approach was adopted with the horizontal separation of the Melbourne urban train system into two franchises (Bayside Trains and Hillside Trains).

17. In Australia, network interface issues are of particular concern in Sydney, where congestion in the urban passenger network restricts the passage of freight trains. Interface issues also arise between the interstate and regional networks, as well as between the main coal lines and regional networks.

toria, there are contractual arrangements between an urban passenger operator in Melbourne, M-Train (formerly Bayside Trains), and interstate and regional operators that allow the use of the urban network by nonurban and freight trains. Similar arrangements also apply in the United States (PC 1999, 110, E24). The balance of evidence indicates that the benefits that can be obtained from horizontally separating urban rail passenger networks outweigh the cost of such contractual arrangements.

11.7.2   Regional Networks

Regional networks in Australia refer to those rail lines that extend from the ports and capital cities into the regional areas as well as lines from regional areas that connect into the interstate network. Within the regional networks of NSW and Queensland are the main coal lines that are discussed separately below. The services provided by regional networks are dominated by the transport of general freight and grains. The financial performance of these networks is mixed. Some networks have been able to generate sufficient revenues to earn a commercial return, while others are reliant on government support. In virtually all instances, the freight carried on regional networks is subject to strong intermodal competition, especially from road transport.

The poorly performing regional networks are confronted with the problems of declining market shares, increasing financial deficits, and a running down of existing infrastructure. These problems have arisen primarily due to these railways' inability to meet new competitive challenges, especially from road transport. This stems mainly from government involvement. In many instances, governments have required railways to pursue a range of conflicting objectives, interfered with their day-to-day operations, and restricted their access to capital. This has reduced the ability of these railways to meet customer needs at competitive prices, which is further compounded by the continual running down of the infrastructure base. At the same time, governments have deregulated freight carried by road, exposing rail to increasing competition.

Regional networks in Australia need to achieve both static and dynamic efficiency gains if they are to survive in the competitive transport markets in which they operate.

As the impediments to improved performance primarily stem from government involvement, the most effective way of overcoming them is to increase the commercial focus of regional networks. This requires that railway managers have the flexibility to make timely decisions, as well as the ability to form strategic alliances, to access capital, and to face no undue restrictions on input choice.

The commercial focus of government-owned railways can be improved through corporatization. However, as noted earlier, there are often limitations on how well the corporatization model is applied. In particular, governments are often unable to maintain an arm's-length relationship from their railway boards because of political and community pressure.

The limitations of government ownership can be overcome through greater private-sector participation by either franchising or full privatization. Privatization of rollingstock and a long-term lease on infrastructure are preferred to franchising in this case because it allows for greater commercial focus and increased flexibility.

Alternatively, the performance of regional railways could be improved by encouraging competition between train operators through vertical separation combined with access arrangements. However, the small volumes of freight carried on regional networks, and the resulting inability to achieve economies of scale, suggest that profitable entry by third-party operators is likely to be limited in most instances. Importantly, as already noted, there is competition from other transport modes, which would encourage improved performance by the incumbent operator. The impediment to improved performance is not a lack of competition but rather an inability to meet existing competitive challenges.

Thus vertical integration appears to be appropriate for regional railways, since vertical separation makes little, if any, contribution to overcoming the main impediments to improved performance.

Regional networks are also particularly suited to horizontal separation. This would clearly delineate those markets where direct government involvement is not required. Rail management would have the freedom to focus on developing new market opportunities and to increase operational efficiency. "Light-handed" access arrangements can be tailored to ensure that noncompeting trains from other networks can gain fair and reasonable access. However, it is expected that access would not be an issue because owners would have incentives to provide access to noncompeting trains as the increased traffic flow could increase profits to the track owner or lessee.

11.7.3   Main Coal Lines

The main coal lines in Australia are defined as the Hunter Valley coal network in NSW and those lines centered on the Goonyella and South Blackwater regions in Queensland. These networks carry high volumes, are highly profitable, and have a natural monopoly in the carriage of almost all coal in these regions (i.e., there is little competition from road or rail-on-rail competition).

Unlike other rail networks in Australia, the main coal lines have maintained their market share in the transport of coal, and investment has been easily justified on a strictly commercial basis. In this instance, the problems associated with the main coal lines are those of market power and the extraction of monopoly rents from mining companies, as well as inefficient operations.

There are two main reform packages the state governments could implement to control the existence of market power on the main coal lines. First, competition between train operators could be encouraged, with monopoly pricing of the track infrastructure addressed through access regulation. Alternatively, franchising of a vertically integrated network may be used to promote competition "for" the market by awarding contracts for the right to supply rail services (track and train). Tenders could be awarded on the basis of the lowest total cost of service provision over a relevant period. Track and rollingstock could be leased to the franchisee and access conditions incorporated into franchise agreements.

The appeal of the first approach is that competition between train operators can control monopoly pricing on the part of operators, while vertical separation can increase the transparency of access-price regulation. However, there are some practical problems with this approach. In the first instance, sunk costs associated with investing in locomotives and wagons can act as a substantial barrier to entry to potential new entrants. This problem is compounded by the fact that the rollingstock used to haul coal (especially the wagons) is specific to the haulage of bulk commodities, reducing its transferability to other rail markets.

In addition, even if effective competition between train operators could be achieved, the issue of monopoly pricing still exists in track infrastructure. The control of such monopoly power requires complex regulation.

Franchising has the advantages that the bidding process can be designed to facilitate the transfer of assets (especially the rollingstock), removing a substantial barrier to entry and making the market more contestable (OECD 1999). The franchisee has commercial incentives to obtain dynamic efficiencies and lower costs by improving the role of railways in the transport logistics chain between the mines and ports. In addition, franchising reduces the need for prescriptive access regulation. Periodic retendering and awarding contracts on the basis of the lowest freight rate can help to reduce monopoly rents (PC 1999).

However, franchising is not a perfect or costless solution to controlling monopoly pricing. The OECD (1999) identified three potential difficulties with the franchising of rail services, including the possibility of uncompetitive bidding when there are insufficient bidders, the difficulties of choosing between bids that offer different packages, and the specification and administration of contracts.

On balance, the economic characteristics of the main coal lines suggest that a process of franchising through competitive tendering is likely to be superior to facilitating rail-on-rail competition. Government involvement continues under both approaches through access regulation or the franchise process and agreements. However, it is less certain that vertical separation and access regulation will lead to new operators' entering the market owing to the sunk costs associated with the rollingstock required. As noted earlier, the franchising process can be designed to overcome this problem, making the market more contestable to potential operators.

To facilitate the franchising process, the main coal lines could be horizontally separated from other networks. The isolation of the network, together with transparent information on the costs and revenues of the franchise, would provide confidence to coal companies that monopoly pricing practices had been eliminated.

11.7.4   Interstate Network

The interstate network can be broadly defined as the standard-gauge track linking all mainland state capital cities. The markets served by the interstate network are varied, including freight (generally containerized) and interstate passenger services.

The financial returns on the interstate network have traditionally been poor. Although never highly profitable, the profitability of the NRC, which carries freight on the interstate network, deteriorated significantly after the introduction of private operators on the network in 1995–1996 (PC 1999, 29).[18] There is strong intermodal competition (from road and coastal shipping) in almost all markets served by the interstate network.[19] The key feature that differentiates the interstate network from regional networks is that for the former there are multiple network owners, responsible for allocating train schedules and undertaking investment.

Currently the ARTC's responsibilities for the interstate network are limited to the track that it owns (i.e., in South Australia and parts of NSW, Western Australia, and Northern Territory) or manages (in Victoria). Operators face significant costs in negotiating access and train schedules with numerous owners.[20]

Figure 11.2 shows that the interstate network initially lost considerable market share to road, in both the transport of nonbulk freight and interstate passengers.[21] The operating deficits of the network have discouraged investment, resulting in a deterioration of the infrastructure, further eroding the competitive position of railways. It has been estimated that more than half the expenditure of the commonwealth from the late 1970s to

18. NRC made operating losses of between A$5 million and A$31 million in the period 1996–1997 to 1999–2000 and recorded a modest profit before tax of A$2.3 million in 2000–2001.

19. For example, in 1994–1995, the interstate transport of bulk commodities was dominated by coastal shipping (95 percent of the market). In contrast, road dominated the transport of nonbulk freight (57 percent of the market, compared to 32 percent for rail).

20. Currently, four authorities are responsible for the administration of access, five authorities have a role in allocating train schedules, and five authorities undertake investment in the network.

21. Rail market share of freight traffic on the east-west corridor reached a low of 65.2 percent in 1995–1996 but has started to rise again, to 77 percent in 1999–2000, the highest level in a decade. This in part reflects the recent growth in rail-on-rail competition from private niche operators (ARTC 2001).

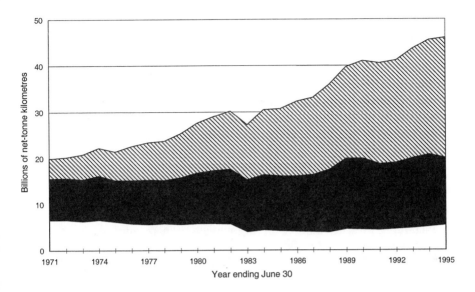

Fig. 11.2   Nonbulk interstate freight, Australia, 1970–1971 to 1994–1995
Source: PC (1999, 15), based on Perry and Gargett (1998).

1996–1997 covered operating losses and historical debt of its railway bodies (HORSCCTMR 1998). This, it has been argued, diverted expenditure from capital works. Some participants to the PC's rail inquiry (1999, 237) noted that there has also been "neglect" of the interstate network by state governments. A number of reports in the 1990s (HORSCCTMR; Maunsell 1998; Booz-Allen and Hamilton 1998) presented evidence of the inadequacy of rail infrastructure. Participants to the PC's inquiry also discussed the inadequacy of investment that contributed to problems in the interstate network and hindered rail's ability to compete (PC 1999, 236–38).

There are two main underlying causes of the loss of competitiveness of rail. First, government ownership and incentive arrangements have impeded the ability of train operators to improve operational efficiency and achieve dynamic efficiency gains through market segmentation and better integration into the transport logistics chain. Second, the multiplicity of network managers imposes costs on train operators in negotiating train schedules and access charges. This impedes the efficient allocation of train schedules, overall use of the network, and investment.

These impediments can in part be overcome through the proposed privatization of NRC and encouragement of more rail-on-rail competition from private niche operators. To overcome the problems associated with multiple owners of the track infrastructure, integrated management of the network is required. This could be achieved by establishing a single network manager to manage the operation of the interstate track on behalf of both train operators and track owners. This approach has a number of possible advantages. For instance, it reduces the coordination issues inherent in having multiple managers of the network. It also avoids the conflicts of interest that could arise if the manager also owned the track or rollingstock. An access regime could allow for train schedules to be allocated by auctioning or other market trading methods. This would maximize the economic value of the network by allocating train schedules to those operators that valued them the highest. Flexible pricing arrangements would facilitate investment.

The successful implementation of this approach would be dependent on the vertical separation of train operations from the track infrastructure. This is to avoid any conflict of interest or difficulties that may arise from one party both owning one segment of the network and providing train services in competition with other operators.

11.8   Implications for Existing Arrangements

The differentiated approach described above has different implications in each Australian jurisdiction because of differences in the characteristics of their railways. The potential for further reform exists in them all.

It has particular implications in states where coal lines are horizontally integrated with the rest of the network (Queensland and NSW), or where freight operations are still government-owned (Queensland and, until the sale of FreightCorp was announced, NSW).

In NSW, consideration could also be given to going further and reintegrating the track and operations. It could adopt the Victorian model such that the privatization of FreightCorp would involve a long-term lease over the nonmetropolitan intrastate track (with appropriate access arrangements). All passenger services could be franchised. The franchisees would buy (or lease) the rollingstock and lease the track from the government.

Further reform of the interstate network has particular implications for the commonwealth, NSW, and Western Australian governments. They are currently owners of parts of the network and have separate access regimes. The single-network-manager approach would be more effective if the interstate network were vertically separated and the manager did not own the track infrastructure. This approach would allow coordinated management and promote competition over the entire interstate network, generating significant benefits and giving rail an opportunity to strengthen its competitive position on this important transport corridor.

Further investigation could also show that the PC's recommended approach may have relevance for some networks in other countries.

The European network, for example, traverses many countries in the same way as Australia's interstate network traverses a number of states. It is used heavily by both freight and passenger trains. This suggests that the approach suggested for Australia's interstate network—involving vertical separation and a single network manager—could be relevant in this context.

Like Australia's regional railways, Eastern European railways are often heavily involved in moving general and bulk freight to ports. Where there is already sufficient intermodal competition, consideration could be given to greater private-sector participation in vertically integrated, horizontally separated railways.

11.9   Conclusion

The Australian Productivity Commission considered that the overarching objective of rail reform should be to improve the efficiency of a country's transport system. It argued that it should not be seen as a means of involving the private sector to compensate for inadequate government investment in loss-making railways.

An important conclusion from the PC inquiry was that the implementation of a common reform package is unlikely to overcome the impediments to improved performance in all markets. Individualized approaches need to be developed on a case-by-case basis for each type of rail network.

Crucial to developing individualized approaches is identifying the characteristics of markets and their boundaries. Even where rail infrastructure is considered a natural monopoly in a technological sense, other characteristics influence the ability of providers to exercise market power and, thus, the appropriate policy approach for a particular network. These characteristics, which will differ across rail networks, include the strength of intermodal competition from air and road, the degree of competition in downstream markets, and traffic density. Hence the appropriate structural and ownership arrangements will differ for long-distance, regional, and urban passenger rail networks.

Trade-offs are inevitable. While vertical separation may assist in promoting competition and reducing monopoly rents, it may result in a lack of accountability, major coordination problems, and significant safety concerns, as evidenced in Great Britain and NSW. In particular, the implementation of strong access regulation to promote competition may diminish incentives for business to invest in maintaining and upgrading the rail infrastructure. Horizontal separation of different networks may promote viable businesses but interface issues between networks may arise. Where viable, however, horizontal separation can allow different policies to be implemented for networks with different characteristics.

Systematic analysis of structural reform and ownership options would involve assessing the relevance and likely magnitude of the associated costs and benefits.

This paper has highlighted considerations that may be relevant to determining the preferred vertical structure of particular networks.

- Where there is sufficient intermodal competition and the possibility of the development of rail-on-rail competition, vertical separation would be appropriate. Benefits are likely to be most significant when infrastructure and operations are relatively independent (OECD 1999).
- Where there is intermodal competition but little possibility of rail-on-rail competition (e.g., where the potential market is small), gains from vertical separation are unlikely to outweigh the costs. In this case, vertical integration and promotion of competition for the market (e.g., through franchising) would be preferred.
- Where there is market power in the network, vertical integration may also be appropriate. Periodic retendering and the awarding of contracts on the basis of the lowest freight rate can help to reduce monopoly rents. Vertical separation, on the other hand, could result in the transfer of monopoly rent from train to track operations. In addition, where there are barriers to entry, such as sunk costs in above-rail operations, rail-on-rail competition is unlikely to develop.

In short, there can be no "one-size-fits-all" approach to rail reform. Care must be taken to ensure that the reform strategy adopted is relevant to the network type, taking into account its economic characteristics, and that it is implemented only when the gains exceed the costs.

11.9.1   Postscript

Since this paper was originally presented, the Australian rail reform process has continued, including the sale of NRC and FreightCorp in January 2002, and the establishment of access arrangements for the parts of the interstate network controlled by the ARTC.

In addition, several developments have highlighted difficulties that can arise in implementing reform.

In December 2002, one of the private operators of the Victorian urban rail passenger network (M-Train), which had incurred large financial losses, withdrew from the system. (Its part of the network is being operated by receivers on behalf of the Victorian government, until a decision is made about longer-term arrangements.) Several factors are likely to have contributed to M-Train's withdrawal. In part, it may reflect problems with horizontal separation within a market (e.g., urban passenger), if it leaves individual providers with a market that is too small or fragmented. Connex, the current operator of the other part of the system, argued that horizontally separating the Victorian urban network has been inefficient, and has expressed interest in operating the whole system (J. Masanauskas, "Train Stations Are Just 'Crap,'" *Herald Sun,* 4 February 2003, p. 8). Thus, the attempt by the Victorian government to adopt a one-size-fits-all approach to its urban network, by emulating the United Kingdom, appears to have failed because it paid insufficient attention to local conditions, particularly the relatively small size of the market. This does not, however, undermine the principle of horizontally separating the urban rail passenger network from other rail networks.

In 2001, investment disincentives—purportedly created by the pricing rules for the rail freight access regimes in Victoria and NSW—were raised as an issue to a PC inquiry into the Australian national access regime (PC 2001). The potential "chilling" effect of access regulation for investment (in all industries) was highlighted as a major concern in the commission's final report (2001). It suggested some general principles that would allow access regimes to facilitate efficient new investment. These included setting regulated access prices to generate expected revenue that at least meets the efficient long-run costs of providing access, that covers the directly attributable or incremental costs of service provision, and that includes a return commensurate with (regulatory and commercial) risk.

References

Asterisis, M. 1994. Rail privatisation: A platform for success. *Economic Affairs* 14 (2): 19–23.

Australian Rail Track Corporation (ARTC). 2001. Interstate rail network audit. Final report prepared by Booz-Allen & Hamilton. Sydney, Australia, April.

Batchelor, Fahey, Anderson, and Egan. 2001. Combined sale of National Rail and FreightCorp under way. Joint media release, 24 August.

Booz-Allen and Hamilton. 1998. *Project evaluation for the Interstate Rail Track Capital Program.* Report for the Commonwealth Department of Transport and Regional Development (Canberra) and the Australian Rail Track Corporation (Adelaide).

Bowers, P. 1996. Railway reform in Germany. *Journal of Transport Economics and Policy* 30 (1): 94–102.

Brooks, M., and K. Button. 1995. Separating transport from track operations: A typology of international experiences. *International Journal of Transport Economics* 12 (3): 235–260.

European Conference of Ministers of Transport (ECMT). 2001. *Railway reform: Regulation of freight transport markets.* Report presented to the Ministers of Transport, Prague Council, May 2000. Paris: Organization for Economic Cooperation and Development Publications Service.

Grayling, T. 2000. "Trouble on the track." In The Guardian (19 October) [online journal]. Available at www.guardian.co.uk/hatfieldtraincrash/story/0,7369,384684,00.html.

Hilmer, F., M. Rayner, and G. Taperell. 1993. *National competition policy.* Report by the Independent Committee of Inquiry. Canberra: Australian Government Printing Service.

House of Representatives Standing Committee on Communications, Transport, and Microeconomic Reform (HORSCCTMR). 1998. *Tracking Australia: An inquiry into the role of rail in the national transport network.* Committee report. Canberra: HORSCCTMR.

Industry Commission (IC). 1991. *Rail transport.* Report no. 13. Canberra: AGPS.

Jansson, J., and P. Cardebring. 1989. Swedish railway policy 1979–88. *Journal of Transport Economics and Policy* 23 (3): 329–337.

Kain, P. 1998. The reform of rail transport in Great Britain. *Journal of Transport Economics and Policy* 32 (2): 247–266.

Kessides, I. N., and R. D. Willig. 1995. Restructuring regulation of the railroad industry. In *Public policy for the private sector,* n. 58. Washington, D.C.: World Bank Group, Private Sector Development Department, October.

King, S. 1994. Competitive tendering and contracting out: An introduction. *Australian Economic Review* 107 (3rd quarter): 75–78.

———. 1997. National competition policy. *The Economic Record* 73 (222): 270–284.

Maunsell Pty Ltd. 1998. *Study of rail standards and operational requirements.* Prepared by Maunsell Proprietary Limited for the Australian Transport Council.

National Rail Corporation (NRC). 2001. *Annual report 2000–01.* Parranatta, NSW, Australia: NRC.

New South Wales Legislative Council. 2001. Second Reading Speech of the Freight Rail Corporation (Sale) Bill. *Hansard,* 27 June, 15424–15434.

Organization for Economic Cooperation and Development (OECD). 1998. *Railways: structure, regulation, and competition policy.* Competition Policy Round Table series, no. 15, DAFFE/CLP(98)1. Paris: OECD.

———. 1999. Competition and railroads. *Journal of Competition Law and Policy* 1 (1): 149–228.

Perry, R., and D. Gargett. 1998. Interstate non-bulk freight. In *Proceedings of the twenty-second Australasian Transport Research Forum,* vol. 22, no. 1, pp. 19–28. Sydney: Transport Data Center of New South Wales, Department of Transport.

Productivity Commission (PC). 1999. *Progress in rail reform.* Report no. 6. Canberra: AusInfo.

———. 2001. *Review of the national access regime.* Report no. 17. Canberra: AusInfo.

Salerian, J. 1999. Australian approach to railway reform, including privatisation of railways. Paper presented at the Regional Conference on Railway Reform and Restructuring, Ministry of Transport of Vietnam and World Bank. 17–18 September, Hanoi, Vietnam.

Scrafton, D. 2001. *Railway reform in Australia: Access regimes, changes in ownership, and structural change. In 2001: A transportation odyssey.* Proceedings of the thirty-sixth annual Canadian Transportation Research Forum, vol. 2, ed. W. G. Waters, 761–776. Saskatoon: University of Saskatchewan.

Thompson, L. 1997. The benefits of separating rail infrastructure from operations. In *Public policy for the private sector,* n. 135. Washington, D.C.: World Bank Group, December.

Trace, K. 1999. Rail privatisation: Lessons from the U.K. In *Regulation, competi-*

tion, and industry structure. Proceedings of the 1999 Industry Economics Conference, 199–218. Melbourne: AusInfo.

Van de Velde, D., and P. van Reeven. 1998. *Railway reform and the role of competition.* Rotterdam, The Netherlands: Erasmus University.

World Bank. 1996. *Argentina transport privatisation and regulation: The next wave of challenges.* Report no. 14469-AR. Latin America and Caribbean Regional Office.

Comment   John McMillan

This paper comprehensively lays out the pros and cons of the alternative mechanisms of railway reform, and gives a useful catalogue of where they apply.

The main point of the paper bears repeating, as it is very important: there is no uniquely right approach to railway reform. What works in one set of circumstances fails in another. One size doesn't fit all.

The approaches to rail reform include downsizing (by means of either horizontal or vertical separation of activities), corporatization, privatization, and offering access to the tracks by competitive service providers. Each of these approaches has its place, as Helen Owens explains.

The bad news, a corollary of one size doesn't fit all, is that any approach to reform necessarily has some shortcomings. Choosing the best feasible solution means making trade-offs and compromises. Whatever solution is adopted, there will always be room for critics to find fault with it.

It is the complexity of the exercise of railway reform that means one size doesn't fit all. The railway industry is harder than most industries to reform successfully, for several reasons.

First, the system of tracks creates a natural-monopoly element, meaning that competition is hard to achieve. One of the main lessons from the post-1980s privatization exercises in many industries around the world is that privatization often fails to bring its intended efficiency gains where the privatized firm remains a monopoly. It is not enough merely to transfer assets to private hands and rely on the profit motive to induce the new owners to improve the firm's efficiency. The discipline of competition is also needed. It is difficult to run a firm as a lean operation if its managers do not feel the continual pressure of competition. In railways, with limited scope for competition, privatization is not guaranteed to bring major efficiency gains.

Second, the policymaker must take account of externalities. Road transportation brings large negative externalities, from congestion, pollution, and accidents. The Federal Highway Administration estimates that the uncompensated negative externalities from driving in the United States come to some $330 billion per year. To the extent that railways reduce these ex-

John McMillan is Jonathan B. Lovelace Professor of Economics at the Graduate School of Business, Stanford University.

ternalities, some form of public support is warranted. Especially for urban commuter rail systems, externality arguments justify public subsidy. This complicates any attempt to privatize or corporatize railways, for simple profitability may not, from a social point of view, be the right criterion for evaluating performance.

Third, the coordination of timetables can be complex, and can raise safety concerns. If multiple rail companies use common tracks, some form of central coordination is needed to avoid crashes.

Finally, technological progress is unlikely to come to the rescue of the reformers. In telecommunications, for instance, technological advances in the 1980s and 1990s reduced the scope of natural monopolies, and made reform easier than it would have been earlier. Such dramatic technological change seems unlikely in railways.

For these reasons it is a delicate matter to judge just which mix of market forces and government control is the right one in any particular set of circumstances, as the paper makes clear.

There is one form of ongoing technological progress, however, that may over time change this mix: the design of market mechanisms. Paul Brewer and Charles Plott designed a mechanism for scheduling the use of the Swedish railways. Multiple rail firms used the common, publicly owned tracks (Brewer and Plott 1996). To generate consistent schedules and avoid train crashes, the traditional approach to scheduling was for a committee to centrally set the timetable. The Brewer-Plott mechanism attempts to capture the informational benefits of decentralized decision making. The rail users bid for the right to use specific lengths of track at specific times. An algorithm first retains only the highest bids. Then it sorts the bids into all possible combinations that are feasible, meaning they respect safety margins for track use. Finally, it computes the bid total for each of the feasible combinations. The combination with the highest bid total is declared the provisional winner. Now a new round of bids is called for, and the process repeats until no one wants to bid higher. In experiments, this mechanism works well, in eliciting close to efficient allocations.

The lesson from the Brewer-Plott mechanism is that we should not underestimate what markets can do. As computing power increases and as economists' ability to design sophisticated bidding mechanisms expands, the balance of the trade-offs Helen Owens analyzes will change.

Reference

Brewer, Paul J., and Charles R. Plott. 1996. A binary conflict ascending price (BI-CAP) mechanism for the decentralized allocation of the right to use railroad tracks. *International Journal of Industrial Organization* 14:857–886.

The Japanese Experience with Railway Restructuring

Fumitoshi Mizutani and Kiyoshi Nakamura

12.1 Introduction

Although many countries privatized their railways after 1987, the privatization of the Japan National Railway (JNR) in that year marked the first sweeping reform of a national railway in the world. Privatization has been accomplished in various ways in different countries. Indeed, railway restructuring in Japan has been markedly different from that in European nations. In this paper, we will explain the Japanese approach to railway reform and discuss the experience gained and lessons learned from the privatization process.

This paper consists of five sections. Section 12.2 summarizes the privatization of the JNR, explaining the impetus for privatization, the steps by which it was achieved, the restructuring options that were available at the time of privatization, and the general characteristics of this privatization. An international comparison is also presented. Section 12.3 describes how the management of the privatized Japan Railways (JRs) differs from that of the former JNR. While most privatization studies focus on regulatory changes, we want to concentrate also on managerial issues such as corporate goals, relationships with interest groups, organizational structure, incentive systems, and task-improving activities. In section 12.4 we show performance results of the regional railway companies after privatization,

Fumitoshi Mizutani is professor of public utility economics in the Graduate School of Business Administration, Kobe University. Kiyoshi Nakamura is professor of industrial economics and associate dean of the School of Commerce, Waseda University.

We would like to thank Mario Lamberte (Philippine Institute for Development Studies), Helen Owens (Productivity Commission, Australia), Takatoshi Ito (University of Tokyo) and the conference participants for valuable suggestions and comments. We also would like to thank an anonymous referee for valuable questions.

discussing not only overall performance but also rail fare, competition, and the operation of local rail service, and presenting an international comparison of these factors. In section 12.5 we consider several policy issues related to rail restructuring, using as a basis for discussion these topics: regional subdivision, functional division, vertical integration, and yardstick competition. Finally, keeping in mind the situation of developing countries, we outline important points related to rail privatization policy in section 12.6.

12.2   A Summary of the Privatization of the Japan National Railway

12.2.1   The Road to Privatization

Reasons for Privatization

Along with two other huge public entities, Nippon Telephone and Telegraph and the Japan Monopoly Public Corporation (Tobacco and Salt), which were privatized in the late 1980s, JNR began the process of privatization in 1987, when it was partitioned into six regional passenger companies (the JRs) and one nationwide freight company.

As a public corporation, the JNR encountered numerous organizational problems, including complacency due to a lack of a sense of crisis, an antagonistic labor-management relationship, and political interference. Reforms were hindered by opposition from politicized labor unions, which were divided into several organizations. The repeated failure of nationalization produced ineffectual alternation between easy dependence on government subsidies and halfway reforms. In 1964, for the first time in its history, JNR showed an operating loss, its competitiveness having been eroded by automation and the failure to reduce its heavy burden of redundant employees. The hostile relationship between management and labor unions profoundly damaged morale in the workplace and lowered productivity and the quality of service.

It gradually became evident to those both inside and outside JNR that divestiture would be necessary to reduce the huge government subsidies supporting JNR, and to enhance its efficiency. The idea that social infrastructure could be paid for not by the government out of strained budgets but with private funding was not new in Japan, since much railway service had been and still is provided by private railway companies. Moreover, since intermodal competition had drastically eroded the domain of JNR as a natural monopoly and the potential for competition in the market was extended, it became obvious that JNR, even though it was such a traditional and politically powerful entity, should be required to work within the framework of a market economy. A divestiture plan was devised by members of a special committee organized by several political entrepreneurs and by proprivatization management inside JNR.

The Process of Privatization

One important fact about the JNR privatization was that it was accomplished not all at once, but rather in a step-by-step manner. When railway reform began in 1987, most stock of the newly established JRs continued to be held by the public sector at Japan National Railway Settlement Corporation (JNRSC), a temporary holding company established for this purpose. Stock was not immediately offered to the public, because the government was concerned that the dismal reputation of the deficit-laden and inefficient JNR would affect stock prices negatively, and embarrassingly few investors would be interested in acquiring stock in the new railway companies. It was necessary to sell the stock at as high a price as possible, to help alleviate some of the immense debt bequeathed by the JNR. The newly created JNRSC would hold railway stocks until the newly privatized companies could establish a reputation worthy of a respectable stock offering, by increasing efficiency and showing profits. Thus, although the date of JNR's privatization is given as 1987, strictly speaking the JNR was not privatized that year but rather was launched onto a course toward privatization.

Among the seven JR companies, the most rapidly privatized proved to be JR East, 62.5 percent of whose stock went on the market in 1993. The subsequent recession delayed the issuance of further stock until 1996, when a portion of JR West's shares went on the market, followed by JR Central's shares in 1997. As of 30 June 2002, all of JR East's, 68.3 percent of JR West's, and 60.4 percent of JR Central's shares were held by the private sector. All shares of the other four JR companies, however, are still held by the government, and a specific plan for their issuance has not been determined (Mizutani and Nakamura 2000). By the end of 2002, the privatization of JNR remained incomplete, with the government still holding portions of the JR companies' stock. There is little doubt, however, that the JR West and JR Central railway companies are headed toward full privatization.

12.2.2   Restructuring Options

General Important Features of Restructuring

As Moyer and Thompson (1992) point out, the restructuring of a railway business must focus on key elements that promote the ability of the railway to meet the needs of its potential users: its assets, liabilities, workforce, management style, and business strategy. As case studies in Europe, North America, and Japan indicate, different prototypes of restructuring have been adopted to enhance the competitiveness of railways. The following are major options for asset restructuring of the railway: geographical division, vertical separation, and functional distinction.

As for geographical division, because of a genetic trait of transport markets, the railway market and physical assets such as the track and terminals can be divided geographically. Geographical market segmentations involve separating freight and passenger markets into several subnetworks. In general, traffic demands on railways are mainly local, or concentrated on specific segments of the networks, so that geographical segmentation may be better suited to offering services to meet local needs.

As for vertical separation, as in telecommunications and other public utilities, the railway business constitutes (1) naturally monopolistic elements, such as track maintenance, and (2) potentially competitive elements, such as train operations and commercial functions. Unbundling track maintenance (the lower part of railways) from train operations (the upper part of railways), at least in theory, is considered one way to sharpen the competitive edge of railways in the transport market. However, as the case of British Rail indicates, the division of track from trains becomes problematic because an adversarial relationship has developed between the central track authorities and the train-operating companies. Problems associated with vertical separation include high transaction costs, a need for monitoring of the other's performance, the difficulty in creating complex performance schedules, and the stimulation of incentives for the track authority to invest in new facilities to increase efficiency and improve safety.

In terms of functional distinctions, railways basically serve two important markets—passenger and freight—each with its own operational and geographical uniqueness. A distinction between passenger and freight markets is logical, because it would make the railway companies more responsive to specific needs of particular users. However, if economies of scope between the related activities are known to be significant, then a horizontal distinction policy is not the best choice.

As far as asset reorganization for debt reduction is concerned, the various mechanisms include selling nonessential assets by auction, offering to the public stock and land (including terminals), franchising or leasing, or selling operating rights.

The Japanese Approach to Restructuring

What would be the best general practice for restructuring any railway? Specific options are most suitable for achieving specific results. Later we will discuss what options other nations have chosen in the restructuring of their railways. In the case of Japan, because of the highly dense population along the major railway lines and the extremely strong commuter demand in metropolitan areas, vertical integration and geographical separation may be the best choices for restructuring. Large economies of scope seem to exist not only between related activities but also between railway and nonrailway activities, including residential development along the lines, tourism, retailing, and so forth. The question of which policies should be applied is perhaps most important for enhancing the efficiency and competitiveness of railways, but there is no clear general answer to this question. One critical question seems to be how structural reforms could include incentive mechanisms, because the structural policy of a railway should go hand in hand with competitive measures for efficiency.

As we discussed in previous work, the Japanese approach to railway privatization has six distinguishing features: (1) horizontal separation (or regional subdivision), (2) functional distinction (or passenger-freight distinction), (3) vertical integration (or operation and infrastructure integration), (4) lump-sum subsidies for low-density JRs, (5) the establishment of an intermediary institution, and (6) allowance of nonrail service (Mizutani and Nakamura 1997). With this study, we add to the list a new distinguishing feature: (7) the yardstick competition scheme. We will briefly explain these characteristics.

The main problem with JNR was that it was too large an organization to be managed properly and it was expected to operate even unprofitable lines built only because of political influence. Thus it was decided that the company would be separated into six regional passenger railway companies, and each company would gain control over decisions about which lines to operate and which lines to close. After consideration of several options for separation, regional subdivision by geographical demand was decided upon. The smaller, subdivided companies would be expected to meet their users' local needs, and to compete with each other to improve their performance. In this subdivision, 95 percent of all trips would be completed within the borders of these regions. In addition to two distinct regional JRs—JR East and JR West in the Tokyo and Osaka metropolitan areas, respectively—JR Central, based in Nagoya, was appointed to be the operator of the most profitable trunk-line, Shinkansen, between Tokyo and Osaka.

Second, because of the growth of the trucking industry, whose increasing success had caused a severe decline in the share of rail freight business, it was decided to separate JR Freight from the passenger JRs. Were JR Freight to remain within the fold of the passenger JRs, it was feared that managerial responsibility for its losses would be vague and its poor performance would damage the morale and the good results the healthier passenger companies were bound to achieve. To avoid an excessive financial burden on JR Freight, however, it would be allowed to borrow tracks from infrastructure-holding passenger JRs, instead of holding the infrastructure itself. Regional separation was not chosen, in order to retain scale merit.

Third, unlike in the European rail industry and in marked contrast to the privatization of British Rail, vertical integration was maintained after privatization. In theory, it was possible to introduce vertical separation of track ownership and rail operation, but this was not seriously discussed before privatization (Suga 1997). Most railways in Japan are privately owned, integrated systems, and their success most likely made vertical separation seem an unattractive and excessively complicated option. Furthermore, since major urban private railways have been increasing profits by diversifying into various businesses—such as running department stores and hotels at stations, developing residential land along the tracks, and promoting tourism—privatized JRs were expected to behave likewise, making the integration of track ownership and train operation desirable in light of the possibility for diversification.

Fourth, in order to stabilize the management situation for smaller JRs, a lump-sum subsidy scheme was implemented through the Management Stabilization Fund (MSF), with interest revenues from the fund to cover these subsidies. Since the three-islands JRs were handicapped by geographical locations with relatively small populations and the rapid development in their regions of highway networks, lump-sum funds (1,278 billion yen) were channeled to these JRs. The fund, which originally took the form of a ten-year debt owned by the JNRSC, was supposed to yield interest and subsidize the operating losses of these JRs. However, the market interest rate decreased so that the interest revenues could not cover the operating deficits of the three-islands JRs. Therefore, a new scheme was implemented in 1997 whereby the Corporation for Advanced Transport and Technology (CATT) borrowed portions of the MSF funds of the three-islands JRs at a fixed interest rate of 4.99 percent, higher than the market rate. Scheduled to be eliminated by the end of fiscal year 2001, this scheme was extended to fiscal year 2006. Without the MSF these JRs will go in the red, making them unattractive candidates for listing on the stock market, so they have postponed plans for issuing their stock.

Fifth, JNRSC was set up as an intermediate institution to repay the debts of the JNR and to find new jobs for its redundant employees. The Japanese government and JNR management placed top priority on facilitating the transfer of dismissed employees to other sectors by enacting a special law for reemployment of former JNR workers in the process of privatization. As a result, in contrast to privatization practices elsewhere in the world, little labor rationalization was undertaken. To avoid sweeping layoffs, every imaginable means of reducing unemployment and social conflict was introduced, including transfers to local governments, public organizations such as the National Tax Administration Agency, the Police Agency, the Meteorological Agency, and the flourishing Nippon Telephone and Telegraph as well. Moreover, the JNRSC was established to transfer these redundant workers smoothly to other sectors. With generous inducements for voluntary retirement, reduction in the workforce had begun well before the implementation of privatization, so that only 1,047 remained to be dismissed in the process of privatization.

The Japanese Experience with Railway Restructuring   311

Sixth, JRs have been allowed to engage in nonrail business, as private rail companies have been doing in Japan for decades. To increase demand for rail transportation, private rail companies conduct such businesses as housing development, tourism, and the operation of other modes of transport such as buses. The JR companies have begun to follow the example of these private railways and tried their luck in various non-rail-related enterprises.

Finally, a yardstick competition scheme was introduced. Under this scheme, rail operators compete with each other to improve performance, and the regulator assesses the operators' performance by using common measures. The results of this assessment are to be used when fare revision is being considered.

Regulatory Changes and Ongoing Plans

Table 12.1 shows regulatory changes and ongoing plans since privatization. First, the organizational form was converted from a public corpora-

Table 12.1   Major Regulatory Changes with Privatization, and Desired Results

	Before Privatization	After Privatization	Desired Result
Organization	Public corporation	Special corporations	Genuinely private companies
Operations	Nationwide service	Six regional passenger companies and one freight company for all Japan	No change
Rail services	Integrated services of passenger and freight	Separation of passenger and freight services	No change, but possibly reorganization of the freight company
Scope of business	Rail-related services only	Nonrail businesses (e.g., residential development, tourism) allowed	More diversification of businesses
Approval of fare	Approval by the Diet	Approval by the Transport Minister	Notification to Ministry of Land, Infrastructure, and Transport
Fare regulation	Strict control by the government	Strict control by the government; installation of yardstick competition scheme in January 1997	Incentive regulations such as price caps
Investment and financing	Capital supplied by the government and investment plan requiring Diet approval	Japan Railway companies allowed to invest without Diet approval but ministerial approval required	No ministerial approval needed on important business matters, including the appointment of top executives, bond issuance, and borrowing

tion, which was one government body, to a special corporation in a stock-company-style commercial body, still regulated by special laws (Mizutani 1999b). These are expected to become fully private corporations, and the special laws related to them are to be abolished.

Second, operations and rail services were divided into six regional passenger companies and one nationwide freight rail company. So far, there are no specific further plans, but freight rail services might be reorganized because of recent concerns about environmental issues and competition with trucks.

Third, as for scope of business, as we mentioned above, JRs have been allowed to be involved in nonrail business since privatization, and these activities continue to expand, with the aim of securing rail ridership and fully utilizing internal resources.

As for fare approval and fare regulation, governmental intervention has been lighter after privatization. Before privatization, rail fare was approved by the Diet but is now regulated by the Transport Ministry, which is still ultimately a division of the national government. However, yardstick regulation has been introduced as an incentive scheme, and quite recently officials have begun to consider a price-cap scheme for determining rail fare.

Since privatization, the government has intervened less in matters of investment and financing, as well as in other areas of corporate management, such as the appointment of directors. Special laws and regulations have been enacted, including guarantees of a certain degree of autonomy in the JRs' management. This contrasts with the situation that existed in the JNR era when there was a great deal of pressure from and tinkering by politicians; their intervention had deleterious effects on the efficiency of JNR management. The full privatization expected to be realized eventually at all the JRs will afford their managers even more freedom to conduct their business as they see fit.

JNR Debts and the JNR Settlement Corporation

The transfer of 37.1 trillion yen of liabilities was supervised by the JNRSC, which itself took on about 60 percent of the total debt and was expected to liquidate this liability by selling JNR-owned real estate (7.7 trillion yen) and stocks (1.2 trillion yen). The remaining 40 percent of the long-term debt was allocated to the three main-island passenger JRs. The three small-island JRs were exempted from liability because their profitability was very uncertain, given the small size of their markets and lower population density. Originally, it was expected that the taxpayer bear the burden of the more than 13.8 trillion yen debt. The JNRSC has sold 6.22 million shares of the three main-island JRs' stock, out of a total of 9.19 million shares. The corporation has paid back 2.7 trillion yen. However, due to the delay in sales of stock and land after the collapse of the asset-inflated bubble economy in the early 1990s, the JNRSC's liabilities have been increasing because of staggering interest payments of about 1 trillion yen annually.

Although the JNRSC was reorganized as a division of the Japan Railway Construction Public Corporation (JRCC) and named the Japan Settlement Headquarters in 1998, there has been no change in the long-term debt issue. In spite of the current plan of JRCC to pay back 3.9 trillion yen by selling JR stocks and land, taxpayers will have to shoulder the 24.1 trillion yen loan, which is to be repaid from the general-account budget over the next sixty years.

The Shinkansen Holding Company

The Shinkansen Holding Company was organized to own and lease infrastructure properties of the Shinkansen and to allocate the resulting profits to the three main-island JRs. It was disbanded because the leasing system would be problematic when Shinkansen assets would be disposed of at the end of the leasing period. The Shinkansen assets were sold to the three main-island JRs through an installment plan, further increasing these JRs' long-term debt. The resulting problem was so severe that even JR Central, although it owns the most profitable Shinkansen line between Tokyo and Osaka, must make annual interest payments worth one-quarter of its yearly earnings.

12.2.3   An International Comparison of Rail Restructuring

For comparative purposes, we consider examples of reform of national railways in three European nations: France, Sweden, and the United Kingdom. Table 12.2 summarizes the main features of the restructuring of these nations' railways.

While the Japanese chose a vertically integrated structure, vertical separation seems more common in Europe, although the adoption schedule differs from country to country. Sweden took a separation policy early on, while France did so more recently, according to the Europe Conference of Ministers of Transport ([ECMT] 1998). Second, ownership of established rail companies is different among countries, with the most radical change occurring in the United Kingdom, where newly established train operating companies (TOCs) and the infrastructure provider Railtrack are all joint stock companies. JR companies also are intended to be joint stock companies, but their evolvement into such is ongoing and less drastic than in the case of the British Rail. In both France and Sweden, state railway companies are still owned by the public sector, although rail operations are provided on a commercial basis.

Presumably, decisions related to structure and ownership reflect the general opinion of a nation as to how involved the public sector should be in the rail industry. In France and Sweden, state influence on investment decisions is still higher than in the United Kingdom. In Japan, while the JNR

Table 12.2   An International Comparison of State Railway Restructuring

	Japan	France	Sweden	United Kingdom
Year of new organizations' start	1987	1997	1988	1993
Organization				
Major companies	JRs (O, I)	SNCF (O), RFF (I)	SJ (O), BV (I)	TOCs (O), Railtrack (I)
Ownership	Joint stock company both privately owned and 100% publicly owned	State enterprise with commercial statutes	State enterprise with commercial statutes (SJ) but with limited commercial freedom (BV)	Joint stock company 100% privately owned
Investment and service obligations				
State influence on investment decisions	Low state influence	High state influence	Intermediate state influence	Low state influence
Public service obligations	None legally, but negotiated with local communities	Imposed by government	Competitive tendering	Competitive tendering
Price regulation				
Passenger tariff control	All passenger services	All passenger services	None	Some specified services
Freight tariff control	Control exists	No control exists	No control exists	No control exists

	Japan	France	Sweden	United Kingdom
Infrastructure				
Separation of infrastructure from operations	No separation for passenger companies	Infrastructure entirely independent	Infrastructure entirely independent	Infrastructure entirely independent
Infrastructure charges	Cover avoidable costs	Determined by RFF	Variable track charges	Cover full infrastructure costs
Infrastructure maintenance	Passenger JRs	SNCF under contract with RFF	BV	Subcontracted by Railtrack
Operation				
Horizontal separation	Separated by regions	Not separated	Not separated	Separated by regions
Design of services	JRs	SNCF	SJ for national profitable lines but BV for nonprofitable lines	TOCs
Production of services	JRs	SNCF	SJ for national profitable lines but operators for nonprofitable lines	TOCs
Traffic control	Passenger JRs	SNCF	BV (since 1996)	Railtrack

Sources: This table has been modified by the authors based on the original sources. ECMT (1998, tables 4 and 5) and van de Velde and van Reeven (1999).

Notes: Symbols for items related to major companies: (O) operator, (I) infrastructure. Companies represented: JRs (Japan Railway companies), SNCF (French National Railways), RFF (French Railway Network), SJ (Swedish State Railways), BV (Banverket), TOCs (train operating companies), and Railtrack.

was interfered with rather heavily by the government, the JRs are relatively free of political interference. As for service obligations to the public, European railways clearly are obliged to maintain service, with services in the United Kingdom and Sweden being decided by competitive tendering. In Japan there is no legal obligation to maintain local services, but depopulated communities often negotiate with JR companies regarding the maintenance of local lines and other matters related to local service. This results in what might be called a type of unofficial social contract between the rail companies and local communities.

Finally, as for rail service operation, horizontal separation was selected in Japan and the United Kingdom, while state railway companies have taken over most services in France and Sweden. Of the four railways under observation here, the United Kingdom's system seems to have undergone the most drastic change, with each regional operating company selected by competitive tendering. In Japan, each regional JR company is given a rail license outright, so that there is no need to compete for infrastructure.

12.3   Managerial Reforms at JR

12.3.1   Management Goals

Sumita (2000) argued from his experience that in state-owned corporations, management responsibility is not clarified, so even if performance targets are not met, there is no need to assume responsibility as long as the best possible efforts have been exerted. One important problem of the JNR was the intervention of many stakeholders: politicians, government officials, unions, and rail users. Intervention from these groups could not be avoided, resulting in a complete loss of independence for JNR. For example, government officials and managers of JNR wishing to manage it more efficiently might deem it necessary to reduce wages and increase fares, while unions and rail users might find these actions unacceptable and put pressure on the government not to change. Conflicting interests led to vague "solutions," and the goals of the JNR became unclear; in fact, its performance goals were drawn up solely for the sake of convenience, in order to have pertinent laws or the budget passed by the Diet. After privatization, the goals of the JRs became clearer.

12.3.2   Relationships with Interest Groups

Massive strikes by labor unions often occurred at the end of the JNR era, and the relationship between management and labor unions was at its worst (Mizutani 1999a). Since then, the situation has improved, mainly because management and labor unions seem to be working toward the same goals, with management now giving rewards in the form of salary increases when performance has improved. This, in turn, seems to lead to further improvement and an increased sense of trust.

It is not clear how relationships with the local community have changed since privatization, but it is certain that before privatization they were not good. Sumita (2000) suggests that the local community was a rather spoiled interest group using private automobiles to distribute petitions demanding extra services from the JNR and protesting loudly when loss-making lines were slated for elimination. A cooperative relationship between communities and the JNR was made difficult mostly because local autonomous municipalities were forbidden by law to furnish subsidies to JNR. In the process of privatization, many local lines were converted to bus services or other rail companies which were owned by both the private and public sectors. As we will explain later, there is still the possibility of future conflict between the two groups with regard to maintaining local service in small communities.

12.3.3 Organizational Structure

Newly established JRs have assumed a structural form designed to facilitate decision making. JNR had been an unwieldy and bureaucratic organization, unresponsive to external change. It was clearly too large to be a single organization and too centralized for efficient decision making. As a result, there were several problems, such as the excessive length of time it took to make a decision and the inability of the organization to meet local needs quickly. To approve a single initiative, it was necessary to circulate documents among twenty to thirty people who would stamp them with their personal seals (Ishi, Okada, and Yada 1994). JNR's reform therefore stipulated not only privatization but also regional subdivision into organizations smaller than JNR. Moreover, the JRs themselves became less centralized organizations in general. For example, branch offices now have more freedom to use their own judgment when making a decision.

Public enterprises lack the will to economize on construction costs or general expenses because generating earnings is not necessarily the first priority of the operation, at least not in Japan. Once agreed upon, budgets, whether at a state or local government level, must be spent in their entirety, and those making efforts to economize and save portions of the budget are regarded as naive. Therefore, almost no efforts are made in these entities to reduce expenditures, and corporate performance is generally poor. On the other hand, private enterprises must generate earnings, or failures would make it impossible to survive in a market where competition from the automobile and airline industries is a constant threat.

As for organizational structure, two kinds of reforms are important: the change to a flat organization and the introduction of an M-form type of structure. First, like most government entities, the JNR was a typical hierarchy with a vertical organization. Government ministries in the past have often been seen as examples of dysfunctional vertical organizations where individual bureaus operated separately but the ministries as a whole failed to function as coordinated units (Sumita 2000). In order to improve upon this kind of organization, first, hierarchy became more flat, evolving from four stages—(1) division manager, (2) section manager, (3) section vice-manager, and (4) subsection—to three stages: (1) division manager, (2) section manager, and (3) subsection. This change shortened decision-making time (Kitani 1997). However, in Mizutani's study (1999a), based on structural maps made available by each JR, the number of divisions increased by about 40 percent from 1987 to 1995. Furthermore, as for characteristics of structural changes, the Honshu JRs show an increase in management divisions and branch offices while the three-islands JRs show an increase in nonmanagement divisions.

Second, the traditional JNR organization was divided into groups with similar job skills, and the decision making of each division was sometimes superior to the decision making of the entire organization. In other words, the old organizational structure encouraged sectionalism and frequently resulted in divisions' consciously thwarting each other, a serious obstacle to getting the entire organization to achieve its full potential. For example, according to Sumita (2000), JNR's civil engineering group was powerful and there were members of the Diet from this group, so that the civil-engineering contingent had a firm hold on a major portion of the budget for many years—a situation that may have accounted for a surfeit of new line construction in the JNR era. To avoid the possibility of a similar problem developing, the M-form type of organization was introduced when the privatization process began. For example, JR East set out to streamline its organization and unify separate departments performing similar work. Sumita reported that integration and unification resulted in information's no longer being restricted to one group exclusive of all others, and in a growing feeling of team spirit throughout the company as a whole.

12.3.4   Incentive Systems

A more private, company-style performance rating system was introduced. The wage system at JNR was based mostly on age and seniority, a system with no built-in incentive to improve performance. However, Sumita (2000) noted that when JR East listed its shares on the stock market in 1993, the majority of its employees opted to become shareholders. Partially owning the company where they work has proved to be a major morale and incentive booster for both management and employees.

12.3.5   Task-Improving Activities

As for task improvement, activities such as the quality control (QC) circle, the suggestion system, and other forms of action have been taken at the initiative of employees. The QC Circle and the suggestion system are very popular among manufacturing and construction companies in Japan and are used to make clear the task responsibility of each employee. In our experience, we cannot state without reserve that these schemes help improve productivity, but Sumita (2000) reported that more than 5 billion yen per year is being saved through the QC Circle, the suggestion system, and other forms of action taken at the initiative of employees.

12.4   The Performance of JRs after Privatization

12.4.1   Overall Performance Changes

Comparisons since Privatization

In this section, we will evaluate the overall performance of JR companies since privatization. For a detailed comparison between before and after privatization, please see our previous research, such as Mizutani and Nakamura (1996, 1997). The overall performance of the six JR companies since privatization is summarized in table 12.3, where we selected nine performance measures and compared three time periods: (1) the beginning of privatization (1987); (2) the fifth year after privatization (1992); and (3) the most recent year (1998). In this analysis, we use as a benchmark the performance results of fifteen large private railways.

Overall performance for most JRs has been improved since privatization. However, compared with the numbers in 1992, the most recent results seem desultory, perhaps due to the recent recession in the Japanese economy. JR Freight's financial performance (operating revenues–cost ratio) was especially dismal, sinking to a level lower than at the beginning of privatization.

Among these measures, efficiency has been much improved since privatization. Certainly, labor productivity has been improving. In our previous study (Mizutani and Nakamura 1996), the JRs' labor productivity after privatization was shown to be still inferior to that of large private railways, but the difference may have disappeared by now. The measure of JR Central was higher than for large private railways in 1998. In fact, when we compared the total productivity growth of JRs with that of private railways, the average annual growth rate of JRs shows much higher values: for 1987–1992, JR (11.40 percent), private (–0.70 percent); and for 1993–1998, (–0.48 percent), private (–0.03 percent). As for the average costs, the level was certainly lower than in 1987. The rate of decrease in average operating cost is higher than that of large private railways. Thus, when we compare the JRs' efficiency measures to those of large private railways, we find that the JRs' measures are improving significantly.

Table 12.3   Overall Performance Changes since Privatization

	Large Private (Benchmark)	JR East	JR Central	JR West	JR Hokkaido	JR Shikoku	JR Kyushu	JR Freight
Operating revenue–cost ratio								
1987	1.172	1.222	1.086	1.091	0.561	0.681	0.810	1.065
1992	1.193	1.284	1.567	1.156	0.632	0.855	0.864	1.024
1998	1.219	1.178	1.429	1.108	0.701	0.812	0.897	0.974
1998/1987	1.040	0.964	1.316	1.016	1.250	1.193	1.108	0.915
Average fare								
1987	9.09	14.68	21.95	16.24	17.39	17.30	15.26	8.57
1992	9.93	13.48	20.46	15.00	15.59	17.12	13.99	7.27
1998	11.76	13.44	21.52	14.95	16.84	18.35	14.86	6.51
1998/1987	1.293	0.916	0.980	0.921	0.969	1.061	0.974	0.760
Average load								
1987	65.96	56.89	51.55	43.56	33.76	31.70	36.61	15.06
1992	61.31	58.74	50.75	44.67	34.82	35.02	31.36	17.04
1998	52.93	57.60	50.98	42.05	28.90	27.13	31.41	17.40
1998/1987	0.802	1.012	0.989	0.965	0.856	0.856	0.858	1.155
Train density								
1987	99,545	30,038	39,406	28,910	10,584	18,217	19,619	7,434
1992	107,299	36,011	49,598	36,512	12,838	23,081	29,245	9,075
1998	109,523	34,305	47,621	38,893	15,231	24,779	29,771	8,544
1998/1987	1.100	1.142	1.208	1.345	1.439	1.360	1.517	1.149
Demand								
1987	101,921	104,491	41,148	45,782	3,920	1,673	7,664	20,026
1992	112,181	128,486	51,201	54,423	4,869	2,068	8,560	26,241
1998	103,792	126,110	48,538	53,526	4,540	1,815	8,280	22,643
1998/1987	1.018	1.207	1.180	1.169	1.158	1.085	1.080	1.131
Labor productivity								
1987	28,250	22,734	39,457	21,070	9,587	14,009	15,354	117,010
1992	32,170	32,717	48,228	26,482	12,945	19,110	26,524	152,970
1998	36,067	34,725	44,463	30,569	16,132	23,138	29,867	166,114
1998/1987	1.277	1.527	1.127	1.451	1.683	1.652	1.945	1.420

	Col 1	Col 2	Col 3	Col 4	Col 5	Col 6	Col 7	Col 8
Monthly wage								
1987	274,565	256,889	264,549	256,617	265,085	234,185	247,844	252,190
1992	286,304	306,487	269,220	302,548	299,103	220,548	260,326	295,486
1998	336,039	360,814	310,362	333,240	318,293	305,127	322,240	275,608
1998/1987	1.224	1.405	1.173	1.299	1.201	1.303	1.300	1.093
Average operating cost								
1987	545	743	1,096	713	1,221	926	817	133
1992	546	670	697	641	1,021	824	608	136
1998	544	717	812	634	817	722	607	138
1998/1987	0.999	0.965	0.741	0.889	0.669	0.780	0.742	1.037
Accident rate								
1987	0.884	1.653	0.883	1.421	1.273	3.489	2.190	0.980
1992	0.584	n.a.	n.a.	n.a.	n.a.	n.a.	n.a.	n.a.
1998	0.520	0.526	0.212	0.810	0.499	1.368	1.182	0.720
1998/1987	0.588	0.318	0.240	0.570	0.392	0.392	0.540	0.734

Notes: All monetary terms are in 1995 values. These figures are all for 1987, 1992, and 1998 fiscal years. JR = Japan Railway companies.
Definition of measures:

Operating revenue–cost ratio = operating revenues/operating costs;
Average fare = fare revenues/passenger kilometer (in yen per passenger-km or per ton-km);
Average load = passenger kilometer (or ton kilometer)/car kilometer (in persons or tons);
Train density = train kilometer/route kilometer (in number of trains per route);
Demand = transported passenger (or ton) kilometer (in millions of passenger-km or millions of ton-km);
Labor productivity = car kilometer/number of employees in rail division (in car-km per person);
Monthly wage = monthly salary per employee in rail division (in yen per person);
Average operating cost = operating cost/car kilometer (in yen per car-km); and
Accident rate = number of all kinds of accidents/million train kilometer,

where fare revenues = total revenues from fare, operating revenues = fare revenues + sales revenues, such as parcel transport and charges to kiosks; and operating costs = labor costs + energy costs + material costs + maintenance costs (tracks and rollingstock) + depreciation + tax.
   Operating revenues do not include subsidies. Operating costs are considered as total costs of rail operation financially defined, which include both variable and fixed components of rail costs.

Table 12.4   The Increasing Percentage of Passenger and Freight Rates since 1980

Date of Revision	Passenger (%)	Freight (%)
Before Privatization		
20 April 1981	9.7	9.7
20 April 1982	6.1	6.3
20 April 1984	8.2	4.2
20 April 1985	4.4	3.1
1 September 1986	4.8	—
After Privatization		
1 April 1989[a]	2.9	3.0
10 January 1996	7.0[b]	3.0
	6.7[c]	
	7.8[d]	
1 April 1997[e]	1.9	1.9

Source: Ministry of Transport (2000, 115).
[a]Enacted consumption tax (3 percent).
[b]JR Hokkaido.
[c]JR Shikoku.
[d]JR Kyushu.
[e]Increased consumption tax rate to 5 percent.

12.4.2   Rail Fare

Rail Revision

Rail fare at JNR was expected to cover all rail costs, but was based on the outcome of political deals, not on sound economic judgment. Political interference in rail operation and investment increased rail costs and led to inefficiency, resulting in a fare increase almost every year from 1981 until 1987, when privatization began. Table 12.4 shows the record of fare revision of the JRs, which, other than the three-islands JRs, did not increase fare level during the ten years after privatization, excepting the two years immediately following the introduction of the consumption tax. Maintaining fare at the same level as at the start of privatization indicates that the real value is decreasing, and an increase in ridership can be expected. In fact, Sumita (2000) reports that JR East has made every effort not to increase rail fare. Thus, one important effect of the privatization of JNR was to stop the almost yearly increase in fare.

Parallel Rail Lines

Rail fare at the JR companies after privatization became more competitive than that of other private rail companies, the most notable case being on JR lines parallel with private rail company lines in large metropolitan areas. Table 12.5 shows a rail fare comparison between JR and large private rail companies along some selected parallel lines. The table shows that in

Table 12.5   **Fare Comparison between Japan Railway Companies (JRs) and Major Private Railways of Selected Competitive Lines**

Section of a Line	Operator	Regular Fare (Yen)		Commuter Rail Pass (Yen per Month)	
		01/04/1986	01/10/2000	01/04/1986	01/10/2000
Tokyo					
Ueno-Narita	JR East	730	890	21,500	26,280
	Keisei	680	810	17,400	21,920
	JR/private	1.07	1.10	1.24	1.20
Shinjuku-Hachioji	JR East	440	460	13,200	13,860
	Keio	290	350	9,300	13,190
	JR/private	1.52	1.31	1.42	1.05
Shinagawa-Yokohama	JR East	260	280	7,800	8,190
	Keikyu	230	290	7,580	11,260
	JR/private	1.13	0.97	1.03	0.73
Nagoya					
Nagoya-Gifu	JR Central	480	450	12,460	13,080
	Meitetsu	480	540	12,460	16,340
	JR/private	1.00	0.83	1.00	0.80
Nagoya-Yokkaichi	JR Central	440	460	13,200	13,860
	Kintetsu	430	610	11,500	19,780
	JR/private	1.02	0.75	1.15	0.70
Osaka					
Tennoji (Nanba)– Wakayama	JR West	730	830	21,500	24,750
	Nankai	700	890	15,500	25,050
	JR/private	1.04	0.93	1.39	0.99
Osaka (Umeda)– Sannomiya	JR West	380	390	11,400	11,960
	Hankyu	230	310	8,780	12,480
	JR/private	1.65	1.26	1.30	0.96
Fukuoka					
Hakata (Fukuoka)– Kurume	JR Kyushu	590	720	16,600	20,750
	Nishitetsu	500	600	14,850	22,280
	JR/private	1.18	1.20	1.12	0.93
Hakata (Fukuoka)– Omuta	JR Kyushu	1,000	1,250	28,760	33,980
	Nishitetsu	850	1,000	22,500	29,480
	JR/private	1.18	1.25	1.28	1.15

Sources: Ministry of Transport (2000, 110–111; 1986, 88–89).

almost all cases the difference in fare level between JRs and large private rail companies became smaller, and in some cases the JRs' fare level became even lower.

The JRs' decreasing relative fare level is certainly due to the increase in productive efficiency caused by the privatization of JNR. Clearly, the unit cost of JR companies has decreased compared with that of JNR, making it a matter of course that JRs' price level has become lower.

Notably, the decrease in JR fare to the level of that of private railways was not the same for all lines. In general, cases in the Nagoya and Osaka areas, where there are more parallel lines, showed larger decreases than cases in the Tokyo area. During the JNR era, JNR lines were not considered serious competition for the private railway lines parallel to them, but after privatization, each regional JR company has aimed to make all regional lines more competitive, with a resulting close in the price gap.

12.4.3 Competition

One important and distinguishing effect of the privatization of the JNR is that competition has worked actively in many ways. First, the Shinkansen became a viable alternative to the airplane along the major long-distance trunk corridor, with popular routes being Tokyo-Osaka, Osaka-Fukuoka, Tokyo-Fukuoka, Tokyo-Yamagata, and Tokyo-Akita. The companies focused mainly on shortening transport time, but attention was paid also to service quality and price. For example, JR West has actively introduced new types of rail cars between Osaka and Fukuoka in order to win business trips from air transportation. The new types of cars provide new amenities such as compartment rooms for meetings, electrical outlets for personal computers, and silent cars for passengers who want to rest. Furthermore, travel time has been reduced by more than 20 percent.

In the medium distance, bus transportation might be a competitive mode. For example, direct service from city center to airport could be a typical case of medium-distance bus service. Although there is no statistical evidence, convenient direct bus services are emerging as strong competitors of privatized JR companies.

The privatization of the JNR has affected other transport organizations, attracting business away from them and reducing their ridership. In the greater Osaka metropolitan area, JR lines run parallel with lines of other private rail companies, giving rail users a choice (Nakamura and Mizutani 1995). Table 12.6 shows trends in the number of passengers and share in rails in the greater Osaka metropolitan area. From this table we can clearly see that the ridership of the JRs after privatization has increased while private rail companies have been gradually losing some of their competitiveness, so that in 1997 their share became less than 50 percent. However, the subway system operated by the local government has not been affected by the privatization of JNR, as its network does not significantly overlap with JR lines.

On 20 March 1996, a new movement was begun in Osaka: a consortium of transport organizations called "Surutto Kansai," ("Go through Kansai"), whose purpose is to increase users' convenience. Under this consortium, rail users can avoid buying separate tickets from separate railway or bus companies along their desired routes by purchasing prepaid cards that can be used on all facilities of the consortium's members. Originally there

Table 12.6   Trends in Number of Passengers and Share in Rails in the Greater
              Osaka Metropolitan Area

	Numbers of Passengers (thousands)			Share of Passengers (%)		
	JR West	Private Rails	Subways	JR West	Private Rails	Subways
1980	1,086,022	2,508,336	813,318	0.246	0.569	0.185
1981	1,079,424	2,515,534	986,452	0.236	0.549	0.215
1982	1,059,261	2,495,711	1,009,021	0.232	0.547	0.221
1983	1,065,140	2,515,052	1,036,329	0.231	0.545	0.224
1984	1,068,560	2,501,624	1,046,038	0.231	0.542	0.227
1985	1,074,479	2,574,773	960,198	0.233	0.559	0.208
1986	1,088,105	2,613,680	975,768	0.233	0.559	0.209
1987[a]	1,145,095	2,623,316	921,938	0.244	0.559	0.197
1988	1,203,132	2,652,969	1,076,853	0.244	0.538	0.218
1989	1,197,248	2,672,564	1,096,877	0.241	0.538	0.221
1990	1,228,650	2,715,036	1,156,811	0.241	0.532	0.227
1991	1,264,666	2,777,166	1,167,219	0.243	0.533	0.224
1992	1,304,737	2,747,929	1,168,136	0.250	0.526	0.224
1993	1,367,843	2,726,708	1,161,090	0.260	0.519	0.221
1994	1,308,396	2,885,756	1,135,110	0.246	0.541	0.213
1995	1,380,645	2,590,129	1,157,746	0.269	0.505	0.226
1996[b]	1,384,975	2,601,995	1,145,749	0.270	0.507	0.223
1997	1,379,976	2,502,765	1,151,611	0.274	0.497	0.229
1998	1,366,037	2,439,685	1,140,150	0.276	0.493	0.231

[a]Privatization.
[b]Consortium.

were five member organizations, such as Hankyu and the Osaka city transport bureau. Four years later, in May 2000, twenty-six transport organizations had joined the consortium, and its network accounted for 792.1 km in rail lines and 2,375.2 km in bus routes. JR West is not specifically excluded from this consortium, but becoming a member would require the installation of ticket gate machines compatible with those of all other members, and JR West has so far opted not to undertake this installation. Whether as a result of this omission or not, an atmosphere of JR-versus-the-Others has taken hold in the Osaka metropolitan area.

The advantages of joining the consortium are as follows. First, an increase in ridership is expected due to expansion of network. Second, investment costs for system development such as for ticket gate machines can be avoided because the system is developed jointly. Third, advertising of the joint network can be expected without loss of management freedom in each organization. An advantage for users is the convenience of not having to buy tickets when changing modes of transportation. The consortium can also be judged to be good for society in that it protects the environment by encouraging the use of public transportation over private cars. According to the administrative office of the consortium, the number of prepaid users has been steadily increasing but a clear effect is not yet evident.

12.4.4   Local Services

Previously, we showed performance results in a profitable market. In this section, we will explain results occurring in an unprofitable market. Before the privatization of JNR, there was considerable debate about whether local rail services in small communities would remain intact. The concern was that newly privatized rail companies would ruthlessly eliminate any unprofitable lines, leaving the transportation-poor, such as children, the elderly, and the handicapped, to fend for themselves. Quite recently, an empirical investigation of this issue was undertaken by Mizutani (1999a).

The methodology is as follows. First, Mizutani selected local rail lines of six passenger JRs. Second, by using timetables, he obtained several service quality measures in both the first year of privatization (1987) and the tenth year after privatization (1997). He then compared these service quality measures for the two time periods. As observations, he chose a total of thirty-five lines from six passenger JRs by considering regional differences and service quality measures such as (1) departure time of the first train, (2) departure time of the last train, (3) operating time per given section of rail line, (4) number of trains per day, (5) number of trains per off-peak hour, and (6) travel time in a given 30 km.

Mizutani's conclusion is that, overall, local rail service in small communities has been maintained since privatization, negating the fear of those who predicted that privatization would damage or even eliminate local rail service. To a certain extent, it is not surprising that local lines have fared so well, considering the financial health of the JRs since privatization. Even the three-islands JRs, which have been less fortunate financially, have managed to maintain their local lines.

However, if the financial situation takes a turn for the worse, the concern remains that the rail companies may at some point choose to abandon service, even though they have so far chosen to keep unprofitable lines despite there being no legal obligation to do so. Quite recently, however, JR West has sent out signals that it is becoming more difficult to maintain several local lines in small communities, and recent drastic reductions in off-peak services found on timetables from April 2001 augur that some sacrifices can be expected in the near future. The deficits of some local lines are being covered by cross-subsidies derived from the JRs' profitable transport operations in major urban areas. Local rail services will be abolished or converted to bus services if the JRs cannot make enough profits from major urban lines or efficiently use internal resources such as employees. According to Sumita (2000), in the future the number of surplus personnel may fall to zero, making it difficult to secure sufficient personnel to operate the local lines.

12.4.5   An International Comparison of Performance Changes

In this section, we will compare performance changes among typical rail companies in which different kinds of railway reform have been undertaken. We selected the same organizations used earlier: the JRs, British Rail (BR), Swedish State Railways (SJ), and French National Railways (SNCF). Table 12.7 gives a summary of performance changes. In this table, the reform of SNCF, in which the French Railway Network (RFF) was established, was accomplished in 1997, so that these numbers are all representative of SNCF. The privatization of BR occurred in 1993, so that the numbers for BR in 1995 are the combined numbers of TOCs and Railtrack. Rail reform in Sweden took place in 1988, so that numbers since 1989 are the combined numbers of SJ and Banverket (BV). Finally, JNR's privatization began in 1987, so that the numbers since 1987 are the total numbers from the seven JR companies. These statistics have been calculated by the authors based on the original from the International Union of Railways.

This table shows, first, that railway reforms commonly lead to an increase in labor productivity, and have certainly done so in the United Kingdom, Sweden, and Japan. The growth ratio of labor productivity of reformed railways is higher than that of nonreformed railways. For example, the growth percentage between 1987 and 1995 for SNCF was 1.179 but was 1.668 for BR, 1.598 for SJ, and 1.255 for the JRs. Labor productivity growth was accomplished mainly through the reduction of employees.

The second benefit of rail reform is the subsequent increase in rail demand. For passenger transport, both the JRs and SJ increased demand between 1987 and 1995. Although the statistics for BR in this table shows a decrease, the demand for passenger transport began an upturn after 1995, according to one source (Preston and Root 1999, 52). However, reform does not seem to affect freight service, with all freight services except SJ continuing to show a decrease. According to one source (Alexandersson and Hulten 1999, 114), even SJ suffered a sharp decline in freight service after 1996: 16.5 billion tons per kilometer in 1996, 14.7 billion tons per kilometer in 1997.

On the other hand, different results were found among railways regarding the operating revenue–cost ratio, a measure that greatly increased for the JRs but that decreased for all other railways. Although both BR and SJ were reformed, this measure worsened, most likely due to an increase in operating costs, with operating costs increasing most drastically in the United Kingdom. We know that operating costs rose both for operation and infrastructure, but due to a lack of available information, we cannot give details.

Table 12.7   An International Comparison of Performance Changes since 1981

	Rail	1981	1983	1985	1987	1989	1991	1993	1995	1995/1987
Operating revenue–cost ratio	SNCF	0.654	0.599	0.612	0.601	0.635	0.648	0.500	0.458	0.762
	BR	0.608	0.603	0.613	0.699	0.751	0.687	0.741	0.357	0.511
	SJ	0.752	0.692	0.673	0.630	0.530	0.578	0.499	0.412	0.654
	JRs	0.614	0.538	0.561	0.892	0.914	1.052	1.087	1.077	1.207
Average operating revenue	SNCF	19.0	12.8	14.5	19.0	17.5	18.8	13.5	15.9	0.837
	BR	12.4	9.4	9.4	13.7	10.5	12.3	8.9	8.9	0.649
	SJ	16.6	11.1	16.6	13.9	12.9	14.9	9.7	12.3	0.885
	JRs	21.4	21.2	27.1	43.1	34.7	40.5	43.8	47.4	1.100
Train density	SNCF	14,368	14,331	13,880	13,547	13,994	14,302	14,340	14,108	1.041
	BR	23,698	23,313	23,399	23,515	26,487	25,807	25,318	24,855	1.057
	SJ	8,780	8,860	9,308	9,054	9,961	8,745	9,417	10,258	1.133
	JRs	30,437	29,475	29,893	30,397	36,687	38,304	38,583	38,801	1.276
Demand (passenger)	SNCF	55,414	58,177	61,828	59,732	64,256	62,081	58,189	55,319	0.926
	BR	30,740	30,100	30,256	33,140	33,323	32,058	30,322	29,216	0.882
	SJ	6,851	6,460	6,586	6,013	6,060	5,524	5,830	6,219	1.034
	JRs	192,115	192,906	197,463	204,679	222,670	247,031	250,013	248,993	1.216
Demand (freight)	SNCF	62,793	57,827	54,225	49,786	51,559	49,397	43,596	46,564	0.935
	BR	17,505	17,144	16,047	17,466	16,742	17,274	13,765	12,537	0.718
	SJ	14,296	14,639	16,863	17,146	18,207	17,974	18,126	18,536	1.081
	JRs	32,927	18,227	10,663	7,981	8,218	7,802	6,632	5,517	0.691

Labor productivity	SNCF	2,000	1,972	1,988	2,110	2,327	2,408	2,432	2,488	1.179
	BR	1,785	1,940	2,204	2,432	3,281	3,106	3,260	4,057	1.668
	SJ	2,619	2,760	2,873	2,901	3,346	3,650	4,029	4,635	1.598
	JRs	1,624	1,755	2,245	3,235	3,787	4,014	4,039	4,059	1.255
Average operating cost	SNCF	29.0	21.4	23.6	31.6	27.5	29.1	27.0	34.7	1.098
	BR	20.4	15.5	15.4	19.5	14.0	17.9	12.0	25.0	1.282
	SJ	22.0	16.1	24.7	22.1	24.3	25.8	19.3	29.9	1.353
	JRs	34.9	39.5	48.2	48.3	38.0	38.5	40.3	44.1	0.913

Source: These numbers were calculated by the authors based on the International Union of Railways' (1997) statistics.

Notes: All monetary terms are in 1990 U.S. dollar values. Numbers for 1995 for BR (British Rail) are combined data of TOCs (train operating companies) and Railtrack. Numbers since 1989 for SJ (Swedish State Railways) are combined data of SJ and BV (Banverket). As for JRs (Japan Railway companies), numbers before 1987 were data for JNR (Japan National Railway). SNCF means French National Railways. Numbers in shaded areas represent cases after large-scale railway reform.

Definition of measures:

Operating revenue–cost ratio = operating revenues/operating costs;

Average operating revenue = operating revenues/train kilometer (in 1990 U.S. dollars per train);

Train density = train kilometer/route kilometer (in number of trains per route);

Demand = transported passenger (or ton) kilometer (in millions of passengers per km or millions of tons per km);

Labor productivity = train kilometer/number of employees (train-km per person); and

Average operating cost = operating cost/train kilometer (in 1990 U.S. dollars per train-km),

where operating revenues = revenues from passenger and baggage traffic + revenues from freight and postal traffic; and operating costs = supplies and external charges + staff costs + taxes + infrastructure levies + valve adjustments, depreciation, provision for contingencies, etc.

In conclusion, we regret that we cannot discern clearly from our results what kind of railway reform works best in every case. Part of our inability to do so is the consequence of a lack of available data. We hope that as railway-reform data accumulate, we will be able by econometric techniques to obtain results that will guide us in making wiser policy decisions in the future.

12.5   Selected Important Lessons

12.5.1   Regional Subdivision: Horizontal Separation

We believe that the policy calling for the subdivision of the nationwide Japanese railway system was correct. The issues are how the system should be divided and how big each organization should be. As for the first question, while other alternatives for dividing the JNR were discussed both officially and unofficially, regional subdivision was selected. At least three other possible options were discussed: four regional subdivisions based on the four main islands (Honshu, Hokkaido, Shikoku, and Kyushu); about twenty regional subdivisions based upon the branch offices of JNR; and division into trunk lines and branch lines. The last two were rejected, first, because there was great financial variation among the twenty subdivisions due to differing rail demand conditions, and second, because branch lines could not be financially independent. As for the proposed four subdivisions, the Honshu region was considered to be too large compared with the other three, thus needing further subdivision. In addition to these three alternatives, a division into urban rail operation and intercity rail operation was suggested, but was rejected as not feasible technically because both operations use the same tracks.

Regional subdivision of the passenger rail service seems to be functioning well so far. First, yardstick competition has improved the overall performance of the JRs. Second, more regional needs have been met, particularly with improvements in frequency. Third, as for the integration of railway services into different regional organizations, not many problems have been reported, although the number of interregional rail services has decreased.

As for the second issue, six regional passenger companies were created. One problem in Japan is the wide variation in the size of the six regional passenger rail organizations, reflecting demand and transportation density. The Honshu JRs (JR East, JR Central, and JR West) are in a highly advantageous position compared with the three-islands JRs (JR Hokkaido, JR Shikoku, and JR Kyushu). As for the size of organization in terms of cost, there is a problem. According to Preston (1996), the optimal railway size for minimizing operating costs might have a network of around 4,000 km and run 120 million train-km per annum. His pioneering results provide useful information for the restructuring of the rail industry but, for us, have the limitation of having been obtained from European state railways. It is necessary to get more precise information about privately owned railways.

Research on the optimal size of rail organizations has recently been done by Mizutani (2001), who estimated the total cost function for pooling data of fifty-nine privately owned urban railways for every five years from 1970 to 1995 in Japan. He calculated the railway size to attain the minimum average cost in terms of service output and network size. That is, he obtained the size by differentiating the average cost function by three measures: service output, number of lines, and average line length. He found the optimal size, which attains the minimum average cost, to be about 128 million vehicle-km per year with a network of 15.0 km per line, and with five lines. In this case, the average costs are 418.8 yen per vehicle-km. The optimal size in terms of output is found to be smaller than Preston's (1996) result, which shows that the optimal size in terms of train-km is 120 million. When we translate Mizutani's result of output to train-km, the result would be about 43 million train-km (= 128 million vehicle-km / 3 cars per train). Furthermore, in terms of network size, Mizutani's result is much smaller than Preston's because the total length is about 75 km (= 15.0 km per line × 5 lines). Presumably, Mizutani's data set is based on urban rail organizations so that the network size would be smaller. In other words, Japanese railway systems are more densely operated than those in other countries.

Based on Mizutani's result, we evaluate the size of the railway organization. His result shows that large private railways, which are considered the most efficient rail operators in Japan, could be approximating optimally sized railways. The Odakyu line operating in Tokyo might be an optimally sized railway operating under ideal conditions. If Mizutani's result is correct, JR Shikoku is perhaps too small and the Honshu JR companies too big in terms of costs.

12.5.2   Functional Division: Passenger and Freight Services

We think that functional division was correct for Japan, where railways are mostly for passenger transport. Freight transport is by either truck or ship, with rail holding only a 4.2 percent share on a ton-kilometer basis. Clearly, before privatization, the freight section of JNR was unprofitable, unable to compete with trucking companies and deficient in marketing skill. In fact, JNR's freight division was one of the main sources of JNR's operating deficits. If such an unprofitable establishment had been attached to any of the JR passenger companies, their prospects for success would have been reduced, and their listing on the stock market would have been less favorable.

We might also cite the argument of scope economies in order to rationalize the separation of passenger and freight service. Several researchers have noted that there are diseconomies of scope with passenger and freight operations in the railway industry (Kim 1987; Preston 1996). From this point of view, it is not necessary to provide both passenger and freight services under the same train company. Instead, the consolidation of freight rail companies with trucking companies may be preferable.

12.5.3   Operation and Infrastructure Integration: Vertical Integration

The issue of vertical integration still stimulates much debate in the rail industry. The relationship between operation and railway infrastructure can take many forms (Brooks and Button 1995). In the European style, for example in the case of the BR privatization, rail operation was separated from infrastructure. In Japan, JR passenger companies hold rail tracks, as most other Japanese private railways do, and cases involving only operation or only ownership of infrastructure are very limited, with Kobe Kosoku and JR Freight being examples of the few.

Empirical results are insufficient to allow a policy judgment on this issue, as a concrete theory has yet to be developed in the rail industry. However, transport economists have discussed advantages and disadvantages, as did the British economist Nash (1997), who wrote of the BR experience. Vertical separation makes it easier to (1) promote a variety of operators, (2) clarify intra-industry relationships, and (3) specialize activities. On the other hand, vertical separation makes it difficult to (1) set up fair prices and monitor performance, (2) organize time-tabling and slot allocation of trains, (3) negotiate arrangements for investment projects, (4) maintain safety of train operation, and (5) provide integrated information and ticketing.

There are two important factors that make a vertically separated system undesirable in Japan. The first factor concerns transaction costs, and the second is the existence of economies of scope between operation and infrastructure providing services. Although we do not have clear evidence, vertical integration or a separation policy is related to these two factors, which may depend on traffic density. For example, under the condition of low traffic density, the integrated system is not efficient because the fixed cost of track maintenance is too high and the rail company could save money by outsourcing with a construction company. Transaction costs related to separation are not significantly large because the traffic is not so heavy that transactions between two companies could not be conducted on an ordinary basis. On the other hand, as traffic density increases, scope economies between the two activities come into play so that the company has an incentive to carry out the two activities. At least, it may be said that there are diseconomies of scale when the two activities are separated. Furthermore, transaction costs related to separation become larger. As many transport economists point out, in the scheduling of track maintenance under heavy operation, and with regard to investment plans for signals and tracks that affect train operation, cost allocation between the two activities will be a considerable issue between the two companies. As a result, transaction costs related to these will increase, such as the opportunity cost of meeting-time, the legal costs of reaching agreements, and the costs of reducing asymmetric information. All these costs make a vertically integrated system seem desirable.

Cost efficiency does not exist in vertical separation in the rail industry. Mizutani and Shoji (2001) attempt to evaluate this subject with a limited data set. Their methodology is straightforward. First, they construct the cost function for track maintenance activities by using a vertically integrated system. Second, they substitute the data of a vertically separated organization, in this case the Kobe Kosoku railway, into the estimated cost function and obtain the infrastructure cost. Finally, they compare these estimated infrastructure costs, which are considered as a case of a vertically integrated system with the actual costs of a vertically separated system. They find that the vertically separated system costs about 5.6 percent more than the vertically integrated system, and thus conclude that there are no significant cost differences between the two systems. This is a just case based on reported accounting costs of railway firms; opportunity costs of transactions, especially time costs of meeting, negotiation, and search, are not included. If we consider these costs, a separated system might be more expensive than an integrated system.

In summary, in the case of low traffic density, a vertically separated system is cheaper than a vertically integrated system but in the case of higher traffic density, the integrated system may be better. The policy option for vertical separation was not considered at all when JNR was privatized (Suga 1997), because when compared with European railways, the much higher traffic volume of the JRs makes it less likely to succeed with a separated system.

12.5.4   Yardstick Competition

A yardstick competition scheme is used for avoiding inefficiency resulting from a too-lenient licensing system. Compared with an open-access system, in which operators are selected by tendering, a yardstick competition scheme is less rigorous but still encourages competition. Shleifer (1985) originally proposed the conceptual framework of yardstick competition, which is considered competition among companies in different markets. The essence of the scheme is for regulators to evaluate companies' performance with selected performance measures. For example, a regulator sets up several performance measures, such as operating costs or productivity, and evaluates companies' performance. If a company can be shown to perform relatively better than other companies in these measures, then the company may receive rewards (e.g., their proposal for increased fares can be accepted). On the other hand, a company that performs less well might be penalized by having its requested fare increase rejected. Thus, this scheme is a kind of incentive regulation in order to improve companies' efficiency by introducing competition. In Japan, yardstick competition has been used since the mid-1970s in reviewing proposals for fare revision among fifteen large private railways. The evaluation measures considered in Japan are productivity growth, cost reduction, and improvement of rail ridership, and if these measures cannot be shown to equal or surpass those of other rail companies, then changes in rail fare are not fully granted by the regulator. While yardstick competition has been used for more than two decades for evaluating large private railways, it has been used at the JRs only since 1997, and cannot yet be shown to have clear effects. Competition certainly works to some degree in the large private railways to which the yardstick competition scheme applies (Mizutani 1997).

In the long run, a licensing system incorporating yardstick competition may attain more efficiency. Long-term commitment to a line is also important. Private rail companies in Japan have traditionally shown this commitment by developing real estate and shopping establishments along rail lines. A company involved only in rail operations might not share this long-term commitment, in the uncertainty that it may lose its operating license at some point. It is conceivable that an operations-only company, with its attention focused only on fulfilling the minimal promises of a written contract, might lose the entrepreneurial behavior characteristic of a major private rail company. Service quality might therefore suffer, ultimately leading to a change in the location of households and further decline in rail business.

In conclusion, a yardstick competition scheme seems a useful part of the licensing system in the long run. So far, the larger private rail companies in Japan that operate within the yardstick scheme have performed well, demonstrating a commitment to the development of a pleasant housing environment along their lines and quality rail service on their trains.

12.6   Concluding Remarks

In conclusion, the Japanese approach to rail restructuring has succeeded in many ways, by improving productivity, cutting operating deficits, decreasing fares, and providing better services. Although political intervention after privatization has lessened, JR companies are not yet totally independent because the privatization process is not yet complete. Local rail services in small communities have been maintained for the past ten years but there are no guarantees that these will survive any serious financial slump the JRs might someday experience.

While the Japanese privatization has been largely a success, there remain a number of problems to be solved in the near future. Care must be taken that privatization should not result in a simple transfer of monopolistic power from a public corporation to the private sector. The main objective of privatization policy is to introduce many kinds of competition, and it is the government's role to create a competitive environment and to promote actual and potential competition in the market and even within the organization itself by using incentive regulations. Furthermore, in Japan the older and very successful large private railways have served as good role models for the newly privatized JRs. The former national railway was conservative, indolent, and fearful of change. The privatization process has served to rouse it from its former, rather inert state into something much more purposeful.

References

Alexandersson, G., and S. Hulten. 1999. Changing trains: Sweden. In *Changing trains,* ed. D. M. van de Velde, 79–141. Aldershot, U.K.: Ashgate.

Brooks, M., and K. Button. 1995. Separating transport track from operations: A typology of international experiences. *International Journal of Transport Economics* 22 (3): 235–260.

Europe Conference of Ministers of Transport (ECMT). 1998. *Rail restructuring in Europe.* Paris: Organization for Economic Cooperation and Development.

International Union of Railways. 1997. *Chronological railway statistics 1970–1995.* Paris: Statistics Centre of the International Union of Railways.

Ishii, Y., K. Okada, and T. Yada. 1994. Henkakuki no tetsudo keiei: Kyushu Ryokyaku Tetsudo Kabushiki Kaisya (Railway management in the age of changes: Kyushu Railway Company). *Unyu to Keizai* 54 (4): 5–40.

Kim, H. Y. 1987. Economies of scale and scope in multiproduct firms: Evidence from U.S. railroads. *Applied Economics* 19 (6): 733–741.

Kitani, S. 1997. JR Nishinihon ni okeru mineika no shinten to sono kouka (Privatization progress and its effects at JR West). In *Mineika no Kouka to Genjitsu,* ed. T. Imamura, 261–287. Tokyo: Chuo Hoki.

Ministry of Transport, Railway Bureau, ed. 2000. *Suji de miru tetsudo 2000* (Rail fact book 2000). Tokyo: Transportation Policy Research Center.

Ministry of Transport, Regional Transport Bureau, ed. 1986. *Suji de miru tetsudo 1986* (Rail fact book 1986). Tokyo: Transportation Policy Research Center.

Mizutani, F. 1994. *Japanese urban railways: A private-public comparison.* Aldershot, U.K.: Avebury.

———. 1997. Empirical analysis of yardstick competition in Japanese rail industry. *International Journal of Transport Economics* 24 (3): 367–392.

———. 1999a. An assessment of the Japan National Railway companies since privatization: Performance, local rail service, and debts. *Transport Reviews* 19 (2): 117–139.

———. 1999b. Changing trains: Japan. In *Changing trains,* ed. D. M. van de Velde, 255–306. Aldershot, U.K.: Ashgate.

———. 2001. Privately owned railways' total cost function, organization size, and ownership. Kobe University, Graduate School of Business Administration. Mimeograph (revised version).

Mizutani, F., and K. Nakamura. 1996. Effects of Japan National Railways' privatization on labor productivity. *Papers in Regional Science* 75 (2): 177–199.

———. 1997. Privatization of the Japan National Railway: Overview of performance changes. *International Journal of Transport Economics* 24 (1): 75–99.

———. 2000. Japan railways since privatisation. In *Privatization and deregulation of transport,* ed. B. Bradshaw and H. Lawton Smith, 205–235. Basingstoke, U.K.: Macmillan.

Mizutani, F., and K. Shoji. 2001. Operation-infrastructure separation in Japanese rail industry: The case of Kobe Kosoku Tetsudo. Paper prepared for the World Conference on Transport Research. 22–27 July, Seoul, Korea.

Moyer, N. E., and L. S. Thompson. 1992. Options for reshaping the railway. Policy Research Working Paper no. 926. Washington, D.C.: World Bank, June.

Nakamura, K., and F. Mizutani. 1995. The effects of railway privatization on competitive performance: A case study of Japanese railways. *Journal of the Eastern Asia Society for Transportation Studies* 1 (1): 85–102.

Nash, M. C. A. 1997. The separation of operations from infrastructure in the provision of railway services: The British experience. In *The separation of operations from infrastructure in the provision of railway services,* ed. European Conference of Ministers of Transport (ECMT), 53–89. Paris: Organization for Economic Cooperation and Development.

Preston, J. 1996. The economics of British rail privatization: An assessment. *Transport Reviews* 16 (1): 1–21.

Preston, J., and A. Root. 1999. Changing trains: Great Britain. In *Changing trains,* ed. D. M. van de Velde, 5–78. Aldershot, U.K.: Ashgate.

Shleifer, A. 1985. A theory of yardstick competition. *Rand Journal of Economics* 16 (3): 319–327.

Suga, T. 1997. The separation of operations from infrastructure in the provision of railway services: Examples in Japan. In *The separation of operations from infrastructure in the provision of railway services,* ed. European Conference of Ministers of Transport (ECMT), 153–176. Paris: Organization for Economic Cooperation and Development.

Sumita, S. 2000. *Success story: The privatisation of Japanese national railways.* London: Profile Books.

Van de Velde, D., and P. van Reeven. 1999. Changing trains: Synthesis and general lessons. In *Changing trains,* ed. D. M. van de Velde, 345–364. Aldershot, U.K.: Ashgate.

Comment   Mario B. Lamberte

This paper discusses the most recent experience of Japan in restructuring and privatizing a rather large and important utility, the Japan Railway. The privatization is still unfinished, yet some lessons already can be drawn from the experience. What I gathered from the paper is that Japan made a very careful plan for and then execution of privatization. For example, JNR was divided into six regional companies (JRs): each one would complete 95

Mario B. Lamberte is president of the Philippine Institute for Development Studies.

percent of all trips within the borders of the region, and there was to be one nationwide freight company. The privatization of each of these companies was done sequentially. The timing of the privatization was as important as the sequence. Rather than copying in toto the railway privatization program implemented in other advanced economies, the Japanese government took a slightly different route that was most suited to Japan's conditions. For instance, it opted for vertical integration instead of vertical separation, allowing the JRs to reduce transaction costs and exploit economies of scope between operation and infrastructure. More importantly, the privatization immediately yielded some benefits to the Japanese society and minimized social costs.

In describing the reasons for privatization, it would help the readers if the authors had started with a discussion about the market structure of the railway industry. I gathered from certain sections of the paper that JNR was facing competition not only from motorization but also from the existence of relatively efficient private railway companies. Do each of the JRs operating in their respective geographical areas face fierce competition with private companies? The presence of vertically integrated private railway companies could have also been a major consideration in opting for vertical integration.

In developing economies, like the Philippines, the railway industry usually is monopolized by state-owned enterprises. Privatization results in a transfer of monopoly power from the government to the private company. Regulation and supervision therefore must be strong. Unfortunately, regulatory capture occurs most of the time. Therefore, this makes the experience of Japan even more interesting, because private companies were allowed to operate in the railway industry even before the privatization of JNR. I am very interested in the legal and regulatory framework that Japan put in place to allow those private railway companies to operate. This could be an alternative route that less developed countries could use when they privatize their railroad companies.

One of the interesting features of the JNR privatization was the setting up of an intermediate institution to repay the debts of JNR and to find new jobs for redundant employees. That feature would make the privatization of JNR acceptable to those who would be adversely affected in terms of employment. However, it is not clear to me what programs the intermediary institution undertook to make the transfer to other government agencies smooth. Were there pressures exerted by the central government on other government agencies to accept the redundant workers of JNR? It could be difficult to transfer redundant workers from JNR to other government agencies, unless these government agencies also are growing and therefore need some additional labor.

Table 12.3 shows the overall performance changes of the JRs since privatization. My understanding is that only JR East, JR West, and JR Central have been privatized so far. It might help if the authors compared the performance of those JRs that already have been privatized with those that have not yet been privatized. More importantly, they should describe the difference in governance structure in these two groups of JRs. They should also describe the extent to which the government formally or informally controls the three privatized JRs, since it still holds at least 30 percent of the total shares outstanding.

In table 12.4, the authors show a comparison of the fares between the JRs and private companies before and after the privatization. Although there seems to be improvement in the price competitiveness of the JRs, we still notice significant differences. Theoretically, the fares of JRs and private companies should converge unless the former have retained some monopoly power. Perhaps the authors can expand more on this issue and speculate when these fares will become approximately the same. It would certainly help the reader if the authors gave an idea of the market shares of the JRs and the private railway companies in the same market.

The privatization plan and sequencing outlined in table 12.1 is something that a country planning to privatize its railway industry must learn. The downloading of fare-setting from the Diet to the regulatory agency certainly depoliticized the process. I wonder if there is a fair and transparent process followed by the regulatory agency in revising rates, because the process itself still could be highly politicized.

Some of the questions that the authors should have answered, which surely will be of interest to those who are looking seriously at the JNR experience as a model, are the following:

1. How is the board of the JRs organized?
2. When should the remaining JRs be privatized? Should the government wait until Japan's stock market recovers?
3. What would be the additional costs to be borne by the government by retaining some JRs?

Comment   Helen Owens

The Mizutani and Nakamura paper provides a clear summary of recent reform initiatives relating to Japanese railways. On many issues it represents a convergence of ideas with those of the Australian Productivity Commission (PC), which were formed while undertaking a major review of Australian railways two years ago (PC 1999).

Helen Owens is a commissioner on the Australian Productivity Commission and presided on the commission's 1999 inquiry into progress in rail reform.

I would like to provide comment on three general matters.

The first is the Japanese approach to rail reform, which has included both structural reform and partial privatization of some railways. There would appear to be a strong case for the horizontal separation, by region, of JNR, which appears to have experienced similar problems to those of other large, publicly owned corporations worldwide. These include complacency, poor management, antagonistic labor relations, overstaffing, huge debts, low morale, political interference, and diseconomies of scale. These problems tend to result in an increased dependence on government subsidies, reduced productivity, poor-quality services, and a reduced ability to compete on an intermodal basis with road and air services.

Horizontal separation holds the promise that rail service providers will be better able to meet different local needs. It can facilitate organizational changes and yardstick competition across businesses. It can also improve the effectiveness of government regulatory regimes and enable government to design contractual arrangements to meet noncommercial objectives (social, regional, and environmental).

On the downside, there may be issues relating to lack of coordination between geographically separated entities and interface issues where the freight operator traverses different passenger networks with multiple owners. On balance, the benefits of horizontal separation by region are likely to far outweigh the costs.

In regard to horizontal separation by product (or function), I would tend to agree with the authors that there are strong arguments for separating passenger from freight operations in Japan. This will ensure management has clear responsibility and that privatization of the more profitable passenger businesses is not undermined by loss-making freight operations. Potentially, the needs of different types of users (passengers, freight forwarders) can be met more effectively. Also, to the extent that the freight company traverses different passenger networks, it would not make sense to link it to one passenger railway.

The authors also cite evidence of diseconomies of scope. Recent experience in New Zealand with the horizontally and vertically integrated, privately owned TranzRail suggests that retaining loss-making urban and long-distance passenger services within a privatized entity can undermine its overall operations, despite regional government subsidies. In 2001 TranzRail repositioned itself as mainly a bulk freight operator, having sold the long-distance passenger service operating between Auckland and Wellington (an intercity commuter operation) as well as two profitable tourist train services on the South Island.

Once again, I agree with the authors that vertical integration of track and operations is the appropriate approach in the Japanese context.

There are a number of possible advantages to vertically separating train operations from track infrastructure services. According to the Organization for Economic Cooperation and Development (1999), economic efficiency can be enhanced by introducing rail on rail competition through vertical separation when

- existing rail operators possess natural monopoly characteristics such as economies of scale and have effective market power;
- other operators can compete on a commercially sustainable basis; and
- track infrastructure and train operations are relatively independent so that the costs of separation are small in relation to the gains from competition and efficient economic regulation.

However, despite the relatively large size of some Japanese passenger markets, market power may not eventuate given the degree of intermodal competition. Thus the opportunities for competitive entry could be limited.

Other problems with vertical separation (and subsequent greater rail-on-rail competition) noted by the authors include the difficulties of monitoring performance; organizing time-tabling and slot allocation; maintaining safety (as evident in United Kingdom); and undertaking long-term investment planning.

In addition, the authors noted that the potential for adversarial relationships to develop between the track owner and operating companies (as manifested in the United Kingdom) may be a problem. In the case of the three Japanese Honshu companies operating high-density services, it is especially important to avoid complications associated with train schedule allocation, time-tabling, and capacity management.

The authors argued that vertical separation may be more appropriate under conditions of low traffic density. However, to the extent that rail businesses encounter high fixed costs associated with inefficient track maintenance, these could be more easily reduced by outsourcing maintenance while maintaining ownership and control. This approach also would avoid any transactions costs of changing ownership.

On balance, the PC review concluded that the benefits and costs of structural separation are likely to differ between network types. It would appear that, in the case of Japan, the characteristics of its transport market would suggest the approach adopted to structural reform is largely appropriate.

The problems encountered by JNR also strongly suggest that privatization or other measures to introduce greater private-sector involvement are appropriate. However, I have some concerns about the privatization process. To date, only three of the seven companies formed from JNR have been partially privatized and the process has been very slow. Six years elapsed from the initial announcement in 1987 until the first partial privatization of JR East in 1993. The partial privatization of JR West and JR Central followed in 1996 and 1997, respectively. The decision to privatize slowly appears to be aimed at giving the companies more time to become more efficient and show a profit in order to increase the sale price and hence government revenue. However, it is unclear why private purchasers would not recognize the potential for future efficiency gains and factor them into the purchase price.

An alternative approach adopted in other countries would be to privatize the businesses as going concerns in order to promote faster efficiency gains, with ongoing community benefits from lower prices probably exceeding any forgone budget revenue.

The danger with the Japanese strategy is that other forces, such as recession or political changes, could cause the process to lose momentum or stall altogether, as appears to be the case. The opportunity for more efficient operations is therefore lost.

Another concern relates to the strategy to privatize the three Honshu rail companies only partially. Again, a danger exists that tensions may arise between the government and private shareholders, as well as that of ongoing political interference in the companies that could restrict organizational and managerial flexibility.

Finally, the authors mention that in privatizing the three Honshu companies, jobs were found for redundant employees with other government agencies, including local governments, the tax office, the police, and the meteorological bureau. If one were to take a whole-government perspective, this may simply shift the inefficiency from one government agency to others.

The second matter on which I would like to comment is the performance of Japanese railways presented in table 12.2 of the paper. It is hard to disentangle the impact of structural reform from privatization as the two processes overlap. Only the data for 1998 relate to the period since privatization of the three Honshu companies (in 1993, 1996, and 1997), so there are insufficient data points to be definitive about the effect of privatization. Further, one year is insufficient time to gauge the impact of the privatization of JR Central. Nevertheless, the data are starting to tell an interesting story.

For the three privatized companies,

- the operating revenue–cost ratio increased between 1987 and 1992 but fell again in 1998 after privatization (this may be due in part to recession);
- average fares fell consistently for JR East and JR West, but rose slightly for JR Central in 1998 (although they were still marginally lower than in 1987); and
- labor productivity rose consistently for JR East and JR West, but increased and then fell for JR Central (although they were still higher than in 1987).

However, labor productivity also rose significantly for the four nonprivatized companies, possibly reflecting the impact of structural reform. The operating revenue–cost ratio also rose for the other passenger companies, but fell for JR Freight. Average operating costs were lower in 1998 than 1987 for all passenger companies but rose for JR Freight. From these results it would appear that any improvements in performance are likely to relate more to structural reform than privatization per se.

My third point is that franchising is an alternative approach to reform that could have been considered. It is clear from the paper that the publicly owned Three-Islands passenger companies are still operating at a loss, as is JR Freight, possibly explaining why they are yet to be privatized under the policy of waiting until they become profitable. This may take a long time, given the slow improvements to date.

Another approach that could be considered for the Three-Islands companies would be to promote "competition for the market" by entering into franchise agreements or contracts with the private sector. To the extent that these services are noncommercial and require continued government support, private companies could tender competitively to operate the service at the lowest subsidy. Investment, quality, and other performance requirements could be incorporated into franchise agreements (or contracts). This would overcome the concerns of the authors with such an approach.

This approach was adopted in the Australian state of Victoria in 1999 for all urban and nonurban passenger services. The urban passenger operations were split into two companies and franchised to separate private companies, one of which also operates the nonurban passenger service. The franchisees lease the track infrastructure. The franchise agreements, which were originally designed to run for ten to fifteen years, specify passenger service levels, maximum fares, and operational performance. Investment commitments are also specified in the contracts, along with subsidy payments.

An approach involving "competition for the market" could be considered for loss-making railways.

References

Organization for Economic Cooperation and Development. 1999. Competition and railways. *Journal of Competition Law and Policy* 1 (1): 149–228.

Productivity Commission (PC). 1999. *Progress in rail reform.* Inquiry Report no. 6. Canberra, Productivity Commission, August.

13

What Has Been Achieved in the Japanese Telecommunications Industry since 1985?

Tsuruhiko Nambu

In this paper I analyze the development of the Japanese telecommunications industry since 1985, when Nippon Telephone and Telegraph (NTT) public corporation—a natural monopoly—was privatized and competition was introduced into long-distance (i.e., interprefecture) markets. At the outset of the analysis I must stress the extreme importance of changes in mode of usage as well as technology over so short a period as fifteen years. This is crucial to the discussion below because there exist some economists who still live in the "medieval" age, when voice telephony was dominant and the market was structured consistent with this technology of the time, namely before 1985. Voice telephony has a history of more than 100 years and the imprints of that age still are so strong as to blind some people to the scope of the new era that started in the early 1990s.

At the same time the nature of competition in telecommunications requires us to conduct a careful examination over the entire period. On the one hand, technological innovation has increased the choices of telecommunications services but it also has blurred the boundary of the market. We have now several telecom carriers and service providers in the local market. Does this mean that the local market has become competitive enough to abolish regulations upon incumbents? Because major telecom carriers are competing in borderless markets, the question arises: should the demarcation of the telecom market be based on a national boundary? Without in-depth empirical analysis we cannot answer either of these questions.

Tsuruhiko Nambu is professor of economics at Gakushuin University.

I am grateful to the comments by Il Chong Nam, Richard Snape, Takatoshi Ito, and Anne Krueger, and especially to Robert Graniere for his thorough reviewing of my paper. Remaining errors are all mine.

From the viewpoint of competition policy, competition authorities like the Japan Fair Trade Commission must accumulate knowledge in the telecommunications industry. In the United States, the Federal Communications Commission (FCC) and the Department of Justice (DOJ) have a long history of regulating AT&T and other telecom carriers on a daily basis or combating AT&T in the court. Consequently they have enough resources and capabilities to deal with the new developments in the telecom industry. In Japan the public monopoly was not subject to regulation and antimonopoly laws until recently. It has only been during the last fifteen years that the government has regulated this industry. It must also be noted that the Japanese regulator is not an independent authority but rather an intraministerial bureau.

The government-business relationship plays an important role in the process of deregulating natural monopoly industries (see Nambu 1997a). The Japanese institutional traits will be the focus of this paper in order to make the last fifteen years of the Japanese telecom industry understandable.

13.1   Introductory Perspective

This introduction clarifies the basic structural changes in technology and demand that have occurred in the telecom industry relatively recently (in the last fifteen years) by dividing those years into three periods. This is necessary because of the many structural changes that have occurred during these years.

13.1.1   Phase I: Up To the Early 1980s

Although optical fiber technology had been commercially developed and was partly introduced, telephone networks were almost exclusively wired with copper technology. Voice traffic was carried over a copper loop and switched at the exchange. In this phase the most striking feature of the industry lay in the fact that telecom services are homogeneous. Of course, there existed an artificial boundary that was set by regulators between local and long-distance services. This boundary reflected a technological hierarchy that was intended to realize economies of scale and scope. Long-distance services are different from local services because they are supplied through a higher hierarchical switching network. But from the viewpoint of economics, they are identical goods except for the illusion that long-distance services used to be regarded as luxuries because they were priced higher than local service in order to realize a cross-subsidy from long-distance to local services. But not withstanding this fact the breakup of AT&T was based on the conviction at that time that long-distance service had a different market structure than local service. In the days of Ma Bell, that is, the days prior to the AT&T breakup, all telephone services were "costed out" on a "station-to-station" basis. However, it had long been thought that the long-distance services were actually "board-to-board" services.

When AT&T was divested, general agreement existed that the long-distance (interstate) market was competitive as a result of technological innovations, whereas the local market was and should remain a natural monopoly. This dichotomy has plagued the dynamic development of the telecom industry in Japan as well as in the United States. Even though this dichotomy was accepted by the majority of economists in both countries, it should not have been treated as a doctrine. However, as a rule, once regulatory agencies accept a certain way of thinking, they usually stick to it until a visible and undeniable change has occurred.

13.1.2   Phase II: From the Middle of the 1980s to the Middle of the 1990s

Structural change came in several ways during this period.

Wireless Technology

Wireless technology is kind of an old technology in a sense that it was used widely in military and some business applications. The problems with this technology are the difficulty of handling wireless equipment and the volatility of communication. Once these difficulties are alleviated, it is obvious that wireless technology has an extreme advantage over wireline services. It is also true that wireless technology has often been utilized by telephone companies as an alternative to wireline technology when short-distance voice services are transmitted to the switches. Under the name of the "geodesic" network, a provocative scenario was presented wherein the telecom industry could be totally restructured by wireless technology and this industry could be contestable.[1]

Cable Television

Cable television (CATV) started as an auxiliary broadcasting service in a limited area where the terrestrial TV radio signal is very weak. Over time, it became apparent that this technology could be used in telecommunications as well. The competitive pressure that CATV exerts against wireline telephony depends on its penetration rate. In the United States, CATV is deemed to be competitive with telephony although the quality of CATV service providers is controversial. In Japan, CATV has not reached this stage. Though the history of CATV is rather short, it has been demonstrated that CATV can effectively compete with local telephone companies and provide broadband services as well.

---

1. The idea was first introduced by Peter W. Huber in a report to the Department of Justice, *The Geodesic Network* (Huber 1987). The second version was published in 1992 (Huber, Kellogg, and Thorne 1992).

Internet

The development of the Internet as a popular data transmission vehicle has changed the telecommunications market as well. It took years for telephone businesspeople to be convinced that the Internet is a new communication device and to dismiss their old paradigm as a result. The difference between the Internet and telephony is especially remarkable at two points. First, routers replace switches but switches are designed to ensure perfect connection among subscribers. Second, Internet users prefer to be continuously connected without having to pick up a phone. These particularities of the Internet have imposed changes upon telephone companies and regulators but there have been noteworthy differences in the speed of compliance with these changes among countries. Although aware that they are challenged by these fundamental structural transformations, the telephone companies and their regulators have not been quick to change their view of the industry.

13.1.3   Phase III: From the Middle of the 1990s to the Present

Faced with revolutionary changes in the telecommunications industry, the legislators set out to initiate a new framework corresponding to the new economic reality. In 1996 the Federal Communications Act of 1934 was amended in the United States and was enacted for the purpose of realizing competition between long-distance carriers and regional Bell operating companies (RBOCs). In Japan the long dispute over the NTT managerial form was settled in 1999 and the reshaping of NTT was realized by creation of a holding company with the three subsidiaries, NTT East and West (which are local companies) and NTT communications (which is a long-distance and international company). However, these two reforms, both in the United States and in Japan, up to now appear not to be fruitful.

It has become clearer during this period that new entrants into the telecom industry found and employed a new strategy: namely, "politicizing" (gaming) entry conditions for the purpose of reducing entry costs and risks. New entrants learned that they could lower entry barriers by arguing to policymakers that incumbents are always trying to preclude entry. This is economically beneficial to the new entrants because they can reduce their entry costs if they do not need to invest in new facilities that might be sunk in the future. At the same time, regulators have learned that they can cater to the public by protecting entrants and quarrelling with incumbents. Their interests coincide to put pressures upon incumbents.

In the case of the United States, the focus of the disputes among regulators, entrants, and incumbents lies in the difficulty of fulfilling the checkpoints imposed on the RBOCs by the 1996 act. Once these checkpoints are fulfilled, the RBOCs can enter the long-distance markets. It is natural that long-distance carriers are fearful of competition from the RBOCs because they face a high probability of losing their customers.

The Tauzin-Dingell bill was discussed in the House of Representatives in the United States in 2001. This bill intends to give RBOCs the freedom to invest in broadband services on an inter–local access and transport area (inter-LATA) basis.

The Japanese government has begun to discuss the possible reshaping of NTT, which was reorganized in 1999.

13.2   Historical Background

13.2.1   The Creation of a Public Monopoly

The Japanese choice of industry structure after privatization in 1985 may be better understood by looking back on the origin of the system of telecommunications service provision established in 1957. After World War II, the Japanese government faced the problem of rebuilding an infrastructure that had been destroyed by the war. This infrastructure was required to support rapid renovation for economic development. There existed conflicting opinions as to how to structure the telecommunications service provider. Japan ultimately chose a public-corporation type of common carrier for telecom services. The public corporation was called Denden Kosha, or the Nippon Telegraph and Telephone public corporation, which was placed under the supervision of the Diet but independent of the regulatory oversight of the Ministry of Posts and Telecommunications (MPT).

The idea of Kosha was to create independence for the investment policy for telecommunications facilities. Denden Kosha succeeded in eliminating the backlog demand for subscription to the telephone network. This objective was accomplished around 1977 or 1978. During this developmental period the Denden Kosha served as a public monopoly with a bureaucratic administration that worked to provide telecommunications services to the public. On top of that, Denden Kosha's board members consisted of carrier bureaucrats who had moved from the Ministry of Communication that existed until 1949. It is often observed that bureaucrats do not initiate new business forms until they are absolutely certain that the old forms are not appropriate any longer. This type of behavior nourished the corporate culture of NTT and it was liable to complaints and criticism directed at its inflexible and slow response to changes in demand, especially from the business world.

Amid the global wave of deregulation in the United States and privatization in the United Kingdom, the Japanese government decided to privatize NTT in 1985. The initial institutional arrangements were as follows:

1. NTT corporation replaced the public monopoly, Denden Kosha. NTT became a private company but was a special entity because more than 51 percent of its shares were held by the government. It also inherited a public obligation as "universal service."

2. Instead of the Public Telecommunications Law, the Telecommunications Business Law became the key determinant of the industrial structure of the telecom industry. Under this law, telecom service providers are classified into two categories, Type I and Type II. The former owns telecom facilities, whereas the latter rents them from Type I carriers.

3. The MPT[2] was put in charge of regulating Type I and Type II carriers. In the day of the public monopoly, Denden Kosha was under the surveillance of the national Diet. At the time of Denden Kosha, regulation by the MPT was rather nominal. Therefore there did not exist any conflict between MPT and NTT. In fact, the Kosha system itself was created in order to encourage and respect the independence of Kosha.

13.2.2   NTT versus MPT: Institutional Stalemate

In this section I analyze the structural difficulty of decision making in Japan from the viewpoint of the Japanese regulatory scheme as compared to the regulatory schemes of the United States and the United Kingdom.

First, the Japanese regulatory scheme might be called a simply unified jurisdiction system, in the contrast to that of the United States, where several agencies are competing with each other (e.g., the FCC, the DOJ, state public-utility commissions, and the court in the case of telecommunications). Contrary to this decentralized system in the United States, there usually exists in Japan one ministry that is in charge of a certain industry or industries. In some cases, this type of centralization has been challenged by other ministries. The Ministry of International Trade and Industry, or MITI, used to challenge MPT because MITI regulated the computer industry. If MITI's challenge had been effective, the concentration of power in MPT would have been weakened. But up to now MPT has not faced a serious challenge. As a result, Japanese telecommunications regulation has been centralized in the hands of MPT.

The difference between a centralized and a decentralized regulatory system seems clear when we compare Japan and the United States. The comparison between Japan and the United Kingdom, however, raises a different problem. These two countries have a centralized bureaucracy in common, although in the case of the United Kingdom, the Office of Telecommunications (OFTEL) was newly created for regulating the telecommunications industry. The creation of telecommunications regulatory pol-

---

2. The name of MPT vanished during the recent restructuring of ministries, and MPT has become a regulatory agency in the Ministry of Public Management, Home Affairs, Posts, and Telecommunications.

icy is in the hands of top executives who are appointed by the government, whereas Japan has a tightly integrated, hierarchical structure of bureaucrats. It is a good contrast that, unlike in Japan, political appointees in the United Kingdom are requested to articulate their own philosophy of regulatory policy.

Second, it is instructive to look at the business-government relationship in Japan as compared to that in the United Kingdom. In Japan, MPT was given jurisdiction over the telecommunications industry for the first time in 1985. NTT public corporation was privatized at that time, but it naturally inherited the bureaucracy created during the days of Kosha. Being ambitious to apply an industrial policy toward the telecommunications industry, MPT invited new entrants into the industry and tried to protect them from the dominance of NTT. The means of protection has been to place NTT under the strict regulation of MPT. As a result, conflicts between MPT and NTT have not been unusual. NTT, being an integrated bureaucracy, had accumulated a deep knowledge of the telecommunications industry and is still the most knowledgeable service provider. MPT was a latecomer that was lacking in industry-specific expertise when it was given the authority to regulate the telecom industry. But MPT took the approach of omnipotent regulator from the outset. As a result, Japan had two bureaucracies that claimed legitimacy.

In the United Kingdom the new regulatory agency, OFTEL, took a different approach toward British Telecom (BT). OFTEL adopted price-cap regulation, which is intended to give positive economic incentives to the incumbent firm. In addition to allowing flexible rate rebalancing by BT, OFTEL admitted one new competitor, Mercury. Price-cap regulation meant that BT did not face the same financial difficulty as NTT because it could rebalance its rates in a few years after privatization in 1984, although BT always claimed the existence of an access deficit. The policy goal of OFTEL had been announced clearly by the director general and the negotiation between OFTEL and BT did not include fatal conflicts such as there used to be in Japan. Sometimes OFTEL was criticized for being too indulgent to BT. This is in contrast to Japan, where MPT protected new entrants by hemming in or handcuffing NTT.

By comparing these cases we can tentatively conclude that "bad" business-government relationships, and conflicts and strains between regulators and the regulated firms, bring about a serious time delay in meeting the challenges of a change in environment. Consider especially the incredibly rapid change of telecommunications technologies. Slow decision making as a result of the regulatory scheme is the greatest obstacle to industrial development. Slow decision making is typically the case in Japan, especially with respect to the introduction of arrangements for new businesses. NTT's business was narrowly restricted to the domestic market, where new entrants were allowed to earn handsome profits from the continuing high prices inherited from the regulatory system. On the other hand, new entrants failed to exhibit innovative marketing to create new services. Next, the difficulties of the Japanese telecommunications industry brought on by a bad business-government relationship are examined.

13.2.3   Dispute over Divestiture

Before privatization of NTT, there was a discussion of the possibility of an NTT divestiture, à la the AT&T breakup in 1984 in the United States. But no conclusion was reached and it was decided that the discussion would be resumed in 1990. At that time, MPT proposed the breakup of NTT based on a report issued by the Telecommunications Council. However, the Ministry of Finance, the Telecommunications Labor Union, and the politicians were against MPT's proposal and no conclusions were reached in 1990. During this second discussion the conflict between NTT and MPT became clearer. NTT refused the idea of divestiture, and MPT refused to abandon it. Although Denden Kosha was privatized, the two bureaucratic systems had reached a stalemate.

The Japanese stock market responded negatively to this situation and the NTT stock price dropped drastically. As a result, any further flotation on NTT stocks became impossible. This induced a huge capital loss for NTT stockholders and had an adverse influence upon the possible flotation of other public corporation stocks, such as the Japan Railways (or JRs; the Japan National Railway was privatized and reshaped into seven JRs). This kind of confrontation between the regulator and the regulated firm inevitably creates uncertainty about the future of the industry.

In 1995 the discussion on the possible divestiture of NTT was resumed, but again, no conclusion was reached. At this point in time, the structural change of the telecom industry appeared clearer. The U.S. government had proposed the National Information Infrastructure scheme to enhance the development of information technology. The National Information Infrastructure anticipated that a new industrial structure might be needed to capitalize on improvements in information technology. It has now become essential to determine how to structure the telecom industry consistent with potential of information technology. The most plausible scheme for facility-based competition in the local telephone market is based on the emergence of new information technologies.

The most likely facility-based entrants into the local market were the long-distance carriers. In 1996 the Federal Communications Law was enacted to break the old boundary between local and long-distance services.

The political situation in Japan at this time was about the same. There were only a few examples of competition in the local market. Tokyo Telecommunication Network Co., Inc. (TTNet), a subsidiary of the Tokyo Electric Power Company, entered the Tokyo area and Osaka MediaPort Corp. (OMC), a consortium of an electric power company and others, entered the Osaka market. But the geographic area covered by the entrants was very limited and accounted for almost nil.

The Japanese government needed to settle the old dispute over NTT's organizational form if it was to foster further competition. At last a compromise was worked out in 1999. A new holding company was created that allowed the old NTT's three divisions to become three separate subsidiaries of the new NTT Holding Company. However, this conclusion to the discussion of the breakup of the old NTT contains inherent contradictions.

13.2.4 Rate Rebalancing and Access Charges

In the United Kingdom, BT was allowed to rebalance its rates as part of the implementation of price-cap regulation, whereas in the United States a brand of new access-charge system was established as a condition of the AT&T divestiture. But in Japan, neither rate rebalancing nor access charges were introduced (fig. 13.1).

This is mainly because NTT and MPT collided on the question of the local and network access deficits. NTT had provided estimates on the size of these deficits but MPT refused to accept them. MPT wanted a structural solution in the form of a structural separation, and to make the industry's cost structure visible to industry observers. NTT complied with MPT's wishes by changing its managerial structure into a long-distance business center and local telephony business centers. This structural division is based upon artificial and arbitrary allocation of the common costs of the whole company. If there had existed mutual confidence and trust between NTT and MPT, the NTT's deficit problem would have been solved earlier. But this was not the case. The delays associated with reaching an agreement have brought about serious economic distortions in the Japanese

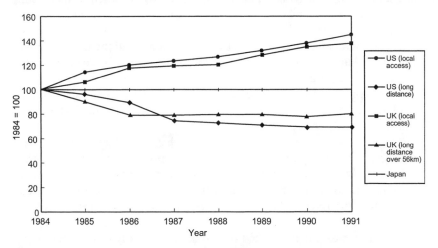

Fig. 13.1   Comparison of rate rebalancing: Japan, U.S., U.K. (1984 = 100)

telecommunications industry. Rate rebalancing is necessary to restore a signaling function of price that is not distorted by the cross-subsidy system of the monopoly era. On top of that, telecom technologies have been ever-changing. If rates continue to be biased by artificial cross-subsidies, the new technology cannot find its suitable place in the market. Consequently the delay caused by the regulatory conflict has inflicted tremendous social cost to Japan from the viewpoint of income distribution as well as efficiency.

It was not until 1994 that an agreement on an access-charge payment was established. The new common carriers (NCCs), which are equal to the other common carriers (OCCs) in the United States, were required to pay about 20 billion yen in addition to the local rate that they already paid to NTT. This additional payment is approximately equal to, say, what NCCs used to be paid in the form subsidy from NTT subscribers. The imposition of a new access charge meant that hidden subsidy was removed. This had a negative impact upon the NCCs' profitability, which, in turn, influenced their investment strategy. If the access-charge arrangement had been realized earlier, then the NCCs' investment behavior might not have been affected so badly. The delay in the resolution of access-charge issues may have given the wrong signal to the NCCs, causing them to invest in low-density areas throughout the country.

13.2.5   Punishing NTT Policy

In the dynamic process of change from monopoly to competition, several structural amendments are necessary to abolish the old institutional restraints. The most basic regulatory framework is based upon a system of cross-subsidy between local and long-distance telephony. As usual, the local telephone rates are maintained at lower levels than their costs on the grounds that local telephone service could not be viable without subsidy.

In preparing for the introduction of competition in the long-distance market, it was deemed necessary in the United States and the United Kingdom to reshape this cross-subsidization mechanism. In contrast with them, Japan was a unique country where no discussion on issues such as access charges or rate rebalancing occurred. The Japanese government simply ordered the newborn NTT to continue to provide local as well as long-distance telephone service without changing its tariff structure. This would mean that new entrants into the long-distance market can earn extraordinary profits by charging slightly lower prices as compared to the NTT tariff. MPT officially admitted that this regulatory policy amounted to cream-skimming by the new entrants. NTT must suffer losses in the long-distance market while it continued to provide below-cost local service.

In Japan it was partly justified on the basis of apathy toward "monopoly" firms. NTT was, in the eyes of the government, an inefficient monopoly and excessive resources were said to be built into the organization. As a result, it was argued, NTT could respond to the competition by reducing its extra costs. In other words, suffering is a necessity for the rebirth of NTT. This point of view is valid as far as there exist extra costs to be removed, but it is a "once-and-for-all" remedy because extra costs must disappear in the process of competition with newcomers. But the reality at that time was that there existed no apparent signal from the government concerning the time horizon of its policy, which resulted in the sharp and sustained decline of NTT's share price ever since the issue of the stock in 1985.

13.3   Competition in the Long-Distance Market

The three NCCs, Daini Denden Incorporated, Japan Telecom, and Teleway Japan, entered and began telephony service in 1987. They successfully competed with NTT because there existed a price differential between NTT and NCCs.

Figure 13.2 shows that the price of an NCC was about 15 to 20 percent lower than NTT's regulated rate. If NTT had been allowed to match the NCCs' price without delay, the advantage of the NCCs may not have been so great. But NTT was not allowed to do so and the price differential accounted for the NCCs' success. In the face of this outcome we must ask whether the NCCs' success was justifiable from the viewpoint of efficiency.

Under the Telecom Business Law, the number of competitors in the market was regulated by MPT pursuant to a supply-and-demand balancing clause. MPT allowed three NCCs to enter and cream-skim the long-distance market. Cream skimming was possible because NTT was not allowed to rebalance its rate or to impose access charges on these NCCs. At least two of three NCCs made huge profits since the early 1990s. Figure 13.3 shows the markup rate differences among carriers. From 1995, the markup of NCCs declined because of the introduction of an access charge and price reductions by NTT.

Another problem with the initial introduction of competition into Japan's long-distance market is a deep concern with dynamic efficiency. No one can know whether newcomers, once selected by MPT, are efficient challengers of NTT. Unlike in the United States, where the number of competitors in the long-distance market was not regulated by the FCC, Japan could not depend upon the usual entry and exit mechanisms to eventually sort out the efficient and inefficient firms. The Japanese style of regulation cannot guarantee the kind of efficiency that should be a trademark of a newly competitive industry.

The advantageous status of NCCs can be justified, in theory, as providing protection to an infant industry. But as is clearly discussed in the economics textbooks, the government cannot protect newcomers forever.

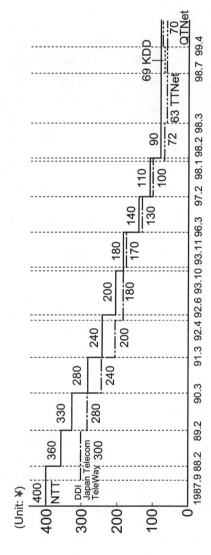

Fig. 13.2   Domestic long-distance call rate history

Notes: The figures are based on "longest call distance" charges. In March 1991, NTT's longest call distance was reduced from 320 km to 160 km and NCCs' longest call distance was reduced from 340 km to 170 km. Since November 1993, NCCs' charges are based on end-to-end charge calculation.

Source: InfoCom Research (2001, 52).

Percentage

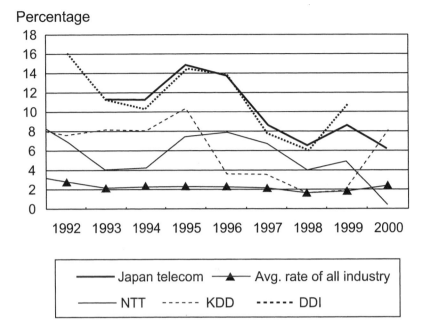

Fig. 13.3   **Make-up rate of carriers**

There must always exist some time limit (sunset) when protection comes to an end and is replaced by the free entry of other firms; otherwise, the wrong signals will be sent to the existing three firms. If MPT had sent a signal to the NCCs in the early stages that it would abandon their protection, the NCCs might not have misunderstood their position as permanent and might not have invested excessively to exploit quasi rent from protection (see fig. 13.4).

It is clear that the NCCs tried to exploit quasi rents in the 1990s. Because of their high profitability on the one hand and mutual competition on the other, they expanded their business areas throughout the country. However, there are diminishing returns when long-distance carriers increase the points of interface since the busiest business areas in Japan are concentrated in a limited number of large cities like Tokyo, Osaka, Nagoya, Fukuoka, and Sapporo. If the NCCs had given proper consideration to the possibility that they would lose their government protection, it is reasonable to conclude that their investment might have been restricted to certain areas. But they were sluggish to change their business policies even in the face of competition from discounters like AT&T that are not Type I carriers.

With the development of price competition in the late 1990s, the three NCCs met financial difficulties in the long-distance market. This was

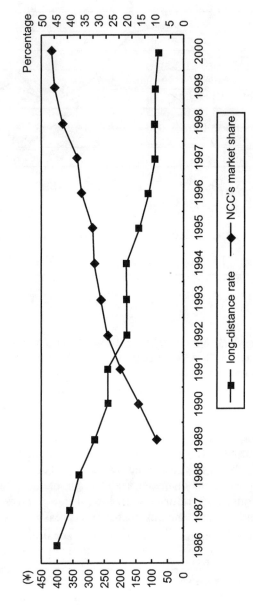

Fig. 13.4   The market share of NCCs in the long-distance market

simply because voice telephony service is homogeneous and, as a result, product differentiation is impossible. This is a common phenomenon in any country. When long-distance rates are approaching their marginal costs, competition may well be ruinous, as was often seen in the past.

Their tenure was ended by the following events (summarized in fig. 13.5):

- Teleway Japan Inc. was established by the Toyota group. This company failed to expand its business nationwide and vanished in December 1998, merging with Kokusai Denshin Denwa Co., Ltd. (KDD).
- KDDI was created by the merger between Daini Denden Inc. (DDI) and KDD; Nippon Idou Tsushin Corp. (IDO) joined KDDI in October 2000.
- Japan Telecom (JT) was created by the Japan National Railways, and International Telecom Japan, Inc. (ITJ) was absorbed into JT in October 1998. Vodaphone owns 45 percent of the JT shares. TU-KA Cellular Tokyo, Inc. (mobile) phones joined Vodaphone in August 1998.
- TTNet is a subsidiary of Tokyo Electric Power Company. It succeeded in acquiring local telephone subscribers in the Tokyo area, and its turnover is nearly 200 billion yen.

Some remarks are possible based on the review of the NCCs' history.

The intent of the regulator to foster long-distance competition has failed in the following sense. The number of entrants had been limited to three. Nobody could know whether these firms were efficient challengers to NTT. Accordingly, Japan needed to introduce a mechanism to examine the efficiency of new entrants into the long-distance market. MPT could abolish entry regulations on the long-distance market, as was done in the United Kingdom in 1990. If entry had been liberalized in the early 1990s, the addition of new long-distance carriers could have been speeded up. The protectionism of MPT invited the efficiency loss.

The entry of NCCs may be regarded as a success in the sense that NTT's long-distance share dropped to almost 50 percent. Without entry pressure, NTT's dominance would have persisted. This argument is well taken, but there still is the question of whether NTT's lost market share was captured by the most efficient entrants. Without free entry, there is no guarantee that the most efficient new entrants absorbed NTT's market share. In fact, it is doubtful whether this kind of substitution happened in the Japanese long-distance market.

13.4 Competition in the Local Market

Although it was generally believed at the time of the codification of the Japanese Telecom Business Law that the local telephone market was a natural monopoly, new legislation allowed competitors into the local market immediately. The first entrants were electric utility companies that created

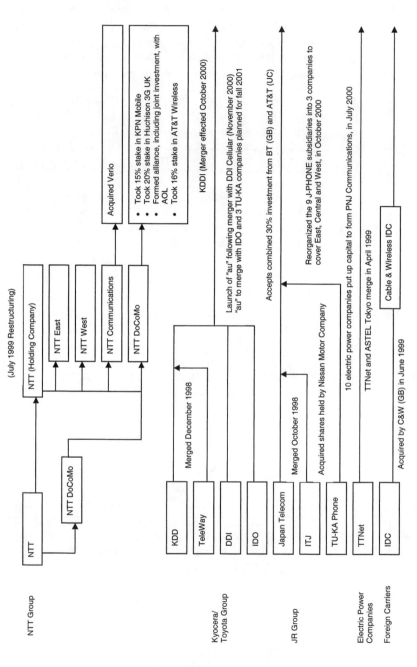

Fig. 13.5 Japan's post-restructuring telecommunications industry

subsidiary companies in each of their franchised regions. In this sense the Japanese institutional framework seems to be progressive in developing local telephony competition, but in reality, local competition has not advanced as expected. There are several reasons for this: Local competitors have been handicapped severely because their interconnection with NTT's local network is asymmetrical. Subscribers to an electricity company's telephone network could telephone and talk to each other but NTT customers could not reach those subscribers. Local rate rebalancing did not occur and below-cost rates remained in force. This made local bypass extremely difficult compared with the United Kingdom or the United States.

In 1995 MPT finally decided to introduce the concept of the interconnection charge (at that time, it was called an access charge). Ten years had already elapsed since the NTT privatization, when the method of calculating the interconnection cost was established.

In order to enhance competition, the interconnection rate has a fundamental importance. At the same time it is quite difficult to interpret that rate in an economic sense. The difficulty comes from the fact that the majority of the embedded local interconnection costs are sunk, whereas the opportunity cost of interconnection is ever-changing because of rapid technological progress. On top of that, there usually exist huge differences in cost structure from district to district that are caused by geographical and demographic factors.

Except for the busiest business districts, the choice of local carrier is very limited. MPT decided to apply the concept of the essential facility to NTT. In each prefecture NTT was regarded as the essential facility and the interconnection rate had to be calculated according to the approved accounting rule. The rate is shown in figure 13.6.

¥/three minutes

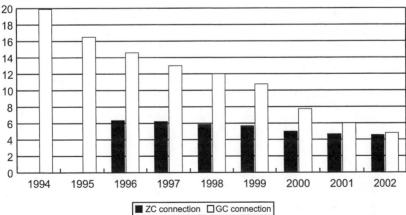

Fig. 13.6   **The interconnection rate**

After the introduction of the interconnection rate, issues concerning the rate level were raised by the NCCs and the United States Trade Representative. In the United States and the United Kingdom, the concept of long-run incremental costs was introduced to calculate the interconnecting cost, because historical cost could not reflect the technological progress that had reduced the cost of local exchange drastically. On the other hand, local carriers have to suffer from the stranded costs, namely, the costs that cannot be recovered because long-run incremental costs are used to calculate the interconnection rate.

In 2000 and 2001, NTT reduced the interconnection rate drastically. The result was as expected. NTT's revenue decreased and its profits went down to their lowest level ever.

The local telephone market experienced a dramatic change in the late 1980s in the United States and the United Kingdom. Local competition was based not upon institutional niches that allowed cream skimming but on bypass technology that was developed by firms that wanted to reduce their payments to the local telephone companies. Rate rebalancing and the imposition of access charges are the most important stimuli for bypassing the local network, because they encourage competition in the local market.

The typical bypass technologies are the mobile telephone and CATV. These technologies challenge the cost structure of the incumbent's old technology. They can realize economies of scale without requiring huge numbers of customers. That is, the critical mass necessary to compete with a local telephone company is not very large.

Japan has been in a strange situation in the context of development of local competition. First, the competition between cellular technology and local telephony has not developed well simply because mobile telephone service had been too expensive. Second, competition was limited among the cellular companies that were not direct competitors to NTT's local network. Third, the regulatory scheme hampered competition once again. Wireless radio-service providers used to be defined as Type I carriers by the Telecom Business Law. As a result, MPT must regulate these carriers with regard to a tariff and to entry and exit conditions. Their rates had to be based upon accounting costs, which cannot be lowered without realizing the critical mass of subscribers. Strategic pricing to combat the local telephone network was not permitted because the requirement for financial stability as a Type I carrier was binding to avoid discontinuity of service.

13.5 Mobile Phones

It was not until the end of 1996 that MPT relaxed its tight policy upon the mobile industry and that industry began to explode. Under the new regime, mobile phone companies were set free to quote their prices, and fierce price competition was invited. Mobile companies were permitted to sell handsets and users could freely choose the style of their handsets. The development of the mobile phone industry in Japan has been characterized by the support of youngsters whose willingness to pay is much higher than that of average consumers. Mobile phones are not the usual telephones that have been regarded as a necessity, but are a kind of luxury item that can serve a large variety of optional demands, from amusements (e.g., games) to business needs. We must also note that the distinction between local and long-distance services has completely disappeared among mobile phone users. This has also happened in the case of the Internet. The development of the number of mobile subscribers is depicted in figure 13.7. The rate of growth represents demand potentials that used to be suppressed by MPT's conservative policies.

The technological advantage of wireless over wireline is obvious. It is predicted that mobile phones can convey broadband services, as well. If this prediction is valid, then the telephone industry must be structured in a manner consistent with the future direction of technology. It may also imply that the old wireline technology can survive only as a supplement to mobiles. Wireline service can be a useful vehicle for providing broadband services at low prices. In any event, wireline is a huge national asset that must be utilized wisely in the future.

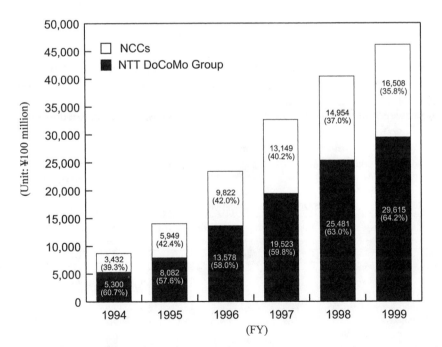

Fig. 13.7   Cellular and car phone revenues
Source: InfoCom Research, 1999 estimates.

13.6 Broadcasting and CATV

The Japanese television industry consists of three types of major broadcasters: terrestrial, satellite, and CATV. The industry has been regulated by MPT. It was, and to a certain extent still is, our tradition that the administration is divided vertically into several jurisdictions. The information industry is under a dramatic structural change and the convergence of broadcasting and telecommunications is obvious. However, in the field of broadcasting there has existed a kind of ideological bias against competition: the freedom of the press, democracy, public order, and morals, to name a few examples.

The Japanese regulatory scheme has an inherent time lag but it is changing very rapidly. In this regard it is very difficult to foresee the future direction of regulation toward broadcasting. MPT is going to review the total regulatory regime for broadcasting and telecommunications. It is recognized that the present laws are preventing a smoother conversion of the two industries whereas, in reality, the NTT group is going to enter broadcasting-satellite data broadcasting and Nippon Hoso Kyokai (NHK) is planning to enter telecommunications.

In this section I describe the industrial structure of the Japanese broadcasting services and discuss the regulatory scheme, which is in transition.

13.6.1 The Market Structure of Terrestrial Broadcasting

Terrestrial broadcasting services have been provided by two types of entities in Japan. One is the government-owned NHK and the others are private companies. There exists competition between NHK and other private broadcasters, although the former can collect fees from the public for signal reception. The private companies depend upon advertising revenues from their television and radio shows. They are shown in table 13.1. The ratio of radio business revenue to total revenue is less than 20 percent over the past ten years.

Table 13.1   Market Share (March of each year; %)

	1990	1991	1992	1993	1994	1995	1996	1997	1998
Nippon Hoso Kyokai (NHK)	17.6	20.2	20.7	21.5	22.6	22.4	21.6	20.7	20.6
Japan News Network	21.8	21.2	20.5	20.0	19.3	19.6	19.7	19.3	20.4
Nippon News Network	19.3	18.5	18.5	18.4	18.4	18.7	19.2	19.7	19.3
Fuji News Network	20.6	19.8	20.0	20.4	19.9	19.6	19.4	19.7	19.5
All Nippon News Network	14.9	14.3	14.1	13.7	13.6	13.9	14.1	14.3	14.0
TV-Tokyo Network	3.9	4.1	4.3	4.1	4.1	4.2	4.2	4.3	4.3
Independent Broadcasters Association (DOKU)	2.0	1.9	1.9	2.0	2.0	1.6	1.7	2.0	1.8
Total	100.0	100.0	100.0	100.0	100.0	100.0	100.0	100.0	100.0

Source: Merrill Lynch.

There are six private broadcasters and they own regional broadcasting stations in each prefecture. Furthermore, there exists vertical integration between the parent broadcasters in Tokyo and their regional broadcasters. The market structure of this industry is oligopolistic: NHK represents 20 percent of the industry, and the other three private companies have comparable shares.

13.6.2   The Development of Satellite Broadcasting

Japan has two types of satellite broadcasters; one relies on broadcasting satellite (BS) technology and the other relies on communications satellite (CS) technology. In the use of BS, Japan has been a leader and has made remarkable progress in its space CATV network. After the industry solved the technical problems of broadcasting satellite–3, this satellite business has been growing.

In the BS broadcasting industry, NHK is in the dominant position, followed by Japan Satellite Broadcasting, Inc., or JSB (WOWOW), as shown in table 13.2.

In contrast to BS, the growth of CS business has been slow.

PerfecTV entered the market in 1996 and merged with J Sky B in 1998 to become SkyPerfecTV. The number of subscribers is 1.73 million. DirecTV started its business in 1997 and has obtained 0.41 million subscribers thus far. DirecTV is far away from the break-even point, however. In 2000, SkyPerfecTV and DirecTV were combined to form a new company that is led by Sony and Fuji TV.

Based on the recent development of the CS broadcasting industry, MPT reportedly wants to deregulate it further. There exists regulation preventing entry by NTT and major terrestrial broadcasters, but MPT is expected to deregulate entry especially with regard to licensing the next generation of CS technology. The focus of regulation will be shifted to the oversight of the capability of program production and finance, which may give more opportunity to the NTT group.

13.6.3   CATV Industry and Deregulation

In 1955 CATV broadcasting started as an auxiliary device of terrestrial broadcasting in areas where radio signals are hard to reach. CATV has become a community media source since the 1970s through the development of multichannel and two-way communications. Although the Japanese CATV industry grew steadily at the rate of 20 percent in the first half of the 1990s, its growth was not so impressive as the growth that occurred in the United States. In the latter half of the 1990s, however, there seems to have been a speeding-up of CATV development. This is due to several factors:

1. The diversification of CATV programming, made possible by the initiation of CS digital broadcast

Table 13.2   Number of Subscribers

	1990	1991	1992	1993	1994	1995	1996	1997	1998	1999	2000 March	2000 July
BS broadcasting (analog)												
NHK	120.4	235.1	380.3	501.5	586.3	658.1	737.5	817.2	879.6	946.4	1,000.7	1,022.0
WOWOW		21.7	80.1	125.7	149.3	174.7	205.5	227.8	240.0	253.4	248.9	251.8
CS broadcasting (digital)												
SkyPerfecTV								23.6	63.1	111.3	188.3	218.0
DirecTV									26.0	29.1	43.5	

Source: InfoCom Research (2001, 85).

Notes: Number of satellite broadcasting subscriptions ($\times$ 10,000) in March of each year, except where noted otherwise. Since DirecTV merged with SkyPerfecTV in April 2000, its number is unknown. See text for explanation of abbreviations.

2. A deregulation policy that made it easier to open up new stations and create a multisystem operator (MSO), which is indispensable to broadcast-area expansion

3. An increase of competition among CATV companies, with a result of increased promotional activity to gain subscribers.

4. The future prospect of providing telecommunications services, especially in the application of the Internet

The effect of the change of the MPT's regulatory regime has been notable. MPT announced deregulation of the joint use of head-ends in 1997 along with abolishing the foreign capital restriction upon CATV and Type I telecom carriers. In 1998 MPT decided to simplify the authorization procedures for starting CATV operations. CATV operators that are permitted to operate as Type I telecom carriers increased dramatically. The development of CATV operators is shown in table 13.3 (parts A and B).

With the increase of full-service operators (CATV plus telecommunications), competition has been accelerated. Two examples are noteworthy in this regard. Jupiter Telecom (located at Suginami-ward) began rate cuts and large volume discounts in 1998. Titus Communications (located in Chiba city) initiated the elimination of the setup charge that used to be a barrier for new subscription. This company also introduced free night service for calls within its telecom network. Furthermore, Titus has become the first CATV operator to offer an integrated service including multichannel, telephony, and Internet services.

Looking back on the development of the CATV industry in Japan, we find several features that are not existent in the United States:

Table 13.3   **CATV Operators**

	1993	1994	1995	1996	1997	1998	1999
A. The Development of CATV Operators							
Number of facilities	625	740	830	937	973	1,030	984
Number of subscribers (× 10,000)	242.2	314.3	363.7	500.1	672.0	793.6	947.1
Household penetration rate (%)	5.6	7.2	8.2	11.2	14.6	17.0	20.0
B. Number of CATV Operators from the Telephone Companies							
NTT			27				
Japan Telecom			27				
KDD			5				
TTNet			5				
NTT Docomo			1				

Source: InfoCom Research (2001).

Note: Penetration rate = subscribed households/registered households. See text for explanation of abbreviations.

1. The terrestrial broadcasting services in Japan are pervasive all through the country. The reason is a geographic difference between the United States and Japan. The United States is a fifty-state country and Japan is a one-state country. Although Tokyo and Osaka are giant cities, they are part of only one state—Japan. This is quite different from the United States. Cities such as Los Angeles, Chicago, Denver, and New York are city centers in each state. In the one-state model, like Japan, it is easier for the incumbent broadcasters to become dominant and the nationwide audience has been more attracted to the information from Tokyo. This has hampered the development of CATV as a community-based broadcaster.

2. The regulation of MPT tended to prevent entry into CATV, especially because of the stress it put upon a close connection between broadcasting and community and local content. These restraints had a negative influence on the potential profitability prospects of the CATV business.

3. Along with the regulation above, ownership of multiple CATV stations was not possible for a long time and this made it difficult for CATV operators to reach a critical mass.

13.7   The Coincidence of Disputes over the Telecommunications Industry

Looking around the developed countries, we notice that each of the associated telecom industries faces the same problems, that is, the delay of development of competition, especially from the viewpoint of regulators. In 1996, the Federal Communications Act of 1934 was amended with the expectation of the rapid emergence of competition between local and long-distance carriers. In 1999, NTT was restructured. A long-distance service provider was separated from local telephone companies in order to enhance competition. The results up to now, however, are rated poor by the regulators and legislators in both countries.

In the United States two things are happening at the same time. The Tauzin-Dingell bill is going to be introduced to let RBOCs invest in inter-LATA broadband services. This is equivalent to opening up a big hole on the 1996 act because legislators are more concerned with the development of broadband services than with the voice telephony. The Tauzin-Dingell bill appears necessary because the examples of entry by long-distance carriers into local markets and the entry of local companies into the long-distance market are scarce. This is a result of the fact that the conditions of the 1996 amendment of the communications act have rarely been met. According to the 1996 act, local carriers must satisfy almost forty checkpoints indicating that they have opened up their local markets before they are permitted to enter into long-distance markets. In typical cases, AT&T and RBOCs do not reach an agreement easily. AT&T argues that RBOCs are always precluding entry by failing to fulfill the checkpoints, whereas the RBOCs reply that the checkpoints are satisfied to a reasonable extent. This is a never-ending dispute because the game is noncooperative, with both players aiming at the lion's share of the entry benefits. The Tauzin-Dingell bill puts aside this stalemate and pushes another type of competition that looks more important for national interests.

At the same time, AT&T has began lawsuits in several states such as Pennsylvania, New Jersey, and Florida. AT&T claims that the structural separation of RBOCs is essential to realize fair competition in the local market. The structural separation is based on a vague distinction between wholesale and retail. However, it is noteworthy that controversy over the industrial structure of local telephony has resumed again.

The situation looks similar in Japan. Except for mobile telephones, the pace of entry into local markets seems slower than expected by regulators. The market share of NTT is 90 percent nationwide. It also is true that local competition has not occurred in every corner of the country. It has been concentrated in large cities and central business districts. This is simply because it is not profitable to enter most of Japanese local markets. Population density is low and few business centers are located in the majority of Japanese cities. This is a reflection of the geological features of Japan. But competitors of NTT never miss the opportunity to accuse NTT of an intent to prevent entry into local markets. The lack of competition in rural areas and small cities cannot be attributed to entry prevention. The news of low penetration rates in local telephony, however, gives suitable credibility to their attack on NTT.

I call this phenomenon "politicizing" entry conditions. Network industries such as telecommunications, gas, and electricity have common characteristics in that entrants rely upon a transmission mechanism that is owned by the incumbents to provide services. As a result, they have two choices. They can construct their own network if the rental prices of the transmission mechanism are higher than the cost of new investment. However, it often occurs that investment in a core network is impossible for entrants because of huge capital costs and their sunk nature. At this time there usually is a heated discussion on the appropriate rental prices for access, interconnection, and transmission or transport services.

New entrants can always benefit from arguing that the rental price imposed by the incumbent is too high to make entry profitable. If we have a neutral authority to judge the fairness of network fees, then the problem can be solved. In some cases the incumbents may be ordered to lower their prices, and in other cases entrants must pay in full the prices set by the incumbents or choose not to enter the market.

In effect, the neutral authority must have the ability to judge the efficacy of new entrants in order to prevent inefficient entry.

The solution to the problem becomes less clear when we do not have this neutral authority but instead have an inherited bureaucracy that usually intends to encourage new competition. The bureaucracy wants to be in the position to point to indicators of vigorous competition. The easiest way to accomplish this task is to blame the incumbent for preventing entry if expected competition does not emerge.

The risks associated with politicization lies in the fear that new entrants are permitted to survive even if they are not efficient. Inefficient entrants may not be able to pay the network fees because they do not have more-efficient equipment than the incumbents, or because they lack the knowledge to make use of the new technologies available. But politicization prevents the exposure of inefficiency. Therefore, no one knows whether the new entrants are efficient. This is not the case when politicization is absent. In this case new entrants may enter and fail because they do not have the opportunity to plea for benevolence.

In network industries the doctrine of "bottleneck" or "essential facility" has become a major source of the phenomenon of politicizing the entry conditions.[3] New entrants can use the doctrine to weaken incumbents in preparation for obtaining greater market share in the future. If these entrants prove to be efficient and compete with the incumbents on an economic basis in the future, people are lucky. But if they are inefficient and collude with incumbents in the future, the result is a total loss to the country. In the name of dynamism some people argue that the expected loss is a fee for the realization of competition. This is true only if we have a fair institution that selects efficient competitions. Here we will turn to the problem of NTT restructuring.

13.8 Future Reforms

In Japan, as in the United States or the United Kingdom, the incumbent problem is likely to be revisited. Before arguing for another reform of the NTT group, I will point out several difficulties inherent in the present form of the restructured NTT. The reshaping of NTT in 1999 was meant to close the long-standing debate begun in 1985 regarding the necessity of breaking up NTT. The present structure of NTT is the result of a pure compromise between NTT and MPT. NTT is satisfied with the present form because it was not divided into independent companies. In theory, the NTT holding company can control their subsidiaries. MPT is satisfied because it can point to the three structurally separated companies (NTT East, NTT West, and NTT Communications) that are independent of each other.

From the viewpoint of economics, however, the new NTT has several basic difficulties. First, as was discussed, the distinction between local and long distance (and international) is nonsense. Second, neither NTT East nor NTT West can provide long-distance or interprefecture services.

---

3. On the economic rationale of the doctrine of "bottleneck" on "essential facility," see Nambu (1997b).

Third, NTT Communications naturally wants to enter the local markets because the roots of business lie in the local market. The conflict of interest within one entity is damaging the efficiency of the holding company. The basic design of the system is an old paradigm of "dichotomy" that has existed since the medieval age of telecommunication.

During the process of the past reform some economists argued that NTT East and NTT West could be allowed to compete with each other. The theory underlying this argument is difficult to understand because we cannot find any incentive for two firms to squeeze into each other's market. From the viewpoint of the NTT holding company, such behavior is a zero-sum game. If NTT East and West are allowed to provide long-distance and international services as well, each would have an incentive to enter the other's market. But this is forbidden. Faced with the slowness of local telephone competition the government may find it necessary to restructure the present NTT system. At this time I must stress several points for the national interest that must not be ignored.

13.8.1   Dividing NTT East and NTT West

The discussion to divide NTT local companies into pieces is economically nonsense. If people think that the obstacle of entry into local markets comes from the fact that NTT East and West are monopolies, then the idea of dividing them into smaller pieces will make the matter even worse. The local companies do not have incentives to enter into a rival market if they are restricted to providing local service. In fact, smaller local companies will have ever stronger incentives to defend their markets. On top of that, some of the new local companies will face additional financial difficulty, even more so in the rural areas since they will be deprived of the capability of cross-subsidy within their territories.

13.8.2   Risks of Mergers and Acquisitions

No Japanese firm is free from the risk of being taken over by the current globalization of mergers and acquisitions. Looking at the share values of NTT subsidiaries, it is obvious that some firms may be acquired by foreign carriers. The idea of further dividing the NTT group will lower their share prices even more. Without an effective countermeasure for the firms in the NTT group, the risk of takeover cannot be neglected.

13.8.3   Plural Eyes upon Wireline and Wireless

Technological change has brought about a new era in which mobile phones play a more important role than wireline service. The advantage of wireless over wireline is obvious, but there also exists a complementary relationship between the two. The main usage of wireline will lie in a continuous, even all-day, interconnection that not possible or desirable for a wireless technology. Therefore, for a telecom enterprise both types of services may be economically combined. The mobile industry will continue to be competitive domestically as well as globally. NTT must be able to provide both services in order to combat global carriers.

13.8.4   Radio Frequency

There exists an institutional problem that needs to be solved concerning the distribution of scarce radio frequency. The United States took the approach of auctioning off radio bandwidth, which resulted in astronomically high prices. Those prices must be charged to the mobile carriers' services but it is not clear whether the mobile carriers will be able to pass these prices on to their customers. Of course, on the other hand, a rationing method overseen by the government results in an arbitrary distribution of scarce resources, which is foreign to efficiency. For the moment nothing has been made clear as to the method of apportioning radio frequency in Japan.

References

Huber, Peter W. 1987. *The geodesic network.* Report on competition in the telephone industry. Washington, D.C.: U.S. Department of Justice.
Huber, Peter W., Michael K. Kellogg, and John Thorne. 1992. *The geodesic network II.* 1993 Report on competition in the telephone industry. Washington, D.C.: The Geodesic Company.
InfoCom Research. 2001. Information and communications in Japan in 2001. Tokyo: InfoCom Research.
Nambu, Tsuruhiko. 1997a. Intervention in Japan's market for infrastructure services: Privatization without full deregulation. In EDI Learning Resources Series, *Infrastructure strategies in East Asia,* ed. Ashoka Mody, 97–107. Washington, D.C.: World Bank.
———. 1997b. Is "bottleneck" a viable concept for the breakup of NTT? *Telecommunications Policy* 21 (2): 113–126.

Comment   Il Chong Nam

Professor Nambu's paper is a very interesting and informative one both as a paper on the Japanese economy and as a paper on the telecommunications industry. A large part of his paper is devoted to the comparative analysis of the Japanese telecommunications industry and those of the United States and United Kingdom. His analysis is quite comprehensive and covers all of the important markets, including broadcasting and Internet mar-

Il Chong Nam is professor at the KDI School of Public Policy and Management, Korea Development Institute.

kets. One can learn a lot from his paper about how the same fundamental change in technology could lead to different evolutionary paths for the same industry in different countries endowed with different infrastructures concerning the way market and government work. As an economist interested in public enterprises, I find this paper especially interesting and quite unique in that it offers a rare opportunity to take a look at how the Japanese MPT bureaucracy responded to the pressure of structural reform caused by technological innovation.

The evolution of the telecommunications industry from a government monopoly to a partially regulated competitive market involved fundamental changes in the corporate governance of former public enterprises, in the industry structure, and in the regulatory regime. It also requires that functions and authorities of the former line ministry, MPT in the case of Japan, must change substantially. Professor Nambu shows that Japan took an approach that is substantially different from those of the United States and United Kingdom on most key issues on liberalization of the telecommunications industry, such as industry structure, corporate governance of the dominant carrier, and regulation on rates and access charges.

I think the most significant difference between the path Japan took and those taken by the United States and United Kingdom lies in the corporate governance of former monopolists and in the role the government plays after liberalization. In the United States, ownership and control have always been in private hands, and regulatory functions were separate from the management of carriers. In the United Kingdom, ownership and governance of BT was handed over to private investors. Regulatory functions were also separated from the management of BT. In Japan, on the other hand, NTT is still majority owned and controlled by the government, and the regulatory regime does not appear to be independent.

I think the public nature of NTT's ownership and control lies at the core of the Japanese telecommunications industry and the policy of the Japanese government thereupon. I also think many of the differences in industry structure and regulation between the Japanese telecommunications industry and those of United States and United Kingdom, listed in Professor Nambu's paper, could be traced to NTT's ownership and control. It seems that a closer investigation of corporate governance of NTT and how it affects the policy functions of the Japanese government could lead to a better understanding of the telecommunications industry and the effectiveness of policy thereupon in Japan.

I have some specific points that I would like to take up.

I think that more detailed information on the ownership and control of NTT will be helpful. Information on actual ownership structure and the legal and policy environments surrounding the nature of government ownership in NTT will clarify the incentives of NTT managers as well as bureaucrats at MPT.

Is NTT subject only to company laws, allowed to seek profits? Or is it subject to some laws that do not apply to the firms owned purely by private investors that make NTT's corporate governance different? Even if NTT is formally subject only to company laws, the question remains as to the nature of the government as the dominant shareholder of NTT. As the dominant shareholder, does the government concern itself only with the commercial performance of NTT or is it interested in using its control over NTT to promote some policy objectives that are not compatible with profit incentives of NTT?

Moreover, it would be interesting to ask what specific mechanisms there are for the government to resort to in trying to force NTT to perform policy functions, which could conflict with its commercial objectives. Which ministry or agency within the government exercises the share-holding right of NTT is also a relevant question because the nature of government involvement in the governance of NTT depends on it. If MPT wields the shareholding right, as it appears, it will be tempted to use its control over NTT to promote its policy objectives toward the telecommunications industry. If this happens, it will affect NTT's incentives and the degree of competition among various carriers that compete with NTT, as well as regulation.

It is also interesting to ask why Japan chose a liberalization path that allowed MPT to continue to play the potentially conflicting roles of "manager of NTT," "maker of industrial policy for the telecommunications industry," and "regulator," even though these roles conflict with each other.

I am also puzzled by the choice of the holding-company system for NTT. NTT East and NTT West are both 100 percent owned by NTT. It would not be easy to induce serious competition between two local monopolies even if they are independent firms. In the case of NTT East and NTT West, both are subsidiaries of NTT. It is not clear to me what incentives the two local monopolies have in competing with each other. If the Japanese government somehow succeeds in forcing NTT East and NTT West to actually compete with each other, there remains the question of why NTT should own NTT East and NTT West. Most major carriers around the world have been adopting holding-company structures in recent times. However, their motive was to raise internal efficiency, not to foster competition among its subsidiaries to increase social welfare.

The evolution of the telecommunications industry in Japan described by Professor Nambu raises more fundamental questions about the way economic systems evolve in different countries. The role of the state, the corporate governance of large firms, and the way the financial market is organized and functions seem to be linked closely with each other and affect the way markets and regulatory functions evolve over time. It seems that the way the market and government are organized and function in Japan makes it difficult to transform a government monopoly into a market-based system in which commercial operation, regulatory functions, and industrial policy objectives are separated.

My last comment is on a trend in the industry that appears irreversible. Mobile services are replacing wired services rapidly. It would be interesting to see how the mobile market has been evolving in Japan; in particular, information about the evolution of the mobile market as well as the dominant player, NTT Docomo, and its relationship with NTT would significantly enhance our understanding of the Japanese telecommunications market. Development in the third-generation market and the policy of the government toward this market also are key to understanding the future direction of the Japanese telecommunications industry.

Comment   Richard H. Snape

I have enjoyed reading Professor Nambu's paper and have learned much from it. Some of the features of Japan's telecom industry are unique to Japan, but many are to be found in other countries also. These relate to problems of transition to competition in an industry in which the incumbent has been a protected, government-owned monopoly and in which there have been many cross-subsidies required by the government for political and social reasons; and in which there is very rapid technological change and convergence of technologies such that in the future there is likely to be an integrated communications, information, and entertainment medium.

There are some points which I would like to take up.

I think there could be more emphasis on the distinction between competition in facilities and in services. At this stage there is still limited competition for the copper local loop (outside central business districts). In many areas and for some services the local loop still has properties of monopoly and essential facility. While mobile phones are booming in Japan and many other countries, a high percentage of such calls still originate or terminate on copper. Outside central business districts, wireless is still not suitable for two-way broadband, and hybrid fiber coaxial (HFC) cable is generally far from ubiquitous in roll-out. So at this stage of development, access and terms of access to the local loop are still relevant for competition in services for much of the population in Japan and elsewhere. As Professor Nambu notes, this leads to the "politicization" of access—good regulation will be aimed at reducing this politicization or gaming.

Professor Nambu notes the bad relations between the incumbent and

Richard H. Snape was deputy chairman of the Productivity Commission, Australia, and emeritus professor at Monash University. He passed away in the fall of 2002.

regulators. Of course, if this reflects ignorance on the part of the regulator, this is bad and should be remedied, though there will always be some asymmetry of knowledge. But I would expect tension between the incumbent (coming from a protected monopoly position) and a regulator trying to bring competition—indeed, I would be worried if there weren't such tension.

In a number of places the paper refers to "fairness" of prices—I would prefer a focus on efficiency of prices.

Professor Nambu very rightly refers to regulations affecting broadcasting—with convergent technologies we also need convergent regulation. In a number of countries we have policies promoting competition in telecoms, but regulations that protect incumbents in broadcasting. Such policy dissonance can only frustrate development.

The paper speaks of the risk of foreign take-overs. Already Vodafone owns a mobile phone company in Japan. I am uncertain as to what the risk is.

I note that new entrants are "selected" by MPT. Why is such selection required? Is it more selective than the "beauty contest" for the allocation of scarce spectrum undertaken in a number of other countries?

The Productivity Commission is undertaking an inquiry into telecom regulation in Australia. We are setting out some principles for regulation. They include:

- Telecom policy should aim at securing efficient outcomes rather than competition in its own right, or the protection of particular competitors.
- Social objectives are best targeted by other policy instruments or by explicit subsidies aimed at the objective.
- Policy should be technologically neutral.
- Regulation should apply only to areas where there are clearly identified problems and where regulation is an effective remedy. It should be transparent, predictable, accountable, and consistent.
- Where there are real bottlenecks justifying regulated access pricing, it is important to encourage efficiency in the use of telecom infrastructure while maintaining incentives for investment.
- Regulation should be such that the incentives for business are to make a better return from procompetitive consumer orientation, than from market foreclosure or regulatory gaming.

How to Restructure Failed Banking Systems
Lessons from the United States in the 1930s and Japan in the 1990s

Charles W. Calomiris and Joseph R. Mason

14.1 Introduction

When banking systems are in distress, should they be rescued? If so, in what form and on what terms should resources be transferred to banks? Is it possible to derive lessons from relatively successful bank rescue efforts of the past that would be useful to Japanese and other would-be bank rescuers? These three questions motivate our attempt to come to grips with the lessons that U.S. bank rescue efforts during the Depression hold for banking policy in Asia today. The key challenge in any bank rescue policy is to design a balanced approach that accomplishes the main objectives of bank rescues—salvaging local information capital about borrowers in the long run and increasing credit flows to worthwhile investments in the short run—while minimizing the damage to market discipline and bank incentives toward risk that comes with government bailouts.

14.1.1 Should Banks Be Helped?

To the first question we posed—whether banks should be rescued—we offer a brief and informal reply. There is certainly a respectable argument in favor of rescuing banking systems from insolvency. Bank finance is cru-

Charles W. Calomiris is Henry Kaufman Professor of Finance and Economics, Columbia University, Graduate School of Business; Arthur F. Burns Scholar and codirector of the Financial Deregulation Project at the American Enterprise Institute for Public Policy Research; and a research associate of the National Bureau of Economic Research. Joseph R. Mason is assistant professor of finance at Drexel University, Le Bow College of Business; Sloan Fellow at the Wharton Financial Institutions Center; and visiting scholar at the Federal Reserve Bank of Philadelphia.

The authors thank Nobu Hibara for his comments and for his help assembling data on Japanese banks.

cial to the process of capital allocation, particularly for investment by small and medium-sized firms for which there are no alternative sources of funding. Smaller firms can be a key source of recovery from recession. That is especially true under current circumstances in Japan, Korea, and elsewhere in Asia. In Japan and Korea, the growth of small firms is needed as part of long-run structural adjustment away from excessive reliance on large-firm conglomerates. Part of that adjustment requires that the financial sector finance the growth of small firms. Thus, in Asia, there may be a particularly strong argument in favor of preserving a viable banking system that can act as a source of finance for smaller firms.

To a large extent the argument in favor of assisting banks relies on attendant reforms in bank lending practices that will ensure that bank credit is channeled to firms on the basis of the merit of their investments. Those incentives are part and parcel of a proper regulatory structure that encourages market discipline, which rewards value creation and prudent risk management by banks. Banks operating under skewed incentives will often make unwarranted, value-destroying loans to insiders or to politically influential borrowers. For example, Krueger and Yoo (2001) show that in Korea resources have been channeled in large part to value-destroying large firms. Thus, bank recapitalization must be combined with effective reforms of lending practices.

To what extent can one argue that bank assistance is unnecessary in a world of free foreign entry by banks? Foreign bank entry is a potential alternative source of funds for small firms, and one that is less likely to be diverted to value-destroying investments. And foreign entrants into distressed banking systems tend to enjoy a relatively low cost of capital, for two reasons: First, they have not suffered capital-destroying loan losses, and second, they are better able to raise new capital because the absence of loan losses also means that markets will impose lower adverse-selection ("lemons") discounts on any new bank capital offerings (Calomiris and Wilson 2003).

While there is substantial evidence that foreign entry enhances the efficiency of banking systems (Demirguc-Kunt, Levine, and Min 1998; Kane 1998), it takes time for foreign entrants to establish information about borrowers and familiarity with local legal and institutional arrangements. Calomiris and Carey (1994) found that foreign bank entrants into the United States during the U.S. bank "capital crunch" of the 1980s tended to lend disproportionately to lower-risk borrowers, tended to purchase rather than originate loans, and tended to act as syndicate participants rather than lead managers. Furthermore, despite their conservative loan purchases and originations, foreign banks tended to suffer worse loan losses than domestic U.S. banks in the early 1990s, which further suggests an information-cost disadvantage. Although relaxing barriers to foreign entry is clearly a crucial part of resolving a credit crunch and reforming long-term lending practices, foreign bank lending may not be a perfect substitute for domestic bank lending in the short run. Thus, it is still potentially beneficial to provide some assistance to the most capable existing domestic banks.

There is, of course, another reason governments wish to protect banks—call it the "dark side" of bank bailouts. Banks are repositories of economic and political power—a source not only of funds but also of substantial discretionary power over the economy. In Asia, as elsewhere, banks have been used as tools of economic planning and also as a primary means of channeling favors to influential parties (so-called crony capitalism). The idea that the banking system should be turned into an efficient, competitive mechanism for attracting and distributing funds may make for a good speech, but it still cannot realistically be described as the sole or overriding purpose of banking policy in most countries. Never mind that the banking crises that gave rise to the losses that now plague virtually every economy in East Asia were the direct result of the perverse incentives of government protection (the so-called moral hazard problem); too many influential people simply have too much at stake to allow banking to be reorganized efficiently. Banks are able to channel such favors only if they themselves are recipients of subsidies from the government; hence the need to preserve banks' (and their related firms') exclusive rights, and the need to offer banks subsidized deposit insurance, subsidized purchases of bad loans, or subsidized capital injections.

Crony capitalists will appeal for bank assistance on the basis of the capital-crunch motive, while in fact hoping to channel government assistance for banks into their own coffers (indeed, there is much anecdotal evidence that aid to Korean banks in 1997–1998 ended up being channeled to distressed *chaebol*). Thus, the central goal of bank bailout policy is to design bank assistance to meet the legitimate goals of mitigating credit supply contraction for value-creating bank-dependent borrowers, while minimizing the potential abuse of assistance.

In this paper, we take it for granted that domestic banking systems will be helped, even if, from the narrow economic standpoint, the likely costs of such assistance exceed the likely benefits. To emphasize the importance of combining aid with proper incentives for banks, however, it is worth pausing a moment to consider how costly assistance to banks can be.

There have been over 100 cases of banking system crises worldwide over the past two decades (where a crisis is defined as losses to insolvent banks that exceed 1 percent of gross domestic product [GDP]—see Beim and Calomiris 2001, chapter 7). The direct costs of bank bailouts are often above 20 percent of GDP and above 30 percent of GDP in the recent Asian-crisis countries of Thailand, Korea, and Indonesia. Estimated resolution costs in Japan are harder to estimate, but likely will exceed 20 percent of GDP. While that cost represents a transfer of resources from taxpayers to bank claimants, rather than a loss to society as a whole, there are significant social losses associated with such an enormous transfer. First, the fiscal consequences of having to finance that transfer are disastrous, and often result in substantial tax increases and severe currency depreciation, both of which are highly distortionary. Furthermore, there are additional economic costs from forgone output in the wake of the economic collapse that accompanies financial crises, and there are additional dead-weight costs from continuing to support inefficient, value-destroying firms via the lifelines that distressed banks provide to distressed borrowers.

The magnitude of the transfers that accompany current-day bailouts is staggering in comparison to historical experience. Waves of bank insolvency used to be far less frequent and far less costly to resolve. The cost of bailing out all the insolvent U.S. banks during the Great Depression would have been roughly 3 percent of GDP. From 1870 to 1913, there were seven major episodes of banking-system insolvency worldwide (defining major episodes as producing negative bank net worth in excess of 1 percent of GDP), and only two of those produced situations where the negative net worth of insolvent banks exceeded 5 percent of GDP; in both of those cases, bank losses did not exceed 10 percent of GDP (Calomiris 2001).

The implication is clear: safety nets themselves, through their effects on bank behavior, have been a significant contributor to the cost of resolving bank distress (Demirguc-Kunt and Detragiache 2000; Demirguc-Kunt and Huizinga 2000; Barth, Caprio, and Levine 2001). And it is worth reiterating that one of the supposed benefits of safety-net assistance—limiting the reduction in bank credit supply in the wake of macroeconomic shocks—is usually illusory: Financial crises produce the worst credit crunches because "resurrection strategies" by banks magnify initial bank losses from macro-economic shocks and ultimately reduce credit supply accordingly. Once banking systems collapse under the weight of safety-net-induced risk taking, the ultimate credit crunch is deeper and lasts longer (Caprio and Klingabiel 1996a,b; Cull, Senbet, and Sorge 2000; Honahan and Klingabiel 2000; Boyd et al. 2000).

14.1.2   Important Policy Choices

The costs of government assistance to banks depend on the way rescues are managed. The central questions of policy relevance do not revolve around whether to bail out banks, but rather around the choice of which banks to rescue and the means for doing so. If a rescue is handled skillfully, the cost can be much reduced.

First, bank rescues need not involve all banks. While new foreign entrants may not be a perfect substitute for existing domestic franchises from the standpoint of allocating loans to small and medium-sized businesses, that does not imply that all, or even most, domestic banks are worth saving. If government can find a way to identify and target relatively solvent banks with relatively high franchise values (a task made easier by the fact that relatively healthy banks also tend to be the ones with higher franchise values), and if it is politically feasible to limit assistance to those banks, then the costs of a partial bailout could be much less than that of a system-wide bailout.

Second, to the extent that the rescue mechanism chosen to assist the designated banks can be designed to minimize moral hazard, the risk of continuing bank weakness (and future government expenses on bailouts) can also be reduced substantially. For example, conditions that limit the ability or incentive of banks to channel credit inefficiently or to take on high risk after receiving infusions of government capital can make assistance much more cost effective.

The history of assistance to U.S. banks during the Great Depression illustrates these themes well, and can provide useful lessons for Asia today. Section 14.2 reviews the history of bank distress and assistance in the United States during the 1930s and examines in detail the role of the Reconstruction Finance Corporation—how it targeted banks, the effects of its assistance, the cost of providing assistance, and the way that it tried to align bank incentives to protect against abuse of government protection. Section 14.3 contrasts that experience with the recent government loans and preferred stock purchases for Japanese banks. Section 14.4 concludes with some specific policy recommendations. We argue that combining subsidized preferred stock purchases with mandatory matching contributions of common stock, limits on bank dividend payments, and reforms of bank capital regulation that credibly incorporate market discipline into the regulatory process would increase the benefits and reduce the costs of government support for banks.

14.2   U.S. Bank Distress during the Great Depression

The banking crisis in the United States during the Great Depression provides a useful historical example of how policymakers can balance the opposing needs of protecting banks and maintaining market discipline over banks. The authorities managed to mitigate the loss of capital in the banking system and its effects on credit supply, while retaining market forces that continued to reward relatively prudent banks.

In this section, we begin with a review of the severity of the shocks banks faced and the extent of bank distress. We show how market discipline transformed the contraction in bank capital into a contraction in credit supply. At the same time, there was an increase in the illiquidity of risky assets as the result of protracted bank asset liquidation.

We then consider the response of the Reconstruction Finance Corporation (RFC) to banking-system distress. Specifically, we present evidence on how the RFC combined assistance with conditions for receiving assistance in a way that preserved market discipline and protected the government from excessive exposure to loss.

14.2.1   The Severity of Bank Distress during the Depression

Measured by bank failure rates, depositor loss rates, or the extent of bank credit contraction, the Great Depression was, and remains, the largest and most persistent shock suffered by the U.S. banking system since (at least) the 1830s. Figure 14.1 presents data on the number of bank suspensions, monthly, from 1921 to 1936, and figure 14.2 reports corresponding data on the deposits of suspended banks. As these figures show, banking collapse during the Great Depression was not a single event, but rather several waves of bank distress. As Wicker (1996) and Calomiris and Mason (2003b) show, these waves of bank failures reflected fundamental shocks that were often region and bank specific—reflecting region-specific shocks to income and bank-specific investment and risk management choices. Contrary to the view espoused by Friedman and Schwartz (1963), which saw the waves of bank failures as the result of autonomous waves of panic in the financial system unrelated to prior fundamental disturbances, Calomiris and Mason find that when one disaggregates by region and bank, it is possible to link prior local and national shocks to subsequent bank failures. Calomiris and Mason find that autonomous sources of bank failure (resulting from either "illiquidity crises" or failure "contagion") were not important prior to January–March 1933 (at the trough of the Depression); thus, bank failures for most of the Depression period (1929–1932) reflected a similar process to that of bank failure during previous economic downturns.

As during previous periods of national depression or regional agricultural distress (e.g., the 1890s and the 1920s), the United States suffered larger numbers of bank failures than countries experiencing comparable shocks. For example, Canada experienced few bank failures in the 1930s (Haubrich 1990). The primary reason that the United States suffered unusual rates of bank failure in response to shocks was the peculiar U.S. "unit banking" system—that is, regulatory limits on bank branching that limited bank opportunities to diversify their loan portfolios across locations (Calomiris 2000).

The consequences of bank distress for credit supply were large and protracted, lasting several years beyond the March 1933 trough of the Depression, as noted by Fisher (1933) and Bernanke (1983). Figures 14.3 and 14.4 show the synchronous contraction in bank capital and bank lending, expressed either as aggregates or as ratios to total assets.

Table 14.1 measures the extent of depositor losses during the period 1921–1942. During the pre-Depression era, losses to depositors in failed banks averaged roughly 5 percent. In contrast, losses suffered by depositors during the Depression were several times larger. Since the 1860s (the period for which data are available), the ratio of negative net worth of banks relative to GDP never exceeded one-tenth of 1 percent of GDP (which it reached in 1893). The combination of the high failure rate and high depositor loss rate during the Depression produced a loss rate on total

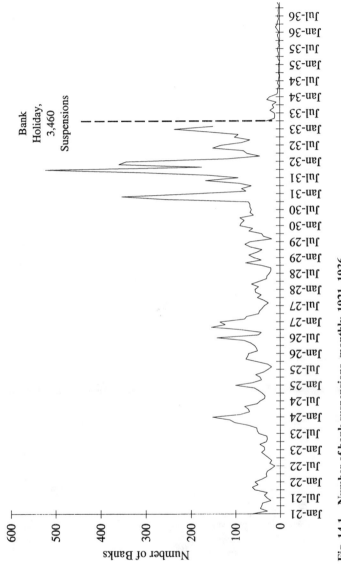

Fig. 14.1   Number of bank suspensions, monthly, 1921–1936

Source: Board of Governors of the Federal Reserve System (1937, 907).

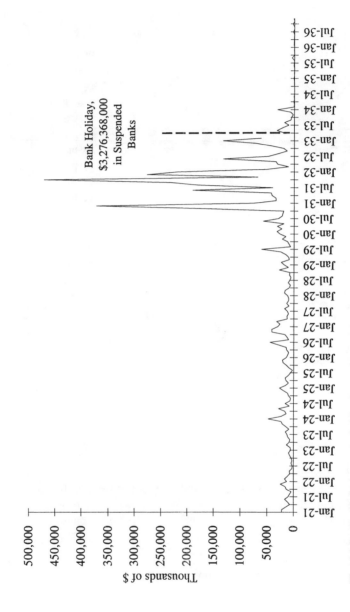

Fig. 14.2 Deposits in suspended banks, monthly flow, 1921–1936 ($ thousands)
Source: Board of Governors of the Federal Reserve System (1937, 909).

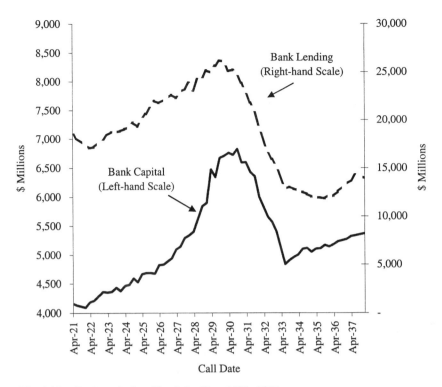

Fig. 14.3   Bank capital and bank lending, 1921–1937
Source: Mason (2001b).

deposits in excess of 2 percent in 1933, and a loss rate relative to GDP of roughly 3 percent for the period 1929–1933 (measured as the ratio of total depositor losses relative to average GDP, for the period 1930–1933).

14.2.2   The Role of Market Discipline in Limiting Bank Distress

Although these losses were large relative to previous U.S. experience, as we noted above, they are quite small relative to the experiences of many countries today, including many cases of countries experiencing much milder shocks than the economic collapse of the Great Depression. The low loss rates of historical banking systems, including that of the United States in the 1930s, reflected the presence of market discipline. Calomiris and Wilson (2003) show that depositors of banks (and to a lesser extent, their minority stockholders) required banks to hold capital commensurate with their portfolio risk, effectively requiring banks to target low levels of default risk. Banks that suffered losses on their investments were required to find ways either to curtail their asset risk (cut credit) or increase capital (cut dividends) to restore their prior low risk of default. Those that failed to do so suffered deposit withdrawals, as funds flowed to lower-risk banks

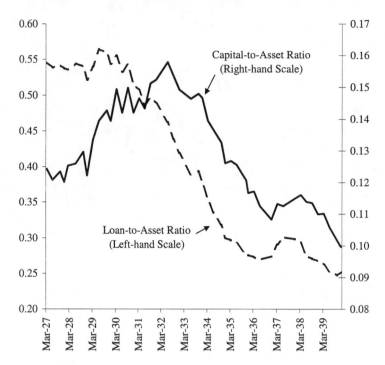

Fig. 14.4 Capital-to-asset and loan-to-asset ratios, all member banks, 1927–1939 call dates

Source: Mason (2001b).

and postal savings. When losses on investments were sufficiently sudden or large, banks that failed to restore market confidence were forced to close.

The existence of deposit market discipline does not imply that all or even most depositors were capable of judging bank balance-sheet condition. Rather, as Calomiris and Kahn (1991) suggest, discipline was concentrated in the hands of a few depositors (often large depositors or interbank depositors) who had the wherewithal and the incentive to monitor bank condition and react to deterioration in that condition. Passive depositors could, of course, magnify the effects of withdrawals from monitoring depositors by reacting with a lag to monitors' withdrawals or other publicly available signals of bank weakness (e.g., stock price declines, or newspaper accounts of bank condition, which were widely available).

This process of market discipline is visible in a variety of facts about bank failure and risk management. Table 14.2 reports the results of the "basic" bank survival model from Calomiris and Mason (2003b). The coefficients in table 14.2—derived from a model of bank survival during the period 1930–1932—show the effects of variation in bank or county characteristics (which are observed periodically) on the predicted survival du-

Table 14.1   **Losses on Deposits in Suspended Banks, Annual, 1921–1942**

| | | | | Losses Relative to Deposits | |
Year	No. of Suspensions	Deposits ($ thousands)	Losses Borne by Depositors ($ thousands)	Suspended Banks (%)	All Commercial Banks (%)
Pre-FDIC					
1921	506	172,806	59,967	34.70	0.21
1922	366	91,182	38,223	41.92	0.13
1923	646	149,601	62,142	41.54	0.19
1924	775	210,150	79,381	37.77	0.23
1925	617	166,937	60,799	36.42	0.16
1926	975	260,153	83,066	31.93	0.21
1927	669	199,332	60,681	30.44	0.15
1928	498	142,386	43,813	30.77	0.10
1929	659	230,643	76,659	33.24	0.18
1930	1,350	837,096	237,359	28.36	0.57
1931	2,293	1,690,232	390,476	23.10	1.01
1932	1,453	706,187	168,302	23.83	0.57
1933	4,000[a]	3,596,708	540,396	15.02	2.15
Post-FDIC					
1934	61	37,332	6,502	17.42	0.0228
1935	31	13,902	600	4.32	0.0018
1936	72	28,100	185	0.66	0.0005
1937	82	33,877	155	0.46	0.0004
1938	80	58,243	293	0.50	0.0008
1939	71	158,627	1,374	0.87	0.0033
1940	48	142,787	57	0.04	0.0001
1941	17	29,797	33	0.11	0.0001
1942	23	19,517	20	0.10	0.0000

Sources: Friedman and Schwartz (1963, 438) and authors' calculations.
[a]Includes banks suspended under Bank Holiday of March 1933.

ration of banks. As table 14.2 shows, banks with lower net worth relative to assets, or with higher portfolio risk, tended to be less likely to survive, ceteris paribus. Portfolio risk is measured here by bank size (smaller banks tend to be less diversified), and by asset composition (riskier banks have higher proportions of noncash assets, higher proportions of risky "ineligible" loans, and higher holdings of dispossessed real estate). Other variables related to the location of the bank (including county unemployment or reliance on crop income) are also important determinants of bank distress.

Interestingly, table 14.2 shows that liability mix is also important for predicting bank survival, a result that echoes similar findings from many other studies of U.S. bank failures in the 1920s and 1930s (Calomiris and Mason 1997). Calomiris and Mason (2003b) interpret the predictive power of liability mix as reflecting the fact that banks that relied heavily on interbank deposits and bills payable for their funding had been rationed from the

Table 14.2   Survival Regression for Individual Fed Member Banks

Variable	Regression	Variable	Regression
Constant	6.044	Bills payable + Rediscounts/	−1.490
	(0.283)	Deposits	(0.146)
Log (total assets)	0.105	Private bills payable/Total bills	−0.126
	(0.011)	payable	(0.050)
State-chartered bank indicator	0.136	Interest paid on debt/Debt	−0.671
	(0.031)		(0.428)
Log (number of branches)	−0.012	Crop Income/Crop + Manufacturing	0.317
	(0.006)	income in county, 1930	(0.093)
Deposit market share of bank	0.259	Pasture share of farm acres in	0.063
	(0.099)	county, 1930	(0.063)
Noncash assets/Total assets	−0.845	Value of grains/Crop value in	−0.016
	(0.124)	county, 1930	(0.058)
Loans/Other noncash assets	−0.229	Unemployment in county, 1930	−1.204
	(0.058)		(0.315)
Loans eligible for discount/Loans	0.115	Percentage of small farms in	−0.075
	(0.054)	county, 1930	(0.052)
Losses on assets and trading/Assets	0.027	(Investment) × (crop income share)	0.139
	(0.049)	in county, 1930	(0.036)
Real estate owned/Noncash assets	−3.415	State bank share in county, 1930	−0.288
	(0.331)		(0.047)
(Change in bond yield) × (securities)	−0.247	Lagged value building permits	0.054
	(0.239)	in state	(0.010)
Net worth/Assets	1.700	Lagged liabilities of failed	−0.005
	(0.184)	businesses/Income in state	(0.004)
Share of demand deposit + Due	−0.164	Growth of agriculture prices	−0.086
to banks	(0.059)	in nation	(0.264)
Share of deposits due to banks	−0.478	Growth of liabilities of failed	−0.057
	(0.203)	businesses in nation	(0.054)
Share of assets due from banks	0.059	Time	0.044
	(0.060)		(0.001)
No. of observations (bank-months)	269,683		
Log-likelihood	−11,704		

Source: Calomiris and Mason (2003b).

Notes: Dependent variable: log probability of survival (daily). Full sample of Fed member banks. Standard errors in parentheses.

consumer deposit market because of their higher-than-average probability of default.

Calomiris and Wilson (2003) model the "capital crunch" phenomenon—the tendency of falling bank capital (due to loan losses) to produce declines in subsequent bank loan supply—and connect that phenomenon to market discipline by depositors. They argue that a bank credit crunch requires two key assumptions: "risk-intolerant" deposits and adverse-selection costs of raising new equity, both of which are the natural result of bank specialization in creating private information about borrowers. Depositor risk intolerance (a form of credit rationing in which depositors withdraw funds in re-

Table 14.3   **Financial Ratios and Default Risk for a Stable Sample of 12 New York City Banks**

Year	MVE/BVE	E/A %	S_A	Bid-Ask %	P	SD P	MVA
1920	1.23	16.73	2.33	2.53	0.00	0.0	306
1921	1.40	18.03	2.78	2.41	0.30	1.0	317
1922	1.51	18.40	4.27	2.09	7.75	26.5	363
1923	1.54	20.25	1.85	1.73	0.00	0.0	352
1924	1.89	21.70	3.72	1.78	0.00	0.0	434
1925	2.36	24.77	5.49	1.47	0.07	0.2	482
1926	2.27	26.10	2.88	1.26	0.00	0.0	530
1927	2.81	32.16	5.89	1.47	0.00	0.0	573
1928	3.82	34.16	8.28	2.58	0.08	0.2	858
1929	2.80	33.10	17.45	2.74	33.46	71.3	1,045
1930	2.06	26.86	8.32	2.05	1.24	2.8	998
1931	1.02	18.54	8.03	4.18	9.18	10.4	739
1932	1.16	19.24	10.62	5.64	34.73	46.8	712
1933	0.88	15.02	6.10	5.41	41.69	112.5	641
1934	0.98	13.88	3.75	5.48	11.72	40.5	781
1935	1.34	16.96	6.32	4.41	23.09	75.4	907
1936	1.32	16.74	4.31	3.66	1.32	4.5	976
1937	0.94	12.95	3.74	4.28	0.60	1.0	863
1938	0.91	12.05	3.49	5.49	7.08	19.5	923
1939	1.39	14.70	5.55	5.63	0.50	1.6	1,133
1940	0.93	9.55	2.01	6.71	2.14	7.4	1,260

Source: Calomiris and Wilson (2003).

Notes: The stable sample is defined as the sample of banks that are present in the database throughout the period. The sample of banks is restricted to banks with available stock prices, as described in Calomiris and Wilson (2003, data appendix). Data are measured at year-end.
  Variable definitions:
MVE = average market value of equity
BVE = average book value of equity
E/A = average market capital-to-asset ratio
S_A = average asset volatility (standard deviation of asset returns)
Bid-Ask = average bid-ask spread as a percentage of share price
P = average deposit default premium in basis points (1.00 = 1 basis point)
SD P = standard deviation of P
MVA = average market value of assets ($ millions)

action to increased default risk) depends on asymmetric information about the quality of the bank loan portfolio. Asymmetric information can motivate deposit rationing for two reasons: agency costs, as in Calomiris and Kahn (1991), or depositors' preferences for claims that are easily accepted in secondary markets, as in Gorton and Pennacchi (1990). Adverse-selection costs of raising equity are also a necessary ingredient to any market-driven capital crunch; without adverse-selection costs of raising equity, banks would typically prefer to respond to capital losses with new stock issues rather than with shrinking credit supply.

Tables 14.3 through 14.5 provide more direct evidence on the relationships among bank capital, loan losses, depositor discipline, and credit con-

Table 14.4   Deposit Growth Regressions

Variable	OLS (1)	2SLS (2)	OLS (3)	2SLS (4)
Constant	9.528*	10.234*	12.526*	14.192*
	(1.038)	(1.093)	(2.415)	(2.547)
P	−0.0497*	−0.1166*	−0.0514*	−0.1293*
	(0.0136)	(0.0289)	(0.0137)	(0.0301)
Trust Co.			−4.476	−5.275
			(2.809)	(2.906)
Nat. Bank			−2.181	−2.995
			(2.998)	(3.094)
Lagged Ind. Prod.			−2.678	−6.689
			(6.594)	(6.915)
Adj. R^2	0.021	0.026	0.021	0.028

Source: Calomiris and Wilson (2003).

Notes: P is the (end-of-year) deposit default premium, derived from the Black-Scholes model, using stock returns and balance-sheet data over the last six months of the year. Nat. Bank and Trust Co. are indicator variables for national banks and state trust companies. In the two-stage least squares (2SLS) regressions, *P* is treated as an endogenous variable, and the list of instruments includes lagged values of the following variables: the market capital-to-asset ratio, the implied standard deviation of returns to assets, and growth in industrial production. Dependent variable is annual percentage change in deposits. Standard errors are in parentheses.

*Significant at below the 5 percent level.

traction from Calomiris and Wilson (2003), using a sample of publicly traded New York City banks for the period 1920–1940. As table 14.3 shows, during the 1920s, as lending opportunities expanded and the economy remained relatively healthy, bank asset risk expanded alongside the market capital ratio. The growth in asset risk and capital ratios reflected substantial increases in banks' loan-to-asset ratios, and frequent bank stock offerings. With the exception of the postrecession year (1922), banks maintained constant and very low default risk during the 1920s, as measured by implied default premiums on bank debt (derived from equity returns and balance sheet data, using the Black-Scholes model). In the wake of the loan losses of 1929–1933, bank default risk rose substantially. In order to reestablish low default risk in the face of declining capital, banks cut loans and accumulated cash to keep asset risk from rising. They also cut dividends to mitigate the decline in their capital ratios. As table 14.3 shows, even as late as 1936 banks had not fully returned to their pre-1929 level of default risk. The recession of 1937–1938 again produced loan losses and further encouraged cuts in lending and dividends.

Table 14.4 reports the findings from an annual panel regression that examines the role of deposit rationing in encouraging banks to adopt this strategy. The dependent variable is individual bank deposit growth. Table 14.4 shows that banks with high default premiums lost more deposits than

Table 14.5   **Dividend Growth Regressions (1929–1939)**

Variable	(1)	(2)	(3)
Constant	3.77	6.75	7.85
	(4.13)	(8.91)	(9.21)
Ba	−1.91*	−1.78*	−1.81*
	(0.65)	(0.67)	(0.75)
P	−0.115*	−0.131*	−0.131*
	(0.055)	(0.057)	(0.061)
Ba_{-1}			−0.225
			(0.684)
P_{-1}			0.02
			(0.08)
Year29		11.31	11.42
		(11.01)	(11.15)
Year30		−22.31*	−22.38*
		(10.75)	(11.00)
Year31		−1.16	−1.35
		(11.12)	(11.27)
Year32		−9.70	−9.74
		(11.76)	(11.90)
Year33		−11.12	−11.16
		(11.75)	(11.87)
Year34		−2.12	−2.55
		(11.81)	(12.00)
Year35		−2.86	−3.09
		(11.81)	(11.91)
Year36		−0.74	−0.65
		(11.69)	(11.81)
Year37		1.89	2.27
		(11.66)	(11.83)
Year38		0.36	0.26
		(11.66)	(11.76)
Adj. R^2	0.05	0.06	0.05

Source: Calomiris and Wilson (2003).

Notes: The variables Ba and P are the end-of-year bid-ask spread and deposit default premium, respectively; 1939 is the omitted year dummy. Dependent variable is annual percentage change in dividends. Standard errors are in parentheses.

*Significant at below the 5 percent level.

other banks. Table 14.5 presents annual panel regressions showing how banks cut dividends in response to capital scarcity. Banks with higher default risk tended to cut dividends more. Banks with higher bid-ask spreads (where the bid-ask spread is expressed as a percentage of stock value) also tended to cut dividends by more. Calomiris and Wilson (2003) use the bid-ask spread as a proxy for high adverse-selection costs of raising capital. They interpret the negative coefficient on the bid-ask spread in table 14.5 as indicating a precautionary demand for preserving capital by banks that knew they faced high costs of raising capital if they were forced to do so.

The evidence in tables 14.2 through 14.5 indicates that during the Great Depression U.S. banks were subject to market discipline, which required them to respond to loan losses with reduced lending and dividends (see also Calomiris and Mason 2003a). Market discipline was able to operate on banks in the 1930s because government assistance to banks was limited, and thus insolvent banks were not protected from market discipline by the various forms of government assistance that banks received. Assistance during the 1930s included loans from the Fed, loans and preferred stock purchases from the RFC, and federal deposit insurance on small deposits. Deposit insurance was limited to small deposits (see Calomiris and White 1994), and banks that were insolvent in 1933 were not permitted to qualify for deposit insurance in 1934. And, as we will discuss in detail below, loans and preferred stock were supplied in a way that limited the potential abuse of such assistance.

In today's world of expanded safety nets and generous bailouts—as, for example, in Japan—credit crunches can (and should) still occur, but typically depend on regulatory, rather than market, discipline to link bank losses to contractions in risk. The creation of a bank safety net makes it necessary to impose risk-based capital regulation to protect against abuse of government protection. Risk-based capital regulation seeks to mimic market discipline by measuring asset risk (e.g., loan default risk and interest rate risk) and linking equity capital requirements to the level of bank risk.

Although this approach is generally not fully effective, and has been the subject of much critical examination (Calomiris 1997; Shadow Financial Regulatory Committee 2000; Barth, Caprio, and Levine 2001), it can serve to limit at least some means of bank risk-taking. For example, Baer and McElravey (1993) examined U.S. bank asset growth in the 1980s (under the new regime of capital regulation and enforcement that was enacted following the loan losses of the post-1986 period). They and others have found that bank asset growth was closely related to the adequacy of regulatory capital. Banks with low capital tended to grow the slowest.

Asset or loan growth, however, do not measure overall bank risk. Others have found substantial evidence that true default risk may be high even when banks reduce their loans to comply with risk-based capital standards. Thus, unlike market discipline (which evaluates the overall riskiness of the bank), regulatory discipline based on rules of thumb that measure bank risk will tend to invite "risk arbitrage" by regulated banks (the search for asset positions whose risks are underestimated by regulatory capital standards). We return to this problem in our discussion of Japan in section 14.3, and in section 14.4's discussion of policy options.

14.2.3   The Cumulative Effects of Banking Distress on Illiquid Asset Markets

Although market discipline was present in the 1930s, and insolvent banks were allowed to fail, the removal of bank assets from bankers' control did not imply the speedy resolution of borrowers' distress. Nonperforming loans of insolvent banks were not liquidated quickly during the Depression. As in many Asian countries today, as the stock of failed banks' loans accumulated, the speed of loan resolution slowed. This loan resolution backlog effect is analyzed by Anari, Kolari, and Mason (2003). They find that this measure of financial-sector distress is a better forecaster of economic activity, and a better explanatory variable for the persistence of output decline during the Depression, than previously used measures of financial sector distress.

Figure 14.5 plots the cumulative "stock" of outstanding (unpaid) deposits in failed national banks over time, their measure of the stock of unresolved bank assets. The authors estimate this quantity using data on the speed of liquidations by receivers and conservators of failed banks. Uninsured depositors were paid on a pro rata basis as the asset liquidation of their failed banks proceeded. The average liquidation time for national banks ran a little more than six years.

Anari, Kolari, and Mason (2003) cite numerous qualitative sources that saw the slow pace of asset liquidation as a source of depositor illiquidity and reduced consumption. Mason (2002) suggests that low liquidation speed was the result of concerns about the real option forgone by selling into a liquidity-depressed market. Observers saw the backlog of unsold assets as depressing investment; the vast supply of property put up for sale depressed property values—which contributed to the unprecedented losses suffered by depositors—and produced a form of gridlock in local markets. Buyers lacked liquidity and sellers trying to realize the full value of assets were reluctant to sell at prices that were perceived as containing a hefty illiquidity discount.

The important implication of this research is that systemwide bank failures pose special costs to society, not just because of the loss of lending capacity by banks that have lost capital, but additionally because of the effects of bank asset liquidation on consumer liquidity and the accentuated liquidity premium in property markets. It follows that an additional benefit of assistance to banks, and countercyclical macroeconomic policy, during a depression is their positive effect on the liquidity of bank assets and liabilities.

14.2.4   The Policy Response to Financial-Sector Distress during the Depression

To understand the way central bankers and government officials responded to the Depression one must be familiar with the histories of previous business cycles, which had produced certain policy rules, and with the ways in which the shocks of the 1930s differed from those of earlier business cycles. Of central relevance was the fact that, prior to the interwar period, the price process under the classical gold standard tended to be mean-reverting. As Eichengreen (1992) and Temin (1989) have noted, the establishment of the interwar gold exchange standard suffered from a

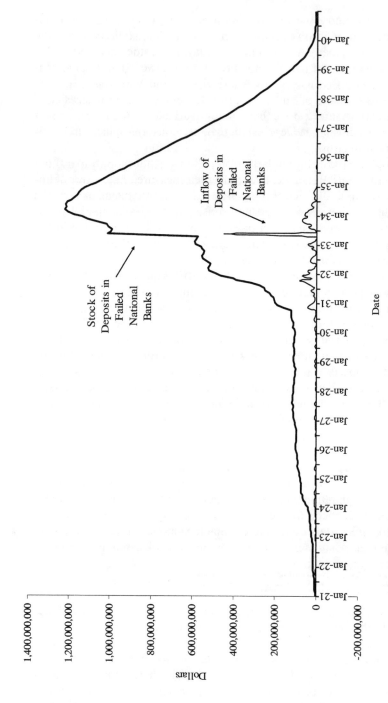

Fig. 14.5 Failed national bank deposit flows and stocks: Monthly, January 1921–December 1940

Source: Anari, Kolari, and Mason (2003).

Notes: The estimated cost of delayed liquidation alone was worth 50 basis points of average 1929–1940 GNP. Maximum stock was $1.217 billion in March 1934.

long-run deflationary bias that was aggravated by the failure of coordination among central banks in response to shocks to global liquidity.

As more and more countries began to return to gold in the mid-1920s, and as income growth further increased the demand for gold, international imbalances produced contractionary monetary policy in some countries (in keeping with the so-called rules of the game for central banks under the gold standard), but that contraction was not offset by appropriate expansion in other countries. World War I had undermined the ability of the major countries to coordinate policy in response to this global deflationary shock. Instead of working together to expand the global supply of money, central banks scrambled for gold and shrank the world money supply, thus driving the price level down and producing a global debt deflation.

The Fed was a relatively new institution as of 1929. It developed an approach to countercyclical monetary policy during the 1920s that reacted to interest rates, free reserves, and gold flows. Those policy-reaction rules of thumb worked reasonably well in the 1920s, but aggravated the contraction in monetary policy in the 1930s (Wheelock 1991; Calomiris and Wheelock 1998). In that deflationary environment, contrary to the Fed's interpretation, low nominal interest rates and high reserve holdings did not imply loose monetary conditions.

The Fed's role as a lender of last resort was ill-defined. The Federal Reserve Act contemplated the role of the Fed as primarily influencing the seasonal availability of reserves, not giving assistance to improve individual banks' chances of survival, and certainly not bailing out insolvent banks. And because the previous macroeconomic environment had never witnessed the like of the monetary policy–induced collapse of the 1930s, the American experience with banking crises had never provided any motive for interventionist policies to prop up banks. Banking panics in 1857, 1873, 1884, 1890, 1893, 1896, and 1907 were short-lived moments of confusion about the incidence of loss, and resulted in few bank failures (Calomiris and Gorton 1991). They were very mild affairs compared to the bank failure waves of the 1930s. Moreover, bank failures in agricultural areas and nationwide bank panics were understood to be closely linked to the fragmented unit banking system; rapid bank industry consolidation during the 1920s seemed to point toward a more stable future.

The bank failures of the 1920s were severe in some agricultural areas, but were directly linked to the post–World War I collapse of prices. That, along with the fact that agricultural states that had enacted deposit insurance in the 1910s and 1920s experienced the worst bank failure waves in the 1920s, led policymakers to view efforts to prop up banks as counterproductive. Deposit insurance had been a disastrous policy when tried at the state level, and the experience was fresh in the minds of policymakers in the late 1920s. The eight state deposit insurance systems lay in ruins at that time, and were clearly and properly understood by observers (including President Roosevelt, who opposed deposit insurance) as examples of what happens to banking systems that relax the discipline of the marketplace (Calomiris 1989, 1990; Calomiris and White 1994).

The banking collapse of the 1930s, however, was simply too severe and too widespread to be ignored, and politicians found in the severity of banking collapse new opportunities. For Congressman Henry Steagall, the Depression offered the chance to pass a long-dormant proposal for federal deposit insurance (which had been understood for fifty years to be special-interest legislation for small agricultural banks). For Senator Carter Glass, the Depression provided the opportunity to push through his decades-long quest to separate commercial banks from capital markets by fostering the now-discredited view that the mixing of commercial and investment banking had caused banks to collapse during the Depression (White 1986; Calomiris and White 1994).

Political opportunism was not the only reason for intervention in the landmark Banking Act of 1933. Banks were collapsing as never before, and even surviving banks were slashing credit. President Hoover's initial reaction to bank collapse in 1930–1932 was understandably reluctant and cautious about federal assistance to distressed banks. By January 1933, however, the financial system was in free-fall. February and March saw most states declaring banking holidays to avoid the runs that were bringing so many banks down so quickly. The Fed and the RFC, both of which had been making collateralized loans to banks, were criticized for failing to provide adequate assistance.

And so, in March 1933, there was a sudden shift: a national bank holiday was enacted, federal deposit insurance (for small deposit accounts) was passed, and the RFC was authorized to purchase preferred stock in banks and other enterprises. Suspended banks would be examined; those that were solvent would be permitted to reopen and join the Federal Deposit Insurance Corporation (FDIC). Some would be nudged to solvency by the RFC, if necessary. Deeply insolvent banks would be shut down. Perhaps even more importantly, President Roosevelt took the country off of the gold standard. Deflation, and deflationary expectations, came to a halt. Industrial production immediately began to recover. That same pattern of immediate recovery was enjoyed by other countries that abandoned the gold standard in 1931, as Eichengreen and Sachs (1985) show.

14.2.5 The Operation of the RFC

Initially (from its founding in February 1932 until 21 July 1932) the RFC operated under the same conservative lending rules as the Fed. After the ouster of its chairman (who also served as chairman of the Federal Reserve Board) in July, RFC collateral standards were relaxed. Lending to banks and other firms grew thereafter. Beginning in March 1933, the RFC's preferred-stock purchase program dominated its assistance to banks, as shown in table 14.6 and figures 14.6 and 14.7.

Table 14.6   Preferred Stock versus Loans, February 1932–December 1936

	Preferred Stock		Notes and Debentures		Loans to All Banks		Loans to Receivers/Conservators	
	No. of Authorizations	Amount of Authorizations ($ millions)	No. of Authorizations	Amount of Authorizations ($ millions)	No. of Applications[a]	Amount of Authorizations ($ millions)	No. of Authorizations	Amount of Authorizations ($ millions)
Jan-28	n.a.	n.a.	n.a.	n.a.	108	45.27	0	0.00
Feb-28	n.a.	n.a.	n.a.	n.a.	821	108.16	3	0.85
Mar-28	n.a.	n.a.	n.a.	n.a.	1,296	153.08	104	5.86
Apr-28	n.a.	n.a.	n.a.	n.a.	1,181	114.50	107	5.95
May-28	n.a.	n.a.	n.a.	n.a.	1,172	236.43	85	11.09
Jun-28	n.a.	n.a.	n.a.	n.a.	1,099	97.37	24	1.23
Jul-28	n.a.	n.a.	n.a.	n.a.	899	85.06	50	7.77
Aug-28	n.a.	n.a.	n.a.	n.a.	515	28.98	46	4.43
Sep-28	n.a.	n.a.	n.a.	n.a.	484	21.45	21	1.67
Oct-28	n.a.	n.a.	n.a.	n.a.	462	22.26	30	2.84
Nov-28	n.a.	n.a.	n.a.	n.a.	633	49.79	57	5.52
Dec-28	n.a.	n.a.	n.a.	n.a.	551	46.92	31	2.82
Jan-29	n.a.	n.a.	n.a.	n.a.	612	89.37	28	3.62
Feb-29	4	13.68	0	0.00	702	74.78	23	4.20
Mar-29	3	7.40	1	0.20	234	60.66	35	46.76
Apr-29	12	9.11	0	0.00	193	64.11	62	35.86
May-29	20	4.84	0	0.00	160	38.84	55	21.47
Jun-29	27	12.73	0	0.00	112	100.91	45	93.89
Jul-29	24	2.90	1	0.50	148	36.18	90	17.38
Aug-29	23	3.76	0	0.00	103	20.97	54	11.81
Sep-29	27	6.33	2	25.04	108	104.57	61	98.34
Oct-29	11	18.07	23	71.70	195	40.54	133	32.47
Nov-29	795	181.15	1,250	129.72	358	109.03	298	101.45
Dec-29	1,063	141.85	1,128	258.54	447	53.06	419	45.14
Jan-30	200	53.50	107	18.25	356	36.67	339	34.34
Feb-30	269	74.96	101	23.28	289	55.48	260	47.86
Mar-30	171	25.71	71	4.05	279	47.61	269	39.06
Apr-30	279	41.56	56	5.43	161	32.70	147	28.62
May-30	234	27.61	45	6.61	138	19.08	124	17.87
Jun-30	158	12.74	55	2.73	111	40.04	95	39.08
Jul-30	127	11.22	41	15.91	90	104.73	84	103.32
Aug-30	106	10.62	26	1.87	63	11.74	60	10.56

(*continued*)

Table 14.6 (continued)

	Preferred Stock		Notes and Debentures		Loans to All Banks		Loans to Receivers/Conservators	
	No. of Authorizations	Amount of Authorizations ($ millions)	No. of Authorizations	Amount of Authorizations ($ millions)	No. of Applications[a]	Amount of Authorizations ($ millions)	No. of Authorizations	Amount of Authorizations ($ millions)
Sep-30	95	20.78	38	2.90	97	26.53	90	26.22
Oct-30	71	9.20	19	1.03	97	20.85	90	19.70
Nov-30	152	16.29	24	1.85	133	22.78	124	21.52
Dec-30	122	13.69	28	1.83	46	12.14	41	11.71
Jan-31	38	2.50	9	0.79	80	9.72	73	8.62
Feb-31	33	1.64	15	1.41	92	15.78	85	11.31
Mar-31	22	2.00	9	0.25	75	10.73	69	7.95
Apr-31	30	5.12	6	0.07	72	21.13	69	21.05
May-31	32	6.36	12	0.44	56	14.10	49	13.97
Jun-31	34	7.03	46	1.17	44	10.05	38	9.18
Jul-31	34	3.11	27	0.84	45	7.04	42	5.87
Aug-31	8	25.12	10	6.18	47	7.45	46	7.42
Sep-31	11	1.20	7	0.31	42	6.23	41	6.23
Oct-31	7	5.78	2	0.07	48	13.49	27	13.42
Nov-31	10	13.75	1	0.01	55	7.68	51	7.30
Dec-31	9	0.53	4	0.05	21	30.11	20	30.11
Jan-32	2	1.03	1	0.03	28	3.96	28	3.96
Feb-32	6	1.59	1	0.01	186	10.30	185	10.29
Mar-32	5	0.85	0	0.00	161	8.26	157	8.08
Apr-32	7	2.30	4	0.07	66	12.77	62	12.70
May-32	3	0.92	1	0.02	50	6.89	50	6.89
Jun-32	0	0.00	2	0.03	16	2.35	16	2.35
Jul-32	1	0.01	0	0.00	42	7.27	42	7.27
Aug-32	3	0.05	1	0.01	41	3.19	41	3.19
Sep-32	1	0.03	1	0.04	24	3.40	24	3.40
Oct-32	2	0.43	0	0.00	23	5.50	22	5.43
Nov-32								
Total	4,291	801.00	3,175	583.22	15,767	2,450.01	4,841	1,168.25

Source: Mason (1996).

Note: Notes and debentures were purchased only in banks in states that prohibited preferred stock investments.

[a]Authorizations used where no data were available on applications.

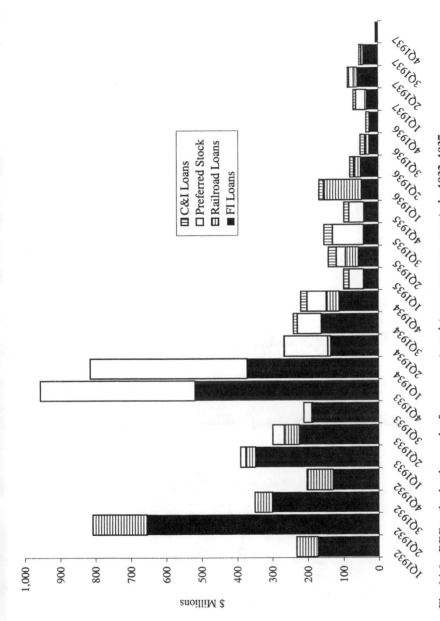

Fig. 14.6   RFC authorizations under four corporate assistance programs, quarterly, 1932–1937

Source: Mason (2001b).

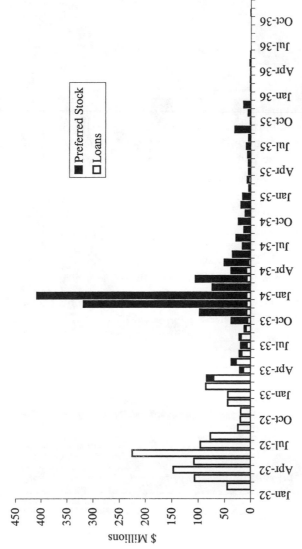

Fig. 14.7   Amounts authorized to open banks under the RFC loan and preferred stock programs, monthly, 1932–1936

Source: Mason (2001b).

Notes: Figure includes only loans to open banks. Does not include loans to receivers or those made on preferred stock. The RFC preferred-stock program began in March 1933. Preferred stock includes investments made through notes and debentures to banks in states that prohibited preferred stock investments.

Table 14.7   **Test of the Difference between the Mean Predicted Probability of Bank Failure Based on Exogenous Characteristics: Banks Receiving RFC Loans and Preferred Stock**

	Banks Receiving Loans	Banks Receiving Preferred Stock	T-Statistic for Difference between Means
Mean	0.31	0.29	1.32
Standard deviation	0.08	0.10	

Source: Mason (1996).

Part of the shift to preferred stock reflected the widespread view that secured loans did not stabilize weak banks (James 1938, 1044). Secured loans represented a senior claim on bank assets relative to deposits, and thus effectively worsened the default risk faced by junior depositors. Olson (1977, 154) writes:

> High collateral requirements forced [banks] to isolate their most liquid assets as security for RFC loans. In April 1932, for example, the Reconstruction Finance Corporation loaned the Reno National Bank over $1,100,000, but in the process took as collateral over $3,000,000 of the bank's best securities. This in itself left the bank unable to meet any future emergency demands for funds by depositors.

In Olson's (1972, 177) view, loans from "the RFC helped only those basically sound enterprises which needed temporary liquidity." It was not a means of reducing default risk for a capital-impaired bank; thus, it provided little relief to banks from default-risk-intolerant market discipline.

Preferred stock, in contrast, was junior to bank deposits, and was not secured by high-quality bank assets. Thus, it offered a means of lowering deposit default risk and thus insulating risky banks from the threat of deposit withdrawal. By March 1934 the RFC had purchased preferred stock in nearly half the commercial banks in the United States. By June 1935, these RFC investments made up more than one-third of the outstanding capital of the banking system (Olson 1988, 82).

Mason (1996, 2001a) examines the relative effectiveness of loans and preferred stock purchases by the RFC, after controlling for differences in the characteristics of banks receiving both kinds of assistance. As table 14.7 and figure 14.8 show, using a model of bank failure risk to compute *exogenous* probabilities of default, Mason found little difference in the exogenous default risk of banks receiving loans versus those receiving preferred stock assistance. Table 14.8 examines the effects of the two types of assistance on the probability of bank failure, after controlling for differences in exogenous characteristics using a Heckman correction. According to these results, receiving a loan from the RFC actually raised the probability of bank failure, while receiving preferred stock assistance reduced the probability of failure.

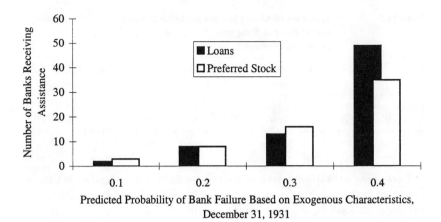

Fig. 14.8   **Distribution of condition of banks receiving assistance**
Source: Mason (1996).

Although this evidence indicates that preferred stock purchases were effective in insulating banks from deposit withdrawal, it is important to emphasize that the RFC preferred-stock program was successful because it was neither too conservative nor too liberal with its assistance. The RFC would have made little difference if it had targeted only the lowest-risk banks for its subsidies. As figure 14.8 and table 14.7 show, that was not the case. At the same time, the RFC did not provide assistance to deeply insolvent banks, nor would its assistance have been a sufficient subsidy to bail out such banks. Moreover, the conditions attached to RFC preferred-stock purchases served to limit bank risk transference to the RFC, which ensured that preferred stock issuers had incentives to limit risk. Thus, capital-impaired (but not deeply insolvent) banks were offered protection from market discipline essentially on condition that they did not abuse such protection by transferring too much risk to the government.

How did RFC conditionality ensure this "happy medium" of controlled risk? First, it offered limited subsidies to banks, and avoided trying to save "basket cases" (see *RFC Circular no. 1, 1932*). The RFC required banks to submit their regulatory examinations for RFC inspection, and banks that were judged as hopelessly insolvent were rejected. Further evidence of the selective nature of assistance is provided in table 14.9, which shows that dividend rates on RFC preferred stock were typically less than 1 percent below those earned in the marketplace, and were above market rates on short-term business loans.

In part, the limited subsidy offered by the RFC reflected its independent corporate status. The RFC was a separately capitalized institution—essentially, a government-sponsored enterprise, not a budget line for the executive branch. Table 14.10 reviews the financing structure of the RFC

Table 14.8   **Accelerated Failure Time Models with RFC Loans and Preferred Stock Purchases**

Variable	(1)	(2)
Constant	11.723***	7.493***
	(1.693)	(1.013)
Illiquid assets/Total assets	−8.220***	−3.564***
	(1.566)	(1.089)
Bonds, stocks, and securities owned/Illiquid assets	3.225***	2.568***
	(1.252)	(1.031)
Real estate owned/Illiquid assets	4.843	3.406
	(3.791)	(3.415)
Loans and discounts/Illiquid assets	3.975***	2.811***
	(0.983)	(0.819)
Paper eligible for rediscount at the Fed/Loans and discounts	1.191**	1.283***
	(0.591)	(0.513)
Net worth/Total assets	2.040*	1.375
	(1.384)	(1.225)
Bills payable and rediscounts/Debt	−3.722***	−2.750***
	(1.378)	(1.145)
Interest and discount on loans/Total earnings	−1.763**	−0.588
	(0.904)	(0.704)
Recoveries/Total earnings	1.187	−0.222
	(1.135)	(1.056)
Losses/Total expenses	−1.058***	−0.586*
	(0.415)	(0.366)
Predicted probability of RFC loan	−3.663***	
	(1.483)	
Predicted probability of RFC preferred stock purchase		6.873***
		(1.276)
No. of individuals in panel	357	327
No. of bank-year observations	979	979
Log-likelihood	−990.9	−971.9
Restricted (slopes = 0) log-likelihood	−1,094.8	−1,094.8
Chi-squared (k − 1 df)	207.9	227.6

Source: Mason (2001a).

Notes: The model measures the determinants of log survival time, measured in days, from 31 December 1931 to 31 December 1935. Both survival models use a Weibull parameterization. Bank financial data are from Federal Reserve *Reports of Condition and Income.* RFC loan and preferred stock data are from monthly *Reports of Activity of the RFC.* The RFC variable in column (1) pertains to loans, while that in column (2) pertains to preferred stock purchases. Standard errors are in parentheses.

***Significant at the 1 percent level.

**Significant at the 5 percent level.

*Significant at the 10 percent level.

Table 14.9   **Rates on RFC Assistance and Selected Private Market Alternatives, 1932–1937 (% per annum)**

Year	RFC Loans to Banks	RFC Loans to Railroads	RFC Preferred Stock in Financial Institutions	RFC Loans to the Commercial and Industrial Sector	Federal Reserve Bank of N.Y. Discount Rate (High)[a]	Moody's Railroad Common Stock Yields[b]	Preferred Stocks[b]	Bank Rates on Short-Term Business Loans[c]
1932	5.77	6.00	n.a.	n.a.	3.50	7.23	6.13	4.70
1933	4.79	5.50	5.10	n.a.	3.50	5.67	5.75	4.30
1934	4.00	5.00	4.92	6.00	2.00	5.75	5.29	3.50
1935	4.00	5.00	3.54	5.42	1.50	4.85	4.63	2.90
1936	4.00	5.00	3.54	5.42	1.50	3.67	4.33	2.70
1937	4.00	5.00	3.54	5.42	1.50	5.26	4.45	2.60

Note: n.a. = not applicable.

[a]From U.S. Bureau of the Census (1975, 1001, data series X 455).

[b]From U.S. Bureau of the Census (1975, 1003, data series X 474–486).

[c]From U.S. Bureau of the Census (1975, 1002, data series X 466).

Table 14.10   **Outstanding Publicly Placed Debt Obligations of the RFC (in addition to those sold to Treasury in Initial Capitalization)**

	Amount Issued
As of December 1932	
Series A	$810,000,000.00
Total	*$810,000,000.00*
As of December 1933	
Series D-1	$475,000,000.00
Series D-2	1,290,000,000.00
Series D-3	230,000,000.00
Series D-4	355,000,000.00
Series Feb. 1, 1934	78,726,187.37
Series E	101,299,666.67
Total	*$2,530,025,854.04*
As of December 1934	
Series D-1	$475,000,000.00
Series D-2	1,290,000,000.00
Series D-3	960,000,000.00
Series D-4	560,000,000.00
Series DA-1	265,000,000.00
Series DA-2	35,000,000.00
Series E	149,621,666.67
Series F	64,093,000.00
Series G	16,000,000.00
Series H	19,622,000.00
Total	*$3,834,336,666.67*
As of December 1935	
Series G	$16,000,000.00
Series H	87,288,000.00
Series J-1	1,715,000,000.00
Series J-2	1,525,000,000.00
Series J-3	635,000,000.00
Series J-4	220,000,000.00
Series K	149,171,666.67
Total	*$4,347,459,666.67*
As of December 1936	
Series H	$86,378,000.00
Series K	165,346,666.67
Series L-1	2,640,000,000.00
Series L-2	1,035,000,000.00
Series L-3	5,000,000.00
Series L-4	5,000,000.00
Total	*$3,936,724,666.67*
As of December 1937	
Series K	$297,272,666.67
Series L-1	2,640,000,000.00
Series L-2	815,000,000.00
Series L-3	25,000,000.00
Series L-4	125,000,000.00
Total	*$3,902,272,666.67*

Source: Mason (1996).

from its inception through the end of 1937. Its financial independence led its chief executive, Jesse Jones, to see a need to make the RFC profitable on a cash flow basis, and he proudly proclaimed that it never saw a year of negative profit under his direction. That constraint, obviously, also limited the potential size of the subsidy the RFC could offer. For this very limited subsidy to have made a difference for bank failure risk (as table 14.8 shows it did), recipients could not have been deeply insolvent.

Second, many restrictions on recipients of RFC assistance ensured that banks would not take advantage of RFC aid by increasing their default risk. The RFC was intended to protect banks from a dramatic decline in their capital, but not to encourage capital-impaired banks from imprudently expanding their portfolio risk. Indeed, the RFC went to great pains to impose conditions that substituted for depositor discipline on bank risk-taking.

Those conditions included seniority of RFC dividends to all other stock dividends and voting rights that effectively gave the RFC the ability to direct institutions toward solvency and profitability and limit excessive risk. In many instances, the RFC used its control rights to replace bank officers and significantly alter business practices (Upham and Lamke 1934, 234; Cho 1953, 29–34; *Commercial and Financial Chronicle* 1933, 1625–26).

The RFC preserved its seniority of claim on bank earnings by limiting common stock dividend payments. Common stock dividends were strictly limited to a specified maximum and remaining earnings were devoted to a preferred stock retirement fund. Some firms avoided applying for RFC preferred-stock purchases out of reluctance to submit themselves to RFC authority.

Finally, although there were numerous attempts by politicians to influence RFC decisions, Mason (2001b, 2003) suggests that the budgetary structure of the RFC and its decentralized process of decision making insulated the RFC from political manipulation. Field offices were given a large degree of autonomy over valuation of collateral and other judgmental decisions, but were held accountable to the central office for having made errors that impacted RFC earnings (Delaney 1954, 47–48). Mason (1996, 2003) shows that objective characteristics of recipients, including their financial condition, their economic importance within their regions, and other reasonable economic criteria, influenced the RFC's choice of recipients; purely political variables (e.g., locations connected to prominent politicians) did not add explanatory power to models explaining the allocation of RFC assistance.

As figure 14.9 and table 14.11 show, bank dividends fell dramatically from 1929 to 1934. To what extent was this decline in dividends, and other measures to limit bank default risk, the result of RFC conditionality? Tables 14.12 and 14.13 examine the extent to which the conditions attached to RFC assistance made a difference for the risk choices of recipient banks. Table 14.12 divides banks into those that received RFC preferred-stock

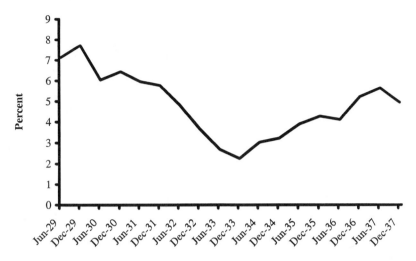

Fig. 14.9 U.S. national bank common dividend payout ratio (as percentage of common capital)

Source: Comptroller of the Currency (various issues).

Table 14.11   **Dividends of U.S. National Banks**

	Common Dividends	Preferred Dividends	Common Dividends/ Common Capital
June 1929	116,254	n.a.	7.14
December 1929	131,643	n.a.	7.72
June 1930	105,386	n.a.	6.04
December 1930	110,091	n.a.	6.44
June 1931	100,400	n.a.	5.95
December 1931	93,623	n.a.	5.77
June 1932	75,532	n.a.	4.81
December 1932	59,849	n.a.	3.66
June 1933	39,247	n.a.	2.68
December 1933	32,391	536	2.24
June 1934	40,027	2,894	3.02
December 1934	42,095	7,209	3.22
June 1935	45,146	8,967	3.90
December 1935	53,640	9,895	4.27
June 1936	51,574	10,570	4.11
December 1936	66,337	7,629	5.22
June 1937	72,642	6,867	5.64
December 1937	64,161	4,665	4.94

Source: Comptroller of the Currency (various issues).

Note: n.a. = not applicable.

Table 14.12 **Univariate Attributes of Banks with and without RFC Preferred Stock, Illinois Sample**

	N	Mean	SD	Min.	Max.
Banks without Preferred Stock, 31 December 1934					
Dividend payout rate, 1934	161	0.008	0.017	0.000	0.080
Change in dividend payout rate, 1931–1934	161	−0.486	5.477	−11.408	11.002
Change in capital/asset ratio					
1929–1934	91	−0.242	0.336	−1.743	0.504
1931–1934	91	−0.345	0.313	−1.701	0.524
1933–1934	146	−0.262	0.180	−0.895	0.104
Asset growth					
1929–1934	91	0.044	0.408	−0.713	1.589
1929–1931	91	0.194	0.336	−0.497	1.725
1929–1933	146	0.270	0.166	−0.116	0.951
Estimated *P* (fail)					
1929	69	0.138	0.145	0.000	0.662
1931	88	0.096	0.129	0.000	0.696
1933	144	0.021	0.064	0.000	0.543
1934	158	0.004	0.014	0.000	0.110
Change in estimated *P* (fail)					
1929–1934	68	−6.640	4.222	−18.602	4.721
1931–1934	86	−5.761	4.012	−16.027	5.233
1933–1934	142	−3.166	5.026	−32.353	9.242
Banks with Preferred Stock, 31 December 1934					
Dividend payout rate, 1934	75	0.001	0.007	0.000	0.050
Change in dividend payout rate, 1931–1934	75	−4.000	5.951	−11.408	10.820
Change in capital/asset ratio					
1929–1934	56	−0.201	0.405	−1.873	0.744
1931–1934	58	−0.317	0.339	−2.049	0.315
1933–1934	63	−0.210	0.266	−1.479	0.338
Asset growth					
1929–1934	56	−0.090	0.349	−0.703	1.078
1929–1931	58	0.098	0.293	−0.374	1.436
1929–1933	63	0.205	0.187	−0.220	1.042
Estimated *P* (fail)					
1929	44	0.165	0.124	0.001	0.656
1931	58	0.147	0.136	0.000	0.536
1933	63	0.056	0.103	0.000	0.420
1934	75	0.011	0.042	0.000	0.342
Change in estimated *P* (fail)					
1929–1934	44	−7.521	5.311	−21.626	0.995
1931–1934	58	−6.526	5.342	−19.975	5.027
1933–1934	63	−4.388	4.998	−19.024	12.349

Note: *N* = number of observations; SD = standard deviation; Min. = minimum; Max. = maximum.

Table 14.13   **Two-Stage Model of the Effects of Preferred Stock on Bank Choices of Capital Ratios and Dividend Payouts**

Dependent Variable	RFC Preferred Stock			
	A. First-Round RFC Preferred stock regression			
Intercept	−9,657,421			
	(1,809,977)			
Size (log of total assets)	633,609			
	(114,548)			
Illiquid assets (loans and discounts over other bonds and securities)	1,279,659 (771,276)			
$P(\text{Fail})_{31}$	1,418,046			
	(1,230,609)			
No. of observations	144			
R^2	0.1809			
Adjusted R^2	0.1635			

	Dividends/ Total Common Capital	Net Worth/ Total Assets	Change in Dividends/ Total Common Capital	Change in Net Worth/ Total Assets
	B. Second-Round Regression of Predicted RFC Preferred Stock and Fundamentals on Capital and Dividends			
Intercept	0.0068	0.1373	−0.0160	−0.0670
	(0.0019)	(0.0066)	(0.0029)	(0.0072)
$P(\text{Fail})_{31}$	−0.0085	0.0029	0.0172	0.0984
	(0.0102)	(0.0363)	(0.0161)	(0.0398)
Predicted preferred stock sold to RFC	1.850E-09 (1.540E-09)	−2.010E-08 (5.484E-09)	−1.244E-08 (2.432E-09)	1.169E-08 (6.012E-09)
No. of observations	144	144	144	144
R^2	0.0155	0.0869	0.1643	0.0624
Adjusted R^2	0.0016	0.074	0.1525	0.0492

Notes: Amounts are coefficients; standard errors are in parentheses.

assistance between March 1933 and December 1934 and those that did not. Most of this assistance was provided in late 1933. Table 14.12 compares mean bank characteristics of recipients and nonrecipients prior to, and subsequent to, preferred stock purchases. Clearly, preferred stock recipients (with average failure probabilities of 0.056) were much more at risk of failure as of 1933 than nonrecipients (with average failure probabilities of 0.021). Recipients' probabilities of failure fell faster than those of nonrecipients from 1933 to 1934, and that relative decline in risk reflected much greater reductions in dividend payout, much greater contraction of total assets in 1934, and a lesser decline in capital-to-asset ratios.

Table 14.13 examines the role of preferred stock conditionality on bank choice of capital ratios and dividend payout more formally. Panel A is a first-stage regression predicting preferred stock assistance. Panel B is the second-stage regression analyzing the effect of preferred stock assistance on banks' choices of dividends and capital ratios (using a Heckman correction to control for the endogeneity of the preferred stock assistance). The last two columns of panel *B* show that receiving preferred stock assistance significantly increases banks' capital ratios and reduces their dividend payout. These results confirm that banks that received preferred stock assistance were effectively constrained in the extent to which their stockholders could transfer risk to the RFC.

RFC preferred-stock assistance was a way to help banks smooth the adjustment process toward low default risk. It insulated banks from the threat of sudden deposit withdrawal by reducing deposit default risk, but substituted RFC discipline for market discipline to ensure that banks adopted prudent long-run risk management and capital accumulation policies.

14.3   Recent Japanese Experience

The Japanese banking collapse of the 1990s occurred in a very different institutional context from that of the U.S. banking collapse of the Great Depression. The existence of implicit deposit insurance protection (which was made explicit in the 1990s) meant that Japanese bank depositors were little concerned about the potential loss of deposits placed in Japanese banks, and therefore had scant incentive to exercise discipline on banks.

Additionally, Japanese banks have much closer relationships with affiliated firms than American banks have had traditionally, and Japanese banks own substantial equity positions in those firms. That complicates the valuation of Japanese bank loan holdings, since banks may have special obligations or incentives to absorb loan losses in ways that are not transparent from an examination of balance sheet data. For example, Sheard (1989) argues that main banks provide implicit insurance to other creditors that participate in loans to their client firms. And there have been some recent claims that equity investments in Japanese banks by client firms may represent "fictitious capital" in the sense that bank borrowers may be encouraged to buy capital in exchange for continuing credit access (which amounts to banks' lending money for the purpose of financing the purchase of bank stock).

Furthermore, reflecting the absence of market pressures on banks to provide informative signals to private debtholders, Japanese accounting practices today are quite different from American banks' accounting practices in the 1930s, and much less informative of actual bank condition. For all these reasons, the value of Japanese bank investments (loans, stocks, and other assets) reported on balance sheets provides a poorer indication of true value than do American bank accounts of the 1930s.

Indeed, the broad range of recent estimates of the amount of bad Japanese bank loans and the likely recovery rates on those loans illustrate how difficult it is to glean reality from reported statistics. As of the end of May 2001, the official estimate of outstanding financial-sector nonperforming loans was ¥34,000 billion, but Goldman Sachs calculated at that time that in the "worst-case scenario" nonperforming loans could be as high as ¥63,000 billion. Bank insolvency and the extent of negative bank net worth in the United States during the 1930s were relatively easy to observe because market discipline forced insolvent banks to fail. In Japan, however, "zombie" banks (to use the expression coined by Ed Kane) can continue almost indefinitely, and it is very hard to measure their insolvency.

Another important difference between the U.S. Depression experience and the current Japanese context is the duration of bank distress, the seemingly endless waves of increasing bank loan losses that plague Japanese banks. By most accounts, Japanese banks have been inadequately capitalized for a decade, and many have been insolvent for more than five years.

Japanese bank loan write-downs totaled ¥10 trillion a year in both 1997 and 1998, when Japanese banks began to write down loan losses in earnest. In 1999, two of the most informed authorities on Japanese bank accounts and solvency, Takeo Hoshi and Hugh Patrick (2000, 20), thought that Japanese banks had turned a corner: "Late 1998 and early 1999 was a significant turning point. The 'crisis' in the banking system is finally over, though most banks still have substantial restructuring problems. Japan is now in the process of building a new financial system." Yet loan write-downs in 1999 and 2000 were roughly ¥4.5 trillion in each year. And despite these formidable write-downs, Japanese bank losses have continued to grow, as new nonperforming loans replace those that were previously written down.

This continuing growth in nonperforming loans reflects new deterioration in asset values and deflationary monetary policy, as well as previously unrecognized earlier losses. After a decade of flat growth and shrinking asset prices, Japan is now seen by many observers as poised at the precipice of economic collapse. Japan, like the United States in the early 1930s, has been caught in a deflationary trap, albeit a much longer-lived one. Deflation weakens firms' and banks' balance sheets, producing further weakening of aggregate demand, and further deflation (Irving Fisher's debt-deflation cycle).

The combination of government protection and a deflationary environment also affects bank strategies toward loan liquidation. In the current environment, the backlog of unresolved loans and weak corporate and bank balance sheets have created a massive liquidity premium in asset pricing. Ten-year bonds yield under 1 percent while stock prices and real estate prices continue to slip. Banks, particularly in a regime of government deposit insurance, have little incentive to hurry to liquidate the assets of their distressed borrowers, especially since banks are shareholders in many of these firms. Making matters worse is the historical absence of bankruptcy or liquidation procedures, which makes orderly liquidation even more challenging. Thus the backlog continues alongside continuing deflation and deepening loan losses.

Banks have received substantial assistance from the government. In addition to anemic early programs to purchase bad loans from banks—an initiative that so far has not produced much incentive for rational disposal of bad loans (see Packer 2000)—the government has offered financial assistance to banks twice, in March 1998 and March 1999. Table 14.14 summarizes the amounts and types of assistance, and the terms and conditions of that assistance. Like the RFC, the Japanese government began to offer assistance primarily in the form of loans and debt purchases, and subsequently came to rely almost exclusively on preferred stock purchases (see also Cargill, Hutchison, and Ito 2000).

The new prime minister, Mr. Koizumi, promises painful structural reform of government expenditure policy, and talks of the need to accelerate bank loan write-downs, which he says are the keys to rebuilding the Japanese economy. Some speculate that more preferred stock assistance will be forthcoming to help spur debt write-downs. But nowhere in sight (given the current Bank of Japan leadership) is there a credible commitment to ending deflationary monetary policy. Without that change, bank balance sheets will continue to deteriorate and banks will continue to postpone liquidation in the hope that they can profit from future improvements in macroeconomic circumstances (the "real option" incentive problem described in Mason 2002).

14.3.1   Regulatory Discipline: a Substitute for Market Discipline?

Figures 14.10 through 14.11 provide a picture of bank capital and lending behavior that differs greatly from the patterns shown in figures 14.3 and 14.4. The differences between Japanese lending behavior and that of the United States in the 1930s is even greater when one takes into account the understatement of Japanese capital losses during the early and mid-1990s. Japanese bank-lending ratios grew substantially from 1995 to 1997 as Japanese bank capital ratios plummeted. The mid-1990s saw substantial increases in Japanese lending elsewhere in Asia, which some observers have characterized as a search for ways to increase loan risk in order to take full advantage of the implicit put option value of government protection. After 1997, bank losses were too large and too visible to continue the masquerade of denial, and international and domestic pressures came to bear on the Japanese government to recognize loan losses and to restrict bank lending accordingly.

Figure 14.12 tells a somewhat similar story through the window of the bank market-to-book value of equity ratio, weighted by bank asset size. The expansion of asset risk in 1996 boosted the market value of bank capital (which incorporates the value of the implicit put option). Since 1997,

Table 14.14 **Approved Conditions for Public Funds Injection into Japanese Banks**

	Total Amount	Convertible Preferred Stock	Period until Conversion Can Be Done (Years)	Dividend Yield (%)	Subordinated Bonds or Loans
		A. March 1999			
Daiwa	408	408	0.25	1.06	0
Chao Trust	150	150	0.25	0.90	0
Mitsui Trust	400.2	250.2	0.25	1.25	150
Sakura	800	800	3.50	1.33	0
Fuji	1,000	250	5.50	0.40	200
		250	7.50	0.55	
		300	(nonconvertible)	2.10	
Sumitomo Trust	200	100	2.00	0.76	100
Mitsubishi Trust	300	200	4.33	0.81	100
Toyo Trust	200	200	0.25	1.15	0
Bank of Yokohama	200	70	2.33	1.13	100
		30	5.33	1.89	
Asahi	500	300	3.25	1.15	100
		100	4.25	1.48	
Tokai	600	300	3.25	0.93	0
		300	4.25	0.97	
Sumitomo	501	201	3.08	0.35	0
		300	6.33	0.95	
DKB	900	200	5.33	0.41	200
		200	6.33	0.70	
		300	(nonconvertible)	2.38	
IBJ	600	175	4.25	0.43	250
		175	4.42	1.40	
Sanwa	700	600	2.25	0.53	100
Total	7,459	6,159			1,300

	Type of Issuance	Amount (Billion Yen)
	B. March 1998	
Nippon Credit Bank	Preferred stock	60
Ashikaga Bank	Perpetual subordinated bonds	30
Daiwa	Perpetual subordinated loans	100
Yasuda Trust	Perpetual subordinated bonds	150
LTCB 1	Perpetual subordinated loans	46.6
LTCB 2	Preferred stock	130
Chuo Trust 1	Perpetual subordinated loans	28
Chuo Trust 2	Preferred stock	32
Hokuriku Bank	Perpetual subordinated loans	20
Mitsui Trust	Perpetual subordinated bonds	100
Sakura	Perpetual subordinated bonds	100
Fuji	Perpetual subordinated bonds	100
Sumitomo Trust	Perpetual subordinated bonds	100
Mitsubishi Trust	Perpetual subordinated bonds	50
Toyo Trust	Perpetual subordinated bonds	50

(*continued*)

Table 14.14   (continued)

	Type of Issuance	Amount (Billion Yen)
Bank of Yokohama	Perpetual subordinated loans	20
Asahi	Perpetual subordinated loans	100
Tokai	Perpetual subordinated loans	100
Sumitomo	Perpetual subordinated bonds	100
Bank of Tokyo–Mitsubishi	Perpetual subordinated bonds	100
DKB	Preferred stock	99
IBJ	Subordinated bonds (fixed periods)	100
Sanwa	Subordinated bonds (fixed periods)	100
Total		1,726

Source: Nikkei Shinbun (13, 18 March 1998, and 5, 13 March 1999)

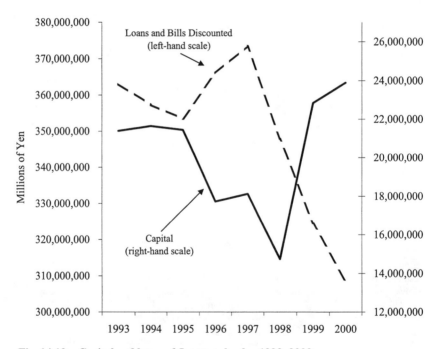

Fig. 14.10   Capital and loans of Japanese banks, 1993–2000
Source: Japanese Bankers Association.

the combination of loan losses and restrictions on bank lending have caused the ratio of the market-to-book value of equity to plummet.

That is not to say that banks have been effectively constrained by regulators in their pursuit of increased asset risk. Nobu Hibara (2001) finds that regulatory capital standards have effectively linked bank loans to the total amount of book capital. Nevertheless, banks in the weakest condition (for

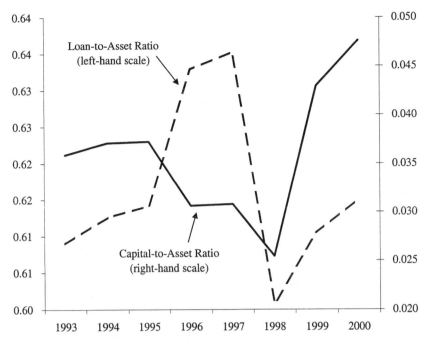

Fig. 14.11   Capital-to-asset and loan-to-asset ratios of Japanese banks, 1993–2000

Source: Japanese Bankers Association.

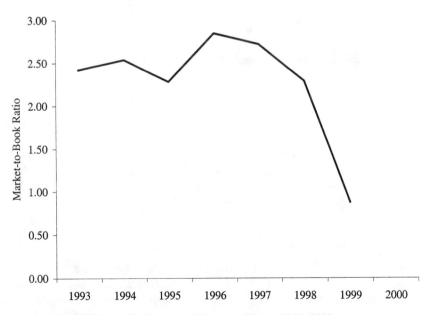

Fig. 14.12   Market-to-book ratios of Japanese banks, 1993–2000

Source: Japanese Bankers Association.

Table 14.15   **Japanese Bank Dividend Payments for Stable Sample of Banks, 1993–2001**

Year	Dividends	Payout Ratio
1993	135,617	0.74
1994	135,108	0.73
1995	134,981	0.74
1996	111,450	0.76
1997	128,939	0.86
1998	147,791	1.15
1999	106,206	0.53
2000	144,486	0.69
2001	156,532	n.a.

Source: Japanese Bankers Association.
Note: n.a. = not available.

whom the put option of government protection is most valuable) gravitate toward the lowest-quality loans, and boost asset risk by increasing the riskiness of their loan portfolios.

To what extent has government assistance in March 1998 and March 1999 been targeted to banks with the best franchises, and to what extent has it been linked to effective conditionality that limits banks' ability to transfer risk to the government? The evidence in table 14.14 indicates that the Japanese government did not try to target assistance selectively. Virtually every bank of any significant size received preferred stock assistance. If anything, it appears that the weakest Japanese banks (Nippon Credit and Long-Term Credit Bank [LTCB]) were the earliest (1998) recipients of preferred stock purchases. Due to the small sample of banks and the uncertain quality of the balance sheet data, we were not able to perform a satisfactory analysis of the differences in condition between banks that received preferred stock assistance and those that did not.

Table 14.15 and figure 14.13 plot dividend payments by banks from 1993 to 2001. Interestingly, dividend payments fell dramatically in 1999, but then more than rebounded. Thus, as Japanese banks continued to experience rising loan losses and declines in equity capital, they kept sending much of the cash inflow that they received from the government in 1998 and 1999 to their shareholders. Clearly, this is at odds with the purpose of a preferred stock purchase program.

14.4 Policy Implications

The essential point of our comparison of U.S. banks in the 1930s and Japanese banks in the 1990s is that, in the historical case, assistance to banks occurred within a context of market discipline, and the conditions attached to government assistance helped to strengthen market discipline.

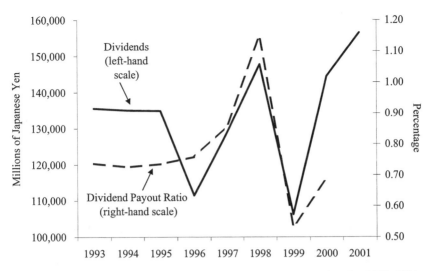

Fig. 14.13   Japanese bank dividend payments for stable sample of banks, 1993–2001
Source: Japanese Bankers Association.

In the current Japanese case, in contrast, assistance was offered within the context of an absence of market discipline, and there is little evidence that conditions attached to assistance have encouraged banks to move toward effective long-run risk management. That failure reflects in part the relative extremity of Japanese bank distress, and in part, the lack of incentives of Japanese banks to limit the transference of risk to the government.

Is it possible, in the current protected environment, for government to find a way of providing a credible combination of financial assistance to banks and conditionality that limits the abuse of that assistance? We think it is possible to apply the lessons of the RFC to contemporary assistance programs.

Doing so requires the adoption of three related and mutually reinforcing means of limiting bank abuse of protection: (1) designing programs of assistance that are selective, and are thus able to target financial assistance to banks that are worth preserving; (2) specifying clear, quantifiable rules that limit access to preferred stock assistance and that tie assistance to effective risk management by recipient banks; and (3) enacting new, ongoing capital regulation that establishes meaningful standards for risk-based capital.

With respect to selectivity, Calomiris (1998, 1999) suggests using a common stock issuance matching requirement to encourage the best banks to "self-select" to participate in subsidized preferred-stock purchases. That approach would attract capital-impaired but relatively healthy banks with high franchise values, but discourage deeply insolvent banks from applying for government subsidies. Those banks' stockholders would be unable to qualify for subsidized preferred-stock purchases because they would be unable to find willing purchasers of new matching common-stock offerings. The beauty of this self-selection mechanism is that it brings market judgments to bear on the allocation of scarce government funds. It does not require the government to pick and choose; the same preferred stock purchase program would be available to all banks, but not all would be able to participate.

Limits on common stock dividend payments, among other conditions attached to preferred stock purchases, are an obvious way to encourage banks to use the new lease on life granted by government protection to rebuild their capital, rather than to engage in strategies that maximize the option value of deposit insurance.

Emergency assistance to banks should be linked to a phasing in of credible capital regulation. Effective risk-based capital regulation would protect taxpayers' investments in bank preferred stock and limit taxpayer liability for insured deposits in rescued banks. It would also restore effective discipline on bank risk management in the future by eliminating incentives for risk arbitrage.

Effective capital regulation must provide a credible and flexible means to measure the riskiness of bank positions and the adequacy of bank capital. Thus, bank capital regulation must focus on ways to incorporate market signals about underlying bank risk into the regulatory process. Calomiris (1997, 1999) and Shadow Financial Regulatory Committee (2000) have argued that a subordinated debt requirement (which can be structured to take account of the particular types of debt instruments that are available in each country) is an essential part of an effective capital requirement (see also Calomiris and Powell 2001). A minimum ratio of subordinated debt relative to bank assets would ensure that, on the margin, someone bears the default risk of bank debt. That would make banks care about limiting their default risk in order to maintain the requisite outstanding issues of subordinated debt. Furthermore, the observed market yield on subordinated debt would be of great value to regulators for measuring and enforcing capital adequacy standards. A visible public signal of bank health would provide supervisors with new information. Even more important, by making bank weakness publicly observable, it would promote greater accountability of supervisors and regulators and undermine the destructive phenomenon of regulatory "forbearance."

Of course, effective bank regulatory policy by itself cannot make a healthy banking system (see Cargill, Hutchison, and Ito 1997). Stable monetary and fiscal policy are necessary preconditions for healthy banks. In some countries, a lack of fiscal discipline makes banks prey to attacks on currency pegs. In other cases, including the United States in the early 1930s and Japan today, banking system recovery is dependent on bringing deflationary monetary policy to an end.

References

Anari, Ali, James Kolari, and Joseph R. Mason. 2003. Bank asset liquidation and the propagation of the Great Depression. *Journal of Money, Credit, and Banking,* forthcoming. Rev. version of Wharton Financial Institutions Working Paper no. 02-35 (August 2002).

Baer, Herbert L., and John N. McElravey. 1993. Capital shocks and bank growth. *Federal Reserve Bank of Chicago Economic Perspectives* 17 (4): 2–21.

Barth, James, Gerard Caprio Jr., and Ross Levine. 2001. Prudential regulation and supervision: What works best? World Bank Working Paper no. 2725. Washington, D.C.: World Bank.

Beim, David O., and Charles W. Calomiris. 2001. *Emerging financial markets.* New York: McGraw-Hill.

Bernanke, Ben S. 1983. Nonmonetary effects of the financial crisis in the propagation of the Great Depression. *American Economic Review* 73 (June): 257–276.

Board of Governors of the Federal Reserve System. 1937. *Federal Reserve bulletin,* September. Washington, D.C.: Federal Reserve.

Boyd, John, Pedro Gomis, Sungkyu Kwak, and Bruce Smith. 2000. A user's guide to banking crises. University of Minnesota, Department of Economics. Working Paper.

Calomiris, Charles W. 1989. Deposit insurance: Lessons from the record. *Federal Reserve Bank of Chicago Economic Perspectives* 13 (3): 10–30.

———. 1990. Is deposit insurance necessary? *Journal of Economic History* 50 (2): 283–295.

———. 1997. *The postmodern bank safety net.* Washington, D.C.: American Enterprise Institute.

———. 1998. Revitalizing ailing banks. *Nikko Capital Trends* 3 (May): 3, 10.

———. 1999. Building an incentive-compatible safety net. *Journal of Banking and Finance* 23 (October): 1499–1519.

———. 2000. *U.S. bank deregulation in historical perspective.* Cambridge: Cambridge University Press.

———. 2001. Victorian perspectives on the banking collapses of the 1980s and 1990s. Columbia University, Graduate School of Business. Working Paper.

Calomiris, Charles W., and Mark S. Carey. 1994. Loan market competition between foreign and domestic banks: Some facts about loans and borrowers. In *Proceedings of the thirtieth annual conference on Bank Structure and Competition,* 331–351. Chicago: Federal Reserve Bank of Chicago.

Calomiris, Charles W., and Gary Gorton. 1991. The origins of banking panics: Models, facts, and bank regulation. In *Financial markets and financial crises,* ed. R. Glenn Hubbard, 109–173. Chicago: University of Chicago Press.

Calomiris, Charles W., and Charles M. Kahn. 1991. The role of demandable debt in structuring optimal banking arrangements. *American Economic Review* 81 (June): 497–513.

Calomiris, Charles W., and Joseph R. Mason. 1997. Contagion and bank failures during the Great Depression: The June 1932 Chicago banking panic. *American Economic Review* 87 (December): 863–883.

———. 2003a. Consequences of bank distress during the Great Depression. *American Economic Review,* forthcoming.

———. 2003b. Fundamentals, panics, and bank distress during the Depression. *American Economic Review,* forthcoming. NBER Working Paper no. 7919, September 2000.

Calomiris, Charles W., and Andrew Powell. 2001. Can emerging market bank regulators establish credible discipline? The case of Argentina, 1992–1999. Chapter 4 in *Prudential supervision,* ed. F. S. Mishkin. Chicago: University of Chicago Press.

Calomiris, Charles W., and David C. Wheelock. 1998. Was the Great Depression a watershed for American monetary policy? In *The defining moment: The Great Depression and the American economy in the twentieth century,* ed. M. Bordo, C. Goldin, and E. N. White, 23–66. Chicago: University of Chicago Press.

Calomiris, Charles W., and Eugene N. White. 1994. The origins of federal deposit insurance. In *The regulated economy: A historical approach to political economy,* ed. Claudia Goldin and Gary Libecap, 145–188. Chicago: University of Chicago Press.

Calomiris, Charles W., and Berry Wilson. 2003. Bank capital and portfolio management: The 1930s "capital crunch" and scramble to shed risk. *Journal of Business,* forthcoming. Rev. version of NBER Working Paper no. 6649, July 1998.

Caprio, Gerard, Jr., and Daniela Klingabiel. 1996a. Bank insolvencies: Cross-country experience. World Bank Working Paper no. 1620. Washington, D.C.: World Bank.

———. 1996b. Bank insolvency: Bad luck, bad policy, or bad banking? Paper prepared for the World Bank's Annual Bank Conference on Development Economics. 10–13 April, Washington, D.C.

Cargill, Thomas F., Michael M. Hutchison, and Takatoshi Ito. 1997. *The political economy of Japanese monetary policy.* Cambridge: MIT Press.

———. 2000. *Financial policy and central banking in Japan.* Cambridge: MIT Press.

Cho, Hyo Won. 1953. The evolution of the functions of the Reconstruction Finance Corporation: A study of the growth and death of a federal lending agency. Ph.D. diss. Ohio State University.

Commercial and Financial Chronicle. 1933. New York: William B. Dana Company.

Comptroller of the Currency. Various issues. *Annual report.* Washington, D.C.: GPO.

Cull, Robert, Lemma W. Senbet, and Marco Sorge. 2000. Deposit insurance and financial development. World Bank Working Paper no. 2682. Washington, D.C.: World Bank.

Delaney, John A. 1954. Field administration in the Reconstruction Finance Corporation. Ph.D. diss. George Washington University.

Demirguc-Kunt, Asli, and Enrica Detragiache. 2000. Does deposit insurance increase banking system stability? World Bank Working Paper no. 2247. Washington, D.C.: World Bank.

Demirguc-Kunt, Asli, and Harry Huizinga. 2000. Market discipline and financial safety net design. World Bank Working Paper no. 2183. Washington, D.C.: World Bank.

Demirguc-Kunt, Asli, Ross Levine, and Hong-Ghi Min. 1998. Opening to foreign banks: Issues of stability, efficiency, and growth. In *Proceedings of the Bank of Korea Conference on the Implications of Globalization of World Financial Markets,* ed. Seongtae Lee, 83–105. Seoul: Bank of Korea.

Eichengreen, Barry. 1992. *Golden fetters: The gold standard and the Great Depression, 1919–1939.* New York: Oxford University Press.

Eichengreen, Barry, and Jeffrey D. Sachs. 1985. Exchange rates and economic recovery in the 1930s. *Journal of Economic History* 45 (December): 925–946.

Fisher, Irving. 1933. The debt-deflation theory of great depressions. *Econometrica* 1 (October): 337–357.

Friedman, Milton, and Anna J. Schwartz. 1963. *A monetary history of the United States, 1867–1960.* Princeton, N.J.: Princeton University Press.

Gorton, Gary, and George Pennacchi. 1990. Financial intermediaries and liquidity creation. *Journal of Finance* 45 (March): 49–72.

Haubrich, Joseph G. 1990. Nonmonetary effects of financial crises: Lessons from the Great Depression in Canada. *Journal of Monetary Economics* 25 (March): 223–252.

Hibara, Nobu. 2001. What happens in banking crises? Moral hazard vs. the credit crunch. Columbia Business School, Department of Economics and Finance. Working Paper, June.

Honohan, Patrick, and Daniela Klingabiel. 2000. Controlling fiscal costs of banking crises. World Bank Working Paper no. 2441. Washington, D.C.: World Bank.

Hoshi, Takeo, and Hugh Patrick, eds. 2000. *Crisis and change in the Japanese financial system.* Boston: Kluwer Academic Publishers.

James, Cyril F. 1938. *The growth of Chicago Banks.* New York: Harper & Brothers.

Kane, Edward. 1998. Capital movements, asset values, and banking policy in globalized markets. NBER Working Paper no. 6633. Cambridge, Mass.: National Bureau of Economic Research.

Krueger, Anne O., and Jungho Yoo. 2001. *Chaebol* capitalism and the currency-financial crisis in Korea. Paper presented at the NBER Conference on Currency Crises Prevention. 11–13 January, Islamorada, Florida.

Mason, Joseph R. 1996. The determinants and effects of Reconstruction Finance Corporation assistance to banks during the Great Depression. Ph.D. diss. University of Illinois, Department of Economics.

———. 2001a. Do lender of last resort policies matter? The effects of Reconstruction Finance Corporation assistance to banks during the Great Depression. *Journal of Financial Services Research* 20 (September): 77–95.

———. 2001b. Reconstruction Finance Corporation assistance to financial intermediaries and commercial and industrial enterprises in the U.S., 1932–1937. In *Resolving financial distress,* ed. Stijn Claessens, Simeon Djankov, and Oshaka Mody, 167–204. Washington, D.C.: World Bank.

———. 2002. A real options approach to bankruptcy costs: Evidence from failed commercial banks during the 1990s. Wharton Financial Institutions Center Working Paper no. 02-20, March. Forthcoming, *Journal of Business.*

———. 2003. The political economy of Reconstruction Finance Corporation assistance during the Great Depression. *Explorations in Economic History* 40 (April): 101–121.

Olson, James S. 1972. The end of voluntarism: Herbert Hoover and the National Credit Corporation. *Annals of Iowa* 41 (Fall): 1104–13.

———. 1977. *Herbert Hoover and the Reconstruction Finance Corporation, 1931–1933.* Ames: Iowa State University Press.

———. 1988. *Saving capitalism.* Princeton, N.J.: Princeton University Press.

Packer, Frank. 2000. The disposal of bad loans in Japan: The case of the CCPC. In *Crisis and change in the Japanese financial system,* ed. Takeo Hoshi and Hugh Patrick, 137–157. Boston: Kluwer Academic Publishers.

RFC Circular no. 1. 1932. Washington, D.C.: GPO.

Shadow Financial Regulatory Committee. 2000. *Reforming bank capital regulation.* Washington, D.C.: American Enterprise Institute.

Sheard, Paul. 1989. The main bank system and corporate monitoring and control in Japan. *Journal of Economic Behavior and Organization* 11:399–422.

Temin, Peter. 1989. *Lessons from the Great Depression.* Cambridge: MIT Press.

Upham, Cyril B., and Edwin Lamke. 1934. *Closed and distressed banks: A study in public administration.* Washington, D.C.: Brookings Institution.

U.S. Bureau of the Census. 1975. *Historical statistics of the United States, colonial times to 1970.* Washington, D.C.: GPO.

Wheelock, David C. 1991. *The strategy and consistency of Federal Reserve monetary policy, 1924–1933.* Cambridge: Cambridge University Press.
White, Eugene N. 1986. Before the Glass-Steagall Act: An analysis of the investment banking activities of national banks. *Explorations in Economic History* 23 (January): 33–55.
Wicker, Elmus. 1996. *The banking panics of the Great Depression.* Cambridge: Cambridge University Press.

Comment   Simon Johnson

This is a thought-provoking paper that should be read carefully by anyone thinking about either banking crises or—topical for the United States today—the causes and effects of collapses in any highly leveraged firm (such as Enron). If anything, the implications of this paper are considerably wider than even the authors realize.

The main focus of the paper is on the canonical case of systemic bank failure: the United States in the 1930s. This rightly remains the benchmark for all models of where collapses come from and how they spread. The authors draw on their important recent papers on this subject and summarize the key findings clearly. At the same time, they extend these ideas to the fascinating case of Japan since the late 1980s.

The authors' argument falls into two parts. First, they argue that there were fewer crises before the advent of bank regulation. In large part this was probably due to better monitoring by the "market," in particular by large depositors who had both a real interest in watching banks carefully and the ability to trigger moves by other, smaller depositors. Particularly intriguing is the idea that banking assistance in the United States during the 1930s had a much greater component of "market discipline" than has been the case in Japan recently.

Second, the authors extend this reasoning to think clearly about the right way to run bank bailouts. In their scheme, the government would buy preferred stock but only if the "market" buys matching common stock. Again, the emphasis is on engaging the private sector in effective monitoring. Their other proposals, such as requiring a minimum ratio of subordinated debt relative to bank assets, are along similar lines.

The evidence in favor of these ideas is strong. For the United States in the 1930s, the authors are fully persuasive. Real shocks hit firms, then spread to banks and created small panics. The problems were exacerbated by deflationary monetary policies, helping to trigger larger bank failures

Simon Johnson is the Ronald A. Kurtz Associate Professor at the Sloan School of Management, Massachusetts Institute of Technology, and a faculty research fellow of the National Bureau of Economic Research.

and a decline in the availability of credit. However, the U.S. authorities were able to develop policies that complemented pressure from the market in forcing banks to improve their performance.

Japan in the 1990s experienced similar problems but developed much less effective solutions. An initial asset price stock had a negative impact on firms and banks. Again, the effects were worsened by a deflationary monetary policy, pushing the economy into a long-term recession. In this case, however, the regulator has repeatedly provided additional capital to banks without sufficient pressure to change performance (or the involvement of any real market forces).

These ideas are relevant to a range of issues around the world today. In particular, the authors highlight the importance of combining market pressure and strong "institutions"—that is, the public regulations that govern private economic relationships. In their scheme, the market needs to know what is really going on at banks. There must be some form of effective securities regulation, forcing the disclosure of information. There must also be sufficiently strong corporate law, in order for shareholders to exercise their rights. There surely also needs to be a judiciary that can enforce contracts. What is the precise combination of institutions necessary, at a minimum, to make market-based restructuring feasible? This is an important issue for further theoretical and empirical work.

Looking at the issues from the other side, what if there is no real regulator or no enforceable regulation? To what extent can the market solve or prevent banking problems completely by itself? For example, in countries such as Russia, Turkey, and Mexico, there has been a real struggle during the 1990s to establish effective securities and banking regulation. Recent Korean experience definitely indicates that "market-based" solutions require strong institutions.

Thinking just about variation within the United States, it seems clear that market pressures are quite effective at controlling the banking system and handling bank-specific difficulties as they arise. The market is much less effective at dealing with highly leveraged nonbanks, such as long-term capital management (LTCM) and Enron. At least in part, this difference must be due to the fact that the disclosure of information and accounting standards are much tougher (in the sense of really being enforced) for banks than for nonbank firms with large-scale investments in derivatives.

In fact, there appears to be a dangerous loophole in current U.S. regulations—pure banks and traditional firms (publicly listed) are well regulated and watched effectively by the market. But hybrid bank-firms can accumulate large levels of leverage, avoid effective regulation, and play the market against itself in ways that prevent effective supervision of any kind. Clearly agency problems inside accounting firms and large investment banks play an important role, although we need more research to understand precisely how.

More generally, how should we think of the Calomiris and Mason line of research? Is it just about banks or are they addressing much bigger issues about the organization of capitalism? In my view, this work should be seen as central to the rapidly developing literature on the real effects of institutions.

Institutions appear to matter for long-term economic development. For example, Acemoglu, Johnson, and Robinson (2001) show that the way in which countries were colonized has had persistent effects on their income per capita over the very long run. Recent work by La Porta et al. (1997, 1998, 1999) has also established that law matters for the level of investor protection, for financial development, and for the quality of governmental institutions. A large finance literature extends and tests these ideas.

The rules governing financial arrangements may also matter for short-run macroeconomic outcomes. Rajan and Zingales (1998) argue that in large part the Asian financial crisis was due to the combination of free capital flows and weak institutions. More generally, Blanchard (2000) suggests that economies with different institutions may experience different short-run macroeconomic patterns, such as more or less severe crises in response to similar shocks (see also Rodrik 1999). In addition, institutions that were once effective in supporting productive activities may decline in relevance or even become a problem, as Olson (1982) argued. Evidence in favor of Olson's idea is growing—see, for example, Morck, Strangeland, and Yeung (2000) and Johnson and Mitton (2003).

Calomiris and Mason's research confirms that financial regulation should be regarded as a central piece of any country's institutions. Their main contribution, in my view, is to emphasize that market-based monitoring can be effective only if combined with effective regulation. Conversely, effective regulation may work only to the extent that it is combined with and builds on what powerful market participants can do and want to do. This fits well with recent evidence from Eastern Europe (see Glaeser, Johnson, and Shleifer 2001).

The research question before us now is precisely how to integrate these literatures. How much regulation is enough for a country like the United States or like Russia? What exactly are the links between institutions in general, corporate governance in particular, and macroeconomic dynamics? In countries with weak institutions, how should the development of financial markets best be integrated with the development of financial regulation?

References

Acemoglu, Daron, Simon Johnson, and Jim Robinson. 2001. The colonial origins of comparative development: An empirical investigation. *American Economic Review* 91 (5): 1369–401.

Blanchard, Olivier. 2000. What do we know about macroeconomics that Fisher and Wicksell did not? *Quarterly Journal of Economics* 115 (November): 1375–410.

Glaeser, Edward, Simon Johnson, and Andrei Shleifer. 2001. Coase versus the Coasians. *Quarterly Journal of Economics* 116 (3): 853–900.

Johnson, Simon, and Todd Mitton. 2003. Cronyism and capital controls: Evidence from Malaysia. *Journal of Financial Economics* 67 (2): 351–382.

La Porta, Rafael, Florencio Lopez-de-Silanes, Andrei Shleifer, and Robert Vishny. 1997. Legal determinants of external finance. *Journal of Finance* 52:1131–50.

———. 1988. Law and finance. *Journal of Political Economy* 106:1113–55.

———. 1999. The quality of government. *Journal of Law, Economics, and Organization* 15:222–279.

Morck, Randall, David Strangeland, and Bernard Yeung. 2000. Inherited wealth, corporate control, and economic growth: The Canadian disease? In *Concentrated corporate ownership,* ed. R. Morck, 319–369. Chicago: University of Chicago Press.

Olson, Mancur. 1982. *The rise and decline of nations.* New Haven, Conn.: Yale University Press.

Rajan, Raghuram G., and Luigi Zingales. 1998. Which capitalism? Lessons from the East Asian crisis. *Journal of Applied Corporate Finance* 11:40–48.

Rodrik, Dani. 1999. Where did all the growth go? External shocks, social conflict, and growth collapses. *Journal of Economic Growth* 4 (4): 385–412.

Banks, Bailout Guarantees, and Risky Debt

Aaron Tornell

15.1 Introduction

During the last decade several emerging markets have experienced twin currency and banking crises. The blame for these crises has been laid at the feet of the policies that have been implemented since the late 1980s. Critics have charged that financial liberalization and bank privatization have been associated with bailout guarantees, and therefore have led to excessive risk taking and overinvestment that have fueled lending booms, inflated asset prices, and rendered economies prone to crises.

The central theme of this paper is that even if we accept that bailout guarantees are the inevitable consequence of financial liberalization, it does not follow that the liberalization policies were doomed to fail. We will argue that in a world where firms are credit constrained, bailout guarantees can be turned into a growth-enhancing vehicle, provided they are accompanied by the right set of policies. Such policies include those aimed at minimizing incentive problems, including rules that ensure bailouts are to be granted only in the event of a systemic crisis and not on an idiosyncratic basis. Also, an efficient regulatory framework is necessary so that banks will perform their monitoring function properly, and connected lending will not exist.

The reforms of the late 1980s liberalized trade and financial markets in many emerging markets. These reforms also brought a significant reduction in the role of the state in the economy. Suddenly, the future looked much brighter than before, and the private sector much smaller than what was desirable. Unfortunately, legal and judicial reform could not be implemented as easily as the other reforms. As a result, many of the institutions

Aaron Tornell is professor of economics at the University of California, Los Angeles, and a faculty research fellow of the National Bureau of Economic Research.

that support the provision of external finance in developed economies did not flourish in emerging markets. Large firms in the tradables sector could finance themselves in international markets. However, this option was not open to the majority of firms.

The policy problem then became how to better promote the fast development of the private sector in an environment where external finance to a majority of firms is constrained by internal funds, and where investment is too low relative to investment opportunities. One is tempted to say that if a government had the appropriate information and correct incentives, the optimal policy would be to transfer resources to those in the population with better entrepreneurial skills, and to let them make the investment decisions. Of course, we now know that this is wishful thinking. After many failed experiments of this sort carried out during the last century, we now know that either governments do not possess the appropriate information, or they are too inclined to crony capitalism and rampant corruption.

Since direct made-to-measure government transfers are not feasible, during the 1990s governments had to design second-best policies to foster the development of the private economy, especially in the nontradables sector. In many countries the decision was made to implement financial liberalization, and to privatize the banks and allow them to be the means through which resources would be channeled to the nascent private sector. A by-product (probably an unintended consequence) of these policies was the appearance of implicit bailout guarantees. As we mentioned earlier, excessive risk-taking and lending booms developed.

We will argue that the policies we have alluded to above can be considered second-best-optimal, in the sense that policymakers took sensible and calculated risks to promote rapid growth, and were unlucky. Crises were thus not the inevitable consequences of bad policy but simply bad draws that did not have to happen. They were the price that had to be paid in order to attain faster growth.[1]

In course of making this argument, we wish to emphasize five main points relating both to policies during a boom, and to policies after a crisis. First, bailout guarantees *can be* a second-best instrument to promote investment in emerging economies. Severe enforceability problems make bank credit practically the only source of external finance for most firms, especially the small ones and those in the nontradables (N) sector. In this environment many profitable investment projects cannot be undertaken because agents are credit constrained. Under some conditions, which we will describe below, bailout guarantees promote investment because they ease these borrowing constraints and provide an implicit subsidy to constrained firms.

---

1. We would like to emphasize that we will not defend some policy measures that simply mask corruption.

It is worth emphasizing that in order to have growth-enhancing effects, bailout guarantees must be "systemic," as opposed to "unconditional." The latter are granted whenever there is an individual default, like in a deposit insurance scheme. In contrast, the former are granted only if a critical mass of agents defaults. That is, it is essential that authorities can commit not to grant bailout guarantees on an idiosyncratic basis, but only in case of systemic crisis.

The second main point is that there are two preconditions for systemic bailout guarantees to have growth-enhancing effects: there must be an efficient regulatory framework in place, and the environment must be "risky" (but not too risky). We consider each in turn.

An efficient regulatory framework is needed because in the presence of bailout guarantees it is very important to limit the extent of connected loans and to prevent fraudulent activities on the part of banks. When these conditions are satisfied systemic bailout guarantees have the advantage of using the monitoring role of banks. This ensures that the implicit subsidy will be directed to those firms with profitable projects. More generally, to the extent that there is an efficient regulatory framework, systemic bailout guarantees will not generate the incentive problems that plague direct-transfer schemes.

A risky environment is necessary because the subsidy implicit in systemic bailout guarantees can be cashed-in only if there exist some states of the world in which there is a systemic crisis. In the absence of exogenous shocks that bankrupt many agents, there must be *endogenous volatility.* Lending booms and risky dollar debt can generate this endogenous volatility by making the economy susceptible to self-fulfilling crises. In fact, as a way of allowing risk into the system, dollar debt has the wonderful feature of being a good coordinating device, as it can be observed by others. It follows that if prudential regulation is introduced with the goal of minimizing risk in the banking system, for instance by forbidding N-sector firms to borrow in dollars, then the investment-enhancing effect of systemic bailout guarantees might be blocked.

However, having a risky environment does not mean that a crisis has to happen during the transition path. In fact, the likelihood of crisis must be small, or otherwise systemic bailout guarantees might have the unintended effect of drastically reducing productive investment. If the environment is too risky, firms will not find it profitable to invest in the first place.

In some policy circles it has been maintained that fixed exchange rate regimes make economies more susceptible to crises, among other things because they provide fewer incentives for agents to hedge their debts. The third point we make is that systemic bailout guarantees can induce the adoption of risky debt structures in fixed as well as in flexible exchange rate regimes. Guarantees may appear under different guises and need not be explicit. The precise form the bailout takes will depend on the regime. For instance, under fixed rates the bailout rate is mostly determined by the amount of reserves authorities are willing to use in order to defend the currency. In contrast, in a pure floating regime the bailout may take the form of direct transfers to agents.

Should an economy experience a bad draw while following policies to promote rapid growth, there is a question about how policymakers should react. This leads us to the fourth point. In the event of a crisis the amount of nonperforming loans increases dramatically. If the bad loans are recognized, the most likely outcome is that the government will have to take over the banking system, make a once-and-for-all bailout payment, and incur a huge fiscal cost up front. This will increase government debt and probably interest rates. On the other hand, if just a small share of nonperforming loans is recognized, the up-front bailout and fiscal cost will be low. However, this strategy might lead to evergreening and generate perverse incentives. Over time the problem might grow and the credit crunch may last longer, as the experiences of Japan and Mexico have shown.

Finally, in the aftermath of crises, countries experienced severe credit crunches. Bailing out lenders and cleaning the balance sheets of banks is not sufficient to reactivate the economy. Since a crisis wipes out a big part of entrepreneurial wealth, it is necessary to implement policies that permit firms to borrow again. Clearly, there are severe incentive problems associated with direct transfers to firms. Systemic bailout guarantees are a second-best instrument to jump-start the economy. To the extent that authorities can commit not to grant bailouts on an idiosyncratic basis and that the regulatory framework works relatively well, systemic bailout guarantees will be immune to incentive problems.

In the next section we present a short description of the Mexican experience. In section 15.3 we present the conceptual framework. Section 15.4, which is the main part of the paper, analyzes the issues we raised above.

15.2   The Mexican Experience

The experience of Mexico during the 1990s illustrates, in a rather sharp way, the dilemma faced by policymakers in the aftermath of reform. It also underlines the importance of distinguishing the differential access to external finance of tradables and nontradables sectors.

In the late 1980s Mexico implemented radical trade and financial liberalization, as well as deregulation and privatization programs. These policy measures generated the expectation of an extraordinary growth in exports after a short transition period. After decades of statism, the private sector was too small and so the relevant policy question was how to promote its rapid growth (as well as the investment in the infrastructure that would provide the services and inputs that the tradables (T) sector would need once the extraordinary future arrived). The decision was made to privatize

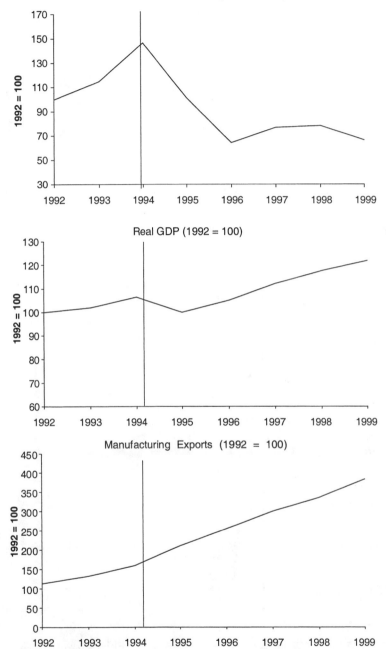

Fig. 15.1   Boom-bust cycle in Mexico

Sources: IMF (2001) and Banco de México.

Notes: Real credit from the banking system to the private sector (1992 = 100); real GDP (1992 = 100); manufacturing exports (1992 = 100).

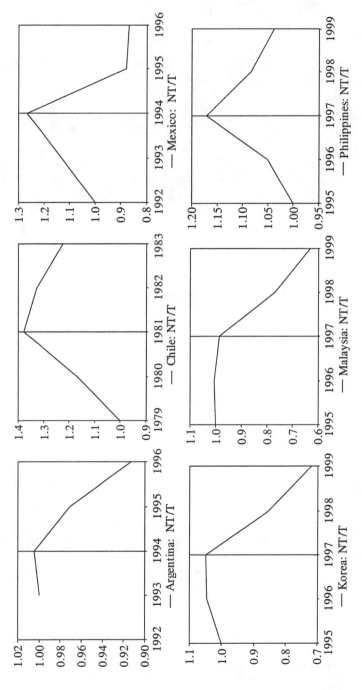

Fig. 15.2   Ratio of nontradables to tradables production

Sources: National institutions of each country.

Notes: A vertical line highlights the year of a crisis. Ratios are calculated as indexed production of construction (nontradables) to indexed production of manufacturing (tradables). The base year is two years before the date of the crisis.

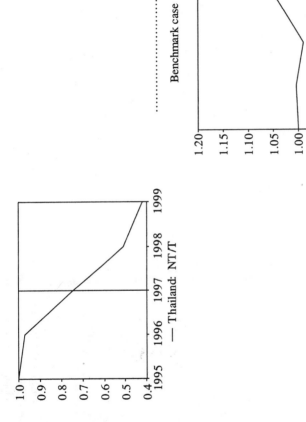

Fig. 15.2 (cont.)

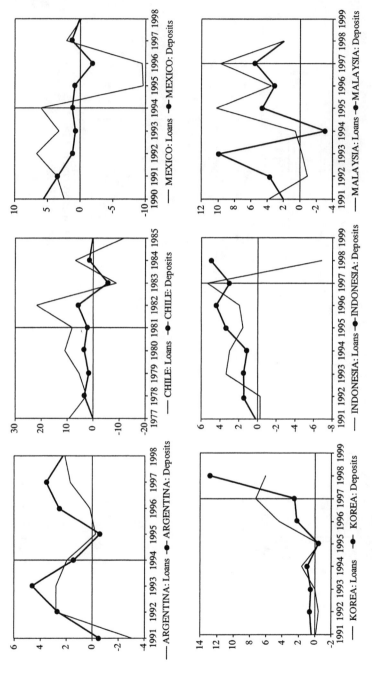

Fig. 15.3   Changes in banks' loans and deposits (percentage of GDP)

Sources: IMF (2001). Loans correspond to line 22d, and deposits is the total of lines 24 and 25.

Notes: A vertical line highlights the year of a crisis.

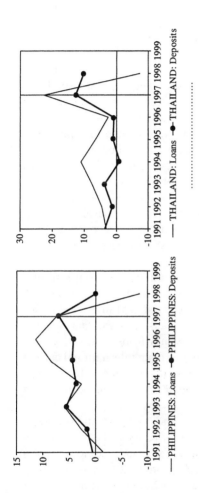

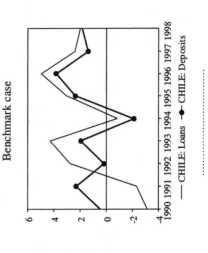

Benchmark case

Fig. 15.3 **(cont.)**

the banks and allow them to be the means through which resources would be channeled to the nascent private sector.

The expectation of an extraordinary growth in exports, as well as implicit bailout guarantees, generated privatization prices for the banks that were way above standard multiples-to-book value. As is well known, Mexico experienced a pronounced lending boom and a severe real appreciation. Between 1992 and 1994, lending from banks to the private sector increased by more than 50 percent in real terms and the real exchange rate appreciated around 15 percent.

In December 1994, the new administration of President Zedillo announced a change in the exchange rate regime and engineered a small depreciation. Although the precrisis estimates of the real appreciation did not exceed 20 percent, Mexico experienced a massive real depreciation of nearly 100 percent. As a result, many firms were unable to repay their dollar-denominated debts and the government had to implement a bailout program, known as the Fobaproa. Current estimates of the Fobaproa's costs are around 20 percent of gross domestic product (GDP).

In the aftermath of the Tequila crisis, real credit from banks to the private sector collapsed and has remained at a depressed level since then (see fig. 15.1). This stands in sharp contrast with the fast recovery of both bank deposits and aggregate real GDP. After a short recession, real GDP started to increase as early as 1996.

Aggregate GDP performance masks an asymmetric sectorial response to the crisis. While the T-sector experienced an acceleration of growth throughout the period, the N-sector experienced a sharp fall and a sluggish recuperation. This asymmetric response was caused by the fact that the credit crunch affected mainly small and medium firms in the N-sector, while firms in the T-sector could obtain finance from international capital markets. As a result, non-oil exports were not affected by the Tequila crisis. In fact, they increased at a faster rate thanks to the real depreciation and to the booming U.S. economy.

The contrasting pattern displayed by the T- and N-sectors and the credit crunch in the aftermath of crisis is not limited to Mexico. Figure 15.2 shows that in several emerging economies, the ratio of nontradables to tradables production increases before a crisis and declines in the aftermath of crisis. Figure 15.3 shows that typically there is a lending boom before a crisis, and a credit crunch in the aftermath of a crisis. This pattern is consistent with the view that the N-sector is more dependent on bank credit than the T-sector, and is prone to "balance sheet" effects induced by real depreciations.[2]

2. The figures include seven emerging economies: Argentina and Mexico, which suffered a crisis in 1995; Korea, Malaysia, the Philippines, and Thailand, which experienced a crisis in 1997; and Chile, which experienced a crisis in 1982, but did not experience any severe crisis during the 1990s, and so can be considered as a benchmark.

15.3   Conceptual Framework

In a perfectly competitive world several of the policies alluded to in the introduction are welfare reducing. However, to make an appropriate assessment one needs to take into account the context in which policies were designed and the imperfections they were supposed to counteract. The conceptual framework that one uses to evaluate policies should allow for the relevant imperfections, and explain the basic features of the boom-bust cycles that characterize emerging economies. In this paper we will use the model developed by Schneider and Tornell (2000) to make such a policy evaluation.

To explain some of the stylized facts, third-generation crisis models have looked to financial market imperfections as key fundamentals. The models are typically based on one of two distortions: either "bad policy," in the form of bailout guarantees, or "bad markets," in the form of an imperfection that induces balance sheet effects, such as asymmetric information, or the imperfect enforceability of contracts.[3] Schneider and Tornell (2000) consider an economy that is *simultaneously* subject to these two distortions: systemic bailout guarantees and the imperfect enforceability of contracts. They also stress the role of the nontradables sector, which is often overlooked in the debate about the causes of recent crises. They show that the interaction of the two distortions generates a coherent account of a complete boom-bust episode.

A simplified version of this model is presented in section 15.3. Here we present an overview. Consider an economy with a tradables (T) and a nontradables (N) sector. In order to explain the facts it is sufficient to consider a simple setup in which T-sector agents are endowed with T-goods, and consume both T- and N-goods. Meanwhile, agents in the N-sector demand T-goods for consumption, and produce nontradables using only nontradables as inputs according to a linear production technology: $q_t = \theta I_t$.

Firms in the T-sector can easily obtain financing in international capital markets either because they can pledge their export receivables as collateral, or because they are closely linked to firms that can secure their debt. In contrast, firms in the N-sector must rely more heavily on domestic bank credit. N-sector financing is subject to two distortions: enforceability problems and bailout guarantees. High enforceability problems imply that lenders will limit the amount they lend regardless of what the interest rate is. As a result, N-sector agents might face borrowing constraints in equilibrium. In the model, like in several financial accelerator models, the amount of credit available to a firm is determined by the level of internal

---

3. See Aghion, Bachetta, and Banerjee (1999); Bernanke, Gertler, and Gilchrist (1999); Burnside, Eichenbaum, and Rebelo (2000); Caballero and Krishnamurthy (1999); Calvo (1998); Chang and Velasco (1998); Corsetti, Pesenti, and Roubini (1998); Krugman (1998); and McKinnon and Pill (1998).

funds. If bailout guarantees are introduced, their interaction with enforceability problems will induce agents to issue risky debt, generating endogenous real exchange rate risk.

In order to explain the fact that in emerging markets debt is often denominated in foreign currency on an unhedged basis, we allow N-sector agents to issue either "risky debt" (denominated in T-goods) or "safe debt" with no real exchange rate risk.

In order to analyze the effect of each distortion we introduce them one by one. Thus, consider an economy in which only enforceability problems are present, as in standard financial accelerator models. If investment has a sufficiently high rate of return, agents will borrow as much as they can. As a result the credit multiplier becomes an investment multiplier:

(1) $$p_t I_t^s = m^s(h) \cdot w_t$$

where w_t denotes internal funds (denominated in T-goods) of a representative N-sector firm; $p_t = p_t^N/p_t^T$ is the inverse of the real exchange rate; $m^s(h)$ is the investment multiplier which is decreasing in the degree of the enforceability problem (indexed by $1/h$); and I_t is physical investment by the N-sector. Although safe debt is more expensive than risky debt, in the presence of bankruptcy costs issuing safe debt is individually optimal. Thus, in the absence of exogenous shocks, the economy will not exhibit susceptibility to meltdowns. Under no circumstances will firms go bust.

Consider now the second distortion: bailout guarantees. There are two types of guarantees: unconditional and systemic. The former are granted whenever there is a default by an individual borrower (e.g., deposit insurance), while the latter are granted only if a critical mass of borrowers goes bust. Clearly, if all debt were covered by unconditional bailout guarantees, then the enforceability problem would become irrelevant and borrowing constraints would not arise in equilibrium. Since a lender would be bailed out in the case of an idiosyncratic default, the lender has no incentives to limit the amount of credit extended to an individual borrower. Hence, in order for bailout guarantees not to neutralize the effect of the enforceability problem, and for borrowing constraints to arise in equilibrium, it is necessary that some part of banks' liabilities be covered only by systemic bailout guarantees.

Systemic bailout guarantees provide an implicit subsidy that eases borrowing constraints. However, this subsidy can be cashed in only if there are some states of nature in which a critical mass of borrowers goes bust. In the absence of exogenous shocks that bankrupt a critical mass of borrowers, the introduction of systemic bailout guarantees will have an effect only if there is aggregate endogenous risk. In our economy, this bankruptcy risk is generated if there exists enough real exchange rate volatility. In this case, the presence of systemic bailout guarantees induces N-sector agents to issue T-debt. This allows agents to reduce the expected value of debt repayments. This reduction, in turn, permits agents to borrow more at each level of internal funds. Therefore, at a given point in time, the "investment multiplier" is greater than that of an economy that features only enforceability problems (m^s). The value of investment by the N-sector is

$$(2) \qquad p_t I_t = m^r(h, F) \cdot w_t, \quad m^s(h) < m^r(h, F),$$

where F stand for the generosity of the bailout guarantee. We now turn to the question of what is the mechanism that generates endogenous risk.

15.3.1   Endogenous Real Exchange Rate Volatility

The first main result is that the *interaction* of systemic bailout guarantees and enforceability problems can generate aggregate endogenous risk. This is because there is a self-reinforcing mechanism at work. If there is sufficient real exchange rate risk, it is individually optimal for an N-sector agent to issue risky T-debt (i.e., to borrow in foreign currency on a short-term and unhedged basis). However, if many N-sector agents gamble by denominating their debt in T-goods, exchange rate risk might be endogenously created, as the economy becomes vulnerable to self-fulfilling meltdowns. If the amount of T-debt is high, a real depreciation can severely squeeze cash flow, or even bankrupt banks altogether. Since they face binding borrowing constraints, they then have to curtail lending to the N-sector. Weak investment demand from the N-sector for its own products in turn validates the real depreciation. The systemic credit risk created by the banking system thus induces endogenous exchange rate risk.[4]

To see why real exchange rate variability can make risky T-debt cheaper than safe debt, suppose that tomorrow's real exchange rate can take on two values: an appreciated value that leaves every firm solvent, and a depreciated one that makes a majority of N-sector firms go bust. In the presence of full bailout guarantees, risk-neutral lenders are willing to fund T-debt at world interest rates because it will be repaid in full in both states of nature. It will be repaid either by the borrowers in the good state, or by the bailout agency in the crisis state. Second, if the probability of crisis is small and real appreciation in the good state is large, it clearly pays N-sector agents to issue T-debt and gamble with the bailout agency's money. This is because the greater the real appreciation, the greater the portion of the debt burden, measured in terms of nontradables, that is inflated away.

To see under which circumstances the existence of T-debt generates volatility we turn to the determination of the equilibrium real exchange rate ($1/p_t$). This price equalizes aggregate demand with the (predetermined) supply of nontradables: $D(p_t) = \theta I_{t-1}$. The aggregate demand for

4. Although there are several ways in which agents can engage in risk taking, risky debt denomination (borrowing in dollars to finance nontradables activities) is a wonderful "coordinating device." Since debt denomination is easily observed, agents can implicitly collude to cash in the subsidy implicit in the bailout guarantee.

N-goods has two components: the demand by the T-sector, and the demand by the N-sector for its own goods. Since at a given point in time supply is given, the key to having multiple equilibria is a backward-bending aggregate demand curve. This is impossible if N-sector firms have only N-debt. In this case, price changes lead to variations in both firms' revenues and their debt payments. In fact, profits (measured in nontradables) are completely insulated against price movements. The upshot is that as long as firms are solvent, demand slopes downward and there is a unique equilibrium real exchange rate.

Multiple equilibria are possible only if N-sector agents have T-debt. In this case real exchange rate movements affect revenues, but keep the debt burden unchanged. Thus, it becomes important to distinguish between insolvent and solvent firms. For real exchange rates more depreciated than a cutoff level $1/p_t^c$, all N-firms go bankrupt because revenues do not cover the debt burden. As a result, internal funds collapse. Total demand in this range is downward sloping. In contrast, for real exchange rates more appreciated than $1/p_t^c$, a further real appreciation is accompanied by a more than proportional increase in internal funds. The reason is that revenues increase while the debt burden remains the same. Equivalently, part of the debt burden measured in terms of nontradables is "inflated away." Consequently, investment demand increases.

It is apparent that if the balance sheet effect is strong enough to make aggregate demand bend backward, as in figure 15.4, multiple market-clearing real exchange rates (and hence self-fulfilling "twin crises") can exist. With identical fundamentals, in terms of supply and debt, the market may clear in one of two equilibria. In a "solvent" equilibrium (point B in fig. 15.4), the price (the reciprocal of the real exchange rate) is high, inflating away enough of firms' debt (measured in nontradables) to allow them to bid

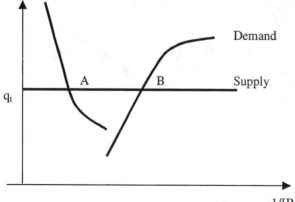

Fig. 15.4   Equilibrium in the nontradables market

away a large share of output from consumers. In contrast, in the "crisis" equilibrium of point A, the price is low, allowing the T-sector and bankrupt N-sector agents with little internal funds to absorb the supply of nontradables. Whichever of these two points is reached depends on expectations. Fundamentals determine only whether the environment is fragile enough to allow two equilibria.

15.3.2   Equilibrium Dynamics

The second main result is that the interaction between systemic bailout guarantees and enforceability problems not only induces endogenous volatility, but also fuels the lending and investment booms as well as the real appreciation. This explains the other stylized facts described in the introduction.

As we have seen, systemic bailout guarantees alleviate the "underinvestment" problem. They permit high leverage with debt denominated in T-goods, and faster credit growth (i.e., $m^r \geq m^s$. As a result, the N-sector grows faster than if guarantees were absent.

Consider now the interplay between the real appreciation and the lending boom. Since N-goods are demanded for investment by the N-sector itself, both output and the relative price of nontradables increase during the boom. Furthermore, since debt is denominated in T-goods, a real appreciation (a relative price increase) reduces the debt burden measured in terms of nontradables. This increases N-sector agents' cash flow. For constrained agents, this translates into more lending through a balance sheet effect. More lending, in turn, permits more investment in N-goods. In order to close the circle, note that if the investment increase is greater than the increase in output, the real exchange rate must appreciate in order to eliminate the excess demand for nontradables.

An economy can follow a risky or safe equilibrium path depending on whether firms' investment plans lead them to go bust in some states. Along the lucky path of a risky equilibrium, credit and investment in the N-sector rise over time while the real exchange rate appreciates. At the same time, demand for N-goods by the T-sector falls. Thus, we have a drastic version of the transfer of resources and the asymmetric sectoral pattern that actually takes place during lending booms. A risky lending-boom equilibrium features two key observed characteristics of credit: debt denomination is used to take on real exchange rate risk and leverage is unusually high. The benchmark is the leverage achieved in a safe equilibrium. The lending boom develops gradually over time. Since the production technology is linear, the relevant "adjustment costs" here are due to the contract-enforceability problem. The N-sector can grow only gradually since it must wait for internal funds to accumulate.

A *self-fulfilling crisis* occurs when the bad state of the sunspot is realized for the first time. The result is a real depreciation and widespread bankruptcies in the N-sector. This depletes the internal funds of the N-sector. Thus, its investment drops and can only gradually recover (due to the financial adjustment costs mentioned above). At the same time, demand by the T-sector jumps up. Again, this highlights the asymmetric patterns followed by the N-sector and the T-sector.

15.3.3   Necessary Ingredients for Boom-Bust Cycles

A key point of Schneider and Tornell (2000) is that the *interaction* of contract enforceability problems and bailout guarantees creates the fragility required for self-fulfilling crises. If there were no guarantees, firms would not be willing to take on price risk to claim a subsidy. Costly enforceability of contracts alone would still imply that the N-sector can only grow gradually and balance sheet effects would play a role during the lending boom. However, there would be no force impetus to makes the boom end in a crisis. Alternatively, if there were only guarantees but no enforceability problems, then there would not be any balance sheet effects that make demand backward-bending, a necessary condition for a sunspot to matter.

Lending booms that feature fragility cannot occur in just any economy with bailout guarantees and enforceability problems. It is also necessary to have a future increase in the demand of the T-sector for nontradables. Otherwise, the N-sector would not be able to repay the accumulated deficits it runs during the lending boom. Backward induction then indicates that the sequence of returns that supports the lending boom would collapse. This suggests that the boom-bust episodes are more likely to occur during a transition period (for instance, following a far-reaching reform or a natural resource discovery).

Even during a transitional period *the likelihood of a self-fulfilling crisis is not a free parameter.* If crises were not rare events, either borrowing constraints would not arise, or they would not be binding in equilibrium if they did arise. In either case, credit would not be constrained by internal funds and balance sheet effects would not exist in equilibrium. Clearly, if this were the case, crises could not occur. If the probability of crises is not small enough, enforceability problems do not generate borrowing constraints.

In conclusion, the introduction of systemic bailout guarantees into an otherwise riskless economy can increase the credit and investment multiplier. However, this occurs only if the economy becomes fragile to self-fulfilling meltdowns. Systemic bailout guarantees induce agents in the N-sector to switch from safe to risky debt, generating aggregate real exchange rate risk.

15.4   Policy Evaluation

An emerging economy is one where the future is much brighter than the present, but where profitable investment projects cannot be undertaken because (1) the private sector is small (i.e., entrepreneurial wealth is low) and (2) the amount of external financing is severely limited, especially for firms in the nontradables sector. The reforms of the late 1980s liberalized trade and financial markets in many emerging markets. These reforms also brought a significant reduction in the role of the state in the economy. Suddenly, the future looked much brighter than before, and the private sector much smaller than what was desirable. Unfortunately, legal and judicial reform could not be implemented as easily as the other reforms. As a result, many of the institutions that support the provision of external finance in developed economies did not flourish in emerging markets. Firms in the tradables sector could finance themselves in international markets. However, this option was not open to N-sector firms.

The policy problem then became how to better promote the fast development of the private sector in an environment where external finance to the nontradables sector is constrained by internal funds of firms, and where N-sector investment is too low relative to investment opportunities (e.g., infrastructure, services, etc.). One is tempted to say that if a government had the appropriate information and correct incentives, the optimal policy would have been to transfer resources to those in the population with better entrepreneurial skills, and to let them make the investment decisions. Of course, we now know that this is wishful thinking. After many failed experiments of this sort carried out during the last century, we now know that either governments do not possess the appropriate information, or they are too inclined to crony capitalism and rampant corruption.

Since direct made-to-measure government transfers are not feasible, during the 1990s governments had to design second-best policies to foster the development of the private economy, especially in the N-sector. In many countries the decision was made to privatize the banks and allow them to be the means through which resources would be channeled to the nascent private sector. The issues described in the introduction should be analyzed from this perspective.

We will analyze these issues by using the framework described in section 15.3. Since this model explains many of the stylized facts that characterize the boom-bust cycles experienced by emerging markets during the 1990s, it is an appropriate framework to evaluate the policies implemented by emerging markets. We will argue that when taking into consideration the distortions that exist in emerging markets, there is a sense in which these policies are second-best-optimal instruments to foster the nontradables sector's growth. We would like to distinguish between these policies and those that are designed to mask corruption. The latter are clearly undefendable.

15.4.1   Policies during a Boom

Consider the two-sector economy described in section 15.3 in which firms in the T-sector can easily obtain financing in international capital markets, while firms in the N-sector must rely more heavily on domestic bank credit. Furthermore, since emerging markets face acute enforceability problems, firms in the N-sector face severe borrowing constraints that limit their ability to undertake profitable projects. As a result, the growth rate of the N-sector is kept below its potential. It follows that a policy-maker, whose objective is to maximize social welfare, must design second-best policies that will ease borrowing constraints and increase investment in the N-sector. Since the N-sector and the T-sector compete for productive resources and since any policies to support the N-sector have implicit fiscal costs, the optimal support level for the N-sector cannot be arbitrarily large.

We have seen that in the presence of severe enforceability problems in financial markets, credit is constrained by internal funds. As a result, profitable investment projects will not be undertaken, especially in the N-sector. Thus, over the medium-run, growth will be significantly lower than its potential. This indicates that systemic bailout guarantees might actually play a socially beneficial role. Systemic bailout guarantees provide an implicit subsidy that reduces the cost at which firms can fund themselves, and that increases the credit multiplier. This increases investment and growth at each level of internal funds. In the absence of better instruments to promote investment and growth of the N-sector, systemic bailout guarantees are a second-best instrument to make transfers to this sector. We would like to emphasize that this mechanism uses the information and monitoring capacity of banks.

Although there are several ways systemic bailouts can be implemented, for simplicity, consider the generosity of bailout guarantees (F) as the policy instrument. An increase in F induces an increase in the investment multiplier in equation (2), which in turn leads to a higher growth rate of the N-sector. Therefore, in an emerging economy it is optimal to set F higher than zero in order to reduce the underinvestment problem. However, there are trade-offs: first, the greater F the greater the contingent fiscal cost; and second, the greater F, the greater the share of resources allocated to the N-sector at the expense of the T-sector. Therefore, the level of F should not be set too high. There is an interior optimum.

We would like to emphasize three points. First, systemic bailout guarantees do not curtail the discipline faced by either individual banks or firms because they are granted only if a critical mass of agents defaults. At the same time, systemic bailout guarantees generate an investment subsidy only if the banks' portfolios are risky, that is, only if there exist states of nature in which there is systemic crisis. In the absence of large exogenous shocks, guarantees will be effective in promoting investment only if the banking system generates risk endogenously (we address this issue below). Second, systemic bailout guarantees imply that the government can credibly commit not to bail out individual agents in the case of idiosyncratic default. Third, if in a given country banks play no monitoring role and are prone to fraud, systemic bailout guarantees will not be socially beneficial.

The experience of Mexico during the 1990s illustrates, in a rather sharp manner, the policy dilemma faced by reformers. Several critics have pointed to the "false rosy expectations" generated by the government, and the promises of bailout guarantees, as the culprits for the Tequila crisis. Certainly, in hindsight this is true, a policymaker would say. However, at that time it seemed a sensible policy. It was a way to avoid low growth and bottlenecks in the N-sector that would otherwise limit the overall future growth of the economy. Plus, from a political standpoint the development of the private sector encouraged by the policy had the added virtue of creating new power bases that would block attempts by statist groups to go back to the old ways. It was a way to ensure the continuity of the reforms.

An important issue that we have not discussed yet is unconditional bailout guarantees, which are granted whenever an individual debtor defaults. Deposit insurance is a prime example. If all guarantees were unconditional, the discipline in the banking system would disappear and guarantees would not play the investment-promoting role we described above.

However, if unconditional bailout guarantees are granted to small bank depositors, they might play a socially beneficial role. This policy avoids bank runs generated by cascading rumors, but does not impinge negatively on the market discipline faced by an individual bank because small depositors typically have very little information regarding the bank's portfolio. As is the case in the United States, market discipline should be imposed by noninsured bank debt, the interest rate of which should serve as an indicator of a bank's health.

The Role of Risky "Dollar" Debt

As mentioned above, systemic bailout guarantees have investment-enhancing effects only in the presence of risk. In the absence of large exogenous shocks, some endogenous volatility must be present if the policy is to be effective. Therefore, outlawing risky dollar debt could undo the investment-enhancing effects of systemic bailout guarantees. Thus, if the conditions of a country call for bailouts as a second-best policy to promote the growth of the private sector, then risky debt (or another way to generate endogenous volatility) must also be allowed. Of course, this does not mean that banks should be allowed to have outrageously risky portfolios. It just means that a naive policy of outlawing risky dollar debt is not correct from a normative perspective.

Since systemic bailout guarantees can be cashed only in states of the world in which there is a systemic crisis, systemic bailout guarantees are effective in increasing investment only if a significant part of the economy is vulnerable to systemic crises. It is only during a systemic meltdown that the bailout agency makes payments to lenders. Thus, the expected value of the subsidy is determined by the likelihood of a crisis and by the generosity of the bailout. The greater the expected value of the subsidy, the lower the interest rates that lenders are willing to accept. Clearly, banks' portfolios cannot be outrageously risky, as the likelihood of crisis must be quite small in order for the mechanism identified in this paper to be operative. Otherwise, firms would not find it profitable to borrow and invest in the first place! Note, however, that *small* is not the same as *zero.* In the absence of major exogenous shocks, the fragility must come from within the system. This is precisely the role of risky debt denomination. As we explained above, if a majority of borrowers have unhedged debt, the economy as a whole can become vulnerable to self-fulfilling crises.

As a way of allowing risk into the economy, dollar debt has the wonderful feature of being a coordinating device, as it can be observed by others. It plays the same role as the real estate buildup on an uninsured basis in catastrophe-prone areas. The principle that "if everyone else does it, then I am safe" reigns.

From a positive perspective it is impossible to outlaw dollar short-term debt. Many firms need such debt in order to carry out their international transactions. Since it is impossible to distinguish what part of dollar debt is used by a given firm to finance international transactions, it is not feasible to enforce a law that forbids dollar debt for uses other than international trade. This lesson has been painfully learned by many countries that have tried to implement dual exchange rates, and then were faced with rampant mis-invoicing of imports and exports.

In conclusion, the degree of banks' and firms' portfolio riskiness should be strictly regulated. However, risky debt should not be outlawed altogether. It is neither socially optimal nor practically implementable.

The Role of Lending Booms and Asset Price Inflation

During a lending boom credit grows unusually fast and, as many observers have pointed out, monitoring effectiveness declines. Thus, it is less likely that unprofitable and white elephant projects will be detected and stopped. At the same time, firms in emerging markets have a very low level of external finance, especially in the N-sector. Thus, a lending boom is a mechanism by which faster growth can be attained. In fact, the lending boom is a transitional phase that is ignited by deep economic reforms that make the future much brighter than the present.

Stopping a lending boom—for example, by increasing reserve requirements—would interrupt the policy of promoting the growth of the private sector. However, allowing the lending boom to continue unchecked increases the debt burden of the economy, which makes it more vulnerable to crises. Hence, it is not clear ex ante at which point a lending boom should be stopped.

It is interesting to note that although crises typically are preceded by lending booms (Tornell 1999), the converse is not true. Gourinchas, Lan-derretche, and Valdes (1999) find that for a large panel of countries the probability that a lending boom ends in a crisis is quite small. That is, in the majority of cases, lending booms end with soft landings. Furthermore, theoretically lending booms can develop only if the probability of crisis is small and they are expected to end with a soft landing if they last long enough (see Schneider and Tornell 1999).

Clearly, India has not experienced lending booms of such magnitude as the ones experienced by Korea. Moreover, India has not suffered currency crises as deep as those endured by Korea. Certainly, this does not mean that over the last half-century the Indian economy has performed better than Korea's. Of course, with hindsight, Korean performance could have been improved on the margin. However, we should beware of fine-tuning policies designed (ex post) to look great ex post.

Prior to several crises it has been observed that some assets, such as real estate, experience a steep price inflation that is followed by a price collapse at the time of crisis. Since real estate is used as collateral, there is a close link between lending and asset price inflation during a boom. Thus, im-plementing policies that would stop asset price inflation will also reduce the growth of credit. Clearly, it might be dangerous to leave asset price in-flation unchecked. However, some degree of inflation might be desirable as a tool to ease borrowing constraints.[5]

What Are the Effects of Reforms That Improve the Contracting Technology in Financial Markets?

During the last decade several countries privatized their banks, liberal-ized their financial markets, and implemented legal reforms that facilitated contracts between private agents. Unfortunately, in several cases these re-forms have lead to an increase in fraud instead of economic growth (see Tornell 2000). The lack of a concurrent improvement in prudential regula-tion is often cited as responsible for this lackluster outcome. Given that the regulatory framework cannot be improved by decree, the question arises as to whether such reforms should be implemented regardless of the regula-tory framework.

To address this issue it is important to note that there is a nonlinearity in the relationship between the degree of contract enforceability and the de-sirability of financial-sector reforms. We will argue that such reforms are socially beneficial only if contract enforceability is very low, or the reforms are radical enough so as to eliminate balance sheet effects.

An improvement in the financial markets' contracting technology has the effect of increasing credit at each level of internal funds. In terms of

5. Schneider and Tornell (1999) study the interplay between asset prices and lending along a boom.

equations (1) and (2), it means a reduction in the parameter h and an increase in the investment multipliers m^s and m^r. In the extreme, if contracts are not enforceable and the legal system is nonfunctional, it will be almost impossible for creditors and lenders to establish a bilateral debt agreement. With certainty borrowers will divert funds and default. As a result, credit to the N-sector will be almost nil, and the economy will not be fragile to crises. In this environment the introduction of systemic bailout guarantees would obviously not induce greater investment as suggested in the previous section. Thus, in these extreme circumstances privatization of the banking system and reforms that improve the contractual environment are clearly socially beneficial.

Consider now the other extreme, in which it is possible to implement legal reforms that reduce the enforceability problem to such a level that it is possible for even small firms in the N-sector to enter into bilateral agreements with foreign lenders. Clearly, in this extreme case borrowing constraints will not be an issue. As a result, firms could borrow up to the level determined by profitability and technological conditions. Therefore, it is socially beneficial to bring the enforceability of contracts to a level where the majority of domestic firms and banks do not face borrowing constraints. Moreover, if this were the case, there would be no role for systemic bailout guarantees. Even if they were put in place, they would be irrelevant!

But, what if contract enforceability (h) is at an intermediate level? Would privatization and financial reforms that improve private contracting unambiguously be socially beneficial? The answer is no. A concurrent improvement in prudential regulation is essential. Recall that it is not socially optimal to increase credit to the N-sector indefinitely at the expense of the T-sector. There is an interior maximum. Taking as given the generosity of bailouts (F), an improvement in contract enforceability ($1/h$) eases borrowing constraints and increases the credit multiplier. However, it does not eliminate borrowing constraints and balance sheet effects altogether. As a result, such an improvement in private contracting might induce more fragility than what is socially desirable. Clearly, if one could fine-tune the generosity of bailout guarantees, one could envision some trade-off. Unfortunately, systemic bailout guarantees are more often than not determined by political forces. Either you have them or you do not!

Another way of stating this argument is that, after some point, a further improvement in contract enforcement will only serve to permit borrowers and lenders to better collude in ripping off the bailout agency and taxpayers. Instead of enhancing the rate of growth of the economy, it will simply facilitate the adoption of white elephant investment projects that mask theft, or might make it easier to design fraudulent lending schemes. If not accompanied by improvements in the regulatory framework, reforms that simply improve contractual arrangements marginally might have the unintended effect of fostering crony capitalism.

The Role of Prudential Regulation

Our previous discussion highlights the need to improve prudential regulation concurrently with privatization and financial reforms. There are two levels at which the regulatory body should act. First, it should ensure that the banking system does not undertake more risk than what is socially desirable. As we discussed in the previous section, a risky debt profile might be necessary for the subsidy implicit in systemic bailout guarantees to have the desired effect of increasing credit and investment. However, this does not mean that anything goes. Appropriate regulation must determine the financial ratios in accordance with the situation of a given country. Blindly applying the Basel accord requirements does not make sense, as the level of risk induced might be greater than the one appropriate for the country in question.

The second level at which the regulatory body should act is in minimizing the extent of fraudulent schemes and adoption of white elephants. The more efficient the regulatory agency is in blocking these manifestations of crony capitalism, the more likely that systemic bailout guarantees will induce fast and sustainable economic growth, and the greater the social payoff associated with reforms that improve contractual enforceability. In the absence of a strong and independent regulatory agency, it becomes important to consider whether the ownership of banks should be strictly separated from ownership of industrial corporations. We will discuss this below.

Reforms that permit better bilateral private contracting should go hand in hand with improvements in regulatory capacity. However, it seems that here lies one of the greatest bottlenecks faced by emerging markets. More often than not, regulatory agencies fall prey to those they regulate. We now know that this is a political distortion that cannot be eliminated by decree.

In the case of banks, at the time of privatization a significant part of de facto nonperforming loans are passed on to the new owners. These invisible nonperforming loans reflect typically past hidden fiscal deficits or political payoffs. At the time of privatization it is politically expedient not to recognize them, and pass them on to the new owners. This has two implications. First, the true capitalization of the newly privatized banks is lower than what the standard ratios indicate. Second, if the privatizers are also the regulators, there is a strong reason for regulators to oversee some future malpractices of the banks: bankers help regulators hide some nonperforming loans to begin with. Both implications make it more likely that the recently privatized banking system will engage in excessively risky lending and even in fraudulent activities.

Even if capture of regulatory agencies is not an issue, one still needs to worry about regulatory forbearance and evergreening. Regulators have incentives to consider the negative shocks that hit banks' balance sheets as more transitory than what they actually are. Doing so avoids forcing banks to recapitalize. Since banks often fail to do so, authorities must seek fiscal resources to recapitalize banks. Since such actions are politically costly, it is always better to ignore the problem, at least for the time being. Thus, with the acquiescence of regulators, banks capitalize the past due interest of de facto nonperforming loans. These loans now become evergreen accounts. Obviously, this is an explosive situation: the capitalization of banks will have to be confronted in the future. There are more perverse situations where evergreen accounts reflect political favors to specific powerful groups.

The FDICIA law implemented in the United States in 1991 has several elements that might be effective ways to improve the regulatory framework in emerging markets (see Kaufman (1997)). This law makes sanctions to banks mandatory and thus lessens political pressure on regulators. This law includes a prompt-corrective-action clause according to which a bank's problems must be solved before effective capital becomes negative. Sanctions are applied in stages depending on the level of effective capital. These sanctions include restrictions on dividend payouts, limits on assets' growth, and losing management rights. Furthermore, new capital must be injected by owners before effective capital becomes negative. With these measures, the resolution of a bank does not imply fiscal costs. International organizations could focus much more attention on this area.

The Role of Foreign Banks

During the last decade the share of the domestic banking system owned by foreigners has increased spectacularly. The accepted wisdom is that foreign ownership of banks brings three main benefits to an emerging market. First, foreign banks improve the banking practice and know-how. Second, since the size of the private sector in emerging markets is too small, the existence of foreign banks makes it easier to separate ownership of banks from ownership of industrial corporations. As we discussed earlier, in the presence of a weak regulatory framework this separation might reduce the likelihood of fraudulent schemes between lenders and borrowers.

Third, in case of a systemic crisis, parents of foreign subsidiaries will inject the resources necessary to withstand a run. Note, however, that in general foreign subsidiaries are legally separate entities from the parents. Thus, subsidiaries can declare themselves in bankruptcy during a crisis, without affecting the parent company. Reputation considerations are frequently invoked to defend the notion that resources would be transferred by the parent in case of a crisis. This argument is far from obvious because in case of a systemic crisis all parent banks can refuse to support their subsidiaries (by invoking some sort of force majeure clause), without losing reputational capital vis-à-vis the other major international banks.

Bailout Guarantees and the Exchange Rate Regime

There are several ways in which systemic bailout guarantees can be implemented. The particulars will of course depend on the exchange rate regime. A nice feature of Schneider and Tornell's framework is that the effects of guarantees and the forces that generate boom-bust cycles are independent of the exchange rate regime or monetary policy rule. This permits us to study how guarantees affect the economy under different regimes.

With fully flexible exchange rates the mechanism is literally the same as the one we consider in section 15.3. If agents are highly leveraged and have risky dollar debt, the economy is vulnerable to self-fulfilling crises in which there is a severe real depreciation and several agents in the N-sector suffer from balance sheet effects and are unable to repay their debts. As a result, creditors get paid a proportion F of the contracted payment. This bailout payment can be financed by an international organization and/or by an increase in future taxes to the rest of the economy. The real depreciation can arise by either a nominal depreciation, a change in nominal prices, or a combination of both.

Consider the other extreme of a fixed exchange rate regime. In the case of an attack the central bank can defend the currency by either running down reserves or increasing the interest rate. If the attack is successful, the reduction in reserves constitutes a bailout payment to bank creditors that withdraw their funds and convert them into foreign currency. Thus, any defense policy has associated with it a bailout rate F. Clearly, the bailout rate need not be 100 percent, as reserves might not suffice to cover all the liabilities of the banking system. We should add that the bailout can be complemented by an explicit transfer, like in Mexico during the Tequila crisis. Again, the real depreciation can come about through a combination of a nominal depreciation and a change in nominal prices.

In the real world we observe a mixture of both regimes. However, it should be clear that the underlying forces are essentially the same in both cases.

15.4.2   Policy in the Aftermath of Crisis

Bailing Out Borrowers versus Bailing Out Lenders

Once a crisis has erupted and a severe real depreciation has taken place, the main objective should be to contain the meltdown and to minimize the number of bankruptcies. This is because inefficient bankruptcy procedures generate deadweight losses. Productive assets are inefficiently liquidated and human capital networks are destroyed. Furthermore, reputational capital in credit markets, which takes a long time to build, is destroyed (Wyne 2000).

Typically, bailouts are granted to lenders, not to borrowers. However, bailing out lenders does not save borrowers from being decapitalized and suffering bankruptcy. Therefore, despite the occurrence of generous bailouts, credit crunches have developed in the aftermath of crises during the 1990s. This has been reflected in three regularities. First, depositors' bank runs have seldom been observed in the crises of the 1990s. Second, in the aftermath of crises the growth rate of bank loans has typically remained below the growth rate of deposits. Since the value of collateral collapses, banks shift their portfolios toward others assets such as government securities. Third, the interest rate spread has typically remained above its precrisis level after GDP growth has returned to its trend.

Ex post, extending some type of bailout to borrowers might avoid bankruptcies and ameliorate the credit crunch. This policy, however, might not be possible to implement because the fiscal cost might be enormous. Furthermore, it has perverse incentives effects. First, many borrowers that have the ability to pay might simply refuse to do so. Since it is extremely difficult to distinguish liquid and illiquid borrowers during a generalized crisis, it is basically impossible to implement a borrower-bailout policy that discriminates among different types of borrowers. Second, market mechanisms might be blocked as borrowers and lenders might delay the resolution of certain loans.

Piecemeal versus All-at-Once Bailouts

In the aftermath of a crisis the share of nonperforming loans increases spectacularly. Both regulators and banks have incentives to underreport the true share of nonperforming loans. This way, bank owners need to inject less capital, and the government needs to spend less fiscal resources up front. In contrast, reporting the true nonperforming loans might force a takeover of several banks by either the government or other banks. As a result, bank owners will lose their franchises, and government officials will face political criticism for their failure to appropriately regulate the banking system.

Thus, bankers and regulators have incentives to "believe" that negative news is more transitory than what it actually is, and to make predictions about the banks' portfolios that are more optimistic than what is warranted by the facts. The effect of this misperception is an evergreening of banks' balance sheets. That is, there is a tendency for banks to classify as performing those loans that are actually never going to be repaid, and for regulators to turn a blind eye to this mistake. The problem with evergreening is that it generally leads to an increase in the share of nonperforming loans over time. This is because interest is not repaid, and because banks have incentives to undertake very risky projects that might have negative expected net present value. Banks might even have incentives to extend outright fraudulent loans.

Evergreening has two negative effects on the economy as a whole. First, the fiscal cost of the bailout grows over time, and it might even grow faster than GDP. Second, the credit crunch suffered by small nontradables firms will be deeper and more persistent, as banks will have more incentives to engage in risky activities than to lend to firms with low internal funds (Krueger and Tornell 2000 analyze the Mexican case).

The alternative policy is to recognize at once all nonperforming loans. Since it is unlikely that bank shareholders will be able to come up with the necessary capital, the government will have to take over all the liabilities of the banking system. This policy implies that government debt must increase by several percentage points of GDP in a single year. This is politically very costly. However, the evergreening alternative is likely to be socially more costly, as the experiences of Japan and Mexico have shown.

Interest Rate and Exchange Rate Responses to Crises

In the standard Mundell-Fleming model, when there is a capital outflow the needed improvement in the current account can be attained with a real depreciation and with no output costs. According to this view, a depreciation induces a shift of resources from the nontradables to the tradables sector, and makes the economy more competitive in world markets. As a result, growth resumes quite fast after the depreciation.

The Mundell-Fleming framework and traditional balance-of-payments crisis models are not appropriate for explaining these new boom-bust episodes because the banking system plays no essential role in these models. Once we move into a world in which bank lending is essential, and debt is denominated in foreign currency, the traditional policy recommendation becomes invalid. As we have seen, allowing the real exchange rate to depreciate in order to close the external gap has perverse effects. Since domestic firms have dollar-denominated debt but their revenues are denominated in domestic currency, a real depreciation will make some domestic firms unable to repay their debts, and will bankrupt them. This in turn, will make the problem even worse. Capital flight will increase, the real exchange rate will depreciate even further, and more firms will go bust. This vicious circle will generate a meltdown of the domestic sector of the economy.

In this situation an increase in interest rates might not be such a bad idea. But does it actually work? It is not clear, whether from an empirical or a conceptual perspective. In a sample of seventy-five countries over the period 1960–1997, Kraay (2000) finds no evidence that interest rates systematically increase during failed speculative attacks, nor that raising interest rates increases the probability that an attack fails.

From a conceptual perspective, an interest rate hike is effective in stemming a crisis only if such an increase does not bankrupt a critical mass of firms. If a critical mass of firms goes bust because they are unable to meet their debt service, then the investment demand will collapse and the real exchange rate will have to depreciate in order to clear the market for nontradables. The end result will be the same as the one in the previous paragraph.

In contrast, if an interest rate hike simply generates a recession but does not induce generalized bankruptcies, then an immediate crisis might be avoided. The question then arises as to whether the time of reckoning will not simply be pushed forward. Will higher domestic interest rates simply induce foreign investors to exploit arbitrage opportunities during a short period until central bank reserves are depleted? Will higher domestic interest rates make several firms insolvent, and lead them to bankruptcy in the near future? It is necessary that the answers to these questions are in the negative in order for an interest rate increase to avoid a crisis.

Clearly, the specific situation of a country will determine what is the correct mix of exchange rate depreciation and interest rate increase.

References

Aghion, Philippe, Philippe Bachetta, and Abhijit Banerjee. 2000. Capital markets and the instability of open economies. Study Center Gerzensee, Switzerland. Mimeograph.

Bernanke, Ben, Mark Gertler, and Simon Gilchrist. 1999. The financial accelerator in a quantitative business cycle framework. In *The handbook of macroeconomics,* ed. J. Taylor and M. Woodford. Amsterdam: Elsevier.

Burnside, Craig, Martin Eichenbaum, and Sergio Rebelo. 2000. On the fundamentals of self-fulfilling speculative attacks. NBER Working Paper no. 7554. Cambridge, Mass.: National Bureau of Economic Research, February.

Caballero, Ricardo, and Arvind Krishnamurthy. 1999. Emerging markets crises: An asset markets perspective. MIT, Department of Economics. Mimeograph.

Calvo, Guillermo. 1998. Capital flows and capital market crises: The simple economics of sudden stops. *Journal of Applied Economics* 1 (1): 35–54.

Chang, Roberto, and Andres Velasco. 1998. Financial crises in emerging markets: A canonical model. NBER Working Paper no. 6606. Cambridge, Mass.: National Bureau of Economic Research, June.

Corsetti, Giancarlo, Paolo Pesenti, and Nouriel Roubini. 1998. Paper tigers. New York University, Department of Economics. Mimeograph.

Gourinchas, Pierre Olivier, Oscar Landerretche, and Rodrigo Valdes. 1999. Lending booms: Some stylized facts. Princeton University, Department of Economics. Mimeograph.

International Monetary Fund (IMF). 2001. International financial statistics yearbook [CD-ROM]. Washington, D.C.: IMF.

Kaufman, George C. 1997. Banking reform: The whys and how tos. Paper presented at the EWC/KDI Conference on Restructuring the National Economy, Honolulu, Hawaii, 7–8 August.

Kraay, Aart. 2000. Do high interest rates defend currencies during speculative attacks? World Bank, Research Department. Mimeograph.

Krueger, Anne, and Aaron Tornell. 1999. The role of bank restructuring in recovering from crises: Mexico 1995–1998. NBER Working Paper no. 7042. Cambridge, Mass.: National Bureau of Economic Research, March.

Krugman, Paul. 1998. Bubble, boom, crash: Theoretical notes on Asia's crisis. MIT, Department of Economics. Working Paper.

McKinnon, Ronald, and Huw Pill. 1998. International overborrowing: A decomposition of credit and currency risks. Stanford University, Department of Economics. Working Paper.

Schneider, Martin. 1999. Borrowing constraints in a dynamic model of bank asset and liability management. University of Rochester, Department of Economics. Mimeograph.

Schneider, Martin, and Aaron Tornell. 1999. Lending booms and asset price inflation. University of California, Los Angeles, Department of Economics. Working Paper.

———. 2000. Balance sheet effects, bailout guarantees, and financial crises. NBER Working Paper no. 8060. Cambridge, Mass.: National Bureau of Economic Research, December.

Tornell, Aaron. 1999. Common fundamentals in the Tequila and Asian crises. NBER Working Paper no. 7139. Cambridge, Mass.: National Bureau of Economic Research, May.

———. 2000. Privatizing the privatized. Chapter 5 in *Economic policy reform: The second stage,* ed. Anne O. Krueger. Chicago: University of Chicago Press.

Wyne, Jose. 2000. Business cycles and firm dynamics in small emerging economies. University of California, Los Angeles, Department of Economics. Mimeograph.

Comment   Kyoji Fukao

Although the major part of this paper is based on a theoretical model, which was originally presented in Schneider and Tornell's (2000) National Bureau of Economic Research (NBER) working paper, the author does not provide substantial explanation of the model in this paper. I found that without reading Schneider and Tornell's working paper, it is very difficult to understand this paper. I would like to ask the author to add sufficient explanation of the background model to this paper.

Let me explain Schneider and Tornell's model, first. Their model is based on two basic assumptions.

First, there are bailout guarantees for systemic risk in the nontradable-goods sector (N-sector). The guarantees make firms choose risky investment plans. The guarantees also work as a kind of investment subsidy.

Second, because of contract-enforceability problems, firms face borrowing constraints. The size of firms' investment is constrained by the amount of their internal funds.

In financial theory, we know these two mechanisms very well. But by combining these two mechanisms and by including several additional as-

Kyoji Fukao is professor at the Institute of Economic Research, Hitotsubashi University.

sumptions, Schneider and Tornell constructed a very interesting general equilibrium model.

The additional assumptions are that firms borrow foreign currency in order to make their investment plans risky, and that the real exchange rate is determined by the equilibrium condition in the nontradable-goods market. Multiple equilibria exist in the model. If the domestic currency depreciates, firms in the nontradable-goods sector go bankrupt and investment demand for nontradable goods declines. In this way a self-fulfilling currency crisis occurs. When there is no crisis, the N-sector will gradually grow. This is the essential part of Schneider and Tornell's model.

In this new paper, the author takes the following strategy. He assumes that Schneider and Tornell's model is completely correct and derives several policy implications from it. His main policy implication is, "The introduction of systemic bailout guarantees can increase the credit and investment multiplier," and that it "can be considered second-best-optimal."

I think that the author's strategy is not very successful. When we construct a model, we can use bold assumptions in order to simplify the model. Schneider and Tornell's paper is excellent. But when we write a paper on economic policy, we need to be more careful about the underlying assumptions. I wished the author would consider the applicability of the model to actual economies, providing more evidence.

Let me provide a few examples.

First, it is assumed that international borrowing is used as a device to create systemic risk by small-sized N-sector firms. But it is not clear why firms do not use other macrovariables to create systemic risk. For example, in many countries, including Japan, investments in real estate created systemic risk.

Second, even if the probability of the occurrence of a currency crisis is low, it is too costly for developing economies to intentionally create risk of currency crisis. There are many other, better policies to enhance the growth of the N-sector. The first-best policy would be to reduce enforcement problems through raising penalties on diversions. The government can use tax incentives to promote investment in N-sector, tax T-sector, or subsidize borrowing by N-sector firms. I would like to ask the author to show why no other policy options are available.

Reference

Schneider, Martin, and Aaron Tornell. 2000. Balance sheet effects, bailout guarantees, and financial crises. NBER Working Paper no. 8060. Cambridge, Mass.: National Bureau of Economic Research, December.

Comment   Sung Wook Joh

The author observes that banks experiencing losses cut credit lending during the economic crisis. Moreover, he notes that the crisis credit crunch affected small and medium-sized firms more than it did large firms. When banks experience losses, there are two major ways of dealing with them: (1) market-based approaches and (2) regulatory authority bailouts. Tornell tries to link bailout policies to an effort to mitigate the credit crunch and avoid underinvestment by small firms. He argues that policymakers can induce banks suffering losses to lend money to small firms producing nontradable goods by giving them bailout guarantees.

This paper provides a different perspective on the currency crisis. Tornell argues that emerging economies pursuing faster growth inevitably risk currency crises. More details on the relationships among exchange market fluctuation, credit lending, and growth would improve this argument.

When a crisis occurs, Tornell argues, credit crunching yields different impacts over different industries and different sectors. His figures show that the ratio of nontradables to tradables production falls in many countries after the crisis. In figure 15.3, he also shows that the percentage of bank loans and deposits over gross national product (GDP) changes after the crisis. More evidence supporting a mechanism by which the credit crunch directly causes a drop in the ratio of nontradable goods to tradable goods would improve this argument.

This paper does not suggest a mechanism to ensure that banks receiving bailout guarantees will lend money to the target firms. Banks can lend money to larger firms rather than small firms. As banks become more cautious on their lending after the crisis, they are likely to be more concerned about the credit risk of borrowers. In general, small firms do not have a strong credit history, so they often lack credit accessibility. Thus, a mechanism that connects bailout policy and lending to small firms is necessary.

Tornell argues that an efficient regulatory framework and a reasonably risky environment are necessary for a successful systematic bailout policy. There are several other factors to consider regarding the government's bailout policy, including (1) adequate fiscal means, (2) bailout size, (3) bailout coverage, and (4) gradual or one-time bailouts. First, does the government or the regulatory authority have sufficient fiscal means for a systemic bailout? If not, what is the next best option? Second, how much money should be given in bailout guarantees for banks to lend to small firms? Without transparency in bank accounting and a well-functioning corporate governance system, measuring the magnitude of banks' losses is difficult. In Korea, after the government initially bailed out banks with

Sung Wook Joh is a research fellow at the Korea Development Institute.

losses, the banks reported new losses and asked for more money. Third, should the bailout program be applied selectively to stronger banks or comprehensively to all banks? In Korea, the government closed down five banks and rescued the rest. Would rescuing all the banks have been better? Fourth, should the bailout occur gradually or at one time? Should the government link improved bank behavior to a gradual bailout?

Incentive problems occur when lenders and borrowers anticipate government bailouts of banks suffering losses. Banks may exacerbate losses to induce government bailouts. Instead of reporting losses early, banks can wait until the losses become large enough to require the government's intervention. Moreover, lenders might allow weak firms to borrow more money to provoke a crisis.

In Korea, large business groups (*chaebol*) are a critical mass of the economy. The failure of a few *chaebol* would trigger systemic bailouts. When *chaebol* suffered large losses, the government did not want to risk economic contraction and high unemployment. Thus, the government repeatedly gave favorable bank loans to *chaebol* experiencing losses. Lenders and borrowers then believed that large firms were too big to fail. Borrowers had an incentive to increase their size (e.g., through cross-debt payment guarantees, creative accounting, etc.). When these firms borrowed enough money, they enjoyed a bailout safety net and no longer needed to pursue profit maximization to survive.

Contributors

Charles W. Calomiris
Graduate School of Business
Columbia University
3022 Broadway Street, Uris Hall
New York, NY 10027

Chen Chien-Hsun
Chung-Hua Institution for Economic
    Research
75 Chang-Hsing Street
Taipei
Taiwan

Kyoji Fukao
Institute of Economic Research
Hitotsubashi University
Naka 2-1, Kunitachi
Tokyo 186
Japan

Takatoshi Ito
Research Center for Advanced Science
    and Technology
University of Tokyo
4-6-1, Komaba, Meguro-ku
Tokyo 153-8904
Japan

Sung Wook Joh
Korea University
College of Business Administration
5Ga 1, Anam-Dong, Sungbuk-Gu
Seoul 136-701
Korea

Simon Johnson
Sloan School of Management
Massachusetts Institute of Technology
50 Memorial Drive, E52-562
Cambridge, MA 02142-1347

Cassey Lee Hong Kim
Department of Applied Economics
Faculty of Economics &
    Administration
University of Malaya
50603 Kuala Lumpur
Malaysia

Anne O. Krueger
International Monetary Fund
700 19th Street, NW
Washington, DC 20431

Mario B. Lamberte
Philippine Institute for Development
    Studies
NEDA sa Makati Building
106 Amorsolo Street, Legaspi Village
Makati
Philippines

David D. Li
Department of Economics
Hong Kong University of Science and
    Technology
Clear Water Bay
Kowloon
Hong Kong

Youngjae Lim
Korea Development Institute
P.O. Box 113, Cheongnyang
Seoul 130-012
Korea

Francis T. Lui
Director, Center for Economic
    Development
Hong Kong University of Science and
    Technology
Clear Water Bay
Kowloon
Hong Kong

Joseph R. Mason
Bennett S. LeBow College of Business
Drexel University
211 Academic Building, 33rd &
    Arch Streets
Philadelphia, PA 19104

John McMillan
Graduate School of Business
Stanford University
518 Memorial Way
Stanford, CA 94305-5015

Fumitoshi Mizutani
Graduate School of Business
    Administration
Kobe University
2-1 Rokkodai, Nada-ku
Kobe 657-8501
Japan

Kiyoshi Nakamura
Graduate School of Commerce
Waseda University
1-6-1 Nishi-Waseda, Shinjuku-ku
Tokyo 169-8050
Japan

Chong-Hyun Nam
Department of Economics
Korea University
1 Anam-Dong, Sungbuk-Ku
Seoul 136-701
Korea

Il Chong Nam
KDI School of Public Policy and
    Management
207-43 Cheongnyang,
    Dongdaemun-Ku
Seoul 130-868
Korea

Tsuruhiko Nambu
Economics Department
Gakushuin University
1-5-1 Mejiro, Toshima-ku
Tokyo 171-8588
Japan

Deunden Nikomborirak
Thailand Development Research
    Institute
565 Ramkhamaeng 39 (Thepleela 1)
Wangthonglang
Bangkok 10310
Thailand

Keijiro Otsuka
Foundation for Advanced Studies on
    International Development
Chiyoda Kaikan Building (5F)
2-2 Wakamatsu-cho, Shinjuku-ku
Tokyo 162-8677
Japan

Helen Owens
Productivity Commission Australia
Level 28
35 Collins Street
Melbourne Victoria 3000
Australia

Shih Hui-Tzu
Chung-Hua Institution for Economic
    Research
75 Chang-Hsing Street
Taipei
Taiwan

Andrei Shleifer
Department of Economics
Harvard University
Littauer Center M-9
Cambridge, MA 02138

Richard H. Snape
formerly of the Productivity
    Commission, Australia

Tetsushi Sonobe
Foundation for Advanced Studies on
    International Development
Chiyoda Kaikan Building (5F)
2-2 Wakamatsu-cho, Shinjuku-ku
Tokyo 162-8677
Japan

Yun-Wing Sung
Department of Economics
The Chinese University of Hong Kong
Shatin, New Territories
Hong Kong

Aaron Tornell
Department of Economics
University of California, Los Angeles
405 Hilgard Avenue, Bunche Hall
    #8283
Los Angeles, CA 90095-1477

Philip L. Williams
Comm Sec
Level 12
385 Bourke Street
Melbourne Victoria 3000
Australia

Graeme Woodbridge
Frontier Economics, Australia
Ground Floor
395 Collins Street
Melbourne Victoria 3000
Australia

Changqi Wu
Department of Economics
Hong Kong University of Science &
    Technology
Clear Water Bay
Kowloon
Hong Kong

Yang Yao
China Center for Economic Research
Beijing University
Beijing 100871
China

Author Index

Subject Index